ROBERT LOWTH

LECTURES

ON

THE SACRED POETRY

OF

THE HEBREWS

TRANSLATED FROM THE LATIN

BY G. GREGORY

TO WHICH ARE ADDED,

THE PRINCIPAL NOTES OF PROFESSOR MICHAELIS,

AND

NOTES BY THE TRANSLATOR AND OTHERS

Elibron Classics
www.elibron.com

LECTURES

ON THE

SACRED POETRY

OF THE

HEBREWS.

Bishop Lowth

London Published by Tho.ᵖ Tegg, 73 Cheapside, 1839.

LECTURES

ON

THE SACRED POETRY

OF

THE HEBREWS.

TRANSLATED FROM THE LATIN OF THE LATE

RIGHT REV. ROBERT LOWTH, D.D. F.R.S.

PRÆLECTOR OF POETRY IN THE UNIVERSITY OF OXFORD, AND
LORD BISHOP OF LONDON;

BY G. GREGORY, F.A.S.

AUTHOR OF ESSAYS HISTORICAL AND MORAL.

TO WHICH ARE ADDED,

THE PRINCIPAL NOTES OF PROFESSOR MICHAELIS,

AND

NOTES BY THE TRANSLATOR AND OTHERS.

THE FOURTH EDITION.

LONDON:

PRINTED FOR THOMAS TEGG, CHEAPSIDE;
TEGG & Co. DUBLIN; GRIFFIN & CO. GLASGOW; AND
JAMES AND SAMUEL AUGUSTUS TEGG,
SYDNEY, AUSTRALIA.

MDCCCXXXIX.

WILLIAM TYLER,
PRINTER,
BOLT-COURT, FLEET-STREET.

TO

THE RIGHT REVEREND

RICHARD,

Lord Bishop of Landaff;

WHOSE GREAT ABILITIES HE HAS ALWAYS ADMIRED,

WHOSE CANDOUR AND LIBERALITY

HE HAS REPEATEDLY EXPERIENCED;

THIS ATTEMPT TO RENDER MORE EXTENSIVELY USEFUL

AN INVALUABLE WORK,

IS RESPECTFULLY INSCRIBED

BY HIS GRATEFUL SERVANT,

THE TRANSLATOR.

TRANSLATOR'S PREFACE.

It may not be improper to apprise the Public, that although the following Lectures be entitled Lectures on the Hebrew Poetry, their utility is by no means confined to that single object: They embrace all THE GREAT PRINCIPLES OF GENERAL CRITICISM, as delivered by the ancients, improved by the keen judgment and polished taste of their Author. In other words, this work will be found an excellent compendium of all the best rules of taste, and of all the principles of composition, illustrated by the boldest and most exalted specimens of genius (if no higher title be allowed them) which antiquity has transmitted to us; and which have hitherto seldom fallen under the inspection of rational criticism.

Lest, from the title of the work, or from the circumstance of being originally published in a learned language, a prejudice should arise in the breast of any individual that these Lectures are addressed only to the learned, I think it a duty to anticipate a misapprehension which might interfere both with his entertainment and instruction. The greatest as well as the most useful works of taste and literature, are those which, with respect at least to their general scope and design, lie most level to the common sense of mankind. Though the learning and genius displayed in the following lectures must ever excite our warmest admiration; though they abound in curious researches, and in refined and exquisite observations; though the splendour of the sentiments and the elegance of the style will necessarily captivate the eye and the ear of the classical reader ; the truth is, THAT THEY ARE MORE CALCULATED FOR PERSONS OF TASTE AND GE- NERAL READING, THAN FOR WHAT IS COMMONLY TERMED THE LEARNED WORLD. Here are few nice philological disquisitions, no abstruse metaphysical speculations ; our Author has built solely upon the basis of common sense, and I know no part of his work which will not be intelligible and useful to almost every under- standing.

A still greater mistake it would be, to suppose any knowledge of the Hebrew necessary to enable us to read these Lectures with profit and pleasure. So happily does the simple genius of the Hebrew language accord with our own ; and so excellent a tran- script of the original (notwithstanding a few errors) is our common translation of the Scriptures ; so completely, so minutely, I might say, does it represent the style and character of the Hebrew writings, that no person who is conversant with it can be at all at a loss in applying all the criticisms of our Author. On this ac- count I will venture to assert, that if the genius of the Translator approached in any degree the clearness, the elegance, the ele- vation of the Author, these Lectures in our own language would exhibit the subject in a much fairer and more advantageous light than in the original form. The English idiom, indeed, has so much greater analogy to the Hebrew, that the advan- tages which it possesses over the Latin must be obvious to any reader who compares the literal translations in each of these languages.

But the utility of these Lectures as a system of criticism, is perhaps their smallest merit. They teach us not only taste, but virtue ; not only to admire and revere the Scriptures, but to profit by their precepts. The Author of the present work is not to be considered merely as a master of the general principles of criticism—he has penetrated the very sanctuaries of Hebrew literature ; he has investigated, with a degree of precision which few critics have attained, the very nature and character of their composition ; by accurately examining, and cautiously compar- ing every part of the sacred writings ; by a force of genius which could enter into the very design of the authors ; and by a comprehensiveness of mind which could embrace at a single view a vast series of corresponding passages—he has discovered the manner, the spirit, the idiom of the original, and has laid down such axioms as cannot fail greatly to facilitate our knowledge and understanding of the Scriptures. The work would amply repay the trouble of perusing it, by the excellent elucidations of particular passages of holy writ which it affords; but when we reflect, that these are connected with such rules and principles as may be applied with the greatest advantage to other difficult passages—with such rules, indeed, as will enable us better to comprehend the whole, surely it must appear inestimable in the eye of any man who has at all at heart his own improvement in religious knowledge. Perhaps the sceptic may learn from the perusal of these Lectures, that the difficulties of which he complains in the Scriptures, are difficulties which might in some measure be removed by a little more knowledge, and a little more diligence in the application of it. Perhaps, too, those profound and learned critics, who quote and censure authors whom they have never read, and talk fluently about languages the rudiments of which they have yet to learn, may find, to their great astonishment, that a degree of penetration superior to their own is able to discover at least a few rays of sublimity in the writings of the Hebrews.

Whatever be the merits or the defects of this Translation, on one account at least I will venture to promise myself the warmest commendations of my readers, namely, for having made them acquainted with the admirable criticisms of the learned Michaelis. I have much reason to regret that the nature of this publication would not permit the insertion of all his observations, and at full length. But the truth is, however suitable they may have been to the work in its original form, some of his remarks are too refined to be generally useful, and some of them too learned to be intelligible to any but those who are familiar with the whole circle of Oriental literature. I have therefore selected such of them as I thought applicable to my present purpose: and as it was my wish to confine this work within as narrow limits as my duty to the public would permit, and to suffer in it nothing but what I esteemed immediately useful, I have taken the liberty of abridging some which

b

I thought, in a literal translation, might appear tedious to the English reader.

Some observations of my own I have also presumed to introduce among the Notes. They were such as to me seemed calculated to render the work a more complete compendium of critical science. As I do not, however, think myself above censure, so I trust I shall not be found too obstinate for correction. Should my indiscretion, therefore, have obtruded any thing which a fair and liberal critic shall deem impertinent or improper, I shall with much cheerfulness, in a future edition, submit to its erasement.

It was not till I had consulted some of the first literary characters concerning the propriety of substituting in the place of our Author's inimitable Latin poems any English versions, that I ventured to appear as a poetical translator. Even then I did not fail to inspect every modern author, who I imagined might furnish me with compositions worthy of appearing among the criticisms of Lowth. I have preferred Mr. Merrick's Psalms to any version which I should have been able to produce, (except indeed in a single instance, where it was necessary that the measure should be elegiac), not only on account of their intrinsic merit, but in consequence of the commendation which our Author has bestowed upon them. By the kindness of Mr. Mason, also, this publication is enriched with one of the most beautiful lyric productions in our language, I mean his Paraphrase of the 14th of Isaiah. When I could find no translation to answer my purpose, I was obliged to attempt the versification of the passages myself. The public will therefore recollect, that I was a poet through necessity, not choice; and will, I flatter myself, receive this as a sufficient apology for the indifferent performance of that part of my undertaking.

Presuming that it would be more agreeable to give the literal translations of the Hebrew from works of established reputation, I have taken many of them from our Author's excellent version of Isaiah, from Mr. Blaney's Jeremiah, from Bishop Newcombe's Minor Prophets, Mr. Heath's Job, and from Dr. Hodgson's translation of the Canticles: and this I trust will be accepted by those gentlemen as a general acknowledgment. Where these did not furnish me with a translation, I have endeavoured myself to produce one as faithful to the original as my knowledge of the language would admit.

Convinced, on the whole, of the utility of this publication, and yet aware of my own inability to do it justice, I dismiss it with that mixed emotion of confidence and humility which such a situation naturally inspires. Imperfect as it appears before the world, if it be the means of imparting to but a few some of that information which all who read the original must regret was not more generally diffused, I am sure I shall have deserved well of the community: at the same time, the reader will do me great injustice if he supposes that I have satisfied myself in the execution of my task. Whatever be its reception, it will disappoint no expectations formed by me of profit or of fame; and if neither ensue from it, I shall have no just cause of complaint. It was impossible to read these Lectures with the attention which even this translation required, and not derive advantages from them far superior to the labour they have cost me; and, whatever may be their effect with others, I am confident they have left me something wiser, and I trust something better, than they found me.

In the prosecution of this work I have incurred a debt of gratitude, which, if I cannot discharge, it is but fair to acknowledge. By the advice and encouragement of Dr. Kippis, I was in a great measure induced to undertake this translation; by a continuance of the same friendly disposition, I was enabled cheerfully to proceed in it. The public will easily perceive a part of their obligation and mine to the ingenious Mr. Henley, of Rendlesham, in the numerous and valuable notes which bear his signature; but I am also indebted to him for many corrections. These are not the only friends to whom I have been obliged on this occasion: I will venture to mention in particular, Mr. Wakefield, of Nottingham, a name sufficiently known in the classical world; and Mr. Foster, of Woolton, near Liverpool, whose careful and laborious revision of my manuscript is the least of the many favours he has conferred upon me. To this companion of my youth I can indeed, with the strictest propriety, apply the language of the Roman poet,—

" Tecum etenim longos memini consumere soles,
   Et tecum primas epulis decerpere noctes.
   Unum opus, et requiem pariter disponimus ambo :
   Atque verecunda laxamus seria mensa.
   Non equidem hoc dubites, amborum fœdere certo
   Consentire dies et ab uno sidere duci.
   Nostra vel æquali suspendit tempora libra
   Parca tenax veri : seu nata fidelibus hora
   Dividit in geminos concordia fata duorum :
   Saturnumque gravem nostro Jove frangimus una.
   Nescio, quod certe est, quod me tibi temperat astrum."

James Street Terrace, Buckingham Gate,
    March 1, 1787.

⁎ The Author's Notes are all particularly distinguished. Those marked **M.** are by Professor Michaelis ; those marked S. H. are by Mr. Henley ; and those marked **T.** by the Translator.

AUTHOR'S PREFACE

SECOND EDITION.

I shall endeavour, in a few words, to explain the additions and improvements which have been made to this Edition.

I have revised the whole work; I have added some things—I have corrected many; and especially in the Notes. I have, however, refrained from all corrections which did not appear absolutely necessary. If any reader should object, that many passages remain which might be amended, as being scarcely established upon the grounds of certainty and conviction; I have only to urge in my own defence, that, on very obscure and difficult subjects, it has always appeared to me sufficient to propose a probable explication; nor can I esteem that to be correction, which only substitutes one conjecture for another.

In other respects this Edition has received considerable improvements. In the first place, I am greatly indebted to the friendly communications of the learned Dr. Kennicott, for the variations of the different copies in several passages of the Old Testament which I have quoted. I have distinguished his notes by inverted commas, and by the letter K. subjoined. The manuscripts are numbered according to the catalogue annexed to that learned author's Dissertation on the Hebrew Text.* I have, moreover, added some observations of the learned Dr. Hunt,

---

* In the Third Edition, the manuscript copies are not cited according to these numbers, which are necessarily changed in the Bible published by Dr. K.; but it is only mentioned in how many manuscripts the different reading occurs. Some different readings also are cited at large.

Professor of the Hebrew and Arabic languages, which he kindly communicated at my request. These, also, I have distinguished by inverted commas, and letter H. subjoined.

After this edition was committed to the press, I was favoured with a sight of the Gottingen edition, published under the inspection of the learned and ingenious Professor of Philosophy in that University, John David Michaelis, and greatly improved and illustrated by him. To this were added his Notes and additions, in which he has with great candour supplied my defects, and corrected my errors. These, with the Preface entire, and with a few additions to the Notes, communicated to me by the author, (who would have added more, but that he was prevented by the increasing business of the University,) I have printed in a separate volume, lest my readers should be deprived of these very learned and excellent illustrations; and I chose to do it in a separate state, that the purchasers of the First Edition might partake equally of the benefit. Whatever some of these Notes may contain repugnant to my own sentiments, I have thought it better to submit them in this form to the judgment of the reader, than, by retracing my former ground, to divert his attention into a controversy, unpleasant, and probably fruitless.

CONTENTS.

THE SECOND PART.

OF THE PARABOLIC OR POETICAL STYLE OF THE HEBREWS.

LECTURE IV.

THE ORIGIN, USE, AND CHARACTERISTICS OF THE PARABOLIC, AND ALSO OF THE SENTENTIOUS STYLE.

LECTURE V.

OF THE FIGURATIVE STYLE, AND ITS DIVISIONS.

LECTURE VI.

OF POETIC IMAGERY FROM THE OBJECTS OF NATURE.

LECTURE VII.

OF POETIC IMAGERY FROM COMMON LIFE.

LECTURE VIII.

OF POETIC IMAGERY FROM SACRED TOPICS.

LECTURE IX.

OF POETIC IMAGERY FROM THE SACRED HISTORY.

LECTURE X.

OF ALLEGORY.

LECTURE XI.

OF THE MYSTICAL ALLEGORY.

LECTURE XII.

OF THE COMPARISON.

LECTURE XIII.

OF THE PROSOPOPŒIA, OR PERSONIFICATION.

LECTURE XIV.

OF THE SUBLIME IN GENERAL, AND OF SUBLIMITY OF EXPRESSION IN PARTICULAR.

LECTURE XV.

OF SUBLIMITY OF EXPRESSION.

LECTURE XVI.

OF SUBLIMITY OF SENTIMENT.

LECTURE XVII.

OF THE SUBLIME OF PASSION.

THE THIRD PART.

OF THE DIFFERENT SPECIES OF POETRY EXTANT IN THE WRITINGS OF THE HEBREWS.

OF PROPHETIC POETRY.

LECTURE XVIII.

THE WRITINGS OF THE PROPHETS ARE IN GENERAL POETICAL.

LECTURE XIX.

THE PROPHETIC POETRY IS SENTENTIOUS.

LECTURE XX.

THE GENERAL CHARACTERISTICS OF THE PROPHETIC POETRY.

OF DRAMATIC POETRY.

LECTURE XXX.

THE SONG OF SOLOMON NOT A REGULAR DRAMA.

LECTURE XXXI.

OF THE SUBJECT AND STYLE OF SOLOMON'S SONG.

CONTENTS.

LECTURE XXXII.

OF THE POEM OF JOB.

In order to criticise the Book of Job with any degree of satisfaction to his auditors, the critic must explain his own sentiments concerning the work in general—The Book of Job a singular composition, and has little or no connexion with the affairs of the Hebrews—The seat of the history is Idumæa; and the characters are evidently Idumæan of the family of Abraham—The author appears to be an Idumæan who spoke the Hebrew as his vernacular tongue—Neither Elihu nor Moses, rather Job himself, or some contemporary —This appears to be the oldest book extant; founded upon true history, and contains no allegory—Although extremely obscure, still the general subject and design are sufficiently evident—A short and general analysis of the whole work; in which the obscurer passages are brought as little as possible in question—The deductions from this disquisition: 1. The subject of the controversy between Job and his friends. 2. The subject of the whole Poem. 3. Its end or purpose—All questions not necessarily appertaining to this point to be avoided . . . . . . *Page* 352

LECTURE XXXIII.

THE POEM OF JOB NOT A PERFECT DRAMA.

The Poem of Job commonly accounted Dramatic; and thought by many to be of the same kind with the Greek Tragedy: this opinion examined—A plot or fable essential to a regular Drama: its definition and essential qualities according to Aristotle—Demonstrated, that the Poem of Job does not contain any plot: its form and design more fully explained—Compared with the Œdipus Tyrannus of Sophocles; with the Œdipus Coloneus: and shown to differ entirely from both in form and manner—It is nevertheless a most beautiful and perfect performance in its kind: it approaches very near the form of a perfect Drama; and, for regularity in form and arrangement, justly claims the first place among the poetical compositions of the Hebrews 370

LECTURE XXXIV.

OF THE MANNERS, SENTIMENTS, AND STYLE OF THE POEM OF JOB.

Though the Poem of Job do not contain a plot or fable, it possesses, nevertheless, some things in common with the perfect Drama—MANNERS or character—The manners of Job; to be distinguished from the passions or emotions—The opinion of Aristotle, that the character of extreme virtue is not proper for Tragedy, demonstrated to be neither applicable to Job, nor true with respect to Tragedy in general—The design of the Poem—The manners of the three Friends: the gradations of passion more strongly marked in them than the diversity of manners—Elihu—The expostulation of God himself—SENTIMENTS; expressive of things and of manners: the latter already noticed; the former consist partly of passion, partly of description: two examples of the softer passions; examples of description —The STYLE of this poem uncommonly elegant and sublime; and the poetic conformation of the sentences extremely correct—Peroration, recommending the study of Hebrew Literature 379

A Brief Confutation of Bishop Hare's System of Hebrew Metre . . 393

LECTURES

ON

THE SACRED POETRY

OF THE

HEBREWS.

LECTURE I.

THE INTRODUCTION.

OF THE USES AND DESIGN OF POETRY.

The purpose of Poetry is to instruct while it gives pleasure; instruction being the end, and pleasure the means—Illustrated by examples from the different species of Poetry—The Didactic—The Epic—Tragic—Lyric—The lighter kinds of Poetry, which are calculated as well for the amusement of our leisure, as for the ornament and improvement of literature—Sacred Poetry; whence a transition to the immediate object of these Lectures.

THOUGH our present meeting be, on some accounts, rather earlier than I could have wished,* yet I cheerfully embrace

---

* The Prælector of Poetry at Oxford is obliged by the statute to read his inaugural lecture the first Tuesday in the Term subsequent to his election; and it appears by the University Register, that Mr. Lowth was elected to the Professorship on the 21st of May, 1741, in the vacation between Easter and Act Term. As this vacation is only thirteen days, commencing the Thursday before Whitsunday, and ending the Wednesday after Trinity Sunday, the longest interval that could possibly happen between his election and his first lecture is somewhat less than three weeks; it might probably be much shorter. Even in his youth Bishop Lowth was distinguished by the cautious accuracy of his judgment; he therefore very properly introduces a plan, upon which he was to work for ten years, (the usual term of the professorship,) with much modesty and reserve; and when he

A

the opportunity which it affords me of assuring you, Gentlemen, that to this undertaking (whether considered as a duty imposed, or as a favour conferred upon me) I bring, if no other accomplishment, at least industry and inclination. I could, indeed, more patiently bear to be accused of wanting genius, fluency, or elegance, than of wanting diligence in the exercise of that office to which your authority has called me, or gratitude in the acceptance of that favour, which (whatever it be in itself) is undoubtedly great, since conferred on me by you. For to judge rightly of obligations of this kind, regard must be had, not only to the favour itself, but to the persons who confer it, and to the person on whom it is conferred. When, therefore, I reflect, that the station to which I am invited, has been adorned by men of the first rank in genius and learning; when I regard you, whose favour can add dignity to the most respectable characters; when, in fine, I consider myself, who could never have expected or hoped from my own merits for any public testimony of your approbation; I receive this appointment as an honour, for which the utmost exertions of labour and assiduity will be but a very inadequate return. This part of my duty, however, though feebly and imperfectly, I would wish you to believe I most willingly perform : for to an ingenuous mind nothing can be more agreeable than the expression, or even the sense of gratitude; and the remembrance of the obligation will rather stimulate than depress. Other considerations have, I must confess, rendered me not a little solicitous : I am appointed to superintend a particular department of science, which you have constantly distinguished by your presence and attention; and a subject is to be discussed, which not only you have judged worthy of your cultivation, and the public countenance of the University, but which has hitherto received in this place all the embellishments of grace and elegance of which it is naturally susceptible. Should it, therefore, fall into neglect or disrepute hereafter, I fear that I shall be compelled to

speaks of meeting his constituents *rather early*, (paulo maturius,) he must be understood as regretting the little time which by the statute was allowed him to prepare his introductory address. This fact will serve also to explain some passages towards the conclusion of the lecture.

For the substance of this note I am indebted to a very intelligent friend at Oxford, and am happy in this opportunity of returning my best acknowledgments.—T.

acknowledge the fault to have been mine, and not that of the institution itself.

Whatever degree of success, indeed, may attend my endeavours, let it not for a moment be suspected, that the design is not altogether deserving of approbation. For, can there be any thing of more real importance to literature itself, can any thing be more consistent with the ends for which this University was founded, than that the art, of whose assistance every other art and profession has so greatly availed itself, should be assigned a place among the rest?—that art, so venerable for its antiquity, so delightful in itself—that art, which is in a manner congenial to humanity, and which sets off Nature by the most agreeable representation of her beauties; which, among the ignorant and the learned, the idle and the studious, has ever obtained favour, admiration, and regard. Nothing surely can be more worthy of a liberal and accomplished mind, than to perceive what is perfect and what is defective in an art, the beauties of which frequently lie beneath the surface; to understand what is graceful, what is becoming, in what its excellences consist; and, in a word, to discover and relish those delicate touches of grace and elegance that lie beyond the reach of vulgar apprehension. From these subtile researches after beauty and taste, there is also the fairest reason to apprehend that the judgment itself will receive some accessions of strength and acuteness, which it may successfully employ upon other objects, and upon other occasions. Such at least appear to have been the sentiments of that excellent person,* to whose munificence Poetry has been long indebted for her admission into the circle of those sciences which are cultivated in this University. For, possessing a mind not only instructed in the most useful branches of knowledge, but adorned with the most elegant arts; and having imbibed the first principles of education in a seminary where the most important and sacred subjects, recommended by all the elegance of polite literature, have been heretofore, and still continue to be, studied with vigour and effect; he saw and experienced how much an attention to these elegancies would contribute to the investigation or illustration of the severer branches of erudition, and how strict the alliance between Philosophy and the Muses.

* The Poetic Lecture was instituted by HENRY BIRKHEAD, LL.D. formerly Fellow of All Souls.—*Author's Note.*

The design, therefore, of the author of this institution, as well as the usual practice on occasions like the present, reminds me, Gentlemen, of the propriety (though a matter already familiar to most of you) of premising a few such observations as appear least exceptionable concerning the end and utility of the poetic art.

Poetry is commonly understood to have two objects in view, namely, advantage and pleasure, or rather an union of both. I wish those who have furnished us with this definition had rather proposed utility as its ultimate object,* and pleasure as the means by which that end may be effectually accomplished. The philosopher and the poet, indeed, seem principally to differ in the means by which they pursue the same end. Each sustains the character of a preceptor, which the one is thought best to support, if he teach with accuracy, with subtlety, and with perspicuity; the other, with splendour, harmony, and elegance. The one makes his appeal to reason only, independent of the passions; the other addresses the reason in such a manner as even to engage the passions on his side. The one proceeds to virtue and truth by the nearest and most compendious ways; the other leads to the same point through certain deflections and deviations, by a winding but pleasanter path. It is the part of the former so to describe and explain these objects, that we must necessarily become acquainted with them; it is the part of the latter so to dress and adorn them, that of our own accord we must love and embrace them.

I therefore lay it down as a fundamental maxim, that Poetry is useful, chiefly because it is agreeable; and should I, as we are apt to do, attribute too much to my favourite occupation, I trust Philosophy will forgive me when I add, that the writings of the poet are more useful than those of the philosopher, inasmuch as they are more agreeable. To

---

* There are, however, poems which only delight, but which are not therefore to be condemned : some, which, though they contain no moral precepts, no commendation of virtue, no sentiment curious or abstruse, yet dress and adorn common ideas in such splendour of diction and harmony of numbers, as to afford exquisite pleasure ; they bring, as it were, before our eyes the woods and streams, and all the elegant and enchanting objects of nature. The excellence of such poems is founded upon the same principle with that of a beautiful picture, which is more valued for contributing to pleasure only, than many other things are for their actual utility. What follows I greatly approve : only, I would not wish it to be denied, that there are some poems which have no design but that of giving pleasure, and that this is even a laudable end; nor, indeed, does our author altogether suppose this impossible. — M.

illustrate this position by well-known examples:—Can it be supposed that the more learned Romans when they became devoted to the doctrine of Epicurus, did not more highly esteem, and more frequently apply to the admirable poem of Lucretius, than to Catius, or Amafanius, or even the commentaries of Epicurus himself? Who can believe that even the most tasteless could peruse the writings on agriculture, either of the learned Varro or (not to mention the elder Cato) of Columella, an author by no means deficient in elegance, with the same pleasure and attention as that most delightful and most perfect work, the Georgics of Virgil? a work in which he has equalled the most respectable writers in the solidity of his matter,* and has greatly excelled the most elegant in the incredible harmony of his numbers. On the contrary, if Manilius, who is numbered (and rightly, if we may credit his own testimony) among the writers of the Augustan age, has treated the engaging science of Astronomy in such low and inelegant verse as even scarcely to excel Julius Firmicus, a prose writer on the same subject in a less polished age, I will allow him the merit of a philosopher and astronomer, but never can account him a poet. For, what is a poet, destitute of harmony, of grace, and of all that conduces to allurement and delight? or how should we derive advantage or improvement from an author whom no man of taste can endure to read? The reason, therefore, why Poetry is so studious to embellish her precepts with a certain inviting sweetness, and, as it were,

—" tincture them with the honey of the Muses,"

is plainly by such seasoning to conciliate favour to her doctrine, as is the practice of even physicians, who temper with pleasant flavours their least agreeable medicines:

---

* Seneca seems to detract from the authority of Virgil's Georgics, describing him as an author " who studied truth less than elegance; and wished rather to delight the reader than to instruct the husbandman." Columella, however, seems to be of a very different opinion; and I cannot help thinking him a much better judge. He continually cites the Georgics, never with any degree of blame, and generally with the greatest applause : " This mode we shall pursue, if we may trust the poet, whose authority on such occasions I esteem little less than an oracle."— Lib. iv. " I shall frequently make use of the authority of this divine poem."— Lib. vii. 3. In the very matter for which Seneca finds fault with Virgil, namely, the time of sowing millet, the reader will see how ignorantly the poet is censured by the philosopher, if he consults Columella, ii. 9. Plin. N. H. xviii. 7. Pallad, iii. 3.—*Author's Note.*

> " Thus, the sick infant's taste disguis'd to meet,
> They tinge the vessel's brim with juices sweet :
> The bitter draught his willing lip receives ;
> He drinks deceiv'd, and so deceiv'd he lives ;"

as Lucretius expresses himself in illustration of his own design, as well as that of poetry in general.

But if it be manifest, even in authors who directly profess improvement and advantage, that those will most effica-
ciously instruct who afford most entertainment ; the same
will be still more apparent in those who, dissembling the
intention of instruction, exhibit only the blandishments of
pleasure ; and while they treat of the most important things,
of all the principles of moral action, all the offices of life, yet
laying aside the severity of the preceptor, adduce at once
all the decorations of elegance, and all the attractions of
amusement : who display, as in a picture, the actions, the
manners, the pursuits and passions of men ; and by the force
of imitation and fancy, by the harmony of numbers, by the
taste and variety of imagery, captivate the affections of the
reader, and imperceptibly, or perhaps reluctantly, impel
him to the pursuit of virtue. Such is the real purpose of
heroic poetry ; such is the noble effect produced by the perusal of Homer. And who so thoughtless, or so callous, as
not to feel incredible pleasure in that most agreeable occupation ? who is not moved, astonished, enraptured, by the
inspiration of that most sublime genius ? who so inanimate
as not to see, not to feel inscribed, or as it were imprinted
upon his heart, his most excellent maxims concerning human
life and manners ? From philosophy a few cold precepts may
be deduced ; in history, some dull and spiritless examples of
manners may be found : here we have the energetic voice of
Virtue herself, here we behold her animated form. Poetry
addresses her precepts not to the reason alone ; she calls the
passions to her aid : she not only exhibits examples, but in-
fixes them in the mind. She softens the wax with her peculiar ardour, and renders it more plastic to the artist's hand.
Thus does Horace most truly and most justly apply this
commendation to the poets :

> " What's fair, and false, and right, these bards describe,
> Better and plainer than the Stoic tribe :"—

Plainer or more completely, because they do not perplex
their disciples with the dry detail of parts and definitions,

but so perfectly and so accurately delineate, by examples of every kind, the forms of the human passions and habits, the principles of social and civilised life, that he who from the schools of philosophy should turn to the representations of Homer, would feel himself transported from a narrow and intricate path to an extensive and flourishing field :—Better, because the poet teaches not by maxims and precepts, and in the dull sententious form; but by the harmony of verse, by the beauty of imagery, by the ingenuity of the fable, by the exactness of imitation, he allures and interests the mind of the reader, he fashions it to habits of virtue, and in a manner informs it with the spirit of integrity itself.

But if from the Heroic we turn to the Tragic Muse, to which Aristotle* indeed assigns the preference, because of the true and perfect imitation, we shall yet more clearly evince the superiority of poetry over philosophy, on the principle of its being more agreeable. Tragedy is, in truth, no other than philosophy introduced upon the stage, retaining all its natural properties, remitting nothing of its native gravity, but assisted and embellished by other favouring circumstances. What point, for instance, of moral discipline have the tragic writers of Greece left untouched or unadorned? What duty of life, what principle of political economy, what motive or precept for the government of the passions, what commendation of virtue is there, which they have not treated of with fulness, variety, and learning? The moral of Æschylus (not only a poet, but a Pythagorean) will ever be admired. Nor were Sophocles and Euripides less illustrious for the reputation of wisdom; the latter of whom was the disciple of Socrates and Anaxagoras, and was known among his friends by the title of the dramatic philosopher. In these authors, surely, the allurements of poetry afforded some accession to the empire of philosophy; nor indeed has any man arrived at the summit of poetic fame who did not previously lay the foundation of his art in true philosophy.

Should it be objected, that some have been eminent in this walk of poetry, who never studied in the schools of the philosophers, nor enjoyed the advantages of an education above the common herd of mankind; I answer, that I am not contending about the vulgar opinion, or concerning the meaning of a word: The man who, by the force of genius

* Poet. cap. ult.

and observation, has arrived at a perfect knowledge of mankind; who has acquainted himself with the natural powers of
the human mind, and the causes by which the passions are
excited and repressed; who not only in words can explain,
but can delineate to the senses, every emotion of the soul;
who can excite, can temper and regulate the passions—such
a man, though he may not have acquired erudition by the
common methods, I esteem a true philosopher. The pas
sion of jealousy, its causes, circumstances, its progress and
effects, I hold to be more accurately, more copiously, more
satisfactorily described in one of the dramas of Shakspeare,
than in all the disputations of the schools of philosophy.

Now, if Tragedy be of so truly a philosophical nature;
and if, to all the force and gravity of wisdom, it add graces
and allurements peculiarly its own—the harmony of verse,
the contrivance of the fable, the excellence of imitation, the
truth of action; shall we not say that philosophy must yield
to poetry in point of utility? or shall we not rather say, that
the former is greatly indebted to the latter, of whose assistance and recommendation it makes so advantageous a use,
in order to attain its particular purpose, utility, or improvement?

"But if the force of imitation and fable be so great, the
force of truth itself must surely appear much greater: we
should therefore apply to history rather than to poetry, for
instruction in morals." This, however, is a mistaken notion. History is confined within too narrow limits; history
is subject to laws peculiar to itself, and too severe to admit
of such an application. It relates things as they really were,
it traces events under the guidance of authority; it must
exhibit what has happened, not what might or ought to have
happened. It must not deviate in quest of reasonable instruction or plausible conjecture, but confine itself to that
path which the stubbornness of fact has prescribed. History
treats of things and persons which have been in actual existence; the subjects of poetry are infinite and universal. The
one investigates causes through the uncertain medium of
conjecture; the other demonstrates them with clearness and
certainty. The one catches the casual glimpses of truth,
whenever they break forth to the view; the other contemplates her unclouded appearance. History pursues her appointed journey by a direct path; poetry ranges uncontrolled
over the wide expanse of nature. The former must make

her precepts subservient to the subject; the latter forms a subject subordinate to her precepts and design. For these reasons poetry is defined by Aristotle to be something of a more serious and philosophical nature than history : * nor is our Bacon (a name not inferior in literature) of a different sentiment. The subject itself, and the authority of so great a man, require that the passage should be quoted in his own words. " Since the sensible world is in dignity inferior to the rational soul, poetry seems to endow human nature with that which lies beyond the power of history, and to gratify the mind with at least the shadow of things where the substance cannot be had. For, if the matter be properly considered, an argument may be drawn from poetry, that a superior dignity in things, a more perfect order, and a more beautiful variety delights the soul of man, than is found in nature since the fall. As, therefore, the actions and events which are the subject of true history, are not of sufficient amplitude to content the mind of man; poetry is at hand, and invents actions of a more heroic nature. Because true history reports the success of events not proportionably to desert, or according to the virtue or vice that has been displayed in them; poetry corrects this, and represents events and fortunes according to justice and merit: Because true history, from the obvious similarity of actions, and the satiety which this circumstance must occasion, frequently creates a distaste in the mind; poetry cheers and refreshes it, exhibiting things uncommon, varied, and full of vicissitude. As poetry, therefore, contributes not only to pleasure, but to magnanimity and good morals, it is deservedly supposed to participate in some measure of Divine inspiration; since it raises the mind, and fills it with sublime ideas, by proportioning the appearances of things to the desires of the mind, and not submitting the mind to things, like reason and history." †

That elevation of sentiment, that inspiration, that usefulness in forming the manners, is, however, by no means so peculiar to the Epic, (to which the great man chiefly refers in this passage,) as to exclude the claim of every other species of poetry: there are others which also deserve to partake in the commendation; and first the Ode,

" With thoughts that breathe, and words that burn ;"

* Και φιλοσοφωτερον και σπυδαιοτερον ποιησις ισοριας εςιν.   Arist. Poet. c. 9.—*Author's Note.*
† De Augm. Scient. l. ii. 13.

which, though in some respects inferior to what are called
the higher species of poetry, yields to none in force, ardour,
and sometimes even in dignity and solemnity.   Every species of poetry has in fact its peculiar mode of acting on the
human feelings; the general effect is perhaps the same.   The
epic accomplishes its design with more leisure, with more
consideration and care, and therefore probably with greater
certainty.   It more gradually insinuates itself—it penetrates,
it moves, it delights; now rising to a high degree of sublimity, now subsiding to its accustomed smoothness; and, conducting the reader through a varied and delightful scene, it
applies a gentle constraint to the mind, making its impression by the forcible nature of this application, but more especially by its continuance.   The ode, on the contrary, strikes
with an instantaneous effect, amazes, and as it were storms
the affections.   The one may be compared to a flame, which,
fanned by the winds, gradually spreads itself on all sides,
and at last involves every object in the conflagration; the
other to a flash of lightning, which instantaneously bursts
forth,

"With instant ruin threats great nature's frame,
And shoots through every part the vivid flame."

The amazing power of Lyric poetry, in directing the
passions, in forming the manners, in maintaining civil life,
and particularly in exciting and cherishing that generous
elevation of sentiment on which the very existence of public virtue seems to depend, will be sufficiently apparent by
only contemplating those monuments of genius which Greece
has bequeathed to posterity.   If we examine the poems of
Pindar, (which though by no means accounted the most excellent of their kind, by some strange fatality are almost the
only specimens that remain,) how exquisite must have been
the pleasure, how vivid the sensation to the Greek, whose
ordinary amusement it was to sing, or hear them sung!
For, this kind of entertainment was not confined to persons
of taste and learning, but had grown into general use.
When he heard his gods, his heroes, his ancestors received
into the number of the gods, celebrated in a manner so
glorious, so divine, would not his bosom glow with the desire
of fame, with the most fervid emulation of virtue, with a patriotism, immoderate perhaps, but honourable and useful in
the highest degree?   Is it wonderful, that he should be so
elevated with this greatness of mind, (shall I call it?) or

rather insolence and pride, as to esteem every other people mean, barbarous, and contemptible, in comparison with himself and his own countrymen? It is almost unnecessary to remind this assembly, that in the sacred games (which afforded so much support to the warlike virtue of Greece*) no inconsiderable share of dignity and esteem resulted from the verses of the poets; nor did the Olympic crown exhibit a more ample reward to the candidate for victory, than the encomium of Pindar or Stesichorus. I wish, indeed, that time had not invidiously deprived us of the works of the latter, whose majesty and excellence commanded universal applause, whom Dionysius† preferred before every other lyric poet, because he made choice of the sublimest and most splendid subjects, and in the amplification of them preserved most completely the manners and the dignity of his characters. To Alcæus, however, the same author attributes the most excellent manner of treating political subjects.‡ As a man, indeed, how great! as a citizen, how strenuous! What a spirited defender of the laws and constitution of his country! what a vigorous opposer of tyrants! who consecrated equally his sword and his lyre on the altar of freedom! whose prophetic muse, ranging through every region, acted as the sacred guardian, not for the present moment only, but for future ages; not of his own city alone, but of the whole commonwealth of Greece. Poetry such as this, so vehement, so animated, is certainly to be esteemed highly efficacious, as well in exciting the human mind to virtue, as in purifying it from every mean and vicious propensity; but still more especially does it conduce to cherish and support that vigour of soul, that generous temper and spirit, which is both the offspring and guardian of liberty. Could an apprehension arise that another Pisistratus would meditate the enslaving of that city, where at every banquet, nay, in the streets and in the meanest assemblies of the common people, that convivial ode was daily sung which bears the name of Callistratus? an author known to us only by this composition, which, however, sufficiently demonstrates him to have been an admirable poet and an excellent citizen:§

---

* Consult the Dissertation of the learned Gilbert West on the Olympic Games, sect. xvii.

† Dion. Halicar. T. ii. p. 123.   Edit. Hudson.   ‡ Ibid.

§ Athenæus, lib. xv.   This *Skolion* (or convivial song) some have attributed to Alcæus; but not conformably with strict chronology, for Alcæus flourished about

" Verdant myrtle's branchy pride
    Shall my thirsty blade entwine :
Such, Harmodius, deck'd thy side ;
    Such, Aristogiton, thine.

Noblest youths ! in islands blest,
    Not like recreant idlers dead ;
You with fleet Pelides rest,
    And with godlike Diomed

Myrtle shall our brows entwine,
    While the Muse your fame shall tell ;
'Twas at Pallas' sacred shrine,
    At your feet the tyrant fell.

Then in Athens all was peace,
    Equal laws and liberty :

eighty years before the death of Hipparchus. But Hesychius has preserved the
name of the author from oblivion, directly assigning the poem to Callistratus. This
poem was so celebrated at Athens, that it was sung at almost every banquet, as we
learn from Aristophanes, Αχαρν. 977.

" Grim-visag'd War shall never be my guest,
    Nor at my table sing Harmodius' praise :
Such lawless riot mars our temp'rate joys."

" He shall never sing Harmodius with me ;" that is, he shall never be my
guest. Upon this passage the Scholiast : " In their convivial meetings they sung a
certain ballad of Harmodius, which begins Φιλτατε 'Αρμοδιε. κ. λ." Also, in the
same comedy, 1092, these songs are enumerated among the other apparatus of the
entertainment :

" The sprightly dance, Harmodius ! thy delight."

There is another allusion to the same, Λυσις. 633.

" My sword I'll bear hid in a myrtle branch ;
    And like Aristogiton walk in arms."

It is evident from this ballad, that the conspirators, when they assaulted Hipparchus, concealed their daggers in those myrtle garlands, which, if I mistake not,
were carried by all who assisted at the sacred rites of the *Panathenaic* sacrifice :
and this is indeed confirmed by the Scholiast upon Aristophanes, in the passage
before referred to : " For these men, Harmodius and Aristogiton, hastily drawing
their swords out of the myrtle boughs, fell furiously upon the tyrant." Hence,
perhaps, arose the custom, that whoever sung any convivial song in company,
always held a branch of myrtle in his hand. See Plutarch, i. *Symp. Quest.* 1.—
Author's Note.

Our Collins, in particular, has attributed this poem to Alcæus, in the following
beautiful lines :

" What new Alcæus, fancy blest,
    Shall sing the sword in myrtles drest,
At Wisdom's shrine awhile its flame concealing,
    (What place so fit to seal a deed renown'd ?)
Till she her brightest lightnings round revealing,
    It leap'd in glory forth, and dealt her prompted wound."

Ode to Liberty.

Nurse of Arts, and eye of Greece,
People valiant, firm, and free !"*

If, after the memorable *Ides of March*, any one of the
tyrannicides had delivered to the populace such a poem as
this, had introduced it to the *suburra*, to the assemblies of
the forum, or had put it into the mouths of the common
people, the dominion of the Cesars and its adherents would
have been totally extinguished: and I am firmly persuaded,
that one stanza of this simple ballad of Hermodius would
have been more effectual than all the Philippics of Cicero.

There are some other species of poetry, which with us
generally appear in an easy and familiar style, but formerly
assumed sometimes a graver and more important character.
Such is the Elegy: I do not speak of the light and amorous
elegy of the moderns, but that ancient, serious, sacred, and
didactic elegy, the preceptress of morals, the lawgiver of
nations, the oracle of virtue. Not to enter into a detail of
authors, of whose works we are not in possession, and of
whose merits we consequently can form no adequate judgment, it will be sufficient to instance Solon, the most venerable character of antiquity, the wisest of legislators, and
withal a poet of no mean reputation. When any thing
difficult or perplexing occurred in the administration of
public affairs, we are informed that he had recourse to
poetry.† Were the laws to be maintained or enforced upon
any particular emergency; was the indolence or licentiousness of the citizens to be reproved; were their minds to be
stimulated to the love of liberty—he immediately attacked
them with some poetical production, bold, animated, and

---

* The above imitation, all but the third stanza, is taken from a paraphrase of
this poem, said to be the production of Sir W. Jones. The following is a more
literal translation, by Mr. Cumberland :

    " He is not dead, our best belov'd,
      Harmodius is not lost ;
    But with Troy's conquerors remov'd
      To some more happy coast.

    Bind then the myrtle's mystic bough,
      And wave your swords around ;
    For so they struck the tyrant low,
      And so their swords were bound.

    Perpetual objects of our love
      The patriot pair shall be,
    Who in Minerva's sacred grove
      Struck and set Athens free."
                     Observer, No. 49.—T.

† See Plutarch and Diog. Laert. *Life of Solon.*

severe; in the highest tone of censorial gravity, and yet in no respect deficient in elegance:

> " Before the awful peal the lightning flies,
>   And gathering clouds impending storms presage ;
> By souls aspiring civil freedom dies ;
>   The people's madness whets the tyrant's rage."

It is a well-known fact, that Athens was altogether in-dobtod for the recovery of Salamis to the verses of Solon, even contrary to their own inclination and intention. After they had, from repeated overthrows, fallen into the deepest despair, insomuch that it was made a capital offence even to propose the renewal of the war, or the reclaiming of the island, such was the influence of that single poem, which begins—" Let us march to Salamis," that, as if pronounced by a prophet instinct with divine enthusiasm, the people, propelled by a kind of celestial inspiration, flew immediately to arms, became clamorous for war, and sought the field of battle with such incredible ardour, that by the violence of their onset, after a great slaughter of the enemy, they achieved a most decisive victory.

We have also some remains of the celebrated Tyrtæus, who

> ——" manly souls to martial deeds
> By verse excited."

The whole scope and subject of his compositions is the cele-bration of valour and patriotism, and the immortal glory of those who bravely fell in battle :—compositions which could impart some degree of courage even to the timid and un-manly; by which, indeed, he elevated the minds of the Lacedemonians, which had been long debilitated and de-pressed, to the certain hope of victory. The fact is well known, and had it not been corroborated by the testimony of so many authors, it would doubtless have been thought by some incredible ; though I confess it appears to me no less supported by the reason of things, than by the authority of the historian. It is impossible that men should act other-wise than with the most heroic ardour, the most undaunted resolution, who sung to the martial pipe, when arranged in military order, marching to the onset, or perhaps actually engaged, such strains as these:

> " Our country's voice invites the brave
>   The glorious toils of war to try ;
> Curs'd be the coward or the slave
>   Who shuns the fight, who fears to die !

Obedient to the high command,
  Full fraught with patriotic fire,
Descends a small but trusty band,
  And scarce restrains th' impatient ire.

Lo! the hostile crowds advance!
  Firmly we their might oppose;
Helm to helm, and lance to lance,
  In awful pomp we meet our foes.

Unaw'd by fear, untaught to yield,
  We boldly tread th' ensanguin'd plain;
And scorn to quit the martial field,
  Though drench'd in blood, though heap'd with slain.

For though stern death assail the brave,
  His virtues endless life shall claim;
His fame shall mock th' invidious grave—
  To times unborn a sacred name!"

Not entirely to omit the lighter kinds of poetry, many
will think that we allow them full enough, when we suppose
their utility to consist in the entertainment which they
afford. Nor is this, Gentlemen, altogether to be despised,
if it be considered that this entertainment, this levity itself,
affords relaxation to the mind when wearied with the laborious investigation of truth; that it unbends the understanding after intense application; restores it when debilitated;
and refreshes it, even by an interchange and variety of
study. In this we are countenanced by the example and
authority of the greatest men of Greece, by that of Solon,
Plato, and Aristotle; among the Romans, by that of Scipio
and Lælius, Julius and Augustus Cesar, Varro and Brutus,
who filled up the intervals of their more important engage-
ments, their severer studies, with the agreeableness and
hilarity of this poetical talent. Nature indeed seems in this
most wisely to have consulted for us, who, while she impels
us to the knowledge of truth, which is frequently remote,
and only to be prosecuted with indefatigable industry, has
provided also these pleasing recreations as a refuge to the
mind, in which it might occasionally shelter itself, and find
an agreeable relief from languor and anxiety.
  But there is yet a further advantage to be derived from
these studies, which ought not to be neglected; for, beside
possessing in reserve a certain solace of your labours, from
the same repository you will also be supplied with many of

the brightest ornaments of literature. The first object is, indeed, to perceive and comprehend clearly the reasons, principles, and relations of things; the next is, to be able to explain your conceptions, not only with perspicuity, but with a degree of elegance. For, in this respect, we are all of us in some measure fastidious: We are seldom contented with a jejune and naked exposition even of the most serious subjects; some of the seasonings of art, some ornaments of style, some splendour of diction, are of necessity to be adopted; even some regard is due to the harmony of numbers, and to the gratification of the ear. In all these respects, though I grant that the language of poetry differs very widely from that of all other kinds of composition, yet he who has bestowed some time and attention on the perusal and imitation of the poets, will, I am persuaded, find his understanding exercised and improved as it were in this Palestra, the vigour and activity of his imagination increased, and even his manner of expression to have insensibly acquired a tinge from this elegant intercourse. Thus we observe in persons who have been taught to dance, a certain indescribable grace and manner; though they do not form their common gesture and gait by any certain rules, yet there results from that exercise a degree of elegance, which accompanies those who have been proficients in it even when they have relinquished the practice. Nor is it the least improbable, that both Cesar and Tully* (the one the most elegant, the other the most eloquent of the Romans) might have derived considerable assistance from the cultivation of this branch of polite literature, since it is well known that both of them were addicted to the reading of poetry, and even exercised in the composition of it.† This too is so apparent in the writings

* " It will not be inconsistent with these studies to amuse yourself with poetry : —Tully, indeed, appears to me to have acquired that luminous and splendid diction which he possessed, by occasionally resorting to such occupations." Quinct. lib. x. 5.—*Author's Note.*

† It may be doubted whether Cicero was indebted for his excellence as an orator to the cultivation of poetry. He would have been accounted but a moderate orator, if his orations had only equalled his poetry—had he spoken as he sung :

" Fortune fortuned the dying notes of Rome :
Till I, thy consul sole, consoled thy doom."

I do not expect from Cicero the polish and perfection of Virgil, but one might at least have hoped to meet in his verse some of that fire and fancy which appears in his oratory. The case, however, is far otherwise; for he appears not deficient in art, but in nature, in that energy and enthusiasm which is called the *poetic furor.*

of Plato, that he is thought not only to have erred in his judgment, but to have acted an ungrateful part, when he excluded from his imaginary commonwealth that art, to which he was so much indebted for the splendour and elegance of his genius, from whose fountains he had derived that soft, copious, and harmonious style, for which he is so justly admired.

But to return to the nobler and more important productions of the Muses.—Thus far poetry must be allowed to stand eminent among the other liberal arts; inasmuch as it refreshes the mind when it is fatigued, soothes it when it is agitated, relieves and invigorates it when it is depressed; as it elevates the thoughts to the admiration of what is beautiful, what is becoming, what is great and noble: nor is it enough to say, that it delivers the precepts of virtue in the most agreeable manner; it insinuates or instils into the soul the very principles of morality itself. Moreover, since the desire of glory, innate in man, appears to be the most powerful incentive to great and heroic actions, it is the peculiar function of poetry to improve this bias of our nature, and thus to cherish and enliven the embers of virtue: and since one of the principal employments of poetry consists in the celebration of great and virtuous actions, in transmitting to posterity the examples of the bravest and most excellent

Upon very mature consideration indeed I will venture to profess that however poetry may contribute to form an accomplished orator, I hardly ever expect to find the same person excellent in both arts. The language of poetry has something in it so different and contrary to that of oratory, that we seldom find those who have applied much to the one rise above mediocrity in the other. The chief excellence of an orator consists in perspicuity; and in such a degree of perspicuity as is necessary to render the composition intelligible even to the common people; but, though obscurity be not a necessary adjunct of a good poem, it must be considerably superior to the language and comprehension of the vulgar to rank above mediocrity. The orator must not deviate from the common and beaten track of language; the poet must aim at a happy boldness of diction, and wander into new paths. The orator, in order to be generally understood, is necessarily more copious and prolix, not only than the poet, but than all other writers: the chief commendation of the poet is brevity. A poem is always enervated by circumlocutions, unless new lights of sentiment and language are thrown in. For these and other reasons I am of opinion, that, if a well cultivated genius for poetry should apply earnestly to oratory, he might indeed prove such an orator as would please a learned audience, and not be unpleasing to the populace; but such a man will never prove a very popular orator, on whom the people shall gaze with admiration and rapture, and who shall acquire a perfect ascendency over all their passions. And he who is by nature an orator, may possibly be a poet for the multitude, or by art and study, and the imitation of the best models, may make a decent proficiency, but never can be a great and divine poet.—M.

B

men, and in consecrating their names to immortality; this praise is certainly its due, that while it forms the mind to habits of rectitude by its precepts, directs it by examples, excites and animates it by its peculiar force, it has also the distinguished honour of distributing to virtue the most ample and desirable rewards of its labours.

But, after all, we shall think more humbly of poetry than it deserves, unless we direct our attention to that quarter where its importance is most eminently conspicuous; unless we contemplate it as employed on sacred subjects, and in subservience to religion. This indeed appears to have been the original office and destination of poetry; and this it still so happily performs, that in all other cases it seems out of character, as if intended for this purpose alone. In other instances poetry appears to want the assistance of art, but in this to shine forth with all its natural splendour, or rather to be animated by that inspiration, which, on other occasions, is spoken of without being felt. These observations are remarkably exemplified in the Hebrew poetry, than which the human mind can conceive nothing more elevated, more beautiful, or more elegant; in which the almost ineffable sublimity of the subject is fully equalled by the energy of the language and the dignity of the style. And it is worthy observation, that as some of these writings exceed in antiquity the fabulous ages of Greece, in sublimity they are superior to the most finished productions of that polished people. Thus, if the actual origin of poetry be inquired after, it must of necessity be referred to religion; and since it appears to be an art derived from nature alone, peculiar to no age or nation, and only at an advanced period of society conformed to rule and method, it must be wholly attributed to the more violent affections of the heart, the nature of which is to express themselves in an animated and lofty tone, with a vehemence of expression far remote from vulgar use. It is also no less observable, that these affections break and interrupt the enunciation by their impetuosity; they burst forth in sentences pointed, earnest, rapid, and tremulous; in some degree the style as well as the modulation is adapted to the emotions and habits of the mind. This is particularly the case in admiration and delight; and what passions are so likely to be excited by religious contemplations as these? What ideas could so powerfully affect a new-created mind, (undepraved by habit or opinion,) as the good-

ness, the wisdom, and the greatness of the Almighty? Is it
not probable, that the first effort of rude and unpolished verse
would display itself in the praise of the Creator, and flow
almost involuntarily from the enraptured mind? Thus far,
at least, is certain, that poetry has been nurtured in those
sacred places where she seems to have been first called into
existence; and that her original occupation was in the temple and at the altar. However ages and nations may have
differed in their religious sentiments and opinions, in this at
least we find them all agreed, that the mysteries of their
devotion were celebrated in verse.* Of this origin poetry
even yet exhibits no obscure indications, since she ever
embraces a divine and sacred subject with a kind of filial
tenderness and affection. To the sacred haunts of religion
she delights to resort as to her native soil: there she most
willingly inhabits, and there she flourishes in all her pristine
beauty and vigour. But to have slightly glanced at the
subject, appears sufficient for the present; we shall soon
perhaps find an opportunity of entering upon a more ample
discussion.

I trust indeed that you will pardon me, Gentlemen, if I
do not as yet venture to explain my future plan of instruction, and the form and method which I think of pursuing.
That man must have too little respect for your judgment,
and by far too high an opinion of his own, who would presume to produce before you matter not sufficiently digested, not sufficiently polished and perfected by study and by
the maturest consideration. I have, therefore, determined
within myself, that nothing shall hastily or prematurely

* The most ancient poetry, as well as music, according to Plato, was "that
which was addressed to the Deity under the appellation of hymns."—*De Leg.* lib.
iii. Suetonius has illustrated this subject in a very elegant manner, though he is
a little unfortunate in his etymology; a circumstance not uncommon with the old
grammarians. "When first," says he, "mankind emerged from a state of barbarism
into the habits of civilised life, and began to be acquainted in some measure with
their own nature and that of the gods, they contented themselves with a moderate
style of living, and a language just proportioned to their wants; whatever was grand
or magnificent in either, they dedicated to their deities. As, therefore, they built
temples more elegant by far than their own habitations, and made the shrines and
images of their divinities much larger than the human form, so they thought it
necessary to celebrate them in a style of greater majesty than common; in language more splendid, harmonious, and agreeable. This species of composition,
because it assumed a certain distinct form, was called a *poem,* from the word
ποιοτης, and those who cultivated it were called *poets.*" From a fragment of a
work not extant concerning Poetry, quoted by Isidorus. Orig. lib. viii. c. 7.—
Author's Note.

proceed from me in this assembly, nothing which is not laboured to the extent of my abilities; and that for what is wanting in genius, in erudition, in fluency, and in every respect in which I feel myself deficient, I shall endeavour to compensate, as much as possible, by care and assiduity. If in these points I shall be enabled to perform my duty, I trust, Gentlemen, that other deficiencies you will be kind onough to excuse; and that the person whom you have honoured with your favour and attention, with your candour and indulgence, you will continue to support.

LECTURE II.

THE DESIGN AND ARRANGEMENT OF THESE LECTURES.

The dignity of the subject, and its suitableness to the design of the institution—That Poetry which proceeds from divine inspiration is not beyond the province of criticism—Criticism will enable us to account for the origin of the art, as well as to form a just estimation of its dignity: that the opinion of the divine origin of Poetry was common in Greece—This work purely critical ; and, consequently, theological disquisitions will be avoided—The general distribution of the subject into three parts—the nature of the verse, the style, and the arrangement.

SOCRATES, as we read in Plato,* having been frequently admonished in a dream to apply to music, and esteeming himself bound to fulfil a duty which appeared to have been imposed upon him by divine authority, began with composing a hymn to Apollo, and afterwards undertook to translate some of the Fables of Æsop into verse. This he did, I apprehend under the persuasion, that the first-fruits of his poetry (which he esteemed the principal branch of the science of music)† ought to be consecrated to the immortal gods ; and that it was not lawful for him, who was but little versed in those studies, to descend to lighter subjects, which perhaps might in the main be more agreeable to his genius, before he had discharged the obligations of religion. It is my intention, Gentlemen, to follow the example of this great philosopher; and since the University has honoured me with this office of explaining to you the nature and principles of poetry, I mean to enter upon it from that quarter whence he thought himself obliged to commence the study and practice of the art. I have determined, therefore, in the first place, to treat of sacred poetry—that species, I mean, which was cultivated by the ancient Hebrews, and which is

---

* In *Phæd.* sub init.

† " What then is education?—As far as respects the body, it consists in the gymnastic exercise ; as far as respects the mind, it consists in harmony." Plato *de Rep.* lib. ii.—*Author's Note.*

peculiarly appropriated to subjects the most solemn and sublime; that, should my endeavours prove unequal to so great a subject, I may, as it were with favourable auspices, descend to matters of inferior importance. I undertake this office, however, with the most perfect conviction, that not only from a regard to duty it ought to be executed with diligence, but, from the respectability of that body, at whose command it is undertaken, it ought to be executed with honour and reputation: nor is it merely to be considered what the intent of the institution, and the improvement of the students may require, but what will be consistent with the dignity of this University. For, since the University, when it gave its sanction to this species of discipline by a special decree, recommended the study of poetry particularly, because it might conduce to the improvement of the more important sciences, as well sacred as profane,* nothing could certainly appear more useful in itself, or more agreeable to the purpose of this institution, and the design of its learned patrons, than to treat of that species of poetry which constitutes so considerable a part of sacred literature, and excels all other poetry, not less in the sublimity of the style, than in the dignity of the subject.

It would not be easy, indeed, to assign a reason, why the writings of Homer, of Pindar, and of Horace, should engross our attention and monopolise our praise, while those of Moses, of David, and Isaiah, pass totally unregarded. Shall we suppose that the subject is not adapted to a seminary in which sacred literature has ever maintained a precedence? Shall we say, that it is foreign to this assembly of promising youth, of whom the greater part have consecrated the best portion of their time and labour to the same department of learning? Or must we conclude, that the writings of those men who have accomplished only as much as human genius and ability could accomplish, should be reduced to method and theory; but that those which boast a much higher origin, and are justly attributed to the inspiration of the Holy Spirit, may be considered as indeed illustrious by their native force and beauty, but not as conformable to the principles of science, nor to be circumscribed by any rules of art? It is indeed most true, that sacred poetry, if we contemplate its origin alone, is far superior to both *nature* and *art;* but if we would rightly estimate its excellences,

* See the Statute relating to the Poetic Lecture.

that is, if we wish to understand its power in exciting the human affections, we must have recourse to both; for we must consider what those affections are, and by what means they are to be excited. Moreover, as in all other branches of science, so in poetry, art or theory consists in a certain knowledge derived from the careful observation of nature, and confirmed by practice and experience; for, men of learning having remarked in things what was graceful, what was fit, what was conducive to the attainment of certain ends, they digested such discoveries as had been casually made, and reduced them to an established order or method: whence it is evident, that art deduces its origin from the works of genius, not that genius has been formed or directed by art; and that it is properly applied in illustrating the works of even those writers, who were either ignorant of its rules, or inattentive to them. Since, then, it is the purpose of sacred poetry to form the human mind to the constant habit of true virtue and piety, and to excite the most ardent affections of the soul, in order to direct them to their proper end; whoever has a clear insight into the instruments, the machinery as it were, by which this end is effected, will certainly contribute not a little to the improvement of the critical art. Now, although it be scarcely possible to penetrate to the fountains of this celestial Nile, yet it may surely be allowed us to pursue the meanders of the stream, to mark the flux and reflux of its waters, and even to conduct a few rivulets into its adjacent plains.

The sacred poetry is undoubtedly entitled to the first rank in this school, since from it we are to learn both the origin of the art, and how to estimate its excellence. The commencement of other arts, however rude and imperfect, and though employed only on light and trivial matters, is an inquiry generally productive of satisfaction and delight. Here we may contemplate poetry in its very beginning—not so much the offspring of human genius, as an emanation from heaven; not gradually increasing by small accessions, but from its birth possessing a certain maturity both of beauty and strength;* not administering to trifling passions,

---

* Our author either affects the orator too much in this passage, or too carelessly follows those Jews and Christians who attribute all the Hebrew writings to the finger of God himself. He seems to forget, that, before the rites of Moses, the Moabites celebrated the victories of their king in a very elegant poem, which Moses himself has preserved, and that there were other historical poems even more ancient

and offering its delicious incense at the shrine of vanity, but the priestess of divine truth, the internunciate between earth and heaven. For this was the first and peculiar office of poetry—on the one hand to commend to the Almighty the prayers and thanksgivings of his creatures, and to celebrate his praises; and on the other to display to mankind the mysteries of the divine will, and the predictions of future events the best and noblest of all employments. It is to this observation, indeed, that I would particularly point your attention; for it is plain from the general tenour of the sacred volume, that the indications of future events have been, almost without exception, revealed in numbers and in verse; and that the same Spirit was accustomed to impart, by its own energy, at once the presentiment of things, and to clothe it in all the magnificence, in all the elegance of poetry, that the sublimity of the style might consist with sentiments so infinitely surpassing all human conception. When considered, therefore, in this point of view, what is there of all which the most devoted admirers of poetry have ever written or fabricated in its commendation, that does not fall greatly short of the truth itself? what of all the insinuations which its bitterest adversaries have objected against it, which is not refuted by simply contemplating the nature and design of the Hebrew poetry? Let those who affect to despise the Muses cease to attempt, for the vices of a few who may abuse the best of things, to bring into disrepute a most laudable talent. Let them cease to speak of that art as light or trifling in itself, to accuse it as profane or impious; that art which has been conceded to man by the favour of his Creator, and for the most sacred purposes; that art consecrated by the authority of God himself, and by his example in his most august ministrations.

than the prophetic blessing of Jacob. To these our author seems not sufficiently to have attended in this place, though he has made some very just remarks on this subject in a succeeding Lecture. I am of opinion, indeed, that the Hebrew poetry originated in the choirs of dancers, (not always, however, of a religious kind,) when the gestures of the dancer accorded with the music. To this I think the present parallelisms of the verses may be referred, of which no man has treated more satisfactorily than our author, Lect. 19. If indeed Moses was not the institutor of a practice totally new to the Hebrews, I mean the accommodation of poetry to music and dancing, it follows that poetry existed long before his time, rustic and uncultivated at first, no doubt, but afterwards more perfect and refined. Nor is it probable that the first essays in poetry were made in the time of Moses, which may be called the golden age of the Hebrew language, and in which we meet with poetry too perfect to have been produced in the infancy of the art.—M.

Whether the Greeks originally derived their poetry from the fountains of nature, or received it through a different channel from a remoter source, appears a question of little importance, and not easy to be determined. Thus far, however, is evident, that an opinion was prevalent in Greece concerning the nature and origin of poetry, which appears most groundless and absurd if we contemplate only the poetry of Greece, though truly and justly applicable to that of the Hebrews. They considered poetry as something sacred and celestial, not produced by human art or genius, but altogether a Divine gift. Among them, therefore, poets were accounted sacred, the ambassadors of Heaven, men favoured with an immediate intercourse and familiarity with the gods. The mysteries and ceremonies of their religion, and the worship of their deities, were all performed in verse; and the most ancient of their compositions, their oracles, always consisted of numbers. This circumstance, I must add, rendered them not only more sublime, but more deserving of credit in the eyes of the common people; for they conceived it equally the effect of Divine inspiration to foresee events, and to express them in extemporaneous verse. Thus, they seemed to have retained some traces of an opinion impressed upon the minds of men in the very earliest ages concerning the true and ancient poetry, even after they had lost the reality itself, and when religion and poetry had by the licentiousness of fiction reciprocally corrupted each other.

Since, therefore, in the sacred writings the only specimens of the primeval and genuine poetry are to be found, and since these are not less venerable for their antiquity than for their divine original, I conceived it my duty in the first place to investigate the nature of these writings, as far as might be consistent with the design of this institution. In other words, it is not my intention to expound to the student of theology the oracles of Divine truth, but to recommend to the notice of the youth who is addicted to the politer sciences, and studious of the elegancies of composition some of the first and choicest specimens of poetic taste. The difficulty of the undertaking ought probably to have discouraged me from the attempt; yet with you, Gentlemen, I trust my temerity will find this excuse, namely, that I have undertaken a subject the most noble in itself, and the best adapted to the circumstances of my office. I trust that you will allow me at least the merit of distinguishing what was most worthy of this place and this assembly; though perhaps I have too rashly engaged, without a due consideration of my own abilities.

In this disquisition it is my intention to pursue that track which the nature of the subject seems to require. Three points are to be considered in every poem: First, the argument or matter, and the manner of treating it; what disposition, what order, and what general form is adapted to each species of composition: Secondly, the elocution and style, in which are comprehended lively and elevated sentiments, splendour and perspicuity of arrangement, beauty and variety of imagery, and strength and elegance of diction: Lastly, the harmony of the verse or numbers is to be considered, not only as intended to captivate the ear, but as adapted to the subject, and expressive of it, and as calculated to excite corresponding emotions in the soul. We shall now consider what is to be performed in each of these departments, and how far we may with safety, and with any prospect of advantage, engage in a critical examination of the Hebrew poetry.

With respect to the nature of the versification, (if I may be allowed to reverse my own arrangement, and to speak of that first which constituted the last division of my subject,) I fear that little can be produced to your satisfaction or my own; since it is manifest, not only from the unsuccessful endeavours of the most learned men, but from the nature of the thing itself, that scarcely any real knowledge of the Hebrew versification is now to be attained; and the only merit to which any modern writer can lay claim, is that of distinguishing certain facts (if any there be) from uncertain conjecture, and demonstrating how imperfect our information must of necessity be upon this topic. Were the inquiry, however, concerning the Hebrew metre to be wholly overlooked, yet, since some vestiges of verse are discernible, a few observations of a general nature will probably occur, which we shall in the first place slightly advert to, and afterwards, as occasion serves, particularize and explain.

That part of these Lectures, on the other hand, which treats of the style of the Hebrew poetry, will afford very ample scope for disquisition, since it possesses not only all the principal excellences which are common to poetry, but possesses many also which are proper and peculiar to itself.

In the remaining part, which, though first in order and dignity, will be the last to be treated of, we must with diligence, (as considering the difficulty of the subject), and at the same time with caution, engage; lest, while we wander too much at large in the ample field of Poetry, we should imprudently break in upon the sacred boundaries of Theology. It will be our business on this occasion to distribute the Hebrew poems, according to their different species, into different classes; to consider in each what is most worthy of attention; and perhaps to compare them with those of Greece and Rome, if there be any extant of the same kind.

THE FIRST PART.

OF THE HEBREW METRE.

LECTURE III.

THE HEBREW POETRY IS METRICAL.

The necessity of inquiring into the nature of the Hebrew verse—The Hebrew poetry proved to be metrical from the alphabetical poems, and from the equality and correspondence of the sentiments; also from the poetical diction—Some of the most obvious properties of the verse—The rhythm and mode of scanning totally lost; proved from facts—The poetical conformation of the sentences—The Greek and Latin Poetry materially different from the Hebrew, from the very nature of the languages—Hence a peculiar property in the prose versions of the Hebrew poetry, and the attempts to exhibit this poetry in the verse of other languages.

On the very first attempt to elucidate the nature of the sacred poetry, a question presents itself uncommonly difficult and obscure, concerning the nature of the Hebrew verse. This question I would indeed gladly have avoided, could I have abandoned it consistently with my design. But since it appears essential to every species of poetry that it be confined to numbers, and consist of some kind of verse, (for, indeed, wanting this, it would not only want its most agreeable attributes, but would scarcely deserve the name of poetry), in treating of the poetry of the Hebrews it appears absolutely necessary to demonstrate, that those parts at least of the Hebrew writings which we term *poetic* are in a metrical form, and to inquire whether any thing be certainly known concerning the nature and principles of this

✳

versification or not. This part of my subject, therefore, I undertake, not as hoping to illustrate it by any new observations, but merely with a view of inquiring whether it will admit of any illustration at all. Even this I shall attempt with brevity and caution, as embarked upon an ocean dishonoured by the shipwreck of many eminent persons, and therefore presuming only to coast along the shore.

In the first place, (notwithstanding that a contrary opinion has been supported by some of the learned,) I think it will be sufficiently apparent, if we but advert to them a little more attentively, that certain of the Hebrew writings are not only animated with the true poetic spirit, but in some degree confined to numbers; for there appear, in almost every part of them, such marks and vestiges of verse, as could scarcely be expected to remain in any language after the sound and pronunciation (as is the case with Hebrew at present) were, through extreme antiquity, become almost totally obsolete.

There existed a certain kind of poetry among the Hebrews, principally intended, it should seem, for the assistance of the memory; in which, when there was little connexion between the sentiments, a sort of order or method was preserved, by the initial letters of each line or stanza following the order of the alphabet. Of this there are several examples extant among the sacred poems;* and in these examples the verses are so exactly marked and defined, that it is impossible to mistake them for prose; and particularly if we attentively consider the verses, and compare them with one another, since they are in general so regularly accommodated, that word answers to word, and almost syllable to syllable. This being the case, though an appeal can scarcely be made to the ear on this occasion, the eye itself will distinguish the poetic division and arrangement, and also that some labour and accuracy has been employed in adapting the words to the measure.

The Hebrew poetry has likewise another property altogether peculiar to metrical composition. Writers who are confined within the trammels of verse, are generally indulged with the license of using words in a sense and manner re-

---

* Psal. xxv., xxxiv., xxxvii., cxi., cxii., cxix., cxlv. Prov. xxxi. from the 10th verse to the end. The whole of the Lamentations of Jeremiah except the last chapter.—*Author's Note.*

mote from their common acceptation, and in some degree
contrary to the analogy of the language; so that sometimes
they shorten them by taking from the number of the syllables, and sometimes venture to add a syllable for the sake of
adapting them to their immediate purpose. This practice
is not only effectual to the facilitating of the versification,
but also to the prevention of satiety, by varying the sounds,
and by imparting to the style a certain peculiar colouring,
which elevates it above the language of the vulgar. Poetry,
therefore, always makes use of some such artifice as accords
best with the genius of each language. This is exemplified
particularly in two respects: first, in the use of glosses or
foreign language; and secondly, in that of certain irregular
or less received forms of common words.* The extreme
liberty which the Greeks allowed themselves in these respects
is remarkable; and their language, beyond every other, because of the variety and copiousness of the different dialects
which prevailed in the several States of Greece, was peculiarly favourable to it. Next to them, none perhaps have
admitted these liberties more freely than the Hebrews, who
not only by the use of glosses, but by that of anomalous language, and chiefly of certain particles† peculiar to metrical

---

* See Aristot. *Poet.* c. 22.

† The poetical particles which the grammarians in general call Paragogic, (or
redundant,) are as follow:—ו added to nouns, Numb. xxiv. 3. Psal. l. 10; lxxix.
2; cxiv. 8; civ. 11, 20. Isa. lvi. 9, (it occurs here twice.) Zeph. ii. 14.

"בנו, Numb. xxiv. 3, as also חיתו, Psal. l. 10, &c., seems to be a pleonasmus
peculiar to the Syriac. For thus it is common for that people to express themselves,
ברה דדויד. The Son of *his* David, Matt. i. 1. פומה דמריא. The countenance of
his Lord, Isa. i. 20, למעינו. Psal. cxiv. 8. It was formerly read למציני, as appears
from the Septuagint, λιμνας ὑδατων."—H.

' Added to nouns, adverbs, prepositions, is common in the poets: also to the
participles, Benoni, sing. masc. and fem. Gen. xlix. 11. Psal. ci. 5. Prov. xxviii.
16. Jer. xxii. 23; xlix. 16; li. 13. Ezek. xxvii. 3. This, however, the Masorites
have sometimes rashly expunged.

Concerning the ', when added to verbs in the second pers. sing. pret. I have sometimes my doubts whether it be an error or not. Certainly the Masorites are of
opinion that it should always be expunged. See Jer. xiii. 21, xxii. 23, xxxi. 21, and
Ezek. xvi., where it occurs eleven times. Now, it is not in the least probable that
in one chapter the same error should so frequently take place. " But in these eleven
places many MSS. confirm the Masoretic Keri,* for the ' is wanting."—K. It may
also be a Syriac gloss, which is the opinion of Cappel; *Crit. Sac.* lib. iii., c. xiii. 8.
Though there is a passage, where it occurs in the same person masc. פי, אמרת, " because thou hast said," Psal. lxxix. 3. So indeed almost all the old interpreters,

* A Masoretic term for a various reading.

composition, and added frequently at the end of words, have
so varied their style, as to form to themselves a distinct

except the Chaldean paraphrast, have taken it; and rightly, indeed, if regard is to be
paid to the context or the parallelism of the sentences.   But this I rather esteem an
error, though the Masorites have not noted it as such.

"Verbs in which the ' is added to the second pers. fem. sing. pret. follow the
Syriac and Arabic form."—H.

מוֹ for ם, or הם, occurs frequently in the Hebrew poetry: see Psal. ii. **3, 4, 5,**
where it appears five times: sometimes in the singular for ו; see Isa. xliv. 15; liii.
8. Job xx. 23; xxii. 2; xxvii. 23. Psal. xi. 7. It is very often merely paragogic,
or redundant. כמוֹ simply seems to be altogether poetical; it occurs in Nehem. ix.
11, and is taken from the Song of Moses, Exod. xv. 5. It is, however, not the same
with præfixes or suffixes.

"Isa. liii. 8. לָמוֹ. The Septuagint in this place is ηχθη εις θανατον (he
was led unto death:) in this it follows the Arabic version, which reads למות."
—H.

Of these particles, which I call poetical, there occur very few examples in the
prose parts of Scripture; indeed I do not know that there are any more than the
following :—ו, Gen. i. 24; but instead of חיתו ארץ, the Samaritan copy has הארץ
חית, as it is also expressed in the Hebrew, in the following verse : ', Gen. xxxi. 39,
twice : but it is also wanting in the Samaritan copy, although it may possibly be
meant for a pronominal affix.   Also in Ruth iii. 3, 4, three times; iv. 5; and in
2 Kings iv. 23.   "But in all these places, many MSS. confirm the Masoretic
Keri; for ' is wanting."— K.   Lastly, מוֹ, Exod. xxiii. 31; but instead of גרשתמו,
the Septuagint and the Vulgate read גרשתים, and the context favours this
reading.

Hitherto, perhaps, might be referred the ה and ן paragogic, and the relative
שׁ, which occur more frequently in the poets than elsewhere.

These are most, if not all of them, examples of anomalies, which serve to distinguish particularly the poetic dialect.   To demonstrate more fully how freely
they are made use of by the sacred poets, I shall annex a specimen, which Abarbanel
exhibits as collected from one short poem, namely, the Song of Moses.   "You
may observe," says he, "in this poem, words sometimes contracted for the sake of
the measure, and sometimes lengthened and extended by additional letters and
syllables, according as the simple terms may be redundant or deficient.   The
letters which in this canticle are superadded, are as follow :—the vau and jod
twice in the word יכסיומו, for in reality כסם would have been quite sufficient: the
jod is also added in נאדרי; the vau in יאכלמו; the vau in תורישמו : the vau also
in כסמו; in תבלעמו; in אחוזת: the thau in אימחה."   (In truth, this form of
nouns appears to be altogether poetical; many examples of which may be found in
Glass. *Phil. Sac.* p. 269; all of them, however, from the poetic and prophetic books.)
"The vau in תביאמו; in תמעמו.   The deficient are jod in יח; ומורת; so in
תמלאמו for תמלא מהם : The vau in נהלת for נהלתו; so also the word לבב is deficient in the verse ישבי כנען; נמוגו כל; for the prince of the prophets cannot be suspected of erring in grammatical or orthographical accuracy; but the necessity of the
verse, and a proper regard to harmony so require it."   Abarb. *in Mantissa Dissert.*
ad Liber. Cosri. a Buxtorfio, edit. *Basil.* 1660, p. 412. To these examples, one might
add from the same canticle, מו twice in כמו, נ epithentic in ארממנהו, paragogic in
ירגזון.

Concerning the glosses or foreign words which occur in the Hebrew poetry, in
the present state of the Hebrew language it is difficult to pronounce on the ruins,

poetical dialect. Thus far, therefore, I think we may with safety affirm, that the Hebrew poetry is metrical. One or two of the peculiarities also of their versification it may be proper to remark, which, as they are very observable in those poems in which the verses are defined by the initial letters, may at least be reasonably conjectured of the rest. The first of these is, that the verses are very unequal in length—the shortest consisting of six or seven syllables, the longest extending to about twice that number; the same poem is, however, generally continued throughout in verses not very unequal to each other. I must also observe, that the close of the verse generally falls where the members of the sentences are divided.*

as it were, of neighbouring and contemporary dialects; since possibly those words which are commonly taken for Chaldaic (for instance) might have been common to both languages; on the contrary, some of those which more rarely occur, and the etymology of which we are ignorant about, may have been borrowed from the neighbouring dialects. Since, however, there are some words which more frequently occur in the poetical remains, and which are not elsewhere to be found but in the Chaldee, we may reasonably conjecture concerning these, that they have been introduced into the Hebrew, or at least, after becoming obsolete in common language, might be again made use of: such are the following, Bar, (a son,) Koshet, (truth,) Seya, (he increased,) Shebach, (he praised,) Zakaph, (he lifted up,) Gnuck, (in the Hebrew tzick,) he pressed, &c. Observe Moses, however, in the exordium of his last benediction, Deut. xxxiii., has he not also frequently admitted of Chaldaisms? What is אתה ? which again occurs ver. 21. What is חבב ? in both form and sense Chaldaic. What דת ? a word scarcely received into common use among the Hebrews till after the Babylonish captivity; especially since the Hebrew abounded in synonymous terms, expressive of the *law of God*. (But perhaps this last word in this place is rightly suspected to be an error. See Kennicott, *Dissert. I. of the Hebrew Text*, p. 427, and Houbigant in loc.) Isaiah, however, elegantly adopts the Chaldaic form speaking of Babylon, in the word מדהבה, which in the Hebrew would be מודבה, ch. xiv. 4. Nor less appositely on the same subject does the Psalmist introduce the word תוללינו, Psal. cxxxvii. 3, which is the Chaldaic for שוללינו, as the Chaldean paraphrast himself allows, who renders it by the synonymous term בוזא, as elsewhere he renders the word שלל ; (see Ezek. xxvi. 12; xxix. 19; xxxviii. 12, 13;) nor indeed do the other interpreters produce any thing to the purpose. Some instances of grammatical anomalies in the glosses have been detected; such are the following Syriac or Chaldaic: כי for כ, Psal. cxvi. thrice; ciii. five times; also in Jer. xi. 15. וחי for וי, Psal. cxvi. 12. ין as a termination plur. nom. masc. for ים, Job iv. 2; xxiv. 22; xxxi. 10, and frequently elsewhere; also Prov. xxxi. 3. Lam. iv. 3. Ezek. xxvi. 18. Mic. iii. 12.

"אתה, the Samaritan, has אתו in the Arabic form. מדהבה, חבב, are Chaldaic as well as Arabic. תולליו, but this word seems to have followed the etymology of the Arabic verb תלל, *he bound, he led captive ;* whence the Septuagint ἀπαγαγοντες ἡμας ; and the Chaldaic בוזא, *he carried away captive.*" H.—*Author's Note.*

* This mode of versification is not altogether foreign to our own language, as is evident from some of our earliest writers, particularly Piers Plowman.— S. H.

As to the real quantity, the rhythm, or modulation, these, from the present state of the language, seem to be altogether unknown, and even to admit of no investigation by human art or industry. It is indeed evident, that the true Hebrew pronunciation is totally lost. The rules concerning it, which were devised by the modern Jews many ages after the language of their ancestors had fallen into disuse, have been long since suspected by the learned to be destitute of authority and truth: for if, in reality, the Hebrew language is to be conformed to the positions of these men, we must be under the necessity of confessing, not only what we at present experience, that the Hebrew poetry possesses no remains of sweetness or harmony, but that it never was possessed of any. The truth is, it was neither possible for them to recall the true pronunciation of a language long since obsolete, and to institute afresh the rules of orthoepy; nor can any person in the present age so much as hope to effect any thing to the purpose by the aid of conjecture, in a matter so remote from our senses, and so involved in obscurity. In this respect, indeed, the delicacy of all languages is most remarkable. After they cease to be spoken, they are still significant of some sound; but that in the mouth of a stranger becomes most dissonant and barbarous—the vital grace is wanting, the native sweetness is gone, the colour of primeval beauty is faded and decayed. The Greek and Latin doubtless have now lost much of their pristine and native sweetness; and as they are spoken, the pronunciation is different in different nations, but everywhere barbarous, and such as Attic or Roman ears would not have been able to endure. In these, however, the rhythm or quantity remains; each retains its peculiar numbers, and the versification is distinct: but the state of the Hebrew is far more unfavourable, which, destitute of vowel sounds, has remained altogether silent, (if I may use the expression,) incapable of utterance, upwards of two thousand years. Thus, not so much as the number of syllables of which each word consisted could with any certainty be defined, much less the length or quantity of the syllable; and since the regulation of the metre of any language must depend upon two particulars, I mean the number and the length of the syllables, the knowledge of which is utterly unattainable in the Hebrew, he who attempts to restore the true and genuine Hebrew versification, erects an edifice without a foundation. To some of those, indeed, who have

c

laboured in this matter, thus much of merit is to be allowed
—that they rendered the Hebrew poetry, which formerly
sounded uncommonly harsh and barbarous, in some degree
softer and more polished; they indeed furnished it with a
sort of versification, and metrical arrangement, when baffled
in their attempts to discover the real. That we are justified
in attributing to them any thing more than this, is neither
apparent from the nature of the thing, nor from the arguments with which they attempt to defend their conjectures.*
Their endeavours, in truth, would rather tend to supersede
all inquiry on a subject which the most learned and ingenious have investigated in vain; and induce us to relinquish
as lost, what we see cannot be retrieved.

But although nothing certain can be defined concerning
the metre of the particular verses, there is yet another artifice
of poetry to be remarked of them when in a collective state,
when several of them are taken together. In the Hebrew
poetry, as I before remarked, there may be observed a certain conformation of the sentences, the nature of which is,
that a complete sense is almost equally infused into every
component part, and that every member constitutes an entire verse: so that, as the poems divide themselves in a
manner spontaneously into periods, for the most part equal;
so the periods themselves are divided into verses, most commonly couplets, though frequently of greater length. This
is chiefly observable in those passages which frequently occur in the Hebrew poetry, in which they treat one subject
in many different ways, and dwell upon the same sentiment;
when they express the same thing in different words, or
different things in a similar form of words; when equals
refer to equals, and opposites to opposites: and since this
artifice of composition seldom fails to produce even in prose
an agreeable and measured cadence, we can scarcely doubt
that it must have imparted to their poetry, were we masters
of the versification, an exquisite degree of beauty and grace.
In this circumstance, therefore, which is common to most
of the Hebrew poems, we find, if not a rule and principle,
at least a characteristic of the sacred poetry; insomuch that
in that language the word *Mizmor*,† (or Psalm,) according

---

* See the Brief Confutation of Bishop Hare's Hebrew Metres.

† *Zamar*, he cut off, he pruned; namely, the superfluous and luxuriant branches
of trees. Hence *Zemorah*, a branch or twig; *Marmarah*, a pruning-hook: also he
sung, or chanted; he cut his voice by the notes in singing, or divided it. *Shur*

to its etymology, is expressive of a composition cut or divided, in a peculiar manner, into short and equal sentences. The nature of the Greek and Latin poetry is, in this respect, directly opposite; and that in conformity to the genius of the different languages. For the Greek, beyond every other language, (and the Latin next to it), is copious, flowing, and harmonious, possessed of a great variety of measures, of which the impression is so definite, the effects so striking, that if one should recite some lame and imperfect portion of a verse, or even enunciate hastily several verses in a breath, the numbers would nevertheless be clearly discernible: so that in these every variety essential to poetry and verse may be provided for almost at pleasure, without the smallest injury to the different metres. But in the Hebrew language the whole economy is different. Its form is simple above every other; the radical words are uniform, and resemble each other almost exactly; nor are the inflexions numerous, or materially different: whence we may readily understand, that its metres are neither complex nor capable of much variety; but rather simple, grave, temperate; less adapted to fluency than dignity and force: so that possibly they found it necessary to distinguish the extent of the verse by the conclusion of the sentence, lest the lines, by running into each other, should become altogether implicated and confused.

Two observations occur in this place worthy of attention, and arise naturally from what has been said. The first is, that a poem translated literally from the Hebrew into the prose of any other language, whilst the same forms of the sentences remain, will still retain, even as far as relates to versification, much of its native dignity, and a faint appearance

---

signifies singing with the voice (vocal music:) *Nazan*, to play upon an instrument. *Zamar* implies either vocal or instrumental melody. Thus, *Bineginoth mismor shir* (see Psal. lxvii. 1,) I think means *a metrical song, accompanied with music.* Thus I suppose *mismor* to denote *measure*, or numbers, what the Greeks called ῥυθμόν (rythmon.) It may also be more immediately referred to the former and original sense of the root, as signifying a poem *cut into short sentences*, and *pruned* from every luxuriancy of expression, which is a distinguishing characteristic of the Hebrew poetry. Prose composition is called *Sheluchah*, loose or free, diffused with no respect to rule; like a wild tree, luxuriant on every side in its leaves and branches. Metrical language is *Zimrah*, cut and pruned on every side into sentences, like branches distributed into a certain form and order; as vines, which the vine-dresser corrects with his pruning-knife, and adjusts into form.—*Author's Note.*

of versification.   This is evident in our common version of
the Scriptures, where frequently

> " The order chang'd, and verse from verse disjoin'd,
>   Yet still the poet's scatter'd limbs we find :"

But the case is very different in literal translations from the
Greek or Latin.*   The other remark which I wished to
recommend to your notice is, that a Hebrew poem, if translated into Greek or Latin verse, and having the conformation of the sentences accommodated to the idiom of a foreign
language, will appear confused and mutilated; will scarcely
retain a trace of its genuine elegance and peculiar beauty.
For, in exhibiting the works of great poets in another language, much depends upon preserving not only the internal
meaning, the force and beauty, as far as regards the sense,
but even the external lineaments, the proper colour and
habit, the movement, and, as it were, the gait of the original.
Those, therefore, who have endeavoured to express the beauties of the sacred poets in Greek or Latin verse, have una-
voidably failed in the attempt to depict them according to
their native genius and character; and have exhibited something, whether inferior or not, certainly very unlike them,
both in kind and form : Whether, on the other hand, they
have been able to approach, in some degree, their energy,
their majesty and spirit, it is not our present object to consider.

* " Nevertheless," (that is, though the sacred poetry be not possessed of metrical
syllables, and divided into feet, which is the opinion of this learned man,) " we
cannot doubt that it has another species of metrical arrangement, which depends
upon the subject.   Is it not evident, that if you translate some of them into another
language, they still retain this metrical form, if not perfect, at least in a great degree? which cannot possibly take place in those poems the metre of which consists
in the number and quantity of syllables."   R. Azarias in *Mantiss. Dissert. ad Libr.
Cosri*, p. 420.—*Author's Note.*

THE SECOND PART.

OF THE PARABOLIC OR POETICAL STYLE OF THE HEBREWS.

LECTURE IV.

THE ORIGIN, USE, AND CHARACTERISTICS OF THE PARABOLIC, AND ALSO OF THE SENTENTIOUS STYLE.

The Poetic style of the Hebrews bears the general title of Parabolic—Its constituent principles are the sententious, the figurative, and the sublime—The source of the Parabolic style, and its original use: among other nations; among the Hebrews— Certain examples of it preserved from the first ages in the writings of Moses.—1. The sententious kind; its nature and effects.

THE subject which next presents itself to our investigation, is the style of the Hebrew poetry. The meaning of this word I do not wish to be restricted to the diction only of the sacred poets, but rather to include their sentiment, their mode of thinking; whence, as from its genuine source, the peculiar character of their composition may be deduced. It will be proper, however, before we proceed, to remark, that as it is the nature of all poetry, so it is particularly of the Hebrew, to be totally different from common language; and not only in the choice of words, but in the construction, to affect a peculiar and more exquisite mode of expression. The truth of this remark will appear from what usually happens to a learner of Hebrew. He, for instance, who is a proficient in the historical books, when he comes to the poetical parts, will find himself almost a perfect stranger. The phraseology, however, peculiar to the poets, the bold ellipses, the sudden transitions of the tenses, genders, and persons, and other similar circumstances, I shall leave to the grammarian; or rather I shall leave (since I do not find that the grammarians acknowledge any distinction

4

between poetical and common language) to be collected
from practice and attentive reading. It would be a no less
indolent and trifling occupation to post through all those
forms of tropes and figures which the teachers of rhetoric
have pompously (not to say uselessly) heaped together;
since there is no necessity of applying to the sacred poetry
for examples of these—every composition, however trite and
barren, abounding in them. Of these, therefore, we shall
be sparing, and use them not as freely as we might, but as
much only as shall appear absolutely necessary: for at
present we are not so much to inquire what are the general
principles of poetical composition, as what are the peculiar
marks and characters of the Hebrew poetry. Let us consider, therefore, whether the literature of the Hebrews will
not suggest some general term, which will give us an opportunity of discussing the subject, so as to bring it under one
comprehensive view; and which, being divided according
to its constituent parts, will prescribe a proper order and
limit to our disquisition.

A poem is called in Hebrew *Mizmor*, that is, as was before
remarked, a short composition cut and divided into distinct
parts.* It is thus called in reference to the verse and numbers. Again, a poem is called, in reference to the diction
and sentiments, *Mashal*;† which I take to be the word

---

* "Agreeable to this is the meaning of the Arabic verb *Zamar, collected*, or
tied up, therefore *rendered smaller*, and *contained* within less space : it also means
to sing," &c.—H.

† Numb. xxi. 27; xxiii. and xxiv. frequently; Mic. ii. 4; Isa. xiv. 4; Psal.
xlix. 5; lxxviii. 2; Job xxvii. 1; xxix. 1.
  Mashal, he *likened*, he *compared*, he *spoke in parables ;* he *uttered proverbs, sentences grave and pointed*, a *composition ornamented with figures* and *comparisons :*
also he *ruled*, he *was eminent*, he *possessed dominion* and authority; delegated, perhaps, and vicarious in its original and restricted sense, whence at last it was taken
more laxly, as referring to any kind of dominion.   The elder servant of Abraham,
who presided over his family, was certainly called Hamashel *be-bal, asher lo*, Gen.
xxiv. 2.   He was, in fact, a steward in the place of his master, and representing
him by a delegated authority ; whence there is evidently a relation between the two
interpretations of this root, consisting in this circumstance, that both the parabolical
image and the steward or deputy are representative.   *Mashal* is therefore a composition elevated and grave, weighty and powerful, highly ornamented with comparisons, figures, and imagery; such is the style of the Psalms, the Prophets, and
the Book of Job ; it is a diction which under one image or examplar includes
many, and may easily be transferred to every one of the same kind—which is
in general the nature of proverbs : it is, in fine, any sentence or axiom excellently or gravely uttered, concise, and confined to a certain form or manner ;
as is evident from 1 Sam. xxiv. 14, and from many examples in the Proverbs
of Solomon.

properly expressive of the poetical style. Many translators render it by the word *parable*, which in some respects is not improper, though it scarcely comprehends the full compass of the Hebrew expression; for, if we investigate its full and proper force, we shall find that it includes three forms or modes of speech,—the sententious, the figurative, and the sublime. To these, as parts or divisions of the general subject, may be referred whatever occurs concerning the parabolic or poetical style of the Hebrews: but the reason of this arrangement will perhaps be better understood, if we premise a short inquiry into the origin and early use of this style of composition.

The origin and first use of poetical language are undoubtedly to be traced into the vehement affections of the mind. For, what is meant by that singular frenzy of poets, which the Greeks, ascribing to Divine inspiration, distinguished by the appellation of *enthusiasm*, but a style and expression directly prompted by nature itself, and exhibiting the true and express image of a mind violently agitated? when, as it were, the secret avenues, the interior recesses of the soul are thrown open; when the inmost conceptions are displayed, rushing together in one turbid stream, without order or connexion? Hence sudden exclamations, frequent interrogations, apostrophes even to inanimate objects: for, to those who are violently agitated themselves, the universal nature of things seems under a necessity of being affected with similar emotions. Every impulse of the mind, however, has not only a peculiar style and expression, but a certain tone of voice, and a certain gesture of the body adapted to it. Some, indeed, not satisfied with that expression which language affords, have added to it dancing and song: and as we know there existed in the first ages a very strict connexion between these arts and that of poetry, we may

---

"In Arabic *Mathal* (for ש, sh, and ת, th, are interchangeable letters) means to *make a likeness*, to *express or imitate a resemblance*, to *dictate a parable or proverb*, to *give an instance*."—H.

With *Mashal*, *Chidah* is frequently joined, and means, *a saying pointed, exquisite, obscure;* such as requires either to the conception or understanding of it considerable ingenuity. It is derived from *Chud*, to propose a *problem* or *enigma*, or *some exquisite and curious saying;* which agrees with *Chedad*, to *sharpen*, or to *be sharp.*

"In the Arabic it signifies *to be bent;* and *Chid*, he *turned out of his way:* whence Schultens (Comment. in Job xvi. 20) deduces the Hebrew word *Chidah;* as it were an *intricate species of composition*, a *riddle.*" H.—*Author's Note.*

possibly be indebted to them for the accurately admeasured verses and feet, to the end that the modulation of the language might accord with the music of the voice and the motion of the body.

Poetry, in this its rude origin and commencement, being derived from nature, was in time improved by art, and applied to the purposes of utility and delight. For, as it owed its birth to the affections of the mind, and had availed itself of the assistance of harmony, it was found, on account of the exact and vivid delineation of the objects which it described, to be excellently adapted to the exciting of every internal emotion, and making a more forcible impression upon the mind than abstract reasoning could possibly effect: it was found capable of interesting and affecting the senses and passions, of captivating the ear, of directing the perception to the minutest circumstances, and of assisting the memory in the retention of them. Whatever, therefore, deserved to be generally known and accurately remembered, was (by those men who on this very account were denominated *wise*)* adorned with a jocund and captivating style, illuminated with the varied and splendid colouring of language, and moulded into sentences comprehensive, pointed, and harmonious. It became the peculiar province of poetry to depict the great, the beautiful, the becoming, the virtuous; to

---

* The bards or poets are enumerated by the Son of Sirach amongst the wise and illustrious men of former times:

> "Wise and eloquent in their instructions,
> Such as found out musical tunes,
> And recited written verses."—Ecclus. xliv. 4.

Observe also, whether those four, whose wisdom is so much celebrated, 1 Kings iv. 31. *Beni Machol*, be not *sons of the Choir*; that is, musicians or poets: for they were (not *sons of Mahol*, as our translators render it, taking an appellative for a proper name, but) sons of *Zerach*, as appears from 1 Chron. ii. 6. " Whence the eldest of them, *Ethan*, was also called *Ha-Ezrachi*, 1 Kings iv. 31, where the Targum expressly has it *Bar Zerach*, son of *Zerach*."—H. Among the Greeks also the poets were anciently called wise men or sophists:

> "Rosy Venus, Queen of all!
> So the *Wise* bright Venus call."—Anacreon.

That is, the poets.—So also Pindar:

> —— "Sung by the *Wise*,
> And honoured by the will of Jove."—*Ist.* v. 36.

Upon which passage the Scholiast:. " The poets are commonly called wise men and sophists." " The poets preceded these (the philosophers) by some ages; and, before the name of *philosopher* was known, were called wise men." Lactantius, lib. v. 5. —*Author's Note.*

embellish and recommend the precepts of religion and virtue; to transmit to posterity excellent and sublime actions and sayings; to celebrate the works of the Deity, his beneficence, his wisdom; to record the memorials of the past, and the predictions of the future. In each of these departments poetry was of singular utility, since, before any characters expressive of sounds were invented, at least before they were commonly received and applied to general use, it seems to have afforded the only means of preserving the rude science of the early times, and in this respect, to have rendered the want of letters more tolerable: it seems also to have acted the part of a public herald, by whose voice each memorable transaction of antiquity was proclaimed and transmitted through different ages and nations.

Such appears by the testimony of authors to have been the undoubted origin of poetry among heathen nations. It is evident that Greece, for several successive ages, was possessed of no records but the poetic; for the first who published a prose oration was Pherecydes, a man of the Isle of Syrus, and contemporary with King Cyrus, who lived some ages posterior to that of Homer and Hesiod; somewhat after that time Cadmus the Milesian* began to compose history. The laws themselves were metrical, and adapted to certain musical notes: such were the laws of Charondas, which were sung at the banquets of the Athenians;† such were those which were delivered by the Cretans‡ to the ingenuous youth to be learned by rote, with accompaniments of musical melody, in order that, by the enchantment of harmony, the sentiments might be more forcibly impressed upon their memories. Hence certain poems were denominated νομοι, (nomoi,) which implied convivial or banqueting

---

* Strabo, *Geog.* lib. i. Plin, *Nat. Hist.* lib. vii. 56, and v. 29. This matter is well explained by Isidorus, however rashly some learned men may have taken it. "It is well known," says he, "that among the Greeks, as well as among the Latins, metrical composition was much more ancient than prose. Every species of knowledge was at first contained in poetry; it was long before prose composition flourished. The first man among the Greeks who composed in prose was Pherecydes Syrius; among the Romans, Appius Cæcus first published a work in prose against Pyrrhus." Isidor. Hispal. *Orig.* lib. i. 27.—*Author's Note.*

† "The laws of Charondas were sung at banquets among the Athenians, as Hermippus relates." Athen. lib. xiv. 3. See Bentley's *Dissertation on Phalaris,* p. 373.—*Author's Note.*

‡ Ælian. *Var. Hist.* i. ii. 39.

songs, as is remarked by Aristotle;* who adds, that the
same custom of chanting the laws to music existed even in
his own time among the Agathyrsi.†   If we may credit
Strabo,‡ the Turdetani, a people of Spain, had laws in
verse.   But the Germans,§ as Tacitus positively asserts,
had no records or annals but the traditional poems in
which they celebrated the heroic exploits of their ancestors.‖   In the same manner, and on the same account, the

---

* "Why are laws called canticles? but that before alphabetical writing was
invented, the laws used to be sung, that they might be preserved in remembrance,
as is the custom still among the Agathyrsi."   Prob. S. 19. Q. 28.—*Author's
Note.*

† Possibly laws, which are in the sententious style, were originally precepts of
equity and morals, and in course of time acquired authority in the courts of justice.
There is much of this proverbial style in the ancient German laws; and, I am
assured by good authority, in those of Sweden also.   Moses himself is so sententious and compact, and pays so much attention to brevity in many of his laws,
that he seems to have adopted into his code some well-known proverbs, containing the general principles of equity.   Of this I think there is an instance in
Exod. xxiii. 5, in which there is a point and antithesis, more resembling the familiarity of a proverb than the dignity of a statute.   To the example of the Lusitanians,
we may add one more recent of the Swedes, who in the year 1748 published laws
in verse.—M.

‡ Geog. lib. iii.

§ After the extraordinary revolution of Germany, and the dispersion of that
people into different colonies, it is not surprising that no monuments of the poetical
records of our ancestors should remain.   Scandinavia and Iceland have been more
fortunate in this respect; there the records of their most ancient transactions are
traditionally preserved to this day.   These instances of a practice so agreeable to
that of the Hebrews, existing among a people so remote, serve to prove the great
similarity in the human mind throughout all the countries of the globe, and show
that the most natural and early mode of preserving facts has been by verses committed to memory, rather than by written documents.   What Pocock relates of
the Arabs, applies perhaps more directly to the present subject: "It seems," he
says, "to be entirely owing to their poetry, that so copious a language is preserved
in a perfect state.   Among other commendations of their poetry, they enumerate this, that both the purity of the Arabic language, and the propriety and
elegance of their pronunciation, have owed their preservation entirely to it.
Ebn Phares observes, that the Arabic poems serve in the place of commentaries, or
annals, in which are recorded the series of their genealogies, and all the facts of history deserving of remembrance, and from which a knowledge of the language is to
be collected." — M.

However the antiquity of Ossian's poems, as exhibited to the public, may be
doubted, it is certain that there exist in the Highlands of Scotland many remains of
the ancient historical ballads, which, though in all probability of a much later date
than the age of Ossian is pretended to be, contain many marks of wild genius, and,
I am informed from good authority, furnished Mr. Macpherson with the bulk of
his materials.—T.

‖ To these testimonies concerning the early use of poetry, I will add a remarkable passage from Plutarch, which states summarily many facts relating to
this circumstance.   "The use of reason seems to resemble the exchange of

Persians, the Arabs, and many of the most ancient of the eastern nations, preserved in verse their history and politics, as well as the principles of religion and morals: Thus all science, human and divine, was deposited in the treasury of the Muses, and thither it was necessary on every occasion to resort.* The only mode of instruction, indeed, adapted to human nature in an uncivilised state, when the knowledge of letters was very little if at all diffused, must be that which is calculated to captivate the ear and the passions, which assists the memory, which is not to be delivered into the hand, but infused into the mind and heart.†

That the case was the same among the Hebrews; that poetry was both anciently and generally known and practised by them, appears highly probable, as well from the analogy of things, as from some vestiges of poetic language extant in the writings of Moses. The first instance occurs in one of the most remote periods of the Mosaic history—I mean the address of Lamech to his wives, which is indeed but ill understood in general, because the occasion of it is very obscurely intimated; nevertheless, if we consider the apt construction of the words, the exact distribution of the period into three distichs, and the two parallel, and as it

money: that which is good and lawful is generally current and well known, and passes sometimes at a higher and sometimes at a lower value. Thus there was a time when the stamp and coin of all reasoning or composition was verse and song. Even history, philosophy, every action and passion which required grave or serious discussion, was written in poetry, and adapted to music. For what at present few will attend to, was then by all men thought an object of importance; *by ploughmen* and *by bird-catchers,* according to Pindar. For, such was the inclination for poetry at that period, that they adapted their very precepts and instructions to vocal and instrumental music, and exhorted, reproved, and persuaded by fables or allegories. The praises also of their gods, their prayers and thanksgivings after victory, were all composed in verse; some through the love of harmony, and some through custom. It is not therefore that Apollo envies the science of divination this ornament, nor did he design to banish from the Tripos his beloved Muse ; he rather wished to introduce her as one who loved harmony and excited to it ; as one who was ready to assist the fancy and conception, and to help to produce what was noble and sublime, as most becoming and most to be admired." Plut. *Inquiry, why the Pythia now ceases to deliver her oracles in verse.—Author's Note.*

See this subject treated at large, *Essays historical and moral,* by G. Gregory, Essay I. *On the Progress of Manners,* p. 81. 37. 39, 40. 43.—T.

* See Chardin's *Travels,* vol. ii. c. 14. Pocock, *Spec. Hist. Arab.* p. 158.

† We may add, that poetry is much less liable to be corrupted than prose. So faithful a preserver of truth is metre, that what is liable to be changed, augmented, or violated, almost daily in prose, may continue for ages in verse, without variation, without even a change in the obsolete phraseology.—M.

were corresponding sentiments in each distich, I apprehend it will easily be acknowledged an indubitable specimen
of the poetry of the first ages:

> " Hadah and Sillah, hear my voice;
> Ye wives of Lamech, hearken to my speech:
> For I have slain a man, because of my wounding;
> A young man, because of my hurt.
> If Cain shall be avenged* seven times,
> Certainly Lamech seventy and seven."†

* " If the murder of Cain shall be avenged."—That is, " If vengeance sevenfold
shall fall upon the head of him that murders Cain, then vengeance seventy times
seven shall fall on him that murders Lamech." Agreeably to what is pronounced
by God in the 15th verse of the same chapter, " Whosoever slaith Cain, vengeance
shall be taken on him sevenfold."—T.

† Gen. iv. 23, 24. The Jews have indulged great liberty of fiction and conjecture concerning this passage, which has answered no other purpose than to
render it more perplexed to others also, who were unable to digest their whimsical
and absurd explications. To me there is very little obscurity in the original; for
though we are necessarily ignorant of the name of the person who was murdered, I
think it is sufficiently plain that some person was murdered by Lamech. I say
person; for what the Jews have feigned concerning the death of two persons, the
one a youth, and the other a man, proceeds entirely from their ignorance of the
nature of the Hebrew poetry, and particularly of the parallelism or repetition of
certain members of the sentences, which our Author has explained in a very masterly manner in the 19th Lecture. Now is there any more reason to distinguish
between the youth and the man, than to suppose Hadah and Sillah other than the
wives of Lamech who are mentioned in the next line:

> " Hadah and Sillah, hear my voice;
> Ye wives of Lamech, attend," &c.

The truth is, Lamech had committed a murder; he repents of the fact, but hopes,
after the example of Cain, to escape with impunity, and with that hope he cheers
his wives, who are anxious for his fate. It is not to be supposed that he addressed
them in verse; the substance of what he said has been reduced to numbers for
the sake of preserving it easily in the memory. This poem therefore constitutes
a part of the history known to the Israelites; and Moses intimates to what Lamech
it relates, namely, not to the Son of Seth, the father of Noah, but to this Lamech
of the seed of Cain: What he adds is to this effect: " This Lamech, who was of
the seed of Cain, is the same who complained to his wives in those well-known traditional verses," &c.
   That Moses has preserved many relics of this kind, is evident from the fragments
of verse which are scattered throughout his writings, and which are very distinguishable from his usual language. Such is that which he relates, Gen. iii. 24, of
the Cherubs placed at the east of the garden of Eden; under which appellation I
understand to be meant, not angels, but the *Equi tonantes* of the Greek and Latin
poets; the reasons for which opinion I have more fully explained in the Commentaries of the Royal Society at Gottingen, T. i. p. 175. The passage is without doubt
poetical: " He placed before the garden Cherubim *(thundering horses)* and a flaming
sword, to keep the way of the tree of life;" in plain terms, the dread of the frequent tempests and daily thunders deterred men from that track in which Paradise
was situated, lest they should eat of the tree of life.—M.

Another example which I shall point out to you, appears no less to bear the genuine marks of poetry than the former;

The former part of the 23rd verse is thus translated by Houbigant:

"I, being wounded, have slain a man,
Being assaulted, a young man."

This translation is ingenious, and I think right : But even it seems to want some further explanation as well as confirmation; which, since he has omitted, I will attempt. The speech of Lamech is an apology for an homicide committed in his own defence, upon some man who violently assaulted him, and it appears struck and wounded him. An homicide in this nature he opposes to the voluntary and inexcusable fratricide of Cain. The phrases which produce the obscurity—*Le-petzangi*, and *Le-chaburathi*, "because of my wound," that is, *a wound which was given me*, and "because of my blows, (or stripes,)" that is, *stripes inflicted upon me*, may, I think, be explained as follows. The affixes to nouns (as Kimchius observes on Isa. xxi. 2) are taken actively as well as passively : thus *Chamasi*, "my violence, or injury," means *a violence committed against me*, Gen. xvi. 31. Jer. li. 35. *Chamas Beni Jehoudah*, "the violence of the sons of Judah," Joel iv. 19. *Chamas Eretz*, "the violence of the land," means *that which they have suffered*. "My servant shall justify many, *Be-deangtli*, in his knowledge," that is, *in their knowledge of him*, Isa. liii. 11. *Reangecha*, "thy thoughts," mean *thoughts concerning thee*, Psalm cxxxix. 17. The preposition ל (*le*) frequently means *because* : "The ships then went to Ophir, *Le-zahab*, because (or for the sake) of gold," 1 Kings xxii. 48. *Le-abiv ve-le-emou*, &c. "because of his father, or because of his mother, or because of his brother, or because of his sister, he shall not pollute himself," Numb. vi. 7. See more in Noldius ad ל, No. 28.—*Author's Note.*

There is nothing in the context to induce a suspicion that Lamech had committed a murder. By taking to himself *two* wives, he first violated the Divine institution of marriage. Such an offence was likely to draw upon him the resentment of his kindred, expose him to a particular quarrel (perhaps with his brother), and fill his wives with fear lest he should be provoked to follow the example of Cain. To remove therefore their apprehensions, he thus expostulates with them, contrasting the offences of polygamy and murder :

Hadah and Sillah, hear my voice;
Ye wives of Lamech, attend to my speech :
Have I slain a man in my contest?
Yea, one born among my kindred ?
If Cain shall be avenged seven times,
Assuredly shall Lamech seventy times seven.

כי in various instances is used interrogatively; 1 Sam. xxiv. 20. 2 Kings xviii. 34. Isa. xxix. 16. Prov. xxx. 4, &c. לפצעי, *in my division* or strife, from פצע, *scidit :* but if the derivative be referred to the secondary sense, *vulneravit*—it may in that case be rendered, *from my wound*, or *the wound that I have inflicted.* ילד signifies *a son*, or *person born*, and ו very frequently occurs in the sense of *yea*, חברת is, in various passages, equivalent to *union*, *alliance*, *affinity*. (In Mal. ii. 14, the same term is applied to *the marriage union.*)—*One born among my kindred* may be considered as synonymous with *my brother.* — S. H.

I did not, however, think myself at liberty to depart, in the text, from that of our Author, though I think this explication exceedingly ingenious. The reader may, for further information on this subject, consult Dawson's Translation of Genesis, c. iv. —T.

and that is, the execration of Noah upon Ham; with the magnificent predictions of prosperity to his two brothers, to Shem in particular, and the ardent breathings of his soul for their future happiness: These are expressed in three equal divisions of verses, concluding with an indignant repetition of one of the preceding lines:

> " Cursed be Canaan !
> A servant of servants to his brothers let him be !
> Blessed be JEHOVAH the God of Shem !
> And let Canaan be their servant.
> May God extend Japheth,
> And may he dwell in the tents of Shem !
> And let Canaan be their servant."*

The inspired benedictions of the patriarchs Isaac and Jacob are altogether of the same kind;† and the great importance of these prophecies, not only to the destiny of the people of Israel, but to that of the whole human race, renders it highly probable that they were extant in this form before the time of Moses; and that they were afterwards committed to writing by the inspired historian, exactly as he had received them from his ancestors, without presuming to bestow on these sacred oracles any adventitious ornaments or poetical colouring.

The matter will appear yet clearer, if we advert to some other verses, a little different in kind, to which the same historian appeals (as well-known and popular) in testimony of the truth of his narration. Thus, when he relates the first incursion of the Israelites into the country of the Amorites, in order to mark more precisely the boundaries of that state, and to explain more satisfactorily the nature of the victories not long before achieved over the Moabites, he cites two fragments of poems; the one from the book of the Wars of Jehovah,‡ the other from the Sayings (*Mashalim*) of those who spoke in parables;§ that is, as appears

---

* Gen. ix. 25—27.   † Gen. xxvii. 27—29. 39, 40.
‡ Numb. xxi. 14, 15.
§ Ibid. 27—30. Compare Jer. xlviii. 45, 46. Αινιγματιϲαι (*ainigmatistai*), Sept. " Who these *Enigmatists* are (says Augustin) is not very plain, since there is no such appellation in our language (Latin); nor indeed is the word elsewhere found in the Holy Scriptures, (that is, in the Septuagint ;) but since they seem to have been employed in singing a poem, in which was celebrated a war that had been carried on between the Amorites and the Moabites, in which Seor king of the Amorites was victorious, it is not improbable that these Enigmatists may have been those whom we now call poets; inasmuch as it is customary with poets to mingle

from the nature of things, from some panegyrical or triumphal poem of the Amorites. To which we may add, what immediately follow, the prophecies of Balaam the Mesopotamian, pronounced also in the parabolic style; as appears from the extreme neatness of the composition, the metrical and parallel sentences, the sublimity of the language and sentiment, and the uncommon elegance of the verse. Hence it is easy to collect, that this kind of poetry, which appears perfectly analogous to all the rest of the Hebrew poetry that still remains, was neither originally the production of Moses, nor peculiar to the Jewish nation; but that it may be accounted among the first-fruits of human ingenuity, and was cultivated by the Hebrews and other Eastern nations from the first ages, as the recorder of events, the preceptor of morals, the historian of the past, and prophet of the future.*

Concerning the utility of poetry, therefore, the Hebrews have maintained the same opinion throughout all ages; this being always accounted the highest commendation of science and erudition, " To understand a proverb and the interpretation; the words of the wise and their dark sayings :"† under which titles two species of poetry seem to be particularly indicated, different indeed in many respects, yet agreeing in some. The one I call *didactic*, which expresses some moral precept in elegant and pointed verses, often illustrated

---

enigmas and fables in their verses, by which they obscurely indicate realities; for an enigma is no other than a figurative mode of expression, upon the explanation of which depends our understanding the author." Quæst. xlv. in Numb.—*Author's Note.*

This matter will appear clearer and more easy of conception, if the distinction be rightly observed between the two different significations of the word *Mashal*: the one more comprehensive, and including all kinds of poetry, on account of the figurative language; the other peculiar to a certain kind of poetry, which is opposed to the canticle or song. Our author, in the following page, seems to apprehend rightly of the word in this double sense; but I thus far differ from him, that I think it is not expressive of two particular species of poetry, but in the one sense it means the whole genus, and in the other the particular species, which I have just, now pointed out. The LXX have rendered this word very ill, αινιγματιϛας. *Mashal*, or *similitude*, may indeed sometimes denote an enigma; and if Augustin has mistaken the meaning of the Septuagint, it is excusable, since, whatever might be his ability in other respects, a profound knowledge of Hebrew was certainly not among his excellences.—M.

* To the above examples from the books of Moses add the following: Gen. xxi. 6, 7; xxiv. 60; xxv. 23; xxviii. 16, 17. Observe also whether the answer of God, Numb. xii. 6—8, be not of the same kind.—*Author's Note.*

† See Prov. i. 6. Wisd. viii. 8. Ecclus. i. 25; vi. 35; xviii. 29; xxxix. 1, 2, 3.

by a comparison either direct or implied; similar to the γνωμαι (gnomai) and adages of the wise men: The other was truly poetical, adorned with all the more splendid colouring of language, magnificently sublime in the sentiments, animated by the most pathetic expression, and diversified and embellished by figurative diction and poetical imagery; such are almost all the remaining productions of the prophets. Brevity or conciseness was a characteristic of each of these forms of composition, and a degree of obscurity was not unfrequently attendant upon this studied brevity. Each consisted of metrical sentences; on which account chiefly the poetic and proverbial language seems to have obtained the same appellation: and in these two kinds of composition, all knowledge human and divine was thought to be comprised.

The sententious style, therefore, I define to be the primary characteristic of the Hebrew poetry, as being the most conspicuous and comprehensive of all. For although that style seems naturally adapted only to the didactic, yet it is found to pervade the whole of the poetry of the Hebrews. There are indeed many passages in the sacred writings highly figurative and infinitely sublime, but all of them manifestly assume a sententious form. There are some too, and those not inelegant, which possess little more of the characteristics of poetry than the versification, and that terseness or adaptation of the sentences which constitutes so important a part even of the harmony of verse. This is manifest in most of the didactic psalms, as well as in some others, the matter, order, diction, and thoughts of which are clearly historical, but the conformation of the sentences wholly poetical. There is indeed so strict an analogy between the structure of the sentences and the versification, that when the former chances to be confused or obscured, it is scarcely possible to form a conjecture concerning the division of the lines or verses, which is almost the only part of the Hebrew versification that remains. It was therefore necessary, before I could explain the mechanism of the Hebrew verse, to remark many particulars which properly belong to the present topic.

The reason of this (not to detain you with what is obvious in almost every page of the sacred poetry) is as follows. The Hebrew poets frequently express a sentiment with the utmost brevity and simplicity, illustrated by no circumstances, adorned with no epithets, (which in truth they sel-

dom use;) they afterwards call in the aid of ornament; they
repeat, they vary, they amplify the same sentiment; and
adding one or more sentences which run parallel to each
other, they express the same or a similar, and often a contrary sentiment, in nearly the same form of words. Of these
three modes of ornament, at least, they make the most frequent use, namely the amplification of the same ideas, the
accumulation of others, and the opposition or antithesis of
such as are contrary to each other: they dispose the corresponding sentences in regular distichs adapted to each other,
and of an equal length, in which, for the most part, things
answer to things, and words to works, as the Son of Sirach
says of the works of God, *two and two, one against the other.**
These forms are again diversified by notes of admiration,
comparison, negation, and more particularly interrogation;
whence a singular degree of force and elevation is frequently
added to the composition.

Each language possesses a peculiar genius and character,
on which depend the principles of the versification, and in
a great measure the style or colour of the poetic diction.
In Hebrew, the frequent, or rather perpetual, splendour of
the sentences, and the accurate recurrence of the clauses,
seem absolutely necessary to distinguish the verse: so that
what in any other language would appear a superfluous and
tiresome repetition, in this cannot be omitted without injury
to the poetry. This excellence, therefore, the sententious
style possesses in the Hebrew poetry, that it necessarily pre-
vents a prosaic mode of expression, and always reduces a
composition to a kind of metrical form. For, as Cicero
remarks, "in certain forms of expression there exists such
a degree of conciseness, that a sort of metrical arrangement
follows of course. For, when words or sentences directly
correspond, or when contraries are opposed exactly to each
other, or even when words of a similar sound run parallel,
the composition will in general have a metrical cadence."†
It possesses, however, great force in other respects, and produces several great and remarkable beauties of composition.
For, as the sacred poems derive from this source a great
part of their elegance, harmony, and splendour, so they are
not unfrequently indebted to it for their sublimity and
strength. Frequent and laconic sentences render the composition remarkably concise, harmonious, and animated;

* Eccles. xxxiii. 15.   † Orator.

D

the brevity itself imparts to it additional strength, and being contracted within a narrower space, it has a more energetic and pointed effect.

Examples sufficient to evince the truth of these remarks will occur hereafter in the passages which will be quoted in illustration of other parts of our subject; and, in all probability, on a future occasion the nature of my undertaking will require a more ample discussion of this subject.*

* See Lect. 19.

LECTURE V.

OF THE FIGURATIVE STYLE, AND ITS DIVISIONS.

2. *The Figurative Style ; to be treated rather according to the genius of the Hebrew poetry than according to the forms and arrangements of Rhetoricians—The definition and constituent parts of the Figurative Style,* METAPHOR, ALLEGORY, COMPARISON, PERSONIFICATION—*The reason of this mode of treating the subject : difficulties in reading the Hebrew poetry which result from the Figurative Style ; how to be avoided.* 1. *Of the* METAPHOR, *including a general disquisition concerning poetic imagery ; the nature of which is explained ; and four principal sources pointed out,—Nature, Common Life, Religion, History.*

In my last Lecture I offered it as my opinion, that the Hebrew word expressive of the poetic style had not one simple and distinct meaning, but might commodiously enough be supposed to admit of three constituent parts or divisions: in other words, that it might imply the *sententious,* the *figurative,* and the *sublime.* On the sententious style, its nature, origin, and effect in the Hebrew poetry, I offered such brief remarks as occurred to me at the time: and now that I am about to treat of the figurative style, I observe before me an infinity of matter and an ample field; in which, lest we should too freely expatiate, or irregularly wander, the scope and order of our journey, the outlets of the road, the circuitous paths, and the most direct avenues, are in the first place to be carefully investigated. In order to the full comprehension also of those matters which will be treated of in this part, for they are in some degree remote from common use, it may not be improper previously to explain as clearly as possible, and therefore with some degree of copiousness, my immediate design ; on what principles, in what order and method, and to what end, I mean to treat of the figures which are chiefly employed in the Hebrew poetry.

The word *Mashal,* in its most common acceptation, denotes resemblance, and is therefore directly expressive of the figurative style, as far as the nature of figures consists in the substitution of words, or rather of ideas, for those which they resemble; which is the case even with most of the figures that have been remarked by the rhetoricians. This definition, therefore, of the figurative style, drawn both from the writings of the Hebrews, and the sense of the word itself, I mean to follow in explaining the nature of their poetry; and this I do the more willingly, because it will enable me to confine our investigation within narrower limits. I shall also venture to omit the almost innumerable forms of the Greek rhetoricians, who possessed the faculty of inventing names in the highest perfection; I shall neglect even their primary distinction between tropes and figures,* and their subdivisions of the figures themselves, denominating some Figures of expression, and some Figures of sentiment. In disregarding these distinctions, I might in my own justification allege the authority of C. Artorius Proculus, who gave the name of *figure* to a trope, as Quintilian informs us; and indeed, the example of Quintilian himself.† I omit them, however, upon a different ground, for I do not pretend to say that in their proper place they are destitute either of reality or use; but our present concern is, not to explain the sentiments of the Greek, but of the Hebrew writers. By figurative language I would be understood to mean, that in which one or more images or words are substituted in the room of others, or even introduced by way of illustration upon a principle of resemblance. That resemblance, if it be only intimated, and confined to a few words, is called a *Metaphor ;* if the figure be continued, it is called an *Allegory ;* if it be directly expressed by comparing the ideas together, and by the insertion of any words expressive of likeness, it is called *Simile* or *Comparison.*‡

---

* This distinction is very judiciously laid aside, since each of these words is but a partial mode of expressing the same thing. A *trope* signifies no more than the *turning* a word from its appropriate meaning; and a *figure*, an appearance incidentally assumed, without the least implication of its being borrowed.— S. H.

† See Quint. lib. ix. 1.

‡ *Comparison* appears to be the first and most natural of all rhetorical figures. When at a loss to explain our meaning, we naturally apply to the associating principle to furnish an illustration : and this seems almost an involuntary act of the mind. A *metaphor* is a comparison, without the words indicating resemblance. When a savage experienced a sensation, for which he had as yet no name, he applied that of the idea which most resembled it, in order to explain himself. Thus the words expressing the faculties of the mind are taken from sensible

On the same principle of resemblance the *Prosopopœia*, or Personification, is also founded, when a character and person is assigned even to things inanimate or fictitious, (which is a bolder species of metaphor,) or when a probable but fictitious speech is attributed to a real personage.

I mean, therefore, to treat of these figures in the order just now proposed; not as supposing them the only figures made use of by the Hebrew poets,* but, in the first place,

images, as *fancy* from *phantasma; idea* in the original language means an *image* or *picture;* and a *way* has always been used to express the mode of attaining our *end* or *desire.*

There is, however, another reason for the use of metaphorical language : when the mind is agitated, the associations are more strongly felt, and the connected ideas will more readily present themselves than at another time. On this account, a man in a passion will frequently reject the words which simply express his thoughts; and, for the sake of giving them more force, will make use of images stronger, more lively, and more congenial to the tone of his mind.

The principal advantages which the metaphor possesses over the simile or comparison, seems to consist in the former transporting the mind and carrying it nearer to the reality than the latter; as when we say, " Achilles rushed like a lion," we have only the idea of a man going on furiously to battle; but when we say, instead of Achilles, " The lion rushed on," the idea is more animated. There is also more of brevity in a style that abounds in metaphors, than in a style which consists more of comparisons; and therefore it proves a better vehicle for the sublime.

The rule which good writers seem to have adopted respecting the use of similes or metaphors is this : Where the resemblance is very strong and obvious, it may be expressed by a simple metaphor, and it will in general be expressed more forcibly; but when the resemblance is not so obvious, it requires to be more expanded, and then a comparison or simile will neither appear formal nor pompous.

There is another observation concerning the use of these figures, which is more common, though I do not think the reason of it is generally understood. Comparisons are unnatural in extremes of *passion,* though metaphors are not. The truth is, the mind when strongly agitated readily catches at slight associations, and metaphors therefore are instantaneously formed; but it is impossible that the mind should dwell upon them with the formality and exactness of a person making a comparison.—T.

* To the figures specified by our author, rhetoricians have added innumerable others of less importance. The principal of these, and the most connected with poetry, are *metonymy, periphrasis, apostrophe,* and *hyperbole.*

In order to explain the nature and origin of these and the other tropes or figures, I must remind the reader, that the associating principle is the true source of all figurative language. I must also remind him, that all ideas are associated or introduced into the mind by one of these three relations—*contiguity in time and place, cause and effect,* or *resemblance.* On the latter of these relations depend *comparisons, metaphors, allegories,* &c.; and on the other relations depend the *metonymy,* the *periphrasis,* the *prosopopœia,* and probably the *apostrophe.*

The word *Metonymy* evidently means a *change of name,* an adoption of some other mark to signify an idea, than that which was originally assigned it. This figure, therefore, is most frequently derived from the relation of *cause and effect,*

because they chiefly come within the definition of the parabolic style; because, too, they most frequently occur in the
sacred poetry, and constitute some of its greatest beauties;
insomuch that their true force and energy is in no other
compositions so apparent.   I must add, that it will not be
sufficient to illustrate them barely by producing a few examples, as if matters uncommon and abstruse were the object of our inquiry, and not such as spontaneously occur on
almost every occasion: it will be necessary to proceed still
further, if possible; it will be necessary to inquire whether
there was any mode of using them peculiar to the Hebrews;
the particular and interior elegancies of them are to be investigated: and to this object of our pursuit we shall not, I

and sometimes from that of contiguity: thus we substitute the cause for the effect,
when we say, "We have read Pope," for "the works of Pope;" and the effect for
the cause, when we say, "The day arose," for "the sun arose." For further illustration I refer to Dr. Priestley's *Institutes of Oratory and Criticism*, p. 238. The
Periphrasis is little else than a species of Metonymy, as, "the lover of Daphne,"
for Apollo. For the connexion between the Metonymy and the Prosopopœia, see
a note on the 13th Lecture. The *Apostrophe* is a more animated Prosopopœia,
when the thing personified is spoken to in the second person, or a distant person or
thing is addressed as present. A most beautiful and pathetic instance is that of
Eve, *Paradise Lost*, B. ii., v. 269.
    The *Hyperbole* is nothing more than an excess of figurative language, the effect of
passion. All the passions are inclined to magnify the objects. Injuries seem
greater than they really are to those who have received them; and dangers, to those
who are in fear. The lover naturally makes a divinity of his mistress: valour and
contempt are equally inclined to degrade and diminish. This figure, therefore, in
particular, requires passion to give it force or propriety; and if this be not the case,
it renders a style very bombastic and frigid. Lucan is too fond of this figure. See
the first six lines of Rowe's Lucan, where "The Sun—

          "—— sicken'd to behold Emathia's plain,
           And would have sought the backward East again."

And in B. vi., v. 329,

          "The missive arms fix'd all around he wears,
           And even his safety in his wounds he bears,
           Fenc'd with a fatal wood—a deadly grove of spears."

Nothing, indeed, can be more bombastic than the whole description of this
warrior's death. The poet calls upon the Pompeians to lay siege to him as
they would to a town; to bring battering-engines, flames, racks, &c., to subdue
him. He is first compared to an elephant, and again to a hunted boar; at
length—

          "—— when none were left him to repel,
           Fainting for want of foes the victor fell."

Some of the extravagance of the above may, however, be the fault of the translator,
but how far I could not determine, as I have not the original by me; nor is it of
any consequence to the English reader.—T.

apprehend, find any easier access, than by that track which the nature of the subject itself obviously indicates to us.

It is the peculiar design of the figurative style, taken in the sense in which I have explained it, to exhibit objects in a clearer or more striking, in a sublimer or more forcible manner. Since, therefore, whatever is employed with a view to the illustration and elevation of another subject, ought itself to be as familiar and obvious, at the same time as grand and magnificent as possible, it becomes necessary to adduce images from those objects with which both the writers and the persons they address are well acquainted, and .which have been constantly esteemed of the highest dignity and importance. On the other hand, if the reader be accustomed to habits of life totally different from those of the author, and be conversant only with different objects; in that case, many descriptions and sentiments, which were clearly illustrated and magnificently expressed by the one, will appear to the other mean and obscure, harsh and unnatural: and this will be the case more or less, in proportion as they differ, or are more remote from each other in time, situation, customs, sacred or profane; in fine, in all the forms of public and private life. On this account difficulties must occur in the perusal of almost every work of literature, and particularly in poetry, where every thing is depicted and illustrated with the greatest variety and abundance of imagery: they must be still more numerous in such of the poets as are foreign and ancient; in the orientals above all foreigners, they being the farthest removed from our customs and manners; and of all the orientals, more especially in the Hebrews, theirs being confessedly the most ancient compositions extant. To all who apply themselves to the study of their poetry, for the reasons which I have enumerated, difficulties and inconveniences must necessarily occur. Not only the antiquity of these writings forms a principal obstruction in many respects; but the manner of living, of speaking, of thinking, which prevailed in those times, will be found altogether different from our customs and habits. There is, therefore, great danger, lest, viewing them from an improper situation, and rashly estimating all things by our own standard, we form an erroneous judgment.

Of this kind of mistake we are to be always aware, and these inconveniences are to be counteracted by all possible diligence: nor is it enough to be acquainted with the language of this people, their manners, discipline, rites, and ceremonies; we must even investigate their inmost sentiments, the manner and connexion of their thoughts; in one word, we must see all things with their eyes, estimate all things by their opinions; we must endeavour as much as possible to read Hebrew as the Hebrews would have read it. We must act as the astronomers with regard to that branch of their science which is called comparative, who, in order to form a more perfect idea of the general system and its different parts, conceive themselves as passing through and surveying the whole universe, migrating from one planet to another, and becoming for a short time inhabitants of each. Thus they clearly contemplate, and accurately estimate, what each possesses peculiar to itself, with respect to situation, celerity, satellites, and its relation to the rest: thus they distinguish what and how different an appearance of the universe is exhibited, according to the different situations from which it is contemplated. In like manner, he who would perceive and feel the peculiar and interior elegances of the Hebrew poetry, must imagine himself exactly situated as the persons for whom it was written, or even as the writers themselves: he must not attend to the ideas which, on a cursory reading, certain words would obtrude upon his mind; he is to feel them as a Hebrew hearing or delivering the same words, at the same time, and in the same country. As far as he is able to pursue this plan, so far he will comprehend their force and excellence. This, indeed, in many cases it will not be easy to do; in some it will be impossible; in all, however, it ought to be regarded, and in those passages particularly in which the figurative style is found to prevail.

In Metaphor, for instance, (and what I remark concerning it may be applied to all the rest of the figures, since they are all naturally allied to each other,) two circumstances are to be especially regarded, on which its whole force and elegance will depend: first, that resemblance which is the groundwork of the figurative and parabolic style, and which will perhaps be sufficiently apparent even from a common and indistinct knowledge of the objects; and, secondly, the beauty or dignity of the idea which is substituted for another; and this is a circumstance of unusual nicety. An opinion of grace and dignity results frequently, not so much from the objects themselves in which these qualities are supposed to exist, as from the disposition of the spectator; or from some slight and obscure relation or connexion which they have with some other things. Thus it sometimes happens, that the external form and lineaments may be sufficiently apparent, though the original and intrinsic beauty and elegance be totally erased by time.

For these reasons it will perhaps not be an useless undertaking, when we treat of the metaphors of the sacred poets, to enter more fully into the nature of their poetical imagery in general, of which the metaphor constitutes so principal a part. By this mode of proceeding we shall be enabled, not only to discern the general beauty and elegance of this figure in the Hebrew poetry, but the peculiar elegance which it frequently possesses, if we only consider how forcible it must have appeared to those for whom it was originally intended, and what a connexion and agreement these figurative expressions must have had with their circumstances, feelings, and opinions. Thus many expressions and allusions, which even now appear beautiful, must, when considered in this manner, shine with redoubled lustre; and many, which now strike the superficial reader as coarse, mean, or deformed, must appear graceful, elegant, and sublime.

The whole course of nature, this immense universe of things, offers itself to human contemplation, and affords an infinite variety, a confused assemblage, a wilderness as it were of images, which, being collected as the materials of poetry, are selected and produced as occasion dictates. The mind of man is that mirror of Plato,* which, as he turns about at pleasure, and directs to a different point of view, he creates another sun, other stars, planets, animals, and even another self. In this shadow or image of himself, which man beholds when the mirror is turned inward towards himself, he is enabled in some degree to contemplate the souls of other men ; for, from what he feels and perceives in himself, he forms conjectures concerning others; and apprehends and describes the manners, affections, conceptions of others from his own. Of this assemblage of images, which the human mind collects from all nature, and even from itself, that is, from its own emotions and operations, the least clear and evident are those which are explored by reason and argument; the more evident and distinct are those which are

* De Rep. lib. x. sub init.

formed from the impressions made by external objects on the senses; and of these, the clearest and most vivid are those which are perceived by the eye. Hence poetry abounds most in those images which are furnished by the senses, and chiefly those of the sight, in order to depict the obscure by the more manifest, the subtile by the more substantial; and, as far as simplicity is its object, it pursues those ideas which are most familiar and most evident, of which there is such an abundance, that they serve as well the purpose of ornament and variety, as that of illustration.

Those images or pictures of external objects which like lights adorn and distinguish the poetic diction, are indeed infinite in number. In an immensity of matter, however, that we may be enabled to pursue some kind of order, and not wander in uncertainty and doubt, we may venture to fix upon four sources of these ideas, whither all that occur may be commodiously referred. Thus, poetical imagery may be derived, first, from natural objects; secondly, from the manners, arts, and circumstances of common life; thirdly, from things sacred; and, lastly, from the more remarkable facts recorded in sacred history. From each of these topics a few cases will be selected, and illustrated by examples, which, though chiefly of the metaphorical kind, will yet be in a great measure applicable to the other figures which have been specified. These we shall afterwards take an opportunity to explain, when not only the figures themselves will be noticed, but also the different forms and rules for their introduction and embellishment.

LECTURE VI.

OF POETIC IMAGERY FROM THE OBJECTS OF NATURE.

The frequent use of the Metaphor renders a style magnificent, but often obscure : the Hebrew poets have accomplished the sublime without losing perspicuity—Three causes assigned for this singular fact : first, the imagery which they introduce is in general derived from familiar objects : again, in the use and accommodation of it they pursue a certain custom and analogy : lastly, they make the most free use of that which is most familiar, and the nature and extent of which is most generally known. These observations confirmed by examples (1.) from natural objects : such as are common to mankind in general ; such as are more familiar to the Hebrews than to others ; and such as are peculiar to them.

" THE great excellence of the poetic dialect," as Aristotle most judiciously remarks, " consists in perspicuity without meanness. Familiar terms and words in common use form a clear and conspicuous, but frequently a low style ; unusual or foreign expressions give it an air of grandeur, but frequently render it obscure." * Of those which he calls foreign, the principal force lies in the metaphor ;. but " as the temperate and reasonable use of this figure enlivens a composition, so the frequent introduction of metaphors obscures it, and if they very commonly occur, it will be little better than an enigma." † If the Hebrew poets be examined by the rules and precepts of this great philosopher and critic, it will readily be allowed that they have assiduously attended to the sublimity of their compositions by the abundance and splendour of their figures, though it may be doubted whether they might not have been more temperate in the use of them.

---

* Poet. c. 22. Modern writers are hardly aware of the ill consequences of what is called far-fetched imagery, or that which is taken from objects not generally known. This was the great error of Cowley, and the metaphysical poets of the last century ; an error for which no beauties can compensate, which always gives a harshness, often a prosaic appearance, to poetry, and never fails to be attended with some degree of obscurity.—T.

† Ib. and Quint. viii. 6.

For in those poems, at least, in which something of uncommon grandeur and sublimity is aimed at, there predominates a perpetual, I had almost said a continued use of the metaphor, sometimes daringly introduced, sometimes rushing in with imminent hazard of propriety. A metaphor thus licentiously intruded, is frequently continued to an immoderate extent. The Orientals are attached to this style of composition; and many flights which our ears, too fastidious perhaps in these respects, will scarcely bear, must be allowed to the general freedom and boldness of these writers. But if we examine the sacred poems, and consider at the same time that a great degree of obscurity must result from the total oblivion in which many sources of their imagery must be involved; of which many examples are to be found in the Song of Solomon, as well as in other parts of the sacred writings; we shall I think find cause to wonder, that in writings of so great antiquity, and in such an unlimited use of figurative expression, there should yet appear so much purity and perspicuity, both in sentiment and language. In order to explore the real cause of this remarkable fact, and to explain more accurately the genius of the parabolic style, I shall premise a few observations concerning the use of the metaphor in the Hebrew poetry; which I trust will be sufficiently clear to those who peruse them with attention, and which I think in general are founded in truth.

In the first place, the Hebrew poets frequently make use of imagery borrowed from common life, and from objects well known and familiar. On this the perspicuity of figurative language will be found in a great measure to depend; for a principal use of metaphors is to illustrate the subject by a tacit comparison; but if, instead of familiar ideas, we introduce such as are new, and not perfectly understood; if we endeavour to demonstrate what is plain by what is occult, instead of making a subject clearer, we render it more perplexed and difficult. To obviate this inconvenience, we must take care, not only to avoid the violent and too frequent use of metaphors, but also not to introduce such as are obscure and but slightly related. From these causes, and especially from the latter, arises the difficulty of the Latin satirist Persius; and but for the uncommon accuracy of the sacred poets in this respect, we should now be scarcely able to comprehend a single word of their productions.

In the next place, the Hebrews not only deduce their metaphors from familiar or well-known objects, but preserve one constant track and manner in the use and accommodation of them to their subject. The parabolic may indeed be accounted a peculiar style, in which things moral, political, and divine, are marked and represented by comparisons implied or expressed, and adopted from sensible objects. As in common and plain language, therefore, certain words serve for signs of certain ideas, so, for the most part, in the parabolic style, certain natural images serve to illustrate certain ideas more abstruse and refined. This assertion, indeed, is not to be understood absolutely without exception; but thus far at least we may affirm, that the sacred poets, in illustrating the same subject, make a much more constant use of the same imagery than other poets are accustomed to: and this practice has a surprising effect in preserving perspicuity.

I must observe, in the last place, that the Hebrews employ more freely and more daringly that imagery in particular which is borrowed from the most obvious and familiar objects, and the figurative effect of which is established and defined by general and constant use. This, as it renders a composition clear and luminous, even where there is the greatest danger of obscurity; so it shelters effectually the sacred poets from the imputation of exuberance, harshness, or bombast.*

In order to confirm and illustrate by examples what has been briefly set forth in the preceding remarks, I shall proceed to consider a few instances of metaphors derived from natural objects†, and such as are most in use: this I shall

---

* It is very observable in our own as well as other languages, how much metaphors lose of the figurative sense by repetition; and it is curious to remark how metaphors are in this manner derived from one another. From the resemblance of a narrow bed of metal running in the earth, to the situation of a vein in the human body, it has taken that name; and hence, I apprehend, are derived the expressions, a *vein of poetry*, a *vein of humour*, &c. – T.

† The frequent recurrence for metaphorical expressions to natural objects, and particularly to plants and to trees, is so characteristic of the Hebrew poetry, that it might be almost called the *botanical* poetry. This circumstance, however, is not at all extraordinary, if we consider that the greater part of that people were occupied with tilling the earth, and keeping their flocks; and further, that the cultivation of poetry, instead of being confined to the learned, was so generally diffused, that every valley re-echoed the songs of the shepherds. Hence, in the very few remains of the Hebrew writings which are come down to us, I mean the Scriptures, there are

do in such a manner, that whatever observations occur upon
one or two of them, may be applied to many other instances.

The images of *light* and *darkness* are commonly made use
of in all languages to imply or denote prosperity and adversity, agreeably to the common sense and perception which
all men have of the objects themselves.   But the Hebrews
employ those metaphors more frequently, and with less variation, than other people : indeed they seldom refrain from
them whenever the subject requires, or will even admit of
their introduction.   These expressions, therefore, may be
accounted among those forms of speech which in the parabolic style are established and defined : since they exhibit the
most noted and familiar images, and the application of them
on this occasion is justified by an acknowledged analogy, and
approved by constant and unvarying custom.   In the use of
images, so conspicuous and so familiar among the Hebrews,
a degree of boldness is excusable.   The Latins introduce
them more sparingly, and therefore are more cautious in the
application of them :—

upwards of 250 botanical terms, which none use so frequently as the poets : and
this circumstance, I think, gives an air of pastoral elegance to their poetry, which
any modern writer will emulate in vain.

It is, however, extraordinary, that the stars should be so seldom mentioned in
the Hebrew poetry, for the names of not more than three or four occur in the whole
Bible.   It has been said, that the patriarchal shepherds applied very much to the
study of astronomy ; but if so, whence is it that we meet with such frequent allusions to botanical subjects, and so few to the heavenly luminaries?   A comet is,
however, I think, spoken of in Numbers xxiv. 17, and in allusion to David ; but it
is by Balaam, who, residing on the borders of the Euphrates, it is reasonable
to . suppose was not altogether unacquainted with the Babylonish sciences.
—M.

There appears but little foundation for this last remark of the learned Professor.
For, in reality, so little are the heavenly bodies subjects of poetic allusion, that we
find them but seldom introduced into any poetry, either ancient or modern.   Our
Annotator seems to forget that poetry is no more than painting in language, and
has not respect to names but appearances.   The appearance of every star is nearly
the same, and consequently they can furnish no great variety of imagery, and that
can only relate to their general qualities, their splendour, &c. ; whereas the nature
and visible qualities of plants are infinitely diversified, and therefore admit of a
much greater variety of allusion.   Indeed a poem, the principal imagery of which
consisted of the names of stars, would be a very strange and a very dull production.
We cannot, therefore, argue from the silence of the Hebrew poetry, that Moses or
the writers of the Scriptures were ignorant of astronomy ; neither is it fair to
suppose that a *nation of shepherds*, in the *serene country* of the East, were unacquainted with the *host of heaven*, which in truth, from these causes, were the
objects of adoration, and even of worship in those parts, as appears from the Preface
to Mr. Wood's *Account of the Ruins of Balbec.*—T.

"Restore, great Chief, thy country's light!
Dispel the dreary shades of night!
Thy aspect, like the spring, shall cheer,
And brighter suns shall gild the year."*

The most respectable of the Roman Muses have scarcely any thing more elegant—I will add at the same time, that they have scarcely any thing bolder—on any similar occasion. But the Hebrews, upon a subject more sublime indeed in itself, and illustrating it by an idea which was more habitual to them, more daringly exalt their strains, and give a loose rein to the spirit of poetry. They display, for instance, not the image of the Spring, of Aurora, of the dreary Night, but the Sun and Stars, as rising with increased splendour in a new creation, or again involved in chaos and primeval darkness. Does the sacred bard promise to his people a renewal of the Divine favour, and a recommencement of universal prosperity? In what magnificent colours does he depict it! such indeed as no translation can illustrate, but such as none can obscure:

"The light of the moon shall be as the light of the sun,†
And the light of the sun shall be sevenfold."‡

But even this is not sufficient:

" No longer shalt thou have the sun for thy light by day;
Nor by night shall the brightness of the moon enlighten thee :
For JEHOVAH shall be to thee an everlasting light,
And thy God shall be thy glory.
Thy sun shall no more decline,
Neither shall thy moon wane ;
For JEHOVAH shall be thine everlasting light ;
And the days of thy mourning shall cease."§

In another place he has admirably diversified the same sentiment:

---

* Hor. *Carm.* iv. 5.
† Hence Milton perhaps adopted his
——" another morning
Ris'n on midnoon," &c.—*Par. Lost*, v. 308.—S. H.
‡ Isa. xxx. 26. These and the following descriptions of the increased splendour of the sun and the stars, are not taken from natural objects, but from fable. The remarkable felicity of the people is compared with that golden age of which the prophets had acquired a knowledge from the Egyptians. Isaiah had expatiated very much upon this image, of which more in the Notes to the 9th Lecture. —M.
§ Isa. lx. 19, 20.

"And the moon shall be confounded, and the sun shall be
    ashamed;
For JEHOVAH God of Hosts shall reign
On Mount Sion, and in Jerusalem;
And before his ancients shall he be glorified."*

On the other hand, denouncing ruin against the proud
king of Egypt:

"And when I shall put thee out, I will cover the heavens,
    And the stars thereof will I make dark;
I will involve the sun in a cloud,
Nor shall the moon give out her light.
All the bright lights of heaven will I make dark over thee,
And I will set darkness upon thy land, saith the Lord JEHO-
    VAH."†

These expressions are bold and daring; but the imagery is
well known, the use of it is common, the signification definite; they are therefore perspicuous, clear, and truly magnificent.

There are, moreover, other images from natural objects,
which, although in some measure common to other nations
as well as the Hebrews, are nevertheless, from the situation
and nature of the country, much better known and more
familiar to them. There is no metaphor more frequent in
the sacred poems, than that by which sudden and great
calamities are expressed under the figure of a deluge of
waters. This metaphor seems to have been remarkably
familiar to the Hebrews, as if directly taken from the nature
and state of the country. The river Jordan was immediately
before their eyes,‡ which annually overflowed its banks; for
the snows of Lebanon and the neighbo ing mountains being
melted in the beginning of the summer, the waters of the
river were often suddenly augmented by the torrents which
burst forth from them. The whole country of Palestine§
indeed was watered by very few perennial currents; but,
being chiefly mountainous, was exposed to frequent floods,
rushing violently along the valleys and narrow passages,
after great tempests of rain, which periodically took place at
certain seasons: and on this account Moses ∥ himself com-
mends to the Israelites the country which they were about

* Isa. xxiv. 33.   † Ezek. xxxii. 7, 8.
‡ Josh. iii. 15; 1 Chron. xii. 15; Ecclus. xxiv. 26.
§ See Sandy's *Travels*, B. iii.   ∥ Deut. viii. 7. xi. 10, 11.

to invade, as being totally different from every thing they had experienced in Egypt, or in the Desert of Arabia. This image, therefore, though known to all poets, and adopted by most, may be accounted peculiarly familiar, local, in a manner, to the Hebrews; and of consequence we cannot wonder at its frequent introduction into their compositions. The prophet seems to have depicted the face of nature exactly as it appeared to him, and to have adapted it to the figurative description of his own situation, when from the banks of Jordan, and the mountains at the head of that river, he pours forth the tempestuous violence of his sorrow with a force of language and an energy of expression which has been seldom equalled;

" Deep calleth unto deep, in the voice of thy cataracts;
  All thy waves and thy billows have gone over me." *

It may not be improper to remark in this place, that though this metaphor is so usual in all the other sacred writers, whenever an occasion presents itself of introducing it, the author of Job, in the whole of that poem, which from the nature of the subject presented excellent opportunities of employing it, has not more than twice,† and then but slightly, made the least allusion to it. Nature, indeed, presented a different aspect to the author, whoever he was, of that most noble poem, if, as many learned men conjecture, it was composed in some part of Arabia—for which, I confess, there is great appearance of argument from that famous simile‡ in which he compares his friends with the perfidious brook; a comparison manifestly taken from the rocky parts of Arabia, and adorned by many images proper to that region.

Finally, there is a species of imagery, derived also from natural objects, altogether peculiar to the Hebrews. Among the mountains of Palestine, the most remarkable, and consequently the most celebrated in the sacred poetry, are Mount Lebanon and Mount Carmel: the one, remarkable as well for its height as for its age, magnitude, and the abundance of the cedars which adorned its summit, exhibiting a striking and substantial appearance of strength and majesty; the other, rich and fruitful, abounding with vines, olives, and delicious fruits, in a most flourishing state both by nature and cultivation, and displaying a delightful

---

* Psal. xcii. 8.   † See Job xxii. 11; xxvii. 20.   ‡ Job vi. 15—20

E

appearance of fertility, beauty, and grace.   The different
form and aspect of these two mountains is most accurately
defined by Solomon, when he compares the manly dignity
with Lebanon,* and the beauty and delicacy of the female
with Carmel.   Each of them suggests a different general
image, which the Hebrew poets adopt for different purposes,
expressing that by a metaphor, which more timid writers
would delineate by a direct comparison.   Thus Lebanon is
used by a very bold figure for the whole people of the Jews,
or for the state of the church;† for Jerusalem;‡ for the
temple of Jerusalem;§ for the king of Assyria ‖ even, and
for his army; for whatever, in a word, is remarkable, august,
and sublime;¶ and in the same manner, whatever possesses
much fertility, wealth, or beauty, is called Carmel.** Thus
too, by the fat rams, heifers, and bulls of Basan,†† by the
wild beast of the reeds,‡‡ or lion of Jordan, are denoted the

---

* Cant. v. 15 ; vii. 5.   † Isa. xxxiii. 9 ; xxxv. 2.

‡ Isa. xxxvii. 24 ; Jer. xxii. 6. 23.   § Zech. xi. 1.

‖ Isa. x. 84.   ¶ Isa. xi. 13.   See Ezek. xxxi.

** See as above, and Isa. x. 18. Mic. vii. 14. Jer. iv. 26.

†† Psal. xxii. 13. Ezek. xxxix. 18. Amos iv. 1.

‡‡ Psal. lxviii. 31. *Chaiah Kaneh*, "The wild beast of the reeds," is a periphrasis for "the lion;" and that by no means obscure, if we bestow upon it a little
attention.   The lions make their dens very commonly among the reeds.   Innumerable lions wander about among the reeds and copses on the borders of the rivers
in Mesopotamia." Am. Mar. lib. xviii. c. 7.   This is so familiar to the Arabs,
that they have a particular name for the *den* or *haunt* of a lion, when it is formed
among the reeds.   Bochart. *Hierog.* Par. I. lib. iii. c. 2.   The river Jordan was particularly infested with lions, which concealed themselves among the thick reeds upon
the banks.   Johan. Phocas, *Descrip. Loc. Sanct.* c. 23.   See also, Maundrel's *Travels*, Jerome upon these words of Zechariah, xi. 3.   "The voice of the roaring of
young lions, for the pride of Jordan is spoiled."   "With the river Jordan, (says
he,) which is the largest in Judea, and near which there are many lions, the Prophet associates the roaring of those animals, on account of the heat of the climate,
the vicinity to the desert, the extent of that vast wilderness, the reeds and the deep
sedge which grow about it."   Hence, in Jer. iv. 7, the lion is said to go forth *Me-
sobechou* (from his thicket;) and, xlix. 19, "to ascend from the overflowing of Jordan."—In this place, therefore, (Psal. lxviii. 31,) the *wild beast* of the *reeds*, the
herd of the *strong*, and the *calves*, are the lions, the bulls, and the beasts wantoning
about, or, in plain terms, the fierce and insolent tyrants : of whom, by a continuation of the metaphor, the Prophet adds, "each of them eagerly" (for there is that
force in the distributive in the singular number, and in the conjugation Hithpael)
"*striking with* their feet, and disturbing the *silver*, or perhaps *desirable, rivers* ; that
is, destroying and laying waste the pleasant places of Judea.   This very image is
adopted by Ezekiel, xxxii. 2, and again xxxiv. 18,19, in which places the verb *raphas*
thrice occurs in that sense : see also Dan. vii. 19.   But whether *rutz* be spoken of
the motion of the river, as in the Latin *currere*, (Virg. *Georg.* i. 132,) so as to signify the river, is not altogether so plain.

insolent and cruel tyrants of the Gentiles. In this and other imagery of the same kind, though the sacred writers presume to attempt what would not be allowed in the Greek and Latin poets, yet they cannot be accused of any deficiency in perspicuity or elegance, especially if it be remembered that the objects which furnished them with this imagery were all familiar, or, if I may be allowed the expression, indigenous to the Hebrews.

In a word, we may generally remark upon this head, that all poetry, and particularly that of the Hebrews, deduces its principal ornaments or imagery from natural objects: and since these images are formed in the mind of each writer, and expressed conformably to what occurs to his senses, it cannot otherwise happen but that, through diversity of situation, some will be more familiar, some almost peculiar to

---

"This word (*retzi*) seems in the Arabic to convey the idea of water. For there is a verb *ruz, to afford plenty of drink;* or *to contain stagnant water,* as *a fish-pond,* or *valley;* and the noun *rutz, a quantity of water lying in the bottom of a lake or cistern.*"—H.

A gentleman of great learning and genius has furnished me with another explication of this passage, which perhaps will attract the attention of the learned reader.

This learned man interprets the whole verse in this manner: "Consume the *wild beast* of the reed; the multitude of those who are strong in the calves of the nations; who excite themselves with fragments of silver: disperse the people who delight in war." The wild beast of the reed is the hippopotamus, which lives among the reeds of the Nile. Under this metaphor the people of Egypt is properly delineated, which of itself opens the way to the explication of the whole verse. For the Egyptians are indeed alluded to through the whole of the passage: they were remarkable for the worship of calves, and that of *Isis* and *Apis* in the form of an ox, and for their religious dances before these idols to the music of timbrels. The Chaldee runs thus: "The assembly of the strong, who put their trust in the calf-idols of the nations."—"Strong in the calves of the nations," is a phrase analogous to that, Eph. vi. 10, "Be *strong in* the Lord," and is an Hebraism. The manner of dancing in the worship of the Egyptian idols is confirmed from Exod. xxxii. 6, 19; also both it and the use of the timbrel, Herod. lib. ii. The word וֹצרפתי is totally different from רפס, which is also found in Prov. vi. 3, where the Vulgate renders it, *hasten thee,* or, better, *excite thee,* since it is in Hithpael. In the Chaldee it means *to trample;* in the Syriac, *to dance;* in the Arabic, *to spurn;* whence in this place, "excite or stimulate themselves to dancing."—"With fragments of silver," (so literally;) that is, with the small pieces or laminæ of metal round the timbrel, which produce the jingling noise when the instrument is beaten. The timbrel was formerly a warlike instrument: "The Queen calls forth the band with warlike timbrels," Virg. Whence Propertius also opposes the Egyptian timbrel to the Roman trumpet in the battle of Actium, (lib. iii., ix. 43.) If we consider it in this light, it will serve much to clear up what follows: "Disperse the people who delight in war." Thus we have not only a clear description of the Egyptians, but one that agrees admirably with the context: "Princes, come out of Egypt," &c.—*Author's Note.*

E 2

certain nations; and even those which seem most general, will always have some latent connexion with their immediate origin, and with their native soil. It is the first duty of a critic, therefore, to remark, as far as possible, the situation and habits of the author, the natural history of his country, and the scene of the poem. Unless we continually attend to these points, we shall scarcely be able to judge with any degree of certainty concerning the elegance or propriety of the sentiments: the plainest will sometimes escape our observation; the peculiar and interior excellences will remain totally concealed.*

* We must not omit noticing, in this place, those images which are derived from rivers and fountains, and the earth recreated with rain; which are indeed used by our poets, but more frequently by the orientals. For the scarcity of water, and the extreme heat of the summer, together with the wonderful fertility of the soil when watered, render this a more elegant and jocund comparison in the East than with us. In spring and summer, if the east wind continues to blow a few days, the fields are in general so parched that scarcely a blade of any thing green remains; many rivers and streams are dried up, the others are rendered briny, and all nature seems at the point of dissolution. After a plentiful shower, however, the fields revive beyond all expectation, the rivers resume their course, and the springs pour forth more delicious water. Mahomet makes use of this idea frequently, as figurative of the resurrection; and in this he shows himself no less of a philosopher than a poet. Dr. Russel has described this regeneration of nature in most lively colours in his *Natural History of Aleppo*, a book which every man ought to read, who wishes not only literally to understand the oriental writers, but to feel them. Indeed, for want of this, many similes appear to us bold and unusual, which among the orientals have a proper and distinct signification. Caab, an Arabic poet, who was contemporary with Mahomet, in one of his poems compares the teeth of a young lady when she smiled, to wine mixed with water, in which remained bubbles of yesterday's rain. In Isaiah there are many allusions of this nature; the favourable or adverse state of the nations being frequently expressed by this image, which many commentators have attempted to explain with more exactness than a poetical idea will bear. They have taken what the poet meant figuratively, sometimes in a literal sense; and at other times they have explained every thing in a mystical manner, and have pretended to define what is meant by the *water*, who are those that are *thirsty*, &c., &c., intermingling many very pious reflections, but utterly foreign to the subject, and such as never once entered the mind of the poet. For it certainly was not the intention of the prophet to write enigmas, but to illustrate and adorn the beautiful figure which he introduces. Thus, ch. xxxv. 6, 7, speaking of the happy state of Palestine, at the time that Idumea was laid waste and subdued:

> " The desert, and the waste, shall be glad;
> And the wilderness shall rejoice and flourish:
> For in the wilderness shall burst forth waters,
> And torrents in the desert:
> And the glowing sand shall become a pool,
> And the thirsty soil bubbling springs:
> And in the haunt of dragons shall spring forth
> The grass, with the reed, and the bulrush."

It is, however, to be remarked, that the level ground suffers most from the intolerable heat, and that the deserts are almost destitute of water. He amplifies the same image in a different manner in ch. xxxv. 17, celebrating the return of the Israelites from the Babylonian exile.

> "The poor and the needy seek for water, and there is none;
> Their tongue is parched with thirst :
> I Jehovah will answer them;
> The God of Israel, I will not forsake them.
> I will open in the high places rivers ;
> And in the midst of valleys, fountains :
> I will make the desert a standing pool;
> And the dry ground streams of waters.
> In the wilderness I will give the cedar;
> The acacia, the myrtle, and the tree producing oil :
> I will plant the fir-tree in the desert,
> The pine and the box together."

This is admirable painting ; and displays a most happy boldness of invention. The trees of different kinds, transplanted from their native soils to grow together in the desert ; the fir-tree and the pine, which are indigenous to Lebanon, to which snow, and rain, and an immense quantity of moisture, seem almost essential; the olive, which is the native of Jerusalem ; the Egyptian thorn, indigenous to Arabia—both of them requiring a dry soil ; and the myrtle, which flourishes most on the sea-shore. The same image occurs, ch. xxxiii. 18— 29, but placed in a different light. The poet feigns in this place, that the wild beasts of the desert, and the dragons themselves, which had been afflicted with thirst, pour forth their nocturnal cries in thankfulness to God for sending rain upon the desert. See also ch. xxxiv. 3, 4. Sometimes in the district of Jerusalem, which by nature is a very dry soil, and in which there are few streams, an immense flood is seen to burst forth, and with irresistible violence fall into the Dead Sea, so that its water, which is more salt than that of any other sea, is rendered sweet. Gihon seems to have afforded the basis of the above description ; a rivulet which proceeds from Sion, when perhaps some uncommon flood had prodigiously increased it. If I am not mistaken, David was the first who made use of this bold figure, but with such a degree of modesty as becomes the author who first introduced it, Psal. xlvi. 2—6. I suspect something of the kind indeed to have happened about the time of his composing that Psalm, for it is usual in earthquakes for some streams to be entirely drained, while others overflow. But his imitators, in their ardour for novelty, have gone far beyond him. Thus Joel intermingles with this figure the picture of the golden age, ch. iii. 18 :

> " The mountain shall drop down new wine,
> And the hills shall flow with milk,
> And all the rivers of Judah shall flow with water,
> And a fountain shall flow from the house of Jehovah,
> And shall water the valley of Shittim."—M.

LECTURE VII.

OF POETIC IMAGERY FROM COMMON LIFE.

Examples of poetical imagery from common life—The habits of life extremely simple among the Hebrews, whose principal employments were agriculture and pasturage —The dignity of these employments; and the splendour of the imagery which is borrowed from them: Threshing, and the threshing instruments—The sublimity of the imagery which is taken from familiar objects results from its propriety—The poetic Hell of the Hebrews explained; the imagery of which is borrowed from their subterraneous sepulchres and funeral rites.

In my last Lecture I explained three causes, which have enabled the Hebrew poets to preserve in their figurative style the most perfect union between perspicuity and sublimity.   I remarked in the first place, that they chiefly employed images taken from familiar objects, such I mean as were generally known and understood; secondly, that, in the use or application of them, they observed a regular track, method, or analogy: and, lastly, that they used most freely that kind of imagery which was most familiar, and the application of which was most generally understood. The truth of these observations will, I think, find further and more decisive confirmation, if those metaphors be considered which are taken from arts, manners, and common life.   These, you will easily recollect, I before pointed out as another source of poetical imagery; and for this part of the subject a few general observations will suffice, with an example or two out of the great number which present themselves in the sacred writings.   The whole course and method of common or domestic life among the Hebrews of the more ancient times, was simple and uniform in the greatest degree.   There existed not that variety of studies and pursuits, of arts, conditions, and employments, which may be observed among other nations who boast of superior civilisation; and rightly, indeed, if luxury, levity, and pride, be the criterions of it.   All enjoyed the same equal liberty; all of them, as being the offspring of the same ancient stock, boasted an equality of lineage and rank: there were no empty titles, no ensigns of false glory; scarcely any distinction or precedence but that which resulted from superior virtue or conduct, from the dignity of age and experience, or from services rendered to their country. Separated from the rest of mankind by their religion and laws, and not at all addicted to commerce, they were contented with those arts which were necessary to a simple and uncultivated (or rather uncorrupted) state of life. Thus their principal employments were agriculture and the care of cattle; they were a nation of husbandmen and shepherds. The lands had been originally parcelled out to the different families; the portions of which (by the laws of the country) could not be alienated by sale,* and therefore descended to their posterity without diminution. The fruits of the earth, the produce of his land and labour, constituted the wealth of each individual. Not even the greatest among them esteemed it mean and disgraceful to be. employed in the lowest offices of rural labour. In the Scripture history, therefore, we read of eminent persons called to the highest and most sacred offices, heroes, kings, and prophets, from the plough, and from the stalls.†

Such being the state of things, we cannot reasonably be surprised to find the Hebrew writers deducing most of their metaphors from those arts particularly, in which they were educated from their earliest years. We are not to wonder that those objects which were most familiar to their senses afforded the principal ornaments of their poetry; especially since they furnished so various and so elegant an assortment of materials, that not only the beautiful, but the grand and magnificent, might be collected from them. If any person of more nicety than judgment should esteem some of these rustic images grovelling or vulgar, it may be of some use to him to be informed, that such an effect can only result from the ignorance of the critic, who, through the medium of his scanty information and peculiar prejudices, presumes to estimate matters of the most remote antiquity;‡ it cannot

---

* Lev. xxv. 13—16, and 23, 24. Compare 1 Kings xxi. 3.

† See Judges iii. 31; vi. 11. 1 Sam. ix. 3; xi. 5. 2 Sam. vii. 8. Psal. lxxviii. 72, 73. 1 Kings xix. 19, 20. Amos i. 1; vii. 14, 15.

‡ One would almost think that this keen remark was prophetically levelled at a late critic of a very extraordinary cast. It was a little unfortunate for that learned gentleman, that these Lectures were not *translated* previous to the publication of

reasonably be attributed as an error to the sacred poets, who not only give to those ideas all their natural force and dignity, but frequently, by the vivacity and boldness of the figure, exhibit them with additional vigour, ornament, and beauty.

It would be a tedious task to instance particularly with what embellishments of diction, derived from one low and trivial object, (as it may appear to some,) the barn or the threshing-floor, the sacred writers have contrived to add a lustre to the most sublime, and a force to the most import-ant subjects: Thus, "Jehovah threshes out the heathen as corn, tramples them under his feet, and disperses them. He delivers the nations to Israel to be beaten in pieces by an indented flail,* or to be crushed by their brazen hoofs. He scatters his enemies like chaff upon the mountains,† and dis-perses them with the whirlwind of his indignation."‡

> " Behold, I have made thee a threshing wain ;
> A new corn-drag armed with pointed teeth :
> Thou shalt thresh the mountains, and beat them small,
> And reduce the hills to chaff.
> Thou shalt winnow them, and the wind shall bear them away ;
> And the tempest shall scatter them abroad."§

Of these quotations it is to be remarked, first, that the nature of this metaphor, and the mode of applying it, are constantly and cautiously regarded by the different authors of the sacred poems; and on this account, notwithstanding the boldness of it, both chastity and perspicuity are pre-served, since they apply it solely to exaggerate the slaughter and dispersion of the wicked. The force and aptness of the image itself in illustrating the subject, will also afford a very proper and ready apology for some degree of freedom in the application of it, particularly if we advert to the nature and method of this rustic operation in Palestine. It was per-formed in a high situation exposed to the wind, by bruising the ear, either by driving upon the sheaves a herd of cattle, or else by an instrument constructed of large planks, and sharpened underneath with stones or iron ; and sometimes by a machine in the form of a cart, with iron wheels or axles.

---

his book : if they had, he certainly would never have laid himself open to the ap-plication of so pointed a sarcasm.—T.

* Hab. iii. 12. Joel iii. 14. Jer. li. 38. Isa. xxi. 10.   † Mic. iv. 13.
‡ Psal. lxxxiii. 14, 16. Isa. xvii. 13.   § Isa. xli. 15, 16.

indented, which Varro calls *Pœnicum,** as being brought to Italy by the Carthaginians from Phœnicia, which was adjacent to Palestine.   From this it is plain (not to mention that the descriptions agree in every particular) that the same custom was common both to the Hebrews and the Romans; and yet I do not recollect that the latter have borrowed any of their poetical imagery from this occupation.   It is proper however to remark, that this image was obvious and familiar to the Hebrews in a high degree, as we learn from what is said of the threshing-floor of Ornan the Jebusite,† which was situated in an open place (as were all the rest) in Jerusalem itself, and in the highest part of the city, in the very place, indeed, where the Temple of Solomon was afterwards erected.

Homer, who was uncommonly fond of every picture of rural life, esteemed that under our consideration so beautiful and significant, that, in a few instances,‡ he draws his comparisons from the threshing-floor (for even he was fearful of the boldness of this image in the form of a metaphor.) Two of these comparisons he introduces to illustrate light subjects, contrary to the practice of the Hebrews; but the third is employed upon a subject truly magnificent; and this, as it approaches in some degree the sublimity of the Hebrew, it may not be improper to recite :—

> " As with autumnal harvests cover'd o'er,
>   And thick bestrown, lies Ceres' sacred floor,
>   When round and round, with never-wearied pain,
>   The trampling steers beat out th' unnumber'd grain ;
>   So the fierce coursers, as the chariot rolls,
>   Tread down whole ranks, and crush out heroes' souls."§

This comparison, however, though deservedly accounted one of the grandest and most beautiful which antiquity has transmitted to us, still falls greatly short of the Hebrew boldness and sublimity.   A Hebrew writer would have compared the hero himself with the instrument, and not his horses with the oxen that are harnessed to it, which is rather too apposite, and too exactly similar.‖   But custom had not given equal license to the Greek poetry : this image had not been equally familiar, had not occupied the same place as with the Hebrews; nor had acquired the same force and authority by long prescription.

---

* De Re Rust. I. 52.'   † 2 Chron. iii. 1.   ‡ See *Iliad*, v. & xiii. 588.
§ Pope's *Iliad*, xx. 577.   ‖ This will be more fully explained in Lect. 12.

I ought not in this place to omit that supremely magnificent delineation of the Divine vengeance, expressed by imagery taken from the wine-press; an image which very frequently occurs in the sacred poets, but which no other poetry has presumed to introduce. But where shall we find expressions of equal dignity with the original in any modern language? By what art of the pencil can we exhibit even a shadow or an outline of that description in which Isaiah depicts the Messiah as coming to vengeance?*

" Who is this that cometh from Edom ?
With garments deeply dyed from Botsra?
This that is magnificent in his apparel;
Marching on in the greatness of his strength?
I who publish righteousness,† and am mighty to save.
Wherefore is thine apparel red;
And thy garments, as one that treadeth the wine-vat ?
I have trodden the vat alone;
And of the peoples there was not a man with me.
And I trod them in mine anger;
And I trampled on them in mine indignation;
And their life-blood was sprinkled upon my garments;
And I have stained all my apparel.''

But the instances are innumerable which might be quoted of metaphors taken from the manners and customs of the Hebrews. One general remark, however, may be made upon this subject, namely, that from one simple, regular, and natural mode of life having prevailed among the Hebrews, it has arisen, that in their poetry these metaphors have less of obscurity, of meanness or depression, than

---

* See Isa. lxiii. 1—3. Our author, in his excellent commentary on Isaiah, has a very long note, proving, against some learned interpreters, (I suppose Jewish,) that Judas Maccabeus could not be the subject of this prophecy. He asserts very properly, that the glorious but fruitless effort of the Maccabees was not an event adequate to so lofty a prediction; and he adds another very material circumstance, which he presumes entirely excludes Judas Maccabeus, and even the Idumeans properly so called; for the Idumea of the prophet's time was quite a different country from that which Judas conquered. To the question, " To whom does it then apply?" he answers, To no event that he knows of in history, unless perhaps the destruction of Jerusalem and the Jewish polity, which in the Gospel is called the coming of Christ, and the days of vengeance. He adds, however, that there are prophecies which intimate a great slaughter of the enemies of God and his people, which remain to be fulfilled: those in Ezekiel and in the Revelation are called Gog and Magog; and possibly this prophecy may refer to the same or the like event. —T.

† In one manuscript this word stands, " the announcer of righteousness." See Bishop Lowth's *Notes on Isaiah.*

could be expected, when we consider the antiquity of their writings, the distance of the scene, and the uncommon boldness and vivacity of their rhetoric. Indeed, to have made use of the boldest imagery with the most perfect perspicuity, and the most common and familiar with the greatest dignity, is a commendation almost peculiar to the sacred poets. I shall not hesitate to produce an example of this kind, in which the meanness of the image is fully equalled by the plainness and inelegance of the expression ; and yet such is its consistency, such the propriety of its application, that I do not scruple to pronounce it sublime. The Almighty threatens the ultimate destruction of Jerusalem in these terms:

> " And I will wipe Jerusalem,
> As a man wipeth a dish :
> He wipeth it, and turneth it upside down."*

But many of these images must falsely appear mean and obscure to us, who differ so materially from the Hebrews in our manners and customs; but in such cases it is our duty neither too rashly to blame, nor too suddenly to despair. The mind should rather exert itself to discover, if possible, the connexion between the literal and the figurative meaning, which, in abstruse subjects, frequently depending upon some very delicate and nice relation, eludes our penetration. An obsolete custom, for instance, or some forgotten circumstance opportunely adverted to, will sometimes restore its true perspicuity and credit to a very intricate passage. Whether the instance I have at present in view may prove of any utility or not in this respect, I will not presume to say ; it may possibly, however, serve to illustrate still further the nature of the Hebrew imagery, and the accuracy of their poets in the application of it.

Either through choice or necessity, the infernal regions and the state of the dead has been a very common topic with the poets of every nation; and this difficult subject, which the most vigorous understanding is unable to fathom by any exertion of reason, and of which conjecture itself can scarcely form any adequate idea, they have ornamented with all the splendour of description, as one of the most important themes which could engage the human imagination. Thus the prompt and fertile genius of the Greeks, naturally adapted

* 2 Kings xxi. 13. This is the answer of some prophet, as related by the historian.

to the fabulous,* has eagerly embraced the opportunity to indulge in all the wantonness of fiction, and has peopled the infernal regions with such a profusion of monsters, as could not fail to promote the ridicule even of the ignorant and the vulgar.† The conduct of the Hebrews has been very different: their fancy was restrained upon this subject by the tenets of their religion; and (notwithstanding the firm persuasion of the existence not only of the soul but of the body after death) we are to remember they were equally ignorant with the rest of mankind of the actual state and situation of the dead. In this case they have acted as in every other:

* I fear our Author, who is not a little indebted to the Greeks, is rather unjustly severe upon them in this passage. The Infernal Regions of the Greeks, which probably they borrowed from the Egyptians, I have little doubt flowed from the very same source ; and the seat of the soul was supposed to be under the earth, because the body was deposited there. Neither can it be denied, that the Hebrew poets also feigned a sort of society or civil community of the departed souls, which without a doubt was utterly fabulous ; though we have none of their authors remaining who describe the fiction in terms equally precise with the Heathen writers, and presume

" Pandere res alta terra et caligine mersas."

They have, moreover, their Elysium, their Styx, &c. of which I shall remark in the notes on Lecture 9. Nor is such a degree of fable inconsistent with poetry even of the most sacred kind ; for, though it be not exactly and literally true, it is yet very far from falsehood. Nay, I find the Hebrew poets more licentious in some respects, as to this matter, than even the Latin or the Greek ; for they not only suppose the human souls to descend to the infernal regions, but those of trees, and even of kingdoms, Isa. xiv. 9—20. Ezek. xxxi. 14. 16, 17, 18 ; xxxii. (where not only they who were slain in battle are supposed to descend to the infernal regions, but the whole army of the vanquished, and the very kingdom itself.) This very bold figure is so usual in the Hebrew writings, that it has been introduced into their prose composition ; and Christ, when he foretels the eternal duration of his Church, says, "the Gates of Hell," or the Kingdom or power of Hell, "shall not prevail against it."—M.

I must caution the reader, in this place, against the enthusiasm of our Annotator for the ancient learning, and particularly for that of Egypt. In this favourite pursuit, of finding out all the Grecian mythology in the Scriptures, he is certainly not less visionary than those commentators whose indiscreet zeal he has on other occasions so ably exposed. That the Hebrew poets have made use of poetical ornaments or fictions on many occasions, I am willing to admit ; and that these should bear some remote resemblance to the poetical ornaments of other nations, is natural enough to suppose ; but it is only such a general resemblance as will frequently occur in writers who treat of the same subjects. For instance, it is a very natural fiction to place the residence of the soul after death beneath the earth, and the association which led to this notion was certainly, as our Author observes, the body's being deposited there ; but there is not the least occasion to recur to the Egyptian rites for this simple and easy fiction. The other instances which our Annotator attempts to produce are very fanciful, as I shall demonstrate in the proper place.—T.

† See Cicero, Quæst. Tusculan. 1. 5, 6.

what was plain and commonly understood concerning the
dead, that is, what happened to the body, suggested the
general imagery to which the Hebrews always resort in describing the state and condition of departed souls, and in
forming what may be termed, if the expression be allowable,
their poetical Hell. It is called *Sheol* by the Hebrews
themselves, by the Greeks *Hades*, and by the Latins *Infer-
num* or *Sepulchrum*. Into the funeral rites or ceremonies
of the Hebrews may be traced all the imagery which their
poets introduce to illustrate this subject; and it must be
confessed that these afforded ample scope for poetical embellishment. The sepulchres of the Hebrews, at least those of
respectable persons, and those which hereditarily belonged
to the principal families, were extensive caves or vaults,*
excavated from the native rock by art and manual labour.
The roofs of them in general were arched; and some were
so spacious as to be supported by colonnades. All round
the sides were cells for the reception of the sarcophagi: these
were properly ornamented with sculpture, and each was
placed in its proper cell. The cave or sepulchre admitted
no light, being closed by a great stone, which was rolled to
the mouth of the narrow passage or entrance. Many of
these receptacles are still extant in Judea: two in particular
are more magnificent than all the rest,† and are supposed
to be the sepulchres of the kings. One of these is in Jeru-

---

* See Gen. xxiii. 2 Kings xiii. 21. Isa. xxii. 16. 2 Chron. xvi. 14. Josh.
x. 27. Lam. iii. 53. John xi. 38, and the Evangelists, concerning the sepulchre
of Christ.

† See a description of these sepulchres, Serlio, *Architettura*, 1. iii. Villapandus,
Apparat. Urb. iii. 16. Maundrel's *Travels*, p. 76.

Josephus makes frequent mention of the sepulchre of David. He calls the
sepulchre itself ταφον or μνημα; and the chambers, into many of which the
sepulchre was divided, οικὸς τὰς εν τῳ μνηματι; the cells, Θηκας. *Antiq.* vii.
15; xv. 7. *Bell.* 1. 2. The sepulchres of the Egyptian monarchs are described by
Strabo, lib. xvii. "About forty cells are cut in the caves." Of the remains of which
see a description, Pocock's *Description of the East*, b. ii. c. 3. There are still
remaining at Naples certain sepulchral vaults called *Catacombs*, which have not
been exceeded in grandeur by any similar work of man. They appear to me, indeed, to be a monument of the most remote antiquity, which, though originally
appropriated to some other use, about the Christian æra were made use of as burial-
places. They are evidently of the same kind with other subterraneous works of
that country, many of which have been destroyed by earthquakes, but many remain
at this day at Cumæ, Misenum, Baiæ, the Lake of Averno, and Mount Posilypo.
I have no doubt but that these works were antecedent to the time of Homer, who
describes them as inhabited by the Cimmerians, a people who live in perpetual
darkness, *Odyss.* ix. sub init. ; as Ephorus in Strabo, lib. v. says of them, "that

salem, and contains twenty-four cells; the other, containing twice that number, is in a place without the city.

If, therefore, we examine all those passages in which the sacred writers have poetically described the infernal regions, we may, if I mistake not, clearly perceive them intent upon this gloomy picture, which their mode of sepulture presented to their view. That which struck their senses they delineated in their descriptions: we there find no exact account, no explicit mention of immortal spirits;—not, according to the notion of some learned persons,* because they disbelieved in the existence of the soul after death, but because they had no clear idea or perception by which they might explain where or in what manner it existed; and they were not possessed of that subtilty of language which enables men to speak with plausibility on subjects abstruse and remote from the apprehension of the senses, and to cover their ignorance with learned disputation. The condition, the form, the habitation of departed spirits, were therefore concealed from the Hebrews equally with the rest of mankind. Nor did revelation afford them the smallest assistance on this subject; not, perhaps, because the Divine Providence was disposed to

they live in certain subterraneous dwellings, which they call *Argillas*, and associate with one another by narrow fosses or passages;" and the remaining monuments demonstrate this account not to be altogether fabulous. These caves are called *Argillas*, from the nature of the soil in which I believe they are usually dug: " *Argil*, or that kind of earth which is used for cleansing, or white clay," Hesych. : whence a hill between Puteoli and Naples was called *Leucogæus*, Plin. *Nat. Hist.* viii. 11, although those mentioned above are all hewn out of the solid grit, in order to resist the injuries of time. Hence *Argiletum*, the name of a street in Rome, taken from some *argil* of this kind, such as formed the cave of Cacus, which was not far from that street; though Virgil does not favour this opinion : see however Varro, *De Ling. Lat.* lib. iv. It is evident that Homer first, and Virgil after him, derived their notions of the infernal regions from these Cimmerian caves of Campania; and when Virgil is describing the cave of Cacus, when forced upon by Hercules, the image of the infernal state immediately occurs :

> " The Court of Cacus stands reveal'd to sight,
> The cavern glares with new-admitted light.
> So pent, the vapours with a rumbling sound
> Heave from below, and rend the hollow ground :
> A sounding flaw succeeds ; and from on high
> The gods with hate behold the nether sky :
> The ghosts repine at violated right ;
> And curse th' invading sun, and sicken at the sight."
>   Dryden's *Virg. Æn.* viii. 321.—*Author's Note.*

* See Le Clerc, *Comment. Hagiographa :* consult the index for the word *Immortalitas.*

withhold this information from them, but because the present condition of the human mind renders it incapable of receiving it: for, when the understanding contemplates things distinct from body and matter, from the want of just ideas, it is compelled to have recourse to such as are false and fictitious, and to delineate the incorporeal world by things corporeal and terrestrial. Thus, observing that after death the body returned to the earth, and that it was deposited in a sepulchre, after the manner which has just been described, a sort of popular notion prevailed among the Hebrews, as well as among other nations, that the life which succeeded the present was to be passed beneath the earth: and to this notion even the sacred prophets were obliged to allude occasionally, if they wished to be understood by the people on this subject.

Hence the meaning is evident, when the deceased are said to " descend into the pit,* to the nether parts of the earth, to the gates and chambers of death, to the stony places, to the sides, to the gates of the caverns;" when it is said, that " the grave has swallowed them up, and closed its mouth upon them;"† that " they lie down in the deep; ‡ immersed in a desert place, in the gulf, in thick darkness, in the land of darkness, and the shadow of death, wild, hideous, where all is disorder and darkness; and darkness, as it were instead of light, diffuseth its beams."§

The poets of other nations, amidst all their fictions, have yet retained a congenial picture of the habitations of the dead: thus the tragic poet has admirably described the deep course of Acheron:

> " Through dreary caves cut in the rugged rock,
> Where reigns the darkness of perpetual hell." ||

---

* שחת, also בור, or באר, Job xxxiii. 18. Psalm xxviii. 1, and passim. ארץ תחתית, or ארץ תחתיות, Ezek. xxxi. 14 ; xxxii. 18, and Psalm passim. שערי שאול, Isa. xxxviii. 10. מות שערי, Job xxxviii. 17. Psalm ix. 14. מות חדרו, Prov. vii. 27. אבני בור, Isa. xiv. 19. ירכתי בור, Isa. xiv. 15. Ezek. xxxii. 23. כדי שאול, Job xvii. 16.

† פי שאול, Psalm cxli. 7. פי באר, Psalm lxix. 16 ; see also Isa. v. 14.

‡ מצולה Psalm lxix. 16 ; lxxxviii. 7. חרבות, Job iii. 14.   Ezek. xxvi. 20.

§ I remember, though I cannot refer to the passage, some Arabian writer considers the nocturnal darkness as an emanation from an opaque body, just as the light of day proceeds from the sun.—S. H.

|| Cic. *Tusc. Quæst.* 1.

But how grand and magnificent a scene is depicted by the Hebrew poets from the same materials, in which their deceased heroes and kings are seen to advance from the earth! Figure to yourselves a vast, dreary, dark, sepulchral cavern,* where the kings of the nations lie, each upon his bed of dust,† the arms of each beside him, his sword under his head,‡ and the graves of their numerous hosts round about them:§ Behold! the king of Babylon is introduced: they all rise and go forth to meet him, and receive him as he approaches! "Art thou also come down unto us? Art thou become like unto us? Art thou cut down and withered in thy strength, O thou destroyer of the nations!"—But I reluctantly refrain.—It is not for me, nor indeed for human ability, to explain these subjects with a becoming dignity. You will see this transcendent imagery, yourselves, better and more completely displayed in that triumphal song which was composed by Isaiah || (the first of all poets for sublimity and elegance) previous to the death of the king of Babylon. Ezekiel¶ also has nobly illustrated the same scene, with similar machinery, in the last prophecy concerning the fall of Pharaoh; that remarkable example of the terrific, which is indeed deservedly accounted the peculiar excellence of this prophet.

---

* Isa. xiv. 9, 18. Ezek. xxxii. 19, 21, &c.

† מִשְׁכָּב, Isa. lvii. 2. Ezek. xxxii. 25, ἡ θήκη, the cell which receives the sarcophagus.

‡ Ezek. xxxii. 27. See 1 Macc. xiii. 29.   § Ezek. xxxii. 22, 23, 24.

|| Isa. xiv. 4—27.   ¶ Ezek. xxxii. 18—32.

LECTURE VIII.

OF POETIC IMAGERY FROM SACRED TOPICS.

Imagery which is borrowed from the rites and ceremonies of religion, peculiarly liable to obscurity and mistake—Instances of expressions which appear uncommonly harsh; and of others, the principal elegance of which would be lost, unless we adverted to the nature of the sacred rites—The exordium of the 104th Psalm explained.

THE present disquisition concerning the poetical imagery of the Hebrews was undertaken, Gentlemen, principally with a view of guarding you against an error which is apt to mislead those who peruse without sufficient attention and information writings of so old a date; namely, that of accounting vulgar, mean, or obscure, passages which were probably regarded among the most perspicuous and sublime by the people to whom they were addressed.   Now, if with respect even to that imagery which is borrowed from objects of nature and of common life (of which we have just been treating) such a caution was proper, it will surely be still more necessary with respect to that which is borrowed from the sacred mysteries of religion.   For, though much of that imagery which was taken by the Hebrew writers from the general face of nature, or from the customs of common life, was peculiar to their own country, yet much, it must be confessed, was equally familiar to the rest of the world; but that which was suggested by the rites and ceremonies of religion was altogether peculiar to themselves, and was but little known beyond the limits of Judea.   Since, therefore, this topic in particular seems to involve many such difficulties and inconveniences, it appears to me deserving of a serious investigation; and such investigation, I flatter myself, will tend to restore in some degree the real majesty of the Hebrew poetry, which seems to have shone forth in former times with no ordinary splendour.

The religion of the Hebrews embraced a very extensive circle of divine and human economy.   It not only included all that regarded the worship of God; it extended even to the regulation of the commonwealth, the ratification of the laws, the forms and administration of justice, and nearly all the relations of civil and domestic life. With them, almost every point of conduct was connected, either directly or indirectly, with their religion. Things which were held least in esteem by other nations, bore among them the sanction of divine authority, and had a very close alliance with both the more serious concerns of life and the sacred ceremonies. On these accounts it happens, in the first place, that abundance of metaphors occur in the Hebrew poetry deduced from sacred subjects; and further, that there is a necessity for the most diligent observation, lest that very connexion with the affairs of religion should escape us. For, should we be mistaken in so material a point; should we erroneously account as common or profane what is in its nature divine; or should we rank among the mean and the vulgar, sentiments and images which are sacred and sublime; it is incredible how much the strength of the language, and the force and majesty of the ideas, will be destroyed. Nothing in nature, indeed, can be so conducive to the sublime, as those conceptions which are suggested by the contemplation of the greatest of all beings; and when the august form of religion presents itself to the mental eye,

> A fervent pleasure, and an awe divine,
> Seizes the soul, and lifts it to its God.

It follows therefore of course, that the dignity of the Hebrew poetry must in some measure be diminished in our eyes, since not only the connexion of the imagery with sacred things must frequently escape our observation, but, even when it is most apparent, it can scarcely strike us with that force and vivacity with which it must have penetrated the minds of the Hebrews. The whole system of the Hebrew rites is one great and complicated allegory, to the study and observance of which all possible diligence and attention were incessantly dedicated by those who were employed in the sacred offices. On this occupation and study, therefore, all good and considerate men were intent: it constituted all their business, all their amusement; it was their treasure and their hope; on this every care and every thought was employed; and the utmost sanctity and reverence distinguished every part of their conduct which had any relation to it. Much dignity and sublimity must also have resulted from the recollection which these allusions produced, of the splendour and magnificence of the sacred rites themselves; the force of which, upon the minds of those who had frequent opportunities of observing them, must have been incredible. Such a solemn grandeur attended these rites, especially after the building of Solomon's temple, that, although we are possessed of very accurate descriptions, our imaginations are still utterly unable to embody them. Many allusions, therefore, of this kind, which the Hebrew poets found particularly energetic, and highly popular among their countrymen, may possibly appear to us mean and contemptible; since many things which were held by them in the highest veneration are by us but little regarded, or perhaps but little understood.

I shall subjoin a few examples of what I have just been remarking; or rather I shall point out a few topics, which will of themselves suggest a variety of examples.

Much of the Jewish law is employed in discriminating between things clean and unclean; in removing and making atonement for things polluted or prescribed; and under these ceremonies, as under a veil or covering, a meaning the most important and sacred is concealed, as would be apparent from the nature of them, even if we had not, besides, other clear and explicit authority for this opinion. Among the rest are certain diseases and infirmities of the body, and some customs evidently in themselves indifferent: these, on a cursory view, seem light and trivial; but when the reasons of them are properly explored, they are found to be of considerable importance. We are not to wonder, therefore, if the sacred poets sometimes have recourse to these topics for imagery, even on the most momentous occasions, when they display the general depravity inherent in the human mind,[*] or exprobrate the corrupt manners of their own people,[†] or when they deplore the abject state of the virgin, the daughter of Sion, polluted and exposed.[‡] If we consider these metaphors without any reference to the religion of their authors, they will doubtless appear in some degree disgusting and inelegant; if we refer them to their genuine source, to the peculiar rites of the Hebrews, they will be found wanting neither in force nor in dignity. Of the same nature, or at least analogous to them, are those ardent expressions of grief and misery which are poured forth by the royal prophet, (who,

---

[*] Isa. lxiv. 6.   [†] Isa. i. 5, 6. 16.   Ezek. xxxvi. 17.
[‡] Lam. i. 8, 9, 17, and ii. 2.

F 2

indeed, in many of those divine compositions, personates a
character far more exalted than his own :) especially when he
complains, that he is wasted and consumed with the loath-
someness of disease, and bowed down and depressed with a
burden of sin too heavy for human nature to sustain.*   On
reading these passages, some, who were but little acquainted
with the genius of the Hebrew poetry, have pretended to
inquire into the nature of the disease with which the poet
was affected; not less absurdly, in my opinion, than if they
had perplexed themselves to discover in what river he was
plunged, when he complains that "the deep waters had
gone over his soul."

But as there are many passages in the Hebrew poets which
may seem to require a similar defence, so there are in all probability many, which, although they now appear to abound
in beauties and elegances, would yet be thought much more
sublime were they illustrated from those sacred rites to
which they allude; and as excellent pictures, viewed in their
proper light.   To this purpose many instances might be
produced from one topic, namely, from the precious and
magnificent ornaments of the priest's attire.   Such was the
gracefulness, such the magnificence of the sacerdotal vestments, especially those of the high priest; so adapted were
they, as Moses says,† to the expression of glory and of beauty, that to those who were impressed with an equal opinion
of the sanctity of the wearer, nothing could possibly appear
more venerable and sublime.   To these, therefore, we find
frequent allusions in the Hebrew poets, when they have occasion to describe extraordinary beauty or comeliness, or to
delineate the perfect form of supreme Majesty.   The elegant
Isaiah‡ has a most beautiful idea of this kind, when he describes, in his own peculiar manner, (that is, most magnificently,) the exultation and glory of the church, after its
triumphal restoration.   Pursuing the allusion, he decorates
her with the vestments of salvation, and clothes her in the
robe of righteousness.   He afterwards compares the church
to a bridegroom dressed for the marriage, to which comparison incredible dignity is added by the word *Ikohen*—a
metaphor plainly taken from the apparel of the priests, the
force of which, therefore, no modern language can express.
No imagery, indeed, which the Hebrew writers could employ, was equally adapted with this to the display (as far

---

* See Psalm xxxviii.   † Exod. xxviii. 2.   See Ecclus. l. 5—13.   ‡ Isa. lxi. 10.

as the human powers can conceive or depict the subject) of the infinite majesty of God. "Jehovah" is therefore introduced by the Psalmist as "clothed with glory and with "strength,"* he is "girded with power;"† which are the very terms appropriated to the describing of the dress and ornaments of the priests.

Thus far may appear plain and indisputable; but, if I mistake not, there are other passages, the beauty of which lies still more remote from common observation. In that most perfect ode, which celebrates the immensity of the omnipresent Deity, and the wisdom of the divine Artificer in forming the human body, the author uses a metaphor derived from the most subtle art of the Phrygian workman :

" When I was formed in the secret place,
When I was wrought with a needle in the depths of the earth." ‡

Whoever observes this, (in truth he will not be able to observe it in the common translations,) and at the same time reflects upon the wonderful mechanism of the human body; the various implications of the veins, arteries, fibres, and membranes; the "undescribable texture" of the whole fabric—may, indeed, feel the beauty and gracefulness of this well-adapted metaphor, but will miss much of its force and sublimity, unless he be apprised that the art of designing in needlework was wholly dedicated to the use of the sanctuary, and, by a direct precept of the divine law, chiefly employed in furnishing a part of the sacerdotal habit,§ and the veils for the entrance of the Tabernacle. Thus, the poet compares the wisdom of the divine Artificer with the most estimable of human arts—that art which was dignified by being consecrated altogether to the use of religion; and the workmanship of which was so exquisite, that even the sacred writings seem to attribute it to a supernatural guidance.||

I will instance also another topic, which, if I am not deceived, will suggest several remarkable examples to this purpose. There is one of the Hebrew poems which has been long since distinguished by universal approbation; the subject is the wisdom and design of the Creator in the formation of the universe : you will easily perceive that I have in view the hundred and fourth Psalm. The exordium is most

* Psal. xciii. 1.   † Psal. lxv. 7.   ‡ Psal. cxxxix. 15.
§ Exod. xxviii. 39; xxvi. 36; xxvii. 16.   Compare Ezek. xvi. 10. 13. 18.
|| See Exod. xxxv. 30—35.

sublime, and consists of a delineation of the Divine Majesty
and power, as exemplified in the admirable constitution of
nature.   On this subject, since it is absolutely necessary to
employ figurative language, the poet has introduced such
metaphors as were accounted by the Hebrews the most
magnificent and most worthy: for all of them are, in my
opinion, borrowed from the Tabernacle: but I find it will
be necessary to quote the passage itself, and I shall endeavour to explain it as briefly as possible.

The poet first expresses his sense of the greatness and
power of the Deity in plain and familiar language ; and then
breaks out in metaphor—

" Thou art invested with majesty and glory :"

Where, observe, the word *labash* (to *invest*) is the word
always used to express the ceremony of putting on the
sacerdotal ornaments.

" Covering thyself with light as with a garment :"

The Light in the Holy of Holies, the manifest symbol of
the Divine Presence, is figured under this idea;* and this

---

* See Exod. xl. 34—38.   Lev. xvi. 2.   Numb. ix. 15, 16.   1 Kings viii. 10,
11.   2 Chron. vii. 1. 2.   A similar allusion, Isa. iv. 5; lx. 2. 19.   Zech. ii. 5.
Rev. xxi. 23.—*Author's Note.*
 I do not know upon what authority our Author has received this fact. The
Rabbies, who talk much about the *Shechina*, could not possibly be witnesses of that
sight, which they themselves confess had disappeared for many ages before their
time, and had never been seen in the second temple. Who, indeed, that is acquainted with the rules which sound reason dictates, and which all who study history
must regard, will give credit, in a matter of so great antiquity, to witnesses whose
faculty in fabricating falsehood has been so frequently exposed, and especially as they
themselves confess that they do not report the fact upon the authority of any books
or records, but merely upon the tradition of their ancestors? and no man can be
ignorant how much such a notion is likely to increase in the different hands through
which it passes.   In reality, I do not suppose our Author took up the matter upon
their representation, but that he founded his opinion upon the passage in Lev. xvi.
2, which, however, the learned Thalcman has asserted, is not to be understood of a
miraculous *Shechina*, but of a cloud of smoke which surrounded the throne consecrated to the Deity, lest the vacant seat should be exposed to the multitude. From
the 13th verse of the same chapter the same author argues, that the cloud upon
the mercy seat was factitious, or arose from the incense which was offered there ;
though I cannot say that I am so entirely of his opinion as to believe, that not
even upon the solemn day of inauguration a cloud of a miraculous nature rested
on the Cherubims. Unless, therefore, we interpret this passage of the Psalmist as
intimating that God is the fountain of all light, I would refer it to that part of
the history of creation which relates the first great display of Almighty power.
—M.

singular example is made use of figuratively to express the universal and ineffable glory of God.

" Stretching out the heavens as a curtain :"

Jeringnah is the word made use of, and is the very name of those curtains with which the Tabernacle was covered at the top and round about.* The Seventy seem to have had this in view, when they render it ὡσει δερριν (as a skin) :† whence the Vulgate *sicut pellem*, (which is a literal translation of the Septuagint;) and another of the old translators δερμα, (a hide or skin.)

" Laying the beams of his chambers in the waters :"

In these words the poet admirably expresses the nature of the air, which, from various and floating elements, is formed into one regular and uniform mass, by a metaphor drawn from the singular construction of the Tabernacle : for it consisted of many different parts, which might be easily separated, but which were united by a curious and artful junction and adaptation to each other.‡ He proceeds —

" Making the clouds his chariot ;
Walking upon the wings of the wind :"

He had before exhibited the Divine Majesty under the appearance which it assumed in the Holy of Holies, that of a bright and dazzling light ; he now describes it according to that which is assumed, when God accompanied the ark in the pillar of a cloud which was carried along through the atmosphere. That vehicle of the Divine Presence is, indeed, distinguished in the sacred history by the particular appellation of *a chariot*.§

" Making the winds his messengers,
And his ministers a flaming fire :"

---

* I do not see why we should suppose the comparison to relate to the tabernacle of Moses more than to any other superb fabric of that kind.—M.

† Compare Exod. xxvi. 7, &c. with the Septuagint.

‡ It is very evident, that if this observation of our Author prove any thing, it proves that any raftered building may be compared to the air. For my own part, I am certain that in this passage there is no allusion at all to the Tabernacle, in which there was no *cœnaculum*, or upper chamber, but rather to the houses in Palestine, at the top of which there was a *cœnaculum*, or chamber, apart from the rest, for the sake of retirement, which has been very accurately described by Shaw. —M.

§ 1 Chron xxviii. 18. See also Ecclus. xlix. 8.

The elements are described as prompt and ready in executing the commands of JEHOVAH, as angels, messengers, or ministers serving at the Tabernacle, the Hebrew word being exactly expressive of the latter sense.

" Who founded the earth upon its bases : "

The following phrase, also, is directly taken from the same ·

" That it should not be displaced for more than ages : "

That is, " for a certain period known only to the infinite wisdom of God." As the situation of both was in this respect nearly the same, so, on the other hand, the permanence of the sanctuary is in other places compared, and in almost the same words, with the stability of the earth.*

Perhaps, in pursuing this investigation with so much subtilty and minuteness, I have scarcely acted consistently with the customs of this place, or the nature of my design : but it appeared absolutely necessary so to do, in order to make myself perfectly understood; and to demonstrate, that it is scarcely, or not at all, possible for any translation fully to represent the genuine sense of the sacred poets, and that delicate connexion which for the most part exists between their poetical imagery and the peculiar circumstances of their nation.† This connexion frequently depends upon the use of certain terms, upon a certain association between words and things, which a translation generally perplexes, and very frequently destroys. This, therefore, is not to be preserved in the most literal and accurate version, much less in any poetical translation, or rather imitation; though

---

* Psal. lxxviii. 69.

† It may be asserted of translations in general, and I am sure I have experienced the truth of the observation in this very attempt, that many of the minuter beauties of style are necessarily lost : a translator is scarcely allowed to intrude upon his author any figures or images of his own, and many which appear in the original must be omitted of course. Metaphors, synecdoches, and metonymies, are frequently untractable; the corresponding words would probably, in a figurative sense, appear harsh or obscure. The observation, however, applies with less justice to our common version of the Bible than to any translation whatever. It was made in a very early stage of our literature, and when the language was by no means formed : in such a state of the language, the figurative diction of the Hebrews might be literally rendered without violence to the national taste; and the frequent recurrence of the same images and expressions serves to familiarise them to us. Time and habit have now given it force and authority; and I believe there never was an instance of any translation, so very literal and exact, being read with such universal satisfaction and pleasure.—T.

there are extant some not unsuccessful attempts of this kind. To relish completely all the excellences of the Hebrew literature, the fountains themselves must be approached, the peculiar flavour of which cannot be conveyed by aqueducts, or indeed by any exertion of modern art.

LECTURE IX.

OF POETIC IMAGERY FROM THE SACRED HISTORY.

The imagery from the sacred history is the most luminous and evident of all—The peculiar nature of this kind of metaphor explained, as used by the Hebrew poets— The order of the topics which commonly furnish them: the Chaos and Creation; the Deluge; the Destruction of Sodom; the emigration of the Israelites from Egypt; the descent of God upon Mount Sinai—This species of metaphor excellently adapted to the sacred poetry, and particularly to the prophetic: not easy to form any comparison between the sacred and profane poetry in this respect.

FOUR distinct classes of imagery have been specified as capable of being introduced in a metaphorical form into the poetry of the Hebrews; the last of these, or that which is suggested by the more remarkable transactions recorded in the sacred history, now remains to be examined. Here, however, since the nature of the subject differs in some degree from the former objects of our investigation, so the manner of treating it must be also different. The principal design of our late disquisition was, by considering the circumstances, customs, opinions, and sentiments of the Hebrews to facilitate our approach to the interior beauties of their poetry; and, by duly examining the nature of the circumstances, to estimate more properly the force and power of each; to dispel as much as possible the mists of antiquity; to restore their native perspicuity to such passages as appear obscure, their native agreeableness to such as now inspire us with sentiments of disgust, their proper allurement and elegance to those which seem harsh and vulgar, and their original dignity to those which the changeableness of custom has rendered contemptible or mean. In this division of our subject, on the contrary, but little will occur either difficult or obscure: nothing which will seem to require explication or defence: all will be at once perspicuous, splendid, and sublime. Sacred history illuminates this class of imagery with its proper light, and renders it scarcely less conspicuous to us than to the Hebrews themselves.   There is, indeed, this difference, that to the Hebrews the objects of these allusions were all national and domestic; and the power of them in moving or delighting the mind was of course proportionably greater; nay, frequently, the very place, the scene of action, certain traces and express tokens of so many miracles lying before their eyes, must have increased the effect.   To us, on the other hand, however we may hold these facts in veneration, however great and striking they may be in themselves, the distance of time and place must of necessity render them less interesting.

The manner in which these metaphors are formed is well deserving of observation, and is in fact as follows.   In describing or embellishing illustrious actions, or future events of a miraculous nature, the Hebrew poets are accustomed to introduce allusions to the actions of former times, such as possess a conspicuous place in their history; and thus they illuminate with colours, foreign indeed, but similar, the future by the past, the recent by the antique, facts less known by others more generally understood: and as this property seems peculiar to the poetry of the Hebrews, at least is but seldom to be met with in that of other nations, I have determined to illustrate this part of my subject with a greater variety of examples than usual.   I mean, therefore, to instance in a regular order certain topics or common-places of Scripture, which seem to have furnished, if not all, at least the principal part of these allusions: it will be necessary at the same time to remark their figurative power and effect, and the regular and uniform method pursued in the application of them, which has been already stated as characteristical of the poetical imagery of the Hebrews.

The first of these topics, or common-places, is the Chaos and the Creation, which compose the first pages of the sacred history.   These are constantly alluded to, as expressive of any remarkable change, whether prosperous or adverse, in the public affairs—of the overthrow or restoration of kingdoms and nations; and are consequently very common in the prophetic poetry, particularly when any unusual degree of boldness is attempted.   If the subject be the destruction of the Jewish empire by the Chaldeans, or a strong denunciation of ruin against the enemies of Israel, it is depicted in exactly the same colours as if universal nature were about to relapse into the primeval chaos.   Thus Jeremiah, in that

sublime, and indeed more than poetical vision, in which is
represented the impending desolation of Judea:

> "I beheld the earth, and lo! disorder and confusion;
> The heavens also, and there was no light.
> I beheld the mountains, and lo! they trembled;
> And all the hills shook.
> I beheld, and lo! there was not a man;
> And all the fowls of the heavens were fled.
> I beheld, and lo! the fruitful field (was become) the desert;
> And all its cities were thrown down,
> Before the presence of JEHOVAH,
> Before the fierce heat of his anger."*

And on a similar subject Isaiah expresses himself with
wonderful force and sublimity:

> "And he shall stretch over her the line of devastation,
> And the plummet of emptiness."†

Each of them not only had in his mind the Mosaic chaos,
but actually uses the words of the divine historian. The
same subjects are amplified and embellished by the prophets
with several adjuncts:

> "The sun and the moon are darkened,
> And the stars withdraw their shining.
> JEHOVAH also will thunder from Sion,
> And from Jerusalem will he utter his voice;
> And the heavens and the earth shall shake."‡

> "And all the host of heaven shall waste away:
> And the heavens shall be rolled up like a scroll;
> And all their host shall wither;
> As the withered leaf falleth from the vine,
> And as the blighted fig from the fig-tree."§

On the contrary, when he foretells the restoration of the
Israelites:

> "For I am JEHOVAH thy God;
> He who stilleth at once the sea,
> Though the waves thereof roar;
> JEHOVAH God of Hosts is his name.
> I have put my words in thy mouth;
> And with the shadow of my hand have I covered thee;

---

* Jer. iv. 23—26. This image, and that which follows from Joel, the learned
Michaelis will not allow to relate to the Mosaic chaos, but supposes them to be no
more than a description of some horrible and desolating tempest. Of this the reader
must judge for himself.—T.

† Isa. xxxiv. 11.   ‡ Joel iii. 15, 16.   § Isa. xxxiv. 4.

To stretch out the heavens, and to lay the foundations of the
　　earth;
And to say unto Sion, Thou art my people."＊

" Thus therefore shall JEHOVAH console Sion;
He shall console her desolations:
And he shall make her wilderness like Eden;
And her desert like the garden of JEHOVAH:
Joy and gladness shall be found in her;
Thanksgiving, and the voice of melody."†

In the former of these two last quoted examples, the universal deluge is exactly delineated, and on similar subjects
the same imagery generally occurs. Thus, as the devastation of the Holy Land is frequently represented by the restoration of ancient Chaos, so the same event is sometimes
expressed in metaphors suggested by the universal deluge:

" Behold, JEHOVAH emptieth the land and maketh it waste;
He even turneth it upside down, and scattereth abroad the
　　inhabitants.
For the flood-gates from on high are opened;
And the foundations of the earth tremble.
The land is grievously shaken;
The land is utterly shattered to pieces;
The land is violently moved out of her place;

＊ Isa. li. 15, 16. *Ragang,* " tranquillizing, (or) instantaneously stilling;" it is
commonly rendered *clearing, dividing,* not only in this but in the parallel places,
Jer. xxxi. 35. Job xxvi. 12. I am, however, of opinion, that the meaning of the
word has been totally mistaken. It denotes strictly something *instantaneous;* a ces-
sation of motion, or a *sudden quieting,*—as when a bird suddenly lights upon a tree.
See Isa. xxxiv. 14. The Septuagint very properly renders it, in the above quoted
passage in Job, κατεπαυσε. Consult the Concordance.
　" If any doubt can remain concerning this translation of the word *Ragang,*
it will meet sufficient confirmation from the Arabic, in which the same verb implies,
to reduce a thing to its former, or a better, state. Whence are derived the following
words, *Regang,* a lake, (as it were a flood of water stopped and confined;)
Ragiang, to stop or confine a flood of water; *Raganjan,* stagnant or confined waters."
—H.
　Concerning the phrase " to stretch out the heavens," consult Vitring. in loc.—
Author's Note.
　Ver. 16. *To stretch out the heavens.*] In the present text it is לנטע, to
plant the heavens: the phrase is certainly very obscure, and in all probability is a
mistake for לנטות. This latter is the word used in ver. 13, just before, in the
very same sentence: and this phrase occurs frequently in Isaiah, chap. xl. 22;
xlii. 5; xliv. 24; xlv. 12. The former in no other place. It is also very remarkable, that in the Samaritan text, Numb. xxiv. 6, these two words are twice changed
by mistake, one for the other, in the same verse."—Bishop Lowth's *Isaiah,* Notes,
p. 356.
　† Isa. li. 3.

The land reeleth to and fro like a drunkard ;
And moveth this way and that, like a lodge for a night."*

These are great ideas: indeed the human mind cannot
easily conceive any thing greater or more sublime.   There
is nothing, however, of this kind more forcible and elevated
than that imagery which is taken from the destruction of
Sodom, that being the next in order of these topics, and
generally applied to express the punishments to be inflicted
by the Almighty on the wicked:

" He shall rain live coals upon the ungodly,
   Fire and sulphur, and a burning storm :† this shall be the
   contents of their cup."‡

---

* Isa. xxiv. 1. 18, 19, 20.   "*Bolekah*, ερημωσει αυτην, (desolateth it), Sept. ;
and in the same sense the Jewish commentators : amongst whom R. D. Kimchi,
having recourse to the Arabic, says, the word *Balokah* signifies in that language, *a
place in which no plant is found to vegetate.*"—H.
   " The word *Melunah* properly signifies *an abode changed nightly from place to
place ;* and it is therefore expressive of the vibrating and unstable situation of the
earth.   The Sept. is οπωροφυλακιον· the Targ. and Syr. עֲרַיְלָא, *a couch for one
night ; a travelling bed.*   See Buxtorf, *Lex Chald.* col. 1670.   Kimchi also explains
the word in the same manner."   H.—*Author's Note.*

   † This is an admirable image, and is taken from the school of nature.   The wind
Zilgaphoth, which blows from the east, is very pestilential, and therefore almost proverbial amongst the orientals.   In the months of July and August, when it happens
to continue for the space of ten minutes, it kills whatever is exposed to it.   Many
wonderful stories are related of its effects by the Arabians, and their poets feign that
the wicked, in their place of eternal torment, are to breathe this pestiferous wind as
their vital air.—M

   ‡ Psal. xi. 6.   *Pachim,* "live coals," ανθρακας, as it is rendered by the old
Translator, Chrys. in loc.   Globes of fire, or meteors, such as Pliny calls *Bolidas,*
Nat. Hist. ii. 26, or simply the lightning, seems to be understood.   Compare Psal.
xviii. 13, 14.   Josephus on *the Destruction of Sodom,* " God assailed the city with
his thunderbolts," *Antiq.* i. 11.   Philo on the same, " Lightning fell down from
heaven," *De Vit. Mos.* i. 12.   This is certainly more agreeable to the context than
snares.   The root is *Puach,* which, though it sometimes means to *insnare,* yet more
frequently means to *breathe forth* or *emit* fire, for instance.   Ezek. xxi. 31.   "*In
the fire of my wrath I will blow upon thee.*"   The Ammonites are spoken of as
thrown into the furnace of the divine wrath : compare ch. xxii. 21, where almost
the same words occur, except that the corresponding (and in this case synonymous)
verb *Napach* is made use of, whence *Mapnach,* a bellows, Jer. vi. 29.   In the same
sense the verb *Puach* is introduced, Prov. xxix. 8.   " Scorners will *inflame* a city."
So also the Sept. Symmachus, the Syriac; and rightly, as appears from the antithetic
member of the sentence, " but *wise men will turn away* wrath."   From this explication of the root *Puach,* the word *Pach,* a *coal blown up,* is rightly derived ;
and *Piach,* (Exod. ix. 8,) *embers,* in which the fire may yet be excited by blowing.
   " The true sense of the word *Pachim* in this place, *burning coals,* will easily be
confirmed from the use of the verb *Puach* in the Arabic, *to boil a pot :* whence

" For it is the day of vengeance to JEHOVAH ;
　The year of recompence to the defender of the cause of Sion.
　And her torrents shall be turned into pitch,
　And her dust into sulphur ;
　And her whole land shall become burning pitch :
　By night or by day it shall not be extinguished ;
　For ever shall her smoke ascend :
　From generation to generation she shall lie desert ;
　To everlasting ages no one shall pass through her."*

The emigration of the Israelites from Egypt, as it affords
materials for many magnificent descriptions, is commonly
applied, in a metaphorical manner, to many events which
bear no unapt resemblance to it.　Does God promise to his
people liberty, assistance, security, and favour? The *Exodus*
occurs spontaneously to the mind of the poet: the dividing
of the sea, the destruction of the enemy, the desert which
was safely traversed, and the torrents bursting forth from
the rocks, are so many splendid objects that force themselves
on his imagination:

" Thus saith JEHOVAH ;
　Who made a way in the sea,
　And a path in the mighty waters ;
　Who brought forth the rider and the horse, the army and the
　　warrior :
　Together they lay down, they rise no more ;
　They were extinguished, they were quenched like tow :
　Remember not the former things ;
　And the things of ancient times regard not :
　Behold, I make a new thing ;
　Even now shall it spring forth ; will ye not regard it ?
　Yea, I will make in the wilderness a way ;
　In the desert, streams of water." †

There is also another prophecy of the same divine poet,
which in one sense (though I think not the principal) is to
be understood as relating to the liberation of the Israelites
from the Babylonish captivity.　In the exordium the same

Puchat, (vehement heat, or burning.) It cannot, however, be denied, that the orientals sometimes call the lightning *snares* or *chains.* The Arabic word סלסלה, (plur.
סלאמל,) according to Golius, not only signifies a *chain*, but also the *track of a thun-
derbolt through the clouds ;* so called, I apprehend, from the continual coruscations
which seem to be connected with each other like a chain." H.—*Author's Note.*
　* Isa. xxxiv. 8, 9, 10.　　　　　† Isa. xliii. 16—19. See also xlviii. 21.

imagery is introduced, but in a very noble personification,
than which nothing can be more sublime :

" Awake, awake, clothe thyself with strength, O arm of JEHO-
    VAH !
    Awake, as in the days of old, the ancient generations.
    Art thou not the same that smote Rahab, that wounded the
        dragon ?
    Art thou not the same that dried up the sea, the waters of the
        great deep ?
    That made the depths of the sea a path for the redeemed to
        pass through ?"*

Of the same kind is the last of these topics which I shall
instance, the descent of JEHOVAH at the delivery of the law.
When the Almighty is described as coming to execute
judgment, to deliver the pious, and to destroy his enemies,
or in any manner exerting his divine power upon earth, the
description is embellished from that tremendous scene which
was exhibited upon Mount Sinai :† there is no imagery
more frequently recurred to than this, and there is none
more sublime. I will only trouble you with two examples :

" For, behold, JEHOVAH will go forth from his place ;
    And he will come down, and will tread on the high places of
        the earth.
    And the mountains shall be molten under him ;
    And the valleys shall cleave asunder ;
    As wax before the fire,
    As waters poured down a steep place." ‡

" The earth shook and was alarmed,
    And the foundations of the hills rocked with terror,
    For the wrath of JEHOVAH was hot against them.
    Before his face a smoke ascended,
    And a flame consumed before his presence ;
    Burning fires were kindled by it.
    He bowed the heavens and came down,
    And clouds of darkness were beneath his feet.
    He rode upon the pinions of the Cherubim,
    And flew on the wings of the wind.
    He concealed himself in a veil of darkness ;
    A pavilion encompassed him
    Of black water, and thick clouds of æther.§

---

* Isa. li. 9, 10.   † See Exod. xix. 16. 18.   Deut. iv. 11, 12.
‡ Mic. i. 3, 4.
§ Ver. 13 and 14. They seem to be corrected by the parallel passage, 2 Sam.
xxii. 13, 14. See Kennicott, Dissert. i. Of the Hebrew Text, p. 464.

From the brightness before him thick clouds passed along,
Hailstones and burning fires.
JEHOVAH thundered in the heavens ;
And the most high God sent forth his voice :
He shot out his arrows and dispersed the enemies,
And he multiplied his thunder and confounded them." *

These examples, though literally translated, and destitute
of the harmony of verse, will I think sufficiently demonstrate
the force, the grandeur and sublimity of these images, which,
when applied to other events, suggest ideas still greater
than when described as plain facts by the pen of the historian, in however magnificent terms: for to the greatness
and sublimity of the images which are alluded to, is added
the pleasure and admiration which result from the comparison between them and the objects which they are brought
to illustrate.

It is, however, worthy of observation, that, since many of
these images possess such a degree of resemblance as renders
them equally fit for the illustration of the same objects, it
frequently happens that several of them are collected together in order to magnify and embellish some particular
event : of this there is an example in that very thanksgiving
ode of David which we have just now quoted.† For, after
describing the wrath and majesty of God, in imagery taken
from the descent upon Mount Sinai, as already explained,
in the very next verse the division of the Red Sea and the
river Jordan is alluded to :

" Then appeared the channels of the waters ;
The foundations of the world were discovered ;
At thy reproofs, O JEHOVAH !
At the breathing of the spirit of thine anger."‡

It is evident, however, as well from the examples which
have been adduced, as from the nature of the thing itself,
that this species of metaphor is peculiarly adapted to the
prophetic poetry. For some degree of obscurity is the

" The words ברר וגחלי אש, which are now repeated in ver. 14, are wanting in four
manuscripts." K.—*Author's Note.*

  * Psal. xviii. 7—14.

  † See also Isa. xxxiv. and what is remarked on that passage, Lect. 20.

  ‡ Psal. xviii. 16. Allusions to the destruction of Nimrod, the first institutor of
idolatry, and his adherents, are, in the Prophets at least, as frequent, if not more so,
than to any other of the topics here noticed.—Examples of this kind I have pointed
out in a Dissertation on Fallen Angels, published by Johnson; and in another
edition shall instance many more.—S. H.

necessary attendant upon prophecy; not that, indeed, which confuses the diction and darkens the style, but that which results from the necessity of repressing a part of the future, and from the impropriety of making a complete revelation of every circumstance connected with the prediction. The event itself, therefore, is often clearly indicated, but the manner and the circumstances are generally involved in obscurity. To this purpose imagery, such as we have specified, is excellently adapted, for it enables the prophet more forcibly to impress upon the minds of his auditors those parts of his subject which admit of amplification, the force, the splendour, the magnitude of every incident; and at the same time more completely to conceal what are proper to be concealed, the order, the mode, and the minuter circumstances attending the event. It is also no less apparent, that in this respect the sacred poetry bears little or no analogy to that of other nations; since neither history nor fable afforded to the profane writers a sufficiently important store of this kind of imagery; nor did their subjects in general require that use or application of it.

This species of metaphor is indeed so adapted, as I before observed, to the nature of prophecy, that even profane poetry, when of the prophetic kind, is not altogether destitute of it; and we find that Virgil himself, in delivering his prophecies, has more than once adopted this method:

> "Simois nor Xanthus shall be wanting there;
> A new Achilles shall in arms appear:
> And he too goddess-born.——
> Another Tiphys shall new seas explore,
> Another Argo land the chiefs upon th' Iberian shore,
> Another Helen other wars create,
> And great Achilles urge the Trojan fate:" *

Though some perhaps will be inclined to interpret this passage literally from the completion of the *Great Year*, and the doctrine of the general restitution of all things.† There is, indeed, this difference between the sacred and profane writers, that among the latter we find frequent examples of metaphors taken from some remarkable person and event, applied to some other event or character;‡ but we never

---

* Dryden's *Virgil*, Æn. vi. 135. Eclog. iv. 41.
† See Origen *contra Celsum*, lib. iv. p. 208. Edit. Spencer.
‡ Allusions to ancient history, both fabulous and authentic, are common with the poets and orators of all nations. There is a very fine one of this kind in the

find from such facts a general or common image derived, which, as an established mode of expression, is regularly applied to the illustration of similar objects, even to the designation of an universal or unlimited idea.

I have classed all these examples under one general head of Metaphor, though many of them might more properly be referred to that of Allegory; but this circumstance is of no importance to the object which I was desirous of elucidating. Many, indeed, of those which I have produced on this last occasion, might more properly be referred to that sublimer kind of allegory, which in its principal view looks forward to a meaning much more important than that which is obvious and literal; and under the ostensible subject, as under a rind or shell, conceals one interior and more sacred. Of this, however, we shall presently have occasion to speak more explicitly; for when we come to treat of the allegory of the Hebrews, it will be necessary to touch upon that species (however difficult and obscure the subject) in which the sublimity of many of the sacred poems will be found chiefly to consist.*

---

second Philippic of Cicero. When he replies to Antony's accusation of being concerned in Cæsar's death, he exclaims, that he glories in the accusation :—" I esteem it," says he, " as great an honour to be accounted a partner in such an action, as if, with the princes of the Greeks, I had been enclosed in the Trojan horse." But I do not recollect a more beautiful instance than one of a contemporary poet :

> " Humility herself, divinely mild,
> Sublime Religion's meek and modest child,
> Like the dumb son of Crœsus, in the strife,
> When force assail'd his father's sacred life,
> Breaks silence, and, with filial duty warm,
> Bids thee revere her parent's hallow'd form ! "
>
> Hayley's *Essay on History*, addressed to
> Mr. Gibbon, Essay iii. v. 379.—T.

* Professor Michaelis makes a very considerable addition to this Lecture, concerning those images or figures which are taken from poetic fable. He asserts, that such fable is essential to all poetry; that whoever has a taste for poetry cannot possibly take it in a literal sense ; and that the sole purpose of it is ornament and pleasure.

He observes, that there are many particulars in which a wonderful agreement may be discovered between the fables of the Greeks and Romans and those of the Hebrews. He is of opinion, that this agreement clearly indicates a common source, which he supposes to be Egypt. From Egypt, Homer and the other Greek poets borrowed the principal of their fables, as we may learn from Herodotus and Heliodorus : nor is it at all improbable, that the Hebrews should do the same, who were for two successive ages the subjects and scholars of the Egyptians. The most ancient Hebrew poem, Job, abounds in Egyptian and fabulous imagery ; as may be seen in the Professor's Dissertation on that subject before the Academy o Sciences.

He begins with instancing a common fabulous notion of the sun retiring to rest in the sea, and there spending the night in the indulgence of the passions. This, he says, is so familiar an idea to the Hebrews, that it occurs even in prose. The setting sun is called בוא, (to enter or come in,) and the moon האספה, (to be received as a guest.) In the 9th Psalm, however, the fiction is expressed in still bolder terms:

> " For he hath set a tabernacle for the sun,
> Who cometh forth as a bridegroom from his chamber,
> And rejoiceth as a strong man to run a race."

Nor is the description of the Atlantic very far distant from this idea, Psal. cxxxix. 9.

> " If I take the wings of the morning,
> And dwell in the uttermost parts of the sea;
> Even there thy hand shall lead me,
> And thy right hand shall hold me."

The resemblance between this image and the fable of Aurora, who was supposed to retire to rest to the borders of the ocean, and there enter the chamber of Tithonus, can scarcely fail to strike every classical reader. There is this difference, however, between the Greek and Hebrew fictions: With the latter, the "Sun runs his race," and Aurora is depicted with wings; with the former, who perhaps might imitate the Persian manner in the description, the Sun has a chariot and horses, which do not occur in the Hebrew poets, though they are mentioned as appendages to the idol of the Sun, 2 Kings xxiii. 11.

The Professor next observes, that the Greek and Latin Poets assigned to their Jupiter a *chariot* and horses of thunder, probably from the resemblance between the noise of a chariot and that of thunder. The Hebrews, he remarks, have a similar fable; and the *cherubim* are expressly the horses of JEHOVAH's chariot. He refers to a dissertation on this subject published by himself in the Gottingen Memoirs, T. i. p. 157—189. He reminds his readers of the common but truly poetical expression, "JEHOVAH of Hosts," and how frequently he is described as " sitting upon the cherubim," Psal. xcix. 1.

> " JEHOVAH reigneth, let the people tremble;
> He sitteth on the cherubim, let the earth be moved."

In plain language, he thunders so that the earth shakes; or, as Horace would have expressed it, —

> " JEHOVAH per coelum tonantes
> Egit equos, volucremque currum:
> Quo bruta tellus, et vaga flumina,
> Quo Styx, et invisi horrida Tænari
> Sedes, Atlanteusque finis
> Concutitur."

> " JEHOVAH, Lord of all above,
> Late through the floating fields of air,
> The face of heaven serene and fair,
> His thundering steeds and winged chariot drove:
> When at the bursting of his flames,
> The ponderous earth, and vagrant streams,

Infernal Styx, the dire abode
Of hateful Tænarus profound,
And Atlas to his utmost bound,
Trembled beneath the terrors of the God."

Francis's *Hor.* B. i. v. 34.

The expression is still bolder in Psal. lxviii. 17, and the same idea is introduced with superior elegance in the lxvth, where God is described as visiting the earth, and dispensing fatness and plenty. He refers also to Psal. xviii. 10 ; civ. 3, 4, and to Habak. iii. 8. He shows that this has not only been a common fiction with the Greeks and Romans, but even with the Swedes and other northern nations. He remarks the admirable use which Milton has made of it, as well as of other poetical fictions applied to sacred subjects.

Another fable which our commentator points out as common to the Hebrews, with the Greeks and Romans, and evidently derived from the same source, is the fiction of a golden age. To this purpose he cites the three prophecies of Isaiah, in which the kingdom of the Messiah is described in almost the same colours as Virgil depicts the happy state of Rome under Augustus.

He proceeds, in the third place, to point out the resemblance between the poetic descriptions of a future state, which are furnished by the Hebrew poets, and those of the Greeks. He is of an opinion contrary to that of many learned men, who have attributed them to the Celts, that the Greeks were altogether indebted to Egypt for their descriptions. He quotes Josephus, who, speaking of the Essenes, a people who, as to country, philosophy, opinions, discipline, were more Egyptian than Jewish, adds, " that in this respect they resemble the Greeks, namely, in asserting that the good shall enjoy another life, in a pleasant situation beyond the ocean, free from storms, tempests, and all excesses of cold or heat, and which is constantly refreshed by a delightful breeze springing from the ocean." —" The Greeks, in the same manner," he observes, " have assigned to their heroes and demigods the happiness of Elysium." The opinion of the Bramins is similar, who, the Professor asserts, have borrowed all their manners and philosophy from the Egyptians, as well as the Gauls, the Greeks, &c. &c. He thinks this hypothesis is clearly demonstrated by the analogy between these opinions, and the rites or ceremonies of sepulture among the Egyptians. *Buto*, the Egyptian goddess who presided over the dead, had a temple built upon some floating islands in the Butic lake. To this the Greeks are, by their own confession, indebted for their fable of Charon, &c.; for, on the day appointed for burial, the name of the deceased being announced, certain judges were convened at the lake, where a boat was ready; the pilot of which, in the Egyptian language, was called Charon. Before the deceased was put on board, full liberty was given to all present of accusing him. But if no accuser was present, or if his accusation was proved groundless, the body was put into the boat, and carried across the lake to the sepulchral fields, (Diod. Sic. l. i. c. 92.) The sepulchres of their kings also were situated on islands formed by art, by admitting the water of the Nile, as Herodotus testifies, (l. ii. c. 124.)

Moses, therefore, being educated among them, and initiated in their hieroglyphic learning, to which the Grecian mythology is under so many obligations, seems to allude to the fable of Elysium, (or the Blessed Isles,) when in that beautiful poem which constitutes the xcth Psalm, at the 10th verse, he thus expresses himself :—

" The strength of our years is labour and sorrow,
    It passeth *over* quickly, and we *fly*."

" The words *we fly*, if I am not mistaken," adds the Professor, " might be rendered *we set sail*, since there is something alike in the actions of sailing and flying, and the one is frequently made use of poetically for the other."

There is another passage of Moses, which, contrary to the opinion of all the commentators, M. Michaelis observes, seems to have been understood by St. Paul alone in the sense he speaks of; namely, the words " beyond the sea," as alluding to the sepulchre, or Elysian fields.   Moses is addressing the Israelites, not as a poet indeed, but as an orator, concerning " the circumcision of the heart," of which the common rite was only an emblem or a type.   *The law*, says he, *which I command thee this day is not hidden from thee, &c.   It is not in heaven, that thou shouldest say, Who shall go up for us to heaven, and bring it down to us?   Neither is it* BEYOND THE SEA, *that thou shouldest say, Who shall go over the sea for us?* &c. Deut. xxx. 11, 12, 13.   St. Paul, after quoting these words, adds, *Who shall descend into the deep? that is, to bring up Christ again from the dead.*   The Professor acknowledges that these words created him no small difficulty, before he could perceive their agreement with the original; until one of his auditors remarked, that " Moses might probably allude to the custom of the Egyptians, who buried their dead on the other side of a lake," &c.   This sentiment, he says, struck him so forcibly, that he immediately adopted it; and, in consequence of it, offers the following paraphrase of the passage already quoted.   " The precept," says Moses, " which I now inculcate, (namely, that of loving and worshipping the one true God, which is the real circumcision of the heart,) is unlike some of my precepts, which have a mystical meaning, not easily understood.   There is no need that some person of uncommon learning should come down from heaven to instruct you in it; no need that some person should cross the lake to the *Isles of the blessed*, to learn from the dead what this obscure precept conceals.   All is easy and obvious," &c.

Our Annotator next refers to a passage in Job, ch. ix. 25, 26.

> " My days are swifter than a courier,
> They flee away, they see no pleasure :
> They are passed away with the swift ships,
> As an eagle rushing on his prey."

This, he allows, might have been said without any allusion to the *Isles of the Blessed*, or Elysium, though the picture is more striking if taken in that view; but he thinks the allusion is clear beyond a doubt, if we regard the answer of Zophar, ch. xi. 16—18.

> " Thou shalt forget thy misery,
> Or remember it as waters passed away ;
> And after the noon-tide thy age shall be happier,
> Thou shalt fly, (*or sail*,) it shall be morning.
> Thou shalt be secure, because there is hope ;
> Thou shalt dig, (*thy sepulchre*,) and calmly lie down."

If any one should doubt of these examples, he thinks there is one still clearer in ch. xxiv. 18—21.

> " He is light upon the waters :
> His portion in the earth is cursed.
> He shall not behold the way of the vineyards," &c.

' That is," as he explains it, " The wicked shall be carried down the rapid stream of Acheron, and shall have their portion in a land which is accursed.   It shall not be permitted them to enter into the gardens of the blessed."

The learned Professor is of opinion, that even the infernal rivers were not unknown to the Hebrews, and that they are mentioned in the xviiith Psalm under the name of the rivers of *Belial*.   He thinks it not fair to interpret Belial in this place *Satan*, into whose power David was not apprehensive of falling, though he complains that the *snares of death* fell upon him, ver. 4—6.   It is rather, he asserts, derived from the negative particle *beli*, (non,) and *jagnal*, (*altus fuit*,) that is, *not high*, or estimable ; whence men of *Belial* are the *vilest* of men ; and the rivers of *Belial*, the rivers of hell.   The following lines in this sense are truly poetical :

" Distracted with evils, I called upon God ;
I am saved from my enemies.
The snares of death were spread over my soul ;
The floods of hell made me afraid ;
The waters of Tartarus encompassed me," &c.—M.

There is something so ingenious in the above observations, that I could not help exhibiting a slight sketch of them to the reader; but, as I before intimated, many of them are too fanciful to challenge any serious attention. It is impossible, for instance, to find the smallest allusion in the passage from Psal. cxxxix. 9, to any fable similar to that of Aurora and Tithonus. I am, on the contrary, inclined to believe, that nothing more is meant by the *wings of the morning* than an allusion to the swift and fleeting nature of time, and particularly the pleasant and jocund hours of morning ; and the poet only means to say, " Had I the swiftness of time, and could transport myself in a few hours to the boundaries of the ocean, even there," &c. If one were even inclined to admit his hypothesis concerning the *Cherubim*, I see no occasion to suppose them to have any kind of relation to the chariot or horses of the heathen Jupiter. The only poetical idea under which the great Governor of the universe can be depicted, is that of a powerful monarch : and under this idea it is as natural for the Hebrew poets to assign him a chariot and other insignia of royalty, as for the Greeks; and this they may do without having the slightest connexion with each other, or without any necessity of studying in the Egyptian school. The supposition that the prophecies of Isaiah, relating to the time of the Messiah's appearing, are borrowed from the fables concerning the golden age, is still more improbable. The Prophet, in those passages, is describing a state of temporal happiness; such is the intention of those poets who have celebrated the golden age : and is it any thing extraordinary that some similar ideas occur upon a subject perfectly similar, and one of so general a nature? The arguments of our Annotator, to prove that the Greeks were indebted to Egypt for their notions of a future state, demonstrate much learning and ingenuity, and are, I confess, satisfactory and convincing to me : but when he endeavours to find the same notions in the Hebrew poets, the reader will, I think, agree with me, that he is altogether visionary, and strains violently a few general expressions, to adapt them to his particular purpose. I must add, that his Latin translations of those passages of Scripture, which I thought myself in some measure obliged to follow in delivering his sentiments, are by no means so faithful to the original as our common version ; and yet on these depends the principal force of his argument.—T.

The wings of the morning, I believe, stripped of their imagery, are *the beams of the rising sun. Wings* are attributed to the moon by Manilius,

" Ultima ad Hesperios infectis volveris alis :"

and if my memory fail me not, in the hymn ascribed to Homer, εἰς Σελήνην.

Instead also of referring to those imaginary *Isles of the Blessed,* which the Professor thinks are alluded to by Moses, it seems far more probable that he had a retrospect to the place where the wicked after death were supposed to be confined ; and which, from the destruction of the old world by the deluge, the covering of the Asphaltic Vale with the Dead Sea, &c., was believed to be situated *under the waters.* To this idea there are allusions in the sacred writings without number. See the second command in the Decalogue, Job xxvi. 5, 6, and many passages in the Psalms and the Prophets ; the story in the Gospel of the demons entering the herd of swine, and urging them into the *sea,* which in the Septuagint version of Job xli. is styled τον ΤΑΡΤΑΡΟΝ της Αβυσσε, *the* Tartarus *of the abyss.*—S. H.

LECTURE X.

OF ALLEGORY.

Three forms of Allegory; 1. Continued Metaphor; which is scarcely worth distinguishing from the simple Metaphor—The freedom of the Hebrews in confounding the forms of the Metaphor, Allegory, and Comparison: a more perfect form also of Allegory instanced.—2. The Parable; and its principal characteristics: that it ought to be formed from an apt and well-known image, the signification of which is obvious and definite; also from one which is elegant and beautiful; that its parts and adjuncts be perspicuous, and conduce to the main object; that it be consistent, and must not confound the literal and figurative meaning—The Parables of the Prophets, and particularly of Ezekiel, examined according to this standard.

ANOTHER branch of the *Mashal,* or figurative style, is Allegory; that is, a figure which, under the literal sense of the words, conceals a foreign or distant meaning.* Three forms of allegory may be observed in the sacred poetry. The first is that which is commonly treated of by rhetoricians, a continuation of metaphor. "When several kindred metaphors succeed one another, they alter," says Cicero, "the form of a composition; for which reason a succession of this kind is called by the Greeks an *Allegory;* and properly, in respect to the etymology of the word: but Aristotle, instead of considering it as a new species of figure, has more judiciously comprised such modes of expression under the general appellation of Metaphors."† I therefore scarcely esteem it worth while to dwell upon this species of allegory, since

---

* The allegorical seems to be one of the first modes of composition adopted by nations emerging from barbarism. Indeed it is only calculated to interest those who have made little progress in intellectual pursuits. It is a mere play of the fancy, and such as requires not enough of exertion to occupy those who have been accustomed to the exercises of reason. This remark, however, must not be extended to the exclusion of allegorical expressions or passages from poetry; but is meant only to be applied to compositions purely allegorical, such as Spenser's *Fairy Queen,* which, notwithstanding some incomparably poetical passages, finds few readers in the present age.—T.

† Orator.

hitherto I have made no distinction between it and the simple metaphor; for many of the examples, which I produced as metaphors, are probably of this class: the principle of each is the same; nor indeed would it be an easy matter to restrict each to its proper limits, or to define where the one ends or the other begins.

It will not, however, be foreign to our purpose to remark the peculiar manner in which the Hebrew poets use the congenial figures, metaphor, allegory, and comparison, and particularly in the prophetic poetry. When they undertake to express any sentiment in ornamented language, they not only illustrate it with an abundance and variety of imagery, but they seldom temper or regulate this imagery by any fixed principle or standard. Unsatisfied with a simple metaphor, they frequently run into an allegory, or mingle with it a direct comparison. The allegory sometimes precedes and sometimes follows the simile: to this is added a frequent change of imagery, and even of persons and tenses; through the whole displaying a degree of boldness and freedom, unconfined by rule or method, altogether peculiar to the Hebrew poetry.

> " Judah is a lion's whelp : " *

This metaphor is immediately drawn out into an allegory, with a change of person:

> " From the prey, my son, thou art gone up ; "

(to the dens in the mountains understood). In the succeeding sentences the person is again changed, the image is gradually advanced, and the metaphor is joined with a comparison, which is repeated:

> " He stoopeth down, he coucheth as a lion,
> And as a lioness ; who shall rouse him ? "

Of a similar nature is that remarkable prophecy, in which the exuberant increase of the gospel on its first dissemination is most explicitly foretold. In this passage, however, the mixture of the metaphor and comparison, as well as the ellipsis of the word to be repeated, creates a degree of obscurity:

> " Beyond the womb of the morning is the dew of thy offspring
> to thee : " †

---

     * Gen. xlix. 9.   † Psal. cx. 3.

That is, "preferable to the dew which proceeds from the womb of the morning; more copious, more abundant."* In the interpretation of this passage, what monstrous blunders has an ignorance of the Hebrew idiom produced!

There is, indeed, a certain form which this kind of allegory sometimes assumes, more perfect and regular, which therefore ought not to be overlooked, and that is, when it occupies the whole compass and argument of the composition. An excellent example of this may be seen in that well-known allegory of Solomon,† in which old age is so admirably depicted. The inconveniences of increasing years, the debility of mind and body, the torpor of the senses, are

---

* Some of the more modern translators seem at length agreed, that this is the proper sense of the passage; none of them, however, as far as I have been able to judge, has hitherto actually explained it at length. I shall, therefore, take advantage of this opportunity to give my sentiments upon it, lest doubts should afterwards arise concerning the meaning of a very important, and (as I think) a very clear passage of Holy Writ. The principal difficulty proceeds from the word *me-racham*, and from the ambiguity of the particle מ and the ellipsis of the word *tal*; which, I think, will be readily cleared up, if we attend to the following examples, the nature and meaning of which are evidently similar. —Psal. iv. 8.

> "Thou hast excited joy in my heart,
> *Beyond* the time in which their corn and wine increased."

That is, "beyond (or superior to) the joy of that time."—Isa. x. 10.

> "Although their shrines are *before* Jerusalem and Samaria;"

That is, "excel the shrines of Jerusalem and Samaria." Job xxxv. 2. "My justice *before* God;" that is, "My justice is greater than the justice of God:" (compare xxxii. 2, and xl. 8.) In the same manner *me-racham*, "*before the womb*," is the same as *me-tal racham*, "*before the dew of the womb*." Nor are there wanting in the Greeks examples of similar ellipses: Μηδ' Ολυμπιας αγωνα φερτερον αυδασομεν· "Neither can we celebrate a contest more noble *than is that* of Olympia:" μηδε τε Ολυμπιακε αγωνος ετερον βελτιονα. Pind. Ολυμπ. A. v. 11. & *Schol.* Edit. Oxon.

> Ὡς ἡ λακαινα των Φρυγων μειων πολις,

"As if the city of the Lacedemonians were smaller *than that* of the Phrygians.
> Eurip. *Androm.* v. 193.

The metaphor taken from the dew is expressive of fecundity, plenty, multitude; (compare 2 Sam. xvii. 11, 12. Micah v. 7.) "A numerous offspring shall be born unto thee, and a numerous offspring it shall produce." *Jaladecha*, "thy youth," or "the youth that are produced from thee;" the abstract for the concrete, as *Shebah*, "whiteness," or being grey-headed, for a grey-headed man, Lev. xix. 32. *Shebi*, "captivity," for a captive, Isaiah xlix. 24; and so the Chaldee Interpreter takes the following, יתבון לרוחצן תולדתך, "Thy offspring shall sit (or remain) in confidence."—*Author's Note.*

† Eccles. xii. 2—6. Concerning this passage, consult the learned Commentary of that excellent physician of the last century, Dr. John Smith. See also what has been lately advanced on the same subject by the first physician of this age, Dr. R. Mead, in his *Medica Sacra.*—*Author's Note.*

expressed, most learnedly and elegantly indeed, but with
some degree of obscurity, by different images derived from
nature and common life : for by this enigmatical composition, Solomon, after the manner of the oriental sages, meant
to put to trial the acuteness of his readers. It has on this
account afforded much exercise to the ingenuity of the
learned, many of whom have differently, it is true, but with
much learning and sagacity, explained the passage.

There is also in Isaiah an allegory, which, with no less
elegance of imagery, is more simple and regular, more just
and complete in the form and colouring : I shall, therefore,
quote the whole passage.* The prophet is explaining the
design and manner of the Divine judgments : he is inculcat-
ing the principle, that God adopts different modes of acting
in the chastisement of the wicked, but that the most perfect
wisdom is conspicuous in all; that " he will," as he had
urged before, " exact judgment by the line, and righteousness by the plummet;"† that he ponders with the most
minute attention the distinctions of times, characters, and
circumstances; all the motives to lenity or severity. All
this is expressed in a continued allegory, the imagery of
which is taken from agriculture and threshing : the use and
suitableness of which imagery, as in a manner consecrated
to this subject, I have formerly explained, so that there is
no need of further detail at present.

" Listen ye, and hear my voice :
   Attend and hearken unto my words.
   Doth the husbandman plough every day that he may sow,
   Opening, and breaking the clods of his field ?
   When he hath made even the face thereof,
   Doth he not then scatter the dill, and cast abroad the
      cummin ;
   And sow the wheat in due measure ;
   And the barley, and the rye, hath its appointed limit ?
   For his God rightly instructeth him ; he furnisheth him with
      knowledge.
   The dill is not beaten out with the corn-drag ;
   Nor is the wheel of the wain made to turn upon the cummin :
   But the dill is beaten out with the staff ;
   And the cummin with the flail ; but the bread-corn‡ with the
      threshing-wain.

---

        * Isa. xxviii. 23—29.   † Isa. xxviii. 17.
    ‡ לחם יורק.]—I have annexed these to the preceding, disregarding the Masoretic
distinction : in this I follow the LXX (though they have greatly mistaken the

"But not for ever will he continue thus to thrash it;
Nor to vex it with the wheel of his wain;
Nor to bruise it with the hoofs of his cattle.
This also proceedeth from JEHOVAH God of Hosts:
He showeth himself wonderful in counsel, great in operation."*

Another kind of allegory is that which, in the proper and restricted sense, may be called Parable, and consists of a continued narration of a fictitious event, applied by way of simile to the illustration of some important truth. The Greeks call these allegories αινοι, (or *apologues*,) the Latins *fabulæ* (or fables;) and the writings of the Phrygian sage, or those composed in imitation of him, have acquired the

---

sense) and Symmachus. I suspect also that the ו before לחם has been obliterated, which Symmachus expressed by the particles δε, the Vulgate by *autem*. The translation will sufficiently explain my reasons. *Lechem*, however, seems to be taken for corn, Psalm civ. 14; and Eccles. xi. 1, "Cast thy bread," that is, "sow thy seed, or corn, upon the face of the waters:" in plain terms, sow without any hope of a harvest; do good to them on whom you even think your benefaction thrown away: A precept enforcing great and disinterested liberality, with a promise annexed to it, "for after many days thou shalt find it again:" at length, if not in the present world, at least in a future, thou shalt have a reward. The learned Dr. George Jubb, the gentleman alluded to in p. 67, suggested this explanation, which he has elegantly illustrated from Theognis and Phocylides, who intimate, that to do acts of kindness to the ungrateful and unworthy, is the same as sowing the sea:—

> "Vain are the favours done to vicious men,
> Not vainer 'tis to sow the foaming deep;
> The deep no pleasant harvest shall afford,
> Nor will the wicked ever make return."
>
> Theog. Γνωμ. v. 105.

> "To befriend the wicked is like sowing in the sea."
>
> Phocyl. v. 141.

These, indeed, invert the precept of Solomon; nor is it extraordinary that they should:

> "The one, frail human power alone produc'd;
> The other, God."   *Author's Note.*

* "Four methods of threshing are here mentioned, by different instruments; the flail, the drag, the wain, and the treading of the cattle. The staff or flail was used for the grain that was too tender to be treated in the other methods. The drag consisted of a sort of frame of strong planks, made rough at the bottom with hard stone or iron: it was drawn by horses or oxen over the corn-sheaves spread on the floor, the drivers sitting upon it. The wain was much like the former, but had wheels with iron teeth, or edges, like a saw; and it should seem that the axle was armed with iron teeth or serrated wheels throughout. The drag not only forced out the grain, but cut the straw in pieces for fodder for the cattle; for in the Eastern countries they have no hay. The last method is well known from the law of Moses, which 'forbids the ox to be muzzled when he treadeth out the corn.'"— Bishop Lowth's *Isaiah*, p. 278.

greatest celebrity. Nor has our Saviour himself disdained
to adopt the same method of instruction, of whose parables
it is doubtful whether they excel most in wisdom and utility,
or in sweetness, elegance, and perspicuity. I must observe,
that the appellation of parable having been applied to his
discourses of this kind, the term is now restricted from its
former extensive signification to a more confined sense.
This species of composition occurs very frequently in the
prophetic poetry, and particularly in that of Ezekiel. But
to enable us to judge with more certainty upon the subject,
it will be necessary to explain in a few words some of the
primary qualities of the poetic parables, that, by considering
the general nature of them, we may decide more accurately
on the merits of particular examples.

It is the first excellence of a parable to turn upon an
image well known and applicable to the subject, the meaning
of which is clear and definite; for this circumstance will give
it perspicuity, which is essential to every species of allegory.
If, therefore, by this rule we examine the parables of the
sacred Prophets, we shall, I am persuaded, find them not in
the least deficient. They are in general founded upon such
imagery as is frequently used, and similarly applied by way
of metaphor and comparison in the Hebrew poetry. Most
accurate examples of this are to be found in the parable of
the deceitful vineyard,* of the useless vine,† which is given
to the fire; for under this imagery the ungrateful people of
God are more than once described. I may instance also
that of the lion's whelps falling into the pit,‡ in which is appositely displayed the captivity of the Jewish princes; or that
of the fair, lofty, and flourishing cedar of Lebanon,§ which
raised its head to the clouds, cut down at length and neglected, exhibiting, as in a picture, the prosperity and the fall
of the king of Assyria. I will add one more example, (there
is, indeed, scarcely any which might not with propriety be
introduced here), I mean that in which the love of God

* Isaiah v. 1–7.   † Ezek. xv. and xix. 10—14.   ‡ Ezek. xix. 1—9.
§ Ezek. xxxi. I take this passage according to the common explanation, disregarding that of Meibomius, which I find is blamed by many of the learned;
and indeed it has some difficulties, which are not easy to clear away. Nor can I
indeed relish that *Assyrian*, who has intruded himself I know not how. In the
10th, for גבהת I think it were better to read גבה with the Syriac and Vulgate,
which reading is adopted by the learned Houbigant. Observe also, that the LXX
have very rightly rendered *Ben Grabathim* by εἰς μεσον των νεφελων, "through
the midst of the clouds."—*Author's Note.*

towards his people, and their piety and fidelity to him, are expressed by an allusion to the solemn covenant of marriage. Ezekiel has pursued this image with uncommon freedom in two parables;* in truth, almost all the sacred poets have touched upon it. There was, therefore, no part of the imagery of the Hebrew poetry more established than this; nor ought it to appear extraordinary, that Solomon, in that most elegant poem the Canticles, should distinguish and depict the most sacred of all subjects, with similar outlines, and in similar colours.

It is not, however, sufficient, that the image be apt and familiar: it must also be elegant and beautiful in itself: since it is the purpose of a poetic parable not to explain more perfectly some proposition, but frequently to give it more animation and splendour. The imagery from natural objects is superior to all other in this respect; for almost every picture from nature, if accurately drawn, has its peculiar beauty. As the parables of the sacred poets, therefore, consist chiefly of this kind of imagery, the elegance of the materials generally serves to recommend them. If there be any of a different kind, such as may be accounted less delicate and refined, it ought to be considered, whether they are not to be accounted among those the dignity and grace of which are lost to us, though they were perhaps wanting in neither to people of the same age and country. If any reader, for instance, should be offended with the boiling pot of Ezekiel,† and the scum flowing over into the fire; let him remember, that the prophet, who was also a priest, took the allusion from his own sacred rites: nor is there a possibility that an image could be accounted mean or disgusting, which was connected with the holy ministration of the Temple.

It is also essential to the elegance of a parable, that the imagery should not only be apt and beautiful, but that all its parts and appendages should be perspicuous and pertinent. It is, however, by no means necessary, that in every parable the allusion should be complete in every part; such a degree of resemblance would frequently appear too minute and exact: but when the nature of the subject will bear, much more when it will even require a fuller explanation, and when the similitude runs directly, naturally, and regularly, through every circumstance, then it cannot be doubted that it is productive of the greatest beauty. Of all these

* Ezek. xvi. and xxiii.   † Ezek. xxiv, 3, &c.

excellences, there cannot be more perfect examples than the parables which have been just specified. I will also venture to recommend the well-known parable of Nathan,* although written in prose, as well as that of Jotham,† which appears to be the most ancient extant, and approaches somewhat nearer to the poetical form.‡

To these remarks I will add another, which may be considered as the criterion of a parable, namely, that it be consistent throughout, and that the literal be never confounded with the figurative sense. In this respect it materially differs from the former species of allegory, which, deviating but gradually from the simple metaphor, does not always immediately exclude literal expressions, or words without a figure.§ But both the fact itself, and this distinction, will more evidently appear from an example of each kind.

---

* 2 Sam. xii. 1—4.   † Judges ix. 7—15.

‡ Poetry seems to me to be often strangely confounded with oratory, from which it is, however, very different. These instances appear to me only the rudiments of popular oratory, the *ancient* and *unrefined mode of speaking*, as Livy calls it : and if the reader will be at the pains to examine Liv. l. ii. c. 32, I dare believe he will be of the same opinion. Poetry, as our Author himself has stated, is one of the first arts, and was in a much more perfect state than we should suppose from the passages in question long before the days of Jotham : oratory is of more recent origin, and was, we may well suppose, at that period in its infancy ; as Cicero remarks, that it was one of the latest of the arts of Greece. *Brut.* c. 7.—M.

See *Essays Historical and Moral*, p. 41.

§ I think there is great judgment and taste in this remark, of which the parable of the Good Samaritan will afford a happy exemplification in the mention of the *man's journeying from Jerusalem to Jericho*, a circumstance that gives substance and reality to the parable.

It may be observed, moreover, that in allegorical writing the literal sense may be sometimes suffered to obtrude itself upon the figurative with very good effect, just as the gold that betrays itself in glimpses from the plumage of the peacock, the scales of the dolphin, or (to illustrate my idea from Spenser) the texture of the loom, augments thereby the splendour of their colours.

> ——" round about the walls yclothed were
> With goodly arras of great maiesty,
> Woven with gold and silk so close and nere
> That the rich metall lurked privily,
> As faining to be hidd from envious eye ;
> Yet here, and there, and every-where, unawares
> It shewed itselfe, and shone unwillingly ;
> Like a discolour'd snake, whose hidden snares
> Through the green grass his long bright burnisht back declares."
> *Faery Queene*, B. iii. c. 11. s. 28.

A fine poetical allegory of this kind may be seen in the first strophe of Gray's Ode on Poesy.—S. H.

The Psalmist, (whoever he was,) describing the people of
Israel as a vine,* has continued the metaphor, and happily
drawn it out through a variety of additional circumstances.
Among the many beauties of this allegory, not the least
graceful is that modesty with which he enters upon and concludes his subject, making an easy and graceful transition
from plain to figurative language, and no less delicately re-
ceding back to the plain and unornamented narrative :

> " Thou hast brought a vine out of Egypt ;
> Thou hast cast out the nations, and planted it,
> Thou preparedst room before it "——

After this follow some figurative expressions less cautiously
introduced ; in which, when he has indulged for some time,
how elegantly does he revert to his proper subject !

> " Return, O God of Hosts !
> Look down from heaven, and behold
> And visit this vine ;
> And the branch which thy right hand hath planted ;
> And the offspring† which thou madest strong for thyself.
> It is burned in the fire, it is cut away ;
> By the rebuke of thy countenance they perish.
> Let thy hand be upon the man of thy right hand ;‡
> Upon the son of man whom thou madest strong for thyself."

You may easily perceive, Gentlemen, how, in this first kind
of allegory, the literal may be mingled with the figurative
sense ; and even how graceful this practice appears, since light
is more agreeably thrown upon the subject in an oblique
manner, without too bare and direct an explication. But it is
different, when the same image puts on the form of the other
sort of allegory, or parable, as in Isaiah.§ Here is no room
for literal, or even ambiguous expressions ; every word is
figurative ; the whole mass of colouring is taken from the
same palette. Thus what, in the former quotation, is expressed in undisguised language, namely, " the casting out
of the nations, the preparation of the place, and its destruc-

---

* Psal. lxxx. 9 – 18.

† If I am not mistaken, all the old translators, the Chaldee excepted, seem
to have read in this place *Ben Adam*, ' the Son of Man,' as in ver. 18. Dr.
Kennicott affirms also that he found this same reading in one manuscript. H.—
Author's Note.

‡ That is, *the man who is joined to thee by a solemn covenant.* The orientals all
swear by lifting up the *right hand.* Hence, also, among the Arabs, *jamin* is to
swear.—M.

§ Chap. v. 1—7.

tion from the rebuke of the Lord," is by Isaiah expressed
wholly in a figurative manner:—"The Lord gathered out
the stones from his vineyard, and cleared it; but when it
deceived him, he threw down its hedge, and made it waste,
and commanded the clouds that they should rain no rain
upon it." Expressions which in the one case possess a peculiar grace, would be absurd and incongruous in the other;
for the continued metaphor and the parable have a very
different aim. The sole intention of the former is to embellish a subject, to represent it more magnificently, or at the
most to illustrate it; that, by describing it in more elevated
language, it may strike the mind more forcibly: but the
intent of the latter is to withdraw the truth for a moment
from our sight, in order to conceal whatever it may contain
ungraceful or disgusting, and to enable it secretly to insinuate itself, and obtain an ascendency as it were by stealth.
There is, however, a species of parable, the intent of which
is only to illustrate the subject: such as that remarkable one
of Ezekiel,* which I just now commended, of the cedar of
Lebanon: than which, if we consider the imagery itself,
none was ever more apt or more beautiful; if the description
and colouring, none was ever more elegant or splendid; in
which, however, the poet has occasionally allowed himself
to blend the figurative with the literal description:† Whether he has done this because the peculiar nature of this
kind of parable required it, or whether his own fervid imagination alone, which disdained the stricter rules of composition, was his guide, I can scarcely presume to determine.

* Chap. xxxi.   † See ver. 11. 14—17.

H

LECTURE XI.

OF THE MYSTICAL ALLEGORY.

The definition of the Mystical Allegory—Founded upon the allegorical or typical nature of the Jewish religion—The distinction between this and the two former species of Allegory; in the nature of the materials: it being allowable in the former to make use of imagery from different objects; in this, only such as is derived from things sacred, or their opposites: in the former, the exterior image has no foundation in truth; in the latter, both images are equally true—The difference in the form or manner of treating them—The most beautiful form is when the corresponding images run parallel through the whole poem, and mutually illustrate each other—Examples of this in the iid and lxxiid Psalms—The parabolic style admirably adapted to this species of allegory; the nature of which renders it the language most proper for prophecy—Extremely dark in itself, but it is gradually cleared up by the series of events foretold, and more complete revelation; time also, which in the general obscures, contributes to its full explanation.

THE third species of allegory, which also prevails much in the prophetic poetry, is when a double meaning is couched under the same words: or when the same prediction, according as it is differently interpreted, relates to different events, distant in time, and distinct in their nature. These different relations are termed the literal and the mystical senses; and these constitute one of the most difficult and important topics of Theology. The subject is, however, connected also with the sacred poetry, and is therefore deserving of a place in these Lectures.

In the sacred rites of the Hebrews, things, places, times, offices, and such like, sustain as it were a double character, the one proper or literal, the other allegorical; and in their writings these subjects are sometimes treated of in such a manner as to relate either to the one sense or the other singly, or to both united. For instance, a composition may treat of David, of Solomon, of Jerusalem, so as to be understood to relate simply either to the city itself and its monarchs, or else to those objects which, in the sacred allegory of the Jewish religion, are denoted by that city and by those monarchs: or the mind of the author may embrace both objects at once, so that the very words which express the one in the plain, proper, historical, and commonly received sense, may typify the other in the sacred, interior, and prophetic sense.

From these principles of the Jewish religion, this kind of allegory, which I am inclined to call *mystical*, seems more especially to derive its origin; and from these we must endeavour at an explanation of it. But its nature and peculiar properties will probably be more easily demonstrable, if we previously define in what respects it is different from the two former species of allegory.

The first remarkable difference is, that in allegories of the kind already noticed, the writer is at liberty to make use of whatever imagery is most agreeable to his fancy or inclination: there is nothing in universal nature, nothing which the mind perceives, either by sense or reflexion, which may not be adapted in the form of a continued metaphor, or even of a parable, to the illustration of some other subject. This latter kind of allegory, on the contrary, can only be supplied with proper materials from the sacred rites of the Hebrews themselves; nor can it be introduced, except in relation to such things as are directly connected with the Jewish religion, or their immediate opposites. For, to Israel, Sion, Jerusalem, in the allegorical as well as the literal sense, are opposed Assyria, Babylon, Egypt, Idumea; and the same opposition exists in other subjects of a similar nature. The two former kinds of allegory are of the same general nature with the other figures, and partake of the common privileges of poetry; this latter, or mystical allegory, has its foundation in the nature of the Jewish economy, and is adapted solely to the poetry of the Hebrews.* Hence that truly Divine

---

* I admire the perspicacity of our Author in discovering this circumstance, and his candour in so freely disclosing his opinion. I am, however, much inclined to suspect those qualities which are supposed to be altogether peculiar to the sacred poetry of the Hebrews; and there is, I confess, need of uncommon force of argument to convince me, that the sacred writings are to be interpreted by rules in every respect different from those by which other writings and other languages are interpreted; but, in truth, this hypothesis of a double sense being applicable to the same words, is so far from resting on any solid ground of argument, that I find it is altogether founded on the practice of commentators, and their vague and tralatitious opinions.—M.

Spirit, which has not disdained to employ poetry as an interpreter of its sacred will, has also in a manner appropriated to its own use this kind of allegory, as peculiarly adapted to the publication of future events, and to the typifying of the most sacred mysteries: so that should it, on any occasion, be applied to a profane and common subject, being diverted from its proper end, and forced, as it were, from its natural bias, it would inevitably want all its power and elegance.

There is likewise this further distinction, that in those other forms of allegory the exterior or ostensible imagery is fiction only; the truth lies altogether in the interior or remote sense, which is veiled as it were under this thin and pellucid covering. But in the allegory of which we are now treating, each idea is equally agreeable to truth. The exterior or ostensible image is not a shadowy colouring of the interior sense, but is in itself a reality: and although it sustain another character, it does not wholly lay aside its own. For instance, in the metaphor or parable, the Lion, the Eagle, the Cedar, considered with respect to their identical existence, are altogether destitute of reality; but what we read of David, Solomon, or Jerusalem, in this sublimer kind of allegory, may be either accepted in a literal sense, or may be mystically interpreted according to the religion of the Hebrews; and in each view, whether considered conjunctly or apart, will be found equally agreeable to truth.

Thus far this kind of allegory differs from the former in the materials, or in the nature of the imagery which it employs; but there is some difference also in the form or manner of introducing this imagery. I had occasion before to remark the liberty which is allowed in the continued metaphor, of mingling the literal with the figurative meaning, that is, the obvious with the remote idea; which is a liberty altogether inconsistent with the nature of a parable. But to establish any certain rules with regard to this point in the conduct of the mystical allegory, would be a difficult and hazardous undertaking. For the Holy Spirit has evidently chosen different modes of revealing his sacred counsels, according to the circumstances of persons and times; inciting and directing at pleasure the minds of his prophets:* at one time displaying with an unbounded liberality the clear

---

* And yet those metaphors and parables, the laws and principles of which our Author has so correctly defined, proceed from the same Holy Spirit; and our Author does not deny his being confined by those laws.—M.

indications of future events; at another, imparting some obscure intimations with a sparing hand. Thus there is a vast variety in the use and conduct of the mystical allegory; in the modes in which the corresponding images are arranged, and in which they are obscured or eclipsed by one another. Sometimes the obvious or literal sense is so prominent and conspicuous, both in the words and sentiments, that the remote or figurative sense is scarcely permitted to glimmer through it:* On the other hand, and that more frequently, the figurative sense is found to beam forth with so much perspicuity and lustre, that the literal sense is quite cast into a shade, or becomes indiscernible. Sometimes the principal or figurative idea is exhibited to the attentive eye with a constant and equal light: and sometimes it unexpectedly glares upon us, and breaks forth with sudden and astonishing coruscations, like a flash of lightning bursting from the clouds. But the mode or form of this figure which possesses the most beauty and elegance, (and that elegance is the principal object of this disquisition,) is when the two images, equally conspicuous, run as it were parallel through the whole poem, mutually illustrating and correspondent to each other. Though the subject be obscure, I do not fear being able to produce one or two undoubted instances of this peculiar excellence, which, if I am not mistaken, will sufficiently explain what I have advanced concerning the nature of the mystical allegory.

The subject of the second Psalm is the establishment of David upon the throne agreeably to the Almighty decree, notwithstanding the fruitless opposition of his enemies. The character which David sustains in this poem is twofold, literal and allegorical. If·on the first reading of the Psalm we consider the character of David in the literal sense, the composition appears sufficiently perspicuous, and abundantly illustrated by facts from the sacred history. Through the whole, indeed, there is an unusual fervour of language, a

---

* When this happens to be the case, how are we to know that the other subject or sentiment, which our Author describes as almost totally eclipsed or extinguished by the superior light, is intended by the writer? If, as I am fully persuaded, a clear and exact picture of the Messiah be exhibited in Psa. cx., what occasion is there to apply it also to David, who never performed the priestly function, nor ever sat at the right hand of God, that is, in the Holy of Holies, at the right of the Ark of the Covenant? On the contrary, if in Psa. xviii. the description of David's victories be so predominant as that it can scarcely be made to speak any other sentiment, what occasion is there to apply it at all to the Messiah?—M.

brilliancy of metaphor; and sometimes the diction is uncommonly elevated, as if to intimate, that something of a more sublime and important nature lay concealed within, and as if the poet had some intention of admitting us to the secret recesses of his subject. If, in consequence of this indication, we turn our minds to contemplate the internal sense, and apply the same passages to the allegorical David, a nobler series of events is presented to us, and a meaning not only more sublime, but even more perspicuous, rises to the view. Should any thing at first appear bolder and more elevated than the obvious sense would bear, it will now at once appear clear, expressive, and admirably adapted to the dignity of the principal subject. If, after having considered attentively the subjects apart, we examine them at length in a united view, the beauty and sublimity of this most elegant poem will be improved.* We may then perceive the vast disparity of the two images, and yet the continual harmony and agreement that subsists between them; the amazing resemblance, as between near relations, in every feature and lineament; and the accurate analogy which is preserved, so that either may pass for the original whence the other was copied. New light is reflected upon the diction, and a degree of dignity and importance is added to the sentiments, whilst they gradually rise from humble to more elevated objects, from human to divine, till at length the great subject of the poem is placed in the most conspicuous light, and the composition attains the highest point of sublimity.

What has been remarked concerning this Psalm, may be applied with propriety to the seventy-second, which exactly resembles it both in matter and form. It might not improperly be entitled the Inauguration of Solomon. The nature of the allegory is the same with the former; the style is something different, on account of the disparity of the subject. In the one, the pomp and splendour of victory is displayed; in the other, the placid image of peace and felicity.

---

* If, as we learn from the authority of the apostle Paul, this Psalm relates chiefly to Christ, his resurrection and kingdom, why should we at all apply it to David? I do not deny that the victories of David, as well as of other kings of Jerusalem, to whom no person has thought of applying the poem in question, might be celebrated in language equally bold and powerful: but let us remember, that we have no right to say a work has relation to every person of whom something similar might be said, but to that person alone who is the actual subject of it. If Christ, therefore, be the subject of this poem, let us set aside David altogether.—M.

The style of the latter is, therefore, more calm and temperate, more ornamented, more figurative; not abounding in the same boldness of personification as the former, but rather touched with the gay and cheerful colouring of nature, in its most flourishing and delightful state. From this example some light will be thrown upon the nature of the parabolic style; in particular, it will appear admirably adapted to this kind of allegory, on account of its abounding so much in this species of imagery. For, as the imagery of nature is equally calculated to express the ideas of divine and spiritual or of human things, a certain analogy being preserved in each; so it easily admits that degree of ambiguity which appears essential to this figure. By these means the composition is at the same time diversified and perspicuous, applicable to both senses, and obscure in neither; and, completely comprehending both parts of the allegory, may clearly and distinctly be referred to either.

Still, however, a degree of obscurity must occasionally attend this style of composition; and this obscurity not only results from the nature of the figure, but is even not without its peculiar utility. For, the mystical allegory is on this very account so agreeable to the nature of prophecy, that it is the form which the latter generally, and I might add, lawfully, assumes, as most fitted for the prediction of future events. It describes events in a manner exactly conformable to the intention of prophecy; that is, in a dark, disguised, and intricate manner; sketching out in a general way their form and outline, and seldom descending to minuteness of description and exactness of detail. If on some occasions it expressly signifies any notable circumstance, it seems to be for two principal reasons:[*] first, that, as generally happens, by suddenly withdrawing from our view the literal meaning, the attention may be excited to the investigation of the figurative sense; and secondly, that certain express marks, or distinguishing features, may occasionally show themselves, which, after the accomplishment of the prediction, may be sufficient to remove every doubt, and to assert and confirm, in all points, the truth and divinity of the prophecy.[†]

---

[*] Psa. xxii. 17, 18, 19; and lxix. 22.

[†] If there be any one prophecy in the Bible comprising a double sense, surely it is that in Isaiah, ch. vii. 15, &c.; but notwithstanding the pretended clue to its two-fold import, which some have flattered themselves with discovering in the separate addresses of the Prophet *to the King*, and *to the House of David;* how

The prophetic, indeed, differs in one respect from every other species of the sacred poetry: when first divulged, it is impenetrably obscure;* and time, which darkens every other composition, elucidates it.   That obscurity, therefore, in which at first this part of the sacred writings was involved, is now in a great measure removed: there are now many things which the course of events (the most certain inter preter of prophecy) has completely laid open; from many the Holy Spirit has itself condescended to remove the veil with which they were at first concealed; many sacred institutions there are, the reason and intent of which are more clearly understood, since the design of the Jewish dispensation has been more perfectly revealed.   Thus it happens, that, instructed and supported by these aids, of which the ancient Hebrews were destitute, and which in truth appear not to have been conceded to the prophets themselves, we come better accomplished for the knowledge and comprehension of that part of the sacred poetry which is the most singular in its nature, and by far the most difficult of explanation.

little room there is for so fanciful an hypothesis, those may see who will refer to Mr. Postlethwaite's elegant discourse on the subject.   [*Cambridge*, 1781.]—S. H.

* What our Author has advanced concerning the language of prophecy, is not quite so satisfactory as I could have wished ; for though the accomplishment of an event predicted be the only certain key to the precise application of every term which the prediction contained, yet if there be not something in the words of the prophecy which at the time of its delivery may serve to mark its general import, how should those to whom it is addressed apply the prediction to its proper object and purpose?   Our Author traces in the prophetic language an assumption of imagery from the Chaos, Creation, Deluge, &c.; surely then, if the application of figures from those topics were apposite and obvious, they must have conveyed the general purport of the prediction which contained them; and, instead of being designed to obscure its real meaning, were doubtless employed for the contrary purpose.   To me the reason of the thing is so clear, and our Saviour's practice of referring to former events with this very intent so certain, (see Matt. xxiv. 15. 37, &c.,) that I cannot but consider it as the most prominent characteristic of the prophetic language.—S. H.

LECTURE XII.

OF THE COMPARISON.

Comparisons are introduced for three purposes; illustration, amplification, and variety—For the first an image is requisite, apt, well-known, and perspicuous; it is of little consequence whether it be sublime or beautiful, or neither: hence comparisons from objects which are in themselves mean and humble, may be sometimes useful—For the purpose of amplification, an image is requisite which is sublime or beautiful, even though it should be less apt and perspicuous: and on this plea, a degree of obscurity, or a remoteness in the resemblance, may sometimes be excused —When variety is the object, splendid, beautiful, and elegant imagery must be sought for; and which has an apt agreement with the object of the comparison in the circumstances or adjuncts, though the objects themselves may be different in kind —The most perfect comparison is that in which all these excellencies are united— The peculiar form of comparisons in the Hebrew poetry; it results from the nature of the sententious style—They are short, frequent, simple, depending often on a single attribute—Different images displayed in the parallel sentences: many comparisons are arranged in this manner to illustrate the same subject; or different attributes of the same comparison are often distributed in the different divisions or parallelisms.

In the following Lecture I shall endeavour to treat of the Comparison, which I have classed the third in order of the poetical figures, with a view of illustrating in some degree both its general properties, and its peculiar application and force in the poetic compositions of the Hebrews.

Comparisons serve three distinct purposes; namely, illustration, amplification, and pleasure or variety.*

* If I am not mistaken, among those writers who enter into the minuteness of criticism, a distinction is observed in the use of the words *Comparison, Simile,* and *Allusion. Comparison* seems to be not only the general term, which includes the whole class, but is more immediately appropriated to a certain species; I mean the most perfect of them, where the resemblance is minutely traced through all the agreeing parts of the objects assimilated.—"Censure," says Dr. Ogden, in one of

In the first place, comparisons are introduced to illustrate a subject, and to place it in a clearer and more conspicuous point of view. This is most successfully effected when the object which furnishes the simile is familiar and perspicuous, and when it exactly agrees with that to which it is compared. In this species of comparison, elevation or beauty, sublimity or splendour, are of little consequence; strict propriety, and a direct resemblance, calculated exactly for the explanation of the subject, is a sufficient commendation. Thus Homer very accurately depicts the numbers of the Grecian army, their ardour and eagerness for battle, by a comparison taken from flies collected about a milk-pail;* and Virgil compares the diligence of the Tyrians in building their city, and the variety of their occupations, with the labours of the bees;† without in the least degrading the dignity of the Epic Muse.

his excellent sermons, "is so seldom in season, that it may not unaptly be compared to that bitter plant which comes to maturity but in the age of a man, and is said to blossom but once in a hundred years."

Simile seems to be a term chiefly appropriated to poetry, and often implies a slighter and more fanciful resemblance than the former word.

A species of *comparison* not extending to a *simile* is called an *allusion*; it chiefly consists in comparing one fact with another. The most fanciful and poetical is, when two facts, bearing a remote resemblance in a few circumstances, are compared; a beautiful example of which may be found in one of Dr. Ogden's sermons.—" If it be the obscure, the minute, the ceremonial parts of religion for which we are contending, though the triumph be empty, the dispute is dangerous : like the men of Ai, we pursue, perhaps, some little party that flies before us, and are anxious that not a straggler should escape ; but when we look behind us, we behold our city in flames."—T.

* ————" thick as insects play,
    The wandering nation of a summer's day,
    That, drawn by milky streams at evening hours,
    In gather'd swarms surround the rural bowers;
    From pail to pail with busy murmur run
    The gilded legions, glittering in the sun."—Pope's *Hom. Il.* ii. 552.

Mr. Pope has considerably elevated this passage by the splendour of his imagery and diction. " The wandering nation," and the " gilded legions ;" each of these expressions raises the image very considerably, (though I do not altogether approve of thus heaping figure upon figure, or rather in this instance reverting in the way of metaphor to the first object of the comparison, for " gilded legions" are here actually compared with " gilded legions.")—The rural scenery also, and the pleasant time of evening, give elegance to an idea very coarse and disgusting in itself.—T.

† *Æn.* i. 432. See the use to which Milton has applied the same diminutive insect, *Paradise Lost*, B. i. 767, and the address with which the simile is introduced by the expressions, *thick-swarm'd*, &c. in the lines immediately preceding. No writer was ever so great a master of amplification as Milton. For proofs of this assertion, in addition to the comparison just referred to, see B. i. v. 196—285, &c. B. ii. v. 285, 485, and other passages without number.—S. H.

I might produce many examples to the purpose from the sacred poetry, but shall content myself with two or three, than which, both as to matter and expression, nothing can be meaner or more vulgar; nothing, however, can be conceived more forcible or expressive. Isaiah introduces the King of Assyria insolently boasting of his victories:

" And my hand hath found, as a nest, the riches of the peoples;
And as one gathereth eggs deserted,
So have I made a general gathering of the earth:
And there was no one that moved the wing,
That opened the beak, or that chirped."*

And Nahum, on a similar subject:

" All thy strong-holds shall be like fig-trees with the first ripe figs;
If they be shaken, they fall into the mouth of the eater."†

There is also another comparison of Isaiah taken from domestic life, very obvious and very common; but which, for the gracefulness of the imagery, the elegance of the arrangement, and the forcible expression of the tenderest affections, has never been exceeded:

" But Sion saith : Jehovah hath forsaken me ;
And my Lord hath forgotten me.
Can a women forget her sucking infant ;
That she should have no tenderness for the son of her womb?
Even these may forget ;
But I will not forget thee."‡

---

* Isaiah x. 14.   † Nah. iii. 12.

‡ Isaiah xlix. 14, 15. This sentiment is most beautifully paraphrased by an elegant poetess of our own times; the excellence of whose poetry is her least commendation. I cannot resist the temptation of transcribing a few lines, which appear to me at once forcible, interesting, and sublime :—

> Heaven speaks ! O Nature, listen and rejoice !
> O spread from pole to pole this gracious voice !
> " Say, every breast of human frame, that proves
> The boundless force with which a parent loves;
> Say, can a mother from her yearning heart
> Bid the soft image of her child depart ?
> She ! whom strong instinct arms with strength to bear
> All forms of ill, to shield that dearest care;
> She! who with anguish stung, with madness wild,
> Will rush on death to save her threaten'd child ;
> All selfish feelings banish'd from her breast,
> Her life one aim to make another's blest ;—

There is another species of comparison, the principal intent of which is the amplification of the subject; and this is

> Will she, for all ambition can attain,
> The charms of pleasure, or the lures of gain,
> Betray strong Nature's feelings ? will she prove
> Cold to the claims of duty and of love ?—
> But should the mother from her yearning heart
> Bid the soft image of her child depart,
> Should she, unpitying, hear his melting sigh,
> And view unmov'd the tear that fills his eye;
> Yet never will the God, whose word gave birth
> To yon illumin'd orbs, and this fair earth;
> Who through the boundless depths of trackless space
> Bade new-wak'd beauty spread each perfect grace;
> Yet, when he form'd the vast stupendous whole,
> Shed his best bounties on the human soul;
> Which reason's light illumes, which friendship warms,
> Which pity softens, and which virtue charms,
> Which feels the pure affections' generous glow,
> Shares others' joy, and bleeds for others' woe—
> Oh ! never will the general Father prove
> Of man forgetful, man the child of love !"
> When all those planets in their ample spheres
> Have wing'd their course, and roll'd their destin'd years;
> When the vast sun shall veil his golden light
> Deep in the gloom of everlasting night;
> When wild, destructive flames shall wrap the skies,
> When Chaos triumphs, and when Nature dies;
> God shall himself his favour'd creature guide
> Where living waters pour their blissful tide;
> Where the enlarg'd, exulting, wondering mind,
> Shall soar, from weakness and from guilt refined;
> Where perfect knowledge, bright with cloudless rays,
> Shall gild Eternity's unmeasur'd days;
> Where friendship, unembitter'd by distrust,
> Shall in immortal bands unite the just;
> Devotion rais'd to rapture breathe her strain,
> And Love in his eternal triumph reign !

Miss Williams's Poems, vol. i. p. 107.—T.

Analogical positions serve for the most part as illustrations, rather than proofs; but no demonstration of reason alone, can so closely take hold on the heart as the images contained in this expostulation.—For a *mother* to *forget* her sucking *infant*, and *feel* no tenderness for the *son* of her womb, is to be *more* unnatural than even a brute : but impossible as it may seem that one such *mother* should exist, yet, were the established order of nature to be so far *subverted* as that every *mother* should become *thus monstrous*, still the Universal Parent will never forget his offspring.

Pliny has mentioned a picture by Aristides of "a town taken by storm, in which was seen an infant creeping to the breast of its mother, who, though expiring from her wounds, yet expresses an apprehension and fear, lest, the course of her milk being stopped, the child should suck her blood."—This picture, it is probable, gave occasion to the following epigram of Æmilianus, which Mr. Webb (see his Beauties of Painting, p. 161) has thus finely translated :—

*

evidently of a different nature from the former; for, in the first place, it is necessary that the image which is introduced for the purpose of amplifying or ennobling a subject be sublime, beautiful, magnificent, or splendid, and therefore not trite or common; nor is it by any means necessary that the resemblance be exact in every circumstance. Thus Virgil has the address to impart even to the labours of his bees a wonderful air of sublimity, by a comparison with the exertions of the Cyclops in fabricating the thunderbolts of Jupiter:* thus he admirably depicts the grace, the dignity and strength of his Æneas, by comparing him with Apollo on the top of Cynthus renewing the sacred chorus;† or with the mountains Athos, Eryx, and Apennine.‡ Thus also Homer,§ in which he is imitated by Virgil,‖ compares two heroes rushing to battle with Mars and his offspring Terror advancing from Thrace to the Phlegyans and Ephyrians. But if it should be objected, that as comparisons of the former kind are wanting in dignity, so these (in which familiar objects are compared with objects but little known, or with objects which have little agreement or resemblance to them) are more likely to obscure than to illustrate; let it be remembered, that each species of comparison has in view a different end. The aim of the poet in the one case is perspicuity, to enable the mind clearly to perceive the subject, and to comprehend the whole of it at one view; in the other, the object is sublimity, or to impress the reader with the idea that the magnitude of the subject is scarcely to be conceived.¶ When considered in this light, it will, I dare

Ἕλκε, ταλαν, παρα μητρος ὁν ουκ ετι μαζον αμελξεις,
Ελκυσον ὑσατιον ναμα καταφθιμενης.
Ηδη γαρ ξιφεεσσι λιποπνοος· αλλα τα μητρος
Φιλτρα και ειν αϊδῃ παιδοκομειν εμαθον.—Antholog. lib. 3.

    Suck, little wretch, while yet thy mother lives,
    Suck the last drop her fainting bosom gives.
    She dies; her tenderness outlasts her breath,
    And her fond soul is provident in death.—S. H.

* Georg. iv. 170.   † Æn. iv. 143.

‡ Æn. xii. 701. Whoever desires to see this accurately and scientifically explained, may consult an excellent work lately published by the learned Mr. Spence, entitled *Polymetis*, p. 37, and 248.—*Author's Note.*

§ Il. xiii. 298.   ‖ Æn. xii. 331.

¶ A simile may, however, be taken from an object really inferior, and yet may serve to elevate the subject; but then the object of the figure must possess some of those qualities which, if they do not heighten our respect, will enlarge or vivify the idea. Thus a field of corn on fire is really a more trifling object than a city in

presume, be allowed, that none of these forms of comparison, when rightly applied, is deficient either in propriety or
elegance.

The Hebrews have nothing that corresponds with those
fables to which the Greek and Roman poets have recourse
when amplification is required; nor can we be surprised
that imagery so consecrated, so dignified by religion and
antiquity, and yet of so obvious and established acceptation
as to be intelligible to the meanest understanding, should
supply abundant and suitable materials for this purpose.
The sacred poets, therefore, resort in this case chiefly to the
imagery of nature; and this they make use of, indeed, with
so much elegance and freedom, that we have no cause to
regret the want of those fictions to which other nations have
recourse.   To express or delineate prosperity and opulence,
a comparison is assumed from the cedar or the palm;* if the
form of majesty or external beauty is to be depicted, Lebanon or Carmel is presented to our view.†   Sometimes they
are furnished with imagery from their religious rites, at once
beautiful, dignified, and sacred.   In both these modes the
Psalmist most elegantly extols the pleasures and advantages
of fraternal concord:

> Sweet as the od'rous balsam pour'd
>   On Aaron's sacred head;
> Which o'er his beard, and down his breast,
>   A breathing fragrance shed:

flames; yet Virgil, Æn. ii. v. 406, introduces it so artfully, that it not only serves
to illustrate, but to raise our idea of the sack of Troy:

> "Thus when a flood of fire by wind is borne,
>   Crackling it rolls, and mows the standing corn," &c.—Dryden.

Of this kind also is that comparison of Milton, in which he likens the spears of the
angels surrounding Satan to a field of corn:

> ————"as thick as when a field
> Of Ceres, ripe for harvest, waving bends
> Her bearded grove of ears, which way the wind
> Sways them," &c.—Par. Lost, B. iv. 983.

The reason why great subjects may thus be elevated by a comparison with smaller,
appears to be, because the latter, being more familiar to our minds, and therefore
easier of comprehension, make a more distinct and forcible impression, and lead
the mind gradually to the contemplation and proper conception of the greater
objects.—T.

* Psalm xcii. 13.   Numb. xxiv. 6.   Hosea xiv. 5, 7, 8.   Amos ii. 9.

† See Lect. 6.

As morning dew on Sion's mount
Beams forth a silver ray;
Or studs with gems the verdant pomp
That Hermon's tops display.*

Let us, however, attend for a moment to Isaiah, whom no writer has surpassed in propriety, when his aim is to illustrate; or in sublimity, when he means to amplify his subject:—

" Woe to the multitude of the numerous peoples,
Who make a sound like the sound of the seas ;
And to the roaring of the nations,
Who make a roaring like the roaring of mighty waters.
Like the roaring of mighty waters do the nations roar;
But he shall rebuke them, and they shall flee far away;
And they shall be driven like the chaff of the hills before the wind,
And like the gossamer before the whirlwind."†

The third species of comparison seems to hold a middle rank between the two preceding: and the sole intent of it is, by a mixture of new and varied imagery with the principal matter, to prevent satiety or disgust, and to promote the entertainment of the reader. It neither descends to the humility of the one, nor emulates the sublimity of the other. It pursues rather the agreeable, the ornamental, the elegant, and ranges through all the variety, all the exuberance of nature. In so extensive a field it would be an infinite task to collect all that might be observed of each particular. I shall remark one circumstance only, which, though it sometimes takes place in the two former species of comparison, may be said, notwithstanding, to be chiefly appropriated to this last.

There are two operations of the mind, evidently contrary to each other. The one consists in combining ideas, the other in separating and distinguishing them. For, in contemplating the innumerable forms of things, one of the first reflections which occurs is, that there are some which

* Psalm cxxxiii. 2, 3. Our Author on this occasion has quoted from Buchanan's translation. In the above attempt I have copied Buchanan as nearly as our language would admit.—T.

† Isaiah xvii. 12, 13. " These five words רבים מים כשאון מים לאמים ישאון are wanting in seven manuscripts; with this difference in two of them, v. 12, for כבירים we read רבים. So also the Syriac version, which agrees with them. These five words are not necessary to the sense; and seem to be repeated only by the carelessness of the transcriber." K.—Author's Note.

have an immediate agreement, and some which are directly
contrary to each other. The mind, therefore, contemplates
those objects which have a resemblance in their universal
nature in such a manner as naturally to inquire, whether in
any respect they so disagree as to furnish any mark of discrimination; on the contrary, it investigates those which
are generally different in such a manner as to remark,
whether, in their circumstances or adjuncts, they may not
possess something in common, which may serve as a bond
of connexion or association to class or unite them. The final
cause of the former of these operations seems to be, to caution and guard us against error, in confounding one with
another; of the latter, to form a kind of repository of
knowledge, which may be resorted to, as occasion serves,
either for utility or pleasure. These constitute the two
faculties which are distinguished by the names of *judgment*
and *imagination*.* As accuracy of judgment is demonstrated by discovering in things which have in general a
very strong resemblance, some partial disagreement; so the
genius or fancy is entitled to the highest commendation,
when in those objects which upon the whole have the least
agreement, some striking similarity is traced out.† In those
comparisons, therefore, the chief purpose of which is ornament or pleasure, thus far may pass for an established principle, that they are most likely to accomplish this end when
the image is not only elegant and agreeable, but is also
taken from an object which in the general is materially
different from the subject of comparison, and only aptly and
pertinently agrees with it in one or two of its attributes.

But I shall probably explain myself better by an example.
There is in Virgil a comparison, borrowed from Homer, of
a boiling caldron.‡ Supposing in each poet the versification and description equally elegant; still, as the relation
between the things compared is different, so the grace and
beauty of the comparison is different in the two poets. In

---

* See Hobbes *of Human Nature*, c. x. sect. 4. and Locke *of Human Understanding*, b. xi. c. 11, sect. 2.

† "Elegance of expression consists in metaphors, neither too remote, which are
difficult to be understood; nor too simple and superficial, which do not affect the
passions." Arist. *Rhet.* iii. 10. "For, as was before observed, metaphors must
be taken from objects that are familiar, yet not too plain and common : as in
philosophy it is a mark of sagacity to discern similitude even in very dissimilar
things." *Ib.* c. ii.—*Author's Note.*

‡ Æn. vii. 462. Iliad, xxi. 362.

Homer, the waters of the river Xanthus boiling in their channel by the fire which Vulcan has thrown into the river, are compared with the boiling of a heated caldron: but Virgil compares with the same object the mind of Turnus agitated by the torch of the fury Alecto. The one brings together ideas manifestly alike, or rather indeed the same, and only differing in circumstances; the other, on the contrary, assimilates objects which are evidently very different in their nature, but aptly agreeing in some of their adjuncts or circumstances. Thus the comparison of the Latin poet is new, diversified, and agreeable; but that of the Greek, although not destitute of force in illustrating the subject, is undoubtedly wanting in all the graces of variety, ornament, and splendour.

For the same reason there is, perhaps, no comparison of any poet extant more ingenious, more elegant or perfect in its kind, than the following of the same excellent poet:

> " The hero, floating in a flood of care,
> Beholds the tempest which his foes prepare :
> To different objects turns his anxious mind ;
> Thinks, and rejects the counsels he design'd ;
> Explores himself in vain, in every part,
> And gives no rest to his distracted heart.
> So when the sun by day, or moon by night,
> Strike on the polish'd brass their trembling light,
> The glittering species variously divide,
> And cast their dubious beams from side to side ;
> Now on the walls, now on the pavement play,
> And to the ceiling flash the glaring day." *

He appears to be indebted for this passage to Apollonius Rhodius:

> " In sad review dire scenes of horror rise,
> Quick beats her heart, from thought to thought she flies :
> As from the stream-stor'd vase with dubious ray
> The sunbeams dancing from the surface play ;
> Now here, now there, the trembling radiance falls,
> Alternate flashing round th' illumin'd walls :
> Thus fluttering bounds the trembling virgin's blood,
> And from her eyes descends a pearly flood."†

In this description, Virgil, as usual, has much improved upon his original; and particularly in that circumstance

---

* Dryd. Virg. Æn. viii. 28.   † Fawkes's *Argonautics*, B. iii. 816.

I

which is the most essential of all, that on which the fitness of the comparison depends, and which forms the hinge, as it were, upon which it turns, he has greatly surpassed the ancient author.

It appears, therefore, that in comparisons, the chief design of which is ornament or variety, the principal excellence results from the introduction of an image different in kind, but correspondent in some particular circumstances. There are, however, two capital imperfections to which this figure is sometimes liable; one, when objects too dissimilar, and dissimilar chiefly in the adjuncts or circumstances, are forced into comparison; the other, and not less common or important, though perhaps less adverted to, when the relation or resemblance is in general too exact and minute. The comparison in the one case is monstrous and whimsical;* in the other, it is grovelling and inanimate.

Examples innumerable in illustration of the present subject might be found in the sacred poetry; I shall, however, produce not more than two from Isaiah. The first, from the historical narration of the confederacy between the Syrians and the Israelites against the kingdom of Judah, "which when it was told unto the king," says the prophet, " his heart was moved, and the hearts of his people, as the trees of the wood are moved with the wind."† The other is a poetical comparison, which is fuller and more diffuse than the custom of the Hebrews generally admits: the subject of correspondent application, however, is perfectly exact.

---

* The principal fault which I have observed in the comparisons of the orientals is, that the resemblance is often too fanciful and remote. They are, however, not singular in this respect : the following occurs in one of our most elegant poems, and in my opinion it is in this respect very reprehensible. Describing the village clergyman, and his care of his flock, the poet proceeds :—

> " His ready smile a parent's warmth express'd,
> Their welfare pleas'd him, and their cares distress'd ;
> To them his heart, his love, his griefs were given,
> But all his serious thoughts had rest in heaven.
> As some tall cliff that lifts its awful form,
> Swells from the vale, and midway leaves the storm,
> Though round its breast the rolling clouds are spread,
> *Eternal sunshine settles on his head.*"—*Deserted Village.* T.

There is another defect in this passage, which perhaps is the real cause of that here pointed out, arising from the use of the term AS, by which the resemblance between the mountain and the man is announced : not to mention the want of the antithetical so, which should necessarily have introduced a further application of the simile.—S. H.

† Isaiah vii. 2.

The divine grace,* and its effects, are compared with showers that fertilise the earth; an image which is uniformly appropriated to that purpose:

" Verily, like as the rain descendeth,
And the snow from the heavens ;
And thither it doth not return ;
But moisteneth the earth,
And maketh it generate, and put forth its increase ;
That it may give seed to the sower, and bread to the eater :
So shall be the word which goeth from my mouth ;
It shall not return unto me fruitless :
But it shall effect what I have willed,
And make the purpose succeed for which I have sent it."†

More examples, and of superior elegance, may be found in the Song of Solomon. ‡ It must not, indeed, be dissembled, that there are some in that ꞏpoem which are very reprehensible, on account of that general dissonance, and fanciful

---

* This passage of the prophet loses much of its poetical beauty if it be not rightly understood. He is not speaking of that *grace* which the school divines treat of, and which has been celebrated since the time of Augustine in so many controversies, nor of the virtue and efficacy of the gospel in correcting the morals of mankind, but of the certain accomplishment of the prophetic word. It was very customary among the Hebrews to compare the word of God, and particularly the word of prophecy, to a shower of rain, Deut. xxxii. 2. Ezek. xxi. 2. Mic. ii. 6. Job xxix. 22, 23. When, therefore, it is their intention to describe the certain and inevitable accomplishment of the divine oracles, they represent the earth as impregnated and fertilised by this refreshing rain. Isaiah has celebrated, in the xlth chapter, as well as the chapter under our consideration, verses 3, 4, and 5, the eternal covenant of God with the Israelites, and the accomplishment of that perpetual and permanent grace which he had sworn to David, namely, that an eternal and immortal king should sit upon his throne ; and that he should rule and direct the heathen. If these should appear to any person above credibility, he advises him to recollect that the divine counsels are far above the reach of the human understanding ; and that those things are easy to him, which appear most difficult to us. He adds, that the sacred oracles, however miraculous, will most assuredly be fulfilled ; *that the word of God may be compared to snow or rain, which does not return* to heaven before it has performed its office of *watering and fecundating the earth:* so it is with *the prophetic decrees,* or the *Divine predictions of future events.* And in this light I understand the passage from the context, both from what precedes and what follows. There is one similar in chapter xlv. 8 ; but the idea is more condensed, assuming rather the form of a metaphor or allegory than of a comparison :

　　　" Drop down, O ye heavens ! the dew from above ;
　　　And let the clouds shower down righteousness :
　　　Let the earth open her bosom, and let salvation produce her fruit ;
　　　And let justice push forth her bud together."—M.

† Isaiah lv. 10, 11.

‡ See Cant. iv. 1—5, farther explained Lect. 31.

agreement, which I have just remarked * as a great imperfection attending the free use of this figure. We must be
cautious, however, lest in some cases we charge the poet
with errors which are in reality our own; since many of
the objects which suggested these comparisons are greatly
obscured, and some of them removed entirely beyond the
sphere of our knowledge, by distance of time and place. It
is the part of a wise man not rashly to condemn what we
are able but partially to comprehend.

These three forms, according to which, for the sake of
perspicuity, I have ventured to class Comparisons in general,
are however not so incompatible that they may not occasionally meet and be variously blended with each other.
That, indeed, appears to be the most perfect comparison,
which combines all these different objects, and, while it explains, serves at the same time to amplify and embellish the
subject; and which possesses evidence and elevation, sea-
soned with elegance and variety. A more complete example is scarcely to be found than that passage in which
Job impeaches the infidelity and ingratitude of his friends,
who in his adversity denied him those consolations of tenderness and sympathy, which, in his prosperous state, and
when he needed them not, they had lavished upon him: he
compares them with streams, which, increased by the rains
of winter, overflow their borders, and display for a little
time a copious and majestic torrent; but with the first impulse of the solar beams are suddenly dried up, and leave
those who unfortunately wander through the deserts of
Arabia destitute of water, and perishing with thirst.†

Thus far of Comparisons in general, and of their matter
and intention: it remains to add a few words concerning
the particular form and manner in which the Hebrews
usually exhibit them.

The Hebrews introduce Comparisons more frequently
perhaps than the poets of any other nation; but the brevity
of them in general compensates for their abundance. The
resemblance usually turns upon a single circumstance; that
they explain in the most simple terms, rarely introducing
any thing at all foreign to the purpose. The following example, therefore, is almost singular, since it is loaded with
an extraordinary accession, or I might almost say a super-
fluity, of adjuncts:—

* See Cant. vii. 2. 4.   † Job iv. 15—20.

> " Let them be as grass upon the house-top,
> Which, before it groweth up, is withered;
> With which the mower filleth not his hand ;
> Nor he that gathereth the sheaves his bosom :
> Nor do they that pass by say,
> The blessing of JEHOVAH be upon you ;*
> We bless you in the name of JEHOVAH."†

The usual practice of the Hebrews is indeed very different from this: sometimes a single word, and commonly a very short sentence, comprehends the whole comparison. This peculiarity proceeds from the nature of the sententious style, which is always predominant in the Hebrew poetry, and, as I before remarked, consists in condensing and compressing every exuberance of expression, and rendering it close and pointed. Thus, in the very parts in which other poets are copious and diffuse, the Hebrews, on the contrary, are brief, energetic, and animated; not gliding along in a smooth and equal stream, but with the inequality and impetuosity of a torrent. Thus their comparisons assume a peculiar form and appearance ; for it is not so much their custom to dilate and embellish each particular image with a variety of adjuncts, as to heap together a number of parallel and analogous comparisons, all of which are expressed in a style of the utmost brevity and simplicity. Moses compares the celestial influence of the divine song which he utters by the command of God, with showers which water the fields; and on an occasion when a Greek or Latin poet would have been contented with a single comparison, perhaps a little more diffused and diversified, he has introduced two pairs of similes exactly expressive of the same thing :

> " My doctrine shall drop as the rain ;
> My language shall alight like the dew :
> As the small rain upon the tender herb ;
> And like the thick drops upon the grass.‡"

The Psalmist makes use of the same form in the following :

> " O my God ! make them as the chaff whirled about ;
> As the stubble before the wind :
> As the fire burneth the forest,
> And as the flame kindleth the mountains ;

---

* A customary expression made use of in this business. See Ruth ii. 4.

† Psalm cxxix. 6—8.   See also Psalm cxxxiii. 3.

‡ Deut. xxxii. 2.

> So do thou pursue them with thy tempests,
> And with thy whirlwind make them afraid."*

This is, indeed, the most common, but by no means the only form which this figure assumes in the Hebrew poetry: there is another, in which the comparison is more diffusively displayed; in which case the equal distribution of the sentences is still strictly adhered to; the image itself, however, is not repeated, but its attributes, which explain one another in two parallel sentences—as Moses has done in a comparison immediately following that which I just now quoted, in which he compares the care and paternal affection of the Deity for his people, with the natural tenderness of the eagle for its young:

> " As the eagle stirreth up her nest;
> Fluttereth over her young;
> Expandeth her plumes, taketh them;
> Beareth them upon her wings."†

The same is observable also in that most elegant comparison of Job, which I formerly commended; and which, for this reason, I shall now quote entire by way of conclusion:

> "My brethren have dealt deceitfully like a torrent,
> As the torrents of the valleys they are passed away;
> Which are congealed‡ by means of the frost;
> The snow hideth itself in their surface:
> As soon as they flow, they are dried up,
> When it is hot they are consumed·from their place;

---

* Psalm lxxxiii. 13—15. Between these two comparisons there exists so nice a relation, that they would form one simple comparison, were it not that the sententious distribution of the verses had disposed the subject in a different form and order. Their threshing-floors were so constructed in open situations, that when the corn was beaten down, the wind carried off the chaff and straw, which being collected together was burnt. See Isaiah v. 24. Matt. iii. 12, and Hammond's *Com.* *Jagnar*, however, is used for any high and uncultivated place, as appears from Mic. iii. 12. " This sense of the word is also confirmed from the Arabic *Vagnar*, a mountain steep and difficult of access." H.—*Author's Note.*

Perhaps it may be thought too free a version to render וּבְסוּפָתְךָ תְבַהֲלֵם,

" And with thy whirlwind involve them in terror;"—

but the words themselves seem to comprise no less.—*Pursue them with thy tempests*, is an evident reference *to the dissipation of chaff*, and what follows relates clearly to *the expansion of the flame.*—S. H.

† Deut. xxxii. 11.

‡ Or, as Dr. Durell proposes, *which stand still;* as though the original had been הַקֹּרִים, instead of הַקָּרִים.—For this elegant emendation the learned Doctor is indebted to Father Houbigant, but he forgot to mention its author: Mr. Heath, however, had a better memory.—S. H.

The paths of their channels are diminished,
They ascend in vapour and are lost.
Look for them, ye troops of Tema :
Ye travellers of Sheba, expect them earnestly.
They made no haste ; because they depended on them :
They came thither, then were they confounded." *

---

* Job vi. 15—20.   "In the fifth line the word חוּרְבּוּ is one of those which only once occur in the Scripture.   In the Arabic and Chaldee the proper force of the verb ורב is *to flow, to flow off*, or *to overflow :* thus the sense will be, In the *time* in *which they flow, or flow off';* that is, are dissolved by the melting of the ice."—H.

In the 20th verse it appears one should read בטחו, with the Syr. and Chald.— *Author's Note.*

LECTURE XIII.

OF THE PROSOPOPŒIA, OR PERSONIFICATION.

Two kinds of Personification: when a character is assigned to fictitious or inanimate objects; and when a probable speech is attributed to a real person—Of fictitious and inanimate characters; of real characters—The prosopopœia of the mother of Sisera (in the song of Deborah) explained: also the triumphal song of the Israelites concerning the death of the King of Babylon, (in Isaiah,) which consists altogether of this figure, and exhibits it in all its different forms.

THE last in order of those figures which I proposed to treat of, as being most adapted to the parabolic style, is the Prosopopœia, or Personification.* Of this figure there are two kinds : one, when action and character are attributed to fictitious, irrational, or even inanimate objects; the other, when a probable but fictitious speech is assigned to a real character. The former evidently partakes of the nature of the metaphor, and is by far the boldest and most daring of that class of figures. Seasonably introduced, therefore, it has uncommon force and expression; and in no hands whatever is more successful in this respect than in those of the

* The passions of resentment and love have been very accurately traced by some late writers on the human mind, into the senses of pain and pleasure : the one arising from the habitual inclination to remove what is hurtful; the other, from that of possessing what is a source of grateful sensations, and a mean of increasing pleasure. (See Hartley *on Man*, and a *Dissertation* prefixed to King's *Origin of Evil*.) The strong expression of these passions is, however, chiefly directed to rational, or at least to animated beings; but this is the effect of reason and habit. The passions are still the same, and will frequently display themselves in opposition to reason. A child turns to beat the ground, or the stone that has hurt him, (see Lord Kames' *Elements of Criticism*;) and most men feel some degree of affection even for the old inanimate companions of their happiness. From these dispositions originates the figure which is the great and distinguishing ornament of poetry, the Prosopopœia. This figure is nearly allied to the metaphor, and still more to the metonymy; it is to the latter what the allegory is to the metaphor. Thus, when we say, " Youth and beauty shall be laid in the dust," for persons possessing youth and beauty, it is hard to determine whether it be a metonymy or a prosopopœia. Lyric poetry, in which the imagination seems to have the fullest indulgence, and which abounds with strong figures, is most favourable to personification.—T.

Hebrew writers; I may add also, that none more frequently or more freely introduce it.

In the first place, then, with respect to fictitious characters, the Hebrews have this in common with other poets, that they frequently assign character and action to an abstract or general idea, and introduce it in a manner acting, and even speaking, as upon the stage.* In this, while they equal the most refined writers in elegance and grace, they greatly excel the most sublime in force and majesty. What, indeed, can be conceived apter, more beautiful, or more sublime, than that personification of Wisdom which Solomon so frequently introduces? exhibiting her not only as the director of human life and morals, as the inventor of arts, as the dispenser of wealth, of honour, and of real felicity; but as the immortal offspring of the omnipotent Creator, and as the eternal associate in the Divine counsels:

> " When he prepared the heavens, I was present;
> When he described a circle on the face of the deep:
> When he disposed the atmosphere above;
> When he established the fountains of the deep:
> When he published his decree to the sea,
> That the waters should not pass their bound;
> When he planned the foundations of the earth:
> Then was I by him as his offspring;
> And I was daily his delight;
> I rejoiced continually before him:
> I rejoiced in the habitable part of his earth,
> And my delights were with the sons of men."†

How admirable is that celebrated personification of the divine attributes by the Psalmist! how just, elegant, and splendid does it appear, if applied only according to the literal sense, to the restoration of the Jewish nation from the Babylonish captivity! But if interpreted as relating to that sublimer, more sacred and mystical sense, which is not obscurely sha-

---

* There is a very animated personification of this kind in one of Dr. Ogden's sermons, though by some it may perhaps be thought too bold for that species of composition. "Truth," says that elegant and sublime writer, "is indeed of an awful presence, and must not be affronted with the rudeness of direct opposition; yet will she sometimes condescend to pass for a moment unregarded, while your respects are paid to her sister Charity." That of Bishop Sherlock, which our Author has quoted in his admirable Introduction to English Grammar, "Go to your natural religion, lay before her Mohammed and his disciples," &c. is well known, and is one of th. finest examples of this figure I have ever seen.—T.

† Prov. viii. 27—31.

dowed under the ostensible image, it is certainly uncommonly noble and elevated, mysterious and sublime:

" Mercy and Truth are met together;
    Righteousness and Peace have kissed each other."

There are many passages of a similar kind, exquisitely imagined, and, from the boldness of the fiction, extremely forcible. Such is that in Habakkuk, of the pestilence marching before JEHOVAH when he comes to vengeance;† that in Job, in which Destruction and Death affirm of Wisdom, that her fame only had come to their ears:‡ in fine, (that I may not be tedious in quoting examples,) that tremendous image in Isaiah, of Hades§ extending her throat, and opening her insatiable and immeasurable jaws.||

* Psa. lxxxv. 11.   † Hab. iii. 5.   ‡ Job xxviii. 22.   § Isa. v. 14.
|| I have not observed, even in the Hebrew poetry, a bolder use of this figure than in a passage of Tacitus, *An.* 16, 21.   *Trucidatis tot insignibus viris, ad postremum Nero Virtutem ipsam exscindere concupivit, interfecto Thrasea,* &c. "After the slaughter of so many excellent men, Nero meditated at length the extirpation of Virtue herself by the sacrifice of Thrasea," &c.
In the opening of Collins's *Ode to Mercy* is a noble example of the prosopopœia :

" Thou, who sitt'st a smiling bride,
    By Valour's arm'd and awful side," &c.

But the whole compass of English poetry cannot furnish a more beautiful specimen than the following:

" Loud howls the storm ! the vex'd Atlantic roars !
    Thy Genius, Britain, wanders on its shores !
    Hears cries of horror wafted from afar,
    The groans of anguish 'mid the shrieks of war !
    Hears the deep curses of the Great and Brave
    Sigh in the wind, and murmur in the wave !
    O'er his damp brow the sable crape he binds,
    And throws his victor-garland to the winds."
                            Miss Seward's *Monody on Major André.*

How different are these instances from the frigid attempts of inferior writers The following personification is completely ridiculous. It is, however, extracted from a poem, which has been highly extolled by one who calls himself a Critic :

" Invidious *Grave,* how dost thou rend in sunder
    Whom love has knit, and sympathy made one !"—*The Grave,* a Poem.

It is a happy thing, that as there are poets of all degrees, there are also critics of taste and judgment exactly equal and correspondent to them.—*Par nobile !* The picture of a *Grave rending a thing in sunder,* can only be matched by the following passage from the same incomparable performance :

—— " But tell us, why this waste,
    Why this *ado* in *earthing* up a carcass
    That's fall'n into disgrace, and to the sense
    Smells horrible ? Ye *undertakers!* tell us "——

There is also another most beautiful species of personification, which originates from a well-known Hebrew idiom, and on that account is very familiar to us; I allude to that form of expression, by which the subject, attribute, accident, or effect of any thing, is denominated the *son*. Hence, in the Hebrew poetry, nations, regions, peoples, are brought upon the stage as it were in a female character:

" Descend, and sit in the dust, O virgin, daughter of Babylon;
   Sit on the bare ground without a throne, O daughter of the
      Chaldeans :*
   For thou shalt no longer be called the tender and the deli-
      cate."†

> " Where are the mighty thunderbolts of war ?
>   Alas ! how *slim, dishonourably slim !* "
>
> " Now tame and humble, *like a child that's whipp'd,*
>   Shake hands with dust," &c.
>
> " Perhaps *some hackney hunger-bitten scribbler*
>   Insults thy memory."
>
> " Here the lank-sided miser—worst of felons!
>   Who meanly stole (discreditable shift!)
>   From back and belly too their proper cheer,
>   Lies cheaply lodg'd."
>
> " O that some courteous ghost would *blab* it out,
>   What 'tis ye are," &c.
>
> ————" O great *Man-eater !*
>   Whose every day is carnival, not sated yet!
>   Like one, whole days defrauded of his meals,
>   On whom lank Hunger lays his skinny hand."

No wonder the above *Critic* could discover nothing sublime in Virgil and the Scriptures.—T.

* " Sitting on the ground was a posture that denoted deep misery and distress. The prophet Jeremiah has given it the first place among many indications of sorrow, in that elegant description of the distress of his country, Lam. ii. 8. 'The elders of the daughter of Sion sit on the ground, they are silent,' &c. *We find Judea,* says Mr. Addison, (on Medals, dial. ii.) *on several coins of Vespasian and Titus, in a posture that denotes sorrow and captivity.—I need not mention her sitting on the ground, because we have already spoken of the aptness of such a posture to represent extreme affliction. I fancy the Romans might have an eye to the customs of the Jewish nation, as well as those of their country, in the several marks of sorrow they have set on this figure. The Psalmist describes the Jews lamenting their captivity in the same pensive posture :* ' By the waters of Babylon we sat down and wept, when we remembered thee, O Sion.' But what is more remarkable, we find Judea represented as a woman in sorrow, sitting on the ground, in a passage of the prophet that foretells the very captivity recorded on this medal."—See Bishop Lowth's *Notes on Isaiah,* c. iii. v. 26.

† Isaiah xlvii. 1, &c.

> Lo ! Sion's daughter, prostrate on the earth,
> All mournful, solitary, weeping, lies !
> In vain her supliant hands to heaven extends;
> She sinks deserted, and no comfort finds.*

Unless we attend to this peculiar phraseology, such expressions as the " Sons of the bow† and of the quiver,"‡ for arrows, will seem extremely harsh and unnatural; as well as that remarkable personification ot Job, denoting the most miserable death, " the first-born of the progeny of Death."§

The parabolic style no less elegantly assigns a character and action to inanimate objects than to abstract ideas. The holy prophets, moved with just indignation against the ungrateful people of God, " obtest the Heavens and the Earth, and command universal Nature to be silent.‖ They plead their cause before the Mountains, and the Hills listen to their voice."¶ All is animated and informed with life, soul, and passion :

> " Let the Heavens rejoice, and let the Earth be glad;
> And let them proclaim through the nations, JEHOVAH reigneth.
> Let the Sea roar, and all that it containeth; **
> The World, and the inhabitants thereof:
> Let the Floods clap their hands;
> Let the Mountains break forth into harmony : ††
> Before JEHOVAH, for he cometh,
> For he cometh to judge the earth." ‡‡

> " The Waters saw thee, O God !
> The Waters saw thee, they were grievously troubled ; §§
> The deep uttered his voice;
> And lifted up his hands on high." ‖‖

And Job admirably in the same style :

> " Canst thou send forth the Lightnings, and will they go ?
> Shall they say unto thee, Behold, here we are ?" ¶¶

With equal success they introduce objects which have no existence in the order and economy of nature ; though it must be confessed, that it is attended with much greater hazard of propriety; for, to those which are within the province of nature, we readily attribute a degree of life and sentiment. Of this the following dialogue in Jeremiah is an admirable specimen :—

* Lam. i. 1, &c.　　　† Job xli. 19.　　　　　　　　‡ Lam. iii. 13.
§ Job xviii. 13.　　　‖ Deut. xxxii. 1.　Isa. i. 2.　¶ Micah vi. 1.
** 1 Chron. xvi. 31.　†† Psalm xcviii. 7, 8.　　　‡‡ Psalm xcvi. 13.
§§ Psalm lxxvii. 16.　‖‖ Habak. iii. 10.　　　　　¶¶ Job xxxviii. 35.

"Ho! Sword of Jehovah!
How long wilt thou not be at rest?
Return into thy scabbard;
Return, and be still.
How can it be at rest,
Since Jehovah hath given it a charge?
Against Askelon, and against the sea-coast,
There hath he appointed it."*

The other kind of prosopopœia, to which I alluded in the former part of this Lecture, is that by which a probable but fictitious speech is assigned to a real person. As the former is calculated to excite admiration and approbation by its novelty, boldness, and variety, so the latter, from its near resemblance to real life, is possessed of great force, evidence, and authority.

It would be an infinite task to specify every instance in the sacred poems, which on this occasion might be referred to as worthy of notice; or to remark the easy, the natural, the bold and sudden personifications; the dignity, importance, and impassioned severity of the characters. It would be difficult to describe the energy of that eloquence which is attributed to Jehovah himself, and which appears so suitable in all respects to the Divine Majesty; or to display the force and beauty of the language which is so admirably and peculiarly adapted to each character; the probability of the fiction, and the excellence of the imitation. One example, therefore, must suffice for the present; one more perfect it is not possible to produce. It is expressive of the eager expectation of the mother of Sisera, from the inimitable ode of the prophetess Deborah.†

The first sentences exhibit a striking picture of maternal solicitude, both in words and actions; and of a mind suspended and agitated between hope and fear:

"Through the window she looked and cried out,
The mother of Sisera, through the lattice:
Wherefore is his chariot so long in coming?
Wherefore linger the wheels of his chariot?"

Immediately, impatient of his delay, she anticipates the consolations of her friends, and her mind being somewhat elevated, she boasts, with all the levity of a fond female,—

(Vast in her hopes and giddy with success;)

* Jer. xlvii. 6, 7.   † Judges v. 28—30.

" Her wise ladies answer her ;
    Yea, she returns answer to herself :
    Have they not found ?   Have they not divided the spoil ? "

Let us now observe, how well adapted every sentiment,
every word is to the character of the speaker.   She takes
no account of the slaughter of the enemy, of the valour and
conduct of the conqueror, of the multitude of the captives,
but

            " Burns with a female thirst of prey and spoils."

Nothing is omitted, which is calculated to attract and engage the passions of a vain and trifling woman—slaves, gold,
and rich apparel.   Nor is she satisfied with the bare enu-
meration of them : she repeats, she amplifies, she heightens
every circumstance ; she seems to have the very plunder in
her immediate possession ; she pauses, and contemplates
every particular :

" Have they not found ?   Have they not divided the spoil ?·
    To every man a damsel, yea a damsel or two ?
    To Sisera a coat of divers colours ?
    A spoil of needle-work of divers colours,
    A spoil for the neck* of divers colours of needlework on either
        side."

To add to the beauty of this passage, there is also an uncommon neatness in the versification, great force, accuracy,
and perspicuity in the diction, the utmost elegance in the
repetitions, which, notwithstanding their apparent redundancy, are conducted with the most perfect brevity.   In the
end, the fatal disappointment of female hope and credulity,
tacitly insinuated by the sudden and unexpected apostrophe,

        " So let all thine enemies perish, O JEHOVAH ! "

is expressed more forcibly by this very silence of the person
who was just speaking, than it could possibly have been by
all the powers of language.

But whoever wishes to understand the full force and excellence of this figure, as well as the elegant use of it in the
Hebrew ode, must apply to Isaiah, whom I do not scruple

---

* לצוארי שלל, "A spoil to ornament the neck," is the constructive for the
absolute. See Mic. vi. 16. Lam. iii. 14, and 66. For further satisfaction on
this subject consult Buxtorf, *Thes. Gram.* ii. 4, who, nevertheless, in the same work
interprets this phrase in a different manner. The Seventy read לצוארו, and
the Syriac שולל ; the context will bear either.—*Author's Note.*

to pronounce the sublimest of poets. He will there find, in one short poem, examples of almost every form of the prosopopœia, and indeed of all that constitutes the sublime in composition. I trust it will not be thought unseasonable to refer immediately to the passage itself, and to remark a few of the principal excellences.*

The prophet, after predicting the liberation of the Jews from their severe captivity in Babylon, and their restoration to their own country, introduces them as reciting a kind of triumphal song upon the fall of the Babylonish monarch, replete with imagery, and with the most elegant and animated personifications. A sudden exclamation, expressive of their joy and admiration on the unexpected revolution in their affairs, and the destruction of their tyrants, forms the exordium of the poem. The earth itself triumphs with the inhabitants thereof; the fir-trees and the cedars of Lebanon (under which images the parabolic style frequently delineates the kings and princes of the Gentiles) exult with joy, and persecute with contemptuous reproaches the humbled power of a ferocious enemy:

> " The whole earth is at rest, is quiet; they burst forth into a
> joyful shout :
> Even the fir-trees rejoice over thee, the cedars of Lebanon:
> Since thou art fallen, no feller hath come up against us."†

This is followed by a bold and animated personification of Hades, or the infernal regions. Hades excites his inhabitants, the ghosts of princes, and the departed spirits of kings: they rise immediately from their seats, and proceed to meet the monarch of Babylon; they insult and deride him, and comfort themselves with the view of his calamity:

> " Art thou, even thou too, become weak as we ?   Art thou made
> like unto us ?
> Is then thy pride brought down to the grave ? the sound of thy
> sprightly instruments ?
> Is the vermin become thy couch, and the earth-worm thy
> covering ? "

---

* Isa. xiv. 4—27.
† Thus spiritedly versified by Mr. Potter :
>   The lordly Lebanon waves high
>   The ancient honours of his sacred head;
>   Their branching arms his cedars spread,
>   His pines triumphant shoot into the sky :
>   " Tyrant, no barb'rous axe invades,
>   Since thou art fallen, our unpierc'd shades."
                    See the conclusion of Lect. 28 —T

Again, the Jewish people are the speakers, in an exclamation, after the manner of a funeral lamentation, which indeed the whole form of this composition exactly imitates.*

* Threnetic strains on the untimely decease of royal and eminent personages were of high antiquity amongst the Asiatics. Thus Euripides, *Iphigenia in Tauris*, v. 177.

> Ch. Αντιψαλμυς ωδας,
> 'ΥΜΝΟΝ Τ' ΑΣΙΗΤΑΝ σοι,
> Βαρβαρον ιαχαν,
> Δεσποινα γ' εξανδασω,
> Ταν εν ΘΡΗΝΟΙΣΙΝ μυσαν,
> Νεκυσιν μελεον·

And again, *Orestes*, v. 1402.

> ΑΙΛΙΝΟΝ, ΑΙΛΙΝΟΝ, ΑΡΧΑΝ, ΘΑΝΑΤΟΥ.
> Βαρβαροι λεγυσιν, ΑΙ, ΑΙ,
> Ασιαδι φωνα ΒΑΣΙΛΕΩΝ
> Ξιφεσι σιδαρεοσιν αϊδα.

Instances of such threnodies often occur in the sacred writings : 2 Sam. i. 18 ; 2 Kings xiii. 30. Amos v. 1, 2. 16. Jer. ix. 17 ; xxii. 18, &c. Many of them are of the proleptic cast, the most conspicuous of which is the denunciation of Isaiah against the king of Babylon. According to the Seventy משל in the fourth verse (which our translators have rendered a *proverb* or *taunting speech*) signifies ὁ ΘΡΗΝΟΣ and ΑΡΧΗ. The same expression, taken conjunctively with מות, hath been also interpreted ΑΡΧΗ ΘΑΝΑΤΟΥ, and coincides with the passage from the Orestes, cited above.—Gray's *Bard* is a composition of the same class, as is evident from the import of ΑΙΛΙΝΟΣ, [— ἡ μεντοι εξ Επιχαρμυ χρησις εθελυσα τον ΑΙΛΙΝΟΝ ΩΔΗΝ των ΙΣΤΟΥΡΓΟΥΝΤΩΝ ΕΙΝΑΙ.—*Eustath.*], when compared with his imagery of weaving——

> " Weave the warp and weave the woof,
>   The winding sheet of Edward's race," &c.

and it is somewhat remarkable, that in his ode from the Norse tongue, entitled the *Fatal Sisters*, the same machinery is more minutely preserved :

> " Now the storm begins to lower,
>   (Haste, the loom of hell prepare ;)
> Iron sleet of arrowy shower
> Hurtles in the darken'd air.
>
> Glittering lances form the loom
> Where the dusky warp we strain ;
> Weaving many a soldier's doom,
> Orkney's woe, and Randver's bane.
>
> See the griesly texture grow,
> ('Tis of human entrails made ;)
> And the weights that play below,
> Each a gasping warrior's head.
>
> Shafts for shuttles," &c.

In his critique upon this sublime ode of Isaiah, the learned Bishop appears to have overlooked a principal source of its beauty, which consists in the happy adaptation of imagery from the history and fate of Nimrod, the founder and

The remarkable fall of this powerful monarch is thus beautifully illustrated:

"How art thou fallen from heaven, O Lucifer, son of the
  morning!*
Art cut down from earth, thou that didst subdue the nations!"

He himself is at length brought upon the stage, boasting in the most pompous terms of his own power, which furnishes the poet with an excellent opportunity of displaying the unparalleled misery of his downfall. Some persons are introduced, who find the dead carcase of the king of Babylon cast out and exposed: they attentively contemplate it, and at last scarcely know it to be his:—

"Is this the man that made the earth to tremble; that shook the
  kingdoms?
That made the world like a desert; that destroyed the cities?"†

They reproach him with being denied the common rites of sepulture, on account of the cruelty and atrocity of his conduct; they execrate his name, his offspring, and their posterity. A solemn address, as of the Deity himself, closes the scene; and he denounces against the king of Babylon, his posterity, and even against the city which was the seat of their cruelty, perpetual destruction; and confirms the immutability of his own counsels by the solemnity of an oath.

How forcible is this imagery, how diversified, how sublime! how elevated the diction, the figures, the sentiments! The Jewish nation, the cedars of Lebanon, the ghosts of departed kings, the Babylonish monarch, the travellers who find his corpse, and last of all JEHOVAH himself, are the characters which support this beautiful lyric drama. One

first king of Babylon, to prefigure the excision of his successor and representative. See *Dissertation on the controverted Passages in St. Peter and St. Jude concerning the Angels that sinned.*—S. H.

* *O Lucifer!* &c.] This is, I think, the most sublime image I have ever seen conveyed in so few words. The aptness of the allegory to express the ruin of a powerful monarch by the fall of a bright star from heaven, strikes the mind in the most forcible manner; and the poetical beauty of the passage is greatly heightened by the personification, "*Son* of the morning." Whoever does not relish such painting as this, is not only destitute of poetical taste, but of the common feelings of humanity.—T.

† Xenophon gives an instance of this king's wanton cruelty in killing the son of Gobrias, on no other provocation than that, in hunting, he struck a boar and a lion, which the king had missed.—*Cyrop.* iv. p. 309, quoted by Bishop Lowth. *Notes on Isaiah*, p. 225.—T.

K

continued action is kept up, or rather a series of interesting actions are connected together in an incomparable whole. This, indeed, is the principal and distinguished excellence of the sublimer ode, and is displayed in its utmost perfection in this poem of Isaiah, which may be considered as one of the most ancient, and certainly the most finished specimen of that species of composition which has been transmitted to us. The personifications here are frequent, yet not confused; bold, yet not improbable: a free, elevated, and truly divine spirit pervades the whole; nor is there any thing wanting in this ode to defeat its claim to the character of perfect beauty and sublimity. If, indeed, I may be indulged in the free declaration of my own sentiments on this occasion, I do not know a single instance in the whole compass of Greek and Roman poetry, which, in every excellence of composition, can be said to equal, or even to approach it.

LECTURE XIV.

OF THE SUBLIME IN GENERAL,[*] AND OF SUBLIMITY
OF EXPRESSION IN PARTICULAR.

3. *In what manner the word* Mashal *implies the idea of Sublimity—Sublimity of language and sentiment—On what account the poetic diction of the Hebrews, either considered in itself, or compared with prose composition, merits an appellation expressive of sublimity—The sublimity of the poetic diction arises from the passions —How far the poetic diction differs from prose among the Hebrews—Certain forms of poetic diction and construction exemplified from Job,* chap. iii.

HAVING, in the preceding Lectures, given my sentiments at large on the nature of the figurative style, on its use and application in poetry, and particularly in the poetry of the Hebrews,—I proceed to treat of the sublimity of the sacred

---

[*] An author, whose taste and imagination will be respected as long as the English language exists, has written a most elegant treatise on the distinction between the *beautiful* and the *sublime*. But after all that has been said, our feelings must be the only criterion. The pleasure which is afforded by the contemplation of beauty, appears to be a pure and unmixed pleasure, arising from the gentler agitation, and is less vivid than that which is produced by the sublime. For, as the latter often borders upon terror, it requires a greater exertion, and produces a stronger, though I think less durable sensation, than the beautiful. We may read an elegant author, and continue for a long time to be pleased with his beauties; a sublime author we shall soon be induced to lay down.

The *sublime* also differs from the *beautiful* in being only conversant with great objects. It differs from the *pathetic* in affording a more tranquil pleasure, if I may so express myself. But though the sublime and beautiful be thus distinguishable, yet they are frequently mixed in the same passage, and seem to run into each other, as is the case in that enchanting simile of Homer, into which Mr. Pope has transfused more of the beautiful than is in the original,

"As when the moon, refulgent lamp of night," &c.

Some descriptions also it is not easy to determine whether to assign to the *sublime* or the *pathetic:* such is that admirable but brief delineation of the feelings of the multitude on the crucifixion of our Lord, Luke xxiii. 48. "And all the people that came together to that sight, beholding the things which were done, smote their breasts, and returned." This may in some measure account for the error of Longinus, who confounds these three different sensations together.—T.

K 2

poets; a subject which has been already illustrated by many
examples quoted upon other occasions, but which, since we
have admitted it as a third characteristic of the poetic style,
now requires to be distinctly explained.   We have already
seen, that this is implied in one of the senses of the word
Mashal, it being expressive of power or supreme authority;
and when applied to style, seems particularly to intimate
something eminent or energetic, excellent or important.
This is certainly understood in the phrase, "to take (or lift)
up his parable;" that is, to express a great or lofty sentiment.
The very first instance in which the phrase occurs will serve
as an example in point. For in this manner Balaam "took
up," as our translation renders it, "his parable, and said:"

> "From Aram I am brought by Balak,
> By the king of Moab from the mountains of the East:
> Come, curse me Jacob;
> And come, execrate Israel.
> How shall I curse whom God hath not cursed?
> And how shall I execrate whom God hath not execrated?
> For from the tops of the rocks I see him,
> And from the hills I behold him;
> Lo! the people, who shall dwell alone,
> Nor shall number themselves among the nations!
> Who shall count the dust of Jacob?
> Or the number of the fourth of Israel?
> Let my soul die the death of the righteous,
> And let my end be as his."*

Let us now consider, on what account this address of the
prophet is entitled *Mashal.*   The sentences are indeed accurately distributed in parallelisms, as may be discovered
even in the translation, which has not entirely obscured the
elegance of the arrangement: and compositions in this form,
we have already remarked, are commonly classed among the
proverbs and adages which are properly called *Mashalim*,
though perhaps they contain nothing of a proverbial or
didactic nature. But if we attentively consider this very passage, or others introduced by the same form of expression,

---

* Numb. xxiii. 7—10. אחרית, here rendered *end*, and in the common version
latter end, properly signifies *posterity*; as in Psalm cix. 13. Amos iv. 2. Daniel
xi. 4. The Seventy translate it by σπερμα. It should be remembered that
Balaam is here speaking of the *righteous* not in their *individual* but in their
aggregate capacity, and therefore had either a retrospect, in his wish, to the promise
which had been made to Abraham concerning his posterity, or else to an immediate
communication on the occasion then present.—S. H.

we shall find, in all of them, either an extraordinary variety of figure and imagery; or an elevation of style and sentiment; or perhaps an union of all these excellences; which will induce us to conclude, that something more is meant by the term to which I am alluding than the bare merit of a sententious neatness. If again we examine the same passage in another point of view, we shall discover in it little or nothing of the figurative kind, at least according to our ideas, or according to that acceptation of the word *Mashal* which denotes figurative language; there is evidently nothing in it of the mystical kind, nothing allegorical, no pomp of imagery, no comparison, and in fourteen verses but a single metaphor: as far, therefore, as figurative language is a characteristic of the parabolic style, this is no instance of it. We must then admit the word *Parable*, when applied to this passage, to be expressive of those exalted sentiments, that spirit of sublimity, that energy and enthusiasm, with which the answer of the prophet is animated. By this example I wished to explain on what reasons I was induced to suppose that the term *Mashal*, as well from its proper power or meaning, as from its usual acceptation, involves an idea of sublimity; and that the Hebrew poetry expresses, in its very name and title, the particular quality in which it so greatly excels the poetry of all other nations.

The word *sublimity* I wish, in this place, to be understood in its most extensive sense: I speak not merely of that sublimity which exhibits great objects with a magnificent display of imagery and diction; but that force of composition, whatever it be, which strikes and overpowers the mind, which excites the passions, and which expresses ideas at once with perspicuity and elevation; not solicitous whether the language be plain or ornamented, refined or familiar. In this use of the word I copy Longinus, the most accomplished author on this subject, whether we consider his precepts or his example.*

The sublime consists either in language or sentiment, or more frequently in an union of both, since they reciprocally assist each other, and since there is a necessary and indissoluble connexion between them: this, however, will not prevent our considering them apart with convenience and advantage. The first object, therefore, which presents itself

* " Whose own example strengthens all his laws,
And is himself the great sublime he draws."—Pope.

for our investigation is, Upon what grounds the poetic diction
of the Hebrews, whether considered in itself, or in comparison with prose composition, is deserving of an appellation immediately expressive of sublimity?

The poetry of every language has a style and form of expression peculiar to itself; forcible, magnificent, and sonorous; the words pompous and energetic; the composition
singular and artificial; the whole form and complexion different from what we meet with in common life, and frequently (as with a noble indignation) breaking down the
boundaries by which the popular dialect is confined. The
language of reason is cool, temperate, rather humble than
elevated, well arranged and perspicuous, with an evident
care and anxiety lest any thing should escape which might
appear perplexed or obscure. The language of the passions
is totally different: the conceptions burst out into a turbid
stream, expressive in a manner of the internal conflict; the
more vehement break out in hasty confusion; they catch
(without search or study) whatever is impetuous, vivid, or
energetic. In a word, reason speaks literally, the passions
poetically. The mind, with whatever passion it be agitated,
remains fixed upon the object that excited it; and while it
is earnest to display it, is not satisfied with a plain and exact
description, but adopts one agreeable to its own sensations,
splendid or gloomy, jocund or unpleasant. For the passions
are naturally inclined to amplification; they wonderfully
magnify and exaggerate whatever dwells upon the mind, and
labour to express it in animated, bold, and magnificent terms.
This they commonly effect by two different methods; partly
by illustrating the subject with splendid imagery, and partly
by employing new and extraordinary forms of expression;
which are indeed possessed of great force and efficacy in this
respect especially, that they in some degree imitate or represent the present habit and state of the soul. Hence those
theories of rhetoricians, which they have so pompously detailed, attributing that to art, which above all things is due
to nature alone:

" For nature to each change of fortune forms
   The secret soul, and all its passions warms;
   Transports to rage, dilates the heart with mirth,
   Wrings the sad soul, and bends it down to earth.
   The tongue these various movements must express."*

* Francis's Hor. Art of Poetry, v. 155, &c.

A principle which pervades all poetry, may easily be conceived to prevail, even in a high degree, in the poetry of the Hebrews. Indeed we have already seen how daring these writers are in the selection of their imagery, how forcible in the application of it: and what elegance, splendour, and sublimity, they have by these means been enabled to infuse into their compositions. With respect to the diction, also, we have had an opportunity of remarking the peculiar force and dignity of their poetic dialect; as well as the artificial distribution of the sentences, which appears to have been originally closely connected with the metrical arrangement, though the latter be now totally lost. We are therefore in the next place to consider, whether there be any other remarkable qualities in the poetical language of the Hebrews, which serve to distinguish it from prose composition?

It is impossible to conceive any thing more simple and unadorned than the common language of the Hebrews. It is plain, correct, chaste, and temperate: the words are uncommon neither in their meaning nor application; there is no appearance of study, nor even of the least attention to the harmony of the periods. The order of the words is generally regular and uniform. The verb is the first word in the sentence, the noun, which is the agent, immediately succeeds, and the other words follow in their natural order. Each circumstance is exhibited at a single effort, without the least perplexity or confusion of the different parts: and, what is remarkable, by the help of a simple particle, the whole is connected from the beginning to the end in a continued series; so that nothing appears inconsistent, abrupt, or confused. The whole composition, in fine, is disposed in such an order, and so connected by the continued succession of the different parts, as to demonstrate clearly the regular state of the author, and to exhibit the image of a sedate and tranquil mind. But in the Hebrew poetry the case is different, in part at least, if not in the whole. The free spirit is hurried along, and has neither leisure nor inclination to descend to those minute and frigid attentions. Frequently, instead of disguising the secret feelings of the author, it lays them quite open to public view; and the veil being, as it were, suddenly removed, all the affections and emotions of the soul, its sudden impulses, its hasty sallies and irregularities, are conspicuously displayed.

Should the curious inquirer be desirous of more perfect

information upon this subject, he may satisfy himself, I apprehend, with no great labour or difficulty. Let him take the book of Job; let him read the historical proem of that book; let him proceed to the metrical parts, and let him diligently attend to the first speech of Job. He will, I dare believe, confess, that, when arrived at the metrical part, he feels as if he were reading another language; and is surprised at a dissimilarity in the style of the two passages much greater than between that of Livy and Virgil, or even Herodotus and Homer. Nor indeed could the fact be otherwise, according to the nature of things; since in the latter passage the most exquisite pathos is displayed, such indeed as has not been exceeded, and scarcely equalled, by any effort of the Muses. Not only the force, the beauty, the sublimity of the sentiments, are unrivalled; but such is the character of the diction in general, so vivid is the expression, so interesting the assemblage of objects, so close and connected the sentences, so animated and passionate the whole arrangement, that the Hebrew literature itself contains nothing more poetical. The greater part of these beauties are so obvious, that they cannot possibly escape the eye of a diligent reader: there are some, however, which, depending chiefly upon the arrangement and construction, are of a more abstruse nature. It also sometimes happens, that those beauties which may be easily conceived, are very difficult to be explained: while we simply contemplate them, they appear sufficiently manifest; if we approach nearer, and attempt to touch and handle them, they vanish and escape. Since, however, it would not be consistent with my duty on the present occasion to pass them by totally unregarded, I shall rely, Gentlemen, upon your accustomed candour, while I attempt to render, if possible, some of these elegances more obvious and familiar.

The first thing that arrests the attention of the reader in this passage is the violent sorrow of Job, which bursts forth on a sudden, and flows from his heart, where it had long been confined and suppressed:

"Let the day perish, I was born in it: (*i.e.* in which I was born;)
And the night (which) said, A man is conceived."*

* Job iii. 3. The learned Bishop follows here the interpretation of Schultens, which Mr. Heath has given a good reason for declining to adopt. He renders the passage thus:—

"May the day perish wherein I was brought forth,
And the night which said, See, a man-child is born!"—S. H.

Observe here the concise and abrupt form of the first verse; and in the second the boldness of the figure, and the still more abrupt conclusion. Let the reader then consider, whether he could endure such a spirited, vehement, and perplexed form of expression in any prose composition; or even in verse, unless it were expressive of the deepest pathos.* He will, nevertheless, 1 doubt not, acknowledge that the meaning of this sentence is extremely clear; so clear indeed, that if any person should attempt to make it more copious and explanatory, he would render it less expressive of the mind and feelings of the speaker. It happens fortunately that we have an opportunity of making the experiment upon this very sentiment. There is a passage in Jeremiah so exactly similar, that it might almost be imagined a direct imitation: the meaning is the same, nor is there any very great difference in the phraseology; but Jeremiah fills up the ellipses, smooths and harmonises the rough and uncouth language of Job, and dilates a short distich into two equal distichs, consisting of somewhat longer verses, which is the measure he commonly makes use of:

" Cursed be the day on which I was born ;
   The day on which my mother bare me, let it not be blessed.
   Cursed be the man who brought the news to my father,
   Saying, There is a male child born unto thee ;
   Making him exceedingly glad."†

Thus it happens that the imprecation of Jeremiah has more in it of complaint than of indignation; it is milder, softer, and more plaintive, peculiarly calculated to excite pity, in moving which the great excellence of this prophet consists; while that of Job is more adapted to strike us with terror than to excite our compassion.‡

* Our author exaggerates a little the boldness and energy of this passage, conceiving that to be an unusual phraseology, which is only uncommon to us. There will be an opportunity of mentioning the *change* or *enallage* of the tenses in the next Lecture   The ellipsis of the relative pronoun *asher* (which) is not at all harsh and unusual ; nothing is more common in the Arabic, it being accounted among the elegances of language, nor is it unusual with the Hebrews.   Even with the English the pronoun *which* is very frequently omitted.—M.

" There are in all languages certain elliptical expressions, which use has established, and which, therefore, very rarely occasion darkness."—Campb. *Phil. of Rhet.*

† Jer. xx. 14, 15.

‡ This is an excellent observation. The grief, or rather despair, of Job, is of the solemn, majestic, and truly tragic kind ; that of Jeremiah has more of

But to proceed. I shall not trouble you with a tedious discussion of those particulars which are sufficiently apparent: the crowded and abrupt sentences, which seem to have little connexion, bursting from the glowing bosom with matchless force and impetuosity; the bold and magnificent expressions, which the eloquence of indignation pours forth, four instances of which occur in the space of twice as many verses,* and which seem to be altogether poetical; two of them indeed are found continually in the poets, and in them only; the others are still more uncommon. Omitting these, therefore, the object which at present seems more worthy of examination is that redundancy of expression which, in a few lines, takes place of the former excessive conciseness:

> "That night—let darkness seize upon it." †

In this also there is the strongest indication of passion, and a perturbed mind. He doubtless intended at first to express himself in this manner:

> " Be that night darkness" ‡——

But, in the very act of uttering it, he suddenly catches at an expression which appears more animated and energetic. I do not know that I can better illustrate this observation than by referring to a passage in Horace, in which a similar transition and redundancy falls from the indignant poet:

> " He who——(bane of the fruitful earth !
> Curst was the hour that gave thee birth !)
> He—O vile, pernicious tree !
> Was surely curst who planted thee.
> Well may I think the parricide
> In blood his guilty soul had dy'd ;
> Or plung'd his dagger in the breast,
> At midnight, of his sleeping guest;
> Or temper'd every baleful juice
> Which poisonous Colchian glebes produce ;
> Or, if a blacker crime be known,
> That crime the wretch had made his own." §

For undoubtedly the poet begun as if he intended to pursue the subject in a regular order, and to finish the sentence

the elegiac tenderness, which raises no greater passion than pity, and is only calculated to excite our tears.—M.

* Ver. 4, 5. 7. גִּלְמוּד, כַּמְרִירֵי, צַלְמָוֶת, תּוֹפַע.   † Ver. 6.

‡ See ver. 4.   § Francis, B. ii. Ode xiii. with some little alteration.

in this form: " He who—planted thee; he was accessory to
the murder of his parents, and sprinkled his chambers with
the blood of his guest; he dealt in the poison of Colchis,"
&c.: but anger and vexation dissipated the order of his
ideas, and destroyed the construction of this sentence. But
should some officious grammarian take in hand the passage,
(for this is a very diligent race of beings, and sometimes
more than sufficiently exact and scrupulous,) and attempt
to restore it to its primitive purity and perfection, the whole
grace and excellence of that beautiful exordium would be
immediately annihilated, all the impetuosity and ardour
would in a moment be extinguished. But to return to
Job:

> "Lo! that night, may it be fruitless!" *

He appears to have a direct picture or image of that night
before his eyes, and to point it out with his finger. " The
doors of my womb," for "the doors of my mother's womb,"†
is an elliptical form of expression, the meaning of which
is easily cleared up, but which no person in a tranquil
state of mind, and quite master of himself, would venture to
employ. Not to detain you too long upon this subject, I
shall produce only one passage more, which is about the
conclusion of this animated speech:

> " Wherefore should he give light to the miserable ?
> And life to those who are in bitterness of soul ?
> Who call aloud for death, but it cometh not ;
> Who dig for it more than for hidden treasures ;
> Who would rejoice even to exultation,
> And be in raptures, if they had found the grave.
> Well might it befit the man whose way is sheltered,
> And whom God hath surrounded with a hedge :
> But my groaning cometh like my daily food,
> And my roarings are poured out like water."‡

The whole composition of this passage is admirable, and
deserves a minute attention. " Wherefore should he give
light to the miserable?" But who is the giver alluded to ?
Certainly God himself, whom Job has indeed in his mind;
but it escaped his notice that no mention is made of him in
the preceding lines. He seems to speak of the miserable
in general, but by a violent and sudden transition he applies

* Ch. iii. ver. 7.   † Ver. 10.   ‡ Ver. 20—24.

the whole to himself, "But my groaning cometh like my daily food." It is plain, therefore, that in all the preceding reflections he has himself only in view. He makes a transition from the singular to the plural, and back again—a remarkable amplification intervening, expressive of his desire of death, the force and boldness of which is incomparable : at last, as if suddenly recollecting himself, he returns to the former subject, which he had apparently quitted, and resumes the detail of his own misery. From these observations I think it will be manifest, that the agitated and disordered state of the speaker's mind is not more evidently demonstrated by a happy boldness of sentiment and imagery, and an uncommon force of language, than by the very form, conduct, and arrangement of the whole.

The peculiar property which I have laboured to demonstrate in this passage, will, I apprehend, be found to prevail as a characteristic of the Hebrew poetry, making due allowance for different subjects and circumstances—I mean that vivid and ardent style which is so well calculated to display the emotions and passions of the mind. Hence the poetry of the Hebrews abounds with phrases and idioms totally unsuited to prose composition, and which frequently appear to us harsh and unusual, I had almost said unnatural and barbarous; which, however, are destitute neither of meaning nor of force, were we but sufficiently informed to judge of their true application. It will however be worth our while, perhaps, to make the experiment on some other passages of this nature, and to try at least what can be done towards the further elucidation of this point.

LECTURE XV.

OF SUBLIMITY OF EXPRESSION.

The character of the Poetic Dialect further illustrated by examples of different kinds from the Song of Moses, Deut. xxxii.—*The frequent and sudden transition from one person to another ; its cause and effects—The use of the tenses in a manner quite different from common language : the reasons of this—The Hebrew language peculiar in this respect—The future is often spoken of in the perfect present, and the past in the future tense : the reason of the former easy to be explained ; the latter is a matter of considerable difficulty, which neither the Commentators, the Translators, nor even the Grammarians have elucidated—Some examples of this, and the explanation of them—The frequent use of this form of construction may be considered as characteristical of the Poetic Dialect.*

In order to demonstrate more completely the sublimity of the Hebrew poetry by a comparison with prose, I referred the student of Hebrew to the Book of Job, convinced that he would easily perceive, both in the manner and diction, a very considerable difference between the historical introduction of that book and the metrical passages immediately succeeding. But lest these passages should be objected to as improper instances for such a comparison, on the supposition that although both of them were written entirely either in verse or prose, yet the different nature of the subjects would require a very different style ; we shall now make the experiment on some other passages, and compare the manner of treating the same subject in verse and prose. The book of Deuteronomy will afford us a convenient instance ; for Moses appears there in the character both of an orator and a poet. In the former character he addresses a very solemn and interesting oration to the people of Israel,[*] exhorting them, by the most inviting promises, to the observance of the covenant, and dissuading them from the violation of it by threats of the most exemplary punishment: and for

---

[*] Deut. xxviii. xxix. xxx. xxxi.

the purpose of impressing the same more forcibly on their minds, he afterwards, by the command of God, embellishes the subject with all the elegance of verse,* in a poem which bears every mark of divine inspiration.   In these two passages is displayed every excellence of which the Hebrew language is capable in both species of composition; all that is grand, forcible, and majestic, both in prose and verse : from them, too, we may be enabled easily to comprehend the difference between the style of oratory among the Hebrews, and that of their poetry, not only in sentiment, but in the imagery, the arrangement, and the language.   Whoever wishes, therefore, to satisfy himself concerning the true character and genius of the Hebrew poetry, I would advise carefully to compare the two passages, and I think he will soon discover that the former, though great, spirited, and abounding with ornament, is, notwithstanding, regular, copious, and diffuse; that, with all its vehemence and impetuosity, it still preserves a smoothness, evenness, and uniformity throughout: and that the latter, on the contrary, consists of sentences, pointed, energetic, concise, and splendid; that the sentiments are truly elevated and sublime, the language bright and animated, the expression and phraseology uncommon; while the mind of the poet never continues fixed to any single point, but glances continually from one object to another.   These remarks are of such a nature, that the diligent reader will apprehend them better by experience and his own observation, than by means of any commentary or explanation whatever.   There are, however, one or two points which have attracted my notice in the perusal of this remarkable poem; and as they are of general use and application, and may serve to elucidate many of the difficult passages of the Hebrew poetry, they appear to me not undeserving of a more particular examination.

Taking, therefore, this poem as an example, the first general observation to which I would direct your attention is, the sudden and frequent change of the persons, and principally in the addresses or expostulations; for enough has been said already concerning the introduction of different characters or personifications. In the exordium of this poem Moses displays the truth and justice of Almighty God, most sacredly regarded in all his acts and counsels: whence he takes occasion to reprove the perfidy and wickedness of his

* Deut. xxxii.

ungrateful people; at first as if his censure were only pointed at the absent—

"Their evil disposition hath corrupted his children, which are indeed no longer his:" *

He then suddenly directs his discourse to themselves:

> " Perverse and crooked generation!
> Will ye thus requite JEHOVAH,
> Foolish people and unwise?
> Is he not thy father and thy redeemer;
> Did he not make thee and form thee?"

After his indignation has somewhat subsided, adverting to a remoter period, he beautifully enlarges upon the indulgence, and more than paternal affection, continually manifested by Almighty God towards the Israelites, from the time when he first chose them for his peculiar people; and all this again without seeming directly to apply it to them.   He afterwards admirably exaggerates the stupidity and barbarity of this ungrateful people, which exceeds that of the brutes themselves.   Observe with what force the indignation of the prophet again breaks forth:

> " But Jeshurun grew fat and resisted;
> Thou grewest fat, thou wast made thick, thou wast covered with fat!
> And he deserted the God that made him,
> And despised the rock of his salvation."

The abrupt transition in one short sentence to the Israelites, and back again, is wonderfully forcible and pointed, and excellently expressive of disgust and indignation.   There is a passage of Virgil, which, though it be less animated, is certainly not unworthy of being compared with this of Moses; it is that in which, by an ingenious apostrophe, he upbraids the traitor with his crime, and at the same time exonerates the king from the imputation of cruelty:

> " By godlike Tullus doom'd the traitor dies;
> (And thou, false Metius, dost too late repent

---

* Ver. 5, 6. I have endeavoured, as far as I am able, to render perspicuous the Hebrew reading; but after all, that which is adopted by the LXX, the Sam. and Syr. is perhaps nearer the truth, שחתו לא לו בני מום; "They are corrupted, they are not his, (they are) sons of error, or blemish." Which is also partly confirmed by Aquila, Vulg. Symmachus.—*Author's Note.*

Thy violated faith !) By furious steeds
In pieces torn, his entrails strew the ground,
And the low brambles drink his streaming blood."*

I might proceed, and produce several examples in point
from the same poem, and innumerable from other parts of
the sacred writings, different from each other both in expression and form.   These, however, are sufficient to demon
strate the force of this kind of composition in expressing the
more vehement affections, and in marking those sudden
emotions which distract the mind and divide its attention.
But whoever will attend with any diligence to the poetry of
the Hebrews, will find that examples of this kind almost
perpetually occur, and much more frequently than could be
endured in the poetry of the Greeks and Romans, or even
in our own: he will find many of these instances not easy to
be understood; the force and design of some of them, when
separately considered, are indeed scarcely to be explained,
or even perfectly comprehended.   The reader will not,
however, be warranted in concluding from this concession,
that those very passages which are most obscure are in themselves absurd, and that they possess no general force or effect
in distinguishing the diction, in sustaining the poetic spirit,
and in forming that peculiar character which, however it
may differ from what we are accustomed to, is in its kind
altogether deserving of applause.   In this case we ought to
consider the proper genius and character of the Hebrew
poetry.   It is unconstrained, animated, bold and fervid.
The orientals look upon the language of poetry as wholly
distinct from that of common life, as calculated immediately
for expressing the passions : if, therefore, it were to be reduced to the plain rule and order of reason, if every word
and sentence were to be arranged with care and study, as if
calculated for perspicuity alone, it would be no longer what
they intended it, and to call it the language of passion would
be the grossest of solecisms.
    The other observation to which I alluded, as relating both
to this poem and to the poetry of the Hebrews in general, is,
that you there find a much more frequent change or variation of the tenses than occurs in common language.   The
chief aim of such a transition is, to render the subject of a
narration or description more striking, and even to embody

* Æn. viii. 642.

and give it a visible existence.* Thus, in all languages, in prose as well as poetry, it is usual to speak of past as well as future events in the present tense, by which means whatever is described or expressed is in a manner brought immediately before our eyes; nor does the mind contemplate a distant object, by looking back to the past or forward to the future. But in this respect there is a great peculiarity in the Hebrew language. For the Hebrew verbs have no form for expressing the imperfect or indefinite of the present tense, or an action which now is performing: this is usually effected by a participle only, or by a verb substantive understood, neither of which are often made use of in such passages as these, nor indeed can be always conveniently admitted. They therefore take another method of attaining this end, and, for the sake of clearness and precision, express future events by the past tense, or rather by the perfect present, as if they had actually taken place; and, on the contrary, past events by the future, as if immediately or speedily to happen, and only proceeding towards their completion. Of the first of these forms of construction, namely, the expressing of the future by the past tense, an instance which we just now quoted will demonstrate both the nature and the effect.

Moses foreseeing, by the impulse of divine inspiration, the miserable neglect of the true worship into which the people of Israel were universally to relapse, reprobates in the following terms the vices of that ungrateful people, as if they had been already committed in his immediate presence:—

---

* The change of tenses here remarked on, is no more a peculiarity of the Hebrew poetry than of our own. Perhaps there does not exist a finer instance of a *past* event rendered *present*, by this means, than in the following description by Dryden:

> "He sung Darius great and good,
>   By too severe a fate,
> Fallen, fallen, fallen, fallen,
>   Fallen from his high estate,
>   And welt'ring in his blood:
> Deserted at his utmost need
> By those his former bounty fed;
> On the bare earth exposed he lies,
>   With not a friend to close his eyes."

Nor is there a less happy example of *future* events made *present*, in the *Bard* of Gray:

> "Visions of glory, spare my aching sight;
>   Ye *unborn* ages, *crowd* not on my soul!" &c, &c.—S. H.

L

"Their evil disposition hath corrupted his children, which are
indeed no longer his."

Thus he speaks as if he were the actual witness of their depravity, and present at those impious rites with which they
were about to violate a religion divinely instituted through
his means. Nothing can be more efficacious than this kind
of anticipation to the clear, evident, and almost ocular demonstration of things. On this account it is a very common
mode of expression in the prophetical writings; and in this,
as in every other excellence, Isaiah particularly challenges
our highest admiration. Observe only with what exactness
and perspicuity he has delineated the journey of Sennache-
rib towards Jerusalem, and the different stages of the army;
insomuch that the light and evidence which the Prophet
throws upon the circumstances of the prediction, falls nothing short of the clearness and accuracy of an historical
narration:

" He is come to Aiath; he hath passed to Migron;
  At Michmas he will deposit his baggage.
  They have passed the strait; Geba is their lodging for the
      night:
  Ramah is frightened; Gibeah of Saul fleeth.
  Cry aloud with thy voice, O daughter of Gallim;
  Hearken unto her, O Laish; answer her, O Anathoth.
  Madmena is gone away; the inhabitants of Gebim flee amain.
  Yet this day shall he abide in Nob;
  He shall shake his hand against the mount of the daughter of
      Sion."*

* Isaiah x. 28—32. In the 29th verse I think with the Chaldee paraphrast,
that for לנו we should read למו. How others, or the greater part, may have read it,
is not sufficiently apparent; but to me it appears of considerable importance, as
well to the sense as the elegance of the passage. *Gnaniah Gnanathoth* in verse 30:
here the epithet alludes to the meaning or etymology of the name, as if he had
said—

        " Alas! thy name is too well founded in truth."

I would remark here, that if the reader desires to understand, how much the
prophets, and particularly Isaiah, are attached to beauties of this kind, he may be
satisfied on consulting the following passages: Isaiah v. 7; xiii. 6; xxiv. 17;
xxvii. 7; xxxiii. 1; lvii. 6; lxi. 3; lxv. 11, 12. Jer. xlviii. 2. Ezek. vii.
6. Hosea ix. 15. Amos v. 5. Mic. i. 10—15. Zeph. ii. 4. See also Gen. ix.
27; xlix. 8—16. 10. Perhaps the Syr. may be right in this passage, *Hear, O
Laisha; and answer, O Anathoth!* It reads *Ve-gnani.* " In the word *Laisha* the
ה is wanting in one manuscript. In verse 32, many manuscripts, and some
editions, read בת; which is one example among many, in which the text of many
manuscripts, and of the oldest editions, agrees with the Keri." K.—*Author's
Note.*

Thus the plague of locusts is denounced and described, as if it had already happened, by the prophet Joel:

" For a nation hath gone up on my land,
  Who are strong and without number;
  They have destroyed my vine, and have made my fig-tree a
    broken branch.
  They have made it quite bare, and cast it away: the branches
    thereof are made white.
  The field is laid waste; the ground, the ground mourneth."*

The Prophet is undoubtedly here speaking of a future event; for the very devastation which, to strike the more forcibly on the mind, he has thus depicted as an event already past, is threatened by him in the sequel under another image to be immediately inflicted,† unless the people repent of their wickedness. Thus far the Hebrew language differs not materially from others; those future actions or events which other writers, for the sake of force and clearness, express in the imperfect present, the Hebrews express in the perfect present with equal effect.

In another point, it must be confessed, they differ essentially from other writers, namely, when they intimate past events in the form of the future tense: and I must add, that this is a matter of considerable difficulty. If we resort to the translators and commentators, so far are they from affording any solution, that they do not so much as notice it, accommodating as much as possible the form of the tenses to the subject and context, and explaining it rather according to their own opinions, than according to the rules of grammar, or any fixed and established principles. If again we apply to the grammarians, we shall still find ourselves no less at a loss: they indeed remark the circumstance: but they neither explain the reason of it, nor yet are candid enough to make a fair confession of their own ignorance. They endeavour to confuse their disciples by the use of a Greek term, and have always at hand a sort of inexplicable and mysterious *enallage* or *change* of the tenses, with which, rather than say nothing, they attempt to evade a closer inquiry, as if the change were made by accident, and from no principle or motive; than which nothing can be conceived more absurd or impertinent.‡ That these apparent anoma-

---

* Joel i. 6, 7. 10, &c.   † Joel ii.
‡ I have no inclination to contradict our Author in this assertion. The grammarians have not been content with defending this phraseology as an enallage,

lies, however, are not without their peculiar force and beauty, I have not a doubt; that many of them should cause difficulty and obscurity, considering the great antiquity of the Hebrew language, is not to be wondered at. Some light may notwithstanding be reflected upon the subject, by a careful attention to the state of the writer's mind, and by considering properly what ideas were likely to be prevalent in his imagination at the time of his writing. There is a remarkable instance of this form of construction in that very Song of Moses to which we have just been alluding. After mentioning the divine dispensation by which the Israelites were distinguished as the chosen people of God, he proceeds to state with what love and tenderness the Almighty had cherished them, from the time in which he brought them from Egypt, led them by the hand through the wilderness, and as it were carried them in his bosom : all these, though past events, are expressed in the future tense :

> " He will find him in a desert land,
> In the vast and howling wilderness :
> He will lead him about, he will instruct him :
> He will keep him as the pupil of his eye."*

but have distinguished it by the name of the *prophetic* preterite. They might as well have called it the *prophetic present*, since, as the Hebrew language wants the *present tense*, the past is always substituted in its room. But however they may choose to distinguish it, whether as a prophetic present, or a prophetic preterite, it is by no means unusual in the more modern languages. Thus in English the author of a poem called Manners :

> " Rapt into thought, lo ! I Britannia see
> Rising superior o'er the subject sea :
> And her gay pennants spread their silken wings
> Big with the fate of empires and of kings."

Thus the Sibyl in Virgil :

> ———" in regna Lavini
> Dardanidæ veniens."—M.

If the learned Professor had been very conversant in our poetry, he might have found many more striking examples than that which he has quoted, and particularly in the poems of Mr. Gray. Indeed this is by no means a favourable specimen of English poetry.—*See* and *sea* is no rhyme, being exactly the same sound.—" The gay pennants and silken wings *big* with the fate of empires," &c. is a false metaphor ; if we even overlook the plagiarism, " *Big with the fate* of Cato and of Rome."

For the information of modern writers, who may choose to make use of this bold figure, I will add a remark, that it is never to be introduced but when the mind is sufficiently warm not to perceive the allusion. The scene must be so interesting that the reader cannot help realising it.—T.

* Deut. xxxii. 10. " In the Samar. copy we read as follows :

יאמצהו בארץ המדבר
ובתהללות ישמנהו :

You will readily judge whether this passage can admit of any other explication, than that of Moses supposing himself present at the time when the Almighty selected the people of Israel for himself; and thence, as from an eminence, contemplating the consequences of that dispensation. The case will be found similar in many other passages; as, in particular, more than once in that historical Psalm which is inscribed with the name of Asaph. After the prophet has exposed the perfidy of the people, their refractory conduct almost in the very crisis of their deliverance from the Egyptian bondage, he in a manner anticipates in his mind the clemency of God and the repeated transgressions of the Israelites, and speaks of them as future events:

" But he, moved with compassion, will pardon their iniquity, and
　　will not destroy them;
　And frequently will turn away his wrath,
　Nor will stir up all his indignation.——
　How often will they rebel against him in the desert,
　And will grieve him in the wilderness !"*

The general disposition and arrangement of the hundred and fourth Psalm affords a most elegant exemplification of this construction. For the prophet, instancing the greatness and wisdom of God in the constitution and preservation of the natural world, speaks of the actions and decrees of the Almighty in the present tense, as if he himself had been a witness when they were brought to light; and displays their consequences and uses, and what are called the final causes, in the future tense, as if looking forward from the beginning through all future time.

But although these and some other passages will admit of this explanation, there are many to which it will not apply. In these, the situation and state of the authors are not so much to be considered, as the peculiar nature or idiom of the language. For the Hebrews frequently make use of the future tense in such a manner, that it appears not to have relation to the present speaker, but to the person or thing which was last spoken of. Thus, when any action is connected with another action, or consequent to it; or when

---

" That is, *He will comfort him in the Land of the Desert, and in rejoicings he
will plentifully sustain him:* this reading is mentioned only that it may be compared and examined with the Hebrew."—H. See Houbigant in loc.—*Author's
Note.*
　　　　　　　* Psalm lxxviii. 38. 40.

the same action is repeated or continued—when a person perseveres in the same action, or performs it with great earnestness or assiduity—this is all expressed as if it were future.* This form is therefore distinguished by the grammarians by the appellation *Gnatid,* which is equivalent to prompt, expedite, or impending. Examples enough to this purpose might be produced from the passages which have been referred to on former occasions: for instance, from that most elegant prosopopœia of the mother of Sisera;† from the allegory of the vine which was brought out of Egypt;‡ from the comparison founded on the maternal piety and solicitude of the eagle:§ the form and manner of all which may be easily perceived by an attentive reader, but cannot be well explained by the most industrious commentator.‖

Now if, as I have stated, this unusual form of construction be the effect either of some sudden emotion in the speaker, of some new and extraordinary state of mind; or if on any other account, from the relation of the subject or the genius of the language, it be possessed of some peculiar force or energy; it will obviously follow, that it must more frequently occur in poetry than in prose, since it is particularly adapted to the nature, the versatility, and variety of the former, and to the expression of any violent passion; and since it has but little affinity to that mildness and temperance of

---

* See 2 Sam. xii. 3.   † Judges v. 29.
‡ Psalm lxxx. 9. 12. 14.   § Deut. xxxii. 11.

‖ I so widely differ from our Author, that I have very little doubt of making this matter, as far as is necessary to understand his meaning, perfectly intelligible to the English reader, by merely exhibiting the passages in question, and comparing the literal with our common translation. In Judges v. 29, our version reads, " Her wise ladies answer her ; yea, she returned answer to herself :" in the original it is, " Her wise ladies *will* answer her; yea, she *will* return answer to herself." In Psalm lxxx. 8. our translation is, " Thou broughtest a vine," &c. : in the original, " Thou *wilt* bring a vine," &c. " Thou *wilt* cast out," &c. In Deut. xxxii. 11, our Bible reads, " As an eagle stirreth up her nest, fluttereth over her young, spreadeth her wings," &c.: in the original it is, " As the eagle *will* stir up, *will* flutter, *will* spread her wings," &c. It is not uncommon in vulgar language, even in this country, and particularly the northern parts of it, when an action is described in the general, as in the above allusion of the eagle, to use the future tense; and if that very passage had been literally translated, the comparison would have been equally intelligible to our common people. But I must confess there is, after all, a most licentious use of the different tenses prevalent in the Hebrew language, which to us, who are unacquainted with the principles of it, creates strange confusion, and obliges us commonly to have recourse to the context, and the apparent design of the passage. Nor do all these very ingenious hypotheses of our Author entirely remove the difficulty, or explain the principles of this form of construction to my satisfaction.—T.

language which proceeds in one uniform and even tenour. Thus, if we attend diligently to the poetry of the Hebrews, and carefully remark its peculiar characteristics, we shall hardly find any circumstance, the regular and artificial conformation of the sentences excepted, which more evidently distinguishes it from the style of prose composition, than the singularity which is now under consideration. For though it be allowed, that this idiom is not so entirely inconsistent with prose but that a few examples of it might be produced,* on the whole I am convinced, that the free and frequent use of it may be accounted as the certain characteristic of poetry.

That the full force of these and other peculiarities, which serve to distinguish the poetical diction of the Hebrews, and to preserve that sublimity and splendour for which it is so remarkable, should be fully apparent from a few examples, is hardly to be expected; nor did I flatter myself with any such expectation, when I entered upon this part of my subject. My intention was only to produce an instance or two, which were most likely to occur to those who enter upon this course of reading, and which appeared to demand particular attention. The perfect character and genius, the whole form, principles, and nature of the poetical diction and ornaments, can neither be comprehended in any minute or artificial precepts whatever, nor perhaps be reduced altogether to rule or method: the complete knowledge and perception of these are only to be attained by reading and investigation, united with acuteness of judgment and delicacy of taste.

* Hitherto I have only met with the following : Judges ii. 1. (see, however, Houbigant in loc.) and xxi. 25. 1 Sam. xxvii. 9. 11. 2 Sam. xii. 31. 1 Kings xxi. 6. 1 Chron. xi. 8. See also Peters on Job, p. 202.—*Author's Note.*

LECTURE XVI.

OF SUBLIMITY OF SENTIMENT.

Sublimity of Sentiment arises, either from elevation of mind, or from some vehement passion : in each, it is either natural, or the effect of divine inspiration—Elevation of mind is displayed in the greatness of the subject, the adjuncts, and the imagery— Examples from the descriptions of the Divine Majesty ; of the works and attributes of the Deity ; also from the display of the Divine Power in the form of Interrogation and Irony—The Hebrew poets attribute the human passions to the Deity without departing from sublimity ; and that frequently when the imagery appears least consistent with the Divine Majesty: the reason of this.

IF we consider the very intimate connexion which on all occasions subsists between sentiment and language, it will perhaps appear, that the peculiar quality of which we have just been treating, under the title of Sublimity of Expression, might ultimately be referred to that of Sentiment. In the strictest sense, however, sublimity of sentiment may be accounted a distinct quality, and may be said to proceed, either from a certain elevation of mind, and a happy boldness of conception, or from a strong impulse of the soul, when agitated by the more violent affections. The one is called by Longinus *Grandeur of Conception,* the other *Vehemence* or *Enthusiasm of Passion.* To each of these we must have recourse in the present disquisition, and, in applying them to the sacred poets, I shall endeavour to detract nothing from the dignity of that inspiration which proceeds from higher causes, while I allow to the genius of each writer his own peculiar excellence and accomplishments. I am indeed of opinion, that the Divine Spirit by no means takes such an entire possession of the mind of the prophet, as to subdue or extinguish the character and genius of the man ; the natural powers of the mind are in general elevated and refined, they are neither eradicated nor totally obscured : and though the writings of Moses, of David, and of Isaiah, always bear the marks of a divine and celestial impulse, we may nevertheless plainly discover in them the particular characters of their respective authors.

That species of the sublime which proceeds from a boldness of spirit and an elevation of the soul, whether inherent in the author or derived from a Divine impulse and inspiration, is displayed, first, in the greatness and sublimity of the subject itself; secondly, in the choice of the adjuncts or circumstances, (by the importance and magnitude of which a degree of force and elevation is added to the description;) and lastly, in the splendour and magnificence of the imagery by which the whole is illustrated.   In all these the Hebrew writers have obtained an unrivalled pre-eminence.   As far as respects the dignity and importance of the subject, they not only surpass all other writers, but even exceed the confines of human genius and intellect.   The greatness, the power, the justice, the immensity of God; the infinite wisdom of his works and of his dispensations—are the subjects in which the Hebrew poetry is always conversant, and always excels.   If we only consider with a common degree of candour how greatly inferior the poetry of all other nations appears, whenever it presumes to treat of these subjects; and how unequal to the dignity of the matter the highest conceptions of the human genius are found to be; we shall, I think, not only acknowledge the sublimity, but the divinity of that of the Hebrews.   Nor does this greatness and elevation consist altogether in the subjects and sentiments, which, however expressed, would yet retain some part at least of their native force and dignity; but the manner in which these lofty ideas are arranged, and the embellishments of description with which they abound, claim our warmest admiration: and this, whether we regard the adjuncts or circumstances, which are selected with so much judgment as uniformly to contribute to the sublimity of the principal subject; or the amplitude of that imagery, which represents objects the most remote from human apprehension in such enchanting colours, that, although debased by human painting, they still retain their genuine sanctity and excellence.   Since, therefore, the sublimity of the sacred poets has been already exemplified in a variety of instances, it will probably be sufficient, in addition to these, to produce a few examples as illustrations of these remarks, chiefly taken from those parts of Scripture in which a delineation of the Divine Majesty is attempted.

In the first place, then, let me recall to your remembrance the solemnity and magnificence with which the power of God in the creation of the universe is depicted. And here I cannot possibly overlook that passage of the sacred historian which has been so frequently commended, in which the importance of the circumstance and the greatness of the idea (the human mind cannot indeed well conceive a greater) are no less remarkable than the expressive brevity and simplicity of the language :—" And God said, Let there be light; and there was light."* The more words you would accumulate upon this thought, the more you would detract from the sublimity of it; for the understanding quickly comprehends the Divine Power from the effect, and perhaps most completely when it is not attempted to be explained; the perception in that case is the more vivid, inasmuch as it seems to proceed from the proper action and energy of the mind itself. The prophets have also depicted the same conception in poetical language, and with no less force and magnificence of expression. The whole creation is summoned forth to celebrate the praise of the Almighty:

> " Let them praise the name of JEHOVAH ;
> For he commanded, and they were created."†

And in another place:

> " For he spoke, and it was ;
> He commanded, and it stood fast."‡

The same subject is frequently treated more diffusely, many circumstances being added, and a variety of imagery introduced for the purpose of illustration. Whether this be executed in a manner suitable to the greatness and dignity of the subject, may be easily determined by a few examples:

> " Where wast thou when I laid the foundations of the earth ?
> If thou knowest, declare.
> Say, who fixed the proportions of it, for surely thou knowest ;
> Or who stretched out the line upon it ?
> Upon what were its foundations fixed ;
> Or who laid the corner-stone thereof?
> When the morning stars sung together,
> And all the sons of God shouted for joy :
> When the sea was shut up with doors,
> When it burst forth as an infant that cometh out of the womb:

---

* Gen. i. 3.   † Psal. cxlviii. 5.   ‡ Psal. xxxiii. 9.

When I placed the cloud for its robe,
And thick darkness for its swaddling-band:
When I fixed my boundary against it,
When I placed a bar and gates :
When I said, Thus far shalt thou come, and not advance,
And here shall a stop be put to the pride of thy waves."*

"Who hath measured the waters in the hollow of his hand ;
And hath meted out the heavens by his span ;
And hath comprehended the dust of the earth in a tierce,
And hath weighed in scales the mountains, and the hills in a
    balance?
Lift up your eyes on high;
And see who hath created these.
He draweth forth their armies by number;
He calleth them each by its name :
Through the greatness of his strength, and the mightiness of his
    power,
Not one of them faileth to appear." †

In these examples, the power and wisdom of the Deity, as demonstrated in the constitution and government of the natural world, you see have suggested a variety of circumstances, a splendid assemblage of imagery, of which it is a sufficient commendation to say, the whole is not unworthy the greatness of the subject. The case is however materially different, when the attributes of God are considered in themselves simply and abstractedly, with no illustration or amplification from their operations and effects. Here the human mind is absorbed, overwhelmed as it were in a boundless vortex, and studies in vain for an expedient to extricate itself. But the greatness of the subject may be justly estimated by its difficulty; and while the imagination labours to comprehend what is beyond its powers, this very labour itself, and these ineffectual endeavours, sufficiently demonstrate the immensity and sublimity of the object. On this account the following passage is truly sublime. Here the mind seems to exert its utmost faculties in vain to grasp an object, whose unparalleled magnitude mocks its feeble endeavours; and to this end it employs the grandest imagery that universal nature can suggest, and yet this imagery, however great, proves totally inadequate to the purpose :

    " O JEHOVAH, thy mercy extendeth to the heavens ;
    And thy truth unto the clouds :

---

* Job xxxviii. 4—11.   † Isa. xl. 12 and 26.

> Thy justice is as the mountains of strength;
> Thy judgment as the vast abyss!"*

But nothing of this kind is nobler or more majestic, than when a description is carried on by a kind of continued negation; when a number of great and sublime ideas are collected, which, on a comparison with the object, are found infinitely inferior and inadequate. Thus the boundaries are gradually extended on every side, and at length totally removed; the mind is insensibly led on towards infinity, and is struck with inexpressible admiration, with a pleasing awe, when it first finds itself expatiating in that immense expanse. There are many such examples in the sacred poetry, one or two of which will probably enable you to recollect the rest.

> "Canst thou explore the deep counsels of God,
> Canst thou fathom the immensity of the Almighty?
> It is higher than heaven, what canst thou do?
> It is deeper than the abyss, what canst thou know?
> The measure thereof is longer than the earth,
> And broader than the expanse of the sea."†

> "Whither shall I go from thy Spirit?
> And whither shall I flee from thy presence?
> If I ascend the heavens, thou art there;
> If I make my bed in the abyss, behold thou art there!
> If I take the wings of the morning,
> And dwell in the extreme parts of the ocean;
> There also thy hand shall lead me,
> And thy right hand shall hold me."‡

---

* Psa. xxxvi. 6, 7.   † Job xi. 7—9.

‡ Psa. cxxxix. 7—10. I am not perfectly satisfied with the commonly received interpretation of the 9th verse; as expressive of the continual motion from east to west, and the velocity of the motion compared with that of the sun's rays. I look upon the two lines of this distich to be in contrast or opposition to each other, and not that the latter is a consequence of the former; and this I think is so apparent from the construction of the sentences, that there cannot remain a doubt concerning it: thus, there is a double transition spoken of, towards the east, and again towards the west; and the length of the flight, and not the velocity of the motion, is the object of amplification. Thus Theodoret upon this passage, " He calls the East *the Morning*, and the West, *the extreme parts of the Sea:* to height and depth he opposes breadth and length, describing and evincing the infinity of the Divine Being."

The author of a very useful collection of Jewish commentaries, the title of which is *Miclol Jophe*, says, This phrase, *If I take the wings of the morning*, should be understood as a common oriental phrase for *departure*, or *flight towards the east*. These are his words, *If I take the wings of the morning, and fly with them;* i. e. *If I go to the extremity of the east.*" H.—Author's Note.

I cannot, after all, give up the beautiful allegory of *taking the wings* (the speed, the swiftness) *of the morning*. It is so much more poetical, so much more agreeable to

Here we find the idea of infinity perfectly expressed, though it be perhaps the most difficult of all ideas to impress upon the mind: for, when simply and abstractedly mentioned, without the assistance and illustration of any circumstances whatever, it almost wholly evades the powers of the human understanding. The sacred writers have, therefore, recourse to description, amplification, and imagery, by which they give substance and solidity to what is in itself a subtile and unsubstantial phantom; and render an ideal shadow the object of our senses. They conduct us through all the dimensions of space, length, breadth, and height: these they do not describe in general or indefinite terms; they apply to them an actual line and measure, and that the most extensive which all nature can supply, or which the mind is indeed able to comprehend. When the intellect is carried beyond these limits, there is nothing substantial upon which it can rest; it wanders through every part, and when it has compassed the boundaries of creation, it imperceptibly glides into the void of infinity—whose vast and formless extent, when displayed to the mind of man in the forcible manner so happily attained by the Hebrew writers, impresses it with the sublimest and most awful sensations, and fills it with a mixture of admiration and terror.

That more vehement species of negation or affirmation which assumes the confident form of interrogation, is admirably calculated to impress the mind with a very forcible idea of the Divine power. This also frequently occurs in the sacred poetry:

" This is the decree which is determined in the whole earth;
And this the hand, which is stretched out over all the nations :
For JEHOVAH God of Hosts hath decreed; and who shall disannul it ?
And it is his hand that is stretched out; and who shall turn it back ? " *

" Hath he said, and will he not do it ?
Hath he spoken, and will he not establish it ? " †

the character and genius of the Hebrew poetry, that I reluctantly differ from our Author, and retain the old interpretation. The passage is, on the whole, the most beautiful instance of the sublime, without any mixture of the terrific, with no images but the placid and tender, that is anywhere to be found. But its great excellence is, that it is no less philosophical than poetical; no less useful for the great truth which it inculcates, than pleasing for the manner in which that truth is conveyed.—T.

* Isa. xiv. 26, 27.   † Numb. xxiii. 19.

Nor is that ironical kind of concession, which is sometimes put into the mouth of the Supreme Being, less energetic. The following passage of Job is an admirable instance :

> " Deck thyself now with majesty and with pride ;
> And array thyself in glory and honour :
> Pour out on every side the furiousness of thy wrath ;
> With a glance humble every one that is proud :
> Look upon every proud thing, and subvert it ;
> And trample down the wicked in their place :
> Overwhelm them also in dust ;
> Bind up their faces, and plunge them into darkness.
> Then will even I confess unto thee,
> That thine own right hand may save thee."*

When the Divine Omnipotence is opposed to human infirmity, the one is proportionably magnified as the other is diminished by the contrast. The monstrous absurdity of a comparison between things extremely unequal, the more forcibly serves to demonstrate that inequality, and sets them at an infinite distance from each other.

Since, however, the sacred poets were under the necessity of speaking of God in a manner adapted to human conceptions, and of attributing to him the actions, the passions, the faculties of man; how can they be supposed ever to have depicted the Divine Majesty in terms at all becoming the greatness of the subject? And are they not in this case more likely to disgrace and degrade it? May not that censure be applied to them, which Longinus so deservedly applies to Homer, that he turned his gods into men, and even debased them beneath the standard of humanity? The case is, however, materially different: Homer, and the other heathen poets, relate facts of their deities, which, though impious and absurd when literally understood, are scarcely or at all intelligible in an allegorical sense, and can by no means be reduced to an interpretation strictly figurative.† On

---

* Job xl. 10—14. Can any one who has duly considered the history of Nimrod, the first revolter against God, and founder of idolatry, and the signal overthrow of his stupendous tower, with the dispersion that immediately ensued—after well weighing the characteristic topics of allusion in the Hebrew poetry (as briefly pointed out in the 9th Lecture,) and the original of this passage from the 6th verse—entertain a doubt to what the figurative terms here used were meant to allude?—I should think it scarcely possible. See a *Dissertation on the Passages in St. Peter and St. Jude concerning the angels that sinned.*—S. H.

† See Fabric. *Biblioth. Græc.* l. v. c. 36. vol. viii. p. 526.

the contrary, in the delineation of the Divine Nature, the sacred poets do indeed, in conformity to the weakness of the human understanding, employ terrestrial imagery; but it is in such a manner, that the attributes which are borrowed from human nature and human action can never in a literal sense be applied to the Divinity. The understanding is continually referred from the shadow to the reality; nor can it rest satisfied with the bare literal application, but is naturally directed to investigate that quality in the Divine Nature which appears to be analogous to the image. This, if I am not mistaken, will supply us with a reason not very obvious, of a very observable effect in the Hebrew writings, namely, why among those sensible images that are applied to the Deity, those principally, which in a literal sense would seem most remote from the object, and most unworthy of the Divine Majesty, are nevertheless, when used metaphorically, or in the way of comparison, by far the most sublime. That imagery, for instance, which is taken from the parts and members of the human body, is found to be much nobler and more magnificent in its effect, than that which is taken from the passions of the mind; and that which is taken from the animal creation, frequently exceeds in sublimity that which the nature of man has suggested. For such is our ignorance and blindness in contemplating the Divine Nature, that we can by no means attain to a simple and pure idea of it; we necessarily mingle something of the human with the Divine. The grosser animal properties therefore, we easily distinguish and separate; but it is with the utmost difficulty that we can preserve the rational, and even some of the properties of the sensitive soul, perfectly distinct. Hence it is, that in those figurative expressions derived from the nobler and more excellent qualities of human nature, when applied to the Almighty, we frequently acquiesce, as if they were in strict literal propriety to be attributed to him : on the contrary, our understanding immediately rejects the literal sense of those which seem quite inconsistent with the Divine Being, and derived from an ignoble source; and, while it pursues the analogy, it constantly rises to a contemplation which, though obscure, is yet grand and magnificent. Let us observe whether this observation will apply to the following passages, in which the Psalmist ascribes to God the resentment commonly experienced by a human creature for an injury unexpectedly

8

received: there appears in the image nothing to excite our admiration, nothing particularly sublime:

> "The Lord heard, and he was enraged;
> And Israel he utterly rejected."*

But when, a little after, the same subject is depicted in figurative terms, derived from much grosser objects, and applied in a still more daring manner, nothing can be more sublime:

> "And the Lord awaked, as out of sleep,
> Like a strong man shouting because of wine."†

On the same principle the sublimity of those passages is founded, in which the image is taken from the roaring of a lion, the clamour of rustic labourers, and the rage of wild beasts:

> "JEHOVAH from on high shall roar,
> And from his holy habitation shall he utter his voice;
> He shall roar aloud against his resting-place,
> A shout like that of the vintagers shall he give
> Against all the inhabitants of the earth."‡

> "And I will be unto them as a lion;
> As a leopard in the way will I watch them;
> I will meet them as a bear bereaved of her whelps;
> And I will rend the caul of their heart:
> And there will I devour them as a lioness;
> A beast of the field shall tear them."§

From ideas, which in themselves appear coarse, unsuitable, and totally unworthy of so great an object, the mind naturally recedes, and passes suddenly to the contemplation of the object itself, and of its inherent magnitude and importance.

* Psal. lxxviii. 59.
‡ Jer. xxv. 30.
† Psal. lxxviii. 65.
§ Hos. xiii. 7, 8.

LECTURE XVII.

OF THE SUBLIME OF PASSION.

Sublimity of Sentiment, as arising from the vehement affections of the mind—What is commonly called Enthusiasm is the natural effect of passion; the true Enthusiasm arises from the impulse of the Divine Spirit, and is peculiar to the sacred poets—The principal force of poetry is displayed in the expression of passion: in exciting the passions poetry best achieves its purpose, whether it be utility or pleasure—How the passions are excited to the purpose of utility; how to that of pleasure—The difference and connexion between the pathetic and the sublime—That sublimity which, in the sacred poetry, proceeds from the imitation of the passions of admiration, of joy, indignation, grief, and terror, illustrated by examples.

WE have agreed with Longinus, that a violent agitation of the mind, or impetuosity of passion, constitutes another source of the sublime: he calls it "the vehemence and enthusiasm of passion." It will be proper, therefore, in the next place, to consider the nature of this enthusiasm; the principles on which the power of exciting or of imitating the passions in poetry may be supposed to depend; and what affinity subsists between passion and sublimity.

The language of poetry I have more than once described as the effect of mental emotion. Poetry itself is indebted for its origin, character, complexion, emphasis, and application, to the effects which are produced upon the mind and body, upon the imagination, the senses, the voice, and respiration, by the agitation of passion. Every affection of the human soul, while it rages with violence, is a momentary frenzy. When, therefore, a poet is able, by the force of genius, or rather of imagination, to conceive any emotion of the mind so perfectly as to transfer to his own feelings the instinctive passion of another, and, agreeably to the nature of the subject, to express it in all its vigour; such a one, according to a common mode of speaking, may be said to

M

possess the true poetic enthusiasm,* or, as the ancients
would have expressed it, "to be inspired; full of the god;"
not, however, implying that their ardour of mind was imparted by the gods, but that this ecstatic impulse became
the god of the moment.†

This species of enthusiasm I should distinguish by the
term *natural*, were it not that I should seem to connect
things which are really different, and repugnant to each
other: the true and genuine enthusiasm, that which alone
is deserving of the name, that I mean with which the sublimer poetry of the Hebrews, and particularly the prophetic,
is animated, is certainly widely different in its nature, and
boasts a much higher origin.

As poetry, however, derives its very existence from the
more vehement emotions of the mind, so its greatest energy
is displayed in the expression of them; and by exciting
the passions, it more effectually attains its end.

Poetry is said to consist in imitation: whatever the human
mind is able to conceive, it is the province of poetry to imitate—things, places, appearances natural and artificial, actions, passions, manners, and customs: and since the human
intellect is naturally delighted with every species of imitation,
that species in particular which exhibits its own image,
which displays and depicts those impulses, inflexions, per-
turbations, and secret emotions, which it perceives and knows
in itself, can scarcely fail to astonish and to delight above
every other. The delicacy and difficulty of this kind of
imitation are among its principal commendations; for to
effect that which appears almost impossible, naturally excites
our admiration. The understanding slowly perceives the
accuracy of the description in all other subjects, and their
agreement to their archetypes, as being obliged to compare
them by the aid, and through the uncertain medium as it
were of the memory: but when a passion is expressed, the
object is clear and distinct at once; the mind is immediately
conscious of itself and its own emotions; it feels and suffers
in itself a sensation, either the same or similar to that which
is described. Hence that sublimity which arises from the
vehement agitation of the passions, and the imitation of them,

---

* Aristotle expresses it μανικον, insane; Plato εκφρονα, out of their common
senses; ενθεον, inspired by a god; ενθαδιαζοντα, enthusiastic.

† Nisus ait, Dîne hunc ardorem mentibus addunt,
   Euryale? an sua cuique deus fit dira cupido?—*Æneid.* ix. 184.

possesses a superior influence over the human mind; whatever is exhibited to it from without, may well be supposed to move and agitate it less than what it internally perceives, of the magnitude and force of which it is previously conscious.

And as the imitation or delineation of the passions is the most perfect production of poetry, so, by exciting them, it most completely effects its purpose. The intent of poetry is to profit while it entertains us; and the agitation of the passions, by the force of imitation, is in the highest degree both useful and pleasant.

This method of exciting the passions is in the first place useful, when properly and lawfully exercised; that is, when these passions are directed to their proper end, and rendered subservient to the dictates of nature and truth; when an aversion to evil, and a love of goodness, is excited. And if the poet deviate on any occasion from this great end and aim, he is guilty of a most scandalous abuse and perversion of his art: For, the passions and affections are the elements and principles of human action; they are all in themselves good, useful, and virtuous; and, when fairly and naturally employed, not only lead to useful ends and purposes, but actually prompt and stimulate to virtue. It is the office of poetry to incite, to direct, to temper the passions, and not to extinguish them. It professes to exercise, to amend, to discipline the affections; it is this which is strictly meant by Aristotle, when he speaks of the *pruning of the passions*, though certain commentators have strangely perverted his meaning.*

But this operation on the passions is also more immediately useful, because it is productive of pleasure. Every emotion of the mind, (not excepting even those which in themselves are allied to pain,) when excited through the agency of the imitative arts, is ever accompanied with an exquisite sensation of pleasure. This arises partly from the contemplation of the imitation itself; partly from the consciousness of our

---

* I think nothing can well be more ridiculous than the established method of rendering παθηματων ΚΑΘΑΡΣΙΝ, *the cleansing or purging of the passions*. Why should a secondary or adventitious sense of a word be adopted, unless its primary signification be incompatible with the context? In the common version of John xv. 2, καθαιρει, a word from the same source with καθαρσις, is translated *he purgeth*, where it evidently signifies *he pruneth*; so παθηματων καθαρσιν, instead of *the cleansing* or *purging of the passions*, should rather be *the checking of their excessive growth*, or *pruning their luxuriances*, that so they might produce their proper fruits.—S. H.

own felicity, when compared with the miseries of others; but principally from the moral sense.*   Nature has endued man with a certain social and generous spirit; and commands him not to confine his cares to himself alone, but to extend them to all his fellow-creatures; to look upon nothing which relates to mankind as foreign to himself.   Thus, "to rejoice with them that do rejoice, and to weep with them that weep;" to love and to respect piety and benevolence; to cherish and retain an indignant hatred of cruelty and injustice; that is, to obey the dictates of nature—is right, is honest, is becoming, is pleasant.

The sublime and the pathetic are intrinsically very different; and yet have in some respects a kind of affinity or connexion.† The pathetic includes the passions which we feel,

---

* See Lord Kames' *Elements of Criticism*, vol. i. ch. 2; Dr. Priestley's *Lectures on Oratory*, p. 137; and Hartley *on the Human Mind*, sect. iv. prop. 49.—T.

† As our author is here treating of that species of the *sublime* which is connected with the *pathetic*, and in a manner depends upon it, it may not be amiss to consider a little the means of exciting this sensation, which have been employed by some of the best writers.

There are two principal modes of producing this mixed sensation.   First, when the story or sentiment is sufficiently striking of itself, by reducing all the circumstances into as narrow a compass as possible, and causing them to flash at once upon the mind; of which Livy's description of the death of Lucretia is a fine example: and this appears the most natural, and is the surest mode of affecting the passions. The second is, by drawing out the description, heaping circumstance on circumstance, and working up the mind by degrees: this, however, is rarely accomplished with sufficient taste and caution.   If I were called upon to specify another historical example, I would refer the reader to the description of Agrippina's return after the death of Germanicus, in Tacitus; or I might add, the example quoted by our Author from the Song of Deborah and Baruch, Lect. 13.   The French dramatic writers generally fail, by attempting this latter mode of affecting the passions: which is only proper when there is not force enough in any single part of a narration, or when a picture cannot be drawn in a few words sufficiently explicit.

Several circumstances, when judiciously introduced, contribute greatly to the pathetic, and consequently to that branch of *sublimity* which is connected with it. 1st. When innocent and helpless persons are involved in ruin.   To introduce an *infant* on the stage in a tragedy, though a common trick, is yet seldom destitute of effect.   I must however remark, that if there be many to participate in the misfortune, the society in sorrow seems to lessen its weight. 2dly. Absence from friends, or persons otherwise very dear.   The whole of that inimitable poem, Mr. Pope's *Eloisa*, affords a strong example of this, and particularly the following lines:

"——No, fly me, fly me, far as pole from pole;
Rise Alps between us! and whole oceans roll!
Ah! come not, write not, think not once of me."—289.

3dly, Exile:

—— " Methinks we wand'ring go
Through dreary wastes, and weep each other's woe,

and those which we excite. Some passions may be expressed without any of the sublime; the sublime also may exist where no passion is directly expressed: there is however no sublimity where no passion is excited. That sensation of sublimity which arises from the greatness of the thoughts and imagery, has admiration for its basis, and that for the most part connected with joy, love, hatred, or fear; and this I think is evident from the instances which were so lately under our consideration.

How much the sacred poetry of the Hebrews excels in exciting the passions,* and in directing them to their noblest

> Where round some mould'ring tower pale ivy creeps,
> And low-brow'd rocks hang nodding o'er the deeps."—*Ib.* 241.

" The world was all before them, where to choose
> Their place of rest, and Providence their guide :
> They hand in hand, with wand'ring steps and slow,
> Through Eden took their solitary way."—*Par. Lost.* xii. 646.

4thly, A sudden abruption from a state of enjoyment:

> " Now warm in love, now with'ring in my bloom,
> Lost in a convent's solitary gloom !
> There stern religion quench'd th' unwilling flame,
> There died those best of passions, love and fame."—Pope's *Eloisa*, 325.

Language cannot express a nobler union of the pathetic and sublime than is contained in the last line.

5thly, The recollection of past happiness is a fine source of the pathetic ; or happiness that might have been attained but for some intervening circumstance that unexpectedly precludes it. On this are founded some of our best tragedies. See the Orphan : also the Fair Penitent, last Act.

6thly, Apparent resignation :

> " O grace serene ! O virtue heav'nly fair !
> Divine oblivion of low-thoughted care ! &c.
> Enter each mild, each amicable guest,
> Receive and wrap me in eternal rest !"—*Eloisa*, 297.—T.

A 7th head may also be added, Inattention to self, and solicitude for others. Thus, Lear to Kent:

> " Pr'ythee, go in thyself ; seek thine own ease——
>
> Poor naked wretches, wheresoe'er you are,
> That bide the pelting of this pitiless storm,
> How shall your houseless heads and unfed sides,
> Your loop'd and window'd raggedness, defend you
> From seasons such as these ?"

And the address of our Saviour—" Daughters of Jerusalem, weep not for me, but for yourselves and your children."—S. H.

* The pathetic is so much the prevailing or distinguishing quality of the Hebrew writings, that I do not hesitate to ascribe much of that superiority which the moderns claim in this respect over the Greeks and Romans, to the free use which they have made of scriptural sentiments and expressions. The reader will easily be

4

end and aim: how it exercises them upon their proper
objects; how it strikes and fires the admiration by the contemplation of the Divine Majesty, and, forcing the affections
of love, hope, and joy, from unworthy and terrestrial objects,
elevates them to the pursuit of the supreme good: how it also
stimulates those of grief, hatred, and fear, which are usually
employed upon the trifling miseries of this life, to the ab-
horrence of the supreme evil, is a subject which at present
wants no illustration, and which, though not unconnected
with sublimity in a general view, would be improperly introduced in this place.   For we are not at present treating
of the general effects of sublimity on the passions, but of
that species of the sublime which proceeds from vehement
emotions of the mind, and from the imitation or representation of passion.

Here, indeed, a spacious field presents itself to our view;
for by far the greater part of the sacred poetry is little else
than a continued imitation of the different passions.   What
in reality forms the substance and subject of most of these
poems but the passion of admiration, excited by the consideration of the Divine power and majesty; the passion of
joy, from the sense of the Divine favour, and the prosperous
issue of events: the passion of resentment and indignation
against the contemners of God; of grief from the consciousness of sin; and terror from the apprehension of the
Divine judgment? Of all these, and if there be any emotions
of the mind beyond these, exquisite examples may be found
in the book of Job, in the Psalms, in the Canticles, and in
every part of the prophetic writings.   On this account my
principal difficulty will not be the selection of excellent and
proper instances, but the explaining of those which spontaneously occur without a considerable diminution of their
intrinsic sublimity.

Admiration, as it is ever the concomitant, so it is frequently
the efficient cause of sublimity.   It produces great and mag-

able to satisfy himself on this subject by a cursory inspection of Milton, Pope, and
even some of our best tragic writers. Mr. Knox has very judiciously pointed out
how greatly Sterne has been indebted to them. That an author, indeed, who has
borrowed from others all the tolerable thoughts which are thinly scattered through
his writings, should resort to the readiest and most copious source of pathetic
imagery, is not surprising. It is only to be lamented, that he has not made the
best use of his plagiarisms; that these noble sentiments are so strangely disfigured
by the insipid frivolity of his style—a style which no classical ear can possibly endure, and which must be confessed to derive its principal embellishments from what
are called the *typographical* figures.—T.

nificent conceptions and sentiments, and expresses them in language bold and elevated, in sentences concise, abrupt, and energetic.

> "Jehovah reigneth ; let the people tremble :
> He sitteth upon the Cherubim ; let the earth be moved."*

> "The voice of Jehovah is upon the waters : ⌡
> The God of Glory thunders :
> Jehovah is upon the many waters,
> The voice of Jehovah is full of power ;
> The voice of Jehovah is full of majesty."†

> "Who is like unto thee among the gods, O Jehovah ?
> Who is like unto thee, adorable in holiness !
> Fearful in praises, who workest wonders !
> Thou extendest thy right hand ; the earth swalloweth them."‡

Joy is more elevated, and exults in a bolder strain : it produces great sentiments and conceptions, seizes upon the most splendid imagery, and adorns it with the most animated language; nor does it hesitate to risk the most daring and unusual figures. In the Song of Moses, in the thanksgiving of Deborah and Baruch, what sublimity do we find, in sentiment, in language, in the general turn of the expression! But nothing can excel in this respect that noble exultation of universal nature, in the psalm which has been so often commended, where the whole animated and inanimate creation unite in the praises of their Maker. Poetry here seems to assume the highest tone of triumph and exultation, and to revel, if I may so express myself, in all the extravagance of joy :

> "Tell in high harmonious strains,
> Tell the world Jehovah reigns !
> He, who fram'd this beauteous whole,
> He, who fix'd each planet's place ;
> Who bade unnumber'd orbs to roll,
> In destin'd course, through endless space.
> Let the glorious Heavens rejoice,
> The hills exult with grateful voice ;
> Let ocean tell the echoing shore,
> And the hoarse waves with humble voice adore !
> Let the verdant plains be glad ;
> The trees in blooming fragrance clad !
> Smile with joy, ye desert lands,
> And, rushing torrents, clap your hands !

---

* Psalm xcix. 1.   † Psalm xxix. 3, 4.   ‡ Exod. xv. 11, 12.

> Let the whole earth with triumph ring ;
> Let all that live with loud applause
> JEHOVAH's matchless praises sing !—
> He comes ! He comes ! Heaven's righteous King,
> To judge the world by Truth's eternal laws."*

Nothing, however, can be greater or more magnificent than the representation of anger and indignation, particularly when the Divine wrath is displayed. Of this the whole of the prophetic Song of Moses affords an incomparable specimen. I have formerly produced from it some instances of a different kind ; nor ought the following to be denied a place in these Lectures :

> " For I will lift my hand unto the heavens,
> And I will say, I live for ever :
> If I whet the brightness of my sword,
> And my hand lay hold on judgment :
> I will return vengeance to my enemies,
> And I will recompense those that hate me :
> I will drench my arrows in blood,
> And my sword shall devour flesh ;
> With the blood of the slain and the captives,
> From the bushy head of the enemy."†

Nor is Isaiah less daring on a similar subject:

> " For the day of vengeance was in my heart,
> And the year of my redeemed was come.
> And I looked, and there was no one to help ;
> And I was astonished that there was no one to uphold :
> Therefore mine own arm wrought salvation for me.
> And mine indignation itself sustained me.
> And I trod down the peoples in mine anger :
> And I crushed them in mine indignation ;
> And I spilled their life-blood on the ground."‡

The display of the fury and threats of the enemy, by which Moses finely exaggerates the horror of their unexpected ruin, is also wonderfully sublime :

> " The enemy said, I will pursue, I will overtake ;
> I will divide the spoil, my soul shall be satiated ;
> I will draw my sword, my hand shall destroy them :
> Thou didst blow with thy breath ; they were covered with the
>   sea."§

---

* Psalm xcvi. 10—13, and xcviii. 7—9.   † Deut. xxxii. 40—42.
‡ Isaiah lxiii. 4—6. See a Note on this passage, Lect. 30.
§ Exod. xv. 9, 10.

Grief is generally abject and humble, less apt to assimilate with the sublime; but when it becomes excessive, and predominates in the mind, it rises to a bolder tone, and becomes heated to fury and madness. We have a fine example of this from the hand of Jeremiah, when he exaggerates the miseries of Sion:

" He hath bent his bow as an enemy, he hath fixed his right hand
    as an adversary;
He hath poured out his anger like fire on the tents of the
    daughter of Sion." *

But nothing of this kind can equal the grief of Job, which is acute, vehement, fervid; always in the deepest afflictions breathing an animated and lofty strain:

" ———for in the conscious bosom flame
Virtue, and grief, and soul-depressing shame."

" His fury rendeth me; he teareth me to pieces;
He gnasheth on me with his teeth:
Mine enemy sharpeneth his eyes upon me.
They run with open mouth upon me,
They smite me reproachfully on the cheek,
They are ready to burst with fury against me.
God hath delivered me over bound to the wicked;
Yea, he hath tumbled me headlong into perdition at the discretion of the impious.
I was in tranquillity, and he rent me asunder;
Yea, he seized me by the neck, and dashed me in pieces;
He hath even set me up as a mark for him,
His archers encompassed me round;
He pierceth through my reins, and spareth not;
He poureth out my gall on the ground.
He breaketh me up breach after breach;
He rusheth upon me like a mighty man."†

---

* Lam. ii. 4.

† Job xvi. 9—14. " Ver. 10. *Jitmalaon*, according to the Sept. ὁμαθυμαδον δε κατεδραμον: R. L. B. Gershom, *They are gathered together:* and the Arabic verb *Mala* denotes in vi. Conjugation, *They assisted one another, and were unanimous,* (as if a great multitude were collected together;) and it is construed with the preposition *gnale*, as in this passage. See also Isaiah xxxi. 4, quoted in Lect. 19, where *Mala* is rendered *a multitude*. This interpretation, however, though sufficiently confirmed by the preceding instances, is, perhaps, not sufficiently forcible and vehement in this place. Ver. 11. *Jarateni, He precipitated me.* This I take to be the true sense of this word, which ought to be enumerated among those that occur but once: for the other place in which it is commonly read, Numb. xxii. 32, is certainly corrupted, and should be corrected from the Samar. which has, *because thy way is evil before me;* with which the answer of Balaam perfectly agrees, ver. 34, *If it be evil in thy sight.* Nor is the construction clear in this phrase *Jarat He-darachecha*, unless we agree

In the same author, with what magnificence and sublimity
are sorrow and desperation expressed !

> " Were but my woes in equal balance weigh'd,
>   Did the vast mass of misery press the scale
>   Against the sands that skirt the ocean round,
>   'Twould far outweigh them : therefore boils my grief !
>   The pointed arrows of th' offended God,
>   Fix'd in my heart, rack every tender nerve;
>   And the slow poison drinks my spirit up ;
>   While hosts of terrors close besiege my soul.
>   O might thy suppliant urge one poor request !
>   Thy wrath, O God ! should loose at once thy arm,
>   (Thy vengeful arm which blasting lightnings wields,)
>   Dash into pieces this imbecile frame,
>   And crush thy suffering creature into nothing."*

The whole poem of Job is no less excellent in the expression and excitation of terror, as the example just now quoted
sufficiently demonstrates. To this commendation, however,
the prophetic writings seem to have the fairest claim ; it
being, indeed, their peculiar province to denounce the divine
judgments upon guilty nations. Almost the whole book of
Ezekiel is occupied with this passion : Isaiah is also excellent in this respect, although he be in general the harbinger
of joy and salvation. The following terrific denunciation
is directed by him against the enemies of Jerusalem :

> " Howl ye, for the day of JEHOVAH is at hand :
>   As a destruction from the Almighty shall it come.

that the true reading is *Jaratah*, &c. Not to dwell upon this, however, the interpretation of the word *Jarateni* appears perfectly just, if we consider that the Arabic
verb *Verat* uniformly means, *he precipitated himself into an affair whence he could not
extricate himself.*" H.—*Author's Note.*

*   Job vi. 2, 3, 4. 8, 9. This passage is thus given by Mr. Scott, with a little
alteration :

> " O for a balance pois'd with equal hand !
>   Lay all my sorrows there 'gainst ocean's sand :
>   Light is the sand whereon the billows roll,
>   When weigh'd with all the sorrows of my soul.
>   Ah ! therefore, therefore does my boiling woe
>   In such a torrent of wild words o'erflow :
>   Rankling I feel th' Almighty's venom'd dart,
>   His arrows fire my veins and rend my heart ;
>   His terrors 'gainst me throng in dire array,
>   War urging war, his boundless wrath display.
>   O that, relenting at my earnest cry,
>   God would extend his thund'ring arm on high ;
>   Ruthless at once his smould'ring trident throw,
>   And, forcing through his mark the vengeful blow,
>   At once destroy me !"

"Therefore shall all hands be slackened;
And the heart of every mortal shall melt; and they shall be
    terrified:
Torments and pangs shall seize them;
As a woman in travail they shall be pained:
They shall look upon one another with astonishment;
Their countenances shall be like flames of fire.
Behold, the day of JEHOVAH cometh inexorable;
Even indignation and burning wrath;
To make the land a desolation:
And her sinners shall he destroy from out of her.
Yea, the stars of heaven, and the constellations thereof,
Shall not send forth their light:
The sun is darkened at his going forth,
And the moon shall not cause her light to shine.
And I will visit the world for its evil,*
And the wicked for their iniquity:
And I will put an end to the arrogance of the proud;
And I will bring down the haughtiness of the terrible.
I will make a mortal more precious than fine gold;
Yea a man than the rich ore of Ophir.
Wherefore I will make the heavens tremble;
And the earth shall be shaken out of her place;
In the indignation of JEHOVAH God of Hosts."†

Jeremiah is scarcely inferior, though perhaps his talents are
better suited in common to the exciting of the softer affections. As an example, I need only refer to that remarkable
vision, in which the impending slaughter and destruction of
Judea is exhibited with wonderful force and enthusiasm:

"My bowels, my bowels are pained, the walls of my heart;
My heart is troubled within me; I cannot be silent;
Because I have heard the sound of the trumpet,
My soul the alarm of war.
Destruction is come upon the heels of destruction;
Surely the whole land is spoiled:
On a sudden have my tents been spoiled,
My curtains in an instant.
How long shall I see the standard?
Shall I hear the sound of the trumpet?
I beheld the earth, and lo! disorder and confusion;
The heavens also, and there was no light."‡

---

* "*I will visit*," &c.]   That is, the Babylonish empire: as *all the world* for the
Roman empire, or for Judea. Luke ii. 1.   Acts xi. 23.—Bishop Lowth's *Isaiah*.
† Isa. xiii. 6—13.   ‡ Jer. iv. 19, &c.

It would be an infinite task to collect and specify all the passages that might be found illustrative of this subject; and probably we shall have more than one opportunity of discoursing upon these and similar topics, when we come to consider the different species of the Hebrew poetry: upon which, after requesting your candour and indulgence to so arduous an undertaking, it is my intention to enter at our next meeting.

THE THIRD PART.

OF THE DIFFERENT SPECIES OF POETRY EXTANT IN THE WRITINGS OF THE HEBREWS.

OF PROPHETIC POETRY.

LECTURE XVIII.

THE WRITINGS OF THE PROPHETS ARE IN GENERAL POETICAL.

The Poetry of the Hebrews classed according to its different characters: this mode of arrangement results rather from the nature of the subject than from any authority of the Hebrews themselves—The PROPHETIC POETRY—*The writings of the Prophets in general poetical and metrical—The opinion of the modern Jews and of Jerome on this point refuted—In the books of the Prophets the same evidences are found of a metrical arrangement as in the poetical books: in the dialect, the style, and poetical conformation of the sentences—Obvious in respect to the two former circumstances; the latter requires a more minute investigation, and also illustration by examples—The intimate relation between Poetry and Prophecy— The College of Prophets; a part of whose discipline it was to sing hymns to the different instruments; and this exercise was called prophecy: the same word, therefore, denotes a prophet, a poet, and a musician—Elisha, when about to pronounce the Oracle of God, orders a minstrel to be brought to him—Poetry excellently adapted to the purpose of Prophecy—A review of the most ancient predictions extant in the historical books, which are proved to be truly poetical.*

O F the general nature and properties of the Hebrew poetry I have already treated—diffusely enough, if the extent of the disquisitions be considered; but too briefly, I fear, and too imperfectly, if respect be had to the copiousness and importance of the subject. My original design, however, extended no farther than to notice the most remarkable passages, and such as I conceived to be immediately illustrative of the peculiarities of the Hebrew style. Even these it was my wish and intention rather to point out and recommend to your own consideration, than minutely to investigate and explain; esteeming it my province rather to exhort and stimulate to these studies, than to intrude upon this audience a formal plan of instruction. It would be superfluous, I am persuaded, to remind you, that the importance of the subject is not to be estimated by the feebleness of my endeavours; and, I trust, it would be still more unnecessary to caution you against a hasty acquiescence in any interpretation of those passages which I have quoted, much less in my own : though I will frankly confess, that I have bestowed no small degree of labour and attention upon this part of my undertaking. What remains at present is, to distribute into its different classes the whole of the Hebrew poetry, and to mark whatever is worthy of observation in each species. In forming this arrangement it will hardly be expected that I should uniformly proceed according to the testimony of the Hebrews, or on all occasions confirm the propriety of my classification by their authority; since it is plain that they were but little versed in these nice and artificial distinctions : It will be sufficient for our purpose; that is, it will be sufficient for the accurate explanation of the different characters of the Hebrew poetry, if I demonstrate that these characters are stamped by the hand of nature, and that they are displayed either in the subject itself, the disposition of its constituent parts, the diversity of style, or in the general form and arrangement of the poem.

The first rank I assign to the PROPHETIC, or that species of poetry which is found to pervade the predictions of the prophets, as well those contained in the books properly called *prophetical*, as those which occasionally occur in other parts of the Scriptures. These, I apprehend, will be generally allowed to be written in a style truly poetical, indeed admirable in its kind; as the many examples which we have already produced will sufficiently demonstrate. I fear, however, it will not be so readily granted, that their claim is equally well founded with that of the books which are commonly called *poetical*, to the other characteristic of poetry, I mean verse, or metrical composition. This fact is denied by the Jews,* and is denied by Jerome,† who was a diligent scholar of the rabbinical writers : after these it is unnecessary to refer to more recent authors, who partly deny that the Hebrews were possessed of any metre at all, and partly allow it to those compositions only which are commonly called poetical, or at most extend the concession to a few canticles scattered through other parts of the Scriptures. A thinking person, however, will not be misled by such authorities as these, before he examines whether they are to be accounted competent judges in this case, and what weight and credit is due to their testimony.

The Jews, by their own confession, are no longer, nor have been indeed for many ages, masters of the system of the ancient metre. All remembrance of it has ceased from those times in which the Hebrew became a dead language ;‡ and it really seems probable that the Masorites, (of whom so little is known,) who afterwards distinguished the sacred volumes by accents and vowel points, as they are now extant, were possessed of so trifling and imperfect a knowledge of this subject, that they were even incapable of distinguishing what was written in metre from plain prose. For when, according to their manner, they marked certain books as metrical, namely, the Psalms, the Proverbs, and the book of Job; they accounted others, which are no less evidently metrical, absolutely prosaic, such as the Song of Solomon, and the Lamentations of Jeremiah, and consequently assigned to them the common prose accent only. In this opinion the

---

* Abarbanel distinguishes three species of canticles. The first is the *rhythmical*, or that with similar endings ; in use among the more modern Hebrews, (who learned it from the Arabic writers,) but which was certainly unknown to the authors of the Holy Scriptures. The second was adapted to music, and sung either alone or accompanied with instruments : such are the songs of Moses, of Deborah, of David. The third species consists of parables, or proverbs; which species, says he, (though by the way absurdly enough, as is not uncommon with the rabbinical writers,) is properly denominated *Shir*. From this class, however, he excludes the parables of the prophets, according to the distinction of Maimonides between prophecy and the Holy Spirit. (See *More Neboc.* ii. 45.) He says they are not canticles, because they are not the work of the prophet himself, but the mere effect of the prophetic inspiration. *Mantissa Dissert. ad Libr. Cosri,* p. 413.—*Author's Note.*

† See Jerome, Preface to Isaiah.

‡ " It cannot be doubted that the canticles of the second species were possessed of a certain melody or metre, which, through the length of the captivity, is become obsolete."—Abarbanel, *ib.* 410.

Jews universally remain, and deny that these books are at all metrical, or to be classed with the three former.* Now the disciple is hardly to be supposed to have more information than his masters; and although Jerome speaks very fluently about the Tetrameters, the Hexameters, the Sapphics, and Iambics of the Hebrews, the very state and circumstances of the case demonstrate how little credit is due to his authority. Indeed his reasoning evidently proceeds from a confused head, when he attempts to trace a sort of remote similarity between the Greek and Hebrew metres; and to explain by some coarse analogies a subject which he appears to have very imperfectly understood: in treating of which, after all, he is not able to preserve even the appearance of consistency. For instance, after Josephus and Origen,

---

* The Song of Solomon is indeed allowed by the Jews to be a poem; not, however, from the nature of the composition, or from its being metrical, but merely because it is of the parabolic kind; and therefore it is referred by Abarbanel to the third species of canticle. Whence it happens, that though in some MS. copies the three metrical books are written in a versified form, the Lamentations and Song of Songs are differently transcribed. This I have observed to be the case with the Vatican MS., which is deservedly accounted one of the most ancient, its date being the year 979 of our Christian æra. The same is observable in many other MSS. as I have been informed by my learned friend Dr. Kennicott, whose Hebrew Bible with the various readings is now published. Indeed it is natural to suppose, that when the Jews exhibit certain canticles, and even whole books, in a poetical or versified order, they followed, or pretended to follow, the true nature of the Hebrew verse, or the proper distribution of the lines. But the great disagreement between them in this respect is a proof of their ignorance; for they seldom agree with one another in the termination of the lines, or follow any determinate rule in this matter. The distribution of the verses is different in different copies, as may be immediately observed on comparing them. In the Song of Moses, Deut. xxxii. in which the different editions agree better than in any other; (and indeed there was but little room for disagreement, the sense always pointing out of itself the order of the sentences;) in this, notwithstanding, the rabbies have contrived to differ, some of them dividing it into 67, and some into 70 verses or lines. See *Annot. ad Bib. Heb.* Edit. Michaelis, *Halæ,* 1720. Among the MS. copies of the metrical books the disagreement is equally manifest, as the above excellent critic proved upon a very strict examination, undertaken at my request. In a very famous MS. which I saw in the Royal Library at Dresden, I remarked a circumstance that clearly demonstrates the perfect ignorance and absurdity of the Jews in this respect. The Chaldee paraphrase was intermingled with the text throughout, in such a manner that we first read the Hebrew, and then the Chaldee, verse by verse alternately: in the metrical books, which were divided into lines or verses, the text and version were so confounded, that the writer, attending only to the equality of his lines, perpetually blended the Hebrew and Chaldee together, in such a manner that where the one ended the other was resumed, and every line partook of both. This is a very elegant copy, and probably five hundred years old. The punctuation is evidently of a more recent date; as in that of the Vatican above mentioned, and in some other copies still older.—*Author's Note.*

he contends * that the Song of Moses in Deuteronomy is composed in hexameter and pentameter verse: in another place, however, he affirms that the very same poem consists of Iambic tetrameters.† In proof of his opinion he appeals to the testimony of Philo, Josephus, Origen, and Eusebius,‡ who were no less ignorant of the nature of the Hebrew metres than himself. Notwithstanding the opinion therefore of Jerome and the rabbinical writers, I shall beg leave to offer a few remarks upon the other side of the question; after which it will not perhaps be thought altogether improbable, that most of the predictions of the prophets, as well as many other of the remains of Hebrew literature, were originally published in a metrical form.

In order to prove that the predictions of the prophets are metrical, I must in part have recourse to the same arguments by which I formerly endeavoured to evince, that the Hebrew poetry in general consisted of a kind of metre; every one of which arguments, I must observe, is strictly applicable to this part of my subject, that alone excepted which regards the alphabetic poems. That it would be unnatural and absurd to look for instances of that kind in the prophetic poetry is evident; since such an artificial arrangement would be utterly repugnant to the nature of prophecy: it is plainly the effect of study and diligence, not of imagination and enthusiasm; a contrivance to assist the memory, not to affect the passions. The other arguments, however, ought to be particularly adverted to upon this subject: the poetic dialect, for instance, the diction so totally different from the language of common life, and other similar circumstances,§ which an attentive reader will easily discover, but which cannot be explained by a few examples; for circumstances which, taken separately, appear but of small account, are in a united view frequently of the greatest importance. To these we may add the artificial conformation of the sentences; which, as it has always appeared to me a necessary concomitant of metrical composition, the only one indeed which is now apparent, I shall afterwards endeavour to explain more at large, having especial regard to the prophetic writers. I must now premise a few other arguments, which will probably lead to the establishment of my opinion.

The prophets were chosen by God himself, and were cer-

* Preface to Chron.   † Epist. clv. ad Paulam Urbicam.
‡ See Jerome, Preface to Job.   § See Lect. 3.

N

tainly excellently prepared for the execution of their office.
They were in general taken from those who had been educated from childhood in a course of discipline adapted to
the ministerial function. It is evident from many parts of
the sacred history, that even from the earliest times of the
Hebrew republic, there existed certain colleges of prophets,
in which the candidates for the prophetic office, removed
altogether from an intercourse with the world, devoted
themselves entirely to the exercises and study of religion:
over each of these some prophet of superior authority, and
more peculiarly under the Divine influence, presided, as the
moderator and preceptor of the whole assembly. Though
the sacred history affords us but little information, and
that in a cursory manner, concerning their institutes and
discipline, we nevertheless understand that a principal part
of their occupation consisted in celebrating the praises of
Almighty God in hymns and poetry, with choral chants
accompanied by stringed instruments and pipes. There is
a remarkable passage* which occurs to this purpose: Saul
being nominated king, and, pursuant to the command of
God, consecrated by a solemn unction, a company of the
prophets, as Samuel had foretold, descending from the
Mount of God, (that being the place in which the sacred
college was situated,) met him; and, preceded by a variety
of musical instruments, *prophesied:* upon hearing which, he
himself, as if actuated by the same spirit, immediately joined
them, and prophesied also. The same thing again occurred
to him, and the persons sent by him to take David prisoner,
at Naioth;† who, when they saw the prophets prophesying,
and Samuel presiding over them, seized with the same
divine spirit and enthusiasm, began to prophesy along with
them. I find no discordance among authors concerning
the nature of this mode of prophesying: all are, I believe,
agreed in this point, and all understand by it the praises of
God celebrated by the impulse of the Holy Spirit, with
music and song. In this they follow the authority of the
Chaldee interpreters, or rather the evidence of reason
itself; for, exactly in the same manner, Asaph, Heman,
Iduthun, who were the chief musicians in the temple, are
said "to have prophesied upon the harp, the psaltery, and
the cymbal, when praise and thanksgiving were offered to
Jehovah."‡ From these instances it is sufficiently apparent,
that the word *Nabi* was used by the Hebrews in an ambi-

* 1 Sam. x. 5—10.   † 1 Sam. xix. 20—24.   ‡ 1 Chron. xxv. 1—3.

guous sense, and that it equally denoted a prophet, a poet,
or a musician, under the influence of Divine inspiration.
To these we may add the prophetesses, Miriam the sister of
Aaron, and Deborah, who were distinguished by that title,
not only because they pronounced the oracles of Jehovah,
but on account of their excellence in music and poetry; for
these sister arts were united by the Hebrews, as well as by
all other nations, during the first stages of society. After
these proofs there can scarcely be any occasion to remark,
that Solomon, or at least the editor or compiler of his proverbs, twice makes use of the word which in its ordinary
sense means prophecy strictly so called, to denote the language of poetry: for he calls the words of Agur and
Lemuel* *Massa*,† which Jerome renders *vision*, the Seventy
Greek translators *an oracle*, the Chaldee *prophecy;* when
in reality those passages have nothing in them which can
be properly said to bear any resemblance to prophecy, but
are mere rhapsodies of morality, ornamented indeed with
the usual embellishments of poetry.‡ The Hebrews certainly did not express by the same word ideas which they
deemed inconsistent, or repugnant to each other; and,
what is remarkable, the same ambiguity prevails, the same
word (and we may well presume for similar reasons) denotes both a prophet and a poet in the Arabic language, in
the Greek, and in the Latin.§

* The late Mr. Hallett of Exeter, in the second volume of his Notes and Discourses, p. 89, &c. hath advanced enough to show that the existence of the two
personages here mentioned is at least problematical. To the reputation of this
excellent man, (and perhaps it was his least praise,) it deserves to be mentioned,
that there is scarcely a conjectural emendation of the Hebrew text proposed by him,
which was not afterwards found by Dr. Kennicott, in one manuscript or another, to
have been an ancient reading.—S. H.

† *Massa*, which, according to its etymology, means *an oracular saying*, λογιον,
is no more peculiar to predictions of future events, than to every species of that
eloquence which is supposed to come by inspiration, including that which teaches
the salutary principles of moral conduct. I do not therefore see much force in
this argument of our Author : for, whatever Lemuel composed under the influence
of the Divine Spirit might properly be called *massa*, whether in verse or not. The
word is derived from *nasa*, he raised, he produced, he spoke ; not, as some of the old
commentators derive it, from *nasa*, he received : though that a divine oracle might, I
confess, take its name with great propriety from *receiving*, as does the Greek word
λημμα, (so the Seventy render this very phrase,) which means being *received*
from God. But the use of the word in 2 Kings ix. 25, militates against this
derivation.—M.

‡ Prov. xxx. 1; xxxi. 1. See also 1 Chron. xv. 22, and 27. שׂר המשׂא,
αρχων των ῳδων, LXX.

§ *Muttenabbi*, Προφητης, Vates. See Joseph Mede's Works, p. 59. Tit. i. 12.
Luke i. 67, and Hammond on the passage.—*Author's Note.*

N 2

Nor is it reasonable to suppose, that Prophecy admitted Poetry and Music to a participation in the name alone; on the contrary we find, that she did not disdain to unite herself with Harmony, and to accept of her assistance. The example of Elisha is remarkable,* who, when about to pronounce the answer of the Most High to the inquiry of the two kings of Israel and Judah, orders a minstrel to be brought to him, and, upon his striking the harp, is immediately agitated by the Holy Spirit.† Many commentators have indeed supposed that the prophet applied to music only to soothe the perturbation of his mind: in this they follow an opinion of some of the more modern rabbies, (an opinion, it may be observed, by no means satisfactorily proved,) that every emotion of a more vehement kind excluded the Holy Spirit, and consequently was totally inconsistent with prophecy;‡ when, on the contrary, we learn from the testimony of the prophets themselves, that the act of prophesying was often, if not always, accompanied with a very violent agitation of the mind.§ Be this as it may, I am inclined to believe, both from this last and the other instances, that the prophet himself accompanied the minstrel, and uttered some hymn, or rather the prediction itself, to the music of the harp; and both the style and the form of this prophetic reply are very much in favour of this opinion. ‖

From all these testimonies it is sufficiently evident, that the prophetic office had a most strict connexion with the poetic art. They had one common name, one common origin, one common author, the Holy Spirit. Those in particular were called to the exercise of the prophetic office, who were previously conversant with the sacred poetry. It was equally a part of their duty to compose verses for the service of the church, and to declare the oracles of God; it cannot, therefore, be doubted, that a great portion of the sacred hymns may properly be termed prophecies, or that many of the prophecies are in reality hymns or poems. Since, as

---

* 2 Kings iii. 15.

† והיה כנגן המנגן ותהי עליו יד יהוה

‡ See Maimon. *More Neboc.* ii. 36. and many others quoted by Smith, *Dissert. of Prophecy*, c. viii.

§ See Jer. xxiii. 9. Ezek. iii. 14, 15. Dan. vii. 28, x. 8. Habak. iii. 2, and 16.

‖ Dryden, in the adjustment of his measures, and Handel of his music, to the diversified strains of Timotheus, seem both to have possessed the same idea.—S. H.

we have already proved, it was from the first a principal end and aim of poetry, to impress upon the minds of men the sayings of the wise, and such precepts as related either to the principles of faith, or the laws of morality, as well as to transmit the same to posterity; it ought not to appear extraordinary, that prophecy, which in this view ranks as a principal, and is of the highest importance, should not disdain the assistance of an art so admirably calculated to effect its purposes. Of this we have an illustrious proof in that prophetic ode of Moses,* which he composed by the especial command of God, to be learned by the Israelites, and committed to memory: " That this song may be," says God himself, " for a witness against the people of Israel, when they shall depart from me : this shall be a testimony in their mouths ; for it shall not be forgotten, nor shall it depart out of the mouths of their posterity for ever."†

But as, on the one hand, this poem of Moses is a clear and remarkable specimen of the prophetic mode of writing; so, on the other, there are many prophecies which are not less conspicuous as poems. It remains, therefore, only to produce a few examples from the prophetic writings. Many of the most ancient of those which are extant in the Mosaic history I have already quoted,‡ as exhibiting the fairest examples of the Hebrew poetry : for instance, the imprecation of Noah, the blessing of Jacob, and the predictions of Balaam ; than all which (and particularly those of Balaam) I do not know that the whole extent of the prophetic writings could afford more pertinent instances. Nay, so eminently distinguished are they by all the characteristics of poetry, that those who are inclined to acknowledge any kind of metre in the Hebrew poetry, must, I am convinced, refer to these as metrical compositions, if they be in the least desirous of maintaining their opinion by fact and argument. Among the prophecies of Balaam I will also venture to class that most elegant poem which is rescued from oblivion by the prophet Micah,§ and which, in matter and diction, in the structure, form, and character of the composition, so admirably agrees with the other monuments of his fame, that it evidently appears to be a citation from the answer of Balaam to the king of the Moabites :‖

* Deut. xxxii.   † See Deut. xxxi. 19. 21.
‡ See Lect. 4.   § Micah vi. 6—8.
‖ See Micah vi. 5, and the late Bishop Butler's Sermon on the character of Balaam.

4

" Wherewith shall I come before JEHOVAH ?
  Wherewith shall I bow myself unto the High God ?
  Shall I come before him with burnt-offerings ;
  With calves of a year old ?
  Will JEHOVAH be pleased with thousands of rams ?
  With ten thousands of rivers of oil ?
  Shall I give my first-born for my transgression ?
  The fruit of my body for the sin of my soul ?
  He hath showed thee, O man, what is good :
  And what doth JEHOVAH require of thee,
  But to do justice, and to love mercy,
  And to be humble in walking with thy God ?"

But if we proceed to other parts of the sacred history,
examples will not be wanting; and among the first of these
is that cygnean song of Moses, as it may properly be called:
I do not speak of the prophetic ode, which has frequently
been distinguished by that title, but of the last blessing of
that divine prophet, in which are predicted the future fortunes of the Israelites:

" JEHOVAH came from Sinai ;
  And rose up unto them from Seir."*

The prophecy is evidently of the same nature with that of
Jacob : both in the exordium and the conclusion it is exquisitely sublime ; and throughout the whole affords an admirable specimen of the prophetic poetry.   In the same class
with these may be ranked the answer of Samuel the prophet to Saul, in which he reproaches him with his disobedience and contumacy, and denounces against him the Divine
decree of expulsion from his kingdom : it consists of four
distichs elegantly corresponding to each other :

" Hath JEHOVAH pleasure in burnt-offerings and sacrifices,
  As in listening to the voice of JEHOVAH ?
  Behold ! to listen is better than sacrifice,
  And to obey than the fat of rams.
  Rebellion is as the sin of divination,
  And contempt as the crime of idolatry.
  Because thou hast rejected the word of JEHOVAH,
  He hath also rejected thee from being king."†

The last words of David‡ afford an evident and illustrious
instance to the same purpose, however difficult and obscure

---

* Deut. xxxiii.
† 1 Sam. xv. 22, 23. All the old translators seem to have read הקשיב for
להקשיב, and הרפים without ו prefixed.
‡ 2 Sam. xxiii. 1—7.

the verbal interpretation of the prophecy may be. I apprehend the examples from sacred history will appear sufficiently
numerous, if I add the prediction of Isaiah concerning Sen-
nacherib, which is inserted in the book of Kings:

" He hath despised thee, he hath mocked thee, O virgin daughter
        of Sion ;
He hath shaken his head at thee, O daughter of Jerusalem."*

The same passage occurs again among the predictions of the
prophet: and this reminds me, that it is now full time to
pass from the historians to the books of the prophets themselves, which will afford us abundant instances to demonstrate that the compositions of the prophets are truly poetical, and at the same time to illustrate the nature of their
poetry.

* 2 Kings xix. 21—34. Isa. xxxvii. 22—35.

LECTURE XIX.

THE PROPHETIC POETRY IS SENTENTIOUS.

The Psalmody of the Hebrews—The manner of chanting the hymns by alternate choirs: whence the origin of the poetical construction of the sentences, and that peculiar form in which verses and distichs run parallel or correspondent to each other—Three species of parallelism; the synonymous, the antithetic, and the synthetic: examples of each; first from the books generally allowed to be poetical, and afterwards from the writings of the Prophets—The sentiments of R. Azarias considered—The great importance of an accurate attention to the poetical conformation of the sentences.

THE origin and earliest application of the Hebrew poetry have, I think, been clearly traced into the service of religion. To celebrate in hymns and songs the praises of Almighty God; to decorate the worship of the Most High with all the charms and graces of harmony; to give force and energy to the devout affections, was the sublime employment of the Sacred Muse. It is more than probable, that the very early use of sacred music in the public worship of the Hebrews, contributed not a little to the peculiar character of their poetry, and might impart to it that appropriate form, which, though chiefly adapted to this particular purpose, it nevertheless preserves on every other occasion. But in order to explain this matter more clearly, it will be necessary to premise a few observations concerning the ancient Hebrew mode of chanting their sacred hymns.

Though we are rather at a loss for information respecting the usual manner and ceremony of chanting their poems; and though the subject of their sacred music in general be involved in doubt and obscurity; thus far at least is evident from many examples, that the sacred hymns were alternately sung by opposite choirs,* and that the one choir usually performed the hymn itself, while the other sung a particular

* See Nehem. xii. 24. 31. 38. 40, and the title of Psa. lxxxviii.

distich, which was regularly interposed at stated intervals, either of the nature of the proasm or epode of the Greeks. In this manner we learn that Moses with the Israelites chanted the ode at the Red Sea; for "Miriam the prophetess took a timbrel in her hand, and all the women followed her with timbrels, and with dances; and Miriam answered them;" that is, she and the women sung the response to the chorus of men :*

> "Sing to JEHOVAH, for he is greatly exalted;
> The horse and the rider he hath cast into the sea."

The same is observable in some of the psalms which are composed in this form. The musical performance was on some occasions differently conducted; for instance, one of the choirs sung a single verse to the other, while the other constantly added a verse in some respect correspondent to the former. Of this the following distich is an example :

> "Sing praises to JEHOVAH, for he is good;
> Because his mercy endureth for ever;"

which Ezra† informs us was sung by the priests and Levites in alternate choirs at the command of David; as indeed may be collected from the psalm itself,‡ in which the latter verse, sung by the latter choir, forms a perpetual epode. Of the same nature is the song of the women concerning Saul and David,§ for "the women who played answered one another;" that is, they chanted in two choirs the alternate song,‖ the one choir singing,—

---

* Exod. xv. 20, 21. See Philo περι γεωργιας, page 199, also περι βιου Θεωρητικου, page 902. Edit. Paris, 1640.

† Ezra iii. 11.   ‡ Psalm cxxxvi.   § 1 Sam. xviii. 7.

‖ It is much to be regretted, that the learned author has not investigated this subject more *fully*, and with his usual precision.—Though the performance of their hymns by two *alternate* choirs was the more usual, it evidently was not the only mode : for as the parallelism of sentences in the Hebrew poetry is not restricted to distichs, but admits a varied form of iteration, so their psalmody, though usually confined to two alternate choruses, was sometimes extended to more. An example of the latter kind will appear in Psalm cxxxv., which was obviously performed by three *different* choirs—the High-priest with the House of Aaron constituting the *first* ; the Levites serving the temple, the *second;* and the Congregation of Israel, the *third;* all having their *distinct* parts, and all at stated intervals *uniting* in full chorus.

The High-priest, accompanied by the rest of the priesthood, began with addressing the Levites :
    Praise ye Jah!
The Levites return the exhortation to the Priests :
    Praise ye the name of Jehovah!

"Saul hath smote his thousands;"

The other answering,

"And David his ten thousands."

The Priests and Levites then joining, address the Congregation:

Praise him, O ye servants of Jehovah!

The Congregation address the Priests—

Ye that stand in the house of Jehovah!

And the Levites—

In the courts of the house of our God!

This may be considered as the first passus of the προασμα, which the *Choir of Priests* resumes by a second exhortation to the *Levites*, and assigning the reason for their praise:

Praise ye Jah, for Jehovah is good.

The Levites then exhort the Congregation:

Sing praises unto his name, for it is pleasant.

And the Congregation joining both, the three choirs unite in full chorus:

For Jah hath chosen Jacob unto himself;
Israel for his peculiar treasure.

The προασμα thus concluding, the *High-priest*, followed by his band, commences in the 5th verse the hymn. The 6th verse belongs to the *Levites*, and the 7th to the *Congregation*, both of whom having, in them, celebrated Jehovah as the *Creator* and *Governor* of the world, the *High-priest* descends, in the 8th verse, to the interpositions of Jehovah in behalf of his chosen people; beginning with the miracle that procured their deliverance from bondage. The *Levites* having adverted to the other miracles wrought in Egypt, in the former clause of the 9th verse, and the *Congregation*, in the latter, pointed out Pharaoh and his servants as those upon whom they, the judgments of Jehovah, were inflicted, the *High-priest* &c. proceed, in the 10th verse, to remark the extension of similar judgments to other nations and kings, whose names and kingdoms the *Levites* enumerate in the 11th verse, whilst the *Congregation*, in the 12th, commemorate the blessings which had thence resulted to them. At the close of this recitative, in the first clause of the 13th verse, follows a chorus of the Priests:

Thy name, O Jehovah! endureth for ever!

And in the second, another, of the Levites:

Thy memorial, O Jehovah! throughout all generations.

The Congregation then striking in with Priests and Levites, all unite in full chorus, as before:

For Jehovah will judge his people;
And will repent him concerning his servants.

This chorus may be considered as closing the first part of the hymn, the concluding clause of which, adverting to the frequent backslidings of the Jewish nation, notwithstanding the blessings, both *ordinary* and *extraordinary* which Jehovah had conferred upon them, and the prosperity they enjoyed in the land promised to their forefathers, notwithstanding their turning aside to the idolatry of the nations that had been cut off from before them, the choir of *Priests*, (referring back to the 5th verse,) as if assured that Israel could revolt no more, breaks out in a second recitative, expressive at once of exultation and contempt:

The idols of the Heathen, silver and gold, &c.

To this the Levites add, in the same indignant strain:

They have mouths, but they speak not, &c.

In the very same manner Isaiah describes the Seraphim chanting the praise of Jehovah:* "They cried alternately,

> Holy, holy, holy, JEHOVAH God of Hosts!
> The whole earth is filled with his glory."

From the Jewish, the custom of singing in alternate chorus was transmitted to the Christian church, and was continued in the latter from the first ages: it was called "alternate or responsive,"† when the whole choir, separated into two divisions, sung the psalm alternately by strophes; and when this was done by single verses or lines, that is, when the same division of the choir always sung the latter part of the distich, they were said to sing the choral response.‡

Now, if this were the ancient and primitive mode of chanting their hymns, as indeed appears highly probable, the proximate cause will be easily explained, why poems of this

The Congregation subjoin:

> *They have ears, but they hear not.*

And the three choirs again uniting:

> *They that make them are like unto them:*
> *Every one that trusteth in them.*

With this exquisite contrast between the gods in whom the heathen confided, and Jehovah the rock of their salvation—the former unable to hear or aid their votaries, and the latter loading benefits on his own – the second part of the hymn is concluded, and the High-priest with his choir, by a graceful transition, renews his exhortation as at first; but now addressing the Congregation:

> *Bless Jehovah, O house of Israel!*

To which the Congregation reply:

> *Bless Jehovah, O house of Aaron!*

The Priests, in like manner, exhorting the Levites:

> *Bless Jehovah, O house of Levi!*

To whom they in their turn rejoin:

> *Ye that fear Jehovah, bless Jehovah!*

All then uniting:

> *Blessed be Jehovah out of Sion!*
> *Who dwelleth in Jerusalem!*

The whole is closed by each choir, in full chorus, exhorting the other two:

> *Praise ye Jah!*

From this analysis it is evident, that the Hebrew Hymn is a composition not less regular than the Grecian Ode, and of a much more varied nature than the Professor had led his audience to suppose.—S. H.

The reader will find the Psalm in an entire state, but divided and apportioned according to the above specimen, in the Appendix.

* Isa. vi. 3. See what Socrates relates of the origin of the ancient hymns, *Hist. Eccl.* vi. 8.

† Plin. lib. x. Epist. 97.—"They repeat alternate verses to Christ, as to a God."

‡ See Bingham's *Antiquities of the Christian Church,* xiv. 1.

kind are disposed in equal stanzas, indeed in equal distichs, for the most part; and why these distichs should in some measure consist of versicles or parallelisms* corresponding to each other. And this mode of composition being admirably adapted to the musical modulation of that kind of poetry which was most in use among them from the very beginning, and at the same time being perfectly agreeable to the genius and cadence of the language, easily extended itself into the other species of poetry, though not designed for the same purpose: in fact, we find that it pervaded the whole of the poetry of the Hebrews, insomuch that what was said of the Heathen Muses may still more strictly be applied to those of the Hebrews,—"they love alternate song." On this occasion also it may not be improper to remark, that the word *gnanah*, which properly signifies to answer, is used more generally to denote any song or poem;† whence we can only infer, either that the word has passed from particular to general use, or that among the Hebrews almost every poem possesses a sort of responsive form.

Such appears to have been the origin and progress of that poetical and artificial conformation of the sentences which we observe in the poetry of the. Hebrews. That it prevailed no less in the Prophetic Poetry than in the Lyric and Didactic, to which it was, in the nature of things, most adapted, is evident from those very ancient specimens of poetical prophecy already quoted from the historical books; and it only remains to show, that it is no less observable in those which are contained in the volumes of the prophets themselves. In order. the more clearly to evince this point, I shall endeavour to illustrate the Hebrew parallelism according to its different species, first by examples taken from those books commonly allowed to be poetical, and afterwards by correspondent examples from the books of the prophets.

The poetical conformation of the sentences which has been so often alluded to as characteristic of the Hebrew

---

* " The correspondence of one verse, or line, with another, I call *parallelism*. When a proposition is delivered, and a second is subjoined to it, or drawn under it, equivalent, or contrasted with it, in sense; or similar to it in the form of grammatical construction—these I call parallel lines; and the words or phrases, answering one to another in the corresponding lines, parallel terms."—Lowth's *Prelim. Disc. to Isa.* p. ix.

† Exod. xxxii. 18. Numb. xxi. 17. Hos. ii. 15. Psa. cxlvii. 7. " Thus the word which in the Arabic answers to *gnanah*, denotes not only to *perform alternately*, but also to *sing*."—H.

poetry, consists chiefly in a certain equality, resemblance, or parallelism, between the members of each period; so that in two lines, (or members of the same period,) things for the most part shall answer to things, and words to words, as if fitted to each other by a kind of rule or measure. This parallelism has much variety and many gradations; it is sometimes more accurate and manifest, sometimes more vague and obscure : it may, however, on the whole, be said to consist of three species.

The first species is the synonymous parallelism, when the same sentiment is repeated in different, but equivalent terms. This is the most frequent of all, and is often conducted with the utmost accuracy and neatness: examples are very numerous, nor will there be any great difficulty in the choice of them : on this account I shall select such as are most remarkable in other respects.

> " When Israel went out from Egypt;
> The house of Jacob from a strange people :
> Judah was as his sacred heritage ;
> Israel his dominion.
> The sea saw, and fled ;
> Jordan turned back :
> The mountains leaped like rams ;
> The hills like the sons of the flock.
> What ailed thee, O Sea, that thou fleddest ;
> Jordan, that thou turnedst back ;
> Mountains, that ye leaped like rams ;
> And hills, like the sons of the flock ?
> At the presence of the Lord tremble thou Earth ;
> At the presence of the God of Jacob !
> Who turned the rock into a lake of waters ;
> The flint into a water-spring."*

The Prophetic Muse is no less elegant and correct:

> " Arise, be thou enlightened : for thy light is come,
> And the glory of JEHOVAH is risen upon thee.
> For, behold, darkness shall cover the earth ;
> And a thick vapour the nations :
> But upon thee shall JEHOVAH arise ;
> And his glory upon thee shall be conspicuous.
> And the nations shall walk in thy light ;
> And kings in the brightness of thy rising."†

---

* Psalm cxiv.
† Isaiah lx. 1—3. " In the brightness of thy rising" is an expression uncommonly beautiful and simple : I never could read it without a glow of tranquil pleasure corresponding to the scene which the image exhibits.—T.

Observe also that famous prophecy concerning the humiliation and expiatory sufferings of the Messiah:

" Who hath believed our report;
   And to whom hath the arm of JEHOVAH been manifested ?
   For he groweth up in their sight like a tender sucker;
   And like a root from a thirsty soil :
   He hath no form, nor any beauty that we should regard him ;
   Nor is his countenance such, that we should desire him.
   Despised, nor accounted in the number of men ;
   A man of sorrows, and acquainted with grief ;
   As one that hideth his face from us :
   He was despised, and we esteemed him not.
   Surely our infirmities he hath borne;
   And our sorrows* he hath carried them.—
   Yet we thought him judicially stricken ;
   Smitten of God and afflicted.
   But he was wounded for our transgressions ;
   Was smitten for our iniquities :
   The chastisement by which our peace was effected was laid
      upon him ;
   And by his bruises we are healed."†

Isaiah is indeed excellent, but not unrivalled, in this kind
of composition: there are abundant examples in the other
prophets; I shall, however, only add one from Hosea,‡ which
is exquisitely pathetic:

" How shall I resign thee, O Ephraim !
   How shall I deliver thee up, O Israel !
   How shall I resign thee as Admah !
   How shall I make thee as Zeboim !
   My heart is changed within me ;
   I am warmed also with repentance towards thee.
   I will not do according to the fervour of my wrath,
   I will not return§ to destroy Ephraim :
   For I am God, and not man ;
   Holy in the midst of thee, though I inhabit not thy cities."‖

---

* Some copies, manuscript as well as printed, point out in the margin the word
הוּא (*he*) to be inserted: (see Bibl. Heb. Edit. Michaelis, Var. Lect. in loc.) The
Syr. and Vulg. certainly express it, and indeed the repetition of the word gives
exquisite force and elegance to the line. " This word occurs in the text of twelve
MS. copies, and in three printed." K.—*Author's Note.*
   † Isaiah liii. 1—5.   ‡ Hosea xi. 8, 9.
   § A beautiful Hebraism to express the repetition of any thing: in this place it
has peculiar force and pathos.—T.
   ‖ There is hardly any thing in which translators have differed more than in the
explanation of this line; which is the more extraordinary when we consider that
the words themselves are so well known, and the structure of the period so plain
and evident. Jerome is almost singular in his explanation : *Comm. in loc.* " I am

There is a great variety in the form of the synonymous parallelism, some instances of which are deserving of remark. The parallelism is sometimes formed by the iteration of the former member, either in the whole or in part:

" Much have they oppressed me from my youth up,
  May Israel now say;
  Much have they oppressed me from my youth,
  Yet have they not prevailed against me."*

" God of vengeance, JEHOVAH;
  God of vengeance, show thyself.
  How long shall the wicked, O JEHOVAH,
  How long shall the wicked triumph!"†

" With the jaw-bone of an ass, heaps upon heaps;
  With the jaw-bone of an ass a thousand men have I
      smitten."‡

Thus Isaiah:

"Because in the night Ar is destroyed, Moab is undone!
  Because in the night Kir is destroyed, Moab is undone."§

So Nahum also, in the exordium of his sublime prophecy:

" JEHOVAH is a jealous and avenging God;
  JEHOVAH avengeth, and is wrathful:

not one of those who inhabit cities; who live according to human laws; who think cruelty justice." Castalio follows Jerome. There is, in fact, in the latter member of the sentence לא אבוא בעיר, a parallelism and synonyme to לא איש in the former. The futuro אבוא has a frequentative power, (see Psalm xxii. 3, and 8.) "I am not accustomed to enter a city; I am not an inhabitant of a city." For there is a beautiful opposition of the different parts: "I am God, and not man." This is amplified in the next line, and the antithesis a little varied: "I am thy God, inhabiting with thee, but in a peculiar and extraordinary manner, not in the manner of men." Nothing I think can be plainer or more elegant than this.—*Author's Note.*

* Psalm cxxix. 1, 2.   † Psalm xciv. 1, and 3.

‡ Judges xv. 16. "It will admit of a doubt whether these words may not be rendered, *With the jaw-bone of an ass, in confusing, I have confused them.* For this seems to be the grammatical construction of the words: and the word *Chamar* commonly signifies to *trouble* or *confuse*. So it is rendered by the LXX, Εν σιαγονι ονε εξαλειφων εξηλειψα αυτες, *With the jaw-bone of an ass, in exterminating, I have exterminated them;* following the same construction, but, taking the more violent sense of the word, *destroying* or *exterminating;* which sense it still retains in the Arabic, for in that language it signifies not only to *trouble* or *disturb,* but also to *overwhelm* or *suppress.* But if in favour of the other interpretation, which is also adopted in our common translation, the passage in Exod. viii. 14, be referred to, (*chomarim, chomarim,* in heaps,) it may be said in answer, that the words in these two passages assume a different form. The verb *chamar* in this place seems most directly suited to express tumult and confusion, and is also introduced for the sake of the paronomasia, and the similarity of sound with the preceding word *chamor,* an ass."—H.

§ Chap. xv. 1.

> JEHOVAH avengeth his adversaries ;
> And he reserveth *indignation* for his enemies."*

There is frequently something wanting in the latter member, which must be repeated from the former to complete the sentence :

> " The king sent and released him ;
> The ruler of the people, and set him free."†

In the same manner Isaiah :

> " Kings shall see him, and shall rise up ;
> Princes, and they shall worship him :
> For the sake of JEHOVAH, who is faithful ;
> Of the Holy One of Israel, for he hath chosen thee."‡

Frequently the whole of the latter division answers only to some part of the former :

> " JEHOVAH reigneth, let the earth rejoice ;
> Let the multitude of islands be glad."§

> " Arise, be thou enlightened ; for thy light is come ;
> And the glory of JEHOVAH is risen upon thee."‖

Sometimes also there are triplet parallelisms. In these the second line is generally synonymous with the first, whilst the third either begins the period, or concludes it, and frequently refers to both the preceding :

> " The floods have lifted up, O JEHOVAH ;
> The floods have lifted up their voice ;
> The floods have lifted up their waves.
> Than the voice of many waters,
> The glorious waves of the sea,
> JEHOVAH on high is more glorious."¶

> " Come and let us return unto JEHOVAH ;
> For he hath torn, and he will heal us ;
> He hath smitten, and he will bind us up :
> After two days he will revive us ;
> On the third day he will raise us up ;
> And we shall live in his sight."**

In stanzas (if I may so call them) of five lines, the nature of which is nearly similar, the line that is not parallel is generally placed between the two distichs :—

---

* Nah. i. 2.   † Psa. cv. 20.   ‡ Isa. xlix. 7.
§ Psa. xcvii. 1.   ‖ Isa. lx. 1.   ¶ Psa. xciii. 3, 4.
** Hos. vi. 1, 2.

" Like as the lion growleth,
Even the young lion, over his prey;
Though the whole company of shepherds be called together
   against him :
At their voice he will not be terrified,
Nor at their tumult will he be humbled."*

" Askalon shall see it, and shall fear ;
Gaza shall also see it, and shall be greatly pained ;
And Ekron shall be pained, because her expectation is put
   to shame :
And the king shall perish from Gaza ;
And Askalon shall not be inhabited."†

Those which consist of four lines generally form two regular
distichs; but there is sometimes a peculiar artifice to be
perceived in the distribution of the sentences :

" From the Heavens JEHOVAH looketh down,
He seeth all the children of men ;
From the seat of his rest he contemplateth
All the inhabitants of the earth."‡

" I will drench my arrows in blood,
And my sword shall devour flesh ;
In the blood of the slain and the captives ;
From the bushy head of the enemies."§

In both the above passages the latter members are to be
alternately referred to the former.   Isaiah too uses with
great elegance this form of composition :

" For thy husband is thy maker ;
JEHOVAH God of Hosts is his name :
And thy Redeemer is the Holy One of Israel ;
The God of the whole earth shall he be called."‖

The sense has an alternate correspondence in these lines.
In the following, the form of the construction is alternate :

" And his land is filled with silver and gold,
And there is no end to his treasures :
And his land is filled with horses,
Neither is there any end to his chariots."¶

The following is perhaps a singular instance :

" Who is like unto JEHOVAH our God ?
Who is exalted to dwell on high,

* Isaiah xxxi. 4.   † Zech. ix. 5.   ‡ Psalm xxxiii. 13, 14.
§ Deut. xxxii. 42.   ‖ Isaiah liv. 5.   ¶ Isaiah ii. 7.

O

> Who humbleth himself to look down,
> In the heavens, and in the earth."*

Here the two members of the latter line are to be referred severally to the two preceding lines; as if it were, " Who is exalted to dwell in the heavens, and who humbleth himself to inspect the things that are in the earth."

The Antithetic parallelism is the next that I shall specify, when a thing is illustrated by its contrary being opposed to it. This is not confined to any particular form; for sentiments are opposed to sentiments, words to words, singulars to singulars, plurals to plurals, &c., of which the following are examples:

> " The blows of a friend are faithful;
> But the kisses of an enemy are treacherous.†
> The cloyed will trample upon an honey-comb;
> But to the hungry every bitter thing is sweet.
> There is who maketh himself rich, and wanteth all things.;
> Who maketh himself poor, yet hath much wealth.
> The rich man is wise in his own eyes,
> But the poor man that hath discernment to trace him out will
>   despise him."‡

There is sometimes a contraposition of parts in the same sentence; such as occurs once in the above, and as appears in the following:

> "I am swarthy but comely, O daughters of Jerusalem;
> As the tents of Kedar, as the pavilions of Solomon."§

The last line here is also to be divided and separately applied to the preceding—" swarthy as the tents of Kedar; comely as the pavilions of Solomon."   So likewise in the enigma of Samson:

> " Out of the eater came forth meat;
> And out of the strong came forth sweetness."||

This form of composition, indeed, agrees best with adages and acute sayings: it is therefore very prevalent in the

---

* Psalm cxiii. 5, 6.

† " To this very day the word עתר is in use in the East, and in an Arabic Lexicon, which is accounted one of the best, it is explained by the word כדב (the same as the Hebrew כזב) *to falsify*. Whence it is evident that there is an antithesis between the two hemistichs, which the LXX have in vain attempted to explain; they have εκουσια, *spontaneous* or *voluntary*. They seem to have read it נעתרות."
—H.

‡ Prov. xxvii. 6, 7; xiii. 7; xxviii. 11.   § Song of Solomon, i. 5.
|| Judges xiv. 14. The solution of the enigma by the Philistines is metrical, as well as the answer of Samson to them. Ib. v. 18.—*Author's Note.*

Proverbs of Solomon, in some of which the principal force and elegance depend on the exactness of the antithesis. It is not, however, inconsistent with the superior kinds of Hebrew poetry; for we meet with it in the thanksgiving ode of Hannah, which is imitated in this particular, as well as in the general form of its composition, in that of the Virgin Mary:

> " The bows of the mighty are broken ;
> And they that stumbled are girded with strength :
> The full have hired themselves for bread ;
> And the hungry have ceased to hunger :*
> The barren also hath borne seven ;
> And she who had many children is become fruitless.
> JEHOVAH killeth and maketh alive ;
> He casteth down to hell and lifteth up.
> JEHOVAH maketh poor, and maketh rich ;
> Depresseth, and also exalteth."†

The sublimer poetry seldom indeed adopts this style. Isaiah, however, by means of it, without departing from his usual dignity, adds greatly to the sweetness of his composition in the following instances:

> " In a little anger have I forsaken thee ;
> But with great mercies will I receive thee again :
> In a short wrath I hid my face for a moment from thee ;
> But with everlasting kindness will I have mercy on thee."‡

> " Behold, my servants shall eat, but ye shall be famished ;
> Behold, my servants shall drink, but ye shall be thirsty ;
> Behold, my servants shall rejoice, but ye shall be confounded ;
> Behold, my servants shall sing aloud for gladness of heart,
> But ye shall cry aloud for grief of heart,
> And in the anguish of a broken spirit shall ye howl."§

There is a third species of parallelism, in which the sentences answer to each other, not by the iteration of the same image or sentiment, or the opposition of their contraries, but merely by the form of construction. To this, which may be called the Synthetic or Constructive Parallelism, may be referred all such as do not come within the two

---

* " There is evidently something wanting after *(chadelu)* *ceased*, in order to complete the sentence. What if we take the word *gnad* from the beginning of the next verse, and so understand it as derived from the verb *gnieved*, *to spoil* or *rob* ? The sense will then be, *the hungry ceased from plundering*, that is, on account of their poverty, as in Job iii. 17."—H.

† 1 Sam. ii. 4—7 ; compare Luke i. 52, 53.

‡ Isaiah liv. 7, 8.   § Isaiah lxv. 13, 14.

former classes.   I shall however produce a few of the most
remarkable instances :

> "The law of JEHOVAH is perfect, restoring the soul ;
>   The testimony of JEHOVAH is sure, making wise the simple :
>   The precepts of JEHOVAH are right, rejoicing the heart ;
>   The commandment of JEHOVAH is clear, enlightening the
>   eyes ;
>   The fear of JEHOVAH is pure, enduring for ever ;
>   The judgments of JEHOVAH are truth, they are just alto-
>   gether :
>   More desirable than gold, or than much fine gold ;
>   And sweeter than honey, or the dropping of honey-combs."*

This kind of parallelism generally consists of verses somewhat longer than usual, of which there are not wanting
examples in the Prophets :

> "How hath the oppressor ceased! the exactress of gold ceased!
>   JEHOVAH hath broken the staff of the wicked, the sceptre of
>   the rulers.
>   He that smote the people in wrath with a stroke unremitted,
>   He that ruled the nations in anger is persecuted, and none
>   hindereth.
>   The whole earth is at rest, is quiet ; they burst forth into a
>   joyful shout ;
>   Even the fir-trees rejoice over thee, the cedars of Lebanon :
>   Since thou art fallen, no feller hath come up against us !
>   Hades from beneath is moved because of thee, to meet thee at
>   thy coming :
>   He rouseth for thee the mighty dead, all the great chiefs of the
>   earth ;
>   He maketh to rise up from their thrones all the kings of the
>   nations."†

Triplets are frequently formed of this kind of parallelism :

> "The clouds overflowed with water ;
>   The atmosphere resounded ;
>   Thine arrows also issued forth ;
>   The voice of thy thunder was in the skies ;
>   The lightnings enlightened the world ;
>   The earth trembled and shook."‡

> "I will be as the dew to Israel :
>   He shall blossom as the lily ;
>   And he shall strike his roots like Lebanon :
>   His suckers shall spread,

---

* Psalm xix. 8—11.   † Isaiah xiv. 4—9.   ‡ Psalm lxxvii. 18, 19.

> And his glory shall be as the olive-tree,
> And his smell as Lebanon."*

Frequently one line or member contains two sentiments :

> " The nations raged ; the kingdoms were moved;
> He uttered a voice; the earth was dissolved :
> Be still, and know that I am God:
> I will be exalted in the nations, I will be exalted in the earth."†

> " When thou passest through waters, I am with thee ;
> And through rivers, they shall not overwhelm thee:
> When thou walkest in the fire, thou shalt not be scorched ;
> And the flame shall not cleave to thee."‡

There is a peculiar figure which is frequently made use of in this species of parallelism, and which seems altogether poetical: that is, when a definite number is put for an indefinite, principally, it should seem, for the sake of the parallelism: for it sometimes happens, that the circumstances afterwards enumerated do not accurately accord with the number specified:

> " In six troubles will he deliver thee ;
> And in seven there shall no evil touch thee."§

> " God hath said once ;
> Twice also have I heard the same."||

That frequently repeated passage of Amos is well known :

> " For three transgressions of Damascus,
> And for four, I will not restore it."¶

The variety in the form of this synthetic parallelism is very great, and the degrees of resemblance almost infinite : so that sometimes the scheme of the parallelism is very subtile and obscure, and must be developed by art and ability in distinguishing the different members of the sentences, and in distributing the points, rather than by depending upon the obvious construction. How much this principle pervades the Hebrew poetry, and how difficult of explication it is, may in some degree be illustrated by one example. This appears to consist of a single line, if the sentiment only be considered:

> " I also have anointed my king on Sion, the mountain of my sanctity."**

---

* Hos. xiv. 6, 7.   † Psa. xlvi. 6. 10.   ‡ Isa. xliii. 2.   § Job v. 19.
|| Psa. lxii. 12.   ¶ Amos i. 3, &c.   ** Psa. ii. 6.

But the general form and nature of the Psalm requires that it should be divided into two parts or versicles: as if it were,

" I also have anointed my king ;
I have anointed him in Sion, the mountain of my sanctity."

Which indeed the Masorites seem to have perceived in this as well as in other places.*

In this peculiar conformation, or parallelism, of the sentences, I apprehend a considerable part of the Hebrew metre to consist; though it is not improbable that some regard was also paid to the numbers and feet. But of this particular we have at present so little information, that it is utterly impossible to determine, whether it was modulated by the ear alone, or according to any settled or definite rules of prosody. Since, however, this and other marks or vestiges, as it were, of the metrical art are alike extant in the writings of the prophets and in the books which are commonly allowed to be poetical, I think there is sufficient reason to rank them in the same class.

Lest I should seem to have attributed too much to this conformation of the sentences, and to have rashly embraced an opinion not supported by sufficient authority, I shall beg leave to quote to you the opinion of Azarias, a Jew rabbi, not indeed a very ancient, but a very approved author.† " Without doubt," says he, " the sacred songs have certain measures and proportions; but these do not consist in the number of the syllables perfect or imperfect, according to the form of the modern verse, but in the number of things, and of the parts of things; that is, the subject and the predicate, and their adjuncts, in every sentence and proposition." (Which words of Azarias are, however, to be understood· with some limitation; nor are they to be literally interpreted according to their sense in logical treatises, for he proceeds,) " Thus a phrase, containing two parts of a proposition, consists of two measures; add another, containing four, and they become four measures; another again containing three parts of a proposition, consists of three measures; add to it another of the like, and you have six

---

* For they mark the word מלכי with the distinctive accent *Athnac*, by which they generally distinguish the members of the distichs. See Psalm xvii. 7 ; xxxii. 3 ; xxxiii. 14 ; cii. 8 ; cxvi. 1. 9. 12. 14, 15. 18; cxxxvii. 2.—*Author's Note.*

† *Mantissa Dissert.* ad Librum *Cosri*, p. 418.

measures; for you are not to number the words or syllables, but the sentences." For instance, "Thy right hand, O JEHOVAH," according to Azarias, consists of two terms, or parts of a proposition; to which is connected, "is all-glorious in power," consisting likewise of two terms: these joined together make a Tetrameter. The following is constructed on a similar principle :

"Thy right-hand, O JEHOVAH, hath crushed the enemy."*

Thus in the following propositions there are three terms or measures :

"My-doctrine shall-drop, as-the-rain; my-word shall-distil, as-the-dew."†

" And thus joined together they form an Hexameter." In fact, what he has here remarked is neither groundless nor altogether just. For, with respect to many passages in which the distribution of the sentences is very unequal, and in which the propositions have but little correspondence with each other, as happens frequently in the Psalms, we must have recourse to some other solution; and when the sentences are most regular and correct, they cannot at all times be reduced to his rules. But although the present question does not depend upon this single point, no man, I think, who reads with attention the poetic books, and especially what may be properly called the prophetic part of them, will entertain a doubt that it is of the utmost importance to distinguish the system of the verses.

But should all that has been remarked concerning the members and divisions of the sentences appear light and trifling to some persons, and utterly undeserving any labour or attention; let them remember, that nothing can be of greater avail to the proper understanding of any writer, than a previous acquaintance with both his general character, and the peculiarities of his style and manner of writing: let them recollect, that translators and commentators have fallen into errors, upon no account more frequently than for want of attention to this article; and indeed I scarcely know any subject which promises more copiously to reward the labour of such as are studious of sacred criticism, than this one in particular.‡

* Exod. xv. 6.   † Deut. xxxii. 2.

‡ Professor Michaelis has subjoined a very considerable addition to this Lecture on the use of the parallelism in the explanation of Scripture, of which he produces several instances.

In Psalm xxii. 3, our English translation runs thus : " They shall come, and shall declare his righteousness unto a people that shall be born, that *he hath done this ;*" and in the Common Prayer, " unto a people that shall be born, *whom the Lord hath made.*" The Professor justly observes, that the word which is here rendered *righteousness,* may, with equal propriety, be translated *truth,* and then, by the assistance of the parallelism, the just sense is restored, and the passage will run thus :

" They shall come, and shall declare his truth ;
    To a people that shall be born (*they shall declare*) that he hath performed *it.*"

That is, that he hath fulfilled his promises and divine predictions.

Psalm xxv. 13.   The literal translation is,
      " His soul shall rest in good,
        And his seed shall inherit the land."

It is not easy to say in what sense we are to take the former part of the sentence. It may either be *to sleep secure from danger;* or, *to enjoy ease and plenty,* i. e. *to remain in a prosperous state ;* or, lastly, it may indicate *the state after death,* or *a happiness beyond the grave.* This last meaning the Professor prefers on account of the parallelism, since the corresponding member of the sentence, *his seed shall inherit the land,* is undoubtedly among those blessings which the Deity promises to the righteous after death.

Psalm cxxx. 20, according to our translation,

      " For they speak against thee wickedly,
        And thine enemies take *thy name* in vain."

The Professor thinks that *nasa lishave* may be translated to *profess* falsely, or to *perjure* themselves. The sense of the second line will therefore run thus : *Who swear falsely by thy cities,* i. e. by Sichem, Bethlehem, Jerusalem, &c. by which it was customary for the Jews to swear, as is plain from Matt. v. 35 ; and this interpretation not only is such as would be suggested by a proper attention to the parallelism, but is perfectly correspondent to the context :

      " I would that thou wouldst slay the wicked, O God ;
        And that the men of blood should depart from me !
      Who use thy name only for deceit,
      And swear falsely by thy cities.
      Do not I hate them who hate thee ?" &c.

Psalm cxxxvii. 9.

      " Who giveth to the beast his food,
        And to the young ravens which cry."

More agreeable to the Hebrew idiom thus :

      " Who giveth to the beast his food,
        And to the young ravens that for which they cry."

But the most complete examples of the use of the parallelism will be found in our Author's Preliminary Dissertation to his *Isaiah.*—T.

LECTURE XX.

THE GENERAL CHARACTERISTICS OF THE PROPHETIC
POETRY.

The whole of the book of Daniel, as well as of Jonah, are to be excepted as not poetical, though of the prophetic kind; also certain historical relations inserted in the books of the Prophets—Some poems occur in the prophetic writings, which properly belong to the other classes of poetry—The remainder constitutes what may be termed a system or code of prophetic poetry—The character of this species of poetry deduced from the nature and design of the prophecy itself—An example of the true style. of prophetic poetry produced from Isaiah, and explained; also another from the prophecies of Balaam, translated into English verse.

In the two last Lectures I endeavoured to explain upon what reasons I was induced to class the predictions of the prophets among the poetical productions of the Hebrews. I speak not of all, but the greater part of the prophetic writings; for there are among them parts which are not prophetic, and even among those which are, there are some passages not poetical. I except, in the first place, those narrations plainly historical, relating to the facts which gave occasion to the prophecies, and which serve to introduce, to explain, and illustrate them: some of this kind occur in Isaiah, and in Jeremiah many more. The whole of what is called the Prophecy of Jonah is the bare recital of a fact, and contains nothing of poetry but the prayer of the prophet, which is an ode. Some of the prophecies themselves must also be excepted, which are indeed sublime and important as to the matter, but not at all poetical as to the style and metrical structure: of this kind many passages occur in Ezekiel, who frequently appears more of the orator than the poet. The whole book of Daniel, too, being no more than a plain relation of facts partly past and partly future, must be excluded the class of poetical prophecy. Much, I confess, of the parabolic imagery is introduced in that book; but the author introduces it as a prophet only—as visionary and allegorical symbols of objects and events, totally untinctured with the true poetical colouring. The Jews, indeed, would refuse to Daniel even the character of a prophet : but the arguments under which they shelter this opinion are very futile; for, those points which they maintain, concerning the conditions on which the gift of prophecy is imparted; the different gradations, and the discrimination between the true prophecy and mere inspiration; are all trifling and absurd, without any foundation in the nature of things, and totally destitute of scriptural authority.* They add, that Daniel was neither originally educated in the prophetic discipline and precepts, nor afterwards lived conformably to the manner of the prophets. I do not, however, comprehend how this can diminish his claim to a divine mission and inspiration : it may possibly enable us, indeed, to assign a reason for the dissimilarity between the style of Daniel and that of the other prophets, and for its possessing so little of the diction and character of poetry, which the rest seem to have imbibed in common from the schools and discipline in which they were educated.†

---

* See Maimon. *More Neboc.* ii. 45. Our Author in this place alludes to the rabbinical notions concerning inspiration, which are explained more at large by Basnage. " They distinguish," says that author, " eleven degrees of prophecy. They reckon among inspired men those who felt some inward emotions, urging them to perform extraordinary actions, as Samson. Those who composed Hymns and Psalms, because they believed themselves inspired with God's Spirit, were accounted so many prophets. However, these prophets are distinguished by the following orders : 1. When Zechariah says, *The word of the Lord came unto me.* 2. Samuel heard a voice, but did not see who spoke. 3. When a man speaks in a dream with a prophet, as it happened to Ezekiel, to whom a man cried, *Son of man.* 4. Angels spoke often in dreams. 5. It was sometimes thought that God himself spoke in a dream. 6. Some mystical objects were discovered. 7. An audible voice was heard from the midst of these objects. 8. A man is seen speaking, as it happened to Abraham under the oak of Mamre, which however was a vision. 9. Lastly, an angel is perceived speaking. Thus Abraham heard one when he was binding Isaac upon the altar to sacrifice him; but that was also a vision." *Hist. of the Jews,* B. iv. ch. xviii. sect. 11.—T.

† We may add the decline of the Hebrew language, which in the Babylonish captivity lost all its grace and elegance. Nor, among so many evils which befell their nation, is it surprising that they should have neither leisure nor spirit for the cultivation of the fine arts. Besides, when a language is confined chiefly to the lowest of the people, it is hardly to be expected that it should produce any poets worthy of the name. Let any man compare what was written in Hebrew before and after the Babylonish exile, and I apprehend he will perceive no less evident marks of decay and ruin than in the Latin language. Wherefore it appears to me very improbable, that any Psalms which breathe a truly sublime and poetical spirit were composed after the return from Babylon, excepting perhaps that elegant piece of poetry the cxxxviith. Certainly nothing can be more absurd than the error, into which some commentators have fallen, in attributing some of the sublimest of the Psalms to

There occur, moreover, in the writings of the prophets, certain passages, which, although poetical, yet do not properly belong to this species of poetry. I allude to some instances in Isaiah, Habakkuk, and Ezekiel, which appear to constitute complete poems of different kinds, odes as well as elegies. These also being excepted, all the other predictions of the prophets (including such as are extant in the historical books, most of which have been occasionally quoted in the course of these Lectures) form a whole, and constitute that particular species of poetry which I distinguish by the appellation of *prophetic.*—I shall now endeavour, in the first place, to offer to your consideration such a description of this species of poetry, as may serve to distinguish it from the rest; and afterwards, to delineate the peculiar character of each of the prophets, as far as may be consistent with the object of these Lectures.

The genius of the prophetic poetry is to be explored by a due attention to the nature and design of prophecy itself. The immediate design of all prophecy is to inform or amend those generations that precede the events predicted; and it is usually calculated either to excite their fears and apprehensions, or to afford them consolation. The means which it employs for the accomplishment of these effects are, a general amplification of the subject, whether it be of the menacing or consolatory kind, copious descriptions, diversified, pompous, and sublime: in this also it necessarily avoids too great a degree of exactness, and too formal a display of the minuter circumstances; rather employing a vague and general style of description, expressive only of the nature and magnitude of the subject; for prophecy, in its very nature, implies some degree of obscurity, and is always, as the apostle elegantly expresses it, "like a light glimmering in a dark place, until the day dawn, and the day-star arise."* But there is also a further use and intention of prophecy, which regards those who live after the prediction is accomplished; and that is the demonstration and attestation which it affords of the Divine veracity: This evidently appears to demand

---

Ezra, than whose style nothing can be meaner or more ungraceful. Indeed I have myself some doubts concerning the cxxxixth, which I am more inclined to attribute to Jeremiah, or some contemporary of his; and I think the taste and spirit of the bard, who sung so sweetly elsewhere the miseries of his nation, may very plainly be discerned in it.—M.

* 2 Peter ii. 9.

a different form of enunciation; for, correct language, apt imagery, and an exact display of circumstances, are peculiarly adapted to this purpose. Since, however, a very plain description would totally withdraw the veil of obscurity, a more sparing use of this liberty of particularising is frequently adequate to that purpose; for the particular notification of one or two circumstances, united with a general propriety in the imagery, the proper adaptation of which shall appear after the event, will afford an accumulation of evidence that cannot be withstood, as might be demonstrated in a number of instances.* The prophetic style, therefore, is chiefly constructed on the former principle; that is, it commonly prefers a general mode of amplifying and elevating the subject, rarely and cautiously descending to a circumstantial detail.

There is also another particular, which must not be omitted. Prophecy frequently takes in, at a single glance, a variety of events, distinct both in nature and time, and pursues the extreme and principal design through all its different gradations. From this cause also it principally employs general ideas, and expresses them by imagery of established use and acceptation; for these are equally capable of comprehending the general scope of the Divine counsels, and of accompanying the particular progressions of circumstances, situations, and events: they may be easily applied to the intermediate relations and ends, but must be more accurately weighed and proportioned to equal the magnitude and importance of the ultimate design.

If such be the genius of prophecy; if it be chiefly employed in describing only the exterior lineaments of events, and in depicting and embellishing general effects; it will not be difficult to understand with how much advantage it may make use of the assistance and ministration of poetry, and in particular of the parabolic style; the nature of which, as I have already copiously stated, is to afford an abundance and variety of imagery of established use and acceptation, from which every subject may receive the most ample and the most proper embellishments. Hence, too, we may easily collect the peculiar character of the prophetic poetry.

This species of poetry is more ornamented, more splendid, and more florid than any other. It abounds more in

---

* See Lect. 9, conclusion.

11

imagery, at least in that species of imagery which, in the parabolic style, is of common and established acceptation, and which, by means of a settled analogy always preserved, is transferred from certain and definite objects to express indefinite and general ideas. Of all the images proper to the parabolic style, it most frequently introduces those which are taken from natural objects, and from sacred history: it abounds most in metaphors, allegories, comparisons, and even in copious and diffuse descriptions. It possesses all that genuine enthusiasm, which is the natural attendant on inspiration; it excels in the brightness of imagination, and in clearness and energy of diction, and consequently rises to an uncommon pitch of sublimity: hence also it often is very happy in the expression and delineation of the passions, though more commonly employed in the exciting of them: this indeed is its immediate object; over this it presides as its peculiar province.

In respect to the order, disposition, and symmetry of a perfect poem of the prophetic kind, I do not know of any certain definition which will admit of general application. Naturally free, and of too ardent a spirit to be confined by rule, it is usually guided by the nature of the subject only, and the impulse of Divine inspiration. There are not wanting, it is true, instances of great elegance and perfection in these particulars. Among the shorter prophecies, I need only mention those of Balaam, each of which is possessed of a certain accuracy of arrangement and symmetry of form: they open with an elegant exordium, they proceed with a methodical continuation of the subject, and are wound up with a full and graceful conclusion. There are many similar instances in the books of the Prophets, and particularly in Isaiah, which deserve the highest commendation, and may with propriety be classed with the most perfect and regular specimens of poetry. I shall select for your consideration one example from that most accomplished writer, which is embellished with all the most striking ornaments of poetry: from this instance I shall not only demonstrate with what accuracy the prophetic Muse sometimes preserves the proper order and arrangement of the parts and circumstances; but I shall be enabled, at the same time, to illustrate most of those positions which I have now laid down, concerning the nature and genius of the prophetic poetry. Such an illustration will probably be not unnecessary; since it is to be apprehended, that what has been remarked only in general terms upon so subtile and difficult a subject, may, without the aid of example, appear not a little perplexed and obscure.

The thirty-fourth and thirty-fifth chapters of Isaiah contain a remarkable prophecy. It is a simple, regular, and perfect poem, consisting of two parts, according to the nature of the subject, which, as to its general properties, is explained with the utmost perspicuity. The first part of the prophecy contains a denunciation of extraordinary punishment, indeed nothing short of total destruction, against the enemies of the church of God; and afterwards, in consequence of this event, a full and complete restoration is promised to the church itself. The prophet introduces the subject by a magnificent exordium, invoking universal nature to the observation of these events, in which the whole world should seem to be interested:

> "Draw near, O ye nations, and hearken;
> And attend unto me, O ye people!
> Let the earth hear, and the fulness thereof;
> The world, and all that spring from it."*

He then publishes the decree of JEHOVAH concerning the extirpation of all those nations against whom " his wrath is kindled:" and he amplifies this act of vengeance and destruction by an admirable selection of splendid imagery, all of which is of the same kind with that which is made use of by the prophets upon similar occasions; the nature of which is to exaggerate the force, the magnitude, atrocity, and importance of the impending visitation; whilst nothing determinate is specified concerning the manner, the time, the place, or other minute circumstances. He first exhibits that truly martial picture of slaughter and destruction after a victory:

> "And their slain shall be cast out;
> And from their carcases their stench shall ascend;
> And the mountains shall melt down with blood.†

He then takes a bolder flight, and illustrates his description by imagery borrowed from the Mosaic chaos, (which is a common source of figurative language on these occasions, and is appropriated to the expression of the downfall of nations,) and as if he were displaying the total subversion of the universe itself:

* Chap. xxxiv. 1.   † Ver. 3.

" And all the host of heaven shall waste away ;
And the heavens shall be rolled up like a scroll :
And all their host shall wither ;
As the withered leaf droppeth from the vine,
And as the blighted fruit from the fig-tree."*

A different image is immediately introduced; a solemn sacrifice is celebrated, and an uncommon number of victims are displayed. JEHOVAH himself takes a part in this magnificent scene, and every circumstance is brought directly before our eyes :

" For my sword is made bare in the heavens ;
Behold, on Edom it shall descend ;
And on the people justly by me devoted to destruction.
The sword of JEHOVAH is satiated with blood ;
It is pampered with fat :
With the blood of lambs and of goats ;
With the fat of the reins of rams :
For JEHOVAH celebrateth a sacrifice in Botzra,
And a great slaughter in the land of Edom.†

The goats, the rams, the bulls, the flocks, and other animals which are mentioned in this passage and those which follow, are commonly used by the prophets to denote the haughty, ferocious, and insolent tyrants and chiefs of those nations which were inimical to God. On the same principle we may explain the allusion to Botzra and Idumea, a city and nation in the highest degree obnoxious to the people of God. These, however, the prophecy seems only slightly or cursorily to glance at : the phraseology is indeed of that kind which expresses generals by particulars ; or consists, as I formerly remarked, of a figure taken from a determinate and definite object, and by analogy applied in a more extensive sense ; in which respect the very words which are made use of have, in this place, a peculiar form and propriety.‡ But the same circumstance is again described by a succession of new and splendid images borrowed

* Chap. xxxiv. 4.
† Ver. 5, 6. In this prophecy Edom is particularly marked out as an object of the Divine vengeance. The principal provocation of Edom was their insulting the Jews in their distress, and joining against them with their enemies the Chaldeans. See Amos i. 11. Ezek. xxv. 12; xxxv. 15. Psalm cxxxvii. 7. Accordingly, the Edomites were, together with the rest of the neighbouring nations, ravaged and laid waste by Nebuchadnezzar. See Jer. xxv. 15—26. Mal. i. 2 —4 ; and see Marsham, *Can. Chron. Sæc.* xviii., who calls this the age of the destruction of cities. Bishop Lowth's *Isaiah,* 298.—T.
‡ See Lowth and Vitringa on the place, and on chap. lxiii. 1.

from the overthrow of Sodom, which, as was formerly demonstrated, may be termed one of the common-places of the inspired poets:

" For it is the day of vengeance to JEHOVAH;
  The year of recompence to the defender of the cause of Sion.
  And her torrents shall be turned into pitch:
  And her dust into sulphur;
  And her whole land shall become burning pitch:
  By night or by day it shall not be extinguished;
  For ever shall her smoke ascend:
  From generation to generation she shall lie desert;
  To everlasting ages no one shall pass through her."*

Lastly, the same event is prefigured under the image of a vast and solitary desert, to which, according to the Divine decree, that region is devoted.† This description the prophet afterwards improves, diversifies, and enlarges, by the addition of several important circumstances, all which, however, have a certain analogy or connexion with each other.

The other part of the poem is constructed upon similar principles, and exhibits a beautiful contrast to the preceding scene. The imagery possesses every possible advantage of ornament and variety: it is, like the former, altogether of a general kind, and of extensive application; but the meaning is plain and perspicuous. Many of the preceding images are taken from the sacred history; the following are almost entirely from the objects of nature:

" The desert and the waste shall be glad;
  And the wilderness shall rejoice and flourish:
  Like the rose shall it beautifully flourish;
  And the well-watered plain of Jordan shall also rejoice:
  And the glory of Lebanon shall be given unto it,
  The beauty of Carmel and of Sharon:
  These shall behold the glory of JEHOVAH,
  The majesty of our God."‡

I formerly remarked the extensive application of Lebanon and Carmel in a figurative sense,§ and that they are sometimes expressive even of the Divine glory and majesty.||

* Chap. xxxiv. 8, 9, 10.

† Ver. 11, &c.—Ver. 16. "For פ׳ הוא three MSS. have פ׳ יהוה: two others have it in a corrected hand. The LXX also read יהוה."—K. Two MSS. *Erfurt*, read פיהו. See Bib. Heb. Michaelis on the place.

‡ Chap. xxxv. 1, 2.   § See Lect. 6. || See Lect. 8.

The cultivation and watering of a barren and rocky soil is so frequently, I might say invariably, in the parabolic style, employed to denote the divine grace and spiritual endowments, that there is no necessity for any further explanation of this symbol; nor is the succeeding imagery, which, according to a similar analogy, seems to illustrate the same event, less clear and perspicuous.

To him who attentively reads and considers the whole poem, the order and arrangement of the subject will be more fully apparent. The passages which I have noted will, however, I apprehend be sufficient to demonstrate the species of imagery, the style and colours, most congenial to the prophetic Muse: they will also, I flatter myself, be sufficient in some measure to explain the manner in which she contrives to display, in the strongest colours, the general nature, magnitude, and importance of events; and at the same time to leave the particular situations, the intermediate gradations, and all the minuter circumstances, concealed under the bold and prominent features of the description, till the accomplishment of the prediction. There are, indeed, one or two passages in this prophecy which would serve to illustrate this position;* in the rest, the circum-

---

* See chap. xxxv. 4, 5, 6. 8, which, without a doubt, in their proximate sense relate to the first coming of the Messiah; to the miracles which were performed by him; to the preaching of the Gospel; and the effusion of the Holy Spirit. In the 8th, the absurd interpunctuation, rendered sacred by the authority of the Masorites, creates a degree of almost impenetrable obscurity. It is, however, a true pentacolon, and ought to be distributed in this manner:

" And an highway shall be there;
And it shall be called the way of holiness :
No unclean person shall pass through it :
But he himself shall be with them, walking in the way,
And the foolish shall not err therein."

HE, that is, our God, spoken of before in the 4th verse; ὃς ἐσκήνωσεν ἐν ἡμῖν, καὶ εἰσῆλθε καὶ ἐξῆλθεν ἐφ ἡμᾶς. Thus the Chal. the Syr. the Vulg. and some of the more modern translators, have distinguished them. Vitringa, who is by far the most learned of commentators, but too much a slave to the authority of the Masorites, has in vain attempted a refutation of them.

Houbigant remarks, that the LXX, in the 2nd verse, for וְרֹכֶן read יָרֹדְ; concerning which reading, conceiving it to be of considerable importance, I consulted Dr. Kennicott. Though the manuscript copies, however, afforded no assistance towards the restoration of this word, he very kindly communicated some critical remarks upon the whole chapter, which I shall endeavour to explain with as much brevity as possible.

Ver. 1. " Jesusom—they will rejoice. The old versions do not allow of the suffix. Perhaps the מ (m) may have been added from the beginning of the next word. It was customary in the Hebrew manuscripts, in order to fill up one line,

P

stances and progress of the particular events are not yet unfolded: for this prophecy is evidently one of those which are not yet completely fulfilled, and of which the greater part at least is yet deposited in the secret counsels of the Most High.

That I may not however conclude this Lecture without exhibiting the form of some prophetic poem complete in all parts, I have selected for this purpose one of the prophecies of Balaam, which I so lately mentioned, and which in the course of these Lectures have more than once deservedly attracted our attention: for, indeed, I do not know that the whole scope of the Hebrew poetry contains any thing more

to take the initial letter or letters of the word that began the next, which, however, they failed not to copy in its proper place."

Ver. 2. It is well observed by Houbigant, that the Seventy read this differently; for, instead of *Gilat-ve-ranen*, with joy and singing, they certainly read other words, which they rendered τα ερημα τε Ιορδανε, the desert places of Jordan; in the same manner also the Arabic; and this reading seems most perfectly to agree with the design of the prophet. He thinks it ought to be read *Galat Jordan*, the marshes of Jordan; I would myself prefer *Gidah Jordan*, the bank of Jordan. In the present reading there is neither meaning nor construction, for an antecedent is wanting to the word לה, to it. "The word *Gedot* occurs in four places, and thrice is joined to Jordan (as in this;) and though the singular *Gidah* does not elsewhere occur, it is found in the Chaldee *Gida*, a bank."

"Six MSS. for לה read לך. If this be admitted, the version will be,

> "And thou also shalt exult, O bank of Jordan;
> The glory of Lebanon shall be given unto thee."

"But perhaps the true reading may be *ve-thagali et*, and thou shalt exult, O bank; for the final *Pe* is often so written that it can scarcely be distinguished from the *Tau*, as is the case with the same word in two MSS."

Ver. 7. "*Rabetzah*, a couching-place, should, it appears, be in the plural to agree with *thanim*, dragons: our most ancient MS. has *mem* for *he*; and another has *rabitzah*, retaining the *jod*, though in a different place. The meaning, however, of this verse is:

> "In the place which was inhabited by dragons,
> Shall grass spring up instead of reeds and rushes."

Ver. 8. "Not only the Syr. but also fourteen MSS. omit the second *ve-derach*. Houbigant thinks, that for לה we ought to read לו; and rightly, for the suffix in the following verse, which relates to the same, is masculine, יערבנו."

Ver. 9. "After *ve-halechu*, shall walk, the word *shom*, there, seems wanting; it is added by the LXX and the Ar."—K.

Vitringa approves of the opinion of the Chaldee paraphrast, who, in ver. 8, thus translates: "And those who pass that way shall not faint." He, however, has not embraced the reading, for it is plain he did not perceive in what manner it had been formed from the Hebrew text. The Chaldean paraphrast, doubtless, instead of ולא חמו read ודוא למי. This remark was furnished me, with many others, by a distinguished character, whose great erudition reflects honour upon a very exalted situation.—*Author's Note.*

exquisite or perfect. This which is at present under our consideration, abounds in gay and splendid imagery copied immediately from the tablet of Nature; and is chiefly conspicuous for the glowing elegance of the style, and the form and diversity of the figures. Though every attempt to display the beauties of the Hebrew imagery in the poetry of another language must fall greatly short of the design, it will yet give a little variety to our studies, to intersperse them occasionally with modern verse. On these occasions, as indeed on every other, I must rely upon the candour of this audience to accept in good part the willing tribute of my faint endeavours.*

> In proud array thy tents expand,
> O Israel, o'er the subject land;
> As the broad vales in prospect rise,
> As gardens by the water spread,
> As cedars of majestic size,
> That shade the sacred fountain's head.
>
> Thy torrents shall the earth o'erflow,
> O'erwhelming each obdurate foe:
> In vain the mind essays to trace
> The glories of thy countless race;
> In vain thy king's imperial state
> Shall haughty Agag emulate.
>
> His mighty God's protecting hand
> Led him from Pharaoh's tyrant land.
> Strong as the beast that rules the plain,
> What power his fury shall restrain?
> Who dares resist, his force shall feel.
> The nations see, and trembling fly,
> Or in th' unequal conflict die;
> And glut with blood his thirsty steel.
>
> With aspect keen he marked his prey,—
> He couched—in secret ambush lay.
> Who shall the furious lion dare?
> Who shall unmov'd his terrors see?
> —Blest, who for thee exalts his prayer!
> And curst the wretch who curseth thee!

* See Numb. xxiv. 5—9.

LECTURE XXI.

THE PECULIAR CHARACTER OF EACH OF THE PROPHETS.

The particular style and character of the different Prophets: what parts of each of them are poetical, and what otherwise—Nothing deserving of notice of this kind in the poetry of Greece—In the Latin poetry the fourth Eclogue of Virgil is remarkable: that poem much more obscure than it is generally accounted, and has not hitherto been properly explained.

" THE Prophets have each their peculiar character," says Jerome, speaking of the twelve minor Prophets.* The same, however, might more properly be affirmed with respect to the three greater: for Isaiah is extremely different from Jeremiah; nor is it easy to conceive any composition of the same denomination more dissimilar to both of them than the book of Ezekiel.

Isaiah, the first of the prophets, both in order and dignity, abounds in such transcendent excellences, that he may be properly said to afford the most perfect model of the prophetic poetry. He is at once elegant and sublime, forcible and ornamented; he unites energy with copiousness, and dignity with variety. In his sentiments there is uncommon elevation and majesty; in his imagery, the utmost propriety, elegance, dignity, and diversity; in his language, uncommon beauty and energy; and, notwithstanding the obscurity of his subjects, a surprising degree of clearness and simplicity. To these we may add, there is such sweetness in the poetical composition of his sentences, whether it proceed from art or genius, that if the Hebrew poetry at present is possessed of any remains of its native grace and harmony, we shall chiefly find them in the writings of Isaiah: so that the saying of Ezekiel may most justly be applied to this prophet,

" Thou art the confirmed examplar of measures,
Full of wisdom, and perfect in beauty."†

* Præf. in xii. Proph.   † Ezek. xxviii. 12.

8

Isaiah greatly excels, too, in all the graces of method, order, connexion, and arrangement; though in asserting this we must not forget the nature of the prophetic impulse, which bears away the mind with irresistible violence, and frequently in rapid transitions from near to remote objects, from human to divine: we must also be careful in remarking the limits of particular predictions, since, as they are now extant, they are often improperly connected, without any marks of discrimination; which injudicious arrangement, on some occasions, creates almost insuperable difficulties. I lately produced a specimen from this Prophet of a complete poem disposed in the most perspicuous order; and in the former part of his volume many instances may be found, where the particular predictions are distinctly marked. The latter part, which I suppose to commence at the fortieth chapter, is perhaps the most elegant specimen remaining of inspired composition, and yet in this respect is attended with considerable difficulty: it is, in fact, a body or collection of different prophecies, nearly allied to each other as to the subject, which for that reason having a sort of connexion, are not to be separated but with the utmost difficulty. The general subject is the restoration of the church: its deliverance from captivity; the destruction of idolatry; the vindication of the Divine power and truth; the consolation of the Israelites, the Divine invitation which is extended to them, their incredulity, impiety, and rejection; the calling in of the Gentiles; the restoration of the chosen people: the glory and felicity of the church in its perfect state; and the ultimate destruction of the wicked—are all set forth with a sufficient respect to order and method. If we read these passages with attention, and duly regard the nature and genius of the mystical allegory, as explained in the eleventh Lecture—at the same time remembering, that all these points have been frequently touched upon in other prophecies promulged at different times—we shall neither find any irregularity in the arrangement of the whole, nor any want of order and connexion as to matter or sentiment in the different parts. I must add, that I esteem the whole book of Isaiah to be poetical, a few passages excepted, which, if brought together, would not at most exceed the bulk of five or six chapters.

Jeremiah, though deficient neither in elegance nor sublimity, must give place in both to Isaiah. Jerome* seems to

* Præf. in Jer.—He probably adopted this opinion from his masters the Jews.

object against him a sort of rusticity of language; no vestige
of which, I must however confess, I have been able to discover.   His sentiments, it is true, are not always the most
elevated, nor are his periods always neat and compact; but
these are faults common to those writers whose principal
aim is to excite the gentler affections, and to call forth the
tear of sympathy or sorrow. This observation is very strongly
exemplified in the Lamentations, where these are the prevailing passions; it is, however, frequently instanced in the
prophecies of this author, and most of all in the beginning
of the book,* which is chiefly poetical.   The middle of it is
almost entirely historical. The latter part, again, consisting
of the six last chapters, is altogether poetical :† it contains
several different predictions, which are distinctly marked;
and in these the prophet approaches very near the sublimity
of Isaiah. On the whole, however, I can scarcely pronounce
above half the book of Jeremiah to be poetical.

Ezekiel is much inferior to Jeremiah in elegance; in sublimity he is not even excelled by Isaiah: but his sublimity
is of a totally different kind.‡ He is deep, vehement, tragi-

---

Of the more modern rabbies, Abarbanel (Præf. in Jer.) complains grievously of the
grammatical ignorance of the prophet, and his frequent solecisms; which he says
Ezra corrected by the Keri or marginal notes, for he remarks that they occur more
frequently in him than elsewhere.   Absurd and ridiculous! to attribute the errors of
transcribers, which occur in almost every part of the Hebrew text, to the sacred
writers themselves.   The greater part of these errors he would indeed have found
scarcely to exist, if he had consulted the more correct copies which remain even at
this day; for among these very marginal readings, there are but few which, in the
more ancient MSS., are not found in the text.   Walton has long since given a remarkable example of this kind, *Prolegom:* iv. 12.   The collations of Dr. Kennicott will
afford many more.—*Author's Note.*

* See the whole of chap. ix; chap. xiv. 17, &c.; xx. 14—18.

† Chap. xlvi.—li. to ver. 59. Chap. lii. properly belongs to the Lamentations, to
which it serves as an exordium.

‡ I must confess that I feel not perfectly satisfied with myself, when, in a matter
entirely dependent upon taste, I can by no means bring myself to agree with our
Author.   So far from esteeming Ezekiel equal to Isaiah in sublimity, I am inclined
rather to think, that he displays more art and luxuriance in amplifying and decorating
his subject than is consistent with the poetical fervour, or, indeed, with true sublimity.
He is in general an imitator; and yet he has the art of giving an air of novelty and
ingenuity, but not of grandeur and sublimity, to all his composition. The imagery
which is familiar to the Hebrew poetry he constantly makes use of; and those figures
which were invented by others, but were only glanced at, or partially displayed by
those who first used them, he dwells upon, and depicts with such accuracy and copiousness, that he leaves nothing to add to them, nothing to be supplied by the reader's
imagination.   On this score his ingenuity is to be commended, and he is therefore of use to his readers, because he enables them better to understand the ancient

cal; the only sensation he affects to excite is the terrible:
his sentiments are elevated, fervid, full of fire, indignant;

poets; but he certainly does not strike with admiration, or display any trait of
sublimity.

Of this I will propose only one example; many of the same kind may be found
in looking over the writings of this prophet. In describing a great slaughter, it is
very common in the best poets to introduce a slight allusion to birds of prey. Thus
in the Iliad:

> Αυτους δ' ἑλωρια τευχε κυνεσσιν
> Οιωνοισι τε πασι——

> " Whose limbs, unburied on the naked shore,
> Devouring dogs and hungry vultures tore."—Pope.

Thus, it is the language of boasting in the historical part of Scripture, " I will give
thy flesh unto the fowls of the air, and unto the beasts of the field," 1 Sam. xvii.
44.   Asaph, also, in Psal. lxxviii. 48, " He shall give their cattle to the hail, and
their flocks to the birds." Moses is still more sublime, Deut. xxxii. 23, 24.

> " I will spend mine arrows upon them.
> *They shall be* eaten up with hunger, a prey unto birds,
> And to bitter destruction !
> I will also send the teeth of beasts upon them,
> With the poison of the reptiles of the earth."

But Habakkuk is more excellent than either of the former : chap. iii. 5, speaking
of the victory of Jehovah over his enemies:

> " Before him went the pestilence,
> And his footsteps were traced by the birds ;"

Doubtless, the *birds of prey.* Isaiah is somewhat more copious, chap. xxxiv. 6, 7.

> " For JEHOVAH celebrateth a sacrifice in Botzra,
> And a great slaughter in the land of Edom.
> And the wild goats shall fall down with them;
> And the bullocks, together with the bulls :
> And their own land shall be drunken with their blood,
> And their dust shall be enriched with fat."

These and other images Ezekiel has adopted, and has studiously amplified with
singular ingenuity ; and by exhausting all the imagery applicable to the subject, has
in a manner made them his own. In the first prediction of the slaughter of Magog,
the whole chapter consists of a most magnificent amplification of all the circumstances and apparatus of war, so that scarcely any part of the subject is left untouched : he adds afterwards, in a bold and unusual style—" Thus, Son of man,
saith JEHOVAH, speak unto every feathered fowl, and to every beast of the field :
Assemble yourselves, and come ; gather yourselves on every side to the banquet
which I prepare for you, a great banquet on the mountains of Israel. Ye shall eat
flesh, and ye shall drink blood : ye shall eat the flesh of the mighty, and drink the
blood of the princes of the earth, of rams, of lambs, of goats, and of bullocks, all of
them fatlings of Bashan. Ye shall eat fat till ye be satisfied, and drink blood till ye
be drunken in the banquet which I have prepared for you. Ye shall be filled at my
table with horses and chariots, with mighty men, and with men of valour, saith the
Lord JEHOVAH ;" Ezek. xxxviii. 17—20. In this I seem to read a poet who is
unwilling to omit any thing of the figurative kind which presents itself to his
mind, and would think his poem deficient if he did not adorn it with every

his imagery is crowded, magnificent, terrific, sometimes
almost to disgust; his language is pompous, solemn, austere,
rough, and at times unpolished: he employs frequent repetitions, not for the sake of grace or elegance, but from the
vehemence of passion and indignation. Whatever subject he
treats of, that he sedulously pursues, from that he rarely
departs, but cleaves as it were to it; whence the connexion is
in general evident and well preserved. In many respects he is
perhaps excelled by the other prophets: but in that species of
composition to which he seems by nature adapted, the forcible,
the impetuous, the great and solemn, not one of the sacred
writers is superior to him. His diction is sufficiently perspicuous; all his obscurity consists in the nature of the subject.
Visions (as for instance, among others, those of Hosea, Amos,
and Jeremiah) are necessarily dark and confused. The greater
part of Ezekiel, towards the middle of the book especially,
is poetical, whether we regard the matter or the diction.

probable fiction which could be added : and for this very reason I cannot help placing
him rather in the middle than superior class. Observe how the author of the Apocalypse, who is in general an imitator, but endued with a sublimer genius, and in
whose prose all the splendour of poetry may be discerned, has conducted these sentiments of Ezekiel: "I saw an Angel standing in the sun ; and he cried with a loud
voice unto the fowls that fly in the midst of heaven, Come and gather yourselves
together unto the supper of the great God ; that ye may eat of the flesh of kings,
and of captains, and the flesh of mighty men, and the flesh of horses, and of them
that sit upon them, and the flesh of all men, both free and bond, both small and
great ;" Rev. xix. 17, 18.

But Ezekiel goes yet further : so delighted is he with this image, so intent is he
upon the by-paths of the Muses, that he gives even the trees, taking them for empires, to the birds, and their shades or ghosts he consigns to the infernal regions.
Thus, chap. xxxi. 13—15, " Upon his trunk shall all the fowls of heaven remain,
and all the beasts of the field shall be upon his branches. To the end that none of
all the trees by the waters shall exalt themselves for their height, nor shoot up their
top among the thick boughs ; neither their trees stand up in their height, all that
drink water : for they are all delivered unto death to the nether parts of the earth
in the midst of the children of men, with them that go down to the pit," &c. In
this we find novelty and variety, great fertility of genius, but no sublimity.

I had almost forgotten to mention, that Ezekiel lived at a period when the Hebrew language was visibly on the decline. And when we compare him with the
Latin poets who succeeded the Augustan age, we may find some resemblance in the
style, something that indicates the old age of poetry.—M.

If I may speak my mind freely of Ezekiel, I must confess I think his fault is
neither a want of novelty nor of sublimity, but of grace and uniformity. There is
so much inequality in his composition, that scarcely any figure is kept up without
sinking into the *bathos* ; and if he introduce in one line a grand image, he pays no
attention to the supporting of it in the next. What the Gottingen Professor remarks
concerning the decline of the Hebrew language, evident in the poetry of this author
is very just.—T.

His periods, however, are frequently so rude and incompact, that I am often at a loss how to pronounce concerning his performance in this respect.

Isaiah, Jeremiah, and Ezekiel, as far as relates to style, may be said to hold the same rank among the Hebrews, as Homer, Simonides, and Æschylus, among the Greeks.

Hosea is the first in order of the minor prophets, and is perhaps, Jonah excepted, the most ancient of them all. His style exhibits the appearance of very remote antiquity: It is pointed, energetic, and concise: it bears a distinguished mark of poetical composition, in that pristine brevity and condensation which is observable in the sentences, and which later writers have in some measure neglected. This peculiarity has not escaped the observation of Jerome: "He is altogether," says he, speaking of this prophet, "laconic and sententious."* But this very circumstance, which anciently was supposed, no doubt, to impart uncommon force and elegance, in the present ruinous state of the Hebrew literature, is productive of so much obscurity, that although the general subject of this writer be sufficiently obvious, he is the most difficult and perplexed of all the prophets. There is, however, another reason for the obscurity of his style. Hosea prophesied during the reigns of the four kings of Judah—Uzziah, Jotham, Ahaz, and Hezekiah ; the duration of his ministry, therefore, in whatever manner we calculate, must include a very considerable space of time: we have now only a small volume of his remaining, which, it seems, contains his principal prophecies; and these are extant in a continued series, with no marks of distinction as to the times in which they were published, or the subjects of which they treat. There is, therefore, no cause to wonder if, in perusing the prophecies of Hosea, we sometimes find ourselves in a similar predicament with those who consulted the scattered leaves of the Sibyl.

The style of Joel is essentially different from that of Hosea; but the general character of his diction, though of a different kind, is not less poetical. He is elegant, perspicuous, copious, and fluent; he is also sublime, animated, and energetic. In the first and second chapters he displays the full force of the prophetic poetry, and shows how naturally it inclines to the use of metaphors, allegories, and comparisons. Nor is the connexion of the matter less clear and evident,

* Præf. in xii. Proph.

than the complexion of the style: this is exemplified in the display of the impending evils which gave rise to the prophecy; the exhortation to repentance: the promises of happiness and success, both terrestrial and eternal, to those who become truly penitent; the restoration of the Israelites; and the vengeance to be taken of their adversaries. But while we allow this just commendation to his perspicuity both in language and arrangement, we must not deny that there is sometimes great obscurity observable in his subject, and particularly in the latter part of the prophecy.

Jerome calls Amos "rude in speech, but not in knowledge;"* applying to him what St. Paul modestly professes of himself.† Many have followed the authority of Jerome in speaking of this prophet, as if he were indeed quite rude, ineloquent, and destitute of all the embellishments of composition. The matter is, however, far otherwise. Let any person who has candour and perspicacity enough to judge, not from the man but from his writings, open the volume of his predictions, and he will, I think, agree with me, that our shepherd "is not a whit behind the very chief of the prophets."‡ He will agree, that as in sublimity and magnificence he is almost equal to the greatest, so in splendour of diction and elegance of expression he is scarcely inferior to any. The same celestial spirit indeed actuated Isaiah and Daniel in the court and Amos in the sheepfolds, constantly selecting such interpreters of the Divine will as were best adapted to the occasion, and sometimes "from the mouths of babes and sucklings perfecting praise;" occasionally employing the natural eloquence of some, and occasionally making others eloquent.

The style of Micah is for the most part close, forcible, pointed, and concise; sometimes approaching the obscurity of Hosea; in many parts animated and sublime, and in general truly poetical.

None of the minor prophets, however, seem to equal Nahum in boldness, ardour, and sublimity. His prophecy too forms a regular and perfect poem: the exordium is not merely magnificent, it is truly majestic; the preparation for the destruction of Nineveh, and the description of its downfall and desolation, are expressed in the most vivid colours, and are bold and luminous in the highest degree.

---

* Prooem. Comment. in Amos.   † 2 Cor. xi. 6.   ‡ 2 Cor. xi. 5.

The style of Habakkuk is also poetical, especially in his ode, which indeed may be accounted among the most perfect specimens of that class.*   The like remark will also apply to Zephaniah; but there is nothing very striking or uncommon either in the arrangement of his matter or the complexion of his style.

Of Obadiah there is little to be said: the only specimen of his genius extant being very short, and the greater part of it included in one of the prophecies of Jeremiah.† Jonah and Daniel I have already considered as mere historical commentaries.

Haggai, Zechariah, and Malachi, are the only remaining prophets.   The first of these is altogether prosaic, as well as the greater part of the second: towards the conclusion of the prophecy there are some poetical passages, and those highly ornamented; they are also perspicuous, considering that they are the production of the most obscure of all the prophetic writers.‡   The last of the prophetical books, that of Malachi, is written in a kind of middle style, which seems to indicate that the Hebrew poetry, from the time of the Babylonish captivity, was in a declining state, and, being past its prime and vigour, was then fast verging towards the debility of age.

Thus far I have thought proper to deliver my sentiments, as distinctly as I was able, concerning the writings of the Prophets, and those parts which are to be accounted poetical or otherwise.   This I did with a view of clearly explaining my conjecture (for I dare not dignify it with any higher appellation) concerning the prophetic poetry;—a conjecture which, though I will confess it is not without its difficulties, and which must, after all, depend in some degree upon opinion, yet I flatter myself you will concur with me in admitting not to be utterly destitute of foundation.

I should now, according to the nature of my plan, proceed to speak of the prophetic poetry of the Greeks, if, indeed, any thing had been transmitted to us, even from

---

* On a very accurate perusal of Habakkuk, I find him a great imitator of former poets, but with some new additions of his own; not, however, in the manner of Ezekiel, but with much brevity, and with no common degree of sublimity. Ezekiel, for the most part, through his extreme copiousness, flags behind those whom he imitates! Habakkuk either rises superior, or at least keeps on an equality with them. —M.

† Compare Obad. 1—9, with Jer. xlix. 14, 15, 16 ; 7. 9, 10.

‡ See chap. ix. x. and beginning of the xith.

their most celebrated oracles, deserving, I will not say to be compared with the sacred prophets, but even to be mentioned at all.   The fact is, there is no such poem now extant, nor do I believe there ever was one of that kind among the Greeks: a few verses there are indeed remaining, and those not above mediocrity; for the Pythian Apollo, if we may credit the Greeks themselves, was not always upon the best terms with the Muses.*   It appears, therefore, that he did not fail to excite the ridicule of sensible persons, not only for his ambiguous and enigmatical divinations, but for ignorance in the art of versification: nay, even the rude and superstitious, who gave him the amplest credit for the veracity of his predictions, could not help confessing that he was a very indifferent poet.†

Among the literature of the Romans, however, there is extant a much celebrated, and indeed admirable poem of this kind, no less remarkable for the elegance and perspicuity of the style, than for the obscurity and darkness of the subject: I speak of the fourth Eclogue of Virgil,‡ which it would be inexcusable to pass unnoticed in this place, since, from the first ages of Christianity, an opinion has prevailed, that this poem bore some remote relation to those genuine remains of prophecy which have been the subject of this Lecture, and indeed that the substance of it was originally

---

* " I find, too, that some of the Oracles of Apollo have not escaped ridicule in this respect, though the obscurity of prophecy renders them in general so difficult to decipher, that the hearers have no leisure to bestow on an examination of the metre."—Merc. in Lucian's Dial. entitled *Jupiter Tragœdus.*

" A response from an Oracle in verse having been recited by one of the company—I have often wondered (says Diogenianus) at the meanness and imperfection of the verses which conveyed the oracular responses; especially considering that Apollo is the president of the Muses, and, one should imagine, would no less interest himself in the style of his own predictions, than in the harmony of odes and other poetry ; besides that he certainly must be superior to Homer and Hesiod in poetic taste and ability.   Notwithstanding this, we find many of the Oracles, both as to style and metre, deficient in prosody, and in every species of poetical merit."—Plutarch, *Inquiry why the Pythia now ceases to deliver her Oracles in Verse.*

† Just as the Bishop's observation is concerning the prophetic Oracles of the Greeks, yet whoever will be at the trouble of considering the predictions of Cassandra in the Agamemnon of Æschylus, may easily perceive a peculiarity of imagery and style that would throw some light on the subject itself, as well as serve to illustrate the prophetic phraseology of the Hebrews.—S. H.

‡ The prophecy of the Sibyl in the 6th Æneid might also be referred to as an example : in it the prophetic ecstasy is so admirably expressed, that the art and imitative powers of Virgil may contribute not a little to enable us to understand the language and manner of true prophecy.—M.

derived from some sacred fountain. The manner in which this could happen, I must confess, is not very easy to be explained—whether to account for the fact we have recourse to the ancient Greek translation of the Scriptures, the publication of which was certainly many years anterior to the Roman poet; or whether we suppose that the author might apply to those translations which were made from the sacred writings by some Hellenistic Jews, and which were handed about as the prophecies of the Sibyls.* However this may have been, there are so many and so manifest indications of the fact in the poem itself, that no person who reads it attentively can retain a doubt upon this head. The sentiments, the imagery, even the language itself, has so direct an agreement with the sacred prophets; the subject has so much of intrinsic sublimity and magnificence; and, on the other hand, it is enlivened with so much boldness and spirit, is indeed so free and elevated, that, considering it as the production of the chastest and most reserved of all the later poets, there is something altogether mysterious in the fact, unless we suppose that he deduced his materials from some higher source than his own genius. Though the subject has engaged the attention of some of the first literary characters in the world, the motive, the scheme, the intention of the poet still remains, and I fear ever will remain, undeveloped. The history and state of the Roman commonwealth at the time point out no circumstance or character which appears to bear a sufficient relation to the subject, or which could afford room for such great and magnificent predictions.† This I

---

* See Bishop Chandler's *Vindication of the Christian Religion*, chap. i.; and Grotius on Matt. ii. 1.

† The learned are generally agreed, that the Eclogue in question cannot relate to Salonius, a son of Pollio, born after the capture of Salona, who is spoken of by Servius, if any such person ever existed, since it appears from Dion and Appian, that the expedition of Pollio to Illyricum took place in the following year. Some have conjectured, that this poem relates to C. Asinius Gallus, a son of the same person, and indeed with much greater appearance of probability ; since Asconius Pedianus reports that he had heard from Gallus himself, that this poem was composed in honour of him. See Serv. *ad Eclog.* iv. 11. But Servius himself affirms, that Gallus was born in the preceding year, while Pollio was consul elect : and although such a boast might very well agree with the vanity of a man, who, Augustus himself said, would be desirous of acquiring the sovereignty after his death, though unequal to it, (Tacit. *An.* i. 13;) yet it is scarcely probable that any poet, in common prudence, would predict any thing so magnificent of a son of Pollio. Further, why has he foretold this divine son to him as a consul only, and not as a father ? which would have reflected much more honour on Pollio. Many, from these difficulties, have

will freely confess, that the more I have contemplated this
extraordinary production in this point of view, the less able

attributed the poet's compliment to Cesar Octavius, and to some child born in his
family, as the certain heir to the empire.　Julia, Marcellus, and Drusus, have all
been mentioned.　As to Drusus, neither his age nor person correspond to the prediction ; and though the age of Marcellus might suit it better, yet the personal
disagreement is the same.　With respect to Julia, the daughter of Octavius, there
can be no objection upon either account, if the Eclogue was written during the
pregnancy of Scribonia ; and that it was written before her delivery is credible from
the invocation it contains to Lucina :—" O chaste Lucina aid !"　But let it be
remembered by those who adopt any of these hypotheses, who, and in what station,
Octavius then was ;—not emperor and Augustus, the sovereign lord of the whole
Roman empire, all which dignities became his only after the battle of Actium, nine
years posterior to the date of this Eclogue ; but a triumvir, equal only in authority
with Antony at least, not to speak of Lepidus.　How then could the poet presume
to predict to any son of Octavius, if at that time any son had been born to him,
the succession to the empire ?　But, if we should even grant what is really true,
that no person more worthy or more proper could be found, or to whom these predictions would be better suited, than to some of the descendants of Octavius ; and
if even we should suppose that a son of his was at that time in being ; still there is
one argument sufficient to overturn the whole, and that is, that the Eclogue is
inscribed to Pollio ; for at that time, and even for some time after, Pollio was of
the party of Antony, and in opposition to Octavius.　Let us with this in our minds
take a summary view of the actions of Pollio after the death of Julius Cesar ; and
let us pay some attention to the chronology of the times.　In the year of Rome
711, C. Asinius Pollio having conducted the war against Sextus Pompeius, on his
return from Spain delivered over his army to Antony, after his flight from Mutina.
In the year 713 Pollio held Cisalpine Gaul as Antony's lieutenant ; and, along
with Ventidius, hovered about the rear of Salvidienus, the lieutenant of Octavius,
who was attempting to annoy Lucius Antonius : Lucius being besieged at Perusia,
Pollio in vain attempted his relief, and afterwards retired to Ravenna.　He held
Venetia a long time subject to Antony ; and after having performed great actions
in that part of the world, joined Antony, bringing over with him, at the same time,
Domitius Ænobarbus, and the fleet under his command.　About the end of the
year 714 the peace of Brundusium took place, the negociators of which were Pollio
as consul, on the part of Antony, and Mæcenas on the part of Octavius, and Cocceius on the part of both, as their common friend ; and about this time the 4th
Eclogue of Virgil was written.　In the year 715 Antony sent Pollio, as his lieutenant, against the Parthini into Illyricum ; who triumphed over them in the
month of October.　Thus far Velleius, Appian, and Dio.　About this time a private disagreement took place between Pollio and Octavius ; and Octavius wrote
some indecent verses against Pollio.　Macrob. *Saturn.* ii. 14.　From this time to
the battle of Actium, which happened in 723, in the beginning of September, Pollio
kept himself perfectly neutral, and took no part in the contest between Antony
and Octavius.　" I must not omit," says Velleius, ii. 86, " a remarkable action
and saying of Asinius Pollio.　After the peace of Brundusium" (he should have
said, after his triumph) " he continued in Italy, nor did he ever see the queen, or,
after the mind of Antony became enfeebled by his destructive passion, take any
part in his affairs ; and when Cesar requested him to accompany him to the battle
of Actium, The kindness, said he, which I have rendered Antony, are greater in
reality than those he has rendered me, but the latter are better known to the world.
I will withdraw myself entirely from the contest, and I shall become the prey of
the conqueror."　From considering these facts, it appears to me altogether incredible,

I have felt myself to comprehend it. There is such a splendour of style, such an elegance in the versification, as deceives us at first respecting the obscurity of the matter. But

that Virgil should send, and inscribe to Pollio, a poem in praise of Octavius, and wholly written in celebration of his family.—*Author's Note.*

Whoever will compare the three prophecies of Isaiah, contained in the second, eleventh, and sixty-fifth chapters, with the fourth Eclogue of Virgil, can hardly doubt whether the same images, united in combinations opposite to the analogies of nature, applied to similar subjects, and by both writers in the way of prediction, must not have ultimately originated in one common source, and the latter have been derived from the former. If so, the agreement in question may be rationally accounted for, especially if it appear that the poet has himself referred to the Jewish Scriptures as the fountain of such images, in the same manner as to the writings of Homer, &c. for others of Grecian origin. [See Georgic. B. iii., l. 12, and the Notes on Vathek, p. 269.] It seems, however, by his Lordship's concession, that the mystery would be in a great measure solved, could it once be shown that the prophecy of Virgil were applicable to any child whose birth was expected at the time of his writing, different from him whom the prophet had foretold. His Lordship having scouted the pretensions of Servius and others in favour of any son of Pollio, and remarked that the poet's prophecy would neither suit the age nor situation of Drusus or Marcellus, readily admits its congruity, so far as a *son* is concerned, to the child with which Scribonia was at that time pregnant. Here the difficulty with his Lordship begins; for how, considering the situation of Octavius at this period, could *his* child be the subject of such a prediction? Why, in predicting the future greatness of a son of Octavius, should Virgil address his prediction to Pollio? And, supposing these difficulties solved, how can the imagery of the prediction itself be reconciled to the subject of it?

Let us take each question in its order. 1. In stating the situation of Octavius, his Lordship has unwarily admitted a succession of facts, which, being posterior to the time when the Eclogue was written, could not have been foreknown by Virgil, and therefore ought not to be brought into question. In the year 714, when all the horrors of a civil war were impending over Italy, a reconciliation was suddenly effected between Antony and Octavius, at the intervention of Pollio, Mæcenas, and Cocceius Nerva. The result of this treaty was a partition of the Roman world between Octavius and Antony (for Lepidus they regarded as a cypher.) When the ratification of this agreement was confirmed, and Antony departed to his province, nothing was left in the west to thwart the aims of Octavius, but what might arise from Pompey, who still commanded a fleet. To guard against any obstacle from this quarter, Octavius, instead of attempting, as had been projected with his colleague, to crush Pompey by violence, chose rather to conciliate his friendship. With this view, therefore, (as the marriage of Octavia with Antony had appeased her husband and brother,) Octavius married Scribonia, the sister of Pompey's wife; and the expedient, for a short time, was not without effect. When this Eclogue then was written, Octavius was master of Italy, and that part of the empire which under his own name comprehended the world. At peace with his colleagues abroad, having nothing to apprehend at home, and invested with absolute power to compose those commotions by which the empire had been so lately convulsed, what might not Octavius hope—or what might not the flattery of a poet, who in circumstances less favourable had styled him a god, now prompt his aspiring mind, and on the ground of a divine prediction, to expect would be the future greatness of his son?

But, 2. It is asked, Why Virgil on such an occasion should address this prediction to Pollio, who had been not the friend of Octavius, but of Antony?

on a nearer inspection of each particular, on a thorough
examination of the nature and force of the imagery and

In answer to this inquiry it may be observed, that the private misunderstanding which his Lordship has alleged to have arisen between Pollio and
Octavius, a year or more *after* Pollio had been consul, is totally beside the
question ; except as it serves to show, that, from the peace of Brundusium till the
rise of this disagreement, Octavius and Pollio were friends.   But whatever political
enmity might have existed between them prior to that treaty, they were both
unanimous in the patronage of genius.   It was whilst Pollio held the territory of
Venice for Antony, that his acquaintance with Virgil commenced; and as the
splendour of the poet's talents, which broke through the obscurity and depression
of his condition, had attracted the notice of Pollio ; so, by his means, they obtained
the favour of Octavius : for it is agreed on all hands, that Pollio, either in person
or by the intervention of some friend, (perhaps Varus, see Ecl. ix.,) brought Virgil
to the knowledge of Octavius, who restored to him his patrimony which the soldiers
had usurped.   Yet, widely as Octavius and Pollio might have differed before the
treaty of pacification, there is no reason to suppose them, after its confirmation, upon
any other than an intimate footing ; at least till that *private* misunderstanding to
which his Lordship has adverted.   Now, what could be more natural, what more
consistent with the nicest address, than that Virgil, whose poetic talents had first
procured him the protection of Pollio, and by his means the munificence of Octavius,
should offer through his first patron, who was not only at this time consul, but had
been chiefly instrumental, by negociating the peace, to the establishment of Octavius
in power, a poetic compliment to his greater benefactor, on a prediction believed to
point out his son ?

Having thus answered two of the questions proposed, it remains to consider the
third.   Virgil, in the first Eclogue, which was written on regaining his estate,
confines himself chiefly to his own concerns and those of his Mantuan neighbours ; but in the present his voice is raised to a loftier strain.   The *arbusta
humilesque myricæ* are the concerns of private life, contrasted with *sylvæ*, such as
belong to the empire at large : thus, Rome is said in the first Eclogue " to rear her
head as high above other cities, as the tall cypress above the lowly shrubs."—*Si
canimus sylvas*, &c.   " If woods be my theme, let the *woods* be worthy of a consul."
This imagery is by no means casual ; for we learn from Suetonius (Jul. Cæs. c.
xix.) that the woods had been lately made a consular care : *Ultima Cumæi venit
jam carminis ætas*, " The last age of the Cumæan prophecy is now come."   It is
highly deserving of notice, that Cicero, in his Treatise on Divination, has not only
referred to the Sibylline verses as containing a divine prediction of some future
king, but also mentioned an expectation that the interpreter of them would apply
that prediction in the senate to Cesar.   This prophecy had possibly its origin in
the Jewish Scriptures, and it is not unlikely that the partiality of Julius towards
the Jews might have concurred with other circumstances to point the application.
But however this were, an expectation had been long prevalent in the East of an
extraordinary personage, who was to establish universal empire ; and the prediction whence this expectation arose, was probably brought to Rome by the
persons whom the senate had deputed to search in different countries for prophetic
verses, to supply the loss of those which had perished in the Capitol.   Such, however, is the affinity between the prediction spoken of by Cicero, and that which
Tacitus (Hist. v. 13) has referred to the Jewish Scriptures as to leave no room
for surprise if we see Virgil, from the notion of both having a common
aim, adopt the one to adorn the other ; for, as the former was thought applicable
to Julius, and the latter to Vespasian or his son, why might not Virgil con-
solidate both, and apply them to the son of Octavius ?   And if Tacitus were
acquainted with the Jewish Scriptures, why might not Virgil be also ?   His writings

diction, so many things occur totally different from the general fashion of the Roman authors, so altogether foreign to the conceptions of the people of that age and nation, that it

show that his researches were universal : and upon every principle of just construction, if *the Muses* and *the Aonian Mount* be emblematical of *the Grecian poesy*, his *Idumæan palms* must equally signify the *poetic scriptures of the Jews*. [See Georg. iii. 12.]—*Ultima ætas*, &c. "The last age of the Cumæan prediction is now come." Whatever were the particulars of this prediction, the *time* set for its completion coincides with *that* in the Scriptures. [The Sibylline oracles in their present condition, by the way, are so sophisticated, that no stress can be rested on their testimony without the support of collateral proof. It will, however, deserve to be considered, If the heathens were ever in possession of a genuine prophecy, which came not from the Jews or the Christians?]—*Magnus*, &c. " The great order of ages again begins : the Virgin is already returning; the Saturnian rule returns." This commencement of the ages perfectly agrees with Isaiah, who styles the child he foretells, " the Father of ages." By the return of Astræa, Virgil alludes to the justice he had himself experienced at the hands of Octavius. The renewal of the Saturnian rule will be best explained by referring to the poet's account of its former state :

> " He [*Saturn*] by just laws embodied all the train
> Who roam'd the hills, and drew them to the plain :
> There fix'd ; and Latium call'd the new abode,
> Whose friendly shores conceal'd the latent god.
> These realms in peace the monarch long controll'd,
> And bless'd the nations with an age of gold."

Jam nova progenies cælo demittitur alto, "A new progeny is now sent down from high heaven." *Sent down*, in opposition to the manner of Saturn's descent :

> " —— Saturn fled before victorious Jove,
> Driven down, and banish'd from the realms above."

The aid of Lucina is invoked in favour, *nascenti puero*, " of the boy when he comes to the birth." It is not improbable that Virgil was induced to transfer the Sibylline prediction from Julius, in whom it had palpably failed, to this expected son of Octavius, from Isaiah's having dwelt so minutely on the infancy of the person foretold.—*Quo ferrea primum*, &c. " With whom the iron age (or *age of war*) shall cease, and the golden age shall rise over the world." Though Virgil, when Scribonia instead of a son was delivered of a daughter, discovered his mistake as to the PERSON *predicted*, he still continued confident in respect to the *events ;* and therefore, when he resumed the prophecy, from a persuasion that he could not a second time err, he makes the Sibyl herself point out Augustus as the person so often promised :

> " Hic Cæsar, et omnis Iüli
> Progenies, magnum cœli ventura sub axem.
> Hic vir, hic est, tibi quem promitti sæpius audis,
> Augustus Cæsar, Divi genus aurea condet
> Secula qui rursus Latio, regnats per arva
> Saturno quondam ; super et Garamantas et Indos
> Proferet imperium," &c.—*Æn.* vi. line 179.

> " Turn, turn thine eyes ! see here thy race divine,
> Behold thy own imperial Roman line :

is not easy to believe it was perfectly understood, even on its
first publication.   But when a foreign interpretation, sug-

> Cæsars with all the Julian name survey;
> See where the glorious ranks ascend to day!—
> This—this is he! the chief so long foretold,
> To bless the land where Saturn rul'd of old,
> And give the Latian realms a second age of gold!
> The promis'd prince, Augustus the divine,
> Of Cæsar's race, and Jove's immortal line!
> This mighty chief this empire shall extend
> O'er Indian realms, to earth's remotest end."

Till, however, a daughter was born, Virgil remained undeceived.   The mention
of the golden age rising again over the world, is sufficient proof that the Virgin before
described as returning was Astræa; and as in the Georgics he asserts that her latest
footsteps on earth were discernible in rural retreats—

> —— "last with you
> Justitia linger'd, ere she quite withdrew;"

so, by adding "Apollo now reigns," he seems to intimate, that the powers of
poetry had triumphed over oppression, and procured him the interposition of justice in the restoration of his pasture and flocks.   But though this interpretation
may agree with the context, the tenth verse will admit of a fuller sense.   After
invoking aid from Lucina, it is added, "Thy own Apollo now reigns;" that is,
the Sibylline prediction is begun to be fulfilled.   As Apollo was the God of prophecy, it was in reference to his reigning under this character that Lucina is
invoked to assist in the fulfilment of the prediction himself had inspired, by grant-
ing to the child a propitious birth.   [It is well known that Augustus afterwards
affected to be patronized by Apollo, to resemble him, to assume his dress, to be
thought his son, and to pay him divine honours as his tutelary deity; now, what
better account of so extraordinary a conduct can be given, than that all was done
with the view of arrogating to himself the Sibyl's prediction, which Virgil in the
Æneid has appropriated to him?]—*Teque adeo,* &c.   "And in thy consulship, O
Pollio, in thine, shall the glory of this age begin to commence, and the great
months thence to proceed."—"The glory of this age (the age *predicted*) shall begin
to commence."   It was in the consulship of Pollio that the marriage of Octavius to
Scribonia took place; the *great months,* therefore, are *the months of her pregnancy,*
which immediately followed her marriage.—*Te duce,* &c.   "Under your manage-
ment, if any vestiges of our wickedness remain, they shall be effaced, and the
world delivered."   This plainly refers to the influence of Pollio in negociating
the treaty at Brundusium, and also to the further exertion of his consular power.
—*Ille Deûm vitam accipiat,* &c.   "He shall receive the life of gods," &c.
Similar, though still bolder, expressions are applied to Augustus in the first
Georgic, verse the 24th.—*Pacatumque, reget patriis virtutibus orbem,* "And shall
govern the world at peace, with his father's virtues."   To whom could this apply
but to a son of Octavius, and the son whom, it was believed, the prediction had foretold?   Hence follows the description of the golden age corresponding with the imagery of Isaiah, to verse 26.—*At simul,* &c.   "But as soon as thou shalt be able to read
the praises of heroes, and the achievements of thy father, and to understand what the
energy of virtue can effect, the spacious field shall by degrees become yellow with the
soft ear;" that is, before you be old enough to view those plains which have so
lately been the theatre of heroism and horror, the devastations of civil discord
shall gradually disappear, and the tranquil occupations of husbandry imperceptibly
change their face: *Pauca tamen suberunt priscæ vestigia fraudis,* &c.   "But there
shall remain beneath the surface some traces of ancient fraud," &c.   This obviously
alludes to Pompey, who still retained the command of his fleet; whilst "the other

gested by the writings of the Hebrews, (the full force and importance of which it is impossible the poet himself could have comprehended,) serves to unravel the difficulties and to enlighten all the obscurities of this extraordinary poem; when I consider this, I own I am at a loss at what point to stop the licentiousness of conjecture upon this subject; and, indeed, what imagination occasionally suggests I dare scarcely express: I will only say, the fact has something in

wars" seem to imply the contests to be looked for in the East, whither Antony was gone; and who, therefore, in compliment to Pollio, is styled "another Achilles." The poet, after this, resumes the images expressive of the golden age as before: *Cara Deûm soboles, magnum Jovis incrementum*, &c.   "O beloved offspring of the gods, great increase of Jove!" &c. is not only consonant to the language of Scriptural prediction, but, in the sense of Virgil, suitable to none but a Cesar.   See the 6th Æneid and 2nd Georgic, before referred to.

There are several other passages of the Eclogue, which, in this attempt at illustration, have been omitted for the sake of brevity, although they would have reflected additional light on the interpretation which is here offered.   Such images of the poet as approach the nearest to those of the prophet are also purposely passed over; because, both in Virgil and Isaiah, they have no specific destination, but are used as generally symbolical of innocence and happiness; and that this was the more obvious mode of explaining the prophetic Scriptures is certain, for the Jews, from those very images in the prophet, have constantly inferred that their promised Messiah would be a *temporal Saviour*.

But there will be no necessity to enlarge on this head; for, notwithstanding what is advanced in the Lecture on the incongruity of Virgil's language to his subject, upon any other idea than that of a mysterious relation to the Messiah and his kingdom, it is the voluntary concession of his Lordship in the note, " that no person could be any where found more worthy of this prophetic Eclogue, nor whom it would more aptly fit, or with whom its contents would better quadrate, than a son of Octavius, provided it could be shown that a *son* was born to him in the year when Pollio was consul."   Now, though it be impossible to supply the proof which his Lordship requires, yet, so far as the spirit of the postulate is concerned, a satisfactory answer can be given.   For, notwithstanding, upon my hypothesis, (which perfectly harmonises with the history of facts,) Octavius had no child till the year *after* Pollio was consul, and then only a *daughter;* yet, as Scribonia became pregnant in the consulship of Pollio, and the Eclogue was written in that very year, Virgil (whatever the coincidences of the time with the Sibylline prediction might have led him to expect) certainly could not know, without the gift of prescience, the sex of this unborn child.

I am duly sensible that an apology is necessary to the reader for so long a detention from the Lectures that follow; but as (notwithstanding his Lordship's opinion, that, " though the subject has engaged the attention of some of the first literary characters in the world, the motive, the scheme, the intention of the poet, still remains undeveloped,") the subject does not seem to have been hitherto discussed with the precision it deserved, I was willing to submit it to the public in a new point of view, with the hope that what appeared convincing to myself might be favourably received by others.—S. H.

Perhaps a still more decisive objection against the hypothesis to which Mr. H. alludes is, that the very prophecies from which Virgil has apparently copied his imagery, do not seem to have any relation to the *first* coming of the Messiah, but seem wholly to relate to that triumphant *second* coming, which is yet unaccomplished.—T.

Q 2

it so extraordinary, so miraculous, to my conceptions, that I am sometimes half inclined to fancy, that what Socrates, in the Io of Plato, says (probably in his usual tone of irony) of poets in general, might have actually come to pass : " Hence," says the philosopher, " the God having, by possessing their minds, deprived them of their natural reason, makes use of them, as well as of the prophets and diviners, as his ministers, to the end that we who hear them should understand, that matters of so great importance are not uttered by men in their sober senses, but that it is the God himself who utters them, and addresses us by their mouths."

OF ELEGIAC POETRY.

LECTURE XXII.

OF THE NATURE AND ORIGIN OF THE HEBREW ELEGY; AND OF THE LAMENTATIONS OF JEREMIAH.

The nature and origin of the Hebrew Elegy traced into the solemn expressions of grief exhibited in their funeral ceremonies—The office and function of professed mourners; the dirges which were sung by them were short, metrical, and sententious; many of the lamentations which are extant in the Prophets were composed in imitation of them—The whole of the Lamentations of Jeremiah constructed upon the same principle—The general conduct and form of that poem; the nature of the verse; the subject and the style.

THAT poetry is indebted for its origin to the more vehement affections of the human mind, has been, I apprehend, very clearly evinced. The distribution of it into its different species is not, however, exactly regulated by the nature and order of the passions; though I think this is a circumstance which ought not entirely to be disregarded. There are, indeed, some species of poetry which admit of every passion, such as the Lyric; and there are some which scarcely admit of any, such as the Didactic: there are others, however, which are peculiarly adapted to particular passions, Tragedy for instance; and we have already had occasion to explain the nature of the passions which are congenial to the Prophetic Muse. There is a distinct species of poetry, which is appropriated solely to one particular passion; and, what is worth remarking, we have never known a people, who might be said to have made any proficiency in poetry, who had not a peculiar form of poem invented purposely for the expression of sorrow, and appropriated wholly to plaintive subjects.*

---

* Λινος, originally, among the Egyptians, a *song* or *ballad.* Herod. ii. 79. "Herodotus remarks, that this kind of song was very common in Phœnicia and Cyprus. Why, therefore, may not the word λινος (linos) be derived from the Arabic *lin, lenis,* to be *tender, soft;* in Conjug. ii. to *soften* or *make tender?*"—H.

This species of poem the Greeks, and most nations after them, distinguished by the name of *Elegy :* the Hebrews call it *Kinah* or *Nehi*, both which are significant of sorrow or lamentation.

The genius and origin of this poem among the Hebrews may be clearly traced into their manner of celebrating their funeral rites. It may indeed more properly be termed the dictate of nature than of custom, to follow to the grave the remains of a friend with grief and lamentation. The ancient Hebrews were not ashamed of obeying the voice of nature on this occasion, and of liberally pouring forth the effusions of a bleeding heart. The language of grief is simple and unaffected: it consists of a plaintive, intermitted, concise, form of expression, if indeed a simple exclamation of sorrow may deserve such an appellation.

> " O father ! O my country ! O house of Priam ! "*

exclaims Andromache in the tragedy; nor less pathetic is the complaint of the tender father in the sacred history, on the loss of his beloved though disobedient son, " O my son Absalom ! O Absalom, my son, my son ! "† There will not, therefore, be occasion for any laboured disquisition concerning that kind of solemn dirge which was used at funerals; but since the sacred writers afford many examples to this purpose, I shall select one or two. The prophet of Bethlehem brought the corpse of the man of God who was slain by the lion, back to the city, that he might mourn over him and bury him. · He placed him in his own sepulchre, and they wept over him, saying, " Alas, my brother ! "‡ So in Jeremiah, JEHOVAH declares of Joachim, the son of Josiah, king of Judah,

> " They shall not lament him, Ah, my brother, or ah, sister !
> They shall not lament him, Ah, Lord, or ah, his glory ! "§

See a note on this subject in Lecture 13, and the passage there cited from the Orestes of Eurip.

ΑΙΛΙΝΟΝ ΑΙΛΙΝΟΝ αρχαν θανατϐ
Βαρβαροι λεγϐσιν ΑΙ, ΑΙ,
Ασιαδι φωνᾳ.—κ. λ.

The Αιλινος (ailinos) in this passage appears to be compounded of the elegiac ΑΙ (ai) and λινος (linos). If so, it will correspond with the λινος (linos) mentioned by Herodotus, and referred to by Dr. Hunt in the above note.—S. H.

* Cicero, *Tusc. Quæst.* lib. iii.   † 2 Sam. xix. 4.   ‡ 1 Kings xiii. 30.

§ Jer. xxii. 18. " In the text it is written הדֹה, with the Arabic suffix, instead of the Hebrew; of which many instances are to be found in the Scriptures. But perhaps the letter ה may be radical, and not the pronominal suffix: *Ah, Lord !* (and not *my* Lord;) *ah, Glory ! Alas ! the vanity of regal splendour*

These and similar exclamations were sufficient for the simple expression of natural and unaffected sorrow. But wayward grief is frequently desirous of a more complete and ostentatious display of its feelings: it studies not only its own alleviation, by publishing its uneasiness, but endeavours to incite and allure others into a society in affliction. Thus, when Abner fell a sacrifice to the treachery of Joab, David not being privy to the action, and in truth extremely afflicted on account of it; yet, from the difficulty of his situation, and the infant state of his authority, not daring to punish the murderer, he fulfils his duty, both to himself and to the deceased, in the eyes of the people, by attending the funeral in the character of chief mourner : " And he lifted up his voice and wept at the sepulchre, and all the people wept with him." And then, by the united aid of poetry and music, he further stimulates their affliction : "And the king lamented Abner, and said,

> " ' Did Abner fall a mean and guilty slave ?
>   With gory fetters were his limbs defil'd ?
> Lo, abject treach'ry snar'd th' incautious brave ;
>   And wily fraud his honest heart beguil'd.'

" And again all the people wept over him."*

Thus a certain ostentatious zeal, which frequently accompanies real sorrow, is apt to persuade men that it is impossible to pay too much respect to the memory of departed friends: that intemperance of passion too, which is always observable in these cases, which is self-indulgent to excess, and is more inclined to irritate than to soothe ; in a word, opinion or fashion, which governs and misleads the bulk of mankind, easily persuades them that it is an indispensable duty incumbent upon the living to afflict themselves for the sake of the dead. Each of these causes has contributed to establish that custom which prevailed in Palestine, in Phrygia,† and afterwards among the Greeks and Romans, of engaging mercenary mourners to weep at their funerals. This office generally fell to the lot of the women, either

---

and majesty ! The LXX and the Vulg. do not acknowledge the suffix, either here or in the preceding member."—H. Three MSS. have יהוה, according to the Masoretic *Keri :* See Bib. Heb. Michaelis, in loc. Codex Orat. 42. In the margin it has יהוה. See Bib. Heb. Houbigant. The LXX omit the word.—*Author's Note.*

* 2 Sam. iii. 33, 34.

† See Jos. Scaliger, Conjectanea in Varronem de Ling. Lat. p. 76, edit. R. Steph.

because it was supposed more congenial to the general im-becility of the female mind, or because, from the flexibility and softness of their nature, and from their tender and plaintive tone of voice, they were supposed more capable of working upon the affections. After the custom was once established, we find no scarcity of these professional mourn-ers, well accomplished in all the discipline of lamentation and woe, and with tears always at command for a reasonable stipend. And in all other arts, so in this, perfection consisted in the exact imitation of nature. The funereal dirges were therefore composed in general upon the model of those complaints which flow naturally and spontaneously from the afflicted heart: the sentences were abrupt, mournful, pathetic, simple, and unembellished; on one account, indeed, more elaborate and artificial, because they consisted of verse, and were chaunted to music.*

Many vestiges of this custom are found in the writings of the prophets; for the predictions of calamity impending over states and empires are often replete with elegance, and gene-rally assume the form of a funereal song. But this remark will be more clearly evidenced by a few examples; and these examples will serve at the same time to illustrate what has been alleged concerning this custom. Hear,† says the pro-phet Amos, addressing the Israelites, and denouncing ven-geance and destruction against them, and their government,

> " Hear my voice, O Israel, hear !
> Whilst I thy fate deplore :
> Thy virgin daughter, Sion ! falls—
> She falls to rise no more !"

And a little after : ‡

> " Through the streets, and through the plains,
> The doleful rumour flies ;
> And skilful mourners raise their voice
> In sad funereal cries."

And in Jeremiah, on a similar occasion, JEHOVAH of Hosts thus addresses his people : §

---

* See Matt. ix. 23, and Lightfoot Exercitat. Hebr. and Talmud. in locum.

† Amos v. 1, 2.

‡ Ib. v. 16. The particle אל in the last clause ought probably to be placed at the beginning of that clause. So the Syr. and Vulg. read it. See Capell, *Sac. Crit.* B. iv., c. xiii. 1.—*Author's Note.*

§ Jer. ix. 17—22.

" Let those well taught in Sorrow's school
  Resound the notes of woe ;
And mournful music through the land,
  In solemn concord flow ;
Till tears shall stream from every eye,
  Till every heart shall fear :—
Hark, 'tis the mourner's voice that sounds !
  'Tis Sion's dirge I hear !
Vanquish'd, enthrall'd, to plunder given,
  The haughty city falls ;
Shrill shrieks of woe aloud resound,
  While ruin shakes her walls :
' We go—deserted and forlorn—
  To rove from shore to shore ;
These long-lov'd seats no more to view,
  These pleasant plains no more.'
Yet hear, 'tis heaven's most high decree !
  The solemn rites prepare !
Let Sion's daughters raise the dirge,
  Replete with wild despair.
The regal dome, the sacred fane,
  Stern Death invades, and wastes the land ;
The pride of Israel strews the plain,
  Like sheaves beneath the reaper's hand.

Many instances of the same kind occur throughout the
Prophets, in which, as in these, there is a direct allusion to
the institution from which they originated. There are also
many other passages, evidently of the same kind, although
the funeral ceremonies be not immediately referred to; and
the peculiar elegance of these we shall not perceive, unless
some regard be paid to the object to which they allude.
The examples that I have produced are, I apprehend, sufficient to indicate the nature and origin of this species of
poetry, and to demonstrate, that these artificial complaints
were originally formed on the model, and expressed in the
language, of real sorrow. Hence also it will be apparent
in what manner, and by what gradations, the *Kinah*, or lamentations of the Hebrews, assumed the form of a regular
poem ; but for the further elucidation of this subject it may
not be improper to examine the Lamentations of Jeremiah,
the most remarkable poem of this kind extant, according to
the principles of these funereal compositions ; for, unless we
examine it in this manner, and by this criterion, it will be
impossible to form a right judgment concerning it.

I shall endeavour to treat of this extraordinary production in the following order: first, Of its nature and form in general; secondly, Of the metre or versification; and, lastly, Of the subject, the sentiments, and imagery.

The Lamentations of Jeremiah (for the title is properly and significantly plural) consist of a number of plaintive effusions, composed upon the plan of the funeral dirges, all upon the same subject, and uttered without connexion as they rose in the mind, in a long course of separate stanzas. These have afterwards been put together, and formed into a collection or correspondent whole. If any reader, however, should expect to find in them an artificial and methodical arrangement of the general subject, a regular disposition of the parts, a perfect connexion and orderly succession in the matter, and, with all this, an uninterrupted series of elegance and correctness, he will really expect what was foreign to the prophet's design. In the character of a mourner, he celebrates in plaintive strains the obsequies of his ruined country: whatever presented itself to his mind in the midst of desolation and misery, whatever struck him as particularly wretched and calamitous, whatever the instant sentiment of sorrow dictated, he pours forth in a kind of spontaneous effusion. He frequently pauses, and as it were ruminates upon the same object; frequently varies and illustrates the same thought with different imagery, and a different choice of language; so that the whole bears rather the appearance of an accumulation of corresponding sentiments, than an accurate and connected series of different ideas arranged in the form of a regular treatise. I would not be understood to insinuate, that the author has paid no regard whatever to order or arrangement; or that transitions truly elegant from one subject, image, or character, to another, are not sometimes to be found; this only I wished to remark, that the nature and design of this poem (being in reality a collection of different sentiments or subjects, each of which assumes the form of a funeral dirge) neither require nor even admit of, a methodical arrangement. The whole poem, however, may be divided into five parts: In the first, second, and fourth, the prophet addresses the people in his own person, or else personifies Jerusalem, and introduces that city as a character: the third part is supposed to be uttered by the chorus of Jews, represented by their leader,*

---

* Thus, in ver. 14, the עָמִי is in the constructive for the absolute form. The Syr. omits the pronoun. See a Note on Lect. 13. So also, it appears, the same word

after the manner of the Greek tragedies; and in the fifth, the whole nation of the Jews, on being led into captivity, pour forth their united complaints to Almighty God. This last, as well as the others, is divided into twenty-two periods, according to the number of the letters of the alphabet; with this difference, that in the four other parts the initial letters of each period exactly correspond with the alphabetical order. And from this circumstance we have been enabled to form some little judgment concerning the Hebrew metres.

The acrostic or alphabetical poetry of the Hebrews was certainly intended to assist the memory, and was confined altogether to those compositions which consisted of detached maxims or sentiments without any express order or connexion.* The same custom is said to have been prevalent, indeed is said still to prevail in some degree among the Syrians, the Persians, and the Arabs.† With how much propriety the prophet has employed this form of composition on the present occasion, is evident from what has been said concerning the nature of this poem. The manner and order of this kind of verse is as follows: Each of the five parts, or grand divisions, is subdivided into twenty-two periods, or stanzas; these periods in the three first parts are all of them triplets, in other words, consist each of three lines only; in each of the two former parts there is one period, consisting of four lines.‡ In the four first parts, the initial letter of each period follows the order of the alphabet; but the third part is so very regular, that every line in the same period begins with the same letter, so as necessarily to ascertain the length of every verse or line in that poem: indeed, even in the others, though the lines are not distinctly marked in this manner, it is no difficult matter to ascertain their limits, by resolving the sentences into their constituent members. By this mode of computation it appears, that in the fourth part all the

ought to be understood Psal. cxliv. 2. Compare likewise Psal. xviii. 48; xlvii. 4. See Pocock *Not. in Port. Mosis.* p. 60. "Lam. iii. 14, two MSS. have עמים. And observe, that in MSS. the plural ם is often expressed ◌, ◌.'" K.—*Author's Note.*

* M. Michaelis very justly remarks, that except the Lamentations of Jeremiah and the xxxviith Psalm, none of the Alphabetic Poems of the Hebrews rise in any degree above mediocrity:—a certain indication, that however useful this kind of discrimination might be on some occasions, in assisting the memory of children and the vulgar, yet such minute arts are in general inconsistent with true genius.—T.

† See Asseman *Bibliothec. Oriental.* vol. iii. p. 63, 180, 188, 328.

‡ In chap. i. ח; in chap. ii. פ.

periods consist of distichs,* as also in the fifth, which is not
acrostic : but in this last part I must remark another peculiarity, namely, that the lines are extremely short, whereas
in all the rest they are long.

The length of these metres is worthy of notice : we find
in this poem lines or verses, which are evidently longer, by
almost one-half, than those which occur usually and on other
occasions.   The length of them seems to be, on an average,
about twelve syllables; there are a few which do not quite
amount to that number, and there are a few which perhaps
exceed it by two or three syllables: for, although nothing
certain can be determined concerning the number of syllables, (in truth I pay no attention to the fictions of the
Masorites,) there is room, nevertheless, for very probable
conjecture.   We are not to suppose this peculiar form of
versification utterly without design or importance ; on the
contrary, I am persuaded that the prophet adopted this kind
of metre as being more diffuse, more copious, more tender,
in all respects better adapted to melancholy subjects.   I must
add, that in all probability the funeral dirges, which were
sung by the mourners, were commonly composed in this kind
of verse ; for whenever, in the Prophets, any funeral lamentations occur, or any passages formed upon that plan, the
versification is, if I am not mistaken, of this protracted kind.
If this then be the case, we have discovered a true legitimate
form of Elegy in the poetry of the Hebrews.   It ought,
however, to be remarked, that the same kind of metre is
sometimes, though rarely, employed upon other occasions by
the sacred poets, as it was indeed by the Greeks and Romans.   There are, moreover, some poems manifestly of the
elegiac kind, which are composed in the usual metre, and
not in unconnected stanzas, according to the form of a
funeral dirge.

Thus far in general as to the nature and method of the
poem, and the form of the versification ;—it remains to offer
a few remarks concerning the subject and the style.

That the subject of the Lamentations is the destruction
of the holy city and temple, the overthrow of the state, the
extermination of the people—and that these events are
described as actually accomplished, and not in the style of
prediction merely—must be evident to every reader ; though

* But the period ב, as it is now read, can neither be conveniently distributed
into two, nor into three verses.—*Author's Note.*

some authors of considerable reputation* have imagined this poem to have been composed on the death of king Josiah. The prophet, indeed, has so copiously, so tenderly and poetically, bewailed the misfortunes of his country, that he seems completely to have fulfilled the office and duty of a mourner. In my opinion, there is not extant any poem which displays such a happy and splendid selection of imagery in so concentrated a state. What can be more elegant and poetical than the description of that once flourishing city, lately chief among the nations, sitting in the character of a female, solitary, afflicted, in a state of widowhood, deserted by her friends, betrayed by her dearest connexions, imploring relief, and seeking consolation in vain? What a beautiful personification is that of " the Ways of Sion mourning, because none are come to her solemn feasts!" How tender and pathetic are the following complaints!

" Is this nothing to all you who pass along the way? Behold and
    see,
  If there be any sorrow like unto my sorrow, which is inflicted
    on me;
  Which Jehovah inflicted on me in the day of the violence of
    his wrath.
  For these things I weep, my eyes stream with water;
  Because the comforter is far away, that should tranquillize my
    soul:
  My children are desolate, because the enemy was strong."†

But to detail its beauties would be to transcribe the entire poem. I shall make but one remark relative to certain passages, and to the former part of the second alphabet in particular. If, in this passage, the prophet should be thought by some to affect a style too bold and energetic for the expression of sorrow, let them only advert to the greatness of the subject, its importance, sanctity, and solemnity; and let them consider, that the nature of the performance absolutely required these to be set forth in a style suitable, in some degree at least, to their inherent dignity;—let them attentively consider these things, and I have not a doubt but they will readily excuse the sublimity of the prophet.

* Josephus, Jerome, Usserius, &c.

† Lam. i. 12 and 16. In the last verse the word עיני is not repeated in the old translations.

LECTURE XXIII.

OF THE REMAINING ELEGIES OF THE HEBREWS.

Many Poems of this kind still extant in the writings of the Hebrews—One collection of Elegies or Lamentations appears to be lost—Elegies in Ezekiel—Many passages in Job may be accounted Elegiac—About a seventh part of the book of Psalms consists of Elegies—A perfect specimen of Elegiac Poetry from the Psalms—The Lamentation of David over Saul and Jonathan explained: attempted in English verse.

In the last Lecture, the nature and origin of the Hebrew Elegy was explained; the form and commencement of that species of poetry was traced into the solemn dirges which were chaunted at funerals by the professed mourners; and this was confirmed by instances taken from those short Elegies or Lamentations which occur in the Prophets, and by an accurate examination of that remarkable poem, The Lamentations of Jeremiah. I shall now treat of some other poems, which, although they do not exactly assume the form of a funeral dirge, are nevertheless to be comprehended in this class.

That the Hebrews were formerly possessed of some collection of Elegies or Lamentations which has not been transmitted to us, we may understand from that passage of sacred history* in which mention is made of the solemn mourning publicly celebrated at the funeral of Josiah, where it appears that a poem, composed for the occasion, by Jeremiah the prophet, amongst others had a place. Though the book which is on this occasion referred to, and which probably contained the most excellent of the Hebrew Elegies, appears to be lost, there are still extant many specimens of this kind of poetry; whence we may reasonably infer that no species of composition was more in use among the Hebrews than the elegiac, the ode perhaps only excepted.

* 2 Chron. xxxv. 25.

In the first place, beside those short dirges which occur in the writings of almost all the prophets, as was before remarked, there are some in Ezekiel which are actually distinguished by the title of Lamentations, and which may with the utmost propriety be referred to the class of Elegies. Among these are the two Lamentations concerning Tyre and the King of Tyre.* In these, though the intent of the prophet be to denounce vengeance and punishment against these objects of the divine wrath, rather than to lament their misfortunes; and though he succeed in his aim of exciting terror instead of pity; yet the mournful nature of the subject fully corresponds with the title, and both the matter and the sentiments bear some degree of resemblance to the funereal songs. According to the custom which prevailed on those solemn occasions, the glory, riches, and power of the deceased are pompously enumerated; and thus, by contrasting his former prosperity with the present calamity, the effect is considerably augmented. As for the two prophecies† in which the destruction of Egypt is predicted, they seem to have been entitled Lamentations merely from the mournful nature of the subject; for they contain nothing of the elegiac form or style, scarcely any sentiment expressive of sorrow, and seem altogether composed for the denunciation of vengeance, and the exciting of terror. Two other Lamentations,‡ the one over the princes of Judah and the other over Jerusalem, may be explained upon similar principles; they are indeed poetical parables, and have been already noticed in their proper place.

There are also many passages in that most admirable poem which bears the name of Job,§ deserving to be accounted legitimate elegies: and indeed I do not know any more perfect specimens of this species of composition; so completely are the inmost recesses of sorrow displayed, and the remotest fountains of pity explored and laid open. But since these are parts of an entire poem, they are not rashly to be detached from the body of the work; and since the elegant disposition, and the extraordinary beauties of this inimitable composition, will deserve a fuller examination, it is sufficient in this place to have mentioned these passages as exquisite treasures, which the Muse of Sorrow might legally claim as her own, were she disposed to assert her rigid rights.

---

* Ezek. xxvii. and xxviii. 12—19.   † Ezek. xxxii.   ‡ Ezek. xix.
§ See Job, chap. iii. vi. vii. x. xiv. xvii. xix. xxix. xxx.

I proceed, therefore, to the book of Psalms, which is a collection, under the general title of hymns to the praise of God, containing poems of different kinds, and elegies among the rest. If indeed the contents of the book were methodically arranged in their proper classes, not less than a sixth or seventh part would appear to be elegiac. Since, however, this is a matter dependent in a great measure upon opinion, and not to be clearly demonstrated upon determinate principles; since the nature of the subject, the complexion of the style, or the general form and disposition of each poem, must decide the question; and since different persons will judge differently upon these points—it will hardly be expected that I should on this occasion proceed to the regular classification of them. It will indeed be more to your advantage, and more to our present purpose, to select an example which may be clearly demonstrated to belong to the elegiac class.

Under this appellation, then, I shall not hesitate to recommend to your notice the forty-second Psalm, since I cannot help esteeming it one of the most beautiful specimens of the Hebrew Elegy. The author of this elegant complaint, exiled from the temple, and from the public exercise of his religion, to the extreme parts of Judea, persecuted by his numerous enemies, and agitated by their reproaches, pours forth his soul to God in this tender and pathetic composition. The ardent feelings of a devout heart are admirably expressed, while the memory of former felicity seems to aggravate his present anguish. The extreme anxiety of a mind depressed by the burden of sorrow, and yet at the same time impatient under it; overcome by an accumulation of evils, yet in some degree endeavouring to resist them, and admitting, through the dark cloud of affliction, a glimmering ray of hope and consolation—is finely depicted. In frequent and almost instantaneous transitions he glows with love and droops with lamentation; he complains, he expostulates; he despairs, and yet hopes; he is afflicted, and again consoled. It is not to be expected that any poetical version should express these sentiments with the force, the energy, and more particularly with the conciseness of the Hebrew, which is indeed not to be imitated in any other language; though it must be confessed, that this poem is more diffuse than the Hebrew poetry in general. The following paraphrase, however, though infinitely short of the

original in sublimity, will perhaps serve to evince the correspondence of the subject and sentiments of this poem, with
the elegiac productions of modern times.

As pants the wearied hart for cooling springs,
    That sinks exhausted in the summer's chase;
So pants my soul for thee, great King of kings!
    So thirsts to reach thy sacred resting-place.

On briny tears* my famish'd soul has fed,
    While taunting foes deride my deep despair;
" Say, where is now thy great Deliverer fled?
    Thy mighty God—deserted wanderer, where?"

Oft dwell my thoughts on those thrice happy days,
    When to thy fane I led the jocund throng;
Our mirth was worship, all our pleasure praise,
    And festal joys still clos'd with sacred song.

Why throb, my heart? Why sink, my sadd'ning soul?
    Why droop to earth with various woes oppress'd?
My years shall yet in blissful circles roll,
    And joy be yet an inmate of this breast.

By Jordan's banks with devious steps I stray,
    O'er Hermon's rugged rocks, and deserts drear;
E'en there thy hand shall guide my lonely way;
    There, thy remembrance shall my spirit cheer.

In rapid floods the vernal torrents roll,
    Harsh-sounding cataracts responsive roar;
Thine angry billows overwhelm my soul,
    And dash my shattered bark from shore to shore.

Yet thy soft mercies, ever in my sight,
    My heart shall gladden through the tedious day;
And 'midst the dark and gloomy shades of night,
    To thee I'll fondly tune the grateful lay.

Rock of my hope! Great solace of my heart!
    Why, why desert the offspring of thy care,
While taunting foes thus point th' invidious dart—
    " Where 's now thy God? abandon'd wanderer, where?"

Why faint, my soul? Why doubt JEHOVAH's aid?
    Thy God, the God of mercy still shall prove!
In his bright fane thy thanks shall yet be paid;
    Unquestion'd be his pity and his love!†

---

* It seems odd to an English reader to represent *tears* as *meat* or *food*; but we
shuold remember that the sustenance of the ancient Hebrews consisted for the most
part of liquids, such as *broths*, *pottages*, &c.—S. H.

† This poem seems to have been composed by David when he was expelled his

Another point to which I would wish every person who reads this Psalm in the original to advert, is the division of the periods, and the resolution of them into their constituent

kingdom by his rebellious son, and compelled to fly to the borders of Lebanon; as it is plain he did from 2 Sam. xvii. 24. 26, 27. Undoubtedly, whoever composed this Psalm was expelled from the sacred city, and wandered as an exile in the regions of Hermon and the heights of Lebanon, whence Jordan is fed by the melting of the perpetual snow, ver. 7. Let it be remembered by the way, that David never betook himself to these places when he fled from Saul, but concealed himself in the interior parts of Judea. Here then he pitched his camp, protected by the surrounding mountains and woods; and hither the veteran soldiers, attached personally to him, and averse to change, resorted from every part of Palestine. Here also, indulging his melancholy, the prospect and the objects about him suggested many of the ideas in this poem. Observing the deer which constantly came from the distant valleys to the fountains of Lebanon, and comparing this circumstance with his earnest desire to revisit the temple of God, and perhaps elevating his thoughts to a higher celestial temple, he commences his poem:

" As the hart panteth after the water-brooks,
So panteth my soul after thee, O God!
My soul thirsteth for God, for the living God:
When shall I enter, and appear before God?"

That is, *enter into the temple*, from which I am now an exile. He adds a bitterer cause of grief than his exile; namely, the reproaches of the multitude, and the cruel taunt that he is *deserted of his God*, and that the Deity, of whom he had boasted, fails to appear to his assistance—than which nothing can be more grating to an honest mind, and a mind conscious of its own piety. Compare 2 Sam. xvi. 7, 8.

" My tears have been my sustenance
By day and by night,
While they continually say unto me,
Where is now thy God?"

The repetition of the name of God raises in him fresh uneasiness, and causes all his wounds to bleed again: this forces him to exclaim, "I remember *God*, and I dissolve in tears." For so the word אלה ought to be translated, and not according to the Masoretic punctuation, "I remember *these things*;" since an obscurity arises from this punctuation, and it is difficult to say what things are referred to:

" I remember God, and pour out myself in tears,
When I went with the multitude to the temple of God,
With the voice of joy and gladness, with the multitude leaping for joy."

He now restrains his tears:

" Why art thou so cast down, O my soul?
And why art thou so disquieted within me?
Hope thou in God, for I still shall praise him."

He again breaks forth into lamentations, with which he elegantly intermingles a poetical description of Lebanon. There are upon those hills frequent cataracts, and, in the spring season, the rivulets are uncommonly turbid by the melting of the snow:

" Deep calleth unto deep at the noise of thy cataracts;
And all thy waves and thy billows are gone over me."

parts or members: he will find, I believe, that the periods spontaneously divide into verses of nearly equal length and measure, exactly similar to those of the four first chapters of the Lamentations of Jeremiah; such as I before remarked appeared to constitute the established metre of the Hebrew Elegy. The whole of the nineteenth Psalm consists also of the same kind of verse, except the epode, which contains two long verses of the same kind, and one shorter; which last is once repeated. The forty-third Psalm too seems to be constructed upon similar principles, containing eight of the same kind of verses, with the same epode. And since it is written in the same train of sentiment, the same style, and even apparently in the same metre, it ought not perhaps to be separated from the preceding Psalm,* but rather to be considered as a part or continuation of the same composition: If this be true, the whole poem consists of three parts almost equal and alike, each of which is concluded by the same intercalary period or stanza.

There is another most beautiful poem of the elegiac kind, which on this occasion solicits our attention—I mean the lamentation of David for Saul and Jonathan;† which appears to have been extracted by the historian from some poetical book, no longer extant, entitled *Jasher.*‡ It will

---

These form the principal imagery of the poem, and I omit the rest, lest I should fatigue the reader by the minuteness of criticism, which is both useless and impertinent when the subject wants no illustration.—M.

* I find Eusebius was formerly of the same opinion :—" This Psalm is without a title in the original, and consequently in all the old translations : there is indeed great reason, from the similarity of thought and expression in both the Psalms, to believe that it originally made a part of the Psalm preceding." In Psalm xliii. this conjecture receives further confirmation from the manuscripts. " The xlii. and xliii. Psalms are united together in twenty-two MSS. The Psalms, however, are distinguished from each other in the MSS. rarely by the numeral letters, but chiefly by these two methods—either by a single word placed in the vacant space between them, which is usually the breadth of one line ; and this word is commonly the last word of the preceding, or the initial word of the succeeding Psalm ; or else by the first word of each Psalm being transcribed in letters of a larger size." K.—*Author's Note.*

† 2 Sam. i. 17—27.

‡ Since so many conjectures have been published concerning the book of *Jasher* and its title, without coming to any certain decision, I will also, without further apology, venture to give my sentiments upon it. The book of *Jasher* is twice quoted, first in Josh. x. 13, where the quotation is evidently poetical, and forms exactly three distichs :

" Sun, stand thou still upon Gibeon ;
And thou, moon, in the valley of Ajalon :

not, I flatter myself, be thought unreasonable to request your attention, while I endeavour to investigate, with some degree of accuracy, the nature and composition of this poem.

The poet treats, though in no common manner, two common topics, and those the best adapted to the genuine elegy; that I mean which was employed in the celebration of the funeral rites; he expresses his own sorrow, and he celebrates the praises of the deceased. Both sentiments are displayed in the exordium; but, as might naturally be expected, sorrow is predominant, and bursts forth with the impetuosity of exclamation:

> " The glory of Israel is slain on the high places :
> How are the mighty fallen ! "

Grief is of a timid and suspicious temper, and always ready at inventing causes for self-torment; easily offended by neglect, and utterly impatient of ridicule or contempt:

> " They heard that I sigh'd, for there was none to comfort me :
> All mine enemies have heard of my calamity, and rejoiced that
>   thou inflictedst it."*

> And the sun stood still, and the moon stayed her course,
> Until the people were avenged of their enemies :
> And the sun tarried in the midst of the heavens,
> And hasted not to go down in a whole day."

And afterwards, in the passage referred to in the text, we find the above lamentation of David extracted from it. The custom of the Hebrews giving titles to their books from the initial word is well known, as Genesis is called *Bereshit*, &c. They also sometimes named the book from some remarkable word in the first sentence : thus the book of Numbers is sometimes called *Bemidbar*. We find also in their writings, canticles which had been produced on important occasions, introduced by some form of this kind : *az jashar* (*then sung*) or *ve-jashar peloni*, &c.; thus, *az jashir Mosheh*, "then sung Moses," Exod. xv. 1, (the Samar. reads *jashar*;) *ve-thashar Deborah*, " and Deborah sang," Judg. v. 1. See also the same inscription of Psa. xviii. Thus I suppose the book of *Jasher* to have been some collection of sacred songs composed at different times and on different occasions, and to have had this title, because the book itself and most of the songs began in general with this word *ve-jashar*. And the old Syriac translator was certainly of this opinion, when in these places he substituted the word *ashir*, he sung; the meaning of which, says the Arabic commentator, is *A book of songs*; in another place he himself explains it by a word expressive of *Hymns*. I however agree in opinion with those who suppose this Lamentation originally to have borne the title of *Keshet*, a bow, either in memory of the slaughter made by the archers of the enemy, or from the *bow* of Jonathan, of which particular mention is made ver. 22. The LXX seem to have favoured this opinion, " *Kosh*, or rather *kos*, signifies in Arabic *to measure*, as is remarked by the learned Michaelis; but I do not remember an instance of this word being used to signify poetic measure (or metre.") H.—*Author's Note.*

* Lam. i. 21.

So Jerusalem complains in Jeremiah, exaggerating in the strongest terms her own misfortunes.   Our poet feels and expresses himself in almost the same manner:

> " Declare it not in Gath,
> Publish it not in the streets of Ascalon,
> Lest the daughters of the Philistines rejoice,
> Lest the daughters of the uncircumcised triumph."

The same passion is also sullen and querulous, wayward and peevish, unable to restrain its impatience, and firing at every thing that opposes it.   " Would ! ne'er that in the Pelian grove," says one of the characters in the Medea of Ennius.*   On another occasion we find a person inveighing against the innocent mountain:

> " Alas ! Betrayer, barren and accurst !
> What men, what heroes hast thou not destroy'd ?
> Fatal alone to those whose patriot worth
> Their noble birth by noblest acts proclaim'd."†

Our poet is not more temperate:

> " O mountains of Gilboa, let there be no dew nor rain upon you !"

If these passages were brought before the severe tribunal of reason, nothing could appear more absurd; but if examined by the criterion of the passions, nothing can be more consonant to nature, more beautiful or emphatic.   Not to refer effects to their real causes is in logic an imperfection, but in poetry often a beauty: the appeal in the one case is to reason, in the other to the passions.   When sorrow has had sufficient vent, there is leisure to expatiate on the accomplishments of the dead.   In the first place they are celebrated for their virtue and heroic actions; next, for their piety and mutual affection; and lastly, for their agility and strength.   Saul is honoured with a particular panegyric, because he had enriched his people, and contributed to the general felicity and splendour of the state.   This passage, by the way, is most exquisite composition; the women of Israel are most happily introduced, and the subject of the encomium is admirably adapted to the female characters.‡

---

* Cicero, *De Fato.* See Euripides, *Medea,* ver. 1.

† Scolion apud Athenæum, lib. xv. See Eustathius *ad Iliad.* Δ. 171. Edit. Alex. Politi, *Florentiæ,* and Herodot. *Terpsichor.* 63, 64.

‡ " Ye daughters of Israel, weep over Saul," &c.

The following passage bears no remote resemblance to this of the sacred writer, and

Jonathan is at last celebrated in a distinct eulogium, which is beautifully pathetic, is animated with all the fervour, and sweetened with all the tenderness of friendship.

I should have made some particular observations on the intercalary period or epode inserted in the Psalm which was lately under our consideration, but that I was aware an opportunity would again present itself during the examination of this poem. This recurrence of the same idea is perfectly congenial to the nature of elegy; since grief is fond of dwelling upon the particular objects of the passion, and frequently repeating them. There is something singular, however, in the intercalary period which occurs in this poem, for it does not regularly assume the same form of words, as is the case in general, but appears with a little variation. It is three times introduced, beautifully diversified in the order and diction: it forms a part of the exordium as well as of the conclusion, and is once inserted in the body of the poem.

Another observation, though it merits no higher title than a conjecture, I do not hesitate to submit to your consideration. There appears to be something singular in the versification of this elegy, and a very free use of different metres. It neither consists altogether of the long verses, nor yet of the short ones, (which are the most usual in the poetry of the Hebrews;) but rather of a very artful and happy mixture of both, so that the concise and pointed parallelism serves to correct the languor and diffuseness of the

I think comes nearer it in sublimity than any thing I have observed in modern poetry :

"Ye, who erewhile for Cook's illustrious brow
Pluck'd the green laurel and the oaken bough,
Hung the gay garlands on the trophied oars,
And pour'd his fame along a thousand shores,
Strike the slow death-bell!—weave the sacred verse,
And strew the cypress o'er his honour'd hearse!"

Miss Seward's *Elegy on Captain Cook.*

A nice ear will discern something peculiar in the structure of the *third* and *fifth* lines of this quotation. Each of these lines, in fact, begins with a Trochaic, followed by Spondees, which, from its abruptness and energy, is admirably adapted to the expression of sorrow :

"Hung the gay garlands," &c.
"Strike the slow death-bell," &c.

In this short elegy specimens may be found of almost every poetical beauty and excellence.—T.

elegaic verse: and this form of versification takes place also
in some of the Psalms.   Certainly there is a great appearance of art and design in this nice and poetical conformation
of the periods; and that no grace or elegance should be
wanting to this poem, it is no less remarkable for the general beauty, splendour, and perspicuity of the style.

To do complete justice to the economy of this excellent
production, it is absolutely necessary to exhibit it in an
entire state.   Not to tire you, therefore, with a repetition of
the verbal translation, I have endeavoured to express the
general sentiments and imagery in elegiac numbers.

> Thy glory, Israel, droops its languid head,
>   On Gilboa's heights thy rising beauty dies ;
> In sordid piles there sleep th' illustrious dead,
>   The mighty victor fallen and vanquish'd lies.
>
> Yet dumb be Grief—hush'd be her clamorous voice !
>   Tell not in Gath the tidings of our shame !
> Lest proud Philistia in our woes rejoice,
>   And rude barbarians blast fair Israel's fame.
>
> No more, O Gilboa ! heaven's reviving dew
>   With rising verdure crown thy fated head !
> No victim's blood thine altars dire imbrue !
>   For there the blood of Heaven's elect was shed.
>
> The sword of Saul ne'er spent its force in air ;
>   The shaft of Jonathan brought low the brave ;
> In life united equal fates they share,
>   In death united share one common grave.
>
> Swift as the eagle cleaves th' aërial way,
>   Through hosts of foes they bent their rapid course ;
> Strong as the lion darts upon his prey,
>   They crush'd the nations with resistless force.
>
> Daughters of Judah, mourn the fatal day,
>   In sable grief attend your monarch's urn ;
> To solemn notes attune the pensive lay,
>   And weep those joys that never shall return.
>
> With various wealth he made your tents o'erflow,
>   In princely pride your charms profusely dress'd ;
> Bade the rich robe with ardent purple glow,
>   And sparkling gems adorn the tissu'd vest.
>
> On Gilboa's heights the mighty vanquished lies,
>   The son of Saul, the generous and the just ;
> Let streaming sorrows ever fill these eyes,
>   Let sacred tears bedew a brother's dust !

> Thy firm regard rever'd thy David's name,
>   And kindest thoughts and kindest acts express'd;
> Not brighter glows the pure and generous flame
>   That lives within the tender virgin's breast.
>
> But vain the tear, and vain the bursting sigh,
>   Though Sion's echoes with our griefs resound;
> The mighty victors fallen and vanquish'd lie,
>   And war's refulgent weapons strew the ground.

OF DIDACTIC POETRY.

LECTURE XXIV.

OF THE PROVERBS, OR DIDACTIC POETRY OF THE HEBREWS.

The ancient mode of instructing by parables or proverbs—The proverbs of Solomon : that work consists of two parts ; the first, which extends to the ninth chapter inclusive, truly poetical, and most elegant in its kind ; the remainder of the book consists of detached maxims—The principal characteristics of a parable or proverb, brevity (which naturally involves in it some degree of obscurity) and elegance—Ecclesiastes: the argument, disposition, and style of that work—All the alphabetical Psalms of this kind, as well as some others—The Wisdom of the Son of Sirach, written originally in Hebrew, in imitation of the Proverbs of Solomon—The fidelity of the Greek translator ; and the great elegance of the work in general—The Wisdom of Solomon written originally in Greek, and in imitation of the Proverbs ; the style and economy of that book—A new translation of the 24th chapter of Ecclesiasticus.

In those periods of remote antiquity, which may with the utmost propriety be styled the infancy of societies and nations, the usual, if not the only mode of instruction was by detached aphorisms or proverbs. Human wisdom was then, indeed, in a rude and unfinished state: it was not digested, methodized, or reduced to order and connexion. Those who by genius and reflection, exercised in the school of experience, had accumulated a stock of knowledge, were desirous of reducing it into the most compendious form, and comprised in a few maxims those observations which they apprehended most essential to human happiness. This mode of instruction was, in truth, more likely than any other to prove efficacious with men in a rude stage of society; for it professed not to dispute, but to command; not to persuade, but to compel; it conducted them not by a circuit of argument, but led immediately to the approbation and practice of integrity and virtue. That it might not, however, be altogether destitute of allurement, and lest it should disgust by an appearance of roughness and severity, some degree of ornament became necessary; and the instructors of mankind added to their precepts the graces of harmony, and illuminated them with metaphors, comparisons, allusions, and the other embellishments of style. This manner, which with other nations prevailed only during the first periods of civilization, with the Hebrews continued to be a favourite style to the latest ages of their literature. It obtained among them the appellation of *Mashalim,* (or parables,) as well because it consisted in a great measure of parables strictly so called, as because it possessed uncommon force and authority over the minds of the auditors.

Of this didactic poetry there are still extant many specimens in the writings of the Hebrews; and among these the first rank must be assigned to the Proverbs of Solomon. This work consists of two parts. The first, serving as a proem or exordium, includes the nine first chapters; and is varied, elegant, sublime, and truly poetical: the order of the subject is in general excellently preserved, and the parts are very aptly connected among themselves. It is embellished with many beautiful descriptions and personifications: the diction is polished, and abounds with all the ornaments of poetry; insomuch that it scarcely yields in elegance and splendour to any of the sacred writings. The other part, which extends from the beginning of the tenth chapter to the end of the book, consists almost entirely of detached parables or maxims, which have but little in them of the sublime or poetical, except a certain energetic and concise turn of expression. Since the didactic poetry of the Hebrews assumes in general this unconnected and sententious form; and since this style intrudes itself into almost all the poetry of the Hebrews, and occurs frequently in poems of a character very different from the didactic; I shall treat principally of this latter part of the book of Proverbs, and endeavour more minutely to investigate the precise nature of a parable or proverb.

Solomon himself, in one of his proverbs, has explained the principal excellences of this form of composition; exhibiting at once a complete definition of a parable or proverb, and a very happy specimen of what he describes :—

> " Apples of gold in a net-work of silver
> Is a word seasonably spoken."*

Thus he insinuates, that grave and profound sentiments are to be set off by a smooth and well-turned phraseology, as the appearance of the most beautiful and exquisitely coloured fruit, or the imitation of it perhaps in the most precious materials, is improved by the circumstance of shining, as through a veil, through the reticulations of a silver vessel exquisitely carved.   Nay, he further intimates, that it is not only a neat turn and polished diction which must recommend them, but that truth itself acquires additional beauty when partially discovered through the veil of elegant fiction and imagery.

To consider the subject in a still more particular point of view, let brevity be admitted as the prime excellence of a proverb.†   This is, indeed, a necessary condition, without which it can neither retain the name nor the nature.   For, if the sentiment be diffusely expressed, if, even when it contains a double image, it exceed ten or at most twelve words, it is no longer a proverb but an harangue.   For the discriminating sentiment must force itself on the mind by a single effort, and not by a tedious process; the language must be strong and condensed, rather omitting some circumstances that appear necessary, than admitting any thing superfluous. Horace himself insists upon this as one of the express rules of didactic poetry; and he has assigned the reason on which it is founded :

> " Short be the precept, which with ease is gain'd
> By docile minds, and faithfully retain'd."‡

Solomon expresses the same sentiment in his own (that is, the parabolic) manner :

> " The words of the wise are like goads,
> And like nails that are firmly fixed,"§

* Prov. xxv. 11.

† " The brevity of this kind of composition, and the condensing of much thought into a small compass, renders it more sententious, more sage and expressive.   As in a small seed, the whole power of vegetation which is to produce a tree, is contained : and if any writer should amplify the sentence, it would be no longer a proverb, but a declamation."—Demet. Phal. Περι Ερμηνειας, sect. ix.

‡ Francis's Horace, *Art of Poetry*, ver. 455.

§ Eccles. xii. 11.   This, I think, is one of the *geminate* proverbs, (or those which " contain a double image," as mentioned before,) and requires a different mode of interpretation for the two images, as having nothing coalescent in their natures.   It is the property of a proverb to *prick sharply*, and *hold firmly :*   The first idea is in-

That is, they instantaneously stimulate or affect the mind; they penetrate deeply, and are firmly retained.

Some degree of obscurity is generally an attendant upon excessive brevity; and the parabolic style is so far from being abhorrent of this quality, that it seems frequently to affect it, and to regard it as a perfection. This obscurity is not indeed altogether without its uses: it whets the understanding, excites an appetite for knowledge, keeps alive the attention, and exercises the genius by the labour of the investigation. The human mind, moreover, is ambitious of having a share in the discovery of truth: excessive indolence or dulness only requires a very open and minute display, or prefers a passive inertness to the exercise and praise of perspicacity and discernment; and that knowledge is ever most delightful, which we have compassed by our own efforts.* Other causes, however, independent of the brevity and conciseness of the language, have, in many cases, contributed to the obscurity of the parabolic style.† In the first place, some degree of obscurity necessarily attends those passages in which different objects are applied in succession to the illustration of each other, without any express marks of comparison: of this we have had an example in the parable just now quoted, and of this there are many other examples in

cluded in the image of a goad: the latter, in the nail *deeply*, and therefore *firmly* driven.—S. H.

In Palestine, it formerly made an essential part of the building of a house, to furnish the inside of the several apartments with sets of spikes, nails, or large pegs, upon which to dispose of, and hang up, the several moveables in common use, and proper to the apartment. These spikes they worked into the walls at the first erection of them—the walls being of such materials, that they could not bear their being driven in afterwards; and they were contrived so as to strengthen the walls by binding the parts together, as well as to serve for convenience.—See Bishop Lowth's *Isaiah*, p. 255.

* So great a portion of human happiness consists in activity and employment, that without at all resorting to the love of fame, we need not wonder that some degree of difficulty interests and engages the mind, and, merely by exciting the faculties to action, affords positive pleasure.—T.

        —— " Pater ipse colendi
    Haud facilem esse viam voluit, primusque per artem
    Movit agros, *curis acuens mortalia corda*:
    Nec torpere gravi passus sua regna veterno."

" Whetting with many a care the human heart."—S. H.

† The *brevity* of the ancient proverbs may, in a great measure, be accounted for, from the want of alphabetical writing, and their being intended to be committed to memory. Much of their *obscurity* may be attributed to our ignorance of many local circumstances to which they allude, and which actually served to assist the memories of those for whom they were designed.—T.

the sacred writings. I will, nevertheless, select one or two which are deserving of our attention for their peculiar propriety and elegance :

> " Clouds and wind without rain,
>   Is a man who glories in a fallacious gift."*

The following is in a different form :

> " Gold, and abundance of rubies,
>   And precious ornaments, are the lips of knowledge."†

Again, obscurity is almost inevitable, when the subject itself, to which the imagery appertains and alludes, is removed out of sight, and the sentiment assumes the form of allegory. Horace expresses a very common precept in plain language :

> " Learn the strong sense of pleasure to control ;
>   With virtuous pride its blandishments disdain :
>   Hurtful is pleasure, when 'tis bought with pain."‡

But with how much more elegance does Solomon deliver the same precept in a figurative manner, and under the veil of allegory !

> " Hast thou found honey? Eat no more than may suffice thee ;
>   Lest thou be satiated, and nauseate it."§

Some obscurity also attends any comparison which is of extensive application ; of this the following seems a pertinent example :

> " As in water face (answers) to face,
>   So doth the heart of man to man."||

This is certainly very difficult to apply or to define, since it may refer, in many different views, to the faculties, genius, affections, will, attachments, manners, virtues, and vices of men, among which there generally subsists a certain agreement or similarity from imitation, and from habits which are insensibly caught in social intercourse. Lastly, not to dwell too long upon this subject, some obscurity succeeds when the principal, or perhaps the whole force of a proverb or parable, does not lie in the direct and literal sense, but in something not immediately expressed, which is, however, concomitant with it :

> " The hearing ear, and the seeing eye,
>   JEHOVAH made them both."¶

---

* Prov. xxv. 14.   † Prov. xx. 15.   ‡ Francis's Horace, B. I. Ep. ii. ver. 78.
§ Prov. xxv. 16. || Prov. xxvii. 19.   ¶ Prov. xx. 12.

To dwell upon the external and literal sense of this proverb, will only bewilder the reader in the dubious turn of the expression; but how sublime, how profitable, is the sentiment, when it comes from the pen of the Psalmist, embellished with his usual perspicuity and animation!

> " He who planted the ear, shall he not hear?
> He who formed the eye, shall he not see?"*

The last quality that I shall mention as essential to a parable or proverb, is elegance; which is not inconsistent with brevity, or indeed with some degree of obscurity. I speak of elegance as it respects the sentiment, the imagery, and the diction; and of its union with all these we have already had sufficient proof in all the parables which have been quoted in the course of this Lecture. It may however be proper to remark in this place, that even those proverbs which are the plainest, most obvious and simple, which contain nothing remarkable either in sentiment or style, are not to be esteemed without their peculiar elegance, if they possess only brevity, and that neat compact form, and roundness of period, which alone are sufficient to constitute a parable. Such is the maxim quoted by David in the sacred history as an ancient proverb,

> "Wickedness will proceed from the wicked."†

Such is that of Solomon,

> " Hate stirreth up strifes;
> But love covereth all transgressions:"‡

and many others which might easily be produced from the same author.

There is another didactic work of Solomon, entitled *Kohelet*, (Ecclesiastes,) or the Preacher; or rather perhaps Wisdom the Preacher; the general tenor and style of which is very different from the book of Proverbs, though there are many detached sentiments and proverbs interspersed: for the whole work is uniform, and confined to one subject, namely, the vanity of the world exemplified by the experience of Solomon; who is introduced in the character of a person investigating a very difficult question, examining the arguments on either side, and at length disengaging himself from an anxious and doubtful disputation. It would be very difficult to distinguish the parts and arrangement of

---

* Psal. xciv. 9.   † 1 Sam. xxiv. 13.   ‡ Prov. x. 12.

this production; the order of the subject and the connexion of the arguments are involved in so much obscurity, that scarcely any two commentators have agreed concerning the plan of the work, and the accurate division of it into parts or sections. The truth is, the laws of methodical composition and arrangement were neither known by the Hebrews, nor regarded in their didactic writings. They uniformly retained the old sententious manner, nor did they submit to method, even where the occasion appeared to demand it. The style of this work is, however, singular: the language is generally low, I might almost call it mean or vulgar; it is frequently loose, unconnected, approaching to the incorrectness of conversation; and possesses very little of the poetical character, even in the composition and structure of the periods—which peculiarity may possibly be accounted for from the nature of the subject. Contrary to the opinion of the rabbies, Ecclesiastes has been classed among the poetical books; though, if their authority and opinions were of any weight or importance, they might perhaps, on this occasion, deserve some attention.*

Some of the Psalms also belong properly to this class— the alphabetical, for instance, with some others. The alphabetical or acrostic form of composition has been more than once alluded to in the course of these Lectures. The chief commendation of these poems is, that they are excellently accommodated to ordinary use; that the sentiments are serious, devout, and practical; the language chaste and perspicuous; the composition neat, and regularly adapted to the sententious form.

There are extant, besides these, two other considerable works of the didactic kind, which the Hebrew poetry may legally claim, though they are not extant in Greek prose: I mean the Wisdom of the Son of Sirach, and that which is entitled the Wisdom of Solomon.

The work of the Son of Sirach, translated from the Hebrew into Greek by one of the descendants of the author, is altogether of the same kind with the Proverbs of Solomon; insomuch that it originally bore the same title, (*Mashalim*,) as we learn from Jerome, who directly asserts that he had

---

* It is the opinion of a very ingenious writer, in a learned work which he has lately produced, that the greater part of this book was written in prose, but that it contains many scraps of poetry, introduced as occasion served; and to this opinion I am inclined to assent. See A. V. Desvoeux, *Tent. Phil. & Crit. in Eccles.* lib. ii., cap. 1.—*Author's Note.*

seen the book in Hebrew :* and I see no reason why his
assertion should not relate to the original Hebrew copy,
rather than to any Syriac version. However this may be, it
is clear, even from the Greek translation which we have, that
the book in every respect resembles the Proverbs of Solomon, as nearly as an imitation can resemble an original.
There is a great similarity in the matter, the sentiments,
and the diction ; the complexion of the style, and the construction of the periods, are quite the same : so that I cannot entertain a doubt, that the author actually adopted the
same mode of versification, whatever it was, if we can admit
that any knowledge of the Hebrew metres was extant at the
time when he is supposed to have written. For all that we
are able to conjecture on this head we are indebted to the
great fidelity of the translator, which is abundantly manifested in every part of the work. He seems, indeed, not at
all to have affected the elegances of the Greek language,
but to have performed his duty with the most religious
regard to the Hebrew idiom : he not only exhibits faithfully
the sentiments, but seems even to have numbered the words,
and exactly to have preserved their order; so that, were it
literally and accurately to be re-translated, I have very little
doubt that, for the most part, the original diction would be
recovered. If any person will make the experiment on a
small scale, he will readily discern the perfect coincidence
of this composition with the most ancient specimens of the
didactic poetry of the Hebrews; so exact indeed is the agreement, both in form and character, that the reader might
without much difficulty be persuaded, that he was perusing
the compositions of another Solomon. This author is however an imitator chiefly of the former part of the book of
Proverbs : for there is more connexion and order in the
sentiments; the style is also more highly coloured, and
abounds more in imagery and figures, than the didactic
poetry of the Hebrews in general requires. As an instance
I need only mention that admirable personification of Wisdom exhibited by him, in which he has so happily adopted
the manner of his great predecessor.†

The Wisdom of Solomon is also composed in imitation of
that prince of didactic writers, but with a degree of success
very unequal indeed to that of the Son of Sirach. It is not,
like the book which bears his name, a translation from the

---

* Præf. in Libros Salomonis.   † Eccl'us. xxiv.

Hebrew, but is evidently the performance of some Hellenistic Jew, and originally written in Greek. The style is very unequal; it is often pompous and turgid, as well as tedious and diffuse, and abounds in epithets, directly contrary to the practice of the Hebrews; it is however sometimes temperate, poetical, and sublime. The construction is occasionally sententious, and tolerably accurate in that respect, so as to discover very plainly that the author had the old Hebrew poetry for his model, though he fell far short of its beauty and sublimity. The economy of the work is still more faulty: he continues the prayers of Solomon from the ninth chapter to the very end of the book; and they consequently take up more than one-half of the whole. But beside the tediousness of such an harangue, he indulges in too great a subtilty of disquisition upon abstruse subjects, and mingles many things very foreign to the nature of an address to the Deity; and, after all, the subject itself is brought to no perfect conclusion. On these accounts I agree with those critics who suppose this book to be a much more modern production than that of the Son of Sirach, and to have been composed in a less enlightened age.

That I may not dismiss the subject without exhibiting a specimen of some complete poem of the kind, such as I have hitherto given, I shall add to this Lecture a translation of a part of Ecclesiasticus, namely, that elegant personification of Wisdom I lately mentioned; in which I have endeavoured as much as possible to preserve, or rather restore, the form and character of the original Hebrew.*

---

* Our Author's observations on the nature and origin of Didactic Poetry are most strikingly just; and, on inspecting the early didactic productions of the Greeks, the old sententious form may be easily discovered: indeed, that pointed and antithetic manner seems (probably by the force of habit and imitation) to have pervaded this kind of poetry, both ancient and modern. To our author's excellent remarks on the subject I will add, that the science of morals appears to be the only branch of discipline which can be successfully treated of in verse. The study of abstract science demands a disposition of mind very different from that which enjoys the playfulness of fancy. In such didactic poetry, therefore, as professes to treat of any subject but morals, the mind is either too much warmed by the language, imagery, and episodes, to think of the main drift of the author, and then he is not understood, as, I believe, is generally found to be the case in reading Dr. Akenside's *Pleasures of Imagination;* or else the attention is fixed upon the matter, and then the poetical style is an unnecessary and meretricious ornament, which only perplexes the mind by diverting it from its object. The reason why ethics may be safely taught in verse seems to be, because that science is conversant chiefly with the human passions, and the delineation of them; and poetry being no other than the language of passion, will, on such a subject, rather illustrate than confuse. I may

S

THE TWENTY-FOURTH CHAPTER OF ECCLESIASTICUS.

" Wisdom shall praise her own spirit,
And shall glory in the midst of her people :
In the congregation of the Most High shall she open her
    mouth ;
And in the presence of his power shall she glory.
I proceeded out of the mouth of the Most High ;
And as a mist I covered the earth.
I dwelt above on high,
And my throne was in the pillar of a cloud.
I compassed the circuit of the heavens alone,
And walked in the depth of the abyss.
In the waves of the sea, and in all the earth,
And in every people, and every nation, I obtained a possession :
With all these I sought rest ;
And in whose inheritance shall I abide ?
Then the Creator of all things commanded me,
And he that created me fixed my tabernacle ;
And said, Let thy dwelling be in Jacob,
And in Israel thine inheritance.
Before the world he created me, from the beginning ;
And I shall never cease.
In the tabernacle of holiness I served before him ;
And so was I established in Sion.
Thus in the beloved city he caused me to rest.
And over Jerusalem was my power ;
I took root in an honourable people,
In the portion of the inheritance of JEHOVAH.
As a cedar in Lebanon was I exalted,
And as a cypress on the mountains of Hermon.
As a palm-tree in Gaddi was I exalted,
And as plants of roses in Jericho :
As a fair olive in a pleasant field,
And as a plane-tree I was exalted above the waters ;
As cinnamon, and as a mass of ointment, I yielded fragrance,

add too, that ethics is a science with which mankind are most generally acquainted,
and therefore can most easily comprehend. I am aware, that on this argument the
success and popularity of some didactic poems will be alleged against me, and particularly that of the Georgics, Lucretius, and Horace's Epistle to the Pisos; but I
must remark, that these very poems owe their whole success to the episodes and the
moral sentiments with which they abound ; and I appeal to any candid reader,
whether, after all, he has not been at some times fatigued with the didactic parts of
even these most elegant productions. I do not indeed approve of long didactic
poems, even upon moral subjects ; for, unless they be enlivened by interesting
episodes and descriptions, they can scarcely fail to appear tedious and dry. — T.

And as choice myrrh I breathed forth a pleasant odour—
As galbanum, and onyx, and storax,
And as the vapour of frankincense in the tabernacle.
I, as the turpentine-tree, sent out my branches,
And my branches are the branches of glory and favour:
I, as the vine, blossomed forth a pleasant smell,
And my flowers are the embryos of honour and wealth.
Come unto me, all ye that desire me,
And with my productions be filled : ·
For my remembrance is sweeter than honey,
And my possession than the comb of the bees.
They that eat me shall yet be hungry;
And they that drink me shall yet be thirsty :
He that obeyeth me shall not be ashamed,
And those that act according to me shall not sin.
All these are in the book of the covenant of God Most High;
The law which Moses commanded,
An inheritance for the generations of Jacob.
Wisdom filleth like Pishon,
And like Hiddekel in the month Abib.
She maketh the understanding to overflow like Euphrates;
And as Jordan in the days of harvest :
She sendeth forth instruction as the river,*
And as Gihon in the days of the vintage.
The first man was not perfect in the knowledge of her,
Neither shall the last search her out :

---

* The grandson of Sirach appears in this place to have fallen into an error, and
to have failed of expressing the sentiment of his ancestor; for, finding the word imperfectly written in his copy, he read it כאר, and rashly translated it ὡς φως, as
the light. Observe also the incongruity of this word with the context, according to
the common reading: Pison, Tigris, Euphrates, Jordan, *the light*, Gihon; in the
place of *the light*, some river must certainly be intended ; and therefore we ought to
read כיאור, ὡς ὁ Ποταμος, *as the river*, that is, the Nile, so called for the sake of
distinction ; and doubtless to a Jew, who resided in its neighbourhood, and who was
a spectator of its wonderful inundations, it would appear worthy of being ranked with
the most noble rivers, and consequently worthy of this distinction. Moreover,
Jablonskius, *Pantheon. Egypt.* lib. iv., cap. 1, sect. 2, is of opinion, that the word
יאר chiefly refers to the Nile in the sacred writers; and supposes יאר, in the
Egyptian *Jaro*, to have been the first and only name of the Nile among the
Egyptians. This word, however, itself is defectively read כאר, Amos viii. 8, ("it
is read כיאר in four MSS."—K.) but being repeated immediately, it is more fully
expressed כיאר, ix. 5. See Cappell. *Crit. Sac.* iv. 2. 11. A learned friend of mine
observed to me, that the great Bochart had long since been of the same opinion,
whose authority I am happy to adduce in favour of what I have here asserted : " אר
is a *river*, as well as יאר. So it occurs Amos viii. 8, where it is spoken of the Nile;
and in the same sense it is used by the Son of Sirach, Eccl'us. xxiv. 27, where it
has been hastily translated *the light*." *Chanaan*, lib. i., chap. 23.—*Author's
Note.*

For her thoughts are more extensive than the sea,
And her counsels than the vast abyss.
I came forth also as a brook from a river,
And as a stream in Paradise welled from its fountain :
I said, I will water my garden,
And I will abundantly water my furrow ;
And behold, my brook became a river,
And my river became a sea.
For I will beam forth instruction as the morning :
I will make it to shine afar off :
For I will pour out doctrine as prophecy,
And bequeath it to all generations for ever.
Behold, I have not laboured for myself alone,
But for all who inquire after the truth."*

* The following translation of this admirable chapter into English verse was furnished me by an ingenious friend ; and I dare believe will prove acceptable to the
reader.—T.

ECCLESIASTICUS—CHAPTER XXIV.

Wisdom shall raise her loud, exulting voice,
And, 'midst her people, glory and rejoice ;
Oft the Almighty's awful presence near,
Her dulcet sounds angelic choirs shall hear.
Wak'd by the breath of heaven's high King to birth,
I seem'd : loud involving skies and earth ;
Aloft on places high was my retreat,
Dark mists encircled my exalted seat ;
Round the broad sky I solitary rov'd,
Or through the mazy depths of ocean mov'd ;
My paths amidst the swelling waves remain'd,
Some power in every changing clime I gain'd ;
With each, with all, I anxious sought repose—
But where, say where, shall Wisdom's wanderings close ?
Hark ! did not He who fram'd the worlds command,
Here shall thy much-lov'd tabernacle stand,
Here on the plains of Jacob shalt thou live,
Thy goodly heritage shall Israel give ?—
Me, before time itself, he gave to day,
Nor shall my spirit faint, or feel decay ;
I bow'd before him in his hallow'd shrine,
And Sion's pride and Sion's strength was mine.
Did I not tall as those fair cedars grow,
Which grace our Lebanon's exalted brow ?
Did I not lofty as the cypress rise,
Which seems from Hermon's heights to meet the skies ?
Fresh as Engaddi's palm that scents the air,
Like rose of Jericho, so sweet, so fair ;
Green as the verdant olive of the groves,
Straight as the plane-tree which the streamlet loves ?
Around soft cinnamon its odour spreads,
Aspalathus perfumes our balmy meads ;
More grateful still does myrrh its fragrance yield,
Sweet to the sense, the glory of the field ;—

In Salem's temple, at JEHOVAH's shrine,
From frankincense ascends a fume divine;
Yet did my breath more precious balms exhale,
And charge with fragrance each auspicious gale.
I the rich produce of the seasons bring,
And grace and honour 'midst my foliage spring;
Richer than vineyards rise my sacred bowers,
Sweeter than roses bloom my vernal flowers:
Fair love is mine, and hope, and gentle fear;
Me science hallows, as a parent dear.
    Come, who aspire beneath my shade to live;
Come, all my fragrance, all my fruits receive!
Sweeter than honey are the strains I sing,
Sweeter than honey-comb the dower I bring:
Me, taste who will, shall feel increas'd desire.
Who drinks shall still my flowing cups require;
He whose firm heart my precepts still obeys,
With safety walks through life's perplexing maze;
Who cautious follows where my footsteps lead,
No cares shall feel, no nightly terrors dread.
    Heaven's book records my ever sacred lore,
Deriv'd from HIM whom earth and seas adore:
His wisdom guides this varying scene below,
(Clear as in spring the streams of Tigris flow;)
His spirit fills with hope th' expanding soul,
Full as the waters of Euphrates roll;
Or as, when harvest swells the golden grain,
Impetuous Jordan rushes o'er the plain.
From him the ray of holy science shines,
Bright as the sun maturing Geon's vines:
Man breath'd at first unconscious of the power,
Nor knows Heaven's wisdom at his latest hour.
Small was my stream, when first I roll'd along
In clear meanders Eden's vales among;
With freshening draughts each tender plant I fed,
And bade each flow'ret raise its blushing head:
But soon my torrent o'er its margin rose,
Where late a brook, behold an ocean flows!
For Wisdom's blessing shall o'er earth extend,
Blessings that know no bound, that know no end—
Each selfish labour Wisdom shall disdain,
My fruit, my treasures, all who seek shall gain.

OF LYRIC POETRY.

LECTURE XXV.

OF THE HEBREW ODE IN GENERAL; AND FIRST OF THAT
CLASS, THE CHARACTERISTICS OF WHICH ARE SWEETNESS
AND ELEGANCE.

*Lyric Poetry originated from the most jocund and pleasing affections of the human
mind—The most ancient species of poetry, and almost coeval with human nature
itself—Particularly cultivated by the Hebrews—The manner, introduced by David,
of singing their odes highly magnificent—The general character of this species
of poetry: its principal distinctions—The first character of the Ode sweetness—
What passions and affections it is intended to express: examples from the Psalms
—The 133rd Psalm in English verse.*

THOSE compositions which were intended for music, whether
vocal alone, or accompanied with instruments, obtained
among the Hebrews the appellation of *Shir*, among the
Greeks that of *Odé ;* and both these words have exactly the
same power and signification. The Hebrew word, as well
as the Greek, appears in course of time to have been appropriated to denote a particular form and species of poetry,
with this difference, however, that it is occasionally used with
greater latitude.

The ode is in its nature sufficiently expressive of its origin.
It was the offspring of the most vivid and the most agreeable
passions of the mind—of love, joy, and admiration. If we
consider man on his first creation, such as the sacred writings
represent him—in perfect possession of reason and speech;
neither ignorant of his own nor of the Divine nature, but
fully conscious of the goodness, majesty, and power of God;
not an unobservant spectator of the beautiful fabric of the
universe; is it not probable, that, on the contemplation of
these objects, his heart would glow with gratitude and love?
And is it not probable, that the effect of such an emotion

would be an effusion of praise to his great Creator, accompanied with a suitable energy and exaltation of voice? Such
indeed were the sensations experienced by the author of that
most beautiful Psalm, in which the whole creation is invited
to celebrate the glory of the most high God :

> " Praise JEHOVAH from the heavens ;
> Praise him in the heights :
> Praise him, all his angels ;
> Praise him, all his hosts."*

This hymn is therefore most elegantly imitated, and put
into the mouth of Adam, by our countryman Milton,† who
is justly accounted the next in sublimity to those poets who
wrote under the influence of Divine inspiration. Indeed, we
scarcely seem to conceive rightly of that original and perfect
state of man, unless we assign him some of the aids of harmony and poetical expression, to enable him to testify, in
terms becoming the dignity of the subject, his devout affections towards his infinite Creator.

Without carrying our researches, however, to objects so
remote from human information, if we appeal only to the
common testimony of history we shall find, that, among
every people not utterly barbarous, the use of music and
poetry, in the celebration of their religious mysteries, has
prevailed from the first periods of society. Of all that sacred
melody which Plato informs us was sometimes established
by the solemn sanction of legal authority,‡ he assigns the
first rank to that which assumed the form of addresses to the
Deity, and was distinguished by the appellation of Hymns.
In all the Latin poetry, there is nothing that can boast equal
antiquity with the Salian poems of Numa, composed by that
wise and learned monarch on the first institution of his religious rites, and sung by the Salii, whom Dionysius styles
" the chorus of the Gods of War,"§ with solemn dancing
and other religious ceremonies. There is scarcely any necessity to mention, that the most ancient of all poems extant
(those I mean of which the date is ascertained, and which
deserve the name of poems) is the thanksgiving ode of Moses
on passing the Red Sea; the most perfect in its kind, and
the true and genuine effusion of the joyful affections. Thus
the origin of the ode may be traced into that of poetry itself,

---

* Psa. cxlviii.　　　　　　　　† Parad. Lost, lib. v.
‡ De Legibus, iii.　　　　　　　§ Antiq. Rom. ii. 70.

and appears to be coeval with the commencement of religion, or more properly the creation of man.*

The Hebrews cultivated this kind of poetry above every other, and therefore may well be supposed to have been peculiarly excellent in it.   It was usual in every period of that nation to celebrate in songs of joy their gratitude to God their saviour for every fortunate event, and particularly for success in war.   Hence the triumphal odes of Moses, of Deborah, of David.   The schools of the prophets were also, in all probability, coeval with the republic; and were certainly antecedent to the monarchy by many years: there, as we have already seen, the youth, educated in the prophetic discipline, applied themselves, among other studies, particularly to sacred poetry, and celebrated the praises of Almighty God in lyric compositions, accompanied with music.   Under the government of David, however, the arts of music and poetry were in their most flourishing state.   By him no less than four thousand singers or musicians were appointed from among the Levites,† under two thousand and eighty-eight principal singers, or leaders of the band, and distributed into twenty-four companies, who officiated weekly by rotation in the temple, and whose whole business was to perform the sacred hymns—the one part chanting or singing, and the other playing upon different instruments.‡   The chief of these were Asaph, Heman, and Iduthun, who also,

---

* This conclusion appears to me neither consonant to reason nor to fact.   The first use of poetry was probably to preserve the remembrance of events, and not the expression of passions; accordingly, the remains of the first poetic compositions appear to have been of the former kind.   One instance was given in a preceding Lecture relative to the history of Lamech, and another may here be added concerning that of Nimrod—"He was a mighty hunter (rather warrior) before the Lord:" wherefore it is said,

" As Nimrod the mighty hunter before the Lord."

Agreeable to this idea is an observation, respecting the Arabians, of the late ingenious but ill-treated Dr. Brown: " *The oldest compositions* are in *rhythm* or *rude verse,* and are often cited as *proofs* of their *subsequent history."*   It is not only evident that Moses applied them in this way, but also that they were long prior to any example of the existence of an ode; which, however, seems to have been in fact, as well as in nature, the next species of poetic composition.—S. H.

The rude poetry of barbarous nations (as far as we can judge from the accounts of those who have visited the South-Sea islands and the Indian nations) relates in general to *love* and *war;* it is employed in cherishing or in exciting the passions.   Notwithstanding, therefore, the ingenuity of the above remark, (which on that account I would not omit,) I am inclined to think there is more foundation for our Author's theory than Mr. H. supposes.   See *Essays Hist. and Mor.* Ess. I. p. 31.—T.

† 1 Chron. xxiii. 5.   ‡ 1 Chron. xxv. 1—7.

as we may presume from the titles of the Psalms, were com-
posers of hymns.* From so very splendid an establishment,
so far surpassing every other appointment of the kind, some
reasonable conjectures may be formed concerning the original dignity and grandeur of the Hebrew ode. We must
remember too, that we at present possess only some ruins
as it were of that magnificent fabric, deprived of every
ornament, except that splendour and elegance which, notwithstanding the obscurity that antiquity has cast over them,
still shine forth in the sentiments and language. Hence, in
treating of the Hebrew ode, we must be content to omit
entirely what relates to the sacred music, and the nature of
the instruments which accompanied the vocal performance;
though there is the utmost probability, that these circumstances were not without their influence as far as respects
the form and construction of the different species of ode.
Our information upon these subjects is, indeed, so very
scanty, that I esteem it safer to be silent altogether concerning them, than to imitate the example of some of the learned,
who, after saying much, have in fact said nothing. I shall
therefore proceed to a brief inquiry into the general nature
and properties of this species of poetry; and after that, we
shall be better qualified to judge of those specimens which
have been transmitted to us by the Hebrew writers.

Of all the different forms of poetical composition, there is
none more agreeable, harmonious, elegant, diversified, and
sublime, than the ode; and these qualities are displayed in
the order, sentiments, imagery, diction, and versification.
The principal beauty of an ode consists in the order and
arrangement of the subject; but this excellence, while it is
easily felt, is difficult to be described, for there is this peculiarity attending it, that the form of the ode is by no means
confined to any certain rule for the exact and accurate distribution of the parts. It is lively and unconstrained: when
the subject is sublime, it is impetuous, bold, and sometimes
might almost deserve the epithet *licentious* as to symmetry
and method; but even in this case, and uniformly in every
other, a certain facility and ease must pervade the whole,
which may afford at least the appearance of unaffected elegance, and seem to prefer nature to art. This appearance
is best preserved by an exordium, plain, simple, and expressive; by a display and detail of incidents and sentiments

* See also 2 Chron. xxix. 30.

rising delicately and artfully from each other, yet without any appearance of art; and by a conclusion not pointed or epigrammatic, but finishing by a gentle turn of the sentiment in a part where it is least expected, and sometimes as it were by chance.* Thus, it is not the metre or versification which constitutes this species of composition; for, unless all these circumstances be adverted to, it is plain, that whatever be the merit of the production, it cannot with any propriety be termed an ode. Many of the odes of Horace are entirely in this form, as well as almost all of those few which our countryman Hannes has left behind him. There are two lyric poems in the Sylvæ of Papinius Statius,† of which the versification is full, sonorous, and flowing; the sentiments elegant; the diction, if not highly polished, yet ardent and glowing—on the whole, however, the form, the grace, the express manner of the ode is wanting.

The sentiments and imagery must be suitable to the nature of the subject and the composition, which is varied and unconfined by strict rule or method. On familiar subjects they will be sprightly, florid, and agreeable : on sublime topics, solemn, bold, and vivid; on every subject, highly elegant, expressive, and diversified. Imagery from natural objects is peculiarly adapted to the ode; historical commonplaces may also be admitted, as well as descriptions lively but short, and (when it rises to any uncommon strain of sublimity) frequent personifications. The diction must be choice and elegant; it must be also luminous, clear, and animated; it must possess some elegances peculiar to itself, and be as distinct from the common language of poetry, as the form and fashion of the production is from the general cast of poetical composition. In this that happiness of expression, for which Horace is so justly celebrated, wholly consists. A sweetness and variety in the versification is indispensable, according to the nature of the language, or as the infinite diversity of subjects may require.

It is much to be lamented, that, in treating of the Hebrew ode, we must of necessity be silent concerning the numbers or versification, which (though we are almost totally ignorant

---

* I do not know any lyric poems to which this commendation is more applicable than the Arabic: I do not speak of all, but the best of them. I have scarcely ever observed happier conclusions to any poems, than to some of the Arabic odes.—M.

† Lib. iv. *Sylv.* 5 & 7.

of its nature and principles) we have the utmost reason to suppose was accommodated to the music, and agreeable to the genius of the language.* In every other respect—as the force and elegance of the language, the beauty and dignity of the sentiments and imagery, the different graces and excellences of order and arrangement—I shall not hesitate to prefer the Hebrew writers to the lyric poets of every other nation. But lest we should dubiously wander in so extensive a field, it will be proper to prescribe some kind of limit to our course, which may be conveniently done by distributing all the diversities of this species of composition into three general classes. Of the first class the general characteristic will be sweetness; of the last, sublimity; and between these we may introduce one of a middle nature, as partaking of the properties of both.† The qualities which may be

---

* This may be presumed from a variety of circumstances, particularly such as might be pointed out in the cxxxvth Psalm, where *Jah* is sometimes used and sometimes *Jehovah*, where either might, for any other than a metrical consideration, have been indiscriminately used.—S. H.

† It will not be unseasonable in this place, perhaps, to offer a few remarks on the peculiar character of the lyric poetry of David. For some commentators, by too indiscriminately praising it, have paid no regard to its peculiar characteristics; and thus, from an intemperate zeal, the poet has even lost a part of that commendation which was justly due to him.

For my part, judging rather by my taste and feelings than by any rules of art, I think David seems to excel in this first species of ode, the characteristic of which is sweetness. He is unequalled when he describes the objects of nature—the fields, the woods, the fountains; and of his other odes those are most excellent which he composed in his exiles: nor is this any thing extraordinary; he had then more leisure for the cultivation of poetry, he experienced more vivid sensations than at other times, and he treated of those objects which, being immediately before his eyes, brought back to his mind the recollection of his youth, and inspired his imagination with fresh vigour. It is however remarkable, that those which he composed in his old age, when he fled from Absalom, not only equal the fruits of his early years, but even surpass them in fire and spirit—if, as I am fully persuaded, the xxiiird and xliind Psalms were produced during that exile.

On the other hand, those Psalms interest me less, in which the more violent affections prevail, whether of sorrow or indignation, not even excepting such as imprecate curses on his enemies. There is in these much of the terrific: but in reading them the heart is not affected, the passions are not vehemently excited. These odes do not possess that general solemnity and awful sublimity which characterise the book of Job; a composition of a different class, but possessing exquisite force in moving the passions. Neither are loftiness of diction, or boldness in describing objects of terror, to be accounted amongst the excellences of David; for in these respects he not only yields, in my opinion, to Job, but also to Moses. I do not except the xviiith Psalm, in the first verses of which I observe more of art and design than of real horror and sublimity: in what follows, the warmth of the composition subsides, and it becomes more temperate than might be expected from such an exordium.

accounted common to all the three classes, are variety and elegance.

Although the lyric poetry of the Hebrews is always occupied upon serious subjects, nor ever descends to that levity which is admitted into that of other nations, the character of sweetness is by no means inconsistent with it. The sweetness of the Hebrew ode consists in the gentle and tender passions which it excites, in the gay and florid imagery, and in the chaste and unostentatious diction which it employs. The passions which it generally affects are those of love, tenderness, hope, cheerfulness, and pensive sorrow. In the sixty-third Psalm the royal prophet, supposed to be then an exile in the wilderness, expresses most elegantly the sentiments of tenderness and love. The voice of grief and complaint is tempered with the consolations of hope in the eightieth Psalm; and the ninety-second consists wholly of joy, which is not the less sincere because it is not excessive. The sweetness of all these in composition, sentiment, diction, and arrangement, has never been equalled by the finest productions of all the heathen Mu es and Graces united. Though none of the above are deficient in imagery, I must confess I have never met with any image so truly pleasing and delightful as the following description of the Deity in the character of a shepherd:

> " The Lord is my shepherd, I shall not want :
> In tender grass he giveth me to lie down :
> He guideth me to streams that gently flow."*

The Mosaic Psalms, I confess, please me more in this respect, and therefore I prefer the xxixth to that in question.—M.

* Psal. xxiii. 1. This Psalm is deserving of all the commendation which our Author has bestowed upon it. If I am not mistaken, it was composed by David, when he was expelled from the holy city and temple; for in the 6th verse he hopes for a return to the house of God. Since of all the divine mercies he particularly commemorates this, that in time of necessity he wants for nothing, and is even received to a banquet in the sight of his enemies, I conceive it to relate to that time, when, flying from the contest with his disobedient son, he pitched his camp beyond Jordan, and was in danger of seeing his little army perish for want of provision in that uncultivated region, or of being deserted by all his friends. Affairs, however, turned out quite different; for what he could not foresee or hope, the Almighty performed for him. The veteran soldiers flowed in to him from every quarter, and his whole camp was so liberally supported by the good and opulent citizens, that in this very situation he was enabled to collect an army, and risk the event of a battle. See 2 Sam. xvii. 26—29.

He therefore compares himself to a sheep, and the Almighty to a shepherd; a very obvious figure, and which every day occurred to his sight during his stay in those desert parts. The sheep, timid, defenceless, exposed to all the beasts

How graceful and animated is that rich and flourishing picture of nature which is exhibited in the sixty-fifth Psalm; when the prophet, with a fertility of expression correspondent to the subject, praises the beneficence of the Deity in watering the earth and making it fruitful. On a sublime subject also, but still one of the gay and agreeable kind, I mean the inauguration of Solomon, which is celebrated in the seventy-second Psalm, there is such variety and beauty of imagery, such a splendour of diction, such elegance in the composition, that I believe it will be impossible in the whole compass of literature, sacred or profane, to find such an union of sublimity with sweetness and grace.

These few select examples of the elegant and beautiful in lyric composition, I have pointed out for your more attentive consideration; and I am of opinion, that in all the treasures of the Muses you will seek in vain for models more perfect. I will add one other specimen, which, if I am not mistaken, is expressive of the true lyric form and character; and compresses in a small compass all the merits and elegance

of prey, and possessed of little knowledge or power of foreseeing or avoiding danger, are indebted for life, safety, and every thing, to the care of the shepherd. We must remember also, that the exiled king had formerly himself been a shepherd. The recollection, therefore, of his past life breaks in upon his mind : " JEHOVAH," says he, " is my shepherd, I shall want nothing." It is his province to provide for my existence, and to procure for me those blessings which I am unable to obtain for myself. The *tender herb* (*dasha*, which is properly the *virgin* herb, or that which has not budded into seed or blossom) is more grateful to sheep than that which is seeded, *gnesch*, Gen. i. 10, 11. In meadows, therefore, covered with the green and tender grass, he supposes JEHOVAH to cause him to rest under his care. He was expelled to Lebanon, from the tops of which cataracts of melted snow are constantly falling : these are dangerous for sheep to approach, nor is the water sufficiently wholesome ; he therefore adds, that he is led to waters gently flowing, where the clear stream meanders through the fertile plain. The scene which was before his eye consisted of rude hills, and valleys deep, gloomy, dark, and horrid, the haunts only of the fiercest animals. I would here remark that the word צלמות, which, according to the Masoretic punctuation, is read *Tzilmavet*, and translated *the shadows of death*, would be better read *Tzilamot*, and translated simply *shades*, or *the valley of the shades;* and I am led to this conclusion by comparing it with the Arabic. There is no safety for the sheep in these valleys, but in the care of the shepherd. You are therefore presented with a great variety of contrasted imagery in this Psalm : on the one hand the open pastures, and the flowing rivulets, the recollection of which never fails to delight; and, on the other hand, the cheerless and gloomy valleys, which inspire the reader with fresh horror. Descending from figurative to plain language, he next celebrates the bounty of God in preparing him a banquet in the face of his enemies, and therefore regales himself with the delicious hope, that he shall once more be restored to his sacred temple.—M.

Mr. Tate (in our common version of the Psalms) has been remarkably fortunate

incidental to that species of composition. It is, if I may be
allowed to use the expression of a very polite writer,

> A drop from Helicon, a flower
> Cull'd from the Muse's favourite bower.*

The Psalmist, contemplating the harmony which pervaded
the solemn assembly of the people at the celebration of one
of their festivals, expresses himself nearly as follows:

PSALM CXXXIII. †

> " How blest the sight, the joy how sweet,
> When brothers join'd with brothers meet
>   In bands of mutual love !
> Less sweet the liquid fragrance, shed
> On Aaron's consecrated head,
>   Ran trickling from above ;
> And reach'd his beard, and reach'd his vest :
> Less sweet the dews on Hermon's breast
>   Or Sion's hill descend :

in his paraphrase of the first verses of this Psalm; so much indeed, that for
simplicity, and a close adherence to the spirit of the original, I cannot help pre-
ferring it to the celebrated translation of Mr. Addison :

> " The Lord himself, the mighty Lord,
>   Vouchsafes to be my guide ;
> The shepherd, by whose constant care
>   My wants are all supplied.
> In tender grass he makes me feed,
>   And gently there repose ;
> And leads me to cool shades, and where
>   Refreshing water flows."

The fifteenth Psalm is also admirably translated by the same hand : the last verse
in particular is beautiful and sublime; though the classical reader will see that the
translator had his eye on the " Si fractus illabatur orbis " of Horace.—T.

* Callimach. *Hymn. in Apoll.* v. 112.

† This Psalm is one of the fifteen which are entitled *Odes of the Ascensions ;* that
is, which were sung when the people *came* up either to worship in Jerusalem at the
annual festivals, or perhaps from the Babylonish captivity.   The *return* is certainly
called " the *ascension,* or *coming up* from Babylon," Ezra vii. 9.   And the old
Syriac translator, who explains the subject of the Psalms by apposite titles, refers
to this circumstance almost all the Psalms that bear this inscription ; some of
them indeed without sufficient foundation, but many of them manifestly have
relation to it.   Theodoret indiscriminately explains them all as relating to the Babylonish captivity; and thus illustrates the title: " Odes of the Ascensions; Theodotion,
Songs of the Ascensions; but Symmachus and Aculas, on the Returns. It is evident
that the coming up, and the ascent, relate to the return of the people from the Babylonish captivity." Theod. in Psa. cxx.   But we must not omit remarking also, that
both in the Old and New Testament there is scarcely a phrase more common than
"to go up to Jerusalem, to go up to the feast," &c. (See John vii. 8.) And observe

> That hill has God with blessings crown'd,
> There promis'd grace that knows no bound,
> And life that knows no end."*

above the rest Psal. cxxii. which can scarcely be applied to any thing but the celebration of some festival. What the Jews say about the steps *ascending* to the
temple is unworthy the attention of any person of common sense. In the last period of this Psalm, the particle שׁם, *shom*, is necessarily to be referred to the word
צִיּוֹן, *tzion;* and there is nothing else to which it can be referred. Besides, to what,
except to *Sion*, can the promises *Berachah* and *Chajom* relate? (See particularly
Psal. cxxxii. 13, and 15.) These words are indeed ambiguous, so that they may
refer either to temporal or eternal happiness, or to both alike. (Compare Deut.
xxviii. 2, &c. with Psal. xxiv. 5; and Prov. xxvii. 27, with Dan. xii. 2.) And in
this place, according to the nature of the mystical allegory, they may be interpreted
in either sense. If these remarks be true, the critics have taken a great deal of
pains about nothing. There is no occasion for emendation. If the ellipsis be only
supplied by the word *ce-tal, as the dew*, or simply by the particle *ve* or *ce, and* or *as*,
before the word *descending*, (or which descends,) the construction will be complete.
In the same manner Hezekiah says in Isaiah,
"As a swallow, (and as) a crane, so I chattered." Chap. xxxviii. 14.—*Author's
Note.*

* On a former occasion I thought it necessary to trouble the reader with an
imitation of Buchanan's version of this beautiful Psalm. I have since endeavoured
to complete it. If the measure should seem in the eyes of some to bear too near a
resemblance to that of their old acquaintance Sternhold, I have only to urge, that
its simplicity seems to be more suitable to the subject than that which Mr. Merrick
has adopted. Notwithstanding our Author's ingenious defence of his own (which is
also Mr. Merrick's) interpretation of the last verse, I am well convinced that Buchanan's version is right, and that the particle *shom* in the last verse relates to the persons, and not to the place; indeed, not only a great part of the general utility, but
even the beauty of this ode is lost, by interpreting it otherwise. The following I
submit, with all humility, to the judgment of the reader, merely that I may not
leave the former stanzas imperfect.

PSALM CXXXIII.

> Sweet is the love that mutual glows
>   Within each brother's breast,
> And binds in gentlest bonds each heart,
>   All blessing, and all blest:
> Sweet as the odorous balsam pour'd
>   On Aaron's sacred head,
> Which o'er his beard, and down his vest,
>   A breathing fragrance shed:
> Like morning dews on Sion's mount,
>   That spread their silver rays,
> And deck with gems the verdant pomp
>   Which Hermon's top displays.
> To such the Lord of life and love
>   His blessing shall extend;
> On earth a life of joy and peace,
>   And life that ne'er shall end.—T.

LECTURE XXVI.

THE INTERMEDIATE OR MIXED STYLE OF THE HEBREW ODE.

The Lyric Poetry of the intermediate or mixed style consists of an union of sweetness and sublimity—The 91st and 81st Psalms explained and critically illustrated—Of the digressions of the Hebrew poets, also of Pindar; not upon the same principle— A criticism upon the 77th Psalm—The 19th Psalm in English verse.

HAVING dismissed the subject of the more beautiful species of ode, in order to proceed by proper stages to what I deem the summit of excellence and sublimity in the lyric poetry of the Hebrews, it will be necessary to rest awhile, and to bestow some little attention upon that middle style of composition, to which I adverted as constituting one of the grand divisions of this order of poems. This again may be considered as admitting of a subdivision, as including both those lyric compositions in which sweetness and sublimity are so uniformly blended, that every part of the poem may be said to partake equally of both; and those in which these qualities separately occur in such a manner, that the complexion of the poem is altogether changeable and diversified. Of each species I shall endeavour to produce an example or two.

The subject of the ninety-first Psalm is the security, the success, and the rewards of piety. The exordium exhibits the pious man placing all his dependence upon Almighty God:

" He that dwelleth in the secret place of the Most High;
  Who lodgeth under the shadow of the Omnipotent;
  Who saith to JEHOVAH, Thou art my hope and my fortress!
  My God, in whom I trust!"*——

---

* This beautiful exordium has been most egregiously mistaken by the Masorites, and by many commentators and translators; whose errors will be most effectually demonstrated by removing the difficulties of which they complain. Thus, the אמר is in *Benoni* as well as ישב; the future יתלונן also has the force of a participle, by the ellipsis of אשר; of which, to go no further, we have three examples in this very Psalm, ver. 5, 6; thus also Symmachus, who has translated the first verse in this manner:

    " He dwelling under the canopy of the Most High,
      Lodging under the shadow of the Mighty One."

And immediately leaving the sentence unfinished, he apostrophises to the same person whom he had been describing:

"He indeed shall deliver thee
From the snare of the fowler, from the destroying pestilence."

The imagery that follows is beautiful and diversified, and at the same time uncommonly solemn and sublime:

" With his feathers will he cover thee;
And under his wings shalt thou find protection:
His truth shall be thy shield and thy defence.
Thou shalt not fear from the terror by night;
From the arrow that flieth by day;
From the pestilence that walketh in darkness;*
From the destruction that wasteth at noon.
A thousand shall fall at thy side;
And ten thousand at thy right hand:
To thee it shall not approach."

How excellent also are the succeeding images—the guard of angels; the treading under foot the fiercest and most formidable animals; and afterwards, that sudden but easy and elegant change of the persons !†

Whence it is plain, that he did not take the verb אמר as if it were the first person of the future, as the Masorites have done; whence principally the error has originated: nor indeed has he compacted into one nugatory proposition the two members of the first verse, which are parallel and synonymous. Then in verse 3, an apostrophe very easy and distinct is made to the person to whom the preceding expressions relate: where it is also to be remarked, that the particle כי is not casual but affirmative, *indeed* or *in fact*, as in Psa. lxxvii. 12. 1 Sam. xiv. 39, and 44, and in many other parts of Scripture. But to demonstrate more clearly this matter by example, the whole form and nature of this exordium is perfectly the same with that of Psa. cxxviii. which has never been considered as involving any obscurity:

" Blessed is every man who feareth JEHOVAH,
And who walketh in his paths:
Thou, indeed, shalt eat the labour of thy hands;
O happy art thou, and well shall it be with thee."

But if, after all, any reader should not be satisfied with the apostrophe formed from the abrupt sentence, he may take the verb אמר for the third person preterite, as the Syr. does. Thus, the first verse will be the subject, and the second the predicate of the proposition. To this explication I am not averse, and it is certainly much better than that which is now generally received. But even in this manner, from the condensing of two verses into one sentence, there will arise a languor in the sentiment, and they will form almost one and the same proposition. *Author's Note.*

  * See a note on the History of the Caliph Vathek, p. 245, and 319.—T.

  † I apprehend there is no change of person till the 14th verse; for the 9th verse I take to be of quite a different nature:

" For thou, JEHOVAH, art my hope:
Very high hast thou placed thy refuge."

T

" Because he hath loved me, therefore will I deliver him:
　I will exalt him, for he hath known my name."

If any reader will carefully weigh and consider the nature
and dignity of this imagery, having due respect at the same
time to the principles of the mystical allegory, I am per-

There are many interpretations of this period, which are differently approved by
different persons. One of these is, that the first member consists of an address
from the believer to God, and the second of a reply from the Prophet to the
believer, which is extremely harsh and improbable, although the plain and obvious
construction of the passage favours this opinion. Others, among which are the old
translators, suppose, that in the second line there is no change of persons at all, but
that JEHOVAH is still spoken of,

" Who hast placed thy dwelling on high;"

which is altogether nothing. Others, in fine, to avoid these absurdities, have fallen
into still greater; for they give quite a new turn to the sentence, altering the
construction in this manner:

" For thou, JEHOVAH, who art my hope,
　Hast placed thy refuge very high."

But this I think will scarcely be endured by a good ear, which is ever so little
accustomed to the Hebrew idiom. Theodoret formerly made a different attempt
upon the passage:—" There is wanting to the construction of the sentence, THOU
HAST SAID, *Thou Lord art my hope.* This is the usual idiom of the prophetic
writings, and especially of the Psalms."

I have very little doubt that this is the true sense of the passage. If, however,
this ellipsis be unpleasing to the reader, (and I confess it is very harsh,) we must, I
believe, at last have recourse to the correction of Bishop Hare, one of the ablest of
critics; who thinks, that for אתה we should read אמרתי. It is indeed rather a
bold conjecture, yet not improbable, if we consider the parallel places, Psalm
xvi. 2, (where אמרתי seems to have been the reading followed by all the old
translators, except the Chald. " and also occurs in three MSS."—K.,) Psalm xxxi.
15; cxl. 7; cxlii. 6. But what if we read, מחסך, with only the change of a
single letter? " For thee (that is, *as to thee,*) JEHOVAH is thy hope." This correction was suggested to me by the ingenious Mr. Merrick, who has lately published a
Translation of the Psalms into English verse; a work of great erudition, of infinite
taste and elegance, and replete with all the choicest beauties of poetry.—*Author's
Note.*

" For thou, JEHOVAH, art my hope;
　Very high hast thou placed thy habitation."

I believe there is no occasion in this instance to practise on the original. The
imagery here remotely alluded to, is placed in a fuller point of view by Habakkuk,
chap. ii. ver. 9.

" Woe unto him who coveteth an evil covetousness for his house;
　That he may set his nest on high;
　That he may be delivered from the power of evil."

And Obadiah, ver. 3.

" He that dwelleth in the clefts of the rock, the height of his habitation,
　Hath said in his heart, Who shall bring me down to the ground?
　Though thou exalt thyself as the eagle,
　And though thou set thy nest among the stars,
　Thence will I bring thee down, saith JEHOVAH."—S. H.

suaded he will agree with me, that something of a mystical design is concealed under the literal meaning of this Psalm. Without a question, the pious person,* the king, or high-priest perhaps, who in the literal sense is the principal character of the poem, is meant in reality to represent some greater and sublimer personage.   But leaving this part of the subject to the investigation of the divine, I submit it to any critic of true taste and discernment, whether the third ode of the fourth book of Horace (the beauty of which has been justly celebrated, and which bears a great resemblance to that under our consideration) is not greatly excelled by the sacred poet, as well in grace and elegance, as in force and dignity. †

* The LXX, Chald. Vulg. Syr. Arab. Æthiop. prefix the name of David to this Psalm.   The Jews suppose it to relate to the Messiah.   See also Matthew iv. 6. Luke iv. 10, 11.—*Author's Note.*

† At a very early period of life I amused myself with translating some of the Odes of Horace into English verse.   The ode alluded to in the text was one of those which I attempted.   I subjoin my translation on this occasion, merely because I think it gives the sense of the original more completely than Francis's version, and the English reader will probably wish to see the ode which is brought into comparison with that of the Psalmist.

TO MELPOMENE.

He, on whose early natal hour
　　Thou, queen of verse ! hast sweetly smil'd,
Breath'd all thy fascinating power,
　　And mark'd him for thy favourite child :

He emulates no victor's place,
　　Nor mixes in the Isthmian games ;
Nor, in the arduous chariot-race,
　　Th' Achaian trophies anxious claims.

He ne'er, adorn'd with conquering bays,
　　And the proud pomp of baneful war,
Shall catch the vagrant voice of praise,
　　While captive kings surround his car ;

But, where the fertile Tiber glides,
　　To secret shades shall oft retire ;
And there shall charm the listening tides,
　　And tune the soft Æolian lyre.

Thy noblest sons, Imperial Rome !
　　Assign to me the laureate crown :
And Envy, now abash'd and dumb,
　　Nor dares to speak, nor dares to frown.

O goddess of the vocal shell !
　　Whose power can sway both earth and sea,
Can the mute fishes teach t' excel
　　The dying cygnet's melody :

T 2

The eighty-first Psalm will serve as another example upon this occasion, being pervaded by an exquisite union of sublimity and sweetness. It is an ode composed for the Feast of Trumpets in the first new moon of the civil year.* The exordium contains an exhortation to celebrate the praises of the Almighty with music and song, and (as is frequent in these productions of the Hebrews) is replete with animation and joy, even to exultation:

> " Sing unto God our strength ;
> A song of triumph to the God of Jacob."

The different instruments of music are named, as is common in the lyric compositions of all other nations :

> "Take the psaltery, bring hither the timbrel,
> The pleasant harp, with the lute."

The trumpet is particularly alluded to, because the solemn use of it on their great festivals was prescribed by the Mosaic law. The commemoration of the giving of the law, associated with the sound of the trumpet, (which was the signal of liberty,)† introduces, in a manner spontaneously, the miseries of the Egyptian bondage, the recovery of their freedom, and the communication with God upon Mount Sinai, (the awfulness of which is expressed in a very few words, "the secret place of thunder,") and finally the contention with their Creator at the waters of Meribah. The mention of Meribah introduces another idea, namely, the ingratitude and contumacy of the Israelites, who appear to have been ever unmindful of the favours and indulgence of their heavenly Benefactor. The remainder of the ode, therefore, contains an affectionate expostulation of God with his people, a confirmation of his former promises, and a tender complaint, that his favourable intentions towards them have been so long prevented by their disobedience. Thus, the object and end of this poem appear to be an exhortation to obedience, from the consideration of the paternal love, the beneficence, and the promises of the Deity; and we have seen with how much art, elegance, variety, and ingenuity, this is accomplished. In order to complete the beauty of this composition,

> To thee, sweet Muse! I owe this fame ;
> That e'er I pleas'd, the gift is thine ;
> That, as I pass, fond crowds exclaim—
> " The Roman bard ! the man divine !"—T.

* See Reland, *Antiq. Heb.* iv. 7.
† See Lev. xxiii. 24.   Numb. xxix. 1, and Lev. xxv. 9, 10.

the conclusion is replete with all the graces of sentiment, imagery, and diction. The sudden and frequent change of persons is remarkable; but it is by no means harsh or obscure. Some allowance is however to be made for the Hebrew idiom, as well as for the state of the author's mind: he is not under the influence of art, but of nature; through the impetuosity of passion, therefore, his transitions are frequent from figure and allusion to plain language, and back again with a kind of desultory inconstancy.

In the last Lecture I treated in general of the disposition and arrangement of lyric composition, and endeavoured, in some degree, to define its usual symmetry and outline. But, on abstruse and difficult subjects, example is of more avail than the utmost accuracy of description. To him, therefore, who wishes to form a correct idea of this kind of poem, I will venture to recommend the Psalm which we have just examined; not doubting, that if he can make himself master of its general character, genius, and arrangement, he will feel perfectly satisfied concerning the nature and form of a perfect ode.

In both these specimens, the style and cadence of the whole poem flows in one equal and uniform tenor; but there are others, which are more changeable and diversified, more unequal both in style and sentiment. These, although they occasionally incline to the character of sweetness, and occasionally to that of sublimity, may nevertheless (though upon a different principle) be properly classed among the odes of this intermediate style. Such are those which, from a mild and gentle exordium, rise gradually to sublimity, both in the subject and sentiments: such also are those which commence in a mournful strain, and conclude with exultation and triumph; such, in fine, are all those in which the style or matter is in any respect diversified and unequal. This inequality of style is perfectly consistent with the nature of lyric composition; for variety is one of the greatest ornaments, if not essentials, of the ode. Since therefore, for the sake of variety, lyric writers in particular are indulged in the liberty of frequent digressions: that boldness in thus diverging from the subject is not only excusable, but on many occasions is really worthy of commendation. Possibly a brief inquiry into the nature of those liberties which the Hebrew poets have allowed themselves in this respect, or rather into the general method and

principles of their lyric compositions, will not be thought
altogether unseasonable in this place.

By far the greater part of the lyric poetry of the Hebrews
is occupied wholly in the celebration of the power and goodness of Almighty God, in extolling his kindness and beneficence to his chosen people, and in imploring his assistance
and favour in time of adversity; in other words, the usual
subjects of these odes are so connected with every part of
the sacred history, as to afford ample scope for those digressions which are most pleasing, and most congenial to this
species of composition. Thus, whether the theme be gay or
mournful; whether the events which they celebrate be prosperous or adverse; whether they return thanks to God their
deliverer for assistance in trouble, or with the humility of
suppliants acknowledge the justice of the Divine correction;
the memory of former times spontaneously occurs, and a
variety of incidents and circumstances, of times, of seasons,
of countries, of nations, all the miracles in Egypt, in the
wilderness, in Judea, are presented to their recollection: and
all these so naturally connect with the subject, that whatever
of ornament is deduced from them, so far from appearing
foreign to it, seems rather an essential part of the principal
matter. It may, therefore, be with modesty asserted of the
Hebrew ode, that, from the nature of the subjects which it
usually embraces, it is possessed of so easy an access to some
of the most elegant sources of poetical imagery, and has
consequently so many opportunities for agreeable digression,
that with unbounded freedom and uncommon variety are
united the most perfect order and the most pleasing uniformity.

The happy boldness of Pindar in his digressions is deservedly celebrated; but as he was very differently situated
from those poets who are at present under our consideration,
so the nature of his subject, and the principles of his
composition, are altogether different from theirs; and a
different reason is to be assigned for the liberties which he
assumed in his lyric productions. We are in no want of
materials to enable us to form a perfect judgment of the
genius of Pindar; there are about forty of his odes remaining, and the subject of them all is exactly similar. They
are all composed in celebration of some victorious chief,
whose praise is heightened and illustrated by the circumstances of his birth, ancestry, manners, or country. Since,

therefore, this poet was professedly the herald of the Olympic conquerors, unless he had determined to assume great liberty in treating of those topics, and even on some occasions to have recourse to topics very foreign to the principal subject, his poems must have been little better than a stale and disgusting repetition. His apology, therefore, is necessity; and on this ground he has obtained not only pardon but commendation; and many things, which in another poet could neither be defended nor probably endured, in Pindar have been approved and extolled. Lest I should seem to assert rashly on this occasion, I will explain myself by an example: The third of the Pythian odes is inscribed to Hiero, at that time labouring under a grievous and chronical disease. The poet, taking advantage of the opportunity to impart a degree of variety to his poem, introduces it with a solemn address, invoking the medical aid of Chiron or Æsculapius, if it be possible for them to revisit the earth. But surely, on such an occasion, it would be excusable in no writer but Pindar to expend more than one hundred verses, that is, above half the poem, on the history of Æsculapius. Nor indeed could we easily pardon it in Pindar himself, but from the consideration that he had already written an ode (the fourth) in praise of the same Hiero, upon a victory obtained in the Olympic games. But we are willing to excuse the boldness of a poet, who, even with a degree of rash impetuosity, escapes from such narrow limits into a more spacious field. It is therefore no discommendation of the Hebrew poets to say, that in this respect they are materially different from Pindar; nor does it detract from the merit of Pindar to assert, that, from the more favourable circumstances of the Hebrews, their lyric poetry is more genuine and perfect.

The seventy-seventh Psalm will afford some illustration of what has been remarked concerning the nature and economy of the Hebrew ode. This Psalm is composed in what I call the intermediate style, and is of that diversified and unequal kind which ascends from a cool and temperate exordium to a high degree of sublimity. The prophet, oppressed with a heavy weight of affliction, displays the extreme dejection and perturbation of his soul, and most elegantly and pathetically describes the conflicts and internal contests to which he is subjected, before he is enabled to rise from the depths of woe to any degree of hope or confidence. In the cha-

racter of a suppliant he first pours forth his earnest prayers
to the God of his hope:

> " I lifted up my voice unto God, and cried ;
> I lifted up my voice unto God, that he should hear me."

But even prayers afford him no sufficient consolation. He
next endeavours to mitigate his sorrow by the remembrance
of former times; but this, on the contrary, only seems to
exaggerate his sufferings by the comparison of his present
adversity with his former happiness, and extorts from him
the following pathetic expostulation:

> " Will the Lord reject me for ever ?
> And will he be reconciled no more ?
> Is his mercy eternally ceased ?
> Doth his promise fail from generation to generation ?
> Hath God forgotten to be merciful ?
> Or hath he in anger shut up his pity ? "

Again, recollecting the nature of the Divine dispensations in
chastising man, "the change of the right hand of the Most
High;" in other words the different methods by which the
Almighty seeks the salvation of his people, appearing frequently to frown upon and persecute those "in whom he
delighteth;" reconsidering also the vast series of mercies
which he had bestowed upon his chosen people; the miracles which he had wrought in their favour; in a word, the
goodness, the holiness, the power of the great Ruler of the
universe—with all the ardour of gratitude and affection he
bursts forth into a strain of praise and exultation. In this
passage we are at a loss which to admire most; the ease and
grace with which the digression is made, the choice of the
incidents, the magnificence of the imagery, or the force and
elegance of the diction.

> " Thy way, O God, is in holiness ;
> What God is great as our God ?
> Thou art the God that doest wonders ;
> Thou hast made known thy strength among the nations ;
> With thy arm hast thou redeemed thy people,
> The sons of Jacob and Joseph.
> The waters saw thee, O God !
> The waters saw thee, and trembled ;
> The depths also were troubled.
> The clouds overflowed with water ;
> The skies sent forth thunder ;

Thine arrows also went abroad:
The voice of thy thunder was in the atmosphere;
Thy lightnings enlightened the world,
The earth trembled, and was disturbed."

The other example to which I shall refer you on this occasion, is composed upon quite a different plan; for it declines gradually from an exordium uncommonly splendid and sublime, to a gentler and more moderate strain, to the softest expressions of piety and devotion. The whole composition abounds with great variety of both sentiment and imagery. You will, from these circumstances, almost conjecture that I am alluding to the nineteenth Psalm. The glory of God is demonstrated in his works both of nature and providence. By exhibiting it, however, in an entire state, though in modern verse, you will more readily perceive the order, method, and arrangement of this beautiful composition.

PSALM XIX.*

" God the heavens aloud proclaim
Through their wide-extended frame,
And the firmament each hour
Speaks the wonders of his power;
Day to the succeeding day
Joys the notice to convey,
And the nights, in ceaseless round,
Each to each repeats the sound;
Prompt, without or speech or tongue,
In his praise to form the song.
Pleas'd to hear their voice extend
Far as to her utmost end,
Earth the heaven-taught knowledge boasts
Through her many-languag'd coasts.
While the sun, above her head,
Sees his tabernacle spread;
And, from out his chamber bright,
Like a bridegroom springs to sight:
See him, with gigantic pace,
Joyous run his destined race;
Now to farthest regions borne,
Onward speed, and now return;

* I have given Mr. Merrick's translation of this Psalm, as more calculated to illustrate the design of our Author in quoting it. I cannot, however, omit mentioning, that Mr. Addison's paraphrase of a part of this Psalm infinitely excels every translation that I have seen, as well in sublimity as elegance; and is indeed, in my opinion, the most beautiful and perfect specimen of sacred poetry extant in English verse.—T.

And to all, with welcome ray,
Life and genial warmth convey.
Warmth and life each thankful heart
Feels thy law, great God! impart;
Clear from every spot it shines,
And the guilt-stain'd thought refines;
Truth's firm base its fame upholds,
While it mysteries unfolds,
Which the child-like mind explores,
And to heavenly science soars
Press'd with sorrows, doubts, and fears,
What like this the spirit cheers?
What so perfect, what so pure?
What to Reason's eye obscure
Can such wond'rous light afford,
As the dictates of thy word?
Where thy fear its fruit matures,
(Fruit that endless years endures,)
There the mind to vice a foe
Pants thy blest decrees to know;
And (its will to thine subdu'd)
Owns them wise, and just, and good.
Nor can gold such worth acquire
From the sev'nth exploring fire;
Nor the labour of the bees
Can in sweetness vie with these:
Taught by them, thy servant's breast
Joys the blessings to attest,
Heap'd on those whose hearts sincere
Learn thy precepts to revere.
Best Instructor, from thy ways
Who can tell how oft he strays?
Purge me from the guilt that lies
Wrapt within my heart's disguise;
Let me thence, by thee renew'd,
Each presumptuous sin exclude;
So my lot shall ne'er be join'd
With the men whose impious mind,
Fearless of thy just command,
Braves the vengeance of thy hand.
Let my tongue, from error free,
Speak the words approv'd by thee;
To thy all-observing eyes
Let my thoughts accepted rise.
While I thus thy name adore,
And thy healing grace implore,
Blest Redeemer, bow thine ear!
God, my strength, propitious hear!"

LECTURE XXVII.

OF THE SUBLIME STYLE OF THE HEBREW ODE.

The third species of the Hebrew Ode, the characteristic of which is Sublimity—This Sublimity results from three sources : From the general form and arrangement of the poem, exemplified in the 50th and 24th Psalms ; from the greatness of the sentiments, and the force of the language—The Ode of Moses on passing the Red Sea explained and illustrated—The brevity of the Hebrew style—The 29th Psalm in English verse.

SUBLIMITY was mentioned as the characteristic of a third species of the Hebrew Ode: But having already treated very copiously of the sublime in general, both as the effect of sentiment and expression, our present investigation must be confined to that which is peculiar to this species of poetry. Now, the sublimity of lyric compositions results either from the plan, the order, and arrangement of the poem; or from those common sources which I formerly specified, the sentiments and the style; or, in some cases, from an union of all, when an aggregate perfection is produced from the beauty of the arrangement, the dignity of the sentiments, and the splendour of the diction. I shall endeavour to exhibit a few examples in each kind: and indeed this subject is every way deserving our attention, since it relates to what may be esteemed the perfection of the Hebrew poetry—for its chief commendation is sublimity, and its sublimest species is the ode.

Let us therefore consider, in the first place, what degree of sublimity the mere form and disposition of a lyric poem can impart to a subject not in itself sublime. We have an example of this in the fiftieth Psalm; the subject of which is of the didactic kind, and belongs to the moral part of theology. It is at first serious and practical, with very little of sublimity or splendour : it sets forth, that the Divine favour is not to be conciliated by sacrifices, or by any of the external rites and services of religion, but rather by sincere piety, and by the devout effusions of a grateful heart ; and yet, that

even these will not be accepted without the strictest attention
to justice, and every practical virtue.   It consists therefore
of two parts: in the first, the devout but ignorant and superstitious worshipper is reproved; and in the second, the hypocritical pretender to virtue and religion.   Each part of the
subject, if we regard the imagery and the diction only, is
treated rather with variety and elegance than with sublimity;
but if the general effect, if the plot and machinery of the
whole be considered, scarcely any thing can appear more
truly magnificent.   The great Author of nature, by a solemn
decree, convokes the whole human race to be witness of the
judgment which he is about to execute upon his people; the
august tribunal is established in Sion:

" JEHOVAH, God of gods,
   Hath spoken, and hath summoned the earth,
   From the rising to the setting of the sun:
   From Sion, from the perfection of beauty, God hath shined,"

The majesty of God is depicted by imagery assumed from
the descent upon Mount Sinai; which, as I formerly observed, is one of the common-places that supply ornaments
of this kind:

"Our God shall come, and shall not be silent;
   A fire shall devour before him,
   And a mighty whirlwind shall surround him."

The heavens and the earth are invoked as witnesses, which
is a pompous form of expression common with the Hebrew
writers:*

"He shall call the heavens from on high;
   And the earth, to the judgment of his people."

At length the Almighty is personally introduced pronouncing
his sentence, which constitutes the remainder of the ode;
and the admirable sublimity and splendour of the exordium
is continued through the whole. There is in Horace an ode
upon a similar subject;† and it is not enough to say, that he
has treated it in his usual manner, with elegance and variety,
for he has done more than could be expected from a person
unenlightened by divine truth—he has treated it with piety
and solemnity.   But that high degree of sublimity to which
the Psalmist rises upon such occasions, is only to be attained
by the Hebrew Muse; for it is a truth universally acknowledged, that no religion whatever, no poetic history, is pro-

---

* Compare Deut. xxxii. 1; Isa. i. 2.   † See Horat. lib. iii. Od. 23.

vided with a store of imagery so striking and so magnificent, so capable of embellishing a scene which may be justly accounted the most sublime that the human imagination is able to comprehend.

The next example which I shall produce, will be found in some measure different from the former, inasmuch as the subject itself is possessed of the highest dignity and splendour, though still no inconsiderable part of the sublimity is to be attributed to the general plan and arrangement of the poem. The induction of the ark of God to Mount Sion by David, gave occasion to the twenty-fourth Psalm.* The removal of the ark was celebrated in a great assembly of the people, and with suitable splendour during every part of the ceremony. The Levites led the procession, accompanied by a great variety of vocal and instrumental music; and this ode appears to have been sung to the people when they arrived at the summit of the mountain. The exordium is expressive of the supreme and infinite dominion of God, arising from the right of creation:

> "The earth is JEHOVAH's, and the fulness thereof;
> The world, and all that inhabit therein :
> For upon the seas hath he founded it,
> And upon the floods hath he established it."

How astonishing the favour and condescension! how extraordinary the testimony of his love, when he selected from his infinite dominion a peculiar seat, and a people for himself! what a copious return of gratitude, of holiness, of righteousness, and of all human virtues, does such an obligation demand! " Behold," says Moses, addressing the Israelites, " The heaven, and the heaven of heavens, is JEHOVAH's, thy God; the earth also, and all that it containeth. Only he had a delight in thy fathers to love them, and their posterity after them, and he chose you above all people, as it is this day."† Such is evidently the reasoning of David in the following passage, though the chain of argument is not quite so directly displayed:

> " Who shall ascend unto the mountain of JEHOVAH ;
> And who shall stand in the seat of his holiness ?
> He, whose hands are innocent, and whose heart is pure ;
> Who hath not put his trust in vanity,‡
> Nor sworn for the purpose of deceit.

---

* See 2 Sam. vi. 1 Chron. xv.   † Deut. x. 14—16.

‡ נשׂא נפשׁו: This phrase denotes confidence, hope, desire. See Psal. xxv. 1.

He shall receive a blessing from JEHOVAH,
And righteousness from the God of his salvation.
This is the generation that seeketh him ;
That seeketh the face of the God of Jacob."*

Thus far is expressive, on the one hand, of the infinite goodness and condescension of God to the children of Israel; and on the other hand, of their indispensable obligation to piety and virtue; since he had deigned to make their nation the peculiar seat of his miraculous providence, and to honour them with his actual presence.— We may now conceive the procession to have arrived at the gates of the tabernacle. While the ark is brought in, the Levites, divided into two choirs, sing alternately the remainder of the Psalm. Indeed, it is not impossible that this mode of singing was pursued through every part of the ode; but towards the conclusion the fact will not admit of a doubt. On the whole, whether we regard the subject, the imagery, or style of this composition, it will be found to possess a certain simple and unaffected (and therefore admirable) sublimity :—

---

lxxxvi. 4 ; cxliii. 8. ; also Deut. xxiv. 15. Jer. xxii. 27. Ezek. xxiv. 25. שָׁוְא, an idol : לַשָּׁוְא יִקְטֹרוּ, " burn incense to vain gods," Jer. xviii. 15.—*Author's Note.*

" Who have not sworn falsely by their life." I offer this translation in preference to our Author's, " Who hath not put his trust in vanity, or in vain gods," on the authority of M. Michaelis; who justly observes, that the translation of the words *nasa lesheva* is to *perjure* or *forswear*, and not to *swear by false gods*, as is evident from Exod. xx. 7 ; and it is properly applied to the naming in a lie the name of JEHOVAH, their *own life*, or the *sacred cities*, Psa. cxxx. 20, or any other thing which was accounted sacred or dear to them.—T.

* It ought to be read either with the LXX, Vulg. Arab. Æthiop. פְּנֵי יַעֲקֹב אֵל ; or with the Syr. פְּנֵי אֵל יַעֲקֹב, which is much the same. " It is פְּנֵי אֱלֹהֵי יַעֲקֹב, in a MS. in possession of Ebner Eschenbach, Norimberg. See Nadleri, *Dissertat. de Ebneri Codicibus MStis.* 1748."—K. The *holy ark*, and the *shechinah* which remained upon it, the symbol of the Divine presence, is called the *face of God:* and to seek the face of God, is to appear before the ark, to worship at the sanctuary of God ; which was required of the Israelites thrice a year. See 2 Sam. xxi. 1. 2 Chron. vii. 14. Psa. xxvii. 8. Exodus xxiii. 17.

" Seek JEHOVAH and his strength,
Seek his face for ever."—Psalm cv. 4.

Where it is worthy of remark, that עֹז, his strength, is parallel and synonymous to פָּנָיו, his face, and signifies the ark of God : compare Psa. lxxviii. 61 ; cxxxii. 8. They but trifle who endeavour to extort any thing reasonable from the common reading. Further, I am of opinion, that in verse 9, the verb וְהִנָּשְׂאוּ in *Niphal* ought to be repeated : so all the old translators seem to have read it.—*Author's Note.*

" Lift up your heads,.O ye gates !
And be ye lift up, ye everlasting doors !*
And the King of Glory shall enter.
Who is this King of Glory ?
JEHOVAH, mighty and powerful,
JEHOVAH, powerful in war.
Lift up your heads, O ye gates !
And be ye lift up, ye everlasting doors !
And the King of Glory shall enter.
Who is this King of Glory ?
JEHOVAH of Hosts, he is the King of Glory."

You will easily perceive, that the beauty and sublimity observable in this Psalm are of such a peculiar kind, as to be perfectly adapted to the subject and the occasion, and to that ·particular solemnity for which it was composed. You will perceive, too, that unless we have some respect to these points, the principal force and elegance will be lost ; and even the propriety of the sentiments, the splendour of the diction, the beauty and order of the arrangement, will be almost totally obscured. If such be the state of the case in this single instance, it is surely not unreasonable to conclude, that it is not the only one which stands in need of the light of history to cast a splendour on its beauties. It is surely not unreasonable to infer, that much of the harmony, propriety, and elegance of the sacred poetry, must pass unperceived by us, who can only form distant conjectures of the general design, but are totally ignorant of the particular application.† Thus, of necessity, much of the delicacy

---

* I would prefer *ye ancient gates*, that is, *long since ennobled* by the worship of the true God. Thus Jacob and Moses speak of the *ancient mountains*, the *everlasting hills*, &c. The meaning of the verse is, " The gates, which were mean and contracted before, and unworthy of JEHOVAH, should now be extended and enlarged."—M.

† I wish, most earnestly, that this observation of our Author might be properly attended to by the commentators upon the Psalms; since whoever neglects it, must of necessity fall into very gross errors. There are some who, attempting to explain the Psalms from the historical parts of Scripture, act as if every occurrence were known to them, and as if nothing had happened during the reign of David which was not committed to writing. This, however, considering the extreme brevity of the sacred history, and the number and magnitude of the facts which it relates, must of course be very far from the truth. The causes and motives of many wars are not at all adverted to, the battles that are related are few, and those the principal. Who can doubt, though ever so inexperienced in military affairs, that many things occurred, which are not mentioned, between the desertion of Jerusalem by David, and that famous battle which extinguished the rebellion of Absalom? The camp must have been frequently removed, as circumstances varied, to places of greater safety ; much trouble must have been had in collecting the veteran soldiers

of sentiment, much of the felicity of allusion and the force of expression, must, by the hand of time, be cast into shade; or rather I should say, totally suppressed and extinguished. The attentive reader will, indeed, frequently feel a want of information, concerning the author, the age, and the occasion of a poem; still more frequently will he find occasion to lament his own ignorance with respect to many facts and circumstances closely connected with the principal subject, and on which, perhaps, its most striking ornaments depend. This we experience in some degree in the admirable poem of Deborah; and this I seem to experience in the sixty-eighth Psalm, though it appears to have some affinity with the subject of that which we have just examined, since it adopts, in the place of an exordium, that well-known form

from different posts; and not a few battles and skirmishes must have occurred, before the exiled king could so far presume upon the strength and increase of his army as to quit the mountains and try the open field. This last battle being fought on this side Jordan, in the forest of Ephraim, is it not natural to suppose that something must have occurred to compel Absalom, whose camp was beyond Jordan, to return into Palestine, properly so called—possibly the preservation of the royal city? Or is it possible to compare the history of 2 Sam. viii. 13, with Psalm lx. and not to perceive, that some unfortunate events must have happened previous to the victories over the Syrians and Idumeans, and that affairs must have been unhappily situated in Palestine itself? that even the royal city must have been in danger; since the Idumeans penetrated even so far as the valley of Salt, which is scarcely distant one day's journey? If all these things be omitted; if, moreover, in the book of Samuel no sufficiently express mention is made of the Assyrians, with whom David certainly waged war, Psalm lxxxiii. 9, why should we not suppose that many lesser facts are omitted in the history, to which, however, a poet might allude, as natural and proper matter of amplification?—But, to return to the point I set out from; those who will not allow themselves to be ignorant of a great part of the Jewish history, will be apt to explain more of the Psalms upon the same principle, and as relating to the same facts, than they ought: whence the poetry will appear tame and languid, abounding in words, but with little variety of description or sentiment.

There are commentators of another class, who take inexcusable liberties of invention, and, instead of resorting to the records of the ancients, endeavour to supply facts from their own ingenuity; in which way some of the biographers of David have greatly indulged themselves, and particularly Delany. For example, in the 7th chap. of the 3rd vol. he takes it for granted, from Psalm xxxviii. and xli. that, at the time when Absalom formed the rebellion, David was ill of the small-pox, (a disease which we cannot pretend to assert from any historical proof to have been known at that period, and from which the king at his time of life could scarcely have recovered;) and to show that nothing could exceed his rashness in inventing, he adds, that by means of the disease he lost the use of his right eye for some time.

Others have recourse to mystical interpretations, or those historical passages which they do not understand they convert into prophecies: into none of these errors would mankind have fallen, but through the persuasion that the whole history of the Jews was minutely detailed to them; and that there were no circumstances with which they were unacquainted.—M.

of expression which was commonly made use of on the removal of the ark,*—

> " Let God arise; let his enemies be scattered;
> And let those that hate him flee from his presence."

But almost every part of this most noble poem is involved in an impenetrable darkness. It would otherwise have afforded a singular example of the true sublime ; the scattered rays of which, breaking forth with difficulty through the thick clouds that surround it, we yet behold with a mixture of admiration and pleasure.†

The most perfect example that I know of the other species of the sublime ode, which I pointed out, (that I mean which possesses a sublimity dependent wholly upon the greatness of the conceptions and the dignity of the language, without any peculiar excellence in the form and arrangement,) is the thanksgiving ode of Moses, composed after passing the Red Sea.‡ Through every part of this poem the most perfect plainness and simplicity is maintained; there is nothing artificial, nothing laboured, either in respect to method or invention. Every part of it breathes the spirit of nature and of passion; joy, admiration, and love, united with piety and devotion, burst forth spontaneously in their native colours. A miracle of the most interesting nature to the Israelites is displayed : The sea divides, and the waters are raised into vast heaps on either side while they pass over ; but their enemies, in attempting to pursue, are overwhelmed by the reflux of the waves. These circumstances are all expressed in language suitable to the emotions which they produced, abrupt, fervid, concise, animated, with a frequent repetition of the same sentiments:

> " I will sing to JEHOVAH, for he is very highly exalted;
> The horse and the rider he hath o'erwhelmed in the sea."

This constitutes the proem of the ode, and is also repeated occasionally by the female part of the band in the manner of a modern chorus, being briefly expressive of the general subject. The same idea, however, occurs in several parts of

---

* Compare Numb. x. 35.

† Having professed above, that I admired not so much the sublimity as the sweetness of David's lyric poetry, I think it my duty to make an exception in favour of this Psalm, than which I do not recollect any thing more sublime in the whole book of Psalms.—M.

‡ Exodus xv.

the poem, with considerable variation in the language and figures:

> " The chariots of Pharaoh and his forces he cast into the sea ;
> And his chosen leaders were drowned in the Red Sea.
> The depths have covered them ;
> They went down into the abyss as a stone."

And again:

> " The enemy said, I will pursue, I will overtake ;
> I will divide the spoil, my soul shall be satisfied ;*
> I will draw the sword, my hand shall destroy them.
> Thou didst blow with thy breath, the sea covered them :
> They sunk like lead in the great waters."

Nor do even these repetitions satisfy the author:

> " Who is like unto thee among the gods, O JEHOVAH !
> Who is like unto thee, glorious in sanctity !
> Fearful in praises, performing miracles !
> Thou extendedst thy right hand, the earth swallowed them."

In these examples is displayed all the genuine force of nature and passion, which the efforts of art will emulate in vain. Here we behold the passions struggling for vent, labouring with a copiousness of thought and a poverty of expression, and on that very account the more expressly displayed. To take a strict account of the sublimity of this ode, would be to repeat the whole. I will only remark one quality, which is indeed congenial to all the poetry of the Hebrews, but in this poem is more than usually predominant, I mean that brevity of diction which is so conducive to sublimity of style. Diffuse and exuberant expression generally detracts from the force of the sentiment; as in the human body excessive corpulency is generally inconsistent with health and vigour. The Hebrews, if we contemplate any of their compositions as a whole, may be deemed full and copious; but if we consider only the constituent parts of any production, they will be found sparing in words, concise and energetic. They amplify by diversifying, by repeating, and sometimes by adding to the subject: therefore it happens, that it is frequently, on the whole, treated rather diffusely ; but still every particular sentence is concise and nervous in itself. Thus it happens in general, that neither copiousness nor vigour is wanting. This brevity of style is in some measure to be

* " This is explained by one of the rabbinical writers, *It will be filled from them* ; that is, says another, *by taking their wealth or substance*."—H.

attributed to the genius of the language, and in some measure to the nature of the Hebrew verse.   The most literal
versions therefore commonly fail in this respect ; and consequently still less is to be expected from any poetical translations or imitations whatever.

Most of those qualities and perfections which have been
the subject of this disquisition, will be found in a very high
degree in the twenty-ninth Psalm.   The supreme dominion
of God, and the awfulness of his power, are demonstrated
from the tremendous noise and the astonishing force of the
thunder, which the Hebrews, by a bold but very apt figure,
denominate "the voice of the Most High."   It is enough
to say of it, that the sublimity of the matter is perfectly
equalled by the unaffected energy of the style.

PSALM XXIX.

" Sing, ye sons of might, O sing
Praise to heaven's eternal King ;
Power and strength to him assign,
And before his hallow'd shrine
Yield the homage that his name
From a creature's lips may claim.
Hark ! his voice in thunder breaks ;
Hush'd to silence, while he speaks,
Ocean's waves from pole to pole
Hear the awful accents roll ;
See, as louder yet they rise,
Echoing through the vaulted skies,
Loftiest cedars lie o'erthrown,
Cedars of steep Lebanon !
See, uprooted from its seat,
Tremblig at the threat divine
Lebanon itself retreat,
And Sirion haste its flight to join
See them, like the heifer borne,
Like the beast whose pointed horn
Strikes with dread the sylvan train,
Bound impetuous on the plain !
Now the bursting clouds give way,
And the vivid lightnings play ;
And the wilds, by man untrod,
Hear, dismay'd, th' approaching God.
Cades ! o'er thy lonely waste
Oft the dreadful sounds have past ;

Oft his stroke the wood invades :
Widow'd of their branchy shades.
Mightiest oaks its fury know ; *
While the pregnant hind her throe
Instant feels, and on the earth
Trembling drops th' unfinish'd birth.
Prostrate on the sacred floor
Israel's sons his name adore ;
While his acts to every tongue
Yields its argument of song.
He the swelling surge commands ;
Fix'd his throne for ever stands ;
He his people shall increase,
Arm with strength, and bless with peace."

* *The oaks are affected with pain, or tremble:* אלה or אילה is *an oak:* and certainly this word frequently occurs in the plural masculine, with the insertion of י. And in this sense the Syr. has taken it, which renders it אילתא דמיע. For the word יור in Syriac, as well as Hebrew, denotes motion or agitation of any kind; nor is its meaning confined to the pains of childbirth. See Isaiah li. 9. "This explanation of the word יחולל in the sense of *moving* or *shaking*, is established beyond a doubt upon the authority of the Arabic verb הול, to *move* or *shake.*—H. Though the word אילתא does not appear in the Syriac Lexicons to signify an oak, yet it occurs four times in this sense in the Syriac version, exactly answering to the Hebrew word אלה, 2 Sam. xviii. 9, 10. 14. as also in this place. The common translations suppose this passage to relate to the *hinds bringing forth young* ; which agrees very little with the rest of the imagery either in nature or dignity : nor do I feel myself persuaded, even by the reasonings of the learned Bochart on this subject, Hieroz. part i. lib. iii. chap. 17 ; whereas the oak struck with lightning admirably agrees with the context. And Bochart himself explains the word אילה, which has been absurdly understood by the Masorites and other commentators as relating to a stag, as spoken of a tree, in a very beautiful explication of an obscure passage in Gen. xlix. 21.—*Author's Note.*

LECTURE XXVIII.

THE SUBLIME STYLE OF THE HEBREW ODE.

The sublime Ode, in which all the constituents of sublimity formerly specified are united—The Prophetic Ode of Moses, Deut. xxxii.—The Triumphal Ode of Deborah; the Prayer of Habakkuk; the Fate of Tyranny, being a poetical imitation of the 14th chapter of Isaiah.

BEFORE we conclude this disquisition concerning the lyric poetry of the Hebrews, it will be proper to produce a few specimens of that kind of ode which derives sublimity from several united causes—from the diction, the sentiments, the form and conduct of the poem; and which accumulates, or in a manner condenses and combines all the beauties and elegances of this style of composition. The poems to which I shall refer on this occasion are too well known to require a minute explanation, and indeed almost too noble and perspicuous in themselves to admit of any illustration from criticism; it will therefore be sufficient to notice them in general terms, or, at most, briefly to recommend a few passages, which are perhaps so eminently beautiful as to deserve particular attention. The first instance I shall mention is that prophetic ode of Moses,* which contains a justification on the part of God against the Israelites, and an explanation of the nature and design of the divine judgments. The exordium is singularly magnificent: the plan and conduct of the poem is just, natural, and well accommodated to the subject; for it is almost in the order of an historical narration. It embraces a variety of the sublimest subjects and sentiments; it displays the truth and justice of God, his paternal love, and his unfailing tenderness to his chosen people: and on the other hand, their ungrateful and contumacious spirit. The ardour of the divine indignation, and the heavy denunciations of vengeance, are afterwards expressed in a remarkable personification, which is scarcely to be paralleled from all

* Deut. xxxii.

the choicest treasures of the Muses. The fervour of wrath
is however tempered with the milder beams of lenity and
mercy, and ends at last in promises and consolation. When
I formerly treated of elevation of sentiment, of the impulse
of the passions, of the force of imagery and diction, I could
scarcely have avoided touching upon this poem, and drawing some of my examples from it.* Not to repeat these, or
accumulate unnecessary matter, I will only add one remark,
namely, that the subject and style of this poem bear so
exact a resemblance to the prophetic as well as the lyric
compositions of the Hebrews, that it unites all the force,
energy, and boldness of the latter, with the exquisite variety
and grandeur of imagery so peculiar to the former.†

Another specimen of the perfectly sublime ode will be
found in the triumphal ode of Deborah.‡ This poem consists of three parts: first, the exordium; next, a recital of
the circumstances which preceded, and of those which
accompanied the victory; lastly, a fuller description of the
concluding event, the death of Sisera, and the disappointed
hopes of his mother, which is embellished with all the
choicest flowers of poetry. Of this latter part I endeavoured to explain at large the principal beauties in a former Lecture. About the middle of the poem, it must be
confessed, some obscurities occur, and those not of a trivial
nature, which impair the beauty of the composition; and
what is worse, I fear they will scarcely admit of elucidation,
unless we were possessed of some further historical lights.
The exordium deserves a particular examination, as well
for its native magnificence and sublimity, as because it will
serve more completely to illustrate my remarks concerning
the digressions of the Hebrew ode. I observed, that the
principal passages in the sacred history, which in general
constitute the materials of these digressions, are so connected
with every subject of sacred poetry, that, even in the most
eccentric excursions of the imagination, there is little danger
of wandering from the main scope and design. The subject of this ode is the triumph of the Israelites over their
enemies through the Divine assistance, and the establishment
of their liberty. At the very opening of the poem this is
proposed as the groundwork of it; and, after inviting the
kings and princes of the neighbouring nations to attend to

this miracle of the Divine goodness, the author proceeds to celebrate the praise of God, not commencing with the benefit so recently received, but with the prodigies formerly exhibited in Egypt:

"O Jehovah, when thou wentest forth out of Seir,
When thou proceedest from the plains of Edom ;
The earth was moved, the heavens dropped,
The clouds also dropped water ;
The mountains melted from before the face of Jehovah,
Sinai itself from before Jehovah, the God of Israel."

The sudden introduction of such important incidents breathes the free and fervid spirit of the lyric Muse. There is, however, no defect in the connexion, nor does any degree of obscurity attend the comparison which is implied between that stupendous deliverance and the benefit so lately received.

On the same principle the prayer of Habakkuk is constructed;* and is a remarkable instance of that sublimity peculiar to the ode, and which is often the result of a bold but natural digression. The prophet foreseeing the judgment of God, and the impending calamities which were to be inflicted upon his nation by the hands of the Chaldeans, as well as the punishments which the latter were themselves to undergo—partly struck with terror, partly cheered with hope, he beseeches Almighty God to hasten the redemption of his people:

"O Jehovah, I have heard thy speech,
I have feared, O Jehovah, thy work.
As the years† approach, thou hast shown it ;
And in thy wrath hast remembered mercy."

In this passage, the resemblance between the Babylonish and Egyptian captivities naturally presents itself to the mind, as well as the possibility of a similar deliverance through the power and assistance of God. With how much propriety, therefore, might the prophet have continued his supplications to that all-powerful and all-merciful God, that, as he had formerly wrought so many miracles in favour of his people, he would afford them relief and consolation on the present occasion? and how efficacious a method would it have been to confirm the fortitude of every pious person, to remind

* Habak. iii.

† See the Vulg. and Theodotion, εν μεσω ετων· Aquila and the LXX, εν τω εγγιζειν τα ετη· Symmachus, εντος των ενιαντων. All of them almost in the same sense, that is, "within a fixed time."

them, that he who had formerly manifested his infinite power in delivering the Israelites from their great afflictions might, in proper time, employ the same means to rescue them from their present state of suffering? He however totally disregards the formality of this method, probably because he supposed all the above ideas would spontaneously occur to the reader; nor does he labour for access by slow and regular approaches to the sacred depository of the most splendid materials, but bursts into it at once and by a sort of unexpected impulse:

> "God came from Teman,
> And the Holy One from Mount Paran :
> His glory covered the heavens ;
> And the earth was full of his praise."

The prophet, indeed, illustrates this subject throughout with equal magnificence; selecting from such an assemblage of miraculous incidents the most noble and important, displaying them in the most splendid colours, and embellishing them with the sublimest imagery, figures, and diction—the dignity of which is so heightened and recommended by the superior elegance of the conclusion, that, were it not for a few shades which the hand of time has apparently cast over it in two or three passages, no composition of the kind would, I believe, appear more elegant or more perfect than this poem.

I will add one remarkable example more of the perfectly sublime ode, which indeed it would be utterly unpardonable to overlook: I mean the triumphal song of the Israelites on the destruction of Babylon. It is almost unnecessary to add, that it is in no respect unworthy of Isaiah, whom I cannot help esteeming the first of poets, as well for elegance as sublimity. Having formerly taken up a considerable portion of your time and attention in a minute investigation of its beauties, it is now presented in the modern form of a lyric composition.

ON THE FATE OF TYRANNY, ISAIAH XIV.

> "Oppression dies; the Tyrant falls;
> The golden city bows her walls :
>   JEHOVAH breaks th' avenger's rod !
> The son of wrath, whose ruthless hand
> Hurl'd desolation o'er the land,
>   Has run his raging race, has clos'd the scene of blood.
> Chiefs arm'd around behold their vanquish'd Lord ;
> Nor spread the guardian shield, nor lift the royal sword.

He falls; and earth again is free.
Hark! at the call of liberty
   All nature lifts the choral song.
The fir-trees, on the mountain's head,
   Rejoice through all their pomp of shade;
   The lordly cedars nod on sacred Lebanon:
Tyrant! they cry, since thy fell force is broke,
Our proud heads pierce the skies, nor fear the woodman's
    stroke.

Hell, from her gulf profound,
Rouses at thine approach; and all around
Her dreadful notes of preparation sound.
   See, at the awful call,
   Her shadowy heroes all,
    Ev'n mighty kings, the heirs of empire wide,
   Rising with solemn state, and slow,
   From their sable thrones below,
    Meet, and insult thy pride!
What, dost thou join our ghostly train,
A flitting shadow, light and vain?
Where is thy pomp, thy festive throng,
Thy revel dance, and wanton song?
Proud King! Corruption fastens on thy breast;
And calls her crawling brood, and bids them share the feast.

O Lucifer! thou radiant star,
Son of the Morn, whose rosy car
   Flam'd foremost in the van of day;
How art thou fall'n thou King of Light!
How fall'n from thy meridian height,
   Who said'st, The distant poles shall hear me and obey;
High o'er the stars my sapphire throne shall glow,
And, as JEHOVAH's self, my voice the heavens shall bow!

He spake—he died.   Distain'd with gore,
Beside yon yawning cavern hoar,
   See where his livid corse is laid.
The aged pilgrim passing by,
Surveys him long with dubious eye;
   And muses on his fate, and shakes his reverend head
Just heavens! is thus thy pride imperial gone?
Is this poor heap of dust the King of Babylon?

   Is this the man, whose nod
Made the earth tremble; whose terrific rod
Levell'd her loftiest cities? Where he trod
   Famine pursu'd, and frown'd;
   Till Nature, groaning round,
Saw her rich realms transform'd to deserts dry;

While at his crowded prison's gate,
Grasping the keys of Fate,
 Stood stern Captivity.
Vain man! behold thy righteous doom ;
Behold each neighbouring monarch's tomb :
The trophied arch, the breathing bust,
The laurel shades their sacred dust ;
While thou, vile outcast, on this hostile plain,
Moulder'st, a vulgar corse, among the vulgar slain.

No trophied arch, no breathing bust,
Shall dignify thy trampled dust ;
 No laurel flourish o'er thy grave.
For why, proud King, thy ruthless hand
Hurl'd desolation o'er the land,
 And crush'd the subject race, whom kings are born to save.
Eternal infamy shall blast thy name,
And all thy sons shall share their impious father's shame.

Rise, purple Slaughter! furious rise ;
Unfold the terror of thine eyes ;
 Dart thy vindictive shafts around :
Let no strange land a shade afford,
No conquer'd nations call them Lord ;
 Nor let their cities rise to curse the goodly ground.
For thus JEHOVAH swears : No name, no son,
No remnant, shall remain of haughty Babylon !

Thus saith the righteous Lord :
My vengeance shall unsheath the flaming sword ;
O'er all thy realms my fury shall be pour'd;
 Where yon proud city stood
 I'll spread the stagnant flood ;
And there the bittern in the sedge shall lurk,
 Moaning with sullen strain ;
 While, sweeping o'er the plain,
  Destruction ends her work.
 Yes, on mine holy mountain's brow,
 I'll crush this proud Assyrian foe !—
 Th' irrevocable word is spoke :
 From Judah's neck the galling yoke
Spontaneous falls ; she shines with wonted state ;
Thus by MYSELF I swear, and what I swear is Fate!"*

---

* Mr. Potter has favoured the world with a very elegant and spirited paraphrase of
this prophetic ode. His description of the reception of the king of Babylon in the
infernal regions is particularly striking :

  "To meet thee, Hades rouses from beneath,
   An iron smile his visage wears ;

He calls through all the drear abodes of death—
   His call each mighty chieftain hears;
And sceptred kings of empires wide
Rise from their lofty thrones, and thus accost thy pride :
   Is this weak form of flitting air
The potent Lord that fill'd the Assyrian throne ?
Thus are thy wonted glories gone ?
   Where thy rich feasts, thy sprightly viols where ?
Beneath thee is corruption spread,
And worms the covering of thy bed.
How art thou fall'n, bright star of orient day !
   How fall'n from thy ethereal height,
Son of the morning ! Thou, whose sanguine ray
   Glar'd terribly a baleful light ;
War kindled at the blaze, and wild
Rush'd Slaughter, Havoc rush'd, their robes with blood defil'd.
I in high heaven will be ador'd,
   Above the stars of God exalt my throne ;
   My power shall sacred Sion own,
The mount of God's high presence hail me Lord.
Such thy vain threats : Death's dark abode
Yawns to receive the vaunting god."

The expostulation of the travellers who find the body exposed, is also expressed in terms truly magnificent :

" Is this the man, whose barb'rous hate
   Bound captive monarchs in his galling chain ;
   While Outrage call'd his loit'ring train,
And Rigour clos'd the dungeon's ruthless gate ?
   How from his high dominion hurl'd
   The spoiler of the ravag'd world ! "

" Shalt thou with honour'd chiefs repose ?
   Her jaws 'gainst thee the Grave shall close ;
For where portentous thy proud banners wav'd,
   Rapine rush'd o'er the wasted land !
Thy country too, her free-born sons enslav'd
   Or slaughter'd, curs'd thy hostile hand."

I close these extracts with the denunciation of JEHOVAH against the Assyrians :

" Dreadful on Sion's sacred brow
   The God of armies shall they know.
Daughter of Sion, let thy joy arise,
   From thy griev'd neck his yoke shall fall ;
Virgin, exult, thy haughty foe despise,
   His chain no more thy arm shall gall !"

OF THE IDYLLIUM, OR HYMN.

—

LECTURE XXIX.

OF THE IDYLLIUM OF THE HEBREWS.

Besides those Poems which may be strictly termed Odes, the general appellation, which in the Hebrew is equivalent to Canticle or Song, includes another species, called by the Greeks the Idyllium—The reason of this name, and the definition of the Poem to which it is appropriated—The historical Psalms in general belong properly to this class—The intercalary stanza, and the nature of it—The elegant plan and arrangement of the 107th Psalm explained: also the 9th chapter of Isaiah, ver. 8, to chap. x. ver. 4.—This passage a perfect specimen of the Idyllium: other examples of the Idyllium no less perfect as to style and form— The Hymn of Cleanthes the Stoic commended—The 139th Psalm in English verse.

AMONGST those poems which by the Hebrews were adapted to music, and distinguished by the general appellation *Shirim*, there are some which differ in their nature from lyric poetry, strictly so called. It will therefore be more regular to class them with those compositions anciently termed Idylliums, the name and nature of which I shall endeavour to explain.

Whether we are to attribute the invention of the name to the poets themselves, or to the grammarians who revised their works, is difficult to say; but we find some of the Greek poems distinguished by the title *Eidé*, which denotes a poem without any certain limitation as to form or subject. Even the Odes of Pindar retain that appellation. But if there were any upon lighter subjects, or in a more humble strain, indeed in any respect of an inferior kind, and such as could not be classed under any of the common divisions, they were entitled *Eidyllia*. Thus the small poems of Theocritus, which consist chiefly of Bucolics, intermingled with others of different kinds, are called Idylliums. In the same manner the Latins preferred the name of *Eclogues*, or poems selected from a number of others; and for a contrary and more modest reason, that of *Sylvæ* (or *woods*) was given to such verses as were hastily composed, and promiscuously thrown together, such as might afford matter for a more accurate revision or for a similar selection. But although the term Idyllium be a vague and general term, which denotes nothing certain relating to the nature of the poem, it still appears by use and custom to have obtained a certain and appropriated destination: and perhaps it may not be improperly defined, a poem of moderate length; of a uniform, middle style, chiefly distinguished for elegance and sweetness; regular and clear as to plot, conduct, and arrangement. There are many perfect examples of this kind of poem extant in the writings of the Hebrews; some of which, I presume, it will not be unpleasing singly to point out and explain.

The first of these poems which attract our notice are the historical Psalms, in celebration of the power and the other attributes of the Deity, as instanced in the miracles which he performed in favour of his people. One of the principal of these, bearing the name of Asaph,* pursues the history of the Israelites from the time of their departure from Egypt to the reign of David, particularizing and illustrating all the leading events. The style is simple and uniform, but the structure is poetical, and the sentiments occasionally splendid. The historical, or rather chronological order, cannot be said to be exactly preserved throughout; for the minute detail of so protracted a series of events could scarcely fail to tire in a work of imagination. The Egyptian miracles are introduced in a very happy and elegant digression, and may be considered as forming a kind of episode. The same subject affords materials for two other Psalms, the hundred-and-fifth, and the hundred-and-sixth—the one including the history of Israel, from the call of Abraham to the Exodus; the other, from that period to the later ages of the commonwealth: both of them bear a strong resemblance to the seventy-eighth, as well in the subject as in the style, (except perhaps that the diction is rather of a more simple cast); the mixture of ease and grace displayed in the exordium is the same in all.

These Psalms, both in plot and conduct, have a surprising analogy to the Hymns of the Greeks. Indeed the Greek translators might very properly have given the title of *Hymns*

* Psal. lxxviii.

to the book of Psalms, as that word agrees much more exactly with the Hebrew title *Tehillim*, than that which they have adopted. This species of poetry was very early in use among the Greeks, and was almost entirely appropriated to the celebration of their religious rites. The subjects in general were the origin of the gods, the places of their birth, their achievements, and the other circumstances of their history. Such are all the poems of this kind now extant in the Greek; such are the elegant hymns of Callimachus, as well as those which are attributed to Homer. The poem of Theocritus, entitled the *Dioskouroi*, or the Praise of Castor and Pollux, is also a genuine hymn, and very elegant in its kind: nor is it improperly classed among the idylliums, which may be said to include all of this species. But the true form and character of the hymn is excellently expressed by the two choirs of Salii (or priests of war) in Virgil:

> " One choir of old, another of the young,
> To dance and bear the burden of the song;
> The lay records the labours, and the praise,
> And all th' immortal acts of Hercules."*

Those ancient hymns which are falsely attributed to Orpheus, are more properly initiatory songs; for they contain " little more than invocations of the gods, which were made use of by those who were initiated in the sacred mysteries of any of the gods."† Ovid, who was both an elegant and a learned poet, united the excellences of both these species of hymns; for the exordium of the hymn to Bacchus contains the invocations of that god, or, in other words, announces solemnly his name and titles; the remainder celebrates his perfections and achievements.‡

There is yet another Psalm which may be enumerated among those of the historical kind, namely, the hundred-and-thirty-sixth. It celebrates the praises of the Almighty, and proclaims his infinite power and goodness; beginning with the work of creation, and proceeding to the miracles of the Exodus, the principal of which are related almost in the historical order. The exordium commences with this well-known distich,

> " Glorify JEHOVAH, for he is good;
> For his mercy endureth for ever:"

---

* Dryd. Virg. *Æneid*. viii. 379.   † Jos. Scaliger. *Annot. in Hymn. Orph.*
‡ Metamorph. iv. 11.

which, according to Ezra,* was commonly sung by alternate choirs. There is, however, one circumstance remarkable attending it, which is, that the latter line of the distich being added by the second choir, and also subjoined to every verse, (which is a singular case,) forms a perpetual epode. Hence the whole nature and form of the intercalary verse (or burden of the song) may be collected : it expresses in a clear, concise, and simple manner, some particular sentiment, which seems to include virtually the general subject or design of the poem; and it is thrown in at proper intervals, according to the nature and arrangement of it, for the sake of impressing the subject more firmly upon the mind. That the intercalary verse is perfectly congenial to the idyllium, is evident from the authority of Theocritus, Bion, Moschus, and even of Virgil. I shall add one or two examples from the sacred poetry, which will not lose in a comparison with the most perfect specimens in this department of poetry which those excellent writers have bequeathed to posterity; and in order to illustrate as well the elegance of the poem in general, as the peculiar force and beauty of the intercalary verse, the order and conduct of the subject must be particularly explained.

The hundred-and-seventh Psalm may undoubtedly be enumerated among the most elegant monuments of antiquity; and it is chiefly indebted for its elegance to the general plan and conduct of the poem. It celebrates the goodness and mercy of God towards mankind, as demonstrated in the immediate assistance and comfort which he affords, in the greatest calamities, to those who devoutly implore his aid :— in the first place, to those who wander in the desert, and who encounter the horrors of famine; next, to those who are in bondage, to those who are afflicted with disease; and, finally, to those who are tossed about upon the ocean. The prolixity of the argument is occasionally relieved by narration; and examples are superadded of the divine severity in punishing the wicked, as well as of his benignity to the devout and virtuous; and both the narrative and preceptive parts are recommended to the earnest contemplation of considerate minds. Thus the whole poem actually divides into five parts nearly equal; the four first of which conclude with an intercalary verse, expressive of the subject or design of the hymn :—

* Ezra iii. 10, 11.

" Glorify JEHOVAH for his mercy,
    And for his wonders to the children of men."

This distich also is occasionally diversified, and another
sometimes annexed illustrative of the sentiment:

" For he satisfieth the famished soul,
    And filleth the hungry with good."

" For he hath broken the brazen gates,
    And the bolts of iron he hath cut in sunder."

The sentiment of the epode itself is sometimes repeated,
only varied by different imagery:

" Glorify JEHOVAH for his mercy,
    And for his wonders to the children of men :
    Let them also offer sacrifices of praise,
    And let them declare his works with melody."

" Let them exalt him in the assembly of the people,
    And in the council of the elders let them celebrate him."

In all these passages, the transition from the contemplation
of their calamities to that of their deliverance, which is made
by the perpetual repetition of the same distich, is truly elegant:

" Let them also cry unto JEHOVAH in their troubles ;
    And from their afflictions he will deliver them."

This, however, does not appear in the least to partake of
the nature of the intercalary verse. The latter part of the
Psalm, which comprehends a vast variety of matter, concludes with two distichs expressive of a sentiment, grave,
solemn, and practical, and in no respect unworthy the rest
of the poem.

There are many other examples to be found in the Psalms ;
but it must be confessed, few of them are equal, and none
of them superior to this. I shall select another specimen
from Isaiah; and the more willingly, because in it, as in
other passages of the same author, the common division into
chapters has greatly obscured that most elegant writer, by
absurdly breaking the unity of a very interesting poem, and
connecting each part with matter which is totally foreign to
the subject. If we unite the conclusion of the ninth chapter
with the beginning of the tenth, we shall find a complete and
connected prophecy against the kingdom of Israel or Samaria.* It is replete with terror and solemnity, and possesses

* Isa. ix. 8—x. 4. " In one MS. a vacant space is left after Isa. x. 4, but no

a degree of force and sublimity to which the idyllium seldom rises; though it preserves the form of the idyllium so perfect and express, that it cannot with propriety be referred to any other class. The poem consists of four parts, each of which contains a denunciation of vengeance against the crimes of this rebellious people, vehemently accusing them of some atrocious offence, and distinctly marking out the particular punishment. In the first, the pride and ostentation of the Israelites is reproved; in the second, the obduracy of their spirit, and the general depravation of their morals; in the third, their audacious impiety, which rages like a flame, destroying and laying waste the nation; and lastly, their iniquity is set forth as demonstrated in their partial administration of justice, and their oppression of the poor. To each of these a specific punishment is annexed; and a clause declaratory of a further reserve of the divine vengeance is added, which forms the epode, and is admirably calculated to exaggerate the horror of the prediction:

> " For all this his anger is not turned away ;
> But his hand is still stretched out."

The examples which I have hitherto produced will, at first view, explain their own nature and kind; there are however others, and probably not a few, (in the book of Psalms particularly,) which may equally be accounted of the idyllium species. I have principally in contemplation those in which some particular subject is treated in a more copious and regular manner than is usual in compositions strictly lyric. Such is the hundred-and-fourth Psalm, which demonstrates the glory of the infinite Creator from the wisdom, beauty, and variety of his works. The poet embellishes this noble subject with the clearest and most splendid colouring of language; and with imagery the most magnificent, lively, diversified, and pleasing, at the same time select, and happily adapted to the subject. There is nothing of the kind extant, indeed nothing can be conceived more perfect than this hymn, whether it be considered with respect to its intrinsic beauties, or as a model of that species of composition. Miraculous exertions of the divine power have something in them which at first strikes the inattentive mind with a strong sentiment of sublimity and awe: but the true subject of praise, the most worthy of God, and the best adapted to impress upon

space of the same kind at the end of chap. ix. In another MS. after chap. x. 4, a space of one line is interposed."—K.

X

the heart of man a fervent and permanent sense of piety, is drawn from the contemplation of his power in the creation of this infinite All; his wisdom in arranging and adorning it, his providence in sustaining, and his mercy in the regulation of its minutest parts, and in ordering and directing the affairs of men. The Greek hymns consisted chiefly of fables; and these fables regarded persons and events, which were neither laudable in themselves, nor greatly to be admired; indeed I do not recollect any that are extant of this sublime nature, except that of the famous stoic Cleanthes, which is inscribed to Jove, that is, to God the Creator, or, as he expresses himself, "to the Eternal Mind, the Creator and Governor of Nature."* It is doubtless a most noble monument of ancient wisdom, and replete with truths not less solid than magnificent. For the sentiments of the philosopher concerning the divine power, concerning the harmony of nature and the supreme laws, concerning the folly and unhappiness of wicked men, who are unceasingly subject to the pain and perturbation of a troubled spirit; and, above all, the ardent supplication for the divine assistance, in order to enable him to celebrate the praises of the omnipotent Deity, in a suitable manner, and in a perpetual strain of praise and adoration; all of these breathe so true and unaffected a spirit of piety, that they seem in some measure to approach the excellence of the sacred poetry.

The hymn of David which I have just mentioned, deservedly occupies the first place in this class of poems: that which comes nearest to it, as well in the conduct of the poem as in the beauty of the style, is another of the same author. It celebrates the omniscience of the Deity, and the incomparable art and design displayed in the formation of the human body: if it be excelled (as perhaps it is) by the former in the plan, disposition, and arrangement of the matter, it is, however, not in the least inferior in the dignity and elegance of the figures and imagery.

PSALM CXXXIX.

" Thou, Lord, hast search'd me out! thine eyes
Mark when I sit, and when I rise:
By thee my future thoughts are read;
Thou, round my path, and round my bed,
Attendest vigilant; each word,
Ere yet I speak, by thee is heard.

* See Cudworth, *Intellect. System*, page 432. or H. Stephan, *Poesim Philosoph.*

" Life's maze, before my view outspread,
Within thy presence rapt I tread,
And, touch'd with conscious horror, stand
Beneath the shadow of thy hand.
How deep thy knowledge, Lord, how wide!
Long to the fruitless task applied,
That mighty sea my thoughts explore,
Nor reach its depths, nor find its shore.
Where shall I shun thy wakeful eye,
Or whither from thy spirit fly?
Aloft to heaven my course I bear—
In vain; for thou, my God, art there:
If prone to hell my feet descend,
Thou still my footsteps shalt attend:
If now, on swiftest wings upborne,
I seek the regions of the morn,
Or haste me to the western steep,
Where eve sits brooding o'er the deep;
Thy hand the fugitive shall stay,
And dictate to my steps their way.
Perchance within its thickest veil
The darkness shall my head conceal;
But, instant, thou hast chas'd away
The gloom, and round me pour'd the day.
Darkness, great God! to thee there's none;
Darkness and light to thee are one:
Nor brighter shines, to thee display'd,
The noon, than night's obscurest shade.
My reins, my fabric's every part,
The wonders of thy plastic art
Proclaim, and prompt my willing tongue
To meditate the grateful song:
With deepest awe my thoughts their frame
Surveys—' I tremble that I am.'
While yet a stranger to the day
Within the burden'd womb I lay,
My bones, familiar to thy view,
By just degrees to firmness grew:
Day to succeeding day consign'd
Th' unfinish'd birth:—Thy mighty mind
Each limb, each nerve, ere yet they were,
Contemplated, distinct and clear:
Those nerves thy curious finger spun,
Those limbs it fashion'd one by one;
And, as thy pen in fair design
Trac'd on thy book each shadowy line,

x 2

" Thy handmaid Nature read them there,
And made the growing work her care ;
Conform'd it to th' unerring plan,
And gradual wrought me into man.
   With what delight, great God ! I trace
The acts of thy stupendous grace !
To count them were to count the sand
That lies upon the sea-beat strand.
When from my temples sloop retires,
To thee my thankful heart aspires ;
And, with thy sacred presence blest,
Joys to receive the awful guest.
Shall impious men thy will withstand,
Nor feel the vengeance of thy hand ?
Hence, murd'rers, hence, nor near me stay !
Ye sons of violence, away !
When lawless crowds, with insult vain,
Thy works revile, thy name profane,
Can I unmov'd those insults see,
Nor hate the wretch that hateth thee ?
Indignant, in thy cause I join,
And all thy foes, my God, are mine !
Searcher of hearts, my thoughts review ;
With kind severity pursue
Through each disguise thy servant's mind,
Nor leave one stain of guilt behind.
Guide through th' eternal path my feet,
And bring me to thy blissful seat."

OF DRAMATIC POETRY.

LECTURE XXX.

THE SONG OF SOLOMON NOT A REGULAR DRAMA.

The Platonic division of Poetry into the narrative, dramatic, and mixed kinds, of little use; but deserves to be noticed on this occasion, as leading to an accurate definition of Dramatic Poetry, and clearing up the ambiguity in which the term has been involved by the moderns—Two species pointed out: the lesser, which possesses only the form of dialogue, without the personal intervention of the poet; and the greater, which contains a plot or fable—There are extant some instances of the former in the writings of the Hebrews; but none of their productions seem to have the least title to the latter character, two perhaps excepted, the Song of Solomon, and the book of Job—Inquiry, whether the Song of Solomon contains a complete plot or fable—It is an Epithalamium: the characters which are represented in it: the poem founded upon the nuptial rites of the Hebrews—The opinion of Bossuet cited and explained; namely, that this poem is a representation of the seven days of festival which succeeded the marriage, and consequently consists of seven parts or divisions—This opinion the most favourable of all, to those who account this poem a regular drama; it however does not prove that it contains a complete plot or fable—Definition of the dramatic Fable—Nothing like it in the Song of Solomon: it is therefore not a perfect drama, but it is of the lesser class of dramatic poems—The chorus of Virgins bears a great analogy to the chorus of the Greek tragedies; but could not serve as a model for them.

THE ancient critics, following the authority of Plato,* have distributed all poetical compositions, according to their form or subject, into three classes: the narrative, the imitative or dramatic, and the mixed. This arrangement is, however, not of much use on the whole; it neither draws a perfect line of distinction between the different species of poems,

* See Plat. *De Rep.* lib. iii.

nor serves to define or explain the nature and form of any.
There is scarcely any species of poem perfectly simple in its
nature, scarcely any which does not occasionally unite these
different modes of expression. The epic indeed may be said
to exhibit almost invariably a narration of the mixed kind;
and the dramatic necessarily assumes the imitative form. But
as other poems may adopt freely the mixed narration, so I
do not see any just reason why they should be absolutely
prohibited from assuming the dramatic form.   Custom,
however, we find, has so far prevailed, that although the
style and manner does not seem necessarily appropriated to
any particular subject whatever, the name at least of *dramatic*
has been generally received as distinguishing a particular
species of poetry.   The present object of inquiry is, therefore, what specimens of this species of composition are extant
in the writings of the Hebrews; and in the very first stage
of our investigation some degree of caution will be required,
lest the ambiguity of the term, as it has been used by the
moderns, should mislead or perplex us.

The term *dramatic poetry*, as I before observed, is now
restricted to two particular species of composition, Tragedy
and Comedy.   It was originally, however, of much more
extensive signification : it regarded simply the external form:
it was properly applied to every poem composed in dialogue,
provided that, throughout the whole, the conversation was
carried on by the characters themselves without the intervention of the poet.*   This mode of composition is exemplified in several of the bucolics of Theocritus and Virgil,

---

* The nature of this appropriation of a general term will perhaps be better
explained, by briefly adverting to the History of the Theatre. In fact, there is
scarcely any circumstance in which the gradual progress of human invention is
more exemplified, than in the origin and improvement of the Greek Drama. It
was originally nothing more than a rude song, exhibited by one or more clownish
minstrels or ballad-singers, who disfigured themselves to excite attention. *Thespis*
collected a company of them together, and transported them from village to village
in a kind of wagon; and something like this state of the drama we see in the
rude exhibitions of *Mummers* and *Morris-dancers* in the inland parts of this kingdom.   Thespis added to the singers an interlocutor, who served to explain the
matter of the songs ; and in this state the drama continued, till an accident brought
it to greater perfection. In the representation of a tragedy, in which the Furies
were exhibited, the barbarous dresses of the chorus (which consisted of fifty
persons) frighted the pregnant women into fits. Hence Æschylus was induced
to retrench the number of the chorus, and, to make up for the deficiency, added to
the actors or interlocutors. He erected a stage, and ornamented it with machinery;
and equipped the actors with the robe, the buskin, and the mask. See more upon
this subject in *Essays Historical and Moral*, by the translator of these Lectures,
Ess. i.—T.

in some of the satires of Horace, and in two of his odes. In order, therefore, to examine the subject more accurately, it will be proper to distinguish two species of dramatic poems: the lesser, in which, by means of dialogue or characters, the manners, passions, and actions of men are imitated or delineated; and the greater, which contains, moreover, a plot or fable, that is, the representation of some incident or transaction of life, regular or complete, in which events succeed each other in a connected series, and which after various and interesting vicissitudes is wrought up to a perfect conclusion. This latter species includes both tragedy and comedy; and as the plot or fable distinguishes them from the inferior species of dramatic poetry, so the perfect form of dialogue serves to draw the line between them and the epic.

There are abundant examples of the former species of dramatic poetry manifestly extant in the writings of the Hebrews; and perhaps there are many others which we have not discovered to be of this kind.* The sudden change

* Our Author has treated with his usual modesty a very difficult subject; on which those who have been more adventurous have been led into great errors. It is certain that many of the Psalms are dramatic, which some commentators observing, delighted with their own discoveries, whenever they met with a passage more difficult than usual, or were able to catch any new and visionary explanation, more agreeable to their theological notions, they have eagerly resorted to the change of the persons or characters, though no such change existed. Such are those commentators who have fancied, in accommodation to the quotation of St. Paul, Heb. i. 10, the spirit and purpose of which they did not understand, that the former part of the ciind Psalm to the 24th verse, "Take me not away in the midst of my age," consisted entirely of a speech of Christ; and that the remainder, "as for thy years, they endure throughout all generations," &c. was the reply of God the Father. Whoever indulges himself in this mode of explication, may easily find out any thing he pleases in the Psalms, and, with little or no philological knowledge, without the smallest assistance from criticism, can give a meaning even to the most difficult or corrupted texts of Scripture—any meaning indeed but the right one.

Our Author very justly suspects, that not a few passages of the dramatic kind are at present unknown; yet we are not allowed to suppose an ode of the dramatic kind, unless it appear so by some decisive proof; nor ought we to fly to this discovery as a refuge for our ignorance. For, as many passages may probably be of the dramatic kind which we do not know to be such, so, many may be accounted dramatic, which a little more philological knowledge, or the true reading, which antiquity may have obscured, would point out to be simple and regular compositions. In order to demonstrate how cautious commentators ought to be in these respects, I shall have recourse to one example, whence we shall be able to judge how uncertain many others are, however they may bear a face of probability.

The second Psalm has been accounted one of the principal of the dramatic kind, and scarcely any person has doubted of its being altogether dramatic. If you attend to some commentators, the holy prophet speaks in the 1st and 2nd verses; in the 3rd, the rebellious princes; in the 4th and 5th, the prophet

of persons, when by the vehemence of passion the author is
led, as it were insensibly, from the narration of an event to
the imitation or acting of it, is frequent in the Hebrew poetry;
but sometimes the genuine dramatic or dialogue form is
quite apparent, and the passage will admit of no other
explanation.   The twenty-fourth Psalm is evidently of this
kind, relating, as I formerly endeavoured to prove, to the
transferring of the ark to Mount Sion: and the whole of the
transaction is exhibited in a theatrical manner, though the
dialogue is not fully obvious till towards the conclusion of
the poem.   That remarkable passage of Isaiah also deserves
notice on this occasion, in whcih the Messiah, coming to vengeance, is introduced conversing with a chorus as on a theatre.

Cho. "Who is this that cometh from Edom?
      With garments deeply dyed from Botsra?
      This, that is magnificent in his apparel;
      Marching on in the greatness of his strength?
Mes. I, who publish righteousness, and am mighty to save.
Cho. Wherefore is thine apparel red?
      And thy garments, as of one that treadeth the wine-vat?
Mes. I have trodden the vat alone;
      And of the peoples there was not a man with me,
      And I trod them in mine anger;
      And I trampled them in mine indignation;
      And their life-blood was sprinkled on my garments;
      And I have stained all mine apparel.
      For the day of vengeance was in my heart;
      And the year of my redeemed was come.
      And I looked, and there was no one to help;
      And I was astonished that there was no one to uphold;
      Therefore mine own arm wrought salvation for me,
      And mine indignation itself sustained me.
      And I trod down the peoples in mine anger;
      And I crushed them in mine indignation;
      And I spilled their life-blood on the ground."*

again; in the 5th, God; in the 7th and 8th, the anointed king; in the 10th, 11th,
and 12th, the holy prophet.   It is very extraordinary that they should not see that
it is not the rebellious princes who speak in the 3rd verse, but that their words are
only referred to by the prophet, and that, according to the manner of the orientals,
without directly identifying the speaker.   Nothing is more common in the Arabic
poetry, than to relate the actions and sentiments of particular persons, and to annex
their very words, without any preface of *saying*, or *he said*, &c.   It does not even
appear that God is introduced as a dramatic character; for, if so, what is the use of
the words, "He shall appear unto them in his wrath," &c.?—M.

* Isa. lxiii. 1—6.   "Ver. 1. after אני in one MS. in the margin יהוה is added.

The hundred-and-twenty-first Psalm is of the same kind; and, as it is both concise and elegant, I shall quote it at large.   The king, apparently going forth to battle, first approaches the ark of God upon Mount Sion, and humbly implores the divine assistance, on which alone he professes to rest his confidence:

> " I will lift up mine eyes unto the mountains,
> Whence cometh my succour.
> My succour is from JEHOVAH,
> Who made the heavens and the earth."

The High-priest answers him from the tabernacle:

> " He will not suffer thy foot to stumble;
> He that preserveth thee will not slumber;
> Behold, he will neither slumber nor sleep:
> He who preserveth Israel,
> JEHOVAH will preserve thee;
> JEHOVAH will shade thee with his right-hand:
> The sun shall not injure thee by day,
> Nor the moon by night.
> JEHOVAH will preserve thee from all evil;
> He will preserve thy soul:
> JEHOVAH will preserve thy going out and thy coming in,
> From this time forth for ever and ever."

This much will suffice for that inferior species of dramatic poetry, or rather that dramatic form which may be assumed by any species of poem.   The more perfect and regular drama, that I mean which consists of a plot or fable, will demand a more elaborate investigation.

There are only two poems extant among the writings of the Hebrews which can, on the present occasion, at all be

---

It is read המדבר in one MS. with the demonstrative article annexed   Also צדקה, without ב prefixed, in one MS.: so the LXX and the Vulg.   It is read ורב, with ו prefixed, in thirty-one MSS.: so the LXX, Syr. Vulg.

" Ver. 2. It is אדום in twenty-eight MSS. and three edit. ללבושיך, plural in twenty-one MSS.: so the LXX, Syr. for the first ל read מ, according to all the old translations.

" Ver. 3. It is read אדרכם, without ו prefixed, in two MSS.: so Syr. Vulg. For אנאלחי, in one MS. אנאלהו.

" Ver. 4. שנת, without ו prefixed, in thirty MSS. and three edit.: so Vulg.

" Ver. 5. For וחמתי seven MSS. and three edit. have וצדקתי.   See chap. lix. 16.

" Ver. 6. For ואשכרם read ואשברם, as occurs in twenty-five MSS. and one edit."—K.

brought into question—the Song of Solomon, and the book of Job; both eminent in the highest degree for elegance, sublimity, and I am sorry to add obscurity also.   The almost infinite labours of the learned have left us but little new to say upon this subject; I shall, however, proceed to inquire, with some degree of minuteness, into the form and structure of each of these poems, and into the reasons which may be alleged in favour of their claim to the appellation of regular dramas.   The opinions of other critics shall not pass unregarded, if any remarks or even conjectures occur, which may be likely to throw any light upon the present subject, or to explain or illustrate their principal beauties.

The Song of Songs (for so it is entitled, either on account of the excellence of the subject or of the composition) is an epithalamium or nuptial dialogue; or rather, if we may be allowed to give it a title more agreeable to the genius of the Hebrew, a *Song of Loves.** It is expressive of the utmost fervour as well as the utmost delicacy of passion; it is instinct with all the spirit and all the sweetness of affection. The principal characters are Solomon himself and his bride, who are represented speaking both in dialogue, and in soliloquy when accidentally separated.   Virgins also, the companions of the bride, are introduced, who seem to be constantly upon the stage, and bear a part in the dialogue: mention too is made of young men, friends of the bridegroom, but they are mute persons.†   This is exactly conformable to the manners of the Hebrews, who had always a number of companions to the bridegroom, thirty of whom were present in honour of Samson at his nuptial feast.‡ In the New Testament, according to the Hebrew idiom, they are called "children (or sons) of the bride-chamber,"§ and "friends of the bridegroom;"‖ there too we find mention of ten virgins, who went forth to meet the bridegroom, and conduct him home:¶ which circumstances, I think, indicate that this poem is founded upon the nuptial rites of the Hebrews, and is expressive of the forms or ceremonial of their marriages.**   In this opinion, indeed, the harmony††

---

* Such is the title of Psalm xlv.   † Cant. v. 1; viii. 13.   See iii. 7 – 11.
‡ Judges xiv. 11.   § John iii. 29.   ‖ Matt. ix. 15.
¶ Lightfoot on Matt. ibid.   ** Psalm xlv. 15.

†† It may seem a bold undertaking to contradict the opinion of all the commentators, which has been so long established, that the principal personages of the Canticles are a bride and bridegroom during the nuptial week. As I cannot, how-

of commentators is not less remarkable than their disagreement concerning the general economy and conduct of the work, and the order and arrangement of the several parts. The present object of inquiry however is only, whether any plot or fable be contained or represented in this poem ? and upon this point the most profitable opinion is that of the celebrated Bossuet,* a critic whose profound learning will ever be acknowledged, and a scholar whose exquisite taste will ever be admired. I shall endeavour, as briefly as possible, to explain his sentiments concerning the form and conduct of this poem, whence we shall probably be enabled to decide in some measure concerning the equity of its claim to the title of a regular drama.

It is agreed on all parts, that the nuptial feast, as well as every other solemn rite among the Hebrews, was hebdomadal.† Of this circumstance M. Bossuet has availed himself

ever, reconcile the matter to my mind, I shall briefly assign the reasons of my dissent from this opinion. The first is, that no direct mention is made, during the course of this long poem, of the ceremony of marriage; nor of any one of the circumstances which attend that ceremony. Again, who can possibly imagine a bridegroom so necessitated to labour, as not to be able to appropriate a few days in his nuptial week to the celebration of his marriage; but be compelled immediately to quit his spouse and his friends for whole days, in order to attend his cattle in the pastures? Nay, at this time of festival, he even does not return at night, but leaves his bride, to whom he appears so much attached, alone and unhappy. Or if such instances might occur in particular cases, certainly they do not afford a proper subject for a nuptial song. At the same time, the bridegroom is supposed to have the care of a vineyard, and his brothers are displeased with him for having neglected it: this is so contrary to every idea of nuptial festivity, that unless we could suppose it meant in the way of burlesque, it is impossible to conceive it to have any relation to the celebration of a marriage.

There is still less reason to think that the poem relates to the state of the parties betrothed before marriage; and there are not the smallest grounds for supposing it the description of any clandestine amour, since the transaction is described as public and legal, and the consent of parents is very plainly intimated.

It remains therefore to explain my own sentiments; and these are, that the chaste passions of conjugal and domestic life are described in this poem, and that it has no relation to the celebration of nuptials. It may seem improbable to some readers, that conjugal and domestic life should afford a subject for an amorous poem; but those readers have not reflected how materially the manners of the orientals are different from ours. Domestic life among us is in general a calm and settled state, void of difficulties, perplexities, suspicions, and intrigues; and a state like this rarely affords matter for such a poem. But in the East, from the nature of *polygamy*, that state admits more of the perplexities, jealousies, plots, and artifices of love; the scene is more varied, there is more of novelty, and consequently greater scope for invention and fancy.—M.

* See Bossuet, *Præf. & Comment in Cant.*

† See Gen. xxix. 27. Judges xiv. 12.

in the analyzation of the poem, and he accordingly divides
the whole into seven parts, corresponding to the seven days
of its supposed duration.* The vicissitudes of day and
night are marked with some degree of distinctness; he
therefore makes use of these as indexes, to point to the true
division of the parts. The nuptial banquet being concluded, the bride is led in the evening to her future husband;
and here commences the nuptial week: for the Hebrews,
in their account of time, begin always at the evening.†
The bridegroom, who is represented in the character of a
shepherd, goes forth early in the morning to the accustomed occupations of a rural and pastoral life; the bride
presently awaking, and impatient of his absence, breaks out
into a soliloquy full of tenderness and anxiety; and this
incident forms the exordium of the poem. The early departure of the bridegroom seems to be according to custom;
hence that precaution, so frequently and so anxiously repeated, not to disturb his beloved:

> "I abjure you, O ye daughters of Jerusalem,
> By the roes and the hinds of the field,
> That ye disturb not, neither awake
> The beloved, till herself be inclined."‡

Nor less frequent is the following exclamation of the virgins:

> "Who is she, rising up out of the desert?
> Who is she, that is seen like the morning?"§

In these terms they seem to greet the bride when she first
comes out of her chamber; and these several expressions
have some allusion to the early time of the morning. The
night is also sometimes mentioned in direct terms,|| and
sometimes it is indirectly denoted by circumstances.¶ If,
therefore, any reader, admitting these indications of time,
will carefully attend to them, he cannot I think but perceive, that the whole of the work consists of seven parts or

---

* In addition to what I remarked above, there is this circumstance, which
militates against the conjecture of Bossuet, namely, that though the nuptial banquet
continues for seven days, no time appears in this poem appropriated to the banquet
itself. Either the bride and bridegroom are separated from, and in quest of each
other, or they are enjoying a wished-for solitude: and whenever they converse with
the virgins, it is in the street or in the field, and never with the guests, or at a
banquet.—M.

† See Gen. i. 5, &c.   ‡ Cant. ii. 7. iii. 5; viii. 4.   § Ch. iii. 6; viii. 5;
vi. 10. || Ch. iii. 1; v. 2.   ¶ Ch. ii. 6; viii. 3.

divisions, each of which occupies the space of a day.*   The
same critic adds, that he can discover the last day to be
clearly distinguished as the Sabbath; for the bridegroom
does not then, as usual, go forth to his rural employments,
but proceeds from the marriage-chamber into public with
his bride.†   Such are the sentiments of this learned person,
to which I am inclined to accede, not as absolute demonstration, but as a very ingenious and probable conjecture
upon an extremely obscure subject; I follow them, therefore, as a glimmering of light which beams forth in the
midst of darkness, where it would be almost unreasonable to
hope for any clearer illumination.

This opinion is the most favourable of all to those who
account the Song of Solomon a regular drama ; for this arrangement seems to display, in some measure, the order and
method of a theatrical representation.   But if they make use
of the term *dramatic* according to the common acceptation
of the word, this poem must be supposed to contain a fable,
or entire and perfect plot or action, of a moderate extent,
in which the incidents are all connected, and proceed regularly from one another, and which, after several vicissitudes,
is brought to a perfect conclusion.   But certainly the bare
representation of a nuptial festival cannot in any respect
answer to this definition.   We are, it is true, very imperfectly instructed in the particular rites and ceremonies of
the Hebrew marriages ; but we have no reason to suppose,
that, in their common and usual form, they were possessed
of such variety and vicissitude of fortunes and events as to
afford materials for a regular plot or fable.   The whole was
one even tenor of joy and festivity.   An unexpected incident might indeed sometimes occur to interrupt the usual
order, and to produce such a change of fortune as might
afford a basis for a dramatic story; and if any such incident is to be found in the poem at present under our
consideration, it will establish its claim to that appellation.
But the truth is, the keenest inspection of criticism can,

---

* The following is the distribution of the work according to Bossuet:

1st Day :	Chap. i.	—— ii.	6.
2nd —	Chap. ii. 7.	——	17.
3rd —	Chap. iii.	—— v.	1.
4th —	Chap. v. 2.	—— vi.	9.
5th —	Chap. vi. 10.	—— vii.	11.
6th —	Chap. vii. 12.	—— viii.	3.
7th —	Chap. viii. 4.	——	14.

† Chap. viii. 5.

throughout the whole, discover no such incident or circumstance: the state of affairs is uniformly the same from the beginning to the end; a few light fluctuations of passion excepted, such as the anxiety of absence, and the amenity and happiness which the lovers enjoy in each other's presence.   The bride laments the absence of her beloved;* she seeks, she finds him, she brings him home: again he is lost, see seeks him again, but with different success; she complains, languishes, indites messages to be delivered to him; she indulges her passion in a full and animated description of his person.   All this, however, bears no resemblance to a regular plot, nor affords the piece any fairer title to the appellation of a perfect drama than the dramatic eclogues of Theocritus and Virgil, in which the loves, the amusements, and the emulations of shepherds are depicted, and which no critic has ever classed with the regular fables of Euripides and Terence.   Thus far, therefore, we may safely admit, that the Song of Solomon possesses indeed the dramatic form, and therefore belongs properly to that inferior species which was mentioned in the former part of this Lecture; but that it cannot, upon any fair grounds of reason, be accounted a regular drama.

There is, however, one circumstance in which this poem bears a very near affinity to the Greek drama—the chorus of virgins seems in every respect congenial to the tragic chorus of the Greeks.   They are constantly present, and prepared to fulfil all the duties of advice and consolation; they converse frequently with the principal characters; they are questioned by them, and they return answers to their inquiries; they take part in the whole business of the poem; and I do not find that upon any occasion they quit the scene.   Some of the learned have conjectured that Theocritus, who was contemporary with the Seventy Greek translators of the Scriptures, and lived with them in the court of Ptolemy Philadelphus, was not unacquainted with the beauties of this poem, and that he has almost literally introduced some passages from it into his elegant Idylliums.†   It might also be suspected, that the Greek tragedians were indebted for their chorus to this poem of Solomon, were not the probabilities on the other side much greater, that the Greeks

---

* Chap. iii. and v.

† Compare Cant. i. 9. vi. 10, with Theoc. xviii. 30. 26.   Cant. iv. 11, with Theoc. xx. 26.   Cant. viii. 6, 7, with Theoc. xxiii. 23—26.

were made acquainted with it at too late a period; and were it not evident that the chorus of the Greeks had a very different origin—were it not evident, indeed, that the chorus was not added to the fable, but the fable to the chorus.*

---

* See Note, p. 326. The uses that certain apologists for the Greek drama have found for the chorus, namely that it heightens the probability, and corrects the ill effects of vicious sentiments in the mouths of the actors, I do not allow. How far the musical part of the chorus might serve to increase the pleasure, or to excite or enliven the passions, is a different question.—T.

LECTURE XXXI.

OF THE SUBJECT AND STYLE OF SOLOMON'S SONG.

The question debated, Whether the Song of Solomon is to be taken in a literal or alle-gorical sense? The allegorical sense defended upon the grounds of the parabolic style—The nature and groundwork of this allegory explained—The fastidiousness of those critics reproved, who pretend to take offence at the freedom of some of those images which are found in the sacred writings ; the nature of those images explained —The allegorical interpretation confirmed by analogical arguments ; not equally demonstrable from the internal structure of the work itself—This allegory of the third or mystical species ; the subject literally relating to the nuptials of Solomon— Two cautions to be observed by commentators—The style of the Poem pastoral ; the characters are represented as pastoral : how agreeable this to the manners of the Hebrews—The elegance of the topics, descriptions, comparisons of this Poem ; illustrated by examples.

HAVING, in my last Lecture, briefly explained what appeared to me most probable, among the great variety of opinions which have prevailed concerning the conduct and economy of the Song of Solomon, a question next presents itself for our investigation, not less involved in doubt and obscurity, I mean the real nature and subject of the poem. Some are of opinion that it is to be taken altogether in a literal sense, and others esteem it wholly allegorical. There is no less disagreement also among those who consider it as allegorical: some conceive it to be no more than a simple allegory, while others place it in that class which I have denominated *mystical*, that, namely, which is founded upon the basis of history. I would gladly, from the first, have considered this question as foreign to my undertaking, and would have avoided it as involved in the deepest obscurity, had I not, in the former part of these Lectures, been under the necessity of remarking the connexion between the different kinds of allegory and the principles of the sacred poetry ; had I not also found it necessary to advert to all the peculiarities of the parabolic style, the most obvious property of which is to express by certain images, chiefly adopted from natural objects, the analogy and application of which is regularly preserved, those ideas and doctrines which are more remote from common apprehension. This I cannot help considering as a matter of the utmost importance, in enabling us to understand properly the poetry of the Hebrews; and upon this point much of the present argument will be found to depend.

I shall on this, as well as upon the last occasion, proceed with that cautious reserve which I think prudent and necessary on so obscure a subject; and since certainty is not to be obtained, I shall content myself with proposing to your consideration what appears least improbable. In the first place, then, I confess, that by several reasons, by the general authority and consent of both the Jewish and Christian churches, and, still more, by the nature and analogy of the parabolic style, I feel irresistibly inclined to that side of the question which considers this poem as an entire allegory. Those, indeed, who have considered it in a different light, and who have objected against the inconsistency and meanness of the imagery, seem to be but little acquainted with the genius of the parabolic diction: for the removal, therefore, of these difficulties, which I find have been the cause of offence to many persons, I shall beg leave to trespass upon your attention, while I explain somewhat more accurately the nature of this allegory, and its analogy with other productions of the Hebrew poets.

The narrowness and imbecility of the human mind being such as scarcely to comprehend or attain a clear idea of any part of the Divine nature by its utmost exertions, God has condescended in a manner to contract the infinity of his glory, and to exhibit it to our understandings under such imagery as our feeble optics are capable of contemplating. Thus the Almighty may be said to descend, as it were, in the Holy Scriptures, from the height of his majesty, to appear on earth in a human shape, with human senses and affections, in all respects resembling a mortal—" with human voice and human form." This kind of allegory is called anthropopathy, and occupies a considerable portion of theology properly so called, that is, as delivered in the Holy Scriptures. The principal part of this imagery is

derived from the passions; nor indeed is there any one
affection or emotion of the human soul which is not, with
all its circumstances, ascribed in direct terms, without any
qualification whatever, to the supreme God; not excepting
those in which human frailty and imperfection is most evidently displayed—anger and grief, hatred and revenge.
That love also, and that of the tenderest kind, should bear
a part in this drama, is highly natural and perfectly consistent. Thus, not only the fondness of paternal affection
is attributed to God, but also the force, the ardour, and the
solicitude of conjugal attachment, with all the concomitant
emotions, the anxiety, the tenderness, the jealousy incidental
to this passion.

After all, this figure is not in the least productive of
obscurity; the nature of it is better understood than that
of most others; and although it be exhibited in a variety
of lights, it constantly preserves its native perspicuity. A
peculiar people, of the posterity of Abraham, was selected by
God from among the nations, and he ratified his choice by
a solemn covenant. This covenant was founded upon reci-
procal conditions: on the one part, love, protection, and
support; on the other, faith, obedience, and worship pure
and devout. This is that conjugal union between God and
his church; that solemn compact so frequently celebrated
by almost all the sacred writers under this image. It is,
indeed, a remarkable instance of that species of metaphor
which Aristotle calls *analogical;** that is, when in a proposition consisting of four ideas, the first bears the same relation to the second as the third does to the fourth, and the
corresponding words may occasionally change their places
without any injury to the sense. Thus, in this form of expression, God is supposed to bear exactly the same relation
to the church as a husband to a wife; God is represented as
the spouse of the church, and the church as the betrothed of
God. Thus also, when the same figure is maintained with
a different mode of expression, and connected with different
circumstances, the relation is still the same: thus, the piety
of the people, their impiety, their idolatry and rejection,
stand in the same relation with respect to the sacred covenant, as chastity, modesty, immodesty, adultery, divorce,
with respect to the marriage-contract. And this notion is
so very familiar and well understood in Scripture, that the

* Poet. chap. xxii. and Rhet. iii. 3.

word adultery, or whoredom, is commonly used to denote idolatrous worship; and so appropriated does it appear to this metaphorical purpose, that it very seldom occurs in its proper and literal sense.

Let us only observe how freely the sacred poets employ this image, how they dwell upon it, in how many different forms they introduce it, and how little they seem to fear exhibiting it with all its circumstances. Concerning the reconciliation of the church to Almighty God, and its restoration to the Divine favour, amongst many images of a similar nature, the elegant Isaiah introduces the following:

> " For thy husband is thy maker;
> JEHOVAH, God of Hosts, is his name:
> And thy Redeemer is the Holy One of Israel;
> The God of the whole earth shall he be called."*

And in another passage, in the form of a comparison:

> " For as a young man weddeth a virgin,
> So shall thy Restorer wed thee ; †

---

* Isa. liv. 5.

† The ambiguity of the word which I translate " thy restorer," has created inextricable difficulties to all the translators and commentators, both ancient and modern. The LXX have mistaken it, and the Masorites have mispointed it. Their authority has consecrated the error, and almost established it. Nothing, however, appears clearer to me than that this word בני is not the plural of the noun בן, *ben*, son, but of the participle *benoni* of the verb בנה, *benah*, to build, and is parallel and synonymous to *thy God* in the alternate member. Compare the above-quoted passage of Isaiah, where also mark that *husbands* and *creators* occur in the plural, with the same relation to the same word. By this explanation every offensive and indelicate idea is taken away from the passage, which I do not wonder proved an impediment in the way of the commentators. There is another passage of Isaiah in which the same word is egregiously misunderstood by the Masorites:

> " They that destroyed thee shall soon become thy builders;
> And they that laid thee waste shall become thy offspring."—Isa. xlix. 17.

Thus, in spite of the Masorites, the sentence ought to be distributed; thus it ought to be explained, conformably to the LXX, who have translated not only this ambiguous word, (as also the Chald. and Vulg.,) but the whole period also, with the greatest accuracy, elegance, taste, and erudition:

> Ταχυ οικοδομηθησῃ ὑφ ὡν καθῃρεθης,
> Και οι ερημωσαντες σε εξελευσονται εκ σȣ.

The Arab. as in general, copies them. See a similar idiom in Psa. cvi. 13. Exod. ii. 18; and the same sense of the verb *jotza*, Jer. xxx. 21. Nahum. i. 11.

In this verse also, for כי יבעל, the LXX, Syr. and Chald. read כי כיבעל. " Before יבעלך one MS. adds כן, so the LXX, Syr. Chald. For ומשוש one MS. has וכמשוש, and another כמשוש." K.—*Author's Note.*

Y 2

> And as the bridegroom rejoiceth in his bride,
> So shall thy God rejoice in thee."*

The same image, a little diversified, and with greater freedom of expression, as better adapted to the display of indignation, is introduced by Jeremiah,† when he declaims against the defection of the Jews from the worship of the true God. Upon the same principle the former part of the prophecy of Hosea ought also to be explained: and whether that part of the prophecy be taken in the literal and historical sense, or whether it be esteemed altogether allegorical, still the nature and principles of this figure, which seems consecrated in some measure to this subject, will evidently appear. None of the prophets, however, have applied the image with so much boldness and freedom as Ezekiel, an author of a most fervid imagination, who is little studious of elegance, or cautious of offending; insomuch, that I am under some apprehension of his incurring no inconsiderable share of censure from those over-delicate critics who have been emitted from the Gallic schools.‡   His great freedom in the use of this image is

---

* Isa. lxii. 5.   See John iii. 29, &c. and Note, p. 342, in answer to Michaelis on the allegorical sense of Solomon's Song.—S. H.
    " Sir John Chardin, in his note on this place, tells us, that it is the custom in the East for youths, that were never married, always to marry virgins; and widowers, however young, to marry widows."—Harmer, *Observ.* ii. p. 482.--T.

† Jer. iii. 1, &c.

‡ Nothing can be more disgusting to any person of common sense, than the arrogant pretences of our neighbours on the continent to superior refinement and civilization: and I confess, on a fair investigation, I am utterly at a loss to find in what this boasted superiority consists. Is it seen in their enlarged and liberal notions of civil government, in their toleration and general information on politics and religion, in the mildness of their punishments, and the equity of their laws? Is it marked by their progress in the great and useful sciences, by their Bacons and their Boyles, their Newtons and their Lockes? Does it appear in the sublimity, the grandeur, the elegance of their poets? Or is it demonstrated by still more certain marks of civilization—by the general cleanliness, decency, and industry of the common people? Is it seen in the convenience and grandeur of their public roads, and the accommodations afforded to travellers in every part of the kingdom? Does it appear in the face of the country, the high state of cultivation, and the success and improvement of agriculture? Or, lastly, is it demonstrable from the morals of the people at large ; from the independence, the dignity, the probity, particularly of the trading classes of society? I know no other marks of civilization than these ; and if the admirers of Gallic frippery cannot answer these questions to my satisfaction, I shall continue to give but little credit to their pretensions to extraordinary refinement and politeness.—T.
    That diversity of manners, that delicacy of conversation, which is observed by some nations, and the coarseness of others, result chiefly from the degree of intercourse which subsists between the sexes. In countries where the intercourse is free and familiar, where the sexes meet commonly in mixed companies, they

particularly displayed in two parables,* in which he describes
the ingratitude of the Jews and Israelites to their great protec-
tor, and their defection from the true worship, under imagery
assumed from the character of an adulterous wife, and the
meretricious loves of two unchaste women. If these parables
(which are put into the mouth of God himself with a direct
allegorical application, and in which it must be confessed
that delicacy does not appear to be particularly studied) be
well considered, I am persuaded that the Song of Solomon
(which is in every part chaste and elegant) will not appear
unworthy of the divine sense in which it is usually taken,
either in matter or style, or in any degree inferior either in
gravity or purity to the other remains of the sacred poets.
To these instances I may add the forty-fifth Psalm, which is
a sacred epithalamium, of the allegorical application of which
to the union between God and the church, I do not find that
any doubt has hitherto been entertained; though many suspect it, and not without good reason, to have been produced
upon the same occasion, and with the same relation to a
real fact,† as the Song of Solomon. Neither ought we to
omit, that the writers of the New Testament‡ have freely
admitted the same image in the same allegorical sense with
their predecessors, and have finally consecrated it by their
authority.§

accustom themselves to a greater modesty and delicacy in their conversation,
which modesty is easily transferred to their composition. Such a people, therefore,
with whom entertainments would seem languid and dull without the company of
young women, though perhaps not free from licentiousness in their manners, will
yet be chaste and delicate in their expressions. Hence arises, in a great degree, that
extreme delicacy in the people of modern Europe, which can scarcely bear some of
the passages in Virgil, and the chastest of the ancient poets. The case is quite
different with the people of the East: for the men having scarcely any society with
the unmarried women, or with the wives of others, converse together without being
restrained by the blushes of females, or with their own wives, whom they regard in
a very inferior light, and consequently treat with all the insolence of familiarity.
The women also converse chiefly with each other; and as they are similarly
situated, are probably not less licentious. It is not extraordinary, therefore, if greater
freedom of speech should prevail in those countries, and if this, when transferred
into their poetry, should be found to offend our ears, which are accustomed to so
much greater delicacy in conversation.—M.

* Ezek. xvi. and xxiii.

† Perhaps the completion and consecration of the temple. See Note, p. 342.
—S. H.

‡ See Matt. ix. 15. John iii. 29. 2 Cor. xi. 2. Eph. v. 23, &c. Rev. xix. 7 ;
xxi. 2 ; xxii. 17.

§ What Chardin relates of the Persian poetry, may perhaps not be unworthy of
the reader's notice in this place. " Debauchery and licentiousness," says he, " are

These reasons appear to me sufficient to remove those objections, founded on the meanness of the imagery, which render many critics averse to the allegorical explanation of this poem. I shall not attempt to confirm this opinion by any internal evidence from the poem itself, as I do not scruple to confess myself deterred by the great difficulty of the undertaking. For though, induced by the most ancient authority, and still more by the analogy of this with other similar allegories contained in the Hebrew writings, I am fully persuaded of the truth of what I have advanced; yet I am still apprehensive that it would be extremely difficult to establish the hypothesis by direct arguments from the internal structure of the work itself.*

the common topics of these compositions; but I must not omit remarking, that the most serious of their poets treat of the sublimest mysteries of theology under the most licentious language, in the way of allegory, as Áfez in his *Kasel*." Voyage de Chardin, 4to. tom. ii. cap. 14. But respecting this matter, see the arguments on both sides elegantly stated by the learned Sir William Jones, *Poes. Asiaticæ Comment.* cap. ix.—*Author's Note.*

* Our Author has treated this very difficult subject with more modesty and more address than any of the commentators; and, indeed, has said all that could be said, exclusive of the theological arguments in favour of the allegorical sense. I question, however, whether he will be able to remove all doubt from the mind of a cool and attentive reader. The reasons of my scepticism on this matter, I will, as a person earnestly desirous of the truth, endeavour briefly to explain; and I shall hold myself greatly indebted to that man who shall, upon rational principles, undertake to remove my scruples.

With regard to the authority of the ancient Christian church, in a question merely depending upon the exposition of a passage in Scripture, I hold it of very little importance, not only because the exposition of Scripture does not depend upon human authority, but because the Fathers, as well on account of their ignorance of the Hebrew language, as of the principles of polite literature in general, were very inadequate to the subject, eagerly pursuing certain mystical meanings, even with respect to the clearest passages, in the explanation of which the most enlightened of the modern commentators have refuted them. The time of the Fathers was so very distant from the period when this poem was composed, that it is impossible they should have been possessed of any certain tradition concerning its purport and meaning. I should entertain very different sentiments, if I could find any mention of the Song of Songs in the New Testament; but, on the most diligent examination, I have not been able to discern the slightest allusion to that poem.

The authority of the synagogue is of still less importance in my eyes, since, in other respects, we have found it so little deserving of confidence in its attempts at expounding the Scriptures. Such of the Jewish writers as have treated of the Canticles lived so many ages after the time of Solomon, after the total destruction of the commonwealth and literature of the Hebrews, that they knew no more of the matter than ourselves.

With regard to the analogy of other poems, all that can be said is, that it was indeed possible enough for Solomon to celebrate the Divine love in terms analogous to those descriptive of the human affections; but it is impossible to determine by that analogy, what kind of love he intended to be the subject of

But if, after all, it be allowed that this work is of the allegorical kind, another question remains, namely, to which

this poem. Shall we pretend to say, that his attention was wholly employed upon sacred poetry, and that he never celebrated in verse any of the human affections? Or, because some of the Hebrew poems celebrate the Divine goodness in terms expressive of the human passions, does it follow, that on no occasion those terms are to be taken in their literal sense?

Our Author has prudently declined examining the arguments which are usually taken from the poem itself, and from its internal structure, for the purpose of establishing the allegory. It is indeed very improbable, that, in so long a poem, if it were really allegorical, no vestiges, no intimation should be found, to direct us to apply it to the Divine love; nothing, which does not most clearly relate to the human passion: and that too, considering it as the production of one of the Hebrew writers, who are accustomed to mix the literal sense with the allegorical in almost all their compositions of this kind. In so long an allegory, one should also expect a deeper moral than usual, and one not generally obvious to be indicated: but no sober commentator has ever been able to deduce from the Canticles any other than this trite sentiment, that God loves his church, and is beloved by it. That this simple sentiment should be treated so prolixly, and nothing more distinctly revealed concerning it, who can credit, but upon the soundest basis of argument or proof? But in support of it we have only the bare position, that the Hebrew writers sometimes make use of allegorical expressions to denote the Divine love.

I am aware of the objections which are started by those who rest the matter upon theological arguments; (though I cannot find that these are of great weight or utility in the present debate: for they seem rather calculated to silence than convince.) They assert, that though the book has never been quoted by Christ or his Apostles, it was yet received into the sacred canon, and is therefore to be accounted of Divine original; and that there does not appear any thing in it divine, or worthy of sacred inspiration, unless it be supposed to contain the mystery of the Divine love. Lest, however, they should seem to have proved too much, and lest they should dismiss the reader prepossessed with some doubts concerning the Divine authority of the book, I will venture to remind these profound reasoners, that the chaste and conjugal affection so carefully implanted by the Deity in the human heart, and upon which so great a portion of human happiness depends, are not unworthy of a muse fraught even with Divine inspiration. Only let us suppose, contrary to the general opinion concerning the Canticles, that the affection which is described in this poem is not that of lovers previous to their nuptials, but the attachment of two delicate persons who have been long united in the sacred bond, can we suppose such happiness unworthy of being recommended as a pattern to mankind, and of being celebrated as a subject of gratitude to the great Author of happiness? This is indeed a branch of morals which may be treated in a more artificial and philosophical manner; and such a manner will perhaps be more convincing to the understanding, but will never affect the heart with such tender sentiments as the Song of Solomon; in which there exist all the fervour of passion, with the utmost chastity of expression, and with that delicacy and reserve which is ever necessary to the life and preservation of conjugal love. Let us remember, however, that Solomon, in his Proverbs, has not disdained very minutely to describe the felicities and infelicities of the conjugal state.—M.

Notwithstanding all that this learned writer has so ably advanced against the allegorical import of this exquisite Idyllium, I cannot be prevailed upon entirely to relinquish the idea. That compositions of a similar kind are still extant amongst

of the three classes of allegory already specified it properly
belongs. The first of these, you will recollect, was the continued metaphor; the second, the parable strictly so called;
and the third, the mystical allegory, which, under the veil
of some historical fact, conceals a meaning more sacred and
sublime. I must confess, that I am clearly of the same
opinion with those who assign this production to the latter
class of allegories; the reason of which will be evident, if it
be admitted that there is any thing in the poem at all allegorical, since there can scarcely be any doubt that it relates
in a literal sense to the nuptials of Solomon. Those also
who are conversant with the writings of the Hebrew poets
will easily perceive, how agreeable the conduct of this poem
is to the practice of those writers, who are fond of annexing

the Asiatics, is certain. The Loves of Megnoun and Leïleh have been celebrated
in the Arabic, Persic, and Turkish languages, with all the charms of poetic
rapture, whilst the impassioned lovers themselves are regarded in the same allegorical light as the bridegroom and bride in the Song of Songs. Exclusive, however,
of this consideration, there appear to stand forth, in the composition itself,
indisputable traits of an allegorical sense. For though (from our imperfect
knowledge of the extraneous manners, arts, local peculiarities, and literature,
of so singular a people at so distant a period) we be now unable to apply the
thing signified to its proper sign, yet a variety of images obtrude themselves upon
us that evidently contain a symbolical meaning.—JEHOVAH having chosen the
Jewish nation as his peculiar people, and being frequently, *by the Prophets after
Solomon,* represented as *their husband,* and they personified as *his wife;* might not
the consecration (2 Chron. vii.) of the temple, as an habitation for the Lord to
dwell in, and there receive them to himself, have suggested to Solomon the idea of
a *conjugal union,* and induced him to adapt an allegory to it?—As to the allegation
that this poem is not cited in the New Testament, it will upon this ground be of
the less weight; for our Saviour, in the parables of the Ten Virgins and the
Marriage Supper, has adopted (if not from it) the same allegory, as well as in other
passages, (Mark ix. 15, &c.,) and is himself not only pointed out to the Jews
expressly in the character of a bridegroom by John Baptist, (John iii,) but referred
to, under it, by St. Paul, (Eph. v. &c.,) and more particularly in the Apocalypse.
How far this conjecture may be supported I will not venture at present to
pronounce, but thus much it may be proper to observe, that such images as the
tents of Kedar compared to the *complexion of a young female;* the *tower of David*
to her *neck; Tirza* to her *beauty,* and *Jerusalem* to her *comeliness;* the *fish-pools of
Heshbon by the gates of Bethrabbin,* to her *eyes;* the *tower of Lebanon looking towards
Damascus,* to her *nose;* the *mount of Carmel,* to her *head;* with others of a
similar kind, would, I think, have never been selected to exemplify the beauties of a
BRIDE, in any composition that was not allegorical.

The idea above suggested will, perhaps, receive no little countenance from the
chapter cited above, 2 Chron. vii. Bossuet's division of the poem into seven days,
is perfectly conformable to the fact mentioned in the 8th and 9th verses, where we
learn, that the dedication of the altar was celebrated by a festival that continued
for the same space of time.—S. H.

a secret and solemn sense to the obvious meaning of their compositions, and of looking through the medium of human affairs to those which are celestial and divine. The subject of the Canticles appears to be the marriage-feast of Solomon (who was, both in name and in reality, the Prince of Peace); his bride is also called *Solomitis*,* the same name with a feminine termination; though the latter Jews have strangely disguised and obscured it by a vicious pronunciation; for Solomon and Solomitis have evidently the same relation to each other as the Latin names Caius and Caia. This circumstance of the names was not to be disregarded, since they seem to have a very strict connexion, and to afford a very distinct intimation of the latent meaning; for, to what purpose innovate the usual practice of the Hebrews, by assigning to the wife of Solomon the same name, unless from a regard to the force and meaning of the word? unless it was meant to indicate, that the name of Solomon himself was not without importance, not without some further aim than merely the distinction of the person? Who this wife of Solomon was, is not clearly ascertained; but some of the learned have conjectured, with an appearance of probability, that she was the daughter of Pharaoh, to whom Solomon was known to be particularly attached. May we not, therefore, with some shadow of reason, suspect, that, under the allegory of Solomon choosing a wife from the Egyptians, might be darkly typified that other Prince of Peace, who was to espouse a church chosen from among the Gentiles?†

Concerning the explanation of this allegory I will only add, that in the first place, we ought to be cautious of carrying the figurative application too far, and of entering into a precise explication of every particular; as these minute

---

* שׁוּלַמִּית שְׁלֹמֹה; which may be expressed in Greek Σολομων, Σωλομιτις. Cant. viii. 1.

† This very nice and remote allusion to Christ is totally destroyed by an unlucky observation of Dr. Hodgson, who very properly remarks, that the Bride, who is the subject of this poem, could not be the daughter of Pharaoh, for in the third chapter, ver. 4, she expressly says,

> " I would not let him go,
> Till I had led him into the house of my mother."

" If, therefore," says the Doctor, " she had been the daughter of Pharaoh, her mother's house would have been in Egypt, whereas the scene of this poem evidently lies at Jerusalem." See Dr. Hodgson's Version of this Poem, Notes on chap. iii.

The quotations from the Canticles in this and the last Lecture are chiefly taken from the above elegant publication.—T.

investigations are seldom conducted with sufficient prudence not to offend the serious part of mankind, learned as
well as unlearned. Again, I would advise that this production be treated according to the established rules of this
kind of allegory, fully and expressly delivered in the sacred
writings, and that the author be permitted to be his own
interpreter. In this respect the errors of critics and divines*
have been as numerous as they have been pernicious. Not
to mention other absurdities, they have taken the allegory
not as denoting the universal state of the church, but the
spiritual state of individuals; than which nothing can be
more inconsistent with the very nature and groundwork of
the allegory itself, as well as with the general practice of the
Hebrew poets on these occasions.

It remains to offer a few remarks upon the style of this
poem. I formerly intimated that it was of the pastoral
kind; since the two principal personages are represented in
the character of shepherds.† This circumstance is by no
means incongruous to the manners of the Hebrews, whose
principal occupation consisted in the care of cattle;‡ nor did
they consider this employment as beneath the dignity of the
highest characters. Least of all could it be supposed inconsistent with the character of Solomon,§ whose father was
raised from the sheepfold to the throne of Israel. The pastoral life is not only most delightful in itself, but, from the
particular circumstances and manners of the Hebrews, is
possessed of a kind of dignity. In this poem it is adorned with
all the choicest colouring of language, with all the elegance
and variety of the most select imagery. "Every part of the
Canticles," says a modern writer, "abounds in poetical
beauties: the objects which present themselves on every side
are, the choicest plants, the most beautiful flowers, the most
delicious fruits, the bloom and vigour of spring, the sweet
verdure of the fields, flourishing and well-watered gardens,
pleasant streams, and perennial fountains. The other senses
are represented as regaled with the most precious odours,
natural and artificial; with the sweet singing of birds, and
the soft voice of the turtle; with milk and honey, and the
choicest of wine. To these enchantments are added all that

---

* Bernard, Durham, Sanctius, Bossuet, &c.   † See chap. i. 7, 8.
‡ See Gen. xlvi. 32—34.
§ Though not inconsistent with Solomon, yet exceedingly so in respect to his
supposed Egyptian bride, as shepherds were held in abomination by the Egyptians.
This confirms Dr. Hodgson's idea in the last note.—S. H.

is beautiful and graceful in the human form; the endear-
ments, the caresses, the delicacy of love: if any object be
introduced which seems not to harmonize with this delightful
scene, such as the awful prospect of tremendous precipices;
the wildness of the mountains; or the haunts of the lions:
its effect is only to heighten by the contrast the beauty of the
other objects, and to add the charms of variety to those of
grace and elegance."*　In the following passage the force
and splendour of description is united with all the softness
and tenderness of passion:

"Get thee up, my companion,
　My lovely one, come away;
For, lo! the winter is past,
　The rain is over, is gone:
The flowers are seen on the earth:
　The season of the song is come,
And the voice of the turtle is heard in our land:
　The fig-tree puts forth its green figs,
And the vine's tender grapes yield a fragrance:
　Arise, my companion, my fair one, and come."†

The following comparisons abound in sweetness and delicacy:

"How sweet is thy love, O my sister, O spouse;
　How much better than wine is thy love,
And the odour of thy perfumes than all spices!
Thy lips, O spouse, distil honey from the comb,
Honey and milk are under thy tongue,
And the scent of thy garments is like the fragrance of
　Lebanon."‡

There are some others which demand a more accurate
investigation:

"Thy hair is like a flock of goats
　That browse upon Mount Gilead."§

* Bossuot, *Pref. to the Cant.*　† Chap. ii. 10—13.　‡ Chap. iv. 10, 11.
§ Chap. iv. 1—5. "It is by no means an easy matter to produce any other explanation of this and the following words than that which had long since been received
by the old translators. The word which is here rendered *browse* denotes in the
Arabic *to ascend,* or *to pass from a lower to a higher situation;* and I scarcely see
how this sense can be admitted in this place. The LXX have it απεκαλυφθησαν,
and in chap. vi. 4, ανεφανησαν, *they appear.* But the word *to shine* will perhaps
agree better, both in this passage and wherever this word occurs. But if the verb
גלש be taken in this passage in the sense of *ascending,* we must take the whole as
it is abore expressed; namely, as descriptive of a flock of goats covering the side of
the mountain from the bottom to the top."—H.
Galash does not mean to *browse* or to *appear,* but to *ascend,* whether we follow
the Septuagint, the Syriac, the Vulgate, or the Arabic copy. The use of the latter
word in this place is not indeed very easy to conceive, as "to ascend from Mount

The hair of the goats was soft, smooth, of a yellow cast, like
that of the bride;* her beautiful tresses are compared with
the numerous flocks of goats which covered this flourishing
mountain from the top to the bottom.

> "Thy teeth are like the shorn flock†
> Which have come up from the washing-place,
> All of which have twins,‡
> And none among them is bereaved."

The evenness, whiteness, and unbroken order of the teeth is
admirably expressed :

> "Like the twice-dy'd thread of crimson are thy lips,
> And thy language is sweet."

That is, thin and ruby-coloured, such as add peculiar graces
to the sweetness of the voice:

> "Like the slice of a pomegranate
> Are thy checks amidst thy tresses."§

Gilead" appears an odd phrase. Possibly the passage ought to be construed, "Thy
locks are as a flock of goats, *ascending, which are seen* from Mount Gilead."—M.

Thy hair is like a herd of goats
That go down from Mount Gilead [in the morning to the watering :]

deriving גלש from an Arabic word, which Schultens explain *to go to be watered in
the morning.*

That browse, is a sense obtained from the Syriac and Chaldee. Those who render
the word *shine* are indebted to a transposition of letters in שלג, *snow,* for this
signification.—S. H.

* See chap. vii. 5, and compare 1 Sam. xix. 13. 16, with xvi. 12. Consult
Bochart, Hieroz. part i. lib. ii. 51.

† "The verb *Katzab* means to *cut off* or *cut down* ; the interpretation, therefore,
of the word *ketzubot,* shorn, which many have adopted, and which is confirmed
by all the old translations, appears to me the most probable. From the same
verb, I think, may be deduced the signification *precisely equal,* intimating
that the sheep were all exactly shorn to one standard as it were. (See Bochart,
Hieroz. part i. lib. ii. 45.) Will not this sense better suit the connexion ?
Is not the *whiteness* and *purity* of sheep (and so of teeth) expressed in these
two lines, rather than their *evenness,* which seems to be included in those that
follow ?"—H.

‡ "The Arabic verb תאם denotes not only *to bring forth twins,* but also *to have
a companion* : whence תואם, *joined,* or *connected in a series* ; and תיאמיה says
Golius, is *a pearl,* from the link or order of the pearls. Nothing can be more
expressive than this image of the beautiful regularity and equality of the teeth.
The learned Michaelis prefers *twins,* referring perhaps to the counterpart in the
next member."—H.

§ *Behind thy veil,* says Michaelis, from the Arabic צמם, *to fasten together* ; and
the well-known מצממה אלראס, Giggeius, to have a *stipated head* ; placed within
small integument."—H.

> "As the opening blossom of the pomegranate are thy cheeks,
> From within thy locks."

3

Partly obscured, as it were, by her hair, and exhibiting a gentle blush of red from beneath the delicate shade, as the seeds of the pomegranate (the colour of which is white tinged with red) surrounded by the rind:

> "Thy neck is like the tower of David
> Built for an armoury;*
> A thousand shields are hung up against it,
> All bucklers for the mighty."

The neck is described as long, erect, slender, according to the nicest proportion; decorated with gold, gems, and large pearls. It is compared with some turret of the citadel of Sion, more lofty than the rest, remarkable for its elegance, and not less illustrious for its architecture than for the trophies with which it was adorned, being hung round with shields and other implements of war:

> "Thy two breasts are like two young kids,
> Twins of the gazal, that browse among the lilies."†

Delicate and smooth, standing equally prominent from the ivory bosom. The animal with which they are compared is an animal of exquisite beauty, and from that circumstance it derives its name in the Hebrew. Nothing can, I think,

---

Simon accurately interprets פלח *by the bursting forth of a flower*, and Guarini by *balaustium*, a word which Pliny will enable us to explain. He observes, that the embryo of the pomegranate, which has its origin in the flower, is called by the Greeks *citynus;* and adds, that the young blossom which breaks forth before the fruit becomes visible, is distinguished by the name *balaustium.* Dioscorides, however, has remarked, that *balaustium* is the blossom of the *wild,* and *cytinus* of the *cultivated* pomegranate. [See Notes on Vatick, p. 309, &c.]--צמה, here translated *locks* in a figurative sense, is properly that radiated down which grows round the blossom of the pomegranate, and partially shades it, as the hair does the cheeks.—S. H.

* "The word הרלפיות, which may be numbered among those that occur but once, certain critics, says R. L. B. Gershom, derive from תלה, to suspend, and פיות, that is, חרבות, of a sword; others from תלה and אלף 1000, suppose of swords: thus, in the following sentence, עליו אלף המגן חלי will afford an etymological explication of this word."—H.

> † " Thy two paps are like two young kids,
> Twins of the gazal,
> That browse amongst the lilies."

The points of similitude between the objects here compared, I apprehend to consist,—

1. In the *colour* of these young animals, which in the original is called עפר, *white deepening into red,* (from an Arabic word of this import,) whence their name is derived.

2. In their *relative height,* as just rising above the growth of lilies: they being compared to " paps *that never gave suck."*

These circumstances are noticed to justify this translation; for the *fawns* of a roe, neither in *colour* nor *height,* at all correspond to the objects compared.—S. H.

be imagined more truly elegant and poetical than all these passages, nothing more apt or expressive than these comparisons.   The discovery of these excellences, however, only serves to increase our regret for the many beauties which we have lost, the perhaps superior graces, which extreme antiquity seems to have overcast with an impenetrable shade.*

* It is much to be lamented, that no commentator has arisen sufficiently qualified to explain this beautiful poem. Those who have attempted it have been scholastic divines, rather indeed mystics, and have entirely overlooked the obvious and more elegant meaning. Indeed the task is by no means easy : besides a very accurate and idiomatical knowledge of the oriental languages, an intimate acquaintance with the manners of antiquity, and no small information concerning natural history, will be requisite : to these must be added a good deal of reading in the Arabic poetry, particularly in their compositions of the amorous kind ; and last of all, a true taste for poetry. Very few of these qualities have existed separately, and never all of them conjunctly in those who have undertaken to illustrate this poem.

In order to exemplify how much might be effected towards clearing up the obscurities of this most elegant composition, by a knowledge of natural history alone, I will endeavour to explain my opinion of some difficult passages, (chap. v. 11. 14; vii. 6. 14.) In chap. v. ver. 6. 11, most people are ignorant, and at a loss to conjecture, what may be the meaning of תלתלים : the Seventy and the Vulgate render it ελαταϛ, elatas, or the downy substance in which the dates are involved : nor is this translation very different from the Arabic, which renders it the *branch of the palm-tree from which the dates depend*. But what relation can this bear to the human hair ? I answer, the resemblance is obvious to any person who has seen the object of the comparison, or has remarked the plate of it annexed to the notes on *Theophrastus's History of Plants* by Jo. Budeus.—But how is Solomon consistent, in the same verse speaking of raven locks and a golden head ?

> " His head is of pure pold,
>   The locks of which resemble the branches of the palm-tree,
>   And black as the raven."

To reconcile this difficulty, it is necessary to know, that although the orientals may possibly admire *raven locks* in their natural state, yet they are accustomed to dye them with *henna,* (so they call the oil of privet,) in order to give them a yellow or golden cast : this is an ancient custom, though the existence of it among the Hebrews may be disputed ; but probably for this same purpose they might make use of gold dust, as the Latins are known to have done.

With the same *henna* they stain the countenance, as well as the hands and arms, which first changes them to an azure blue, and they grow yellow by degrees ; and this they esteem a great object of beauty, though it would be accounted deformity with us. This observation will enable us to understand better some phrases in the 14th and 15th verses of the same chapter :

> " His hands are as gold rings
>   Inlaid with chrysolite :
>   His belly as plates of ivory
>   Inclosed in sapphire :
>   His legs are as columns of marble
>   Upon a base of gold."

The fingers being stained with *henna,* appeared as if they had gold rings on, set with chrysolite ; which gem was *formerly* of a yellow colour.   I say formerly, because the same stone which we call the *topaz* was the ancient chrysolite.   (See

Hill's *Hist. of Fossils.*) But if by the word *tarshish* we understand the ancient hyacinth or amethyst, an azure colour will then be alluded to, which the same henna produces on the skin. The whiteness of the body, covered with a delicate purple vest, is finely compared to ivory overlaid with sapphire. *Shesh* is without doubt figured marble ; to which the legs and thighs are compared, from the blue and serpentine veins which run along them, and which are more pellucid in proportion to the fineness of the skin. The bases are golden slippers.

The 5th verse of the viith chapter is among the most difficult. The head of the king's daughter is compared to the pyramidal top of Carmel, covered with thick trees; by which simile is, I apprehend, intimated the quantity and beauty of her hair. The word *dallat* also occurs for hair, in the explanation of which commentators have been greatly perplexed : some, led away by a whimsical etymology, have supposed it to mean *thin hair*, as if this could possibly be a subject of flattery to a young lady. In my opinion, the word is derived from the Arabic as well as the Chaldaic word דלּיל, the fringe of a garment or tent, and means any thing pendant, or hanging loose. The hair is compared to purple, not however, I think, on account of the colour ; for the henna, with which they stained their hair, makes it yellow, not purple : I suspect some allusion is rather intended to the animal which produces purple. That animal is of a pyramidal form, rising beautifully in a spiral cone, whence it is called *aregman*, from its likeness to the stone monuments. There follows מלך אסור ברהטים, which, with some degree of hesitation, I venture to translate, "as a king encircled with a diadem :" the Septuagint has it ὡς πορφυρα βασιλεως, περιζεμενη ειλημασι. The upright oriental tiara is alluded to, the mark of royalty, which is more noble the higher it is. Thus the verse may be explained, and it will then be found to present a just picture of the oriental head-dress :

> " Thine head resembles Carmel ;
> And thine hair is raised like the shell of the purple,
> Like a king encircled with diadems."

In the latter verses of the same chapter there is an elegant description of Spring ; but what chiefly creates difficulty is the *dudaim*, which are said to *produce odours*. The famous Celsius, in his *Sacred Botany*, seems to have been peculiarly unfortunate on this subject. The word is translated *mandragoræ* (or mandrake) on the most ancient authority ; but Celsius cannot allow this plant any place in a love-poem, because it has in reality a bad smell. The text explained from the Arabic is, " The mandrakes produce a *strong* odour." We must remember, that it was the opinion of all the orientals that the mandrake was of especial efficacy in love-potions ; the truth of which opinion is of no concern to us, if we only allow it to have been the general opinion of the eastern nations. The text therefore implies, " The mandrake will breathe its strong and somniferous odours, and provoke to love."—M.

LECTURE XXXII.

OF THE POEM OF JOB.

In order to criticise the Book of Job with any degree of satisfaction to his auditors, the critic must explain his own sentiments concerning the work in general—The Book of Job a singular composition, and has little or no connexion with the affairs of the Hebrews—The seat of the history is Idumæa; and the characters are evidently Idumæan of the family of Abraham—The author appears to be an Idumæan, who spoke the Hebrew as his vernacular tongue—Neither Elihu nor Moses, rather Job himself, or some contemporary—This appears to be the oldest book extant: founded upon true history, and contains no allegory—Although extremely obscure, still the general subject and design are sufficiently evident— A short and general analysis of the whole work; in which the obscurer passages are brought as little as possible in question—The deductions from this disquisition: 1. The subject of the controversy between Job and his friends. 2. The subject of the whole poem. 3. Its end or purpose—All questions not necessarily appertaining to this point to be avoided.

SUCH a diversity of opinions has prevailed in the learned world concerning the nature and design of the poem of Job, that the only point in which commentators seem to agree is the extreme obscurity of the subject.   To engage, therefore, in an undertaking on which so much erudition has been expended, to tread the same paths which so many have already traversed in vain, may seem to require some apology for the temerity, not to say the presumption, of the attempt. Though I might allege, that the authority of the most learned men is lessened in some measure by the discordance of their opinions, and that, therefore, the failure of others is the more readily to be excused; I will, however, make use of no such defence, but will entrench myself rather in the necessity and in the nature of my present undertaking.   I pretend not to any new discoveries; I presume not to determine the subtile controversies of the learned; I scarcely venture to indulge the hope of being able to illustrate any obscurities. My sole intention is to collect, from such passages as appear the least intricate, the most probable conjectures: and what I conceive to have any tolerable foundation in fact, that I mean to propose, not as demonstration, but as opinion only. I proceed in this manner upon the principle, that, considering the great discordance of sentiments upon this subject, it would be impossible for any man to discourse with a sufficient degree of accuracy and perspicuity upon the structure and parts of this poem, unless he previously explained his own ideas concerning the scope and purport of the work in general.

The book of Job appears to me to stand single and unparalleled in the sacred volume. It seems to have little connexion with the other writings of the Hebrews, and no relation whatever to the affairs of the Israelites. The scene is laid in Idumæa;* the history of an inhabitant of that

---

* The information which the learned have endeavoured to collect, from the writings and geography of the Greeks, concerning the country and residence of Job and his friends, appears to me so very inconclusive, that I am inclined to take a quite different method for the solution of this question, by applying solely to the sacred writings: the hints with which they have furnished me towards the illustration of this subject, I shall explain as briefly as possible.

The land of *Uz* or *Gnutz*, is evidently *Idumæa*, as appears from Lam. iv. 21. *Uz* was the grandson of Seir, the Horite; Gen. xxxvi. 20, 21. 28. 1 Chron. i. 38. 42. Seir inhabited that mountainous tract which was called by his name antecedent to the time of Abraham, but his posterity being expelled, it was occupied by the Idumæans; Gen. xiv. 6. Deut. ii. 12. Two other men are mentioned of the name *Uz*; one the grandson of Shem, the other the son of Nachor, the brother of Abraham: but whether any district was called after their name is not clear. Idumæa is a part of Arabia Petræa, situated on the southern extremity of the tribe of Judah; Numb. xxxiv. 3. Joshua xv. 1. 21 : the land of Uz therefore appears to have been between Egypt and Philistia, Jer. xxv. 20, where the order of the places seems to have been accurately observed in reviewing the different nations from Egypt to Babylon ; and the same people seem again to be described, in exactly the same situations, Jer. xlvi. – l.

Children of the East, or *Eastern people*, seems to have been the general appellation for that mingled race of people (as they are called, Jer. xxv. 20.) who inhabited between Egypt and the Euphrates, bordering upon Judea from the south to the east; the Idumæans, the Amalekites, the Midianites, the Moabites, the Ammonites: See Judges vi. 3, and Isaiah xi. 14. Of these the Idumæans and Amalekites certainly possessed the southern parts: See Numb. xxxiv. 3; xiii. 29. 1 Sam. xxvii. 8. 10. This appears to be the true state of the case : the whole region between Egypt and the Euphrates was called the East, at first in respect to Egypt, (where the learned Jos. Mede thinks the Israelites acquired this mode of speaking; Mede's *Works*, p. 580,) and afterwards absolutely, and without any relation to situation or circumstances. Abraham is said to have sent the sons of his concubines, Hagar and Keturah, " eastward, to the country which is commonly

Z

country is the basis of the narrative; the characters who
speak are Idumæans, or at least Arabians of the adjacent

called the East," Gen. xxv. 6, where the name of the region seems to have been
derived from the same situation. Solomon is reported " to have excelled in wisdom
all the Eastern people, and all Egypt," 1 Kings iv. 30, that is, all the neighbouring
people on that quarter; for there were people beyond the boundaries of Egypt, and
bordering on the south of Judea, who were famous for wisdom, namely, the
Idumæans, (see Jer. xlix. 7. Obad. 8,) to whom we may well believe this passage
might have some relation. Thus JEHOVAH addresses the Babylonians, " Arise,
ascend unto Kedar, and lay waste the children of the East," Jer. xlix. 28, notwithstanding these were really situated to the west of Babylon. Although Job,
therefore, be accounted one of the orientals, it by no means follows that his
residence must be in Arabia Deserta.

Eliphaz the Temanite: Eliphaz was the son of Esau, and Teman the son of
Eliphaz, Gen. xxxvi. 10, 11. The Eliphaz of Job was without a doubt of this
race. Teman is certainly a city of Idumæa, Jer. xlix. 7. 20. Ezek. xxv. 13.
Amos i. 11, 12. Obad. 8, 9.

Bildad the Shuhite: Shuah was one of the sons of Abraham by Keturah,
whose posterity were numbered among the people of the East, and his situation
was probably contiguous to that of his brother Midian, and of his nephews
Shebah and Dedan; see Gen. xxv. 2, 3. Dedan is a city of Idumæa, Jer.
xlix. 8, and seems to have been situated on the eastern side, as Teman was on
the west, Ezek. xxv. 13. From Sheba originated the Sabæans in the passage
from Arabia Felix to the Red Sea: Sheba is united to Midian, Isaiah lx. 6;
it is in the same region, however, with Midian, and not far from Mount Horeb,
Exod. ii. 15; iii. 1.

Zophar the Naamathite: Among the cities which by lot fell to the tribe of
Judah, in the neighbourhood of Idumæa, Naama is enumerated, Josh. xv. 21.
41. Nor does this name elsewhere occur: this probably was the country of
Zophar.

Elihu the Buzite: Buz occurs but once as the name of a place or country,
Jer. xxv. 23, where it is mentioned along with Dedan and Thema: Dedan, as was
just now demonstrated, is a city of Idumæa; Thema belonged to the children of
Ishmael, who are said to have inhabited from Havilah even to Shur, which is in
the district of Egypt, Gen. xxv. 15. 18. Saul, however, is said to have smitten
the Amalekites from Havilah even to Shur, which is in the district of Egypt,
1 Sam. xv. 7. Havilah cannot, therefore, be very far from the boundaries of the
Amalekites; but the Amalekites never exceeded the boundaries of Arabia Petræa.
(See Reland, Palæstin. lib. i. c. 14.) Thema therefore lay somewhere between
Havilah and the Desert of Shur, to the southward of Judea. Thema is also
mentioned in connexion with Sheba, Job vi. 19.

Upon a fair review of these facts I think we may venture to conclude, still
with that modesty which such a question demands, that Job was an inhabitant
of Arabia Petræa, as well as his friends, or at least of that neighbourhood.
To this solution one objection may be raised: it may be asked, how the
Chaldeans, who lived on the borders of the Euphrates, could make depreda-
tions on the camels of Job, who lived in Idumæa at so great a distance?
This, too, is thought a sufficient cause for assigning Job a situation in
Arabia Deserta, and not far from the Euphrates. But what should prevent
the Chaldeans, as well as the Sabæans, a people addicted to rapine, and roving
about at immense distances for the sake of plunder, from wandering through
these defenceless regions, which were divided into tribes and families rather
than into nations, and pervading from Euphrates even to Egypt? Further, I
would ask, on the other hand, whether it be probable that all the friends of Job,

country, all originally of the race of Abraham. The language is pure Hebrew, although the author appears to be an Idumæan; for it is not improbable that all the posterity of Abraham, Israelites, Idumæans, and Arabians, whether of the family of Keturah or Ishmael, spoke for a considerable length of time one common language. That the Idumæans, however, and the Temanites in particular, were eminent for the reputation of wisdom, appears by the testimony of the prophets Jeremiah and Obadiah: * Baruch also particularly mentions them amongst "the authors (or expounders) of fables, and searchers out of understanding."† The learned are very much divided in their sentiments concerning the author of this book. Our Lightfoot conjectures that it is the production of Elihu; and this conjecture seems at first sight rather countenanced by the exordium to the first speech of Elihu,‡ in which he seems to assume the character of the author, by continuing the narrative in his own person. That passage, however, which appears to interrupt the speech of Elihu, and to be a part of the narrative, is, I apprehend, nothing more than an apostrophe to Job, or possibly to himself; for it manifestly consists of two distichs; while, on the contrary, it is well known that all the narrative parts, all in which the author himself appears, are certainly written in prose. Another opinion, which has been still more generally received, attributes the work to Moses. This conjecture, however, for I cannot dignify it with any higher appellation, will be found to rest altogether upon another, namely, that this poem was originally a consolatory address to the Israelites, and an allegorical representation of their situation: and I must confess I can scarcely conceive any thing more futile than such an hypothesis, since it is impossible to trace, throughout the whole book, the slightest

who lived in Idumæa and its neighbourhood, should instantly be informed of all that could happen to Job in the Desert of Arabia and on the confines of Chaldea, and immediately repair thither? Or whether it be reasonable to think, that, some of them being inhabitants of Arabia Deserta, it should be concerted among them to meet at the residence of Job; since it is evident that Eliphaz lived at Theman, in the extreme parts of Idumæa? With respect to the *Aisitas* of Ptolemy, (for so it is written, and not *Ausitas*,) it has no agreement, not so much as in a single letter, with the Hebrew *Gnutz*. The LXX indeed call that country by the name *Ausitida*, but they describe it as situated in Idumæa; and they account Job himself an Idumæan, and a descendant of Esau. See the Appendix of the LXX to the book of Job, and Hyde, Not. in *Peritzol.* chap. xi.——*Author's Note.*

    * Jer. xlix. 7.   Obad. 8.   † Baruch iii. 22, 23.   ‡ Job xxxii. 15, 16.
                                    z 2

allusion to the manners, customs, ceremonies, or history of the
Israelites. I will add, moreover, that the style of Job appears to me materially different from the poetical style of
Moses; for it is much more compact, concise, or condensed,
more accurate in the poetical conformation of the sentences:
as may be observed also in the prophecies of Balaam the
Mesopotamian—a foreigner indeed with respect to the Israelites, but neither unacquainted with their language, nor
with the worship of the true God. I confess myself, therefore, on the whole, more inclined to favour the opinion of
those who suppose Job himself, or some contemporary, to be
the author of this poem: for that it is the most ancient of all
the sacred books, is, I think, manifest from the subject, the
language, the general character, and even from the obscurity
of the work.* Concerning the time also in which Job lived,

---

* In opposition to the antiquity of the poem, and to what I have urged above,
that it appears to have no connexion with, or relation to, the affairs of the
Israelites, appeals have been made to Job xxxi. 28. See *A free and candid
Examination of the Bishop of London's Sermon*, Anonymous, p. 165, in which
the author inquires " In what nation upon earth idolatry was ever accounted
a crime but under the Jewish economy?" His argument is proposed as unan-
swerable, and is thought to be sufficiently confirmed by the authority of Mr.
Locke. I will, however, appeal to a higher authority than that of Locke, namely,
that of reason and the sacred writings; and will answer the question in a few
words: under the Patriarchal economy, in every tribe and family under Abraham, Melchizedec, Job, and the rest. On the increase of idolatry Abraham
was called by the divine command from Chaldea, to the end that from him
should proceed a nation separate from all others, who should worship the true
God, should afford a perfect example of pure religion, and bear testimony
against the worship of vain gods. Was it not, therefore, the duty of Abraham,
who in his own tribe or family possessed all the attributes of sovereignty, to
punish idolatry as well as homicide, adultery or other heinous crimes? Was
it not the duty of Melchizedec, of Job, of all those patriarchal princes who
regarded the worship of the true God, sedulously to prevent every defection
from it; to restrain those who were disposed to forsake it, and to punish the
obstinate and the rebellious?· In fact, in this allusion to the exertion of the
judicial authority against idolatry, and against the particular species which is
mentioned here, namely, the worship of the Sun and Moon, (the earliest species
of idolatry,) consists the most complete proof of the antiquity of the poem, and
the decisive mark of the patriarchal age. But if it should be suspected, that the
ingenuity of the poet might lead him to imitate with accuracy the manners of
the age which he describes, this indeed would be more to the purpose, and a more
plausible argument against the antiquity of the poem: but I cannot possibly
attribute such address and refinement to a poet in a barbarous age, and after
the Babylonish captivity. Further than this, the style of the poem savours
altogether of the antique; insomuch, that whoever could suppose it written after
the Babylonish captivity, would fall little short of the error of Hardouin, who
ascribed the golden verses of Virgil, Horace, &c. to the *iron age* of monkish
pedantry and ignorance.

With regard to the other difficulty, the solution of which appears so embarrassing,

although not directly specified, I see no great room for
doubt. The length of his life evinces that he was before
Moses, and probably contemporary with the patriarchs.
Not, however, to dwell upon the innumerable hypotheses of
the learned on this subject, I will only mention, that there
is the utmost probability of his having lived prior to the
promulgation of the Law, from the nature of the sacrifice
which he institutes conformably to the command of God,
namely, seven oxen and seven rams; for it is plain, from
the example of Balaam, that a respect for that number
prevailed in those countries and at that period, from the
traditional accounts which were still preserved among them
of the seven days of creation.* The truth of the narrative
would never, I am persuaded, have been called in question,
but from the immoderate affection of some allegorising
mystics for their own fictions, which run to such excess as to
prevent them from acceding to any thing but what was visionary and typical. When I speak of the poem as founded
in fact, I would be understood no further than concerns the
general subject of the narrative; for, I apprehend, all the
dialogue, and most likely some other parts, have partaken
largely of the embellishments of poetry; but I cannot allow
that this has by any means extended so far as to convert the
whole into an allegory. Indeed, I have not been able to
trace any vestige of an allegorical meaning throughout the
entire poem. And should even the exordium be suspected
to be of this nature,† we must recollect, that the historical
books are not destitute of similar narratives.‡ The exor-

namely, how any person not acquainted with the Jewish economy could assert that
" God visits the sins of the fathers upon the children," Job xxi. 19, let the *candid
observer* for the present content himself with this verse of Horace :—

" Delicta majorum immeritus lues,
Romane."

" Though guiltless of thy father's crimes,
Roman, 'tis thine, to latest times,
The vengeance of the gods to bear." Francis.—*Author's Note.*

* Job xliii. 8.   Compare Numb. xxiii. 1, &c.
There seems to be but little weight in this reasoning, because Job, as an Idumæan,
might have been a worshipper of the true God, like Balaam the Mesopotamian ;
and therefore, though the law had been given to the Israelites, continued, notwithstanding, to offer sacrifice according to the traditionary mode of his progenitors.—
S. H.
† Job i. 6, &c. ii. 1, &c.   Compare 1 Kings xxii. 19—22.
‡ It has long been a dispute among the learned, whether the poem of Job
consists of fable or a true history : this question, if authority alone be applied

dium and conclusion, I agree, are distinct from the poem itself, and stand in the place of an argument or illustration:

to, must long since have been decided in favour of those who assert it to be a real history.

With me I confess, on the other hand, it is no longer matter of opinion, but I feel very little doubt that the subject of the poem is altogether fabulous, and designed to teach us, that "the rewards of virtue being in another state, it is very possible for the good to suffer afflictions in this life; but that, when it so happens, it is permitted by Providence for the wisest reasons, though they may not be obvious to human eyes." But before I proceed to examine the grounds of this opinion, it may be necessary to premise a few remarks in reply to those who may think the Divine authority of the book affected by the supposition of its not being founded in fact. For my own part, I cannot conceive that the sanctity, the dignity, or the utility of that book will be in the least affected, though we should suppose no such person as Job had ever existed.

If moral precepts, conveyed in the garb of fabulous narrations, allure the hearers by the pleasure they afford; if they strike the mind more forcibly, are more easily understood, and better retained, than abstract sentiments—I see no reason why this mode of writing should be deemed unworthy of inspiration. Indeed, on the contrary, we find it made use of by Christ himself; nor does it at all derogate from his force as a moral teacher, that the good Samaritan, the rich man and Lazarus, &c. were not real persons.

I shall not, however, rest here; for I assert further, that the book of Job is more instructive as a fable, than it could possibly be as a true history. Taken as a mere relation of a matter of fact, it is necessary to suppose that the sentiments and conversations are exhibited exactly as they were spoken, and are the sentiments of mere mortals not actuated by the Spirit of God: for we find that God has reproved both Job and his friends as being severally mistaken. It would then be impossible to determine what was true or what false: no doctrine of religion, no precept of morality, could with certainty be deduced from these conversations. In the whole book, the historical part, (and how short is that!) and the words attributed to God himself, would be alone divine, or of Divine authority; the rest would be all human. Considered as a fable, the case is different. The author, composing under the influence of Divine inspiration, we may reasonably suppose has attributed to the fictitious characters such sentiments as were proper and natural to their state and circumstances: We have then, in the first place, a picture of the human mind drawn by the finger of God; and, in the next, we may rest satisfied that Job and his friends err only in the principal matter upon which they dispute, and only on the points for which God has reproved them; but that whatever is said exclusive of this is founded on divine truth: such is the mention of the angels by Eliphaz, and the assertion of Job, that there is none pure among mortals. Finally, we are by these means enabled both to determine what are the sentiments which immediately meet with the approbation of God, and what are the errors which are intended to be exposed. An able writer in dialogue never fails to discover his own sentiments: as from the books of Cicero on *the Nature of the Gods*, we may collect with ease what the author thought, or rather doubted upon the subject; which would have been impossible if he had only reported the actual words of the philosophers who are supposed to have conversed on that subject.

I will now proceed freely to explain what at first I undertook to prove concerning the book in question. It is surely more becoming to consider the exordium, in which Satan appears as the accuser of Job, rather in the light of a fable than of a true narrative. It is surely incredible that such a conversation ever took place between the Almighty and Satan, who is supposed to return with *news* from the

that they are, however, coeval with the poetical part, and the work of the same author, is evident, since they are

terrestrial regions. Indeed the commentators who have undertaken to vindicate this part of the book, have done it with so much asperity, that they seem conscious of the difficulty under which it labours.

Nor will it suffice to answer, as some temperate and rational commentator like our Author probably will, and indeed as he himself hints, that the great outline of the fact only is true; and that the exordium is set off with some poetical ornaments, among which is to be accounted the conversation between God and Satan : for on this very conversation the whole plot is founded, and the whole story and catastrophe depends. One of the best of men is thrown into so many unexpected and undeserved evils, that neither he nor his adversaries are able to conceive how it can be consistent with a benevolent Being to plunge a good man into so great afflictions; nor has God condescended to explain the motives of it to them, but reproves them all for investigating matters beyond their reach. But the author of the book undoes the knot which is left unresolved in these conversations, and gives the reader to understand how indifferently those reason concerning the Divine providence, and the happiness or misery of mankind, who are only partially informed of causes and events. The Almighty acts for the honour of Job, of human nature, and of piety itself; he permits Job to be unhappy for a time, and refutes the accusations of Satan even by the very means which he himself pointed out. Suppose, therefore, that what is thus related of Satan be fictitious, and all the rest true, instead of the difficulty being done away, the consequence will be, that the whole plot remains without any solution whatever. What our Author has added concerning one of the historical books of Scripture, in which a similar passage occurs, 1 Kings xxii. 19—22, appears not at all to the purpose. It is not a history related by the author, nor does the author speak in his own person, but a prophet explains a vision which he has had. But those who suppose the book of Job to be founded upon fact, allow that the historian speaks in the first and second chapters, who, if he did invent, would certainly, one would think, take that liberty only in matters which did not affect the great scope of the history, and not in a matter which, if it be supposed fictitious, reduces the whole book to nothing.

Moreover, the style of the whole book being poetical, and so sublime, that I defy any man to imitate it in any extempore effusion, is an irrefragable proof in favour of my opinion. Our Author, indeed, pleads a very specious excuse : he thinks that the conversation and speeches of the different characters have been poetically ornamented. And this argument I do not wish to confute. There are however, others, who defend the historical truth of the poem in a manner not quite so modest. Among the rest, the famous Schultens alleges it not to be incredible that these are the actual words of the disputants, if we consider the amazing faculty which the Arabians possess of making extempore verses. In answer to this I must confess, that all he can urge on this subject will never persuade me, that poetry, which is confessedly superior to all that human genius has been able to produce, is nothing more than an extempore effusion. Indeed, nothing can be more ridiculous than to suppose men in circumstances of so great distress, in the midst of difficulties and afflictions, capable of amusing themselves with making extempore verses.

These objections which I have just stated are well known to the commentators ; but there are others not quite so common, which induce me to suppose the subject of this poem not historical but fabulous. So many round numbers and multiplications of them occur in the life of Job, as to be quite incompatible with mere chance. *Ten* children perish, *seven* sons (which, though it be not a round number,

indispensably necessary to the unravelling of the plot, which
is not developed in the body of the poem.   There are, it is

is yet held sacred and mysterious by the orientals) and *three* daughters ; 7000
sheep, 3000 camels, 1000 oxen, and exactly half the number of asses.   In lieu of
these, there are restored to him 14,000 sheep, 6000 camels, 2000 oxen, and
1000 asses, exactly the duplicate of the former numbers; together with exactly the
same number of children as he had lost, seven sons and three daughters, and these
from one wife.   The same principle is found to extend to the years of Job's prosperity, which are multiplications of the number 70.   These circumstances betray art
and fiction in the narrator who has introduced these round numbers, which we
know are the first to present themselves to the mind ; it bears no appearance of
chance or casualty, which, when it predominates in a series of events, produces a
wonderful variety, but very little of regularity or equality.   The name of JOB, too,
which, in the Arabic, means returning to God, and loving him, and hating whatever
is contrary to him, is so adapted to the character of his latter years, that we can
never suppose it a name given to him by his parents, but invented by the author
of the story.

A fourth argument is, that the scene is laid in Arabia, yet the poem abounds so
much in imagery borrowed from Egypt, that it is plain that country must have been
extremely well known to the author, and indeed predominant in his mind, as I
have endeavoured to prove in a Dissertation recited before the R. S. of Gottingen.

But the most powerful of all proofs is, that some things appear in the book of
Job which could not possibly have place in a true history.   At a period when the
longevity of the Patriarchs was reduced within the limit of two hundred years, Job
is said to have lived 140 years after his malady, and therefore could not be very
ancient when he fell into this malady : nevertheless he upbraids his friends with
their youth, (who, by the way, could not be very young, since Elihu, ch. xxxii.
6, 7. 9, reverences their hoary age,) and adds, that " he would have disdained to set
their *fathers* with the dogs of his flock," ch. xxx. 1.   But what is more extraordinary, these same men boast of their own age, and seem to exact a degree of
reverence from Job as their junior : thus Eliphaz, ch. xx. 10, " With us are both
the grey-headed and the very aged men much older than thy father."   These
passages, therefore, so directly contradict each other, that they cannot be connected
with true history.   The opprobrium which he casts upon the birth of his friends
seems also an inconsistency, ch. xxx. 1—6, as it is incredible that so noble and rich
a man should ever have chosen his friends from the meanest of the people.

It remains only to remove one objection, with which those who contend for the
historical truth of the book of Job may press us.   Job is quoted by Ezekiel along
with Noah and Daniel, whom we know to have been real persons, and they are
proposed by James as an example of patience, (Ezek. xiv. 14—20.   James v. 11 ;)
as if it were improper or indecent to recommend the virtues of fictitious characters to our imitation, or as if this were not in fact the end of delineating such
characters.   Neither is there the least impropriety in instancing the same virtues in
real and fictitious characters.   Suppose a father to recommend to his daughters the
examples of Lucretia and Pamela, as models of chastity and virtue, who would
esteem such a discourse reprehensible, or think that it either took from the truth of
the history, or gave a reality to the fiction ?

To return to the point from which we set out : This poem seems to treat of
the affliction which may sometimes happen to good men, at the same time that
the author seems to wish to accommodate the consolation to the people of God,
and to represent their oppression under the character of Job.   To this opinion

true, phrases extant in the exordium, in which some critics
have pretended to discover the hand of a later writer: the

it is objected by our Author, that there appears nothing in the book like an allusion
to the manners, rites, or affairs of the Israelites. Of the latter I shall treat,
when we come to speak of the application of this poem to the history of tho
Israelites. As to the manners, they are what I called *Abrahamic*, or such as were
at that period common to all the seed of Abraham at that time, Israelites,
Ishmaelites, and Idumæans. But perhaps it may be thought necessary to instance
those customs which were peculiar to the Israelites, and by which they were
distinguished from the Arabians : this, however, would not display much judgment
in the author of a poem, the scene of which lies in Arabia; besides, that most of
the peculiar customs of the Israelites, those I mean which distinguished them from
the other descendants of Abraham, were either derived from the Egyptians, or were
taught them by Moses : and who would require, that such things as the paschal
lamb, and the Mosaic feasts and priesthood, should be introduced into such a poem?
The frequent allusions, however, to the country and the productions of Egypt
abundantly answer this objection; insomuch, that though the scene is laid in
Arabia, one would imagine the actors had been Egyptians. Nor are there wanting
allusions to the circumstances of the Israelites. These, like Job, lost their children
and possessions by the tyranny of Pharoah ; and, if I am not mistaken, the disease
is the same which affected Job, with that which prevailed among the Egyptians by
the command of Moses.

From these circumstances I am much inclined to the opinion which attributes
this book to Moses. For is it to be imagined, that a native of Idumæa should crowd
his poem with images and figures borrowed from Egypt? Or what native of
Arabia (for it must be allowed that the book of Job has some allusions peculiar to
Arabia) was so likely to intermingle the imagery of both countries as Moses? To
these may be added the allusions to the *Isles of the Blessed*, which are common to
the book of Job and the Mosaic writings. I am well aware that there is more of the
tragic, more of the strong poetic feeling in this book, than in the other relics of
Mosaic poetry, which has induced our Author to remark the discrepancy of style.
But how different are the language and sentiments of a man raging in the heights of
despair, from those which are to be sung in the temple of God ? We must also
remember that the poetic style of an author in the flower of his youth is very different from that of his latter days. If Moses were really the author of this poem, he
composed it about the age of forty years ; but the rest of his poems were written
between the 85th and 120th year of his age : at which period I am often surprised to
meet with so much vigour of language and sentiment ; and no other difference of
style have I been able to discover.—M.

If I might flatter myself that the reader would not be wearied with replications
and rejoinders, I would request his attention to a few animadversions on these
remarks of the Gottingen Professor. For, though I thought it my duty to state his
arguments as fully as I could, consistently with the limits of this work, I must confess that I do not myself feel by any means convinced ; nor dare I venture to
affirm, upon any such presumptive proofs, that the book of Job is altogether
fabulous. I think it by no means follows, that because a book contains some things
which may with propriety be termed poetical fictions, it has no foundation whatever
in fact. The poems of Homer contain more fictions of this kind than any commentator has pretended clearly to discover in the book of Job ; and yet no sober
critic has denied that there ever was such an event as the Trojan war, on which
those poems are founded.

I cannot help thinking with our Author, that such a man as Job might very

arguments however of these critics I cannot esteem of any great force or importance.

That these points should be accounted of a very ambigu-

possibly have existed, and that the leading facts concerning his sudden depression and consequent misfortunes might really have happened; and yet that the poet, in relating these facts, may have added such machinery, and other poetical ornaments, as appeared necessary to enliven the story and illustrate the moral. Though we should not contend with the learned Professor for the literal acceptation of the exordium; though we should even admit with him that it is not probable any such conversation ever took place between the Almighty Governor of the universe and the great enemy of mankind, as is related in the first chapter; yet it by no means follows that the inspired writer had no grounds whatever for what he describes perhaps poetically. The manner in which the Deity and the other celestial intelligences are spoken of in this poem appears necessary, when the human mind is called upon to contemplate their actions; and may be considered as a kind of personification in accommodation to our limited faculties, and is common in many other parts of Scripture.

With regard to the objection founded on the round numbers, I think it very weak when applied to the children of Job; and as to the cattle, the event being recorded some time after it took place, it is hardly reasonable to expect that the number should be specified with the utmost exactness: indeed, nothing could be more awkward or ungraceful, in a poetical narration, than to descend to units; and when the numbers are doubled at the conclusion, I look upon it as no more than a periphrasis, expressing, that the Lord gave to Job twice as much as he had before.

As to the name; it is well known that all the names of the ancients were derived from some distinguishing quality, and not always given at their birth, as with us. (See *Essays Historical and Moral*, Ess. vi. p. 119.) Nay, the objection, if admitted, would strike at the authority of a considerable part of Holy Writ; for not only many of the persons recorded there take their names from circumstances which occurred late in life, but, in some instances, from the very circumstances of their deaths, as *Abel* from *Habal*, vanity or nothingness, because he left no offspring.

There appears, at first sight, something more formidable in the argument founded on the inconsistencies which he boasts of having detected; nevertheless, I can by no means grant it all the credit which its author seems to claim. Both the expressions of Elihu and those of the other friends are very general, and I think improperly applied by the Professor; for the passage referred to, chap. xv. 10, by no means proves that the friends of Job were older than he: "*with us* or *among us*," seems to imply no more than this, "older persons than either you or we are *with us*, or of our sentiments." Still more general is the complaint of Job, chap. xxx. 1; indeed, so general, that to a fair examiner it is impossible it should appear to have any relation at all to the friends of Job, as he is simply complaining of his altered state, and among other evils mentions the loss of that respect which he was accustomed to receive from all ranks of people, insomuch, that now even the *young*, the *children*, presume to hold him in derision. The other argument is by no means conclusive, namely, that which is founded on the supposed opprobrium on the birth of his friends, as really I cannot conceive any part of this speech to have the least reference to them; or, if it have, it is easy enough to suppose, that their fathers or themselves might have been raised to opulence from a mean station: and indeed such a supposition is absolutely necessary to give any point to the sarcasm of Job, admitting that it ought to be understood in the light our commentator seems to intend.—T.

ous nature, and should cause much embarrassment and controversy in the learned world, is nothing extraordinary; but
that the main object and design of the poem should ever have
been called in question, may justly excite our astonishment.
For, though many passages be confessedly obscure; though
there be several which I fear no human skill will ever be able
to unravel; and though the obscurity consist chiefly in the
connexion of the incidents and the sentiments, it by no means
necessarily follows that the whole is involved in impenetrable
darkness. The case, indeed, is far otherwise; for one and the
same light, though at intervals overcast, shines on through
the whole, and, like a conducting star, uniformly leads to
the same point. If, then, any person will follow this guidance without perplexing himself with obscurities which he
will occasionally meet, I have very little doubt but that he
will clearly discern the end, the subject, the connexion, and
arrangement of the whole work. It will, perhaps, be worth
while to put to trial the efficacy of this maxim: let us therefore, for the present, pass over those obscurities which might
impede our progress; and, making the best use of those
lights which are afforded by the more obvious passages, proceed with an attentive eye through the whole of the work,
and observe whether something satisfactory is not to be
discovered relating to the subject of the narrative, and the
design and intent of the poem.

The principal object held forth to our contemplation in
this production is, the example of a good man, eminent for
his piety, and of approved integrity, suddenly precipitated
from the very summit of prosperity into the lowest depths
of misery and ruin; who, having been first bereaved of his
wealth, his possessions, and his children, is afterwards afflicted with the most excruciating anguish of a loathsome disease
which entirely covers his body. He sustains all, however,
with the mildest submission, and the most complete resignation to the will of Providence: " In all this," says the historian, " Job sinned not, nor charged God foolishly."*
And, after the second trial, " In all this did not Job sin
with his lips."† The author of the history remarks upon
this circumstance a second time, in order to excite the observation of the reader, and to render him more attentive to
what follows, which properly constitutes the true subject of
the poem: namely, the conduct of Job with respect to his

* Job i. 22.   † Job ii. 10.

reverence for the Almighty, and the changes which accumu-
lating misery might produce in his temper and behaviour.
Accordingly we find, that another still more exquisite trial
of his patience yet awaits him, and which, indeed, as the
writer seems to intimate, he scarcely appears to have sustained with equal firmness; namely, the unjust suspicions,
the bitter reproaches, and the violent altercations of his
friends, who had visited him on the pretence of affording
consolation.   Here commences the plot or action of the
poem; for when, after a long silence of all parties, the grief
of Job breaks forth into passionate exclamations, and a
vehement execration on the day of his birth; the minds of
his friends are suddenly exasperated, their intentions are
changed, and their consolation, if indeed they originally
intended any, is converted into contumely and reproaches.
The first of these three singular comforters reproves his impatience : calls in question his integrity, by indirectly insinuating that God does not inflict such punishments upon
the righteous; and finally, admonishes him, that the chastisement of God is not to be despised.   The next of them,
not less intemperate in his reproofs, takes it for granted that
the children of Job had only received the reward due to
their offences; and with regard to himself, intimates, that
if he be innocent, and will apply with proper humility to
the divine mercy, he may be restored.   The third upbraids
him with arrogance, with vanity, and even with falsehood,
because he has presumed to defend himself against the unjust accusations of his companions; and exhorts him to a
sounder mode of reasoning, and a more holy life.   They all,
with a manifest, though indirect allusion to Job, discourse
very copiously concerning the divine judgments which are
always openly displayed against the wicked, and of the
certain destruction of hypocritical pretenders to virtue and
religion.   In reply to this, Job enumerates his sufferings,
and complains bitterly of the inhumanity of his friends,
and of the severity which he has experienced from the hand
of God: he calls to witness both God and man, that he
is unjustly oppressed; he intimates, that he is weak in
comparison with God, that the contention is consequently
unequal, and that, be his cause ever so righteous, he cannot hope to prevail.   He expostulates with God himself
still more vehemently, and with greater freedom; affirming, that he does not discriminate characters, but equally

afflicts the just and the unjust. The expostulations of Job serve only to irritate still more the resentment of his pretended friends; they reproach him in severer terms with pride, impiety, passion, and madness; they repeat the same arguments respecting the justice of God, the punishment of the wicked, and their certain destruction after a short period of apparent prosperity. This sentiment they confidently pronounce to be confirmed both by their experience and by that of their fathers; and they maliciously exaggerate the ungrateful topic by the most splendid imagery and the most forcible language. On the part of Job, the general scope of the argument is much the same as before, but the expression is considerably heightened: it consists of appeals to the Almighty, asseverations of his own innocence, earnest expostulations, complaints of the cruelty of his friends, melancholy reflections on the vanity of human life, and upon his own severe misfortunes, ending in grief and desperation : he affirms, however, that he places his ultimate hope and confidence in God; and the more vehemently his adversaries urge, that the wicked only are objects of the Divine wrath, and obnoxious to punishment, so much the more resolutely does Job assert their perpetual impunity, prosperity, and happiness, even to the end of their existence.* The first of his opponents, Eliphaz, incensed by this assertion, descends directly to open crimination and contumely; he accuses the most upright of men of the most atrocious crimes, of injustice, rapine, and oppression; inveighs against him as an impious pretender to virtue and religion; and, with a kind of sarcastic benevolence, exhorts him to penitence. Vehemently affected with this reproof, Job, in a still more animated and confident strain, appeals to the tribunal of All-seeing Justice; and wishes it were only permitted him to plead his cause in the presence of God himself. He complains still more intemperately of the unequal treatment of Providence; exults in his own integrity; and then more tenaciously maintains his former opinion concerning the impunity of the wicked. To this another of the triumvirate, Bildad, replies by a masterly though concise dissertation on the majesty and sanctity of the Divine Being, indirectly rebuking the presumption of Job, who has dared to question his decrees. In reply to Bildad, Job demon-

* Chap. xxi. and xxiv. are indeed obscure; the opinion, however, of Schultens on this subject appears to me more than probable.—*Author's Note.*

strates himself no less expert at wielding the weapons of
satire and ridicule than those of reason and argument; and,
reverting to a more serious tone, he displays the infinite
power and wisdom of God more copiously and more poetically than the former speaker. The third of the friends
making no return, and the others remaining silent, Job at
length opens the true sentiments of his heart concerning the
fate of the wicked: he allows that their prosperity is unstable, and that they and their descendants shall at last experience on a sudden, that God is the avenger of iniquity.
In all this, however, he contends that the divine counsels do
not admit of human investigation; but that the chief wisdom
of man consists in the fear of God. He beautifully descants
upon his former prosperity: and exhibits a striking contrast
between it and his present affliction and debasement.
Lastly, in answer to the crimination of Eliphaz, and the
implications of the others, he relates the principal transactions of his past life; he asserts his integrity as displayed in
all the duties of life, and in the sight of God and man; and
again appeals to the justice and omniscience of God in
attestation of his veracity.

If these circumstances be fairly collected from the general
tenor and series of the work, as far as we are able to trace
them through the plainer and more conspicuous passages, it
will be no very difficult task to explain and define the subject of this part of the poem, which contains the dispute
between Job and his friends. The argument seems chiefly
to relate to the piety and integrity of Job, and turns upon
this point, whether he, who by the Divine providence and
visitation is severely punished and afflicted, ought to be
accounted pious and innocent? This leads into a more extensive field of controversy; into a dispute indeed, which less
admits of any definition or limit, concerning the nature of
the divine counsels in the dispensations of happiness and
misery in this life. The antagonists of Job in this dispute
observing him exposed to such severe visitations, conceiving
that this affliction has not fallen upon him unmeritedly,
accuse him of hypocrisy, and falsely ascribe to him the guilt
of some atrocious but concealed offence. Job, on the contrary, conscious of no crime, and wounded by their unjust
suspicions, defends his own innocence before God with
rather more confidence and ardour than is commendable;
and so strenuously contends for his own integrity, that he

seems virtually to charge God himself with some degree of injustice.

This state of the controversy is clearly explained by what follows; for, when the three friends have ceased to dispute with Job, "because he seemeth just in his own eyes,"* that is, because he has uniformly contended that there was no wickedness in himself which could call down the heavy vengeance of God; Elihu comes forward, justly offended with both parties—with Job, because "he justified himself in preference to God,"† that is, because he defended so vehemently the justice of his own cause that he seemed in some measure to arraign the justice of God;—against the three friends, because, "though they were unable to answer Job, they ceased not to condemn him;"‡ that is, they concluded in their own minds that Job was impious and wicked, while, nevertheless, they had nothing specific to object against his assertions of his own innocence,· or upon which they might safely ground their accusation.

The conduct of Elihu evidently corresponds with this state of the controversy: he professes, after a slight prefatory mention of himself, to reason with Job, unbiassed equally by favour or resentment. He therefore reproves Job from his own mouth, because he had attributed too much to himself; because he had affirmed himself to be altogether free from guilt and depravity; because he had presumed to contend with God, and had not scrupled to insinuate that the Deity was hostile to him. He asserts, that it is not necessary for God to explain and develop his counsels to men; that he nevertheless takes many occasions of admonishing them, not only by visions and revelations, but even by the visitations of his providence, by sending calamities and diseases upon them, to repress their arrogance and reform their obduracy. He next rebukes Job, because he had pronounced himself upright, and affirmed that God had acted inimically, if not unjustly towards him; which he proves to be no less improper than indecent. In the third place, he objects to Job, that from the miseries of the good, and the prosperity of the wicked, he has falsely and perversely concluded that there was no advantage to be derived from the practice of virtue. On the contrary he affirms, that when the afflictions of the just continue, it is because they do not place a proper con-

* Chap. xxxii. 1.   † Chap. xxxii. 2.   Compare xxxv. 2; xl. 8.
‡ Chap. xxxii. 3.

fidence in God, ask relief at his hands, patiently expect it,
nor demean themselves before him with becoming humility
and submission.   This observation alone, he adds very properly, is at once a sufficient reproof of the contumacy of
Job, and a full refutation of the unjust suspicions of his
friends.*   Lastly, he explains the purposes of the Deity in
chastening men, which are in general to prove and to amend
them, to repress their arrogance, to afford him an opportunity of exemplifying his justice upon the obstinate and rebellious, and of showing favour to the humble and obedient.
He supposes God to have acted in this manner towards
Job: on that account he exhorts him to humble himself
before his righteous Judge, to beware of appearing obstinate
or contumacious in his sight, and of relapsing into a repetition of his sin.   He entreats him, from the contemplation
of the Divine power and majesty, to endeavour to retain a
proper reverence for the Almighty.   To these frequently
intermitted and often repeated admonitions of Elihu, Job
makes no return.

The oration of God himself follows that of Elihu, in which,
disdaining to descend to any particular explication of his
divine counsels, but instancing some of the stupendous effects
of his infinite power, he insists upon the same topics which
Elihu had before touched upon.   In the first place, having
reproved the temerity of Job, he convicts him of ignorance,
in being unable to comprehend the works of his creation,
which were obvious to every eye; the nature and structure
of the earth, the sea, the light, and the animal kingdom.
He then demonstrates his weakness, by challenging him to
prove his own power by emulating any single exertion of
the divine energy; and then, referring him to one or two of
the brute creation with which he is unable to contend—how
much less, therefore, with the omnipotent Creator and Lord
of all things, who is or can be accountable to no being whatever !†   On this Job humbly submits to the will of Providence, acknowledges his own ignorance and imbecility, and
"repents in dust and ashes."

On a due consideration of all these circumstances, the
principal object of the poem seems to be this third and last
trial of Job, from the injustice and unkindness of his accusing
friends.   The consequence of which is, in the first place, the
anger, indignation, and contumacy of Job, and afterwards

* Chap. xxxv. 4.   † See chap. xli. 2, 3.

his composure, submission, and penitence. The design of the poem is therefore to teach men, that, having a due respect to the corruption, infirmity, and ignorance of human nature, as well as to the infinite wisdom and majesty of God, they are to reject all confidence in their own strength, in their own righteousness, and to preserve on all occasions an unwavering and unsullied faith, and to submit with becoming reverence to his decrees.

I would wish it, however, to be carefully observed, that the subject of the dispute between Job and his friends differs from the subject of the poem in general; that the end of the poetical part is different from the design of the narrative at large. For although the design and subject of the poem be exactly as I have defined them, it may nevertheless be granted, that the whole history, taken together, contains an example of patience, together with its reward. This point not having been treated with sufficient distinctness by the learned, I cannot help esteeming it the principal cause of the perplexity in which the subject has been involved.

I am not ignorant, that to those who enter upon this inquiry, some questions will occur, which appear to require a separate examination: since many of them, however, are chiefly connected with those passages which are acknowledged to be obscure, which have not yet been clearly explained, and which, whatever they may hereafter be found to import, are not likely to affect the truth of our conclusion, I have thought proper to omit them. Nor will I allow, that because many things yet remain ambiguous and perplexed, we are therefore to doubt of those which are more open and evident. In regard to certain more important doctrines, which some persons of distinguished learning have thought to be established by this extraordinary monument of ancient wisdom, as they either depend in a great degree on the obscure passages above mentioned, or do not seem to contribute in the least to the main design of the poem, nor to be consistent with the object of it, which I just now pointed out, I thought it still more unnecessary to introduce them in this disquisition. What I have advanced, I conceived fully adequate to the purpose of this undertaking, and a sufficient introduction to a critical examination of the composition and beauties of the poem.

LECTURE XXXIII.

THE POEM OF JOB NOT A PERFECT DRAMA.

The poem of Job commonly accounted Dramatic; and thought by many to be of the same kind with the Greek Tragedy: this opinion examined—A plot or fable essential to a regular Drama: its definition and essential qualities according to Aristotle—Demonstrated, that the poem of Job does not contain any plot: its form and design more fully explained—Compared with the Œdipus Tyrannus of Sophocles; with the Œdipus Coloneus; and shown to differ entirely from both in form and manner—It is nevertheless a most beautiful and perfect performance in its kind: it approaches very near the form of a perfect Drama; and, for regularity in form and arrangement, justly claims the first place among the poetical compositions of the Hebrews.

WHEN I undertook the present investigation, my principal object was to enable us to form some definite opinion concerning the poem of Job, and to assign it its proper place among the compositions of the Hebrew Poets. This will possibly appear to some a superfluous and idle undertaking, as the point seems long since to have been finally determined, the majority of the critics having decidedly adjudged it to belong to the dramatic class. Since, however, the term *dramatic*, as I formerly had reason to remark, is in itself extremely ambiguous, the present disquisition will not be confined within the limits of a single question; for the first object of inquiry will necessarily be, what idea is affixed to the appellation by those critics who term the book of Job a dramatic poem. And after we have determined this point, (if it be possible to determine it, for they do not seem willing to be explicit,) we may then with safety proceed to inquire whether, pursuant to that idea, the piece be justly entitled to this appellation.

A poem is called dramatic either in consequence of its form—the form I mean of a perfect dialogue, which is sustained entirely by the characters or personages without the intervention of the poet; and this was the definition adopted by the ancient critics; or else, according to the more modern acceptation of the word, in consequence of a plot or fable being represented in it.   If those who account the book of Job dramatic adhere to the former definition, I have little inclination to litigate the point; and indeed the object of the controversy would scarcely be worth the labour; though a critic, if disposed to be scrupulously exact, might insist that the work, upon the whole, is by no means a perfect dialogue, but consists of a mixture of the narrative and colloquial style; for the historical part, which is all composed in the person of the writer himself, is certainly to be accounted a part of the work itself, considered as a whole.   Since, however, on the other hand, the historical or narrative part is all evidently written in prose, and seems to me to be substituted merely in the place of an argument or comment, for the purpose of explaining the rest, and certainly does not constitute any part of the poem; since, moreover, those short sentences which serve to introduce the different speeches, contain very little more than the names—I am willing to allow that the structure or form of this poem is on the whole dramatic.   But this concession will, I fear, scarcely satisfy the critics in question; for they speak of the regular order and conduct of the piece, and of the dramatic catastrophe; they assert, that the interposition of the Deity is a necessary part of the machinery of the fable; they even enumerate the acts and scenes, and use the very same language in all respects as if they spoke of a Greek tragedy; insomuch that when they term the poem of Job dramatic,* they seem to speak of that species of drama which was cultivated and improved in the theatre of Athens.   It appears therefore a fair object of inquiry, whether the poem of Job be possessed of the peculiar properties of the Greek drama, and may with reason and justice be classed with the theatrical productions of that people?

We have already agreed, that the greater and more perfect drama is peculiarly distinguished from the lesser and more common species, inasmuch as it retains not only the dramatic form, or the perfect dialogue, but also exhibits some entire action, fable, or plot.   And this is perfectly agreeable to the definition of Aristotle; for, although he points out many parts or constituents in the composition of

* See Calmet, *Preface sur Job.*   Hare, Not. ad Psal. cvii. 40.   Carpzovii, *Introduct. in Libros Biblicos*, part ii. p. 76.

a tragedy, he assigns the first place to the plot or fable.* This he says is the beginning, this the end, this is the most important part, the very soul of a tragedy, without which it is utterly undeserving of the name, and indeed cannot properly be said to exist. A plot or fable is the representation of an action or event, or of a series of events or incidents tending all to one point, which are detailed with a view to a particular object or conclusion. A tragedy, says the same author, is not a representation of men, but of actions, a picture of life, of prosperity and adversity: in other words, the business of the poem is not merely to exhibit manners only, nor does the most perfect representation of manners constitute a tragedy; for, in reality, a tragedy may exist with little or no display of manners or character; its business is to exhibit life and action, or some regular train of actions and events, on which depends the felicity or infelicity of the persons concerned. For human happiness or prosperity consists in action; and action is not a quality, but is the end of man. According to our manners we are denominated good or bad; but we are happy or unhappy, prosperous or unsuccessful, according to actions or events. Poets therefore do not form a plot or action merely for the sake of imitating manners or character; but manners and character are added to the plot, and, for the sake of it, are chiefly attended to. Thus far he has accurately drawn the line between the representation of action and that of manners. He adds, moreover, that unity is essential to a regular plot or action, and that it must be complete in itself, and of a proper length.† But to comprehend more perfectly the nature of a plot or fable, it must be observed, that there are two principal species;

* Arist. *Poet.* cap. vi.

† Arist. *Poet.* cap. vii. It is evident that the human mind can dwell on one object only at a time, and whenever it takes more into its view, it is by combination, as forming *one* object out of many, or as many objects contributing to *one* action. Painters observe this rule so minutely, that they will not suffer *attention* to be *divided* by two equal groups, by two principal figures, two equal lights or colours, or even two equal folds of drapery. I flatter myself in the above translation I have not obscured the meaning of Aristotle, so as to bring upon him the charge of inconsistency. When he speaks of unity being essential to a dramatic fable or action, he means it, I apprehend, as speaking of a whole. When, therefore, he speaks afterwards of plots or fables as simple or complex, by the latter term he must mean one plot or story which consists of several incidents or vicissitudes: and by the former, a plot founded upon one simple and uninterrupted action: and so our Author indeed explains him.—T.

for they are either complex or simple :* the former contains some unexpected vicissitude of fortune, such as the recognition of a person at first unknown, the recovery of a lost child, or a sudden change in the situation of the parties, or perhaps both; the latter contains nothing of the kind, but proceeds in one uniform and equal tenor.   In every plot or fable, however, be it ever so simple, and though it contain nothing of the wonderful or unexpected, there is always a perplexity or embarrassment, as also a regular solution or catastrophe :† the latter must proceed from the former, and indeed must depend upon it; which cannot be the case, unless there be a certain order or connexion in the incidents and events which inclines them towards the same end, and combines them all in one termination.

On fairly considering these circumstances I have no hesitation in affirming, that the poem of Job contains no plot or action whatever, not even of the most simple kind: it uniformly exhibits one constant state of things, not the smallest change of fortune taking place from the beginning to the end; and it contains merely a representation of those manners, passions, and sentiments, which might actually be expected in such a situation.   Job is represented as reduced from the summit of human prosperity to a condition the most miserable and afflicted; and the sentiments of both Job and his friends are exactly such as the occasion dictates. For here a new temptation falls upon him, by which the constancy of Job is put to the severest trial; and this circumstance it is that constitutes the principal subject of the poem.   Job had, we find, endured the most grievous calamities, the loss of his wealth, the deprivation of his children, and the miserable union of poverty and disease, with so much fortitude, and with so just a confidence in his own integrity, that nothing could be extorted from him in the least inconsistent with the strictest reverence for the Divine Being: he is now put to the proof, whether, after enduring all this with firmness and resignation, he can with equal patience endure to have his innocence and virtue (in which perhaps he had placed too much confidence) indirectly questioned, and even in plain terms arraigned.   Job, now sinking under the weight of his misery, laments his condition with more vehemence than before.   His friends reprove his impatience, and drop some dark insinuations to the apparent disparagement of his virtue and integrity, by

* Arist. *Poet.* cap. x.   † Ibid. cap. xviii.

entering into very copious declamations concerning the justice of God in proportioning his visitations to the crimes of men. Job is still more violently agitated; and his friends accuse him with less reserve. He appeals to God, and expostulates with some degree of freedom. They urge and press him in the very heat of his passion; and, by still more malignant accusations, excite his indignation and his confidence, which were already too vehement. Elihu interposes as an arbiter of the controversy; he reproves the severe spirit of the friends, as well as the presumption of Job, who trusted too much in his own righteousness. Job receives his admonitions with mildness and temper, and, being rendered more sedate by his expostulation, makes no reply, though the other appears frequently to expect it. When the Almighty, however, condescends to set before him his rashness, frailty, and ignorance, he submits in perfect humility, and with sincere repentance. Here the temptation of Job concludes, in the course of which there was great reason to apprehend he would be totally vanquished: at the same time the poem necessarily terminates, the state of things still remaining without any change or vicissitude whatever. The poem indeed contains a great variety of sentiment, excellent representations of manners and character, remarkable efforts of passion, much important controversy; but no change of fortune, no novelty of incident, no plot, no action.

If indeed we rightly consider, we shall, I dare believe, find that the very nature of the subject excludes even the possibility of a plot or action. From that state of settled and unvarying misery in which Job is involved, arises the doubt of his integrity, and those insinuations and criminations which serve to exasperate him, and by which he is stimulated to expostulate with God, and to glory in his own righteousness. It was proper therefore, that, by a continuance of the same state, and condition, he should be recalled to an humble spirit, and to a proper reverence for the Almighty Providence: For it would have been altogether contrary to what is called poetical justice, if he had been restored to prosperity previous to his submission and penitence. The repentance of Job, however, we find concludes the poem. Nor was it at all necessary that the question concerning the Divine justice should be resolved in the body of the work, either by the fortunate issue of the affairs of Job, or even by the explication of the Divine intentions:

this, in fact, was not the primary object, nor does it at all constitute the subject of the poem; but is subservient, or in a manner an appendage to it. The disputation which takes place upon this topic is no more than an instrument of temptation, and is introduced in order to explain the inmost sentiments of Job, and to lay open the latent pride that existed in his soul. The Almighty, therefore, when he addresses Job, pays little regard to this point; nor indeed was it necessary, for neither the nature nor the object of the poem required a defence of the Divine providence, but merely a reprehension of the over-confidence of Job.

If, indeed, we suppose any change to have taken place in the state of affairs, the nature and subject of the poem will also be changed. If we connect with the poetical part either the former or the latter part of the history, or both, the subject will then be the display of a perfect example of patience in enduring the severest outward calamities, and at length receiving an ample reward at the hands of the Almighty: from this, however, the universal tenor of the poem will be found greatly to differ. It will be found to exhibit rather the impatience of Job in bearing the reproaches and abuse of his pretended friends: and this appears to lead to the true object of the poem: for Job is irritated, he indulges his passion, he speaks too confidently of his own righteousness, and in too irreverent a style concerning the justice of God: in the end, he is converted by the admonitions of Elihu, and the reproofs of his omnipotent Creator. The true object of the poem appears therefore to be, to demonstrate the necessity of humility, of trust in God, and of the profoundest reverence for the Divine decrees, even in the holiest and most exalted characters.

Should it be objected, that I have contended with a scrupulous perverseness concerning the meaning of a word; and should it, after all, be affirmed, that this very temptation of Job, this dispute itself, possesses in some degree the form or appearance of an action: I am content to submit the trial to another issue, and to be judged by a fair investigation of the practice of the Greek poets upon similar occasions. There is no necessity to remind this assembly, with how much art and design the fable or plot of the Œdipus Tyrannus of Sophocles appears to have been constructed; with what powers of imagination and judgment the process of the drama is conducted: and in what manner, by a regular

succession of events arising naturally from each other, the
horrid secret is developed, which, as soon as disclosed, pre-
cipitates the hero of the tragedy from the summit of human
happiness into the lowest depths of misery and ruin. Let
us only suppose Sophocles to have treated the same subject
in a different manner, and to have formed a poem on that
part of the story alone which is comprised in the last act.
Here Œdipus would be indeed exhibited as an object of the
most tender compassion, here would be a spacious field for
the display of the most interesting and tragical affections:
the fatal catastrophe would be deplored; the blindness, disgrace, exile of the hero, would enhance the distress of the
scene; and to the bitterness of present calamity would be
added the still more bitter remembrance of the past. The
poet might copiously display the sorrow and commiseration
of his daughters, his detestation of himself, and of all that
belong to him; and more copiously, of those who had preserved him when exposed, who had supported and educated
him; all these topics the poet has slightly touched upon in
these lines,

> "O curst Cithæron! why didst thou receive me?
> Or, when thou didst, how couldst thou not destroy me?"

The succeeding passages are also extremely pathetic. These
would easily admit of amplification, and, when the ardour
of grief was a little abated, he might have added his vindication of himself, his asseverations of his innocence, his plea
of ignorance, and fatal necessity, and his impassioned exclamations against Fortune and the Gods. From all this might
be constructed a poem, great, splendid, copious, diversified;
and the subject would also furnish a topic of disputation not
unlike that of Job. It might also assume in some measure
the dramatic form: the same characters that appear in the
tragedy might be introduced; it might possess the exact
proportions and all the requisites of a drama, fable alone
excepted, which indeed constitutes the very essence of a
dramatic poem, and without which all other qualities are of
no avail; for the Greeks would have called such a production
a monody, or elegiac dialogue, or any thing but a tragedy.
  This opinion receives still further confirmation from the
example and authority of Sophocles himself in another instance. For, when he again introduces the same Œdipus
upon the stage in another tragedy, though the groundwork

of the piece be nearly that which we have been describing, the conduct of it is totally different. This piece is called Œdipus Coloneus: the plot or fable is quite simple; on which account it is a fairer object of comparison with the poem of Job than any the plot of which is more complex. Œdipus is introduced blind, exiled, and oppressed with misery: none of these circumstances above mentioned have escaped the poet; such as the lamentation of his misery, the passionate exclamations against Fate and the Gods, and the vindication of his innocence. These, however, do not form the basis of the poem; they are introduced merely as circumstances which afford matter of amplification, and which seem to flow from that elegant plot or action he has invented. Œdipus, led by his daughter, arrives at Colonus, there to die and be interred according to the admonition of the Oracle; for upon these circumstances the victory of the Athenians over the Thebans was made to depend. The place being accounted sacred, the Athenians are unwilling to receive him; but Theseus affords him refuge and protection. Another of his daughters is introduced, who informs him of the discord between her brothers; also that Creon is coming, with an intention of bringing him back to his own country in pursuance of a decree of the Thebans. After this Creon arrives: he endeavours to persuade Œdipus to return to Thebes; and, on his refusal, attempts to make use of violence. Theseus protects Œdipus: and in the mean time Polynices arrives, with a view of bringing over his father to his party in the war against the Thebans; this being the only condition on which he was to hope for victory. Œdipus refuses, and execrates his son in the severest terms: in conclusion, the answer of the oracle being communicated to Theseus, Œdipus dies, and is secretly buried there. In this manner is constructed a regular, perfect, and important action or plot; all the parts of which are connected together in one design, and tend exactly to the same conclusion, and in which are involved the fates of both Thebes and Athens. The manners, passions, characters, and sentiments, serve to adorn, but not to support the fable. Without any striking representation of these the plot or action would still remain, and would of itself sustain the tragedy; but if the action be removed, though all the rest remain, it is evident that the tragedy is totally annihilated.

From these observations it will, I think, be evident, that the poem of Job cannot properly be brought into comparison with either the Œdipus of Sophocles, or with any other of the Greek tragedies. It will be evident, I think, that this poem ought not to be accounted of the same kind; nor can possibly be classed with them, unless the whole nature and form of either the Greek or the Hebrew poem be changed: or unless the plot or action be taken from the one, or added to the other: for, without this great essential, no poem can indeed be accounted a perfect drama.

But though I have urged thus much against its claim to that title, let it not be understood that I wish to derogate from its merits. That censure will rather apply to those who, by criticising it according to foreign and improper rules, would make that composition appear lame and imperfect, which, on the contrary, is in its kind most beautiful and perfect. If indeed the extreme antiquity of this poem, the obscurity and the difficulty that necessarily ensue from that circumstance, be considered; and if allowance be made for the total want of plot and action, we shall have cause to wonder at the elegance and interest which we find in its form, conduct, and economy. The arrangement is perfectly regular, and every part is admirably adapted to its end and design. The antiquary or the critic, who has been at the pains to trace the history of the Grecian drama, from its first weak and imperfect efforts, and has carefully observed its tardy progress to perfection,* will scarcely, I think, without astonishment, contemplate a poem produced so many ages before, so elegant in its design, so regular in its structure, so animated, so affecting, so near to the true dramatic model: while, on the contrary, the united wisdom of Greece, after ages of study, was not able to produce any thing approaching to perfection in this walk of poetry before the time of Æschylus. But however this be—whatever rank may be assigned to Job, in a comparison with the poets of Greece, to whom we must at least allow the merit of art and method, amongst the Hebrews it must certainly be allowed, in this respect, to be unrivalled. It is of little consequence whether it be esteemed a didactic or an ethic, a pathetic or dramatic poem, only let it be assigned a distinct and conspicuous station in the highest rank of the Hebrew poetry.

---

* See Note, p. 326

LECTURE XXXIV.

OF THE MANNERS, SENTIMENTS, AND STYLE OF THE POEM OF JOB.

Though the Poem of Job do not contain a plot or fable, it possesses, nevertheless, some things in common with the perfect drama—Manners or character—The manners of Job; to be distinguished from the passions or emotions.—The opinion of Aristotle, that the character of extreme virtue is not proper for Tragedy, demonstrated to be neither applicable to Job, nor true with respect to Tragedy in general—The design of the Poem—The manners of the three Friends; the gradations of passion more strongly marked in them than the diversity of manners —Elihu—The expostulation of God himself—Sentiments; expressive of things and of manners: the latter already noticed; the former consist partly of passion, partly of description: two examples of the softer passions: examples of description —The style of this Poem uncommonly elegant and sublime, and the poetic conformation of the sentences extremely correct—Peroration, recommending the study of Hebrew literature.

WHEN I contended that the poem of Job ought not to be accounted a true and regular drama, such as are the tragedies of the Greeks, I was far from insinuating that it did not possess the dramatic form. I not only allowed that in its general conduct and economy it exhibited a similitude, an anticipation, as it were, of genuine tragedy; but that it contained also all the principal requisites of a dramatic poem, fable alone excepted : of these the first and most important is, the imitation of manners or character.

The manners are what serve to mark or discriminate the different persons who take a part in the action of the poem ; to declare and express each character's peculiar mode of speaking, thinking, and acting ; and compose, as it were, the intellectual image of the man. The principal personage in this poem is Job, and in his character is meant to be exhibited (as far as is consistent with human infirmity) an example of perfect virtue. This is intimated in the argument or introduction, but is still more eminently displayed by his own actions and sentiments. He is holy, devout, and most piously and reverently impressed with the sacred awe of his Divine Creator: he is also upright, and conscious of his own integrity; he is patient of evil, and yet very remote from that insensibility, or rather stupidity, to which the Stoic school pretended. Oppressed therefore with unparalleled misfortunes, he laments his misery, and even wishes a release by death; in other words, he obeys, and gives place to the dictates of nature: irritated, however, by the unjust insinuations and the severe reproaches of his pretended friends, he is more vehemently exasperated; and the too great confidence in his own righteousness leads him to expostulate with God in terms scarcely consistent with piety and strict decorum.

It must be observed, that the first speech of Job, though it burst forth with all the vehemence of passion, consists wholly of complaint—"the words and sentiments of a despairing person, empty as the wind;"* which is indeed the apology that he immediately makes for his conduct—intimating, that he is far from presuming to plead with God, far from daring to call in question the Divine decrees, or even to mention his own innocence in the presence of his all-just Creator: nor do I see any good reason for the censure which has been passed by some commentators upon this passage. The poet seems, with great judgment and ingenuity, to have performed in this what the nature of his work required. He has depicted the affliction and anguish of Job, as flowing from his wounded heart, in a manner so agreeable to human nature, (and certainly so far venial,) that it may be truly said, "in all this Job sinned not with his lips." It is, nevertheless, embellished by such affecting imagery, and inspired with such a warmth and force of sentiment, that we find it afforded ample scope for calumny; nor did the unkind witnesses of his sufferings permit so fair an opportunity to escape. The occasion is eagerly embraced by Eliphaz, to rebuke the impatience of Job; and, not satisfied with this, he proceeds to accuse him in direct terms of wanting fortitude, and obliquely to insinuate something of a deeper dye. Though deeply hurt with the coarse reproaches of Eliphaz, still, however, when Job afterwards complains of the severity of God, he cautiously refrains from violent expostulations

* Job vi. 26.

with his Creator, and, contented with the simple expression
of affliction, he humbly confesses himself a sinner.* Hence,
I think, it is evident, that those vehement and perverse at-
testations of his innocence, those murmursa gainst the Divine
providence which his tottering virtue afterwards permits,
are to be considered merely as the consequences of momentary passion, and not as the ordinary effects of his settled
character or manners.   They prove him at the very worst
not an irreligious man, but a man possessed of integrity and
too confident of it; a man oppressed with almost every ima-
ginable evil, both corporal and mental, and hurried beyond
the limits of virtue by the strong influence of pain and
affliction.   When, on the contrary, his importunate visitors
abandon by silence the cause which they had so wantonly
and so maliciously maintained, and cease unjustly to load
him with unmerited criminations; though he defends his
argument with scarcely less obstinacy, yet the vehemence
of his grief appears gradually to subside; he returns to himself, and explains his sentiments with more candour and
sedateness: and however we may blame him for assuming
rather too much of arrogance in his appeals to the Almighty,
certainly his defence against the accusations of Eliphaz is
no more than the occasion will strictly justify.   Observe, in
the first place, how admirably the confidence and persever-
ance of Job is displayed in replying to the slander of his
false friends:

" As God liveth, who hath removed my judgment;
    Nay, as the Almighty liveth, who hath embittered my soul:
    Verily as long as I have life in me,
    And the breath of God is in my nostrils,
    My lips shall not speak perversity;
    Neither shall my tongue whisper prevarication.
    God forbid that I should declare you righteous!
    Till I expire I will not remove my integrity from me.
    I have fortified myself in my righteousness,
    And I will not give up my station:
    My heart shall not upbraid me as long as I live.
    May mine enemy be as the impious man,
    And he that riseth up against me as the wicked."†

But how magnificent, how noble, how inviting and beautiful, is that image of virtue in which he delineates his past
life! What dignity and authority does he seem to possess!

---

* See chap. vii. 20.   † Chap. xxvii. 2—7.

" If I came out to the gate, nigh the place of public resort,
   If I took up my seat in the street,
   The young men saw me, and they hid themselves ;
   Nay, the very old men rose up and stood.*
   The princes refrained talking ;
   Nay, they laid their hands on their mouths.
   The nobles held their peace,
   And their tongue cleaved to the roof of their mouth."†

What liberality ! what a promptitude in beneficence !

" Because the ear heard, therefore it blessed me ;
   The eye also saw, therefore it bare testimony for me,
   That I delivered the poor who cried,
   The orphan also, and him who had no helper.
   The blessing of him who was ready to perish came upon me.
   And I caused the heart of the widow to sing for joy."‡

What sanctity, what integrity in a judicial capacity !

" I put on righteousness, and it clothed me like a robe ;
   My justice also was a diadem.
   I was a father to the poor,
   And the controversy which I knew not, I searched it out.
   Then brake I the grinders of the oppressor,
   And I plucked the prey out of his teeth."§

But what can be more engaging than the purity of his devotion, and his reverence for the Supreme Being, founded
upon the best and most philosophical principles ? besides that
through the whole there runs a strain of the most amiable
tenderness and humanity :

" For what is the portion which God distributeth from above,
   And the inheritance of the Almighty from on high ?
   Is it not destruction to the wicked,
   And banishment‖ from their country to the doers of iniquity ?

---

* " This is a most elegant description, and exhibits most correctly that great
reverence and respect which was paid even by the old and decrepit to the holy man
in passing along the streets, or when he sat in public. They not only rose, which
in men so old and so infirm was a great mark of distinction, but they stood : they
continued to do it, though even the attempt was so difficult."—H.

† Chap. xxix. 7—10.   ‡ Chap. xxix. 11—13.   § Chap. xxix. 14. 16, 17.

‖ "Abalienation ; or reprobation, repudiation : so the word signifies in the
Arabic dialect. Abalienation agrees with the Sept. version, and perfectly expresses
the force of the Hebrew word."—H.
   This passage appears to have a manifest relation to the history of Nimrod and his
adherents, and may be added to the others which have been already mentioned, in
proof of their story having been one of the common-place topics of the Hebrew
poets.—S. H.

Doth he not see my ways ?
And numbereth he not all my steps ?
If I should despise the cause of my servant,
Or my maid, when they had a controversy with me,
What then should I do when God ariseth ?
And when he visiteth, what answer could I make him ?
Did not he who formed me in the belly form him,
And did not one fashion us in the womb ?"*

Aristotle has remarked, that the example of a singularly
good man falling from prosperous circumstances into misfortune, is by no means a proper subject for a tragedy;† since
it is offensive and indecent, rather than piteous or terrible.‡
This remark, though consistent enough with the Greek
drama, and with the sentiments and manners of the heathens,
is scarcely applicable to our tragedy, and still less to the poem
of Job. "Pity," says the same author on another occasion,
"is excited when adversity falls upon those who are undeserving of it." Great virtue, therefore, plunged into great
misfortunes, so far from being an unsuitable subject, ought
to be the most direct and proper means of moving compassion. "Terror is excited by a representation of the misery
of such persons as bear the nearest resemblance to ourselves:"
the misfortunes therefore of those who are vicious in an
extreme, are not much calculated to excite terror; but this
is by no means the case with regard to the misery of such
as are eminently good; for, if we fear for ourselves when we
see moderate virtue in affliction, much more, surely, when a
superior degree of it is in that state.§ It appears to me,
therefore, that Aristotle was not of opinion that the example
of a very good man in extreme affliction is ill calculated to
excite either pity or terror; but rather it is a spectacle likely
to prove injurious to the cause of virtue, and therefore disgusting and detestable, and consequently unfit to be produced

---

* Chap. xxxi. 2—4. 13—15.   † De Poet. cap. xiii.

‡ The opinion of Aristotle appears to be, that such a representation is calculated
to excite our indignation, (possibly against the gods;) and consequently that this
passion is likely to counteract the sentiments of pity and terror.— T.

§ "Men also pity their equals in age, manners, rank, situation, and birth: this
indeed brings the evil nearer to themselves; and the obvious reflection is, that they
are equally exposed to it: for it is an established maxim, that men pity others on
the same accounts, and in the same proportion, as they fear for themselves—
especially if the sufferers be esteemed good men; for the misery is brought
immediately before their eyes, and is consequently rendered more glaring and
apparent."—Arist. Rhet. ii. 8.

upon the stage.   This opinion of the philosopher seems to
result from an unjust and visionary estimation of human
virtue, to repress which appears to have been the very design and object of the book of Job.   The character of Job
indeed, though approaching so near to the perfection of virtue, seems, notwithstanding, to have a considerable alloy of
human infirmity, so as neither to want probability, nor to
lose its effect in exciting terror. For, if it be extreme wickedness in the most upright of men, when oppressed with the
severest misery, to murmur at all against the Divine justice,
who then shall stand before God? who shall expect to pass
through the pilgrimage of life without his portion of evil and
of sin?   The end of the poem is moreover by no means ill
calculated to excite terror; since this moral is particularly
inculcated in it, "Be not high-minded, but fear:" and Job
himself sets before us what impression the example of his
misfortunes ought to make upon our minds in this respect:

"The upright will be astonished at this !
 Then the innocent will surely rise up against the profligate;
 The righteous man will also hold on his way,
 And he that hath clean hands will gather strength."*

The three friends are exactly such characters as the nature
of the poem required.   They are severe, irritable, malignant
censors, readily and with apparent satisfaction deviating from
the purpose of consolation into reproof and contumely. Even
from the very first they manifest this evil propensity, and
indicate what is to be expected from them.   The first of
them, indeed, in the opening of his harangue, assumes an
air of candour:

"Wouldst thou take it unkindly that one should essay to speak
    to thee?"†

Indignation is, however, instantly predominant:

"But a few words who can forbear?"

The second flames forth at once:

"How long wilt thou trifle in this manner?
 How long shall the words of thy mouth be as a mighty wind?"‡

But remark the third:

"Shall not the master of words be answered?
 Or shall a man be acquitted for his fine speeches?

* Chap. xvii. 8, 9.   † Chap. iv. 2.   ‡ Chap. viii. 2.

> Shall thy prevarications make men silent ;
> Shalt thou even scoff, and there be no one to make thee
>   ashamed ?"*

They are represented as illiberal, contentious, inclined to torture every thing to the worst of purposes:

> " Doth God pervert judgment ?
>   Doth the Almighty pervert justice ?"†

Where observe, Job has not as yet uttered an intemperate expression in disparagement of Divine justice.

> " Nay, thou castest off fear,
>   And thou restrainest prayer before God :"‡

Such is the invective of the other of them. They are also proud, contemptuous, and arrogate too much to their own wisdom :

> " Why are we accounted as beasts ;
>   Why are we vile in your eyes ?
>   Let him tear himself in his fury :
>   What, shall the earth be forsaken for thee ?§
>   Or shall the rock be outrooted from its place ?
>   Rather let the light of the wicked be extinguished."‖

Nor is Zophar, who takes up the subject after Bildad, more modest :

> " Verily the impulse of my thoughts incites me to reply,
>   Even because there is some resentment within me :
>   I hear the ignominious reproof that is aimed at me,
>   And the spirit within me compels me to answer."¶

The conduct of all these malicious censors is much the same through the whole piece. Eliphaz indeed, who begins in the mildest terms, descends afterwards to the severest reproaches; and he directly charges Job with the most

---

* Chap. xi. 2, 3.   † Chap. viii. 3.   ‡ Chap. xv. 4.

§ " So the LXX. *What ! if thou diest, shall the whole earth be desolate ?* Which version, or rather paraphrase, is most elegant, and in my opinion finely accommodated to the purpose of the sacred writer. When the orientals would reprove the pride or arrogance of any person, it is common for them to desire him to call to mind how little and contemptible he and every mortal is, in these or similar apothegms :

> What though Mohammed were dead ?
> His *Imauns* (or ministers) conducted the affairs of the nation.

> The universe shall not fall for his sake.

> The world does not subsist for one man alone.

Nay, this very phrase is still in use among the Arabic writers, אל ארץ עובת, " the earth is desolate." Gol. col. 1570.—H.

‖ Chap. xviii. 3—5.   ¶ Chap. xx. 2, 3.

2 B

atrocious offences: from which intemperance of language, it must be confessed, the others refrain. Bildad, not to be silent, repeats in a brief and florid manner the subject which had already been twice treated of by the others, namely, the majesty and holiness of God; and Zophar, withdrawing from the contest, deserts entirely the cause of his companion, and leaves the field to Job. The business of defamation indeed seems, with great propriety, committed to three persons. It would have been too confined and trivial in the hands of one; and, amongst a crowd of accusers, too confused and clamorous. There appears, however, but little difference in the manners of the three friends; for in them the poet has rather studied to display the progress of the passions than any diversity of character. But though the nice and fastidious criticism of the moderns demand variety in this respect, the simplicity of infant poetry will be excused by every person of real judgment; and I think this deficiency (if such it may be called) is amply compensated by the gravity and importance of the subject and sentiments.

The lenity and moderation of Elihu serves as a beautiful contrast to the intemperance and asperity of the other three. He is pious, mild, and equitable; equally free from adulation and severity; and endued with singular wisdom, which he attributes entirely to the inspiration of God: and his modesty, moderation, and wisdom, are the more entitled to commendation when we consider his unripe youth. As the characters of his detractors were in all respects calculated to inflame the mind of Job, that of this arbitrator is admirably adapted to soothe and compose it: to this point the whole drift of the argument tends; and on this the very purport of it seems to depend.

The interposition of the Deity, and its connexion with the general design of the poem, I have formerly noticed. I will only add, that although some critics have really thought the whole address inconsistent, and foreign to the subject, no man has ever accounted it in any respect unworthy of that supreme Majesty to which it is ascribed.

Another circumstance deserving particular attention in a poem of this kind, is the sentiment; which must be agreeable to the subject, and embellished with proper expression. It is by Aristotle enumerated among the essentials of a dramatic poem; not indeed as peculiar to that species of poetry alone, but as common, and of the greatest importance to all.

Manners or character are essential only to that poetry in which living persons are introduced; and all such poems must afford an exact representation of human manners; but sentiment is essential to every poem, indeed to every composition whatever.   It respects both persons and things: as far as it regards persons, it is particularly concerned in the delineation of the manners and passions; and those instances to which I have just been adverting, are sentiments expressive of manners.   Those which relate to the delineation of the passions, and to the description of other objects, yet remain unnoticed in this Lecture.   As I formerly, however, treated of these subjects in general, I could scarcely avoid producing some examples from this poem; for, in demonstrating the power of the poetic diction in exciting the passions, I could not possibly deduce my instances from a better source.*   On the present occasion, therefore, I shall study brevity, and avoid as much as possible the tediousness of repetition.

The poem of Job abounds chiefly in the more vehement passions, grief and anger, indignation and violent contention. It is adapted in every respect to the incitement of terror; and, as the specimens already quoted will sufficiently prove, is universally animated with the true spirit of sublimity.   It is, however, not wanting in the gentler affections; the following complaints, for instance, are replete with an affecting spirit of melancholy:

" Man, the offspring of a woman,
Is of few days, and full of inquietude;
He springeth up, and is cut off like a flower;
He fleeteth like a shadow, and doth not abide :
Upon such a creature dost thou open thine eyes ?
And wilt thou bring even me into judgment with thee ?
Turn thy look from him, that he may have some respite,
Till he shall, like a hireling, have completed † his day."‡

The whole passage abounds with the most beautiful imagery, and is a most perfect specimen of the Elegiac.   His grief afterwards becomes more fervent; but is at the same time soft and querimonious.

* See Lect. 14, 15, 16, 17.
† " Or until he *shall acquiesce*, or *shall make satisfaction*, (the original will bear either interpretation;) for the word in the Arabic dialect sometimes signifies, He *did or afforded to another, what he held to be agreeable to himself*."—H .
‡ Chap. xiv. 1, 2, 3. 6.

" How long will ye vex my soul,
　And tire me with vain harangues ?
　These ten times have ye loaded me with reproaches ;
　Are ye not ashamed that ye are so obstinate against me ?*
　Pity me, O pity me, ye are my friends,
　For the hand of God hath smitten me.
　Why will you be my persecutors as well as God,
　And wherefore will ye not be satisfied with my flesh ? " †

That self-indulgence which is so natural to the passion of
Hope; its ingenuity in drawing pictures of future felicity;
its credulity in cherishing these ideas, and the gaiety and
elevation of mind with which it describes them—are finely
expressed by Job in the passage immediately following the
relation of his past life :

"Therefore I said, I shall die in my nest ;
　I shall multiply my days like the sand :
　My root was spread abroad nigh the waters,
　And the dew lay all night on my branches :
　My glory was fresh within me,
　And my bow gained strength in my hand.
　They hearkened to me, nay they waited for me ;
　They were silent also, they approved my counsel.
　After I had spoken they replied not ;
　For my words dropped upon them ;
　They waited also for me as the rain ;
　And their mouths were open as for the latter rain."‡

To this part of the subject, which relates to the delineation of the passions, may be referred those delicate touches
which animate almost every description, and which are drawn
from the most intimate knowledge of the genuine emotions
of the human soul.　I shall content myself with one example out of the many which the compass of the work affords.
It is exactly copied from nature; for, when events take place

---

* " I think the word תזהכרו occurs but this once in the Scriptures, and (as is my
usual practice when I meet with any such words or phrases) I consulted the Arabic
lexicographers.　They explain it by two other words ; the one is עבב, *to admire*, the
other is חאר, *to wonder, to be astonished*.　Whence הכר, *to wonder in amazement*, (to be
overcome with astonishment, as Giggeius explains it;) and the sense of the passage
will be, *Are you not ashamed to gaze at me?* Kimchi says his father affirmed, that
the word הכר signifies in Arabic *impudence* or *forwardness :* I do not however find
this interpretation confirmed by the lexicons which I have consulted.　But still if
we suppose that the word תזהכרו is derived from נכר, the explication of Kimchi may
be accepted, but the form of the verb will be anomalous.　It is, however, safest perhaps to adhere to the common translation."—H.

† Chap. xix. 2, 3, 21, 22.　　　　　　‡ Chap. xxix. 11—23.

according to our ardent wishes, but quite contrary to our expectations, we have the utmost difficulty to believe them real. Job thus expresses himself respecting God:

> " If I called upon him, and he should answer me,
> Yet could I scarcely believe that he had heard my voice."*

This is admirably expressive both of the majesty of God and of the severity which he exercised towards Job: it is also no less descriptive of the humiliation and despair of the sufferer.

> " If I were merry with them, they would not believe it,"†

says Job of his dependents; in which is expressed his own dignity and gravity united with urbanity, and at the same time their unviolated attachment to him. Thus too, by the same circumstance, is depicted both the ardour and alacrity of the war-horse and his eagerness for the battle:

> " For eagerness and fury he devoureth the very ground,
> He believeth it not when he heareth the trumpet.
> When the trumpet soundeth, he saith, Aha!
> Yea he scenteth the battle from afar,
> The thunder of the chieftains, and their shouts."‡

This passage, which has indeed always attracted general admiration, will also serve to exemplify the excellence of the descriptive parts of this poem: and from the same circumstance we may fairly conjecture, that the pictures which are exhibited in other parts of the work would appear no less striking resemblances of the realities, were we equally well acquainted with the originals. To judge rightly of a description, we ought to have as clear and distinct ideas of the thing itself as the author. The idea of thunder is familiar to all mankind; observe, therefore, how it is depicted by Elihu:

> " At this my heart trembleth,
> And is ready to bound from its place.
> Hearken attentively, and tremble at his voice;
> Even at the sound that goeth out of his mouth.
> Its flash is beneath the whole heavens,
> And its blaze to the ends of the earth.
> After it a voice roareth;
> He thundereth with the voice of his majesty;
> He deceiveth them not when his voice is heard."§

* Chap. ix. 16.   † Chap. xxix. 24.   ‡ Chap. xxxix. 24, 25.
§ That is, " they cannot mistake his voice for any thing beside." Heath. Job xxxvii. 1—4.

It would be superfluous to insist any longer on a minute detail, since the most splendid examples of every beauty and elegance of sentiment, of imagery, and of diction, meet the eye of the attentive reader in every part of the poem. Let it suffice to say, that the dignity of the style is answerable to that of the subject; its force and energy to the greatness of those passions which it describes; and as this production excels all the other remains of the Hebrew poetry in economy and arrangement, so it yields to none in sublimity of style, and in every grace and excellence of composition. Among the principal of these may be accounted the accurate and perfectly poetical conformation of the sentences, which is, indeed, generally most observable in the most ancient of the poetical compositions of the Hebrews. Here, however, as is natural and proper in a poem of so great length and sublimity, the writer's skill is displayed in the proper adjustment of the period, and in the accurate distribution of the members rather than in the antithesis of words, or in any laboured adaptation of the parallelisms.

———

HAVING now gone through the several topics of which I purposed to treat in my investigation of the nature of the Hebrew Poetry, it is time that my present undertaking should draw towards a conclusion. If, in the prosecution of my design, I have by my industry been able to accomplish any thing that may be deemed satisfactory, it is but common justice to attribute the greatest part of my success to you, Gentlemen, who have condescended to look with a propitious

---

In the last line it seems as if we should read יעקב, he will not deceive, with the Vulg. and Symmachus. For this correction I am indebted to the learned Richard Grey, who has paid a very critical attention to this poem.

"The true sense is, perhaps, *he does it not at intervals, or by fits,* i. e. *thunders, &c.* but *continually;* which, among others, is the sense of the word in the Arabic dialect. And the exposition of R. L. B. Gershom, *he does not defer* or *delay,* agrees very well with this opinion; as well as our common English translation, which is thus far preferable to that of the Vulgate and Symmachus, namely, that it requires no change of the text. This also, in all probability, is the meaning of the Septuagint version, Ουκ ανταλλαξει αυτες; though this seems to relate to the hearers, when in reality it should relate to the things heard." H.—*Author's Note.*

"See whether the verb *shemang* be ever construed with *beth,* except in the sense *obeying,* which does not agree with the context in this place. It seems better, therefore, to construe the verb with *kolu,* and to render the sentence in this manner —*Hear his voice attentively, and with trembling.*"—H.

eye upon my endeavours, and to invigorate my application
by your attention and partiality.   When, indeed, I first
meditated this system of instruction, I foresaw, as well from
the native sublimity and obscurity of the subject, as from
the extreme antiquity of the Hebrew writings, much subtile
investigation, much difficult explication, much doubtful
assertion, and dangerous error.   I foresaw too, and daily
experience confirmed my apprehensions, that in this maze of
science the vestiges and the documents of the learned would
be frequently found but imperfect guides.   That my courage
did not utterly forsake me in the course of my undertaking,
is to be attributed entirely to the favour and encouragement
which I received from you.   I had the satisfaction to find
my plan meet with the approbation of some of the greatest
and most eminent characters in the learned world, as being
neither inconsistent with the design of this institution, the
dignity of this University, nor the profit and utility of the
students.   I had often the singular pleasure of seeing among
my auditors many persons, to whom it would better become
me to apply for instruction in this and in every other branch
of literature ; and the young men for whose benefit this
institution was established, I have found ever diligent and
constant in their attendance : all which testimonies of your
favour, unless I accounted as obligations, I should think
either too arrogantly of myself, or too disrespectfully of you.
To all of you, therefore, I feel, and shall for ever feel myself obliged : the remembrance of your kindness will, in every
vicissitude of my condition, be pleasing to me; nor is there
any danger of my suffering that to escape my memory,
which I must ever esteem the great ornament of my life.

But to return to a point which is of more importance, and
which has indeed been the principal object of all my endeavours—I should now think myself called upon, in the last
place, to exhort this assembly of accomplished youths to an
assiduous application to these studies, but that I confess I
think you rather demand commendation than advice.   For
the Hebrew language, which was for a series of years in a
manner obsolete and neglected, has been lately cultivated by
you with such attention and application, and has obtained so
respectable a place among the other branches of erudition,
that it seems through your means to have recovered, after a
tedious exile, all its former dignity and importance.   Proceed,
therefore, in the same career with the same ardour and suc-

cess, and consider it as a work worthy of your utmost exertions to illustrate and cultivate this department of literature. You will find it no less elegant and agreeable than useful and instructive; abounding in information no less curious for its extent and variety, than for its great importance and venerable sanctity; deserving the attention of every liberal mind; essential to all who would be proficients in theology; a branch of literature, in a word, which will confer credit upon yourselves, will be an honour to the University, and an advantage to the Church. I congratulate you, Gentlemen, on having an Instructor,* who, from his authority, example, assiduity, and information, will be found in no respect wanting to your profit and accommodation; a gentleman no less eminent for his abilities and profound erudition, than for the candour, urbanity, and gentleness of his manners. He will unfold to you the inexhaustible treasures of oriental literature: he will open to your view an unbounded field of science and of fame. It is sufficient for me to have discovered to you a few of the more delightful retreats of this paradise: and could I flatter myself that my endeavours have been so fortunate as to allure or excite any to these studies, or even to stimulate and keep alive your attention to this department of literature, I should think that I had received the most honourable, the most grateful reward of my labours.

* Dr. Thomas Hunt, King's Professor of Hebrew, and Laudian Professor of the Arabic language.

A

BRIEF CONFUTATION

OF

BISHOP HARE'S SYSTEM

OF

HEBREW METRE.

It is well known that an hypothesis was invented by the late Bishop Hare concerning the Hebrew Metres; and the arguments which he had advanced in its favour appeared so conclusive to some persons of great erudition, as to persuade them that the learned Prelate had fortunately revived the knowledge of the true Hebrew versification, after an oblivion of more than two thousand years; and that he had established his opinion by such irresistible proofs, as to place it beyond the utmost efforts of controversy. Whoever, indeed, encounters it in such a manner as only to call in question some particular part, to intimate only an occasional scruple, or to attack but one or two of his arguments, will, doubtless, "attempt in vain* to root out of their minds an opinion which has been so deeply implanted and established by the authority of so great a man; much less will any person obtain credit who shall affirm that he has discovered what was not discovered by the learned Prelate, unless by the strongest arguments he not only overthrows the hypothesis which he rejects, but confirms his own. Avoiding, therefore, every subterfuge, I shall come immediately to the point, and demonstrate by the clearest and most decisive instances, which is the only method of extorting assent from the incredulous, that I have actually discovered the nature and principles of this poetry," and those directly contrary to the system which he has adopted. I shall, on this occasion, make use of the same example that Bishop Hare himself has chosen, which, when properly considered, will, I think, sufficiently explain and prove my opinion, and at the same time effectually overturn his hypothesis.

* See Hare's Preface to the Psalms, at the beginning.

PSALM CXI.

1. odéh javóh becól lebáb,   i.
2. besód jesárim véyedáh.
3. gédolím mayasé javóh,   ii.
4. dérusím lecól chepzéhem.
5. hód vehádar póyaló,   iii.
6. vezidkathó yomédeth láyad.
7. zecér yasáh leníphlotháv ;   iv.
8. chánun vérachúm Javóh.
9. téreph náthan líreáv,   v.
10. jízcor léyolám berítho.
11. coách mayasáv higíd leyámo,   vi.
12. lathéth lahém nachálath góim.
13. mayasé jadáv eméth umíspat ;   vii.
14. neemánim cól pikdúav :
15. semúcim láyad léyolám,   viii.
16. yásuím beeméth vejásar.
17. pedúth salách leyámo,   ix.
18. zívah léyolám berítho.
19. kâdos vénorá semó ;   x.
20. resíth chocmáh jiráth javoh.
21. sécel tób lecól yoséhem,   xi.
22. tehíllathó yomédeth láyad.

From this alphabetic Psalm, which is divided into its proper verses according to the initial letters, and restored to its proper numbers without any violation of the text, without even any change of the Masoretic vowels, (except that, with Bishop Hare, I read *javoh*,) the canons of the Hebrew metre are to be collected and established.

*I. In the first place, then, in the Hebrew poetry the feet are not all dissyllables; for in verse 3. 11. 16.—lím maya—cóach maya—ím be—are Dactyls; in verse 13, 14, mayasé,

---

* The following are the principal rules or canons of Bishop Hare :—
1. In Hebrew poetry all the feet are two syllables.
2. No regard is paid to the quantity of the syllables.
3. When the number of the syllables is even, the verse is trochaic, placing the accent on the first syllable.
4. If the number of syllables be odd, they are to be accounted iambics, and the accent is to be placed on the second syllable, in order to preserve the rhythm.
5. The periods mostly consist of two verses, often three or four, and sometimes more.
6. The verses of the same period, with few exceptions, are of the same kind.
7. The trochaic verses mostly agree in the number of feet : there are, however, a few exceptions.

ncemá—are Anapæsts: contrary to the first canon of Bishop Hare.

II. Attention must always be paid to the quantity of the syllables; for the same word, as often as it occurs, is always of the same quantity; for instance, javóh, lecól, are constantly Iambics, lávad is always a Trochaic, mavasé an Anapæst; lévolám is uniformly an Amphimaser; berítho, vomédeth, is an Amphibrachis: contrary to the second canon of Bishop Hare.

III. The verses are either Trochaic, which admit a Dactyl; or Iambic, which admit an Anapæst; but it by no means follows that a verse is either the one or the other from its consisting of an even or odd number of syllables. Those indeed which consist of an even number of syllables, are for the most part Iambic, as verse 1, 2, 7, 13, 14, 15, 20; but they are also sometimes Trochaic, as verse 3, 4, 10, 18, 21; and those which consist of an odd number of syllables are mostly Trochaic, as verse 5, 8, 9, 11, 16, 19; they are however sometimes Iambic, as verse 6, 12, 17, 22: contrary to the third and fourth canons.

IV. The verses of the same period are of different kinds, period iii. iv. vi. viii. ix. x. xi. a few only excepted, as period i. ii. v. vii; and those which are of the same kind seldom agree in the number of syllables and feet: for instance, in period ii. and v. the first verse is a Trochaic Dimeter Catalectic, the second a Trochaic Dimeter Acatalectic; in period vii. the first is an Iambic Dimeter Hypercatalectic, the second an Iambic Dimeter Catalectic; the only instance of verses agreeing in kind, agreeing also in syllables and feet, is in period i., and those are Iambics: and this is contrary to the sixth, seventh, and eighth canons.

V. All the periods consist of only two verses; for, properly, *koph* and *resh* constitute the penultimate, and *shin* and *tau* the ultimate period; as also appeared to the learned Cappell:* this is contrary to the fifth canon.

VI. Each verse has one particular sense: contrary to the ninth canon.

" That what I have advanced as true and indisputable, is most true, appears from the examples which I have adduced;

---

8. In the iambic verses the feet are mostly unequal, though in some instances they are equal.

9. Each verse does not contain a distinct sense.—See Hare's *Pref.* p. 27.

* See Cappell, Crit. Sac. lib. i. cap. xii. 11.

and whoever reads attentively the book of Psalms will find similar instances in almost every page."*

* See Hare's Preface, p. 31. The reader has doubtless observed, that, to establish our two last canons, and perhaps the others, a general proposition is deduced from a particular instance; viz. so it is in this Psalm, and so, therefore, it must be in all Hebrew poems whatever: in this, however, I only copy Bishop Hare; for to say the truth, upon this mode of reasoning, and begging the question at the same time, depends his whole hypothesis.

I find these observations have greatly displeased Dr. Thomas Edwards, a strenuous advocate for Bishop Hare's metres. Towards the conclusion of his Dissertation lately published he asserts, that I did not understand what I presumed to censure: And to this accusation I indeed plead guilty; for I will freely confess, that I neither did understand, nor do I yet understand, what metre can exist without any distinction of long and short syllables, or what can be meant by trochaic, iambic, and anacreontic feet and verses, where no regard is paid to the quantity of the syllables. Nor do I understand any better, what purpose the confutation of my hypothesis can answer, since I gave it myself as futile and false, and since the futility of it was one of the strongest arguments against the hypothesis of Hare. This argument can only be done away by proving that my hypothesis is not founded upon the same, or upon principles equally clear and certain with Bishop Hare's: this unfortunately his defender has not done, nor indeed can he do.

With regard to his accusation, that I have acted dogmatically, and that I have upon my own authority, and without any regard to reason, affirmed, that the hypothesis of Bishop Hare depends altogether upon his taking for granted the very point to be proved; in order to exonerate myself from so invidious an imputation, and in order to confirm what I before had advanced, I must request the reader's attention to the following particulars.

The 111th Psalm is proposed as an example, and is divided into verses, whence the laws of Hebrew versification are to be deduced. We grant that in this Psalm the verses are rightly distinguished, since it is alphabetical, and the members of each period are nearly equal. But what is this to the establishment of a certain rule for the division of others, which are neither alphabetical nor seem capable of a regular and equal distribution of the sentences and members? Indeed, such is the difficulty of Bishop Hare's hypothesis in this respect, that, according to it, a number of the Psalms are divided, not only arbitrarily and oddly, but inelegantly, injudiciously, contrary to the genius of the Hebrew poetry, and contrary to every appearance of truth. We will take for an example the 1st Psalm, on which the Author prides himself not a little. But when divided into verses, by what rule is it accented? Why in this rather than any other manner? How is it proved, that, when the number of syllables is even, the verse is trochaic, when odd, iambic? From the nature and principles of trochaic and iambic verse? By no means; for, in the Greek and Latin trochaics and iambics the case is directly contrary; but merely from the pleasure and will of the Author. Why then may not I, or any other person, affix different accents to this 111th or any other Psalm, and so turn the trochaics of Bishop Hare into iambics, and his iambics into trochaics? By what rule too are the syllables numbered? According to the Masoretic punctuation? By no means; for the Masoretic number of syllables is altered, and that, as by a previous rule, or according to an established system of metre, which existed before the punctuation; as from this Psalm, so ordered and illustrated, the rules of metre are afterwards to be collected. "But I do not desert the Masoretic punctuation, unless an erroneous punctuation interferes with the metre." This would be a sound argument, if it were previously determined what these rules

Since this is the case; since I have deduced happily the abstruse principles of the Hebrew metre from this Psalm, or rather explained clearly such as readily presented themselves, and have reduced them to an art easy, perfect, and consistent—depending upon principles certain and self-evident; but not taking those liberties in which Bishop Hare has prolixly indulged himself, so as to make the same word sometimes trochaic, sometimes iambic, sometimes a dissyllable, and sometimes a trisyllable; I may reasonably indulge myself in that hope, that the candid reader will prefer my hypothesis to that of Bishop Hare. This at least I trust I may expect, that he will treat them upon equal terms, and allow to each the same authority, that is—NONE AT ALL.

In the same manner, every hypothesis which pretends to define the laws of Hebrew Metre, and to prescribe the numbers, the feet, the scanning of the lines, may, I think, be easily overset; for to that hypothesis another directly contrary, yet confirmed by arguments equally forcible, may, I am persuaded, be successfully opposed.

With regard to the opinion of those who suppose the whole art of Hebrew metre to consist in a similarity of termination to each verse; though it has acquired some popu-

of metre were. But for what good reason are all trisyllabic metres excluded from the Hebrew poetry? " Because truly, if the trisyllabic feet were admitted, a distinction of long and short syllables would have place necessarily in the Hebrew poetry." And why should it not? "In Hebrew poetry there is no respect at all to the quantity of the syllables." A most extraordinary assertion, and scarcely credible! But that so it might be, learn from the testimony of your eyes and ears. "For from this Psalm it is evident, that no regard is paid to quantity in the Hebrew poetry; since in the 4th and 5th verses, not to mention other instances, the *lc* and *ve* are long. On the other hand, in the fifteenth and twenty-second, *mu* in *semucion*, and *hil* in *tehillatho*, are short." That is, according to Hare, the shortest syllable may be made use of instead of the longest (such indeed he acknowledges them to be) in his trochaic and iambic measures; and on the other hand, the longest may be introduced instead of the shortest—of which this Psalm affords the precedent; and, on the authority of this precedent, a law is framed to serve in all other cases: and when we ask, upon other evidence, the reason of the fact, he refers us to his own authority and his own example. For indeed, says he, this is the plain state of the case : " That this, and all that I have urged upon this subject, is undoubtedly fact, is plain from the examples which I have produced ; and must strike every reasonable person who only looks into a single page of the book of Psalms." I confess it, indeed, most learned Prelate, if we look into your Psalms; but I fear we shall then be very little nearer the truth, since it is by no means a decided point that your Psalms are rightly and judiciously divided into verses, feet, and syllables.

See " A larger Confutation of Bishop Hare's Hebrew Metres, in a Letter to Dr. Edwards, Lond. 1764."—*Author's Note.*

larity and authority in the learned world, I think it by far the most ill-founded of all; and I think its absurdity so obvious, that with the utmost ease it may be detected. Since the endings of the verses are defined in some of the alphabetical poems, and since it is manifest that in these the verses do not end alike, that no art or attention has been bestowed upon that point, it follows of course that the art of Hebrew versification does not consist in making verses with similar endings.

APPENDIX,

REFERRED TO FROM PAGE 203.

PSALM CXXXV.

ΠΡΟΑΣΜΑ, or *Prelude.*—Part I.

High-Priest and Priests, to the Levites :
Praise ye Jah !

Levites, to the Priests :
Praise ye the name of Jehovah !

Priests and Levites, to the Congregation :
Praise him, O ye servants of Jehovah !

The Congregation to the Priests :
Ye that stand in the house of Jehovah !

The Congregation to the Levites :
In the courts of the house of our God !

ΠΡΟΑΣΜΑ.—II.

Priests, to the Levites :
Praise ye Jah, for Jehovah is good.

Levites to the Congregation :
Sing praises unto his name, for it is pleasant.

Congregation, joining both Priests and Levites :
For Jah hath chosen Jacob unto himself,
Israel for his peculiar treasure.

HYMN.

High-Priest, followed by the Priests :
For I know that Jehovah is great,
Even our Lord above all Gods.

Levites :
Whatsoever Jehovah pleased,
He did in heaven, and in earth,
In the seas, and in deep places.

Congregation :
He causeth the vapours to rise from the ends of the earth ;
He maketh lightnings for the rain ;
He bringeth the wind out of his treasuries.

High-Priest, accompanied by the Priests :
Who smote the first-born of Egypt,
Both of man and of beast.

Levites :
Sent tokens and wonders into the midst of thee, O Egypt ;

Congregation :
Upon Pharaoh, and upon all his servants.

High-Priest and Priests :
Who smote great nations, and slew mighty kings :

Levites :
Sihon, king of the Amorites,
And Og, king of Basan,
And all the kingdoms of Canaan.

Congregation :
And he gave their land an heritage,
An heritage with Israel his people.

Priests ;
Thy name, O Jehovah, endureth for ever :

Levites :
Thy memorial, O Jehovah, throughout all generations.

Priests, Levites, and Congregation in full chorus :
For Jehovah will judge his people ;
And will repent him concerning his servants.

II.

High-Priest, accompanied by the Priests :
The idols of the Heathen—silver and gold !
The work of mortal hands.

Levites :
They have mouths, but they speak not ;
Eyes have they, but they see not.

Congregation :
They have ears, but they hear not ;
Neither is there any truth in their mouths.

Priests, Levites, and Congregation, in full chorus :
They that make them are like unto them ;
Every one that trusteth in them.

ΑΝΤΙΦΩΝΗΣΙΣ.

High-Priest and Priests, to the Congregation :
Bless Jehovah, O house of Israel !

Congregation, to the High-Priest and Priests :
Bless Jehovah, O house of Aaron !

High-Priest and Priests, to the Levites :
Bless Jehovah, O house of Levi !

Levites, to High-Priest and Priests :
Ye that fear Jehovah, bless Jehovah !

Priests, Levites, and Congregation, in full chorus :
Blessed be Jehovah out of Sion,
Who dwelleth in Jerusalem !

Full chorus, continuing each division to both the rest :
Praise ye Jah !

The praising the name JEHOVAH, so often mentioned in Scripture, arises from the answer to the question of Moses, Exod. iii. 13.—S. H.

*

AN

INDEX

PASSAGES OF THE OLD TESTAMENT,

WHICH ARE

CITED, EXPLAINED, OR REFERRED TO

IN THE

LECTURES.

GENESIS.	Page
i. 3	170
5	332
24	31
iii. 24	44
iv. 23, 24.	ib.
ix. 25—27	46, 197
27	162
xiv. 6	353
xvi. 31	45
xxi. 6, 7	47
xxiii.	77
xxiv. 2	38
60	47
xxv. 2, 3	354
6	353
15 and 18	354
23	47
xxvii. 27—29	46
39, 40	ib.
xxviii. 16, 17	47
xxix. 27	331
xxxi. 39	31
xxxvi. 10, 11	354
20, and 28	353
xlvi. 32 – 34	346
8. 16, and 19	162
9	105
11	30
21	308

EXODUS.	
ii. 15	354
18	339
iii. 1	354
viii. 14	207

EXODUS.	Page
ix. 8	94
xv. 1—21	280, 305, 31
1	260
5	31
6	215
9, 10	184
11, 12	183
20, 21	201
xix. 16 and 18	96
xx. 7	302
xxiii. 5	40
17	302
31	31
xxvi. 7, &c.	87
36	85
xxvii. 16	ib.
xxviii. 2	84
39	85
xxxii. 6 and 19	67
18	204
xxxv. 30—35	85
xl. 34—38	86

LEVITICUS.	
xvi. 2	86
xix. 32	106
xxiii. 24	292
xxv. 9, 10	ib.
13—16	71
23, 24	ib.

NUMBERS.	
vi. 7	45
ix. 15, 16	86
x. 35	305

2 c

INDEX

OF

REMARKABLE CIRCUMSTANCES

NOTICED IN THE

LECTURES AND NOTES.

Description, to judge rightly of, it is necessary to have as distinct and clear
ideas of the thing itself as the author, 389.

Divine Spirit never takes such entire
possession of the mind of the prophet, as to subdue or extinguish the
character and genius of the man,
168.

Dramatic exhibitions, their commencement and progress, 326.

E.

Edom, why particularly marked as an
object of divine vengeance, 223.

Elegance not inconsistent with brevity
and obscurity, 270.

Elegy, the ancient, 13. Not only the
Lamentations of Jeremiah, but parts
of the prophecy of Ezekiel, of the
book of Job, and of the Psalms, are
elegiac, 255, 256.

Elihu, his character, 386.

Eliphaz, who he was, and where he
dwelt, 354.

Enallage of the tenses ought never to be
introduced but when the mind is sufficiently heated not to perceive the il-
lusion, 164.

Enthusiasm, poetical, 39.

Epic Poetry, its character and effects, 9.

Euripides known amongst his friends by
the appellation of the Dramatic Philosopher, 9.

Ezekiel inferior in elegance to Isaiah,
230. His character as a prophet, *ib.*
Not excelled by Isaiah in sublimity,
ib.

F.

Figures, congenial, of Metaphor, Allegory, and Comparison, used by the
Hebrew poets in a peculiar manner,
105.

Firmicus, Julius, an astronomical writer, 5.

G.

Georgics of Virgil, a delightful and perfect work, 5.

Glosses in the Hebrew language, 30.

Greeks indebted to the Egyptians for
their notions of a future state, 101.
Arguments in support of the Hebrews
deriving theirs from the same source,
visionary, 103.

II.

Habakkuk, character of his style, 235.

Haggai, the Prophet, his style altogether prosaic, 235.

Happiness, human, consists in action,
390.

Hebrews, opinion of M. Michaelis, that
they as well as the Greeks and Romans borrowed their poetical imagery from the Egyptians, 99. This
hypothesis ingenious but fanciful,
103.

Hebrew Metre, a considerable part of it
probably consisted in the parallelism
of the sentences, 213.

Hebrew Poets, their peculiar commendation, 74.

Hebrew Poetry possesses excellences peculiar to itself, 26. Its opposition
to the Greek and Latin poetry, 35.
Its dialect distinctly poetical, 30.
Greatly superior to the Grecian, 18.

Hebrew versification, little knowledge of
it now to be attained, 26, 33.

Hebrew word expressive of the poetic
style admits of three significations,
38. The same used to denote a
Prophet, a Poet, and a Musician,
194.

Heroic Poetry, its character, 6.

History inferior to Poetry as a means of
instruction, 8.

Homer, his excellence, 6.

Hosea, characteristics of his style, 233.

Horace, the 3d ode of the 4th book
commended, 291.

Hyperbole requires passion to give it
force or propriety, 53.

I.

Idumæans eminent for wisdom, 355.

Jeremiah probably the author of the
139th Psalm, 219.

Jews, futility of their opinions respecting Daniel, 218.

Images, sensible, reason why, amongst
such as are applied to the Deity,
those principally which seem most
remote from the object, and most
unworthy of the Divine Majesty, are,
when used metaphorically, the most
sublime, 175.

Images of Light and Darkness commonly used in all languages to denote
Prosperity and Adversity, 62.

THE END.

W. Tyler, Printer, Bolt-court, Fleet-street.

LONDON, No. 73, CHEAPSIDE, 1845.

MR. TEGG HAS JUST ISSUED THE FOLLOWING NEW PUBLICATIONS,

OF SUPERIOR CHARACTER, GENERAL UTILITY, AND POPULAR INTEREST, ON THE MOST INTERESTING SUBJECTS OF LITERATURE AND SCIENCE.

*** *Orders from Merchants, for Exportation, of whatever magnitude, executed with Correctness and Despatch.*

BIBLICAL CRITICISM AND INTERPRETATION.

	£	s.	d.
BOOTHROYD'S FAMILY BIBLE. 3 vols. 4to.	3	3	0
BROWN'S SELF-INTERPRETING BIBLE. 4to. Maps, &c.	1	10	0
————— DICTIONARY OF THE HOLY BIBLE. 8vo.	0	9	0
————— CONCORDANCE OF THE HOLY SCRIPTURES. 18mo.	0	2	0
BURDER'S ORIENTAL CUSTOMS. New Edition. By GROSER. 8vo.	0	9	0
CAMPBELL'S NOTES ON THE GOSPELS. 2 vols. 8vo.	0	16	0
CALVIN'S COMMENTARY ON THE PSALMS. 3 vols. 8vo.	1	10	0
CARPENTER'S BIBLICAL COMPANION. Imperial 8vo.	0	12	0
CLARKE'S (DR. ADAM) COMMENTARY ON THE OLD AND NEW TESTAMENTS. 6 vols. Imperial 8vo.	6	8	0
————— SUCCESSION OF SACRED LITERATURE. 2 vols. 8vo.	0	15	0
DODDRIDGE'S FAMILY EXPOSITOR. Imperial 8vo.	1	1	0
FLEURY'S MANNERS OF THE ANCIENT ISRAELITES. By A. CLARKE. 12mo.	0	6	0
GRAY AND PERCY'S KEY TO THE OLD AND NEW TESTAMENTS. 8vo.	0	8	0
HENRY'S COMMENTARY ON THE SCRIPTURES. By BLOMFIELD. 4to.	1	10	0
HORNE'S (Bp.) COMMENTARY ON THE PSALMS. 8vo.	0	8	0
JENNINGS'S JEWISH ANTIQUITIES. 8vo.	0	7	0
JONES'S BIBLICAL CYCLOPÆDIA. 8 vo.	0	16	0
LELAND'S DIVINE AUTHORITY OF THE OLD AND NEW TESTAMENTS. 8vo.	0	7	0
LOCKE AND DODD'S COMMON-PLACE BOOK TO THE BIBLE. 8vo.	0	9	0
LOWTH'S (Bp.) LITERAL TRANSLATION OF ISAIAH. 8vo.	0	7	0
————— LECTURES ON HEBREW POETRY. 8vo.	0	8	0
LUTHER ON THE GALATIANS. 8vo.	0	10	6
NEWTON'S (Bp.) DISSERTATION ON THE PROPHECIES. 8vo.	0	8	0
OWEN'S EXPOSITION OF THE HEBREWS. 4 vols. 8vo.	2	16	0
————— EXERCITATIONS PREFIXED TO THE HEBREWS. 8vo.	0	14	0
PATRICK, LOWTH, WHITBY, AND LOWMAN'S COMMENTARY ON THE OLD AND NEW TESTAMENTS. 4 vols. Imperial 8vo.	4	10	0
STACKHOUSE'S HISTORY OF THE BIBLE, New Edit. By D. DEWAR, D.D. Imp. 8vo.	1	10	0
STUART'S COMMENTARY ON THE ROMANS. 8vo.	0	9	0
————— HEBREWS. 8vo.	0	9	0
WHITBY AND LOWMAN'S COMMENTARY ON THE NEW TESTAMENT. Impl.	1	5	0
WINTLE'S TRANSLATION OF DANIEL, with Notes. 8vo.	0	8	0

LIGHT READING & BOOKS IN THE PICKWICK STYLE.

	£	s.	d.
ADVENTURES OF CAPTAIN BOLIO. 32 Engravings. 12mo.	0	7	0
————— PAUL PERIWINKLE, OR THE PRESS-GANG. 40 Engravings by PHIZ. 8vo.	1	1	0
————— GRACE DARLING. A Tale. 20 Engravings. 8vo.	0	5	0
ARABIAN NIGHTS, 3 vols. 32mo.	0	12	0
CHRONICLES OF CRIME, by CAMDEN PELHAM, Esq. Plates by PHIZ. 2 vols. 8vo.	1	8	0
COLMAN'S BROAD GRINS, with Cuts, Cloth, Gilt Edges	0	1	6
DOINGS IN LONDON. 30 Engravings. 10th Edit. 8vo.	0	7	0
EGAN'S PILGRIMS OF THE THAMES. 26 Plates. 8vo.	0	8	0
————— BOOK OF SPORTS AND MIRROR OF LIFE. Cuts, 8vo.	0	7	0
GIDEON GILES THE ROPER. By MILLER. Plates. 8vo.	0	13	0
GODFREY MALVERN. By MILLER. Plates. 8vo.	0	14	0
GRANT'S SKETCHES IN LONDON. 24 Engravings by PHIZ. 8vo.	0	8	0
HONE'S STRUTT'S SPORTS OF THE PEOPLE OF ENGLAND. 8vo.	0	10	6
————— EVERY-DAY BOOK AND TABLE BOOK. 3 vols. 8vo.	1	4	0
————— YEAR BOOK. New Edition. Cuts. 8vo.	0	8	0
MORNINGS AT BOW-STREET. Cuts by CRUIKSHANK. Fcap. 8vo.	0	5	0
ODDITIES OF LONDON LIFE. 77 Cuts. 2 vols. post 8vo.	1	1	0
PICKWICK ABROAD. By REYNOLDS ; Plates by PHIZ, &c. 8vo.	0	14	0
PICTURES OF THE FRENCH. Royal 8vo.	0	6	0
PARTERRE OF HISTORICAL ROMANCE, ANECDOTE, &c. 4 vols. 8vo.	0	16	0
PUNCH AND JUDY, with 24 Plates, by CRUIKSHANK. Post 8vo.	0	4	0
ROBERT MACAIRE. 18 Plates, by Phiz. Post 8vo.	0	10	6
TITMARSH'S COMIC TALES. 20 Plates. 2 vols. post 8vo.	1	1	0
WORLD (THE) OF LONDON. By JOHN FISHER MURRAY, Esq. 12mo.	0	5	0

GEOGRAPHY, HISTORY, AND BIOGRAPHY.

ADDISON'S DAMASCUS & PALMYRA, 2 vols. 8vo. 14s.

ADVENTURES in ALGIERS, 3 vols. 8vo. 15s.

BARROW'S PETER THE GREAT, 5s.

BLUNT'S REFORMATION, 5s.

BREWSTER'S (SIR DAVID) LIFE OF SIR ISAAC NEWTON, 5s.

BROOKES'S GENERAL GAZETTEER, New Edition, by FINDLAY, 8vo, 12s.

BROOKES'S GENERAL GAZETTEER IN MINIATURE, by FINDLAY, 18mo, 7s.

BROWN'S LIFE OF HOWARD THE PHILANTHROPIST, 8vo, 15s.

CAMPBELL'S LIVES OF BRITISH ADMIRALS, fcap. 8vo. 7s. 6d.

CAVE'S LIVES OF THE FATHERS, New Edition, by CARY, 3 vols. 8vo, 1l. 4s.

CAVE'S LIVES OF THE APOSTLES, New Edition, by CARY, 8vo, 8s.

CECIL'S LIFE OF NEWTON, 32mo, 2s.

CONDER'S MODERN TRAVELLER; each Work sold separately, viz. :—

AMERICA, 2 vols. 10s.

ARABIA, 5s.

AFRICA, 3 vols. Maps & Plates, 15s.

SIAM AND ASSAM, 5s.

BRAZIL & BUENOS AYRES, 2 vols. 10s.

COLUMBIA, 5s.

EGYPT, NUBIA, and ABYSSINIA, 2 vols. 10s.

GREECE, 2 vols. 10s.

INDIA, 4 vols. 1l.

ITALY, 3 vols. 15s.

MEXICO and GUATEMALA, 2 vols. 10s.

PALESTINE, 5s.

PERSIA and CHINA, 2 vols. 10s.

PERU AND CHILI, 5s.

RUSSIA, 5s.

SPAIN & PORTUGAL, 2 vols. 10s.

SYRIA & ASIA MINOR, 2 vols. 10s.

TURKEY, 5s.

MODERN TRAVELLER, 33 vols., Maps and Plates, 8l. 5s.

CUNNINGHAM'S (ALLAN) LIVES OF BRITISH PAINTERS, SCULPTORS, &c. 6 vols. 1l. 10s.

DAVENPORT'S LIFE OF ALI PACHA, VIZIER OF EPIRUS, 5s.

DAVENPORT'S HISTORY OF THE BASTILE, 5s.

DE FOE'S VOYAGE ROUND THE WORLD BY A COURSE NEVER SAILED BEFORE, 5s.

DE FOE'S HISTORY OF THE PLAGUE OF LONDON, 5s.

DE FOE'S HISTORY OF THE DEVIL, AND VISION OF MRS. VEAL, 5s.

DRUMMOND'S AUTOBIOGRAPHY OF A. H. ROWAN, ESQ., 8vo. 7s. 6d.

EDMONDS'S LIFE AND TIMES OF WASHINGTON, 2 vols. 10s.

EUSTACE'S CLASSICAL TOUR IN ITALY. Seventh Edition, 3 vols. 15s.

FULLER'S CHURCH HISTORY of BRITAIN, by NICHOLS, 3 vols. 8vo. 1l. 7s.

FULLER'S WORTHIES OF ENGLAND, by NUTTALL, 3 vols. 8vo. 1l. 7s.

FULLER'S HISTORY OF CAMBRIDGE, WALTHAM - ABBEY, AND INJURED INNOCENCE, by NICHOLS. 8vo. 14s.

GIBBON'S DECLINE and FALL of the ROMAN EMPIRE, Imperial 8vo. 1l. 4s.

GOLDSMITH'S HISTORY of ENGLAND, (Chiswick,) 12mo. 6s.

HISTORY OF THE JEWS, by MILMAN, 3 vols. 18mo. 15s.

HOLLINGS' LIFE of GUSTAVUS ADOLPHUS. 18mo. 5s.

IRVING'S LIFE and VOYAGES of CHRISTOPHER COLUMBUS, 18mo. 5s.

JOHNSON'S HIGHWAYMEN, &c. 9s.

JOSEPHUS'S HISTORY OF THE WARS OF THE JEWS, 3 vols. 8vo. 1l. 7s.

JOSEPHUS'S HISTORY OF THE WARS. Complete in 1 vol. 7s. 6d.

LANDER'S DISCOVERIES to the NIGER, 2 vols. 18mo. 10s.

LANGHORNE'S PLUTARCH, 8vo. 9s.

LIFE OF CICERO, by HOLLINGS, 18mo. 5s.

LIFE OF RICHARD I., 18mo. 5s.

LIFE OF MAHOMMED ALI, 18mo, 3s.

LIFE OF MAHOMET, by REV. S. GREEN, 5s.

LIFE OF BRUCE, by MAJOR HEAD, 18mo. 5s.

LIVES OF EMINENT PHYSICIANS, 18mo. 5s.

M'CRIE'S LIFE OF KNOX, 12mo, 4s.

MEMOIRS OF THE LIFE OF DR. ADAM CLARKE, by One of the Family, 8vo. 7s. 6d.

MEMOIRS of JOHN SHIPP, New Edit. 5s.

M'FARLANE'S LIVES AND EXPLOITS OF BANDITTI AND ROBBERS, 18mo. 5s.

MITFORD'S HISTORY OF GREECE, by DAVENPORT, 8 vols. 1l. 1s.

NAPOLEON BUONAPARTE'S LIFE and ADVENTURES, 2 vols. 18mo. 10s.

NAPOLEON BUONAPARTE, THE CAMP AND COURT OF, 18mo. 5s.

NEAL'S HISTORY OF THE PURITANS, by TOULMIN, 3 vols. 8vo. 1l. 16s.

PALGRAVE'S ANGLO-SAXONS, 18mo, 5s.

PILKINGTON'S DICTIONARY OF PAINTERS. By ALLAN CUNNINGHAM. 8vo. 21s.

ROLLIN'S ANCIENT HISTORY, 6 vols. 8vo. Maps, 1l. 12s.

SEGUR'S NARRATIVE of NAPOLEON'S EXPEDITION IN RUSSIA, 2 vols. 18mo. 10s.

SKETCHES FROM THE HISTORY OF VENICE, Maps and Cuts, 2 vols. 18mo. 10s.

SOUTHEY'S LIFE of NELSON, Cuts, &c. 5s.

TOUR THROUGH SOUTH HOLLAND AND UP THE RHINE, 18mo. 5s.

TYTLER'S LIVES OF SCOTTISH WORTHIES, 3 vols. 18mo. 15s.

TYTLER'S UNIVERSAL HISTORY, 18mo, 6 vols. 1l. 10s.

WATSON'S LIFE OF PHILIP II. 8vo. 9s.

WATSON'S LIFE OF PHILIP III. 8vo. 9s.

WELLS'S GEOGRAPHY OF THE OLD AND NEW TESTAMENTS, Maps, 12s.

WILLIAMS'S LIFE AND ACTIONS OF ALEXANDER THE GREAT, 18mo. 5s.

WILSON'S MISSIONARY VOYAGE TO THE SOUTH SEAS, 2s.

NOVELS AND ROMANCES.

ADVENTURES OF CAPTAIN BONNE-
VILLE, by Irving, 3 vols. 8vo. 10s. 6d.
CAVENDISH, OR THE PATRICIAN AT
SEA, 12mo. 6s.
CŒLEBS IN SEARCH OF A WIFE,
by Hannah More, 12mo. 3s.
DE FOE'S LIFE AND ADVENTURES of
ROBINSON CRUSOE, 2 vols. (Oxford) 10s.
DE FOE'S LIFE AND ADVENTURES of
CAPTAIN SINGLETON, 5s.
DE FOE'S LIFE AND ADVENTURES of
COLONEL JACK, 5s.
DE FOE'S MEMOIRS of a CAVALIER, 5s.
DE FOE'S FORTUNATE MISTRESS, or
LIFE OF ROXANA, 5s.
DE FOE'S CARLTON'S MEMOIRS and
LIFE OF MOTHER ROSS, 5s.
EDINBURGH CABINET NOVELS, 2 vols.
5s.

FLYING DUTCHMAN, by the Author of
" Cavendish," 3 vols. 1l. 11s. 6d.
COOPER'S LIONEL LINCOLN, 12mo. 3s.
IRVING'S KNICKERBOCKER'S HIS-
TORY OF NEW YORK, 5s.
JACK TENCII, MIDSHIPMAN TURNED
IDLER, 18 Plates, 8vo. 10s. 6d.
LIFE AND TIMES OF DICK WHIT-
TINGTON, 22 Plates, 8vo. 8s.
PORTER'S (MISS) LAKE OF KILLAR-
NEY, a Tale, 12mo. 4s. 6d.
ROBERT MACAIRE in ENGLAND, Plates
by Phiz, 10s. 6d.
WORTLEY MONTAGUE, 3 vols. 10s. 6d.
TITMARSH'S COMIC TALES AND
SKETCHES, 12 Plates. 2 vols. 21s.
TREASURY of WIT and ANECDOTE,
32mo, 2s. 6d.

BOOKS FOR CHILDREN AND YOUNG PEOPLE.

ABBOTT'S ROLLA AT SCHOOL, Royal
18mo, cloth, 2s. 6d.
———— ROLLA'S VACATION, Royal
18mo, cloth, 2s. 6d.
ÆSOP'S FABLES (Whittingham), 32mo. 3s.
AIKIN'S CALENDAR OF NATURE, 2s. 6d
BOY'S OWN BOOK, 19th Edit. square, 6s.
BARBAULD'S EVENINGS AT HOME, 4s.
BREAKFAST-TABLE SCIENCE, 2s. 6d.
BREWSTER'S NATURAL MAGIC, 5s.
BOY'S BOOK OF SCIENCE, 16mo, 7s. 6d.
CHESTERFIELD'S ADVICE to HIS SON
ON MEN AND MANNERS, 18mo. 1s. 6d.
CHILD'S (MRS.) STORIES FOR HOLI-
DAY EVENINGS, half-bound, 2s. 6d.
CHILD'S (THE) OWN BOOK, 6th Edition,
Cuts, square 16mo. 7s. 6d.
CHILD'S (THE)BOTANY, square 16mo, 2s.
COPLEY'S (ESTHER) EARLY FRIEND-
SHIP, a Tale, 2s. 6d.
COPLEY'S POPLAR GROVE, 2s. 6d.
EARLY IMPRESSIONS, by a Lady, 1s. 6d.
EDGEWORTH'S EARLY LESSONS,
2 vols. 18mo. 5s.
EDGEWORTH'S ROSAMOND, 2 vols.
18mo, cloth, 5s.
ENDLESS AMUSEMENTS, 18mo, 2s.
ENTERTAINMENT for the NURSERY,
155 Cuts, 4s.
FISHER'S YOUNG MAN'S COMPA-
NION, 2s. 6d.
GIRL'S OWN BOOK, by Mrs. Child, 144
Cuts, square, 4s. 6d.
GRIFFIN'S BOOK OF TRADES, 4s. 6d.
HISTORY OF SANDFORD and MERTON,
12mo. 4s. 6d.
HOME, by Sedgwick, 2s.
MARY HOWITT'S JUVENILE BOOKS,
18mo. Sold separately at 2s. 6d.
1. STRIVE AND THRIVE.
2. HOPE ON HOPE EVER.
3. SOWING AND REAPING.
4. ALICE FRANKLIN.
5. WHO SHALL BE GREATEST.
6. WHICH IS THE WISER.
7. LITTLE COIN MUCH CARE.
8. WORK AND WAGES.
9. NO SENSE LIKE COMMON
SENSE.
10. LOVE AND MONEY.

MARY HOWITT'S WORKS—continued.
11. MY UNCLE, the CLOCK-MAKER.
12. THE TWO APPRENTICES.
13. MY OWN STORY.
JANEWAY'S TOKEN FOR CHILDREN,
32mo. 6d.
JUVENILE SCRAP-BOOK, TALES,&c. 4s.
JUVENILE EVERY-DAY BOOK, 3s. 6d.
LOOKING-GLASS FOR THE MIND,2s.6d.
LOVE TOKEN FOR CHILDREN, by Miss
Sedgwick, 2s.
MOTHER'S STORY BOOK, by Mrs. Child,
18mo. 3s. 6d.
PETER PARLEY'S GRAMMAR OF GEO-
GRAPHY, 4s. 6d.
PETER PARLEY'S LIVES OF FRANK-
LIN AND WASHINGTON, 4s. 6d.
PETER PARLEY'S TALES ABOUT
Europe, Asia, Africa, and America, 7s. 6d.
The Sea and Pacific | Animals, Cuts, 7s. 6d.
Ocean, 4s. 6d. | The United States of
The Sun, Moon, and | America, 4s. 6d.
Stars, 4s. 6d. | Rome and Modern Italy,
England, Ireland, and | 4s. 6d.
Scotland, 7s. 6d. | Mythology of Greece
Ancient and Modern | and Rome, 4s. 6d.
Greece, 4s. 6d. | Plants, edited by Mrs.
Christmas and Its Fes- | Loudon, 7s. 6d.
tivals, 7s. 6d. | Universal History,7s.6d.
PHILIPS'S CONVERSATIONS ABOUT
THE WHALE FISHERY, 4s. 6s.
PHILIPS'S CONVERSATIONS ABOUT
the TOOLS and TRADES of ANIMALS, 4s. 6d.
RICH POOR MAN AND POOR RICH
MAN, by Miss Sedgwick, 2s.
STORIES ABOUT POLAND, 2s. 6d.
TEGG'S PRESENT FOR AN APPREN-
TICE. New Edition, 4s. 6d.
TOM TELESCOPE'S NEWTONIAN PHI-
LOSOPHY. Cuts, 4s. 6d.
VILLAGE AND THE VICARAGE, 2s. 6d.
WATTS'S DIVINE SONGS, 6d.
WATTS'S DIVINE SONGS ; with Essay
by Scott. 6d.
WHITE'S NATURAL HISTORY OF
SELBORNE, by Lady Dover, 3s. 6d.
WRIGHT'S OCEAN WORK, 18mo. 2s. 6d.
YOUNG MAN'S AID TO KNOWLEDGE.
24mo. 2s. 6d.
YOUNG LADIES' STORY-TELLER, by
Miss Leslie, 2s.

THEOLOGY AND ECCLESIASTICAL HISTORY.

	£	s.	d
JENKS'S FAMILY DEVOTION. By SIMEON. 12mo.	0	3	0
LAWS OF CHRIST RESPECTING CIVIL OBEDIENCE, &c. 8vo.	0	16	0
LEIGHTON'S (ARCHBISHOP) WORKS. 8vo.	0	8	0
———— LECTURES, THEOLOGICAL, &c.	0	2	6
MASON'S HELP TO FAMILY AND PRIVATE DEVOTION	0	3	0
——— SPIRITUAL TREASURY FOR THE CHILDREN OF GOD. 8vo.	0	7	0
MASSILLON'S SERMONS. New Edition. 8vo.	0	9	0
MILNER'S CHURCH HISTORY. By HAWEIS. 8vo.	0	12	0
MORE'S (HANNAH) PRACTICAL PIETY. 32mo.	0	2	6
MORNING EXERCISES AT CRIPPLEGATE, AND GILES-IN-THE-FIELDS.			
New Edition. By J. NICHOLS. 6 vols. 8vo.	3	14	0
MOSHEIM'S ECCLESIASTICAL HISTORY. 2 vols. 8vo.	1	1	0
NEWTON'S (REV. JOHN) THEOLOGICAL WORKS. 8vo.	0	10	6
OLNEY HYMNS. By COWPER and NEWTON. 32mo.	0	1	6
ORTON'S (REV. JOB) PRACTICAL WORKS. 2 vols. 8vo.	1	4	0
PALEY'S WORKS. New Edition. 8vo.	0	12	0
——— NOTES AND ILLUSTRATIONS. By PAXTON. 5 vols. 8vo.	2	5	0
PASCAL'S THOUGHTS ON RELIGION. 18mo.	0	2	6
PEARSON ON THE CREED. A New Edition. By NICHOLS. 8vo.	0	10	6
PITMAN'S SERMONS FOR EVERY SUNDAY IN THE YEAR. 2 vols.	1	1	0
——— SECOND COURSE. 2 vols.	1	1	0
PORTEUS'S (BISHOP) LECTURES ON ST. MATTHEW. 8vo.	0	7	0
QUESNEL'S REFLECTIONS ON THE GOSPELS. Essay by WITMAN, 3 vols. 12mo.	1	1	0
ROBERT'S ORIENTAL ILLUSTRATION OF THE SCRIPTURE, 8vo.	0	12	0
ROBINSON'S SCRIPTURE CHARACTERS. 8vo.	0	9	0
ROMAINE'S THEOLOGICAL WORKS. 8vo.	0	9	0
ROWE'S DEVOUT EXERCISES OF THE HEART	0	1	6
SAURIN'S SERMONS. New Edition. By BURDER. 3 vols.	1	16	0
SCOTT'S (REV. THOMAS) THEOLOGICAL WORKS. CHISWICK.	0	8	0
SIMPSON'S PLEA FOR RELIGION AND THE SACRED WRITINGS. 12mo.	0	4	6
SPRING'S OBLIGATIONS OF THE WORLD TO THE BIBLE. 32mo.	0	3	0
STURM'S REFLECTIONS ON THE WORKS OF GOD. By Dr. CLARKE. 2 vols.	0	6	0
THE SABBATH SCHOOL AS IT SHOULD BE. Royal 32mo.	0	2	6
TODD'S SABBATH SCHOOL TEACHER	0	3	0
——— WORKS ON SUNDAY TEACHING, &c. 8vo.	0	8	0
VENN'S COMPLETE DUTY OF MAN. 12mo.	0	4	0
WAKE'S (BISHOP) GENUINE APOSTOLICAL EPISTLES. 12mo.	0	5	0
WARDEN'S SYSTEM OF REVEALED RELIGION. By NICHOLS. 8vo.	0	10	0
WATTS' PSALMS AND HYMNS. 32mo. Pocket Edition.	0	1	6
——— (BARFIELD's Edition.) 8vo. cloth	0	10	6
——— SCRIPTURE HISTORY. 12mo.	0	4	0
——— HOPEFUL YOUTH FALLING SHORT OF HEAVEN	0	1	0
——— GUIDE TO PRAYER. 32mo.	0	1	6
——— DEATH AND HEAVEN. 32mo.	0	1	6
WESLEY'S SERMONS, Edited by DREW. 2 vols. 8vo.	0	15	0
——— JOURNAL OF HIS LIFE AND TRAVELS. 8vo.	0	9	0
WHEATLEY ON THE COMMON PRAYER. 8vo.	0	8	0
WILBERFORCE'S PRACTICAL VIEW OF CHRISTIANITY. 32mo.	0	2	0
WILLIAMS'S CHRISTIAN PREACHER. By JACKSON. 12mo.	0	4	6
WITSIUS ON THE COVENANT BETWEEN GOD AND MAN. 2 vols.	1	4	0

CHEMISTRY, NATURAL HISTORY, BOTANY, MEDICINE, &c.

ABERCROMBIE'S POCKET GARDEN-ER'S CALENDAR, 18mo. 2s.

BERTHOLLET ON DYEING, by URE, 12s.

BEST'S ART OF ANGLING, by JACKSON, 32mo. 2s. 6d.

BUCHAN'S DOMESTIC MEDICINE, 8vo. 7s. 6d.

BUFFON'S NATURAL HISTORY, New Edition, by WRIGHT, 466 Cuts, 4 vols. 1l. 4s.

CREAM OF SCIENTIFIC KNOWLEDGE; A NOTE-BOOK OF GENERAL INFORMATION, 18mo. 3s.

DAVY'S AGRICULTURAL CHEMISTRY, 8vo. 9s.

GARDENS & MENAGERIE OF THE ZOOLOGICAL SOCIETY. 222 Cuts. 2 vols. 1l. 1s.

GRIFFIN'S SCIENTIFIC MISCELLANY, 8vo. 1l. 1s.

HUBER'S OBSERVATIONS ON THE HONEY-BEE, 12mo, 6s.

MAWE'S EVERY MAN HIS OWN GARDENER, 6s.

NATURAL HISTORY OF INSECTS. Cuts. 2 vols. 10s.

PARKE'S CHEMICAL CATECHISM, 5s.

RYDGE'S VETERINARY SURGEONS' MANUAL, 4th Edition, 6s.

THOMSON'S INORGANIC CHEMISTRY, 2 vols. 8vo. 1l. 5s.

WHITE'S NATURAL HISTORY OF SELBORNE, by Lady DOVER, 3s. 6d.

MISCELLANEOUS ENGLISH LITERATURE.

ABBOT'S HOARY HEAD AND THE VALLEY
  BELOW, 2s. 6d.
ABBOT'S (JACOB AND JOHN) WORKS.
  11 vols. 64mo. Cloth, Gilt, 1l.
ANECDOTE BOOK, OR FIVE HUNDRED
  CURIOUS NARRATIVES, &c. 12mo, 3s.
BARROW'S HISTORY OF THE MUTINY OF
  THE BOUNTY, 5s.
BUCK'S ANECDOTES, MORAL, RELIGIOUS,
  AND ENTERTAINING. 12mo, 5s.
BUCKE'S HARMONIES AND SUBLIMITIES
  OF NATURE. 3 vols. 8vo, 1l. 11s. 6d.
BUCKE'S RUINS of ANCIENT CITIES. 2 vls. 10s.
BURTON'S ANATOMY OF MELANCHOLY.
  New Edition, Plates, 8vo. 12s.
CAMPBELL'S PHILOSOPHY OF RHETORIC.
  8vo, 9s.
CHANNING'S (DR. W. E.) WORKS. New Edit.
  2 vols. 8vo, 12s.
CHILD'S (MRS.) FRUGAL HOUSEWIFE. New
  Edition, 2s.
CHILD'S (MRS.) FAMILY NURSE. Companion
  to the above, 3s. 6d.
CHILD'S (MRS.) MOTHER'S BOOK. 32mo, 2s.
COLERIDGE'S SIX MONTHS' RESIDENCE
  IN THE WEST INDIES, 5s.
COMMON SENSE FOR COMMON PEOPLE.
  By MARTIN DOYLE, 1s.
COWPER'S LIFE AND WORKS. By GRIM-
  SHAWE. 8 vols. 2l.
COWPER'S POEMS. 18mo, cloth, 2s.
CROKER'S FAIRY LEGENDS, &c. OF THE
  SOUTH OF IRELAND, 5s.
CYCLOPÆDIA OF POPULAR SONGS. New
  Edition, 5s.
DE FOE'S NOVELS AND MISCELLANEOUS
  WORKS, 20 vols., Separately at 5s.

  Robinson Crusoe complete, 2 vols.—Life and Adventures of Captain Singleton.—Fortunes and Misfortunes of the famous Moll Flanders.—Life and
  Adventures of Colonel Jack.— Memoirs of a
  Cavalier. — New Voyage Round the World. —
  Memoirs of Captain Carleton and Mrs. Davies.
  —History of the Plague; and the Consolidator.
  —History of the Devil.—Roxana; or, the Fortunate Mistress.—A System of Magic.—History
  and Reality of Apparitions.—Religious Court-
  ship, with an Appendix.—Family Instructor,
  complete, 2 vols.—Complete English Tradesman,
  2 vols.—Memoirs of Duncan Campbell.—Life of
  De Foe, &c.

DE FOE'S SYSTEM OF MAGIC AND HIS-
  TORY OF THE BLACK ART, 5s.
DE FOE'S SECRETS OF THE INVISIBLE
  WORLD, AND HISTORY OF APPARI-
  TIONS, 5s.
DIARY OF AN AMERICAN PHYSICIAN, 2s.
DOUCE'S ILLUSTRATIONS OF SHAK-
  SPEARE. 40 Engravings. 8vo, 14s.
ELEGANT EXTRACTS, PROSE. 6 vols. 18mo,
  1l. 10s.
ELEGANT EXTRACTS, VERSE. 6 vols. 18mo,
  1l. 10s.
ENFIELD'S HISTORY OF PHILOSOPHY.
  8vo, 14s.
EPHRAIM HOLDING'S DOMESTIC AD-
  DRESSES, 32mo, 2s.
FERGUSSON'S LECTURES ON MECHANICS,
  &c., 8vo. 10s.
FOX'S BOOK OF MARTYRS. New Edition.
  By MILNER. 8vo, 15s.
FOX'S BOOK OF MARTYRS Abridged. 16mo, 2s. 6d.
FAMILY LIBRARY, THE, IN EIGHTY VOLS.
  Sold Separately at 5s.

  Life of Buonaparte, 2 vols.—Life of Alexander the
  Great.—Lives of British Artists, 6 vols.—History
  of the Jews, 3 vols.—Insects, 2 vols.—Court and
  Camp of Buonaparte.—Life and Voyages of

Columbus.—Life of Nelson, by Southey.—Lives
  of British Physicians.—History of British India,
  4 vols.—Demonology and Witchcraft, by Scott.—
  Life and Travels of Bruce.—Voyages of Colum-
  bus's Companions.—Venetian History, 2 vols.—
  History of the Anglo-Saxons.—Lives of Scottish
  Worthies, 3 vols.—Tour in South Holland.—Life
  of Sir Isaac Newton.—Mutiny of the Bounty.
  —Reformation in England.—Lander's Travels
  in Africa, 2 vols.—Salmagundi, by Washington
  Irving.—Trials of Charles I. and the Regicides.
  —Brewster's Natural Magic.—Life of Peter the
  Great.—Six Months in the West Indies.—Sketch
  Book, by Irving, 2 vols. — Taytler's General
  History of the Crusades.—Fairy Legends.—Me-
  moirs of the Plague, by De Foe and Brayley.—
  Life and Times of General Washington, 2 vols.
  — Knickerbocker's History of New York. —
  Wesley's Philosophy, 3 vols.—Segur's Narrative
  of Napoleon's Expedition to Russia, 2 vols.—
  Life of Ali Pasha.—Lives of Banditti and Rob-
  bers.—Sketches of Imposture, Deception, and
  Credulity.—History of the Bastille.—History of
  Gustavus Adolphus. — Chronicles of London
  Bridge.—Life of Duke of Marlborough.—Life of
  Cervantes, by Roscoe.—Life of Cicero.—Ruins
  of Cities, 2 vols.—Life of Richard Cœur de
  Lion.—Life of Mahomet.—Peril and Suffering,
  2 vols.—Eustace's Classical Tour in Italy, 3 vols.
  —Lives of Eminent Men.—Mutiny at the Nore.

HAND-BOOK OF HORSEMANSHIP. 12 plates,
  18mo. 2s. 6d.
HISTORY OF THE MUTINY AT THE NORE.
  By W. J. NEALE, 5s.
HONE'S EVERY-DAY BOOK. Numerous Cuts.
  2 vols. 8vo. 16s.
HONE'S TABLE BOOK, 8vo. 8s.
HONE'S YEAR-BOOK, 8vo. 8s.
HOLLAND'S DOMESTIC COOKERY. 12mo, 3s.
HOWARD'S BEAUTIES OF BYRON. 18mo, 2s.
INCHBALD'S BRITISH THEATRE. 20 vols. 30s.
  Any Play separately at 1s.
IRVING'S (WASHINGTON) SKETCH-BOOK.
  2 vols. 10s.
KAMES'S ELEMENTS OF CRITICISM, 8vo. 7s.
LELAND'S VIEW OF DEISTICAL WRITERS.
  By EDMONDS. 8vo, 12s.
LIVE AND LET LIVE. By Miss SEDGWICK, 2s. 6d.
LOCKE'S ESSAY ON THE HUMAN UNDER-
  STANDING. 8vo, 9s.
LOCKE'S EDUCATION. With Notes. By ST.
  JOHN, 12mo, 6s.
MANUAL OF ASTROLOGY. New Edition. By
  RAPHAEL. 8vo, 5s.
MASON'S TREATISE ON SELF-KNOWLEDGE.
  32mo, 2s.
MILITARY REMINISCENCES. By COL. WELSH.
  2 vols. 8vo. 16s.
MILTON'S POETICAL WORKS. By SIR
  EGERTON BRYDGES. 1 vol. 8vo, 16s.
MILTON'S POETICAL WORKS. 18mo, 3s. 6d.
————— PARADISE LOST. 18mo, 2s.
————— SELECT PROSE WORKS AND
  NOTES. By ST. JOHN. 2 vols. 12s.
MORE (HANNAH) ON FEMALE EDUCATION.
  18mo, 2s.
MORE'S (HANNAH) TALES FOR THE COM-
  MON PEOPLE, 32mo, 2s. 6d.
MORE'S (HANNAH) STORIES FOR THE MID-
  DLE RANKS, 32mo, 2s. 6d.
MORE'S (MRS. HANNAH) MISCELLANEOUS
  WORKS. 2 vols. 8vo, 1l. 4s.
MORE'S DRAMAS, SEARCH, & ESSAYS, 2s. 6d.
NARRATIVES OF PERIL AND SUFFERING.
  By DAVENPORT. 2 vols. 10s.
OWEN'S BOOK OF ROADS. 18mo. New Edition, 2s.
PATTERSON'S BOOK OF ROADS. 8vo, 18s.
PHILOSOPHY OF COMMON SENSE, 32mo. 2s.
POST CAPTAIN, OR THE WOODEN WALLS
  WELL MANNED. Royal 32mo, 2s. 6d.

REID'S ESSAYS ON THE INTELLECTUAL POWERS OF THE HUMAN MIND, with Examination Questions, &c. by the Rev. G. N. WRIGHT, 8vo, 12s.

REID'S ESSAY ON THE ACTIVE POWERS OF MAN, AND INQUIRY INTO THE HUMAN MIND; Essay on Quantity, &c. New Edition, by the Rev. G. N. WRIGHT, 8vo, 12s.

RICHMOND'S ANNALS OF THE POOR. 32mo, 2s.

SCENES IN SCOTLAND. By LEIGHTON. 12mo, 5s.

SCENES FROM THE LIFE OF EDWARD LAS-CELLES, GENT., with Illustrations by G. CRUIKSHANK, 1 vol. 12mo, 12s.

SCOTT'S LETTERS ON DEMONOLOGY AND WITCHCRAFT. 12mo, 5s.

SCOTT'S MINSTRELSY OF THE SCOTTISH BORDER. 8vo, 7s. 6d.

SHAKSPEARE'S DRAMATIC WORKS. Diamond Edition, 7s.

SHAKSPEARE'S DRAMATIC AND POETIC WORKS. 8vo, 10s. 6d.

SIGOURNEY'S LETTERS TO MOTHERS, 2s.

SIMPSON AND WISE'S READIEST READY RECKONER ever invented, 12mo, bound, 5s.

SKETCHES OF IMPOSTURE, DECEPTION, AND CREDULITY, 5s.

STEWART'S (DUGALD) PHILOSOPHY OF THE HUMAN MIND. New Edition, with the Latin Quotations, translated by the REV. G. N. WRIGHT. 8vo, 10s. 6d.

SPHINX. A COLLECTION OF 400 ENIGMAS, &c., 1s. 6d.

THREE EXPERIMENTS OF LIVING. 32mo, 2s.

TODD'S STUDENT'S MANUAL. 32mo, 3s.

TODD'S LECTURES TO CHILDREN. 32mo, 2s.

—— TRUTH MADE SIMPLE. 32mo, 2s.

—— SIMPLE SKETCHES. 32mo, 2s.

TREASURY OF WIT AND ANECDOTE. Royal 32mo, 2s. 6d.

TRIALS OF CHARLES THE FIRST AND THE REGICIDES. 12mo, 5s.

TWO YEARS BEFORE THE MAST. 24mo, 2s.

VOCAL COMPANION, OR SINGER'S OWN BOOK, 12mo, 3s. 6d.

WARTON'S HISTORY of ENGLISH POETRY. New Edition. 3 vols. 8vo, 1l. 16s.

WATTS ON THE IMPROVEMENT OF THE MIND. 18mo, 2s.

WESLEYANA, A SELECTION FROM WES-LEY'S WRITINGS. 18mo, 3s.

WESLEYAN METHODIST CONFERENCE. By RYERSON. 8vo, 2s.

WESLEY'S NATURAL PHILOSOPHY. By ROBERT MUDIE. 3 vols. 15s.

WESLEY FAMILY. By DR. A. CLARKE, 2 vols. 12s.

WONDERS OF HUMAN NATURE. 12mo, 5s.

YOUNG ENTHUSIAST IN HUMBLE LIFE, 14mo, 2s. 6d.

YOUNG'S NIGHT THOUGHTS ON LIFE, DEATH, AND IMMORTALITY, 18mo, 2s.

SCHOOL BOOKS.

ADAM'S ROMAN ANTIQUITIES. New Edition, by BOYD, with Questions, 12mo, 7s.

ÆSCHYLUS, a New Translation. 18mo, 5s.

ÆSOP'S FABLES. (Chiswick Press.) 3s. 6d.

AINSWORTH'S LATIN-ENGLISH DICTION-ARY, by DYMOCK, 18mo, 7s.

ALEXANDER THE GREAT, LIFE OF, by Rev. J. WILLIAMS, 5s.

ALDERSON'S ORTHOGRAPHICAL EXER-CISES, 1s.

ANTHON'S HORACE, with English Notes. A New Edition, by BOYD, 7s. 6d.

ANTHON'S SALLUST, with English Notes. A New Edition, by BOYD, 12mo, 5s.

ANTHON'S CICERO'S ORATIONS, with English Notes. A New Edition, by BOYD, 12mo, 6s.

ANTHON'S GREEK READER, with English Notes. A New Edition, by BOYD, 12mo, 7s. 6d.

ANTHON'S CÆSAR'S COMMENTARIES, with Maps and Plates, 12mo, 6s.

ANTHON'S GREEK GRAMMAR. New Edition, by DR. MAJOR, King's College. 12mo, 4s.

ANTHON'S GREEK PROSODY. New Edition, by DR. MAJOR, King's College, 12mo, 2s. 6d.

ANTHON'S LATIN GRAMMAR. New Edition. by Rev. W. HAYES, King's College, 12mo, 4s.

BALDWIN'S ROME. 12mo. 3s. 6d.

BALDWIN'S GREECE. 12mo. 4s.

BALDWIN'S PANTHEON OF THE HEATHEN DEITIES. 12mo, 5s. 6d.

BALDWIN'S FABLES. Cuts. 12mo. 4s.

BARROW'S PETER THE GREAT, 5s.

BLAIR'S LECTURES ON RHETORIC, by Rev. T. DALE. 8vo. 12s.

BONNYCASTLE'S SCHOOL BOOKS, edited by Rev. E. C. TYSON, viz.—

Arithmetic, 3s. 6d.	Key to Algebra, 4s. 6d.
Key to Ditto, 4s. 6d.	Introduction to Mensu-
Introduct. to Algebra,	ration, 5s.
4s.	Key to Mensuration, 5s.

BOWEY'S FRENCH DICTIONARY, 8vo. 12s.

BURGESS'S (BISHOP) HEBREW ELEMENTS. 12mo, 6s.

BURGESS'S (BISHOP) RUDIMENTS OF HE-BREW GRAMMAR. 7s.

CARR'S MANUAL OF ROMAN ANTIQUITIES. 12mo, 6s. 6d.

CICERO'S EPISTOLÆ AD ATTICUM. 2 vols. 12mo, 12s.

CRABB'S DICTIONARYOFGENERAL KNOW-LEDGE. Fourth Edition. 7s.

CUDWORTH'S INTELLECTUAL SYSTEM, 4 vols. 8vo.

DAVENPORT'S WALKER'S DICTIONARY IN MINIATURE. 18mo, 5s.

DUNCAN'S (Rev. Dr.) HEBREW LEXICON AND GRAMMAR. 18mo, 7s.

ENFIELD'S SPEAKER. A New Edition. 3s. 6d.

ENFIELD'S PROGRESSIVE SPELLING-BOOK. New Edition. 1s. 3d.

ETON GREEK GRAMMAR, by HOMER, 12mo, 4s.

FINLAY'S GENERAL SCHOOL ATLAS. Royal 8vo. Coloured 12s.

—— OUTLINE MAPS. Royal 8vo. 5s.

FRENCH CLASSICS FOR SCHOOLS, edited by VENTOUILLAC, 18mo, viz.—

Elisabeth. MME. COT-TIN. 2s. 6d.	LaChaumière Indienne. ST. PIERRE. 2s. 6d.
Numa Pompilius. By FLORIAN. 5s.	Choix des Contes Moraux de Marmontel. 2s. 6d.
Nouveaux Morceaux Choisis de Buffon. 2s. 6d.	Histoire de Pierre le Grand. VOLTAIRE. 5s. Pensées de Pascal. 2s.6d.

ELLIS'S LATIN EXERCISES. New Edition. By WRIGHT. 3s. 6d.

GUY'S SCHOOL BOOKS—

British Primer, 12mo. half-bound, 6d.	with Chart, 12mo. roan, 4s. 6d.
Spelling Book, 12mo. sheep, 1s. 6d.	SchoolArithmetic,12mo. sheep, 2s.
Expositor, 12mo, shp, 1s. 6d.	Key to ditto, 12mo.roan sheep, 4s. 6d.
British Reader, 12mo, roan, 3s. 6d.	Pocket Cyclopædia, 12mo. cloth, 10s. 6d
School Question Book,	

GEOGRAPHY AND HISTORY. By a Lady.
New Edition. By WRIGHT. 12mo, 4s. 6d.
GOLDSMITH'S GRAMMAR OF GEOGRAPHY.
New Edition. By WRIGHT. 18mo, 3s. 6d.
HUTTON'S MATHEMATICS. A New Edition.
By RUTHERFORD. 8vo, 16s.
HUTTON'S MATHEMATICAL RECREA-
TIONS. By RIDDLE. 8vo, 16s.
JOHNSON'S ENGLISH DICTIONARY. (Pocket
Size.) 2s.
JONES'S SHERIDAN'S PRONOUNCING DIC-
TIONARY, square, 3s. 6d.
JOYCE'S COMMERCIAL ARITHMETIC, by
WRIGHT, 12mo, 3s.
JOYCE'S INTRODUCTION TO THE ARTS
AND SCIENCES. 18mo, 3s. 6d.   [2s. 6d.
JOYCE'S SCIENTIFIC DIALOGUES. 12mo,
KEITH ON THE USE OF THE GLOBES.
New Edition, by WRIGHT, 12mo, 6s. 6d.
LEMPRIERE'S CLASSICAL DICTIONARY.
By PARK. 18mo, 7s.
LENNIE'S ENGLISH GRAMMAR. 18mo, 1s. 6d.
MADAN'S JUVENAL. 2 vols. 8vo, 14s.
MANGNALL'S HISTORICAL AND MISCEL-
LANEOUS QUESTIONS. 12mo, 4s. 6d.
MAVOR'S SPELLING-BOOK. 12mo.   1s.
MEADOWS'S ITALIAN AND ENGLISH DIC-
TIONARY. 18mo, 7s.
MEADOWS'S FRENCH AND ENGLISH PRO-
NOUNCING DICTIONARY. 18mo. 7s.
MEADOWS'S SPANISH AND ENGLISH DIC-
TIONARY. 18mo, 7s.
MORRISON'S BOOK-KEEPING. 8vo, 8s.
MURRAY'S (LINDLEY) SCHOOL-BOOKS,
edited by TYSON, viz.—

English Gram. 4s.
——— (Abridged). · 4s.
18mo, 1s.
——— Exercises.
12mo, 2s. 6d.
Key to the Exercises.
12mo, 2s. 6d.

English Reader. 12mo,
4s.
Introduction to the En-
glish Reader. 12mo,
2s.
Grammar & Exercises.
By GARTLEY.18mo,2s.

NEWTON'S PRINCIPIA MATHEMATICA. 2
vols. Royal 8vo, 1l. 5s.
NOVUM TESTAMENTUM GRÆCE. 32mo, 5s.
PARLEY'S UNIVERSAL HISTORY. 4s. 6d.
PARLEY'S GRAMMAR OF GEOGRAPHY,
4s. 6d.
PARLEY'S TALES ABOUT GREECE. 4s. 6d.
PARLEY'S TALES ABOUT ROME. 4s. 6d.
PARLEY'S MYTHOLOGY OF GREECE. 4s. 6d.
PERRIN'S ELEMENTS OF FRENCH CON-
VERSATION. By WRIGHT. 12mo, 1s. 6d.
PERRIN'S FRENCH FABLES. 12mo, 2s. 6d.
PERRIN'S FRENCH SPELLING-BOOK. By
WRIGHT. 12mo, 2s.
PINDARI CARMINA. HEYNE. 32mo. 4s.
PINNOCK'S ENGLAND. New Edit. 12mo, 3s. 6d.
POTTER'S ANTIQUITIES OF GREECE. By
BOYD. 12mo. 9s.
QUESTIONS ON ADAM'S ROMAN ANTIQUI-
TIES. By BOYD. 1s. 8d.
RAMSHORN'S DICTIONARY OF LATIN
SYNONYMES. 8vo. 7s.
SEPTUAGINT (The GREEK). 2 vols. 32mo, 12s.
SIMSON'S EUCLID, by RUTHERFORD. 18mo, 5s.
TEGG'S FIRST BOOK FOR CHILDREN, 6d.
TOM TELESCOPE'S NEWTONIAN PHILOSO-
PHY. Cuts. 4s. 6d.
TOOKE'S (HORNE) DIVERSIONS OF PUR-
LEY. New Edition, by TAYLOR. 8vo. 14s.
TROLLOPE'S (Rev.) GREEK TESTAMENT,
8vo. 21s.
VALPY'S LATIN DELECTUS, by WRIGHT. 2s. 6d.
WALKINGAME'S TUTOR, 12mo. 2s.
WANOSTROCHT'S RECUEIL CHOISI, New
Edit. by WRIGHT, 12mo. 3s.
WATTS'S VIEW OF SCRIPTURE HISTORY.
12mo, 4s. 6d.
WRIGHT'S COMMENTARY ON NEWTON'S
PRINCIPIA. 2 vols. 1l. 8s.
WRIGHT'S GREEK-ENGLISH LEXICON.—
18mo, 7s.

DICTIONARIES, LEXICONS, &c.

BROOKES'S GENERAL GAZETTEER, OR
GEOGRAPHICAL DICTIONARY. 8vo. 12s.
BROOKES'S GENERAL GAZETTEER IN
MINIATURE, New Edition, by FINDLAY, 7s.
BROWN'S (REV. JOHN) DICTIONARY
OF THE HOLY BIBLE, 8vo. 9s.
BUCK'S THEOLOGICAL DICTIONARY,
New Edition, by HENDERSON, 8vo. 14s.
CALMET'S DICTIONARY OF THE HOLY
BIBLE, by TAYLOR, Imperial 8vo. 1l. 4s.
CARPENTER'S DICTIONARY OF SY-
NONYMES, 3rd Edition, 18mo, 2s. 6d.
CRABB'S DICTIONARY OF GENERAL
KNOWLEDGE, 4th Edition, 12mo, 7s.
CRUDEN'S CONCORDANCE OF THE OLD
AND NEW TESTAMENT, Imperial 8vo. 18s.
CUNNINGHAM'S (A.) PILKINGTON'S
DICTIONARY OF PAINTERS, 8vo, 21s.
DAVENPORT'S WALKER'S PRONOUN-
CING DICTIONARY, 18mo. 5s.
DOLBY'S SHAKSPEARIAN DICTION-
ARY, an Index to Shakspeare, 12mo, 7s. 6d.
DUNCAN'S (REV. DR.) HEBREW LEXI-
CON AND GRAMMAR, 18mo. 7s.
DYMOCK'S AINSWORTH'S LATIN-
ENGLISH DICTIONARY, 18mo. 7s.
GORTON'S TOPOGRAPHICAL DIC-
TIONARY OF GREAT BRITAIN, & Atlas, 4 v. 72s.
GURNEY'S DIAMOND DICTIONARY
OF THE BIBLE, 24mo. 3s. 6d.

GUTHRIE'S GEOGRAPHY IN MINIA-
TURE, by DAVENPORT, 18mo, 7s.
JOHNSON'S DIAMOND DICTIONARY
OF THE ENGLISH LANGUAGE, 32mo. 2s.
JOHNSON'S DICTIONARY OF THE
ENGLISH LANGUAGE, 2 vols. 4to. 2l. 2s.
JONES'S (STEPHEN) BIOGRAPHICAL
DICTIONARY, 18mo. 6s.
JONES'S BIBLICAL CYCLOPÆDIA, 16s.
LEMPRIERE'S CLASSICAL DICTION-
ARY, by PARK, 18mo, 7s.
MEADOWS'S ITALIAN-ENGLISH DIC-
TIONARY, 18mo. 7s.
MEADOWS'S FRENCH-ENGLISH PRO-
NOUNCING DICTIONARY, 18mo. 7s.
MEADOWS'S SPANISH-ENGLISH DIC-
TIONARY, 18mo. 7s.
MITCHELL'S PORTABLE CYCLOPÆ-
DIA, 60 Plates, 8vo. 1l. 1s.
NUTTALL'S CLASSICAL AND ARCHÆ-
OLOGICAL DICTIONARY, 8vo. 16s.
ROBINSON'S GREEK AND ENGLISH
LEXICON OF THE TESTAMENT, 8vo. 15s.
TEGG'S DICTIONARY OF CHRONO-
LOGY. 12mo. 6s.
WALKER'S CRITICAL PRONOUNCING
DICTIONARY, 8vo. 7s.
WALKER'S PRONOUNCING DICTION-
ARY, and the Key to Proper Names, 8vo. 9s.